THE EXCELLENT

PUB QUIZ

BOOK

MORE THAN
10,000 QUESTIONS

THIS IS A CARLTON BOOK

Published by Carlton Books Limited
20 Mortimer Street
London W1T 3JW

A CIP catalogue record for this book is available from
the British Library

ISBN: 978-1-78097-889-5

Printed and bound in Great Britain

This book is a compilation of sections taken from *The Best Football
Pub Quiz Book Ever!*, *The Best Pop Pub Quiz Book Ever!*, *The Best
Movie Pub Quiz Book Ever!* and *The Best TV Pub Quiz Book Ever!*, plus
additional material from *The Best Formula One Quiz Book Ever!*, *The
Best Irish Pub Quiz Book Ever!* and *The Best Australian Quiz Book Ever!*

THE EXCELLENT PUB QUIZ BOOK

MORE THAN 10,000 QUESTIONS

CARLTON
BOOKS

Contents

Introduction

Over the past decade snugs and lounges in pubs the length and breadth of the country have become, if not seats of learning at least seats of intellect. Which makes a change from seats of worn leatherette (although these still prevail in some areas). The pub quiz has transformed the bar into an arena of knowledge where beery brethren battle to the final bell. The format is simple: some friends, acquaintances, even complete strangers, will do, a questioner, some paper, a collection of ragged Biros and a surfeit of beer and questions are all that is needed to create the perfect evening's entertainment. Wits are challenged, heads are huddled and patience is tested as teams attempt to outdo each other in their show of trivia retention. At these events you will learn that no fact is too small, no sport star too obscure and no war too insignificant to test the pub crowd's grey matter. In fact, the more obscure and wide-ranging the questions the greater the chance of involving the entire barroom – nothing will gain the pub idiot greater respect than showing that they have the entire cast, storyline and signature tune of "Emergency Ward 10" lodged in their head, except perhaps their switching from slip-ons to lace-ups. So take heart, and a copy of this book to the boozer and have a few warm-up sessions and see if you can't organize your own pub quiz. You know it makes sense; it's the only way you'll know all the answers.

The main aim of this book is to entertain, so it is important that you retain a sense of humour and good sportsmanship as you play along, whether you are testing friends at home or setting a quiz for your local hostelry. That aside, you also have to ensure that you are fully in control of your questions and players: remain calm, speak in a steady voice and be constantly unflapped when challenged by any of the more heavily imbibed, as indeed you will be.

This book is divided into three sections: Easy, Medium and Hard questions, which are all subdivided by specialist and pot-luck rounds. The former can be chosen either to help or hinder your players; giving Easy sports questions to the literature fanatics is bound to reveal some interesting answers but it is possibly more challenging to tailor your questions so that the experts receive the brain-wracking Hard questions and the novice the stupefyingly simple Easy questions. Nothing hurts a fanatic more than being beaten on their specialist subject and the division of questions gives you the chance to employ a handicap system. Other handicap systems will also become apparent as you continue as quiz master.

In the interest of further clarification there follows a brief run-down of each section:

Easy

In this primary round the main objective is to keep breathing; these questions are so easy that anyone in the pub could gurgle their way through them in the time it takes to down a pint and still have time left to knock over the stack of pennies on the bar.

Medium

On your toes people, things are getting tricky. By now even the ringers on the out-of-towners' team will be sweating. These questions make for a challenge, but you are bound to get the odd smug bar steward who will fancy his chances, for which you should continue on to the last section.

Hard

Ask a full thirty of these questions and only the shrill wail of the pub cat fighting in the yard will be heard, brows will be furrowed, glances exchanged and beer stared into. To set an entire quiz using just these questions is a form of evil so dark-hearted Fu Manchu would blanch.

All that is left to say is good luck with your testing and if you can't keep your spirits up at least try to keep them down.

The Easy Questions

If you think that Louis Armstrong was the first man on the moon or that Billy Shears played centre-forward for Newcastle United then you will no doubt struggle through the next few questions terribly. For the rest of us though these are the EASY questions, so called because if the quizzee falters on these they are either three sheets to the wind or far too young to be in the pub – either state rendering them toddling buffoons whose social graces will equal their breadth of knowledge. So beware their flailing arms as you attempt to collect the answers.

These questions are perfect when used in the first round of an open entry quiz as they lull everyone into a false sense of security, although you must ensure that contestants don't shout answers out, which creates a problematic precedent for the later, harder questions. Another way of placing these questions is to dot them about throughout the quiz, thus making sure that on every team everyone should know the answer to at least one question despite their age.

If you are running a league quiz then some of your team members may heap derision on such obvious questions, but don't worry: even the cleverest quiz team member can come a cropper, as was noted in a championship final when a contestant was asked to name the continents. He deliberated before eventually beaming out the answer, "A, E, I, O, U!"

1   Which continent's soccer does the CAF association govern?
2   In which French stadium did the UEFA Euro 2016 final take place?
3   Which annual match takes place between the winners of the Champion's League and the Europa League?
4   Which English player earned a red card during UEFA Euro 2012?
5   Which president of FIFA left office in 2015?
6   How many English football clubs are typically given entry to the UEFA Champion's League?
7   How is the Confederation of North, Central American and Caribbean Association Football better known?
8   Sevilla FC won which UEFA tournament in 2014, 2015 and 2016?
9   Which English team reached the semis of the 2016 Champion's League?
10 In 2010, FIFA selected which country for to host the 2022 World Cup?
11 AFC Ajax is based in which Dutch city?
12 Which stadium was due to host the 2017 UEFA Champion's League final?
13 As of June 2016, the record for most appearances in the UEFA Champion's League was held by Iker Casillas?
14 In which city is the football club Celtic FC based?
15 How many teams are in the group stage of the Champion's League?
16 Which country did Germany wallop 13-0 in 2006?
17 Which nation won UEFA Euro 2016?
18 Who was the highest goal-scorer of the 2016 Champion's League?
19 FK Partizan are a leading football club in which nation?
20 CONMEBOL is the association in charge of soccer for which region?
21 Which team knocked England out of Euro 2016?
22 Which London stadium will host the EURO 2020 semi-finals and final?
23. Which nation has won the Champion's League the most?
24. In 1996, England reached which round of the European Championships?
25. Which nation won UEFA Euro 2012?
26 The UEFA Europa League was known as what between 1971 and 2008?
27 Which British team got to the semi-finals of UEFA Euro 2016?
28 Which English football club won the 2012 UEFA Champion's League?
29 In 2016, Sergio Ramos was the captain of which football club?
30 In 2010, FIFA selected which country for the 2018 World Cup?

1 Which folksy American singer/songwriter was born Robert Zimmerman?
2 Which Canadian singer had a major hits with "The Power of Love"?
3 Which singer/songwriter had smash hits including "Like a Virgin"?
4 Which three-letter pop band had huge hits with "Waterfalls"?
5 Which crooner Barry is known for hits including "Copacabana"?
6 Which band had a hit with "When Will I Be Famous"?
7 Which Californian band defined the 'Surf Pop' sound?
8 Which girl band had top ten hits with "Black Coffee", and "Never Ever"?
9 Which trio of brothers had hits in the 70s including "Stayin' Alive"?
10 Which Canadian popster debuted with "Sk8er Boi"?
11 Which singer and dancer recorded *Thriller*?
12 Which singer was born Stefani Germanotta?
13 Which singer/songwriter shot to fame with *Jagged Little Pill*?
14 Which group had hits with "Venus" and "Really Saying Something"?
15 Which heartthrob has fans known as "Beliebers"?
16 Which singer had smash hits with "Umbrella" and "Diamonds"?
17 Which TV-show band had hits with "I'm a Believer" and "Daydream Believer"?
18 Which singer is usually known as 'The King'?
19 Which boy-had had hits, including "Flying Without Wings" and "You Raise Me Up"?
20 Which iconic American singer was known as "Ol' Blue Eyes"?
21 Which band consisted of John, Paul, George, and Ringo?
22 Which Colombian singer released "Hips Don't Lie"?
23 Which trio of Sisters had a 1940s hit with "Boogie Woogie Bugle Boy"?
24 Which American singer had huge hits including "Shake it Off"?
25 Which former Disney star recorded the hit "Oops! I Did It Again"?
26 Which boy-band originally included Robbie Williams?
27 Which trio of brothers had hits with "S.O.S." and "Burnin' Up"?
28 Which band had the smash hit "Nights in White Satin"?
29 Which British pop band, had hits with "Yellow" and "In My Place"?
30 Which American singer LeAnn had hits with singles including "Can't Fight the Moonlight", "How Do I Live", and "I Need You"?

Answers | **World Football** *(see Quiz 1)*

1 Africa. 2 Stade de France. 3 Super Cup. 4 Wayne Rooney. 5 Sepp Blatter. 6 Four. 7 CONCACAF. 8 Europa League. 9 Manchester City. 10 Qatar. 11 Amsterdam. 12 Millennium Stadium. 13 Porto. 14 Glasgow. 15 32. 16 San Marino. 17 Portugal. 18 Cristiano Ronaldo. 19 Serbia. 20 South America. 21 Iceland. 22 Wembley. 23 Spain. 24 Semi-finals. 25 Spain. 26 UEFA Cup. 27 Wales. 28 Chelsea. 29 Real Madrid. 30 Russia.

1 *Anna Christie* was the first talkie for which Swedish star?
2 *The Blue Angel* with Marlene Dietrich was shot in English and which other language?
3 Which "modern" film was Chaplin's last silent movie?
4 In *Stagecoach* which actor John played the Ringo Kid?
5 Which 1939 movie featured a Yellow Brick Road?
6 Which dancers appeared in *The Story of Vernon and Irene Castle*?
7 *Mr Smith Goes to* where in the title of the 1939 movie?
8 Which Laurence played Heathcliff to Merle Oberon's Cathy in *Wuthering Heights*?
9 What were Katharine Hepburn and Cary Grant *Bringing Up* in the 1938 comedy?
10 Which King was a successful ape?
11 Which Clark Gable film, the name of a city, was about a Californian earthquake at the beginning of the 20th century?
12 *The Adventures of* which English hero was the title of a 1938 movie with Errol Flynn?
13 What type of character did James Cagney play in *Angels with Dirty Faces*?
14 *Thoroughbreds Don't Cry* teamed Judy Garland with which Mickey?
15 Which Busby did the choreography for *Footlight Parade*?
16 Which *Hotel* was the title of a Garbo movie?
17 Which zany brothers made *Animal Crackers* in 1930?
18 In which city is *The Hunchback of Notre Dame* set?
19 Bela Lugosi starred as the first sound version of which character?
20 Where was it *All Quiet* in the movies in 1930?
21 The movie *Scarface* was based on the life of which gangster?
22 Which 1939 movie was about a schoolmaster called Mr Chipperfield?
23 What was the heroine of *Gone with the Wind* called?
24 Boris Karloff starred in one of the first horror movies about which Mary Shelley character?
25 What completes the title of the Mae West movie, *She Done Him ____*?
26 Who released *Snow White and the Seven Dwarfs* in 1938?
27 Which future US President began his acting career in the 1930s?
28 The soldiers of which country's army are depicted in *All Quiet on the Western Front*?
29 In which film is Rufus T. Firefly the lead character?
30 Who hoofs it with Fred Astaire in *Follow the Fleet*?

Answers	**TV Pot Luck 1** *(see Quiz 4)*

1 Horrid. **2** Gisele Bundchen. **3** Riley. **4** 2013. **5** The Avengers. **6** Snowy River. **7** Neighbours. **8** Keeping Up Appearances. **9** Brian Wilde. **10** James Bolam. **11** John Arlott. **12** A pickle factory. **13** Moonlighting. **14** Hannah Gordon. **15** Caroline Ahern. **16** This Is Your Life. **17** Shooting Stars. **18** Space 1999. **19** Montel. **20** Jon Snow. **21** Cilla Black. **22** Timecop. **23** Highway to Heaven. **24** The Octonauts. **25** Airwolf. **26** Claudia Winkleman. **27** Channel 5. **28** Armistead Maupin. **29** Edward Woodward. **30** David Frost.

1 What adjective describes Henry in his television series?
2 Which model played the "Girl from Ipanema" at the opening ceremony of the 2016 Olympic Games in Rio?
3 What was Mavis Wilton's maiden name in *Coronation Street*?
4 Which year did Malcolm Tucker's alter ego become *Doctor Who*?
5 Which series featured Tara King and Mother?
6 Which Australian series was subtitled *The McGregor Saga*?
7 Which soap featured the character Rick Alessi?
8 What is the name of Roy Clarke's sitcom about a snobbish woman and her embarrassing relations?
9 Who played Foggy in *Last of the Summer Wine*?
10 Who played a woodwork teacher in *The Beiderbecke Tapes*?
11 Who was the voice of cricket and did television commentaries?
12 What was the family business in *Nearest and Dearest*?
13 In which series did David Addison and Maddie Hayes appear?
14 Who hosts *Watercolour Challenge*?
15 In 2016, Mrs Merton died. What was the name of her real life alter ego?
16 Which series has been hosted by Eamonn Andrews and Michael Aspel?
17 On which series were Mark Lamarr and Ulrika Jonsson team captains?
18 Which S.F. series featured Martin Landau as John Koenig?
19 In the US, Which Williams hosts his own chat show?
20 What is Kit Harington's most famous character called?
21 Who hosted the 1998 game show *The Moment of Truth*?
22 Which S.F. series features the character Jack Logan?
23 In which feelgood series did Victor French play Mark?
24 What is the children's tv show programme featuring Captain Barnacles?
25 Which action show had a super-helicopter hidden by its pilot, Stringfellow Hawke?
26 Which comedian succeeded Bruce Forsyth as host of *Strictly Come Dancing*?
27 Which channel shows *Xena: Warrior Princess* and *Hercules: The Legendary Journeys*?
28 Whose *Tales of the City* were a Channel 4 series?
29 Who presented *In Suspicious Circumstances*?
30 Which knight presents his *Sunday Morning Breakfast Show*?

Quiz 5

1 In 2013, Gareth Bale went overseas to play for which team?
2 Which country did John McGinlay play for?
3 Which was Dennis Bergkamp's first club in England?
4 Which club have played Sutton, Gallacher and Wilcox in the same side?
5 Tony Cottee was a favourite with which London club?
6 Who got in a tabloid tangle in 2016 about his taxes?
7 Jose Mourinho joined Manchester United from which club, in 2016?
8 Which country did Gerd Müller play for?
9 What was the nickname of William Ralph Dean?
10 Milosevic and Yorke played together for which team?
11 Which Everton striker spent time in jail in 1995?
12 Malcolm Macdonald and Jackie Milburn have been famous strikers for which club?
13 Which former England striker is known as "Bully"?
14 Which country did Mick Channon play for?
15 Wright and Bright formed a strike force for which London side?
16 Which Scottish team did Mark Hateley play for?
17 Which Dean played in Turkey before joining Nottingham Forest?
18 Which country did Joe Jordan play for?
19 Which club had Kennedy and Radford as a deadly double act?
20 Which Scottish player Gordon is known as "Juke-Box"?
21 Who was transferred from Tottenham Hotspur to Liverpool in July 2008?
22 Which club did Thierry Henry leave to join Barcelona?
23 Who scored the winning goal of the 2016 FA Cup Final?
24 Who missed AC Milan's final penalty in the 2005 Champions League Final?
25 Which country did Nuno Gomes represent in Euro 2008?
26 Which Chelsea striker caused a rumpus by throwing a coin back into the crowd?
27 Which team won the Euros in 2016 against host nation, France?
28 Which Luton striker scored a league record 10 goals in a game?
29 Who is England's top international goal scorer?
30 Who was the top goal scorer at the 2014 World Cup finals?

1 Which band released an album in 2016 called *A Head Full of Dreams*?
2 Which musical instrument does Elton John play?
3 Who was Siouxsie's group?
4 What is the home country of A-Ha?
5 Which Buddy Holly group shares its name with insects?
6 Which Bob sang with the Wailers?
7 Which part did David Essex play in the musical *Godspell*?
8 What goes with Shake and Rattle in the 50s song?
9 Who led the Pacemakers?
10 Which song title gave No. 1 hits to Jennifer Rush and Frankie Goes to Hollywood?
11 Which late zany DJ was born Maurice Cole?
12 For which sport was "Nessun Dorma" used as a theme in 1990?
13 What goes after Hillbilly Rock in the title of the Woolpackers' hit?
14 Which surname is shared by the singer Michael and bandleader Kenny?
15 What was A Boy Named according to Johnny Cash in 1969?
16 Which Heartbreak place did Elvis stay at in 1956?
17 Who was the original lead singer with the Supremes?
18 In 1978 Gerry Rafferty was in which London street?
19 How is Priscilla White better known?
20 Whose first hit was "Waterloo"?
21 Who sang on the 2016 hit "Try Everything" from the film *Zootopia*?
22 Which Sisters sang "I Don't Feel Like Dancing"?
23 Which group did Axl Rose bring back to life in 2015?
24 Who was the youngest of the Gibb brothers, who died in 1988?
25 How many Steps to Heaven did Eddie Cochran sing about?
26 Which Georgie's backing group were called the Blue Flames?
27 Which Billy, who died in 1983, was a former schoolmate of Ringo Starr?
28 Which group included brothers Ray and Dave Davies?
29 Who was Billy J. Kramer's backing group?
30 How many Tops sang "Reach Out"?

| **Answers** | **Strikers** *(see Quiz 5)* |

1 Real Madrid 2 Scotland. 3 Arsenal. 4 Blackburn Rovers. 5 West Ham Utd. 6 Lionel Messi. 7 Chelsea. 8 West Germany. 9 Dixie. 10 Aston Villa. 11 Duncan Ferguson. 12 Newcastle Utd. 13 Steve Bull. 14 England. 15 Crystal Palace. 16 Rangers. 17 Saunders. 18 Scotland. 19 Arsenal. 20 Durie. 21 Robbie Keane. 22 Arsenal. 23 Jesse Lingard. 24 Andriy Schevchenko. 25 Portugal. 26 Didier Drogba. 27 Portugal. 28 Joe Payne. 29 Bobby Charlton. 30 James Rodríguez.

1 Which actor voiced Nick the fox in 2016's *Zootopia*?
2 Who did Nick Park create as Wallace's faithful hound?
3 Who bought the Lucasfilm company in 2012?
4 Which movie has the cub Simba and his evil uncle Scar?
5 Which Robin was the voice of the genie in *Aladdin*?
6 Dan Stevens will star as which character in a 2017 Disney remake?
7 Which alter ego of Mr Bean was the voice of Zazu in *The Lion King*?
8 Which Tarzan mate did Minnie Driver provide the voice for in *Tarzan*?
9 Who featured in *Knighty Knight Bugs* in 1958?
10 In which decade was *Fantasia* released?
11 Who swung into action as *The Legend of Tarzan* in the 2016 reboot?
12 Pongo and Perdita were which types of black-and-white dog in the 1961 Disney movie?
13 Which "Book" movie featured a jazz-loving bear, Baloo?
14 In which decade was *Jungle Book* released?
15 What type of creature was Felix, an early animation character?
16 Ellen Degeneres provided whose voice in 2016's *Finding _____*?
17 Which felines were the stars of a 1970 Disney classic?
18 In which canine caper was there a "Twilight Bark"?
19 Which cartoon duck was usually dressed in blue and white?
20 In which decade was *Snow White and the Seven Dwarfs* released?
21 Which Bunny did Mel Blanc provide the voice for?
22 In which decade was *The Lion King* released?
23 Which film featured the song "The Bare Necessities"?
24 Which English actor Jeremy was the voice of Scar in *The Lion King*?
25 Which movie featured Buzz Lightyear and Mr Potato Head?
26 Which cartoon movie series has Mike Myers and Eddie Murphy as lead voices?
27 Which rare Chinese mammal becomes a kung fu expert in the 2008–2016 trilogy?
28 Who wrote the music for the 1994 version of *Thumbelina*?
29 Who voices the part of Barry in *The Bee Movie*?
30 Which 2007 animated film had a French culinary term as its title?

---

1 In which country was Kirsty Young born?
2 What is the name of the dog who lives with Garfield the cat?
3 What was the BBC2 comedy starring Steve Coogan as an ex-roadie?
4 What was the title of Joanna Lumley's desert island documentary?
5 Which famous magician, married to a McGee, passed away in 2016?
6 In which 2003–2016 TV show did Michael Cera play George Michael?
7 Who played Elizabeth in *Hawkeye*?
8 Which Clunes stars in *Nativity 3: Dude, Where's My Donkey*?
9 Who plays DC Isobel de Pauli in the crime series *Liverpool One*?
10 Which chat show hostess has the christian name Sally?
11 Which Freeman was in 2015's *Fargo*?
12 In which series is Reg a 1940s policeman?
13 Which soap features the character Toadfish?
14 Which series features Darryl and Chris as convicted armed robbers?
15 Which series starred Rudolph Walker and Jack Smethhurst?
16 Which character was Gordon Brittas's wife in *The Brittas Empire*?
17 Which children's series had a postmistress named Mrs Dingle?
18 Which soap had an omnibus edition on a Saturday evening?
19 What does the H stand for in *M*A*S*H*?
20 What nationality is Ulrika Jonsson?
21 In which sitcom does Roger Lloyd Pack portray a plumber named Jake the Klingon?
22 Which star of *Ballykissangel* appeared in *Goodnight Sweetheart*?
23 Which series features DCI Jack Meadows?
24 Which series set in Alaska features the characters Holling, Maurice and Ed?
25 On which channel would you have found *He-Man and The Masters of the Universe*?
26 Who was the titular "Gadget Man" for Channel 4 in 2015?
27 Who presented *The X Creatures* on BBC1?
28 Which US crime series features detectives Pembleton and Bayliss?
29 Which animated series features Hank, Peggy and Bobby?
30 In 2015, which famous female comedian was appointed Visiting Professor in Mental Health Nursing at the University of Surrey?

Answers | Movies: Animation *(see Quiz 7)*

1 Jason Bateman. 2 Gromit. 3 Disney. 4 The Lion King. 5 Williams. 6 The Beast. 7 Rowan Atkinson. 8 Jane. 9 Bugs Bunny. 10 1940s. 11 Alexander Skarsgård. 12 Dalmatians. 13 Jungle Book. 14 1960s. 15 Cat. 16 Dory. 17 The Aristocats. 18 101 Dalmatians. 19 Donald. 20 1930s. 21 Bugs Bunny. 22 1990s. 23 Jungle Book. 24 Irons. 25 Toy Story. 26 Shrek. 27 Panda. 28 Barry Manilow. 29 Jerry Seinfeld. 30 Ratatouille.

1 Which Brazilian star found his wife could not settle in Middlesbrough?
2 Which London club signed Slaven Bilic?
3 Which club did John Hartson leave to join Arsenal?
4 The first half-a-million-pound deal involving a British club involved which player going from Liverpool to Hamburg ?
5 Who became England's keeper in 2008 and still held the title in 2016?
6 Which club did Darren Peacock join on leaving QPR?
7 Which club has Mark Hughes joined on two separate occasions?
8 Which international fullback Denis got a free transfer from Leeds before a move to Old Trafford?
9 Which Frenchman prompted "Frog on the Tyne" headlines on his move to Newcastle?
10 Which club did Gareth Southgate leave to join Aston Villa?
11 Which Dutchman joined Arsenal for £7+ million in 1995?
12 Which fullback Warren cost Newcastle £4 million?
13 Which club did Nigel Clough join on first leaving Nottingham Forest?
14 Who moved from Argentina to Barcelona then to Napoli?
15 Which club did Duncan Ferguson leave to join Everton?
16 Which manager brought Fabrizio Ravanelli to England?
17 Who became the world's first £15 million player?
18 Which club did Niall Quinn join on leaving Manchester City ?
19 Which Spanish club signed Ronaldo for over £13 million?
20 England's first £1 million transfer involved which Trevor?
21 Which ex-World Player of the Year spurned Manchester City for AC Milan in 2008?
22 In 2011 which long-haired player went on *Strictly Come Dancing*?
23 England goalkeeper Paul Robinson was transferred to which club in 2008?
24 Which former Arsenal player joined Tottenham after three years at Blackburn?
25 In which country did Robbie Keane play in 2000–01?
26 Who was signed for a British record fee of £32.5 million in 2008?
27 From which club was Juan Sebastian Veron signed by Manchester United in 2001?
28 Which goalkeeper moved from Parma to Juventus for £32.6 million in 2001?
29 Which striker was signed by Manchester United for around £30.75 million in 2008?
30 Who did Arsenal sell Patrick Vieira to in 2005?

Answers	**Pop Pot Luck 3** *(see Quiz 10)*

1 Canada. 2 Eileen. 3 Day. 4 Air Supply. 5 Easton. 6 Frank. 7 Tennessee. 8 Yes.
9 Doop. 10 The Wonder Stuff. 11 His Master's Voice. 12 Stock, Aitken and Waterman.
13 Eternal. 14 Marc Bolan. 15 The Tardis. 16 Dippy. 17 Four. 18 Mick Hucknall.
19 Writing on the Wall. 20 Breaking. 21 Jason Orange 22 Kanye West. 23 Slade.
24 Madonna. 25 Adele. 26 Courtney Love. 27 Bono. 28 Iceland. 29 Manic Street
Preachers. 30 Bryan Ferry.

1 What is the home country of Justin Bieber?

2 Who did Dexy's Midnight Runners tell to Come On in 1982?

3 Which surname is shared by the musical star Darren and the 50s singer Doris?

4 Which Supply's first hit was "All Out of Love"?

5 Which Sheena was a Modern Girl in 1980?

6 What is the first name of the New Orleans rock star Ocean?

7 In which US state are music towns Memphis and Nashville?

8 Were the Isley Brothers really brothers?

9 Who had a 1994 No. 1 with "Doop"?

10 Who were Vic Reeves's backing band?

11 What do the letters HMV stand for?

12 Which trio of record producers are credited on the 1989 "Ferry 'Cross the Mersey"?

13 What was the Bangles' Flame like in 1989?

14 How is Mark Feld better known?

15 Which "Doctor Who" machine were the Timelords Doctorin' in 1988?

16 Right Said Fred were Deeply what in 1992?

17 How many members of Abba were there?

18 Who is lead singer with Simply Red?

19 In 1967 the Beatles were in which Lane?

20 Which Hearts did Elton John sing about in 1985?

21 Who was missing from Take That when the band toured in 2015?

22 Which rapper had a 2007 hit with "Stronger"?

23 Which 1970s glam rock band included Noddy Holder and Dave Hill?

24 Which singer released *Rebel Heart* in 2015?

25 Levi Stubbs was the lead singer of which top Motown group?

26 Which American rock singer married Kurt Cobain?

27 How is Paul David Hewson better known?

28 Which country does Bjork come from?

29 Who wrote and sang Wales' Euros 2016 campaign anthem?

30 Who was the lead singer of Roxy Music?

1 In which city is the 2011 Woody Allen *Midnight in _____* filmed?
2 In 2016, which *Mamma Mia!* supergroup reformed to open a restaurant?
3 Gene Autry was usually billed as a singing what?
4 Which Newman/Redford movie featured "Raindrops Keep Falling on My Head"?
5 John Barry is linked with the music for films about which celebrated secret agent?
6 "Colours of the Wind" was from which movie about a native North American heroine?
7 "When You Wish upon a Star" was from which film about a puppet?
8 Which Mrs was a character and the theme song in *The Graduate*?
9 "Can You Feel the Love Tonight" came from which Disney movie?
10 "Whole New World" was heard in which Disney hit about a genie?
11 "Bright Eyes" from *Watership Down* was about which animals?
12 Which "Top" 80s movie had the hit song "Take My Breath Away"?
13 "Up Where We Belong" was used in which movie with Richard Gere and Debra Winger?
14 Which French-Canadian sang the theme from *Titanic*?
15 Who sang "You Must Love Me" from *Evita*?
16 Which "Cowboy" movie provided the hit "Everybody's Talkin'" for Nilsson?
17 Which Oscar-winner featured "My Heart Will Go On"?
18 Who wrote the music for *Evita*?
19 Which *Spectre* song did Sam Smith win a 2016 Best Song Oscar?
20 Which Shirley sang the title song for the 007 movie *Goldfinger*?
21 What type of "River" was the theme from *Breakfast at Tiffany's*?
22 Scott Joplin's music for *The Sting* is played on which musical instrument?
23 Which "Melody", a hit for the Righteous Brothers, featured in *Ghost*?
24 How is composer and Oscar-winner Hoagland Howard Carmichael better known?
25 Which BRIT school singer sang 2012 *Skyfall's* theme?
26 Which Hugh Grant/Julia Roberts movie set in London featured "She"?
27 Who first sang "Somewhere over the Rainbow"?
28 What is the theme song of *Quantum of Solace*?
29 Who sings "Meet Me in St Louis" in the 1944 film of the same name?
30 Which animated film features the song "Whistle While You Work"?

Answers | **TV Pot Luck 3** *(see Quiz 12)*

1 Kerry Katona. 2 Shilpa Shetty. 3 Chris Evans. 4 Anderson. 5 Boston. 6 Finlay. 7 Absolutely Fabulous. 8 The Golden Girls. 9 And Mother Makes Five. 10 The Brittas Empire. 11 TW Time Machine. 12 Matthew Willows. 13 Eric Bana. 14 KYTV. 15 Cricket. 16 Melbourne. 17 Jennifer Ehle. 18 Steve Coogan. 19 Common as Muck. 20 Will. 21 On an Oil Rig. 22 Cadfael. 23 The Muppet Show. 24 Saturday. 25 Blackadder The Third. 26 Tim Spall. 27 Cardiac Arrest. 28 Chigley. 29 Cinders. 30 Open All Hours.

1 Which Atomic Kitten won *I'm a Celebrity: Get Me Out of Here!* in 2004?
2 Who was the winner of the controversial *Celebrity Big Brother* series in 2007?
3 Who was the presenter of *Don't Forget Your Toothbrush*?
4 Which Clive chaired *Whose Line is It Anyway*?
5 In which US city did *Cheers* take place?
6 Which doctor set aside his Casebook in the 90s revival of the series?
7 In 2016, Patsy and Eddy got a film version of which hit TV show?
8 Which American sitcom, set in Miami, was made into a British version *Brighton Belles*?
9 What was the sequel from *And Mother Makes Three*?
10 In which series were Gavin and Tim gay lovers?
11 Which series highlights technological milestones from *Tomorrow's World*?
12 Who was Henry's son in *Home to Roost*?
13 Who starred opposite Ricky Gervais in 2016's *Special Correspondents*?
14 What was the name of the spoof TV station in the series starring Angus Deayton?
15 Which sport was featured in the sitcom *Outside Edge*?
16 In *Neighbours*, Erinsborough is a suburb of which city?
17 Who played Elizabeth Bennet in *Pride and Prejudice*?
18 Who starred as the host of *Scissored Isle* in 2016?
19 What was the name of the series about dustmen starring Edward Woodward and Roy Hudd?
20 What is Commander Riker's christian name in *Star Trek: The Next Generation*?
21 Where is the drama series *Roughnecks* set?
22 In which series does Michael Culver play Prior Robert and Sean Pertwee play Hugh Beringer?
23 Which comedy series featured *The Veterinarians Hospital*, a place for old jokes?
24 On which night does *Noel's House Party* take place?
25 What was the full title of the comedy starring Rowan Atkinson set in Regency times?
26 Who played Barry the Brummie in *Auf Weidersehen Pet*?
27 Which medical series featured the characters Dr Andrew Collin and Dr Rajah?
28 What is the name of the hamlet near *Camberwick Green*?
29 In *Roughnecks* what is the nickname of the cook played by Ricky Tomlinson?
30 Which series, in 2013, got a sequel called *Still Open All Hours*?

Answers	**Music on Film** *(see Quiz 11)*

1 Paris. 2 Abba. 3 Cowboy. 4 Butch Cassidy and the Sundance Kid. 5 James Bond. 6 Pocahontas. 7 Pinocchio. 8 Robinson. 9 The Lion King. 10 Aladdin. 11 Rabbits. 12 Top Gun. 13 An Officer and a Gentleman. 14 Celine Dion. 15 Madonna. 16 Midnight Cowboy. 17 Titanic. 18 Andrew Lloyd Webber. 19 Philadelphia. 20 Bassey. 21 "Moon River". 22 Piano. 23 "Unchained Melody". 24 Hoagy Carmichael. 25 Jones. 26 Notting Hill. 27 Judy Garland. 28 "Another Way to Die". 29 Judy Garland. 30 Snow White and the Seven Dwarfs.

Quiz 13 Football: Three Lions

Answers – page 24

1 Which club was Steve Stone with when he made his international debut?
2 Which player opened England's account in Euro 2016?
3 Who is England's all-time record goalscorer?
4 Which 20-year-old winger scored a wonder goal for England in Brazil in 1984?
5 Which forward Peter had an England career stretching from 1986 to 1996?
6 Terry Butcher and Paul Mariner were colleagues at which club?
7 Who was England's first-choice goalkeeper in the 1990 World Cup in Italy?
8 What is the first name of 80s striker Blissett?
9 Who was known as "The Wizard of the Dribble"?
10 Who burst into tears after the World Cup semi-final defeat in 1990?
11 Which captain married one of the Beverley Sisters?
12 What forename was shared by Francis and Brooking?
13 Which club did Ronnie Clayton play for?
14 Which club was Bobby Moore with when he became England captain?
15 Which Liverpool fullback Rob made his international debut while still 20?
16 Which David made his debut against Moldova?
17 Which Kenny made 86 appearances at fullback?
18 Which striker hit five goals in one game in the 70s?
19 Which club was Steve Coppell with during his international career?
20 What forename links Bull and McManaman?
21 Whose back pass became an own goal when England lost 2–0 to Croatia in 2007?
22 Who were England's first opponents at the new Wembley Stadium?
23 What was the final score in England's last qualifying match for Euro 2008?
24 Which Caribbean team did England play in the summers of 2006 and 2008?
25 Who scored England's last goal of the 2006 World Cup competition?
26 Who succeeded Steve McClaren as England manager?
27 Who scored a hat-trick against Croatia in 2008?
28 Against whom did David Beckham make his 100th international appearance?
29 Against which team did England play their first international?
30 When did England first appear in a World Cup finals?

Answers	Pop Pot Luck 4 *(see Quiz 14)*

1 Cilla Black. 2 Debbie Harry. 3 Mae. 4 Roxy Music. 5 Shapiro. 6 Paul Anka. 7 Cockney Rebel. 8 Neil Diamond. 9 Australia. 10 Guitar. 11 Joseph. 12 k. d. 13 Greece. 14 Turner. 15 Yates. 16 Philadelphia. 17 Softly. 18 Starr. 19 Miss Molly. 20 Abbey Road. 21 X-Factor. 22 Madonna. 23 Tuesday. 24 Jackie Trent and Tony Hatch. 25 Mathis. 26 Marilyn Manson. 27 Dusty Springfield. 28 California. 29 The Sex Pistols. 30 Five.

1 Which Liverpool lady had a No. 1 with "Anyone Who Had a Heart" in 1963 and died in 2015?

2 Who was lead singer with Blondie?

3 Which Vanessa's album was called *The Violin Player*?

4 Which Music group was Bryan Ferry lead singer with?

5 Which Helen was Walking Back to Happiness in 1961?

6 Whose first hit was "Diana" in 1957?

7 Who were Steve Harley's backing group?

8 How is Noah Kaminsky better known?

9 What is the home country of 5 Seconds of Summer?

10 Which musical instrument does Queen's Brian May play?

11 Which character with a Technicolor Dreamcoat did Jason Donovan play on the London stage?

12 What are the initials of the Canadian Ms Lang?

13 Which country is Lordi from?

14 Which Tina's life story was in the film *What's Love Got to Do with It?*?

15 Which Paula was the daughter of Peaches, who died in 2015?

16 Which US city is mentioned with Freedom in a hit from 1975?

17 How were the Fugees Killing Me in 1996?

18 Which surname is shared by Edwin and Ringo?

19 Who did Little Richard say Good Golly to back in 1958?

20 Which Road famous for its recording studios is the title of a Beatles album?

21 Which show did Louisa Johnson win in 2016?

22 Which No. 1 singer/actress/dancer divorcd Guy Ritchie in 2008?

23 Which Ruby gave Melanie a 70s hit?

24 Which singer/songwriters were nicknamed Mr and Mrs Music?

25 Which Johnny joined Deneice Williams on "Too Much Too Little Too Late"?

26 Which male vocalist shared his name with late actress Miss Monroe?

27 Who had an album called Everything Comes Up Dusty?

28 Which US state were the Mamas and Papas Dreamin' of in 1966?

29 Which punk band was Malcolm McLaren manager of in the 70s?

30 How many members of the Hollies were there?

Answers	**Football: Three Lions** *(see Quiz 13)*

1 Nottingham Forest. 2 Eric Dier. 3 Bobby Charlton. 4 John Barnes. 5 Beardsley. 6 Ipswich Town. 7 Peter Shilton. 8 Luther. 9 Stanley Matthews. 10 Paul Gascoigne. 11 Billy Wright. 12 Trevor. 13 Blackburn Rovers. 14 West Ham Utd. 15 Jones. 16 Beckham. 17 Sansom. 18 Malcolm Macdonald. 19 Manchester Utd. 20 Steve. 21 Gary Neville. 22 Brazil. 23 England 2, Croatia 3. 24 Trinidad and Tobago. 25 David Beckham. 26 Fabio Capello. 27 Theo Walcott. 28 France. 29 Scotland. 30 1950.

1 In which European country was he born?
2 What was he "Pumping" in the 1977 documentary film about himself?
3 What was the name of "the Barbarian" he played in 1982?
4 Which 2015 movie gave him the line "I'll be back" for the last time (?).
5 What colour went before "Sonja" in his 1985 movie?
6 Which Danny was his co-star in *Twins*?
7 What type of "Recall" was the 2014 remake of his 1990 movie?
8 In 1990 which Republican President made him chairman of the Council on Physical Fitness?
9 In which Californian city was *The Terminator* set?
10 Which muscleman relative of Jayne Mansfield did he play in the TV biopic?
11 What was *Conan the Destroyer* the sequel to?
12 Who starred opposite him in 2013's *Escape Plan*?
13 Which journalist Ms Shriver divorced him?
14 Which James, later famous for *Avatar*, directed *The Terminator*?
15 What very unmasculine condition was he in *Junior*?
16 In weightlifting circles he was billed as what type of Austrian tree?
17 Which *Terminator* film was subtitled "Judgment Day"?
18 What sort of "Lies" did he make for James Cameron in 1994?
19 What sort of "Action Hero" was he in 1993?
20 In which decade was he born?
21 What sort of "Cop" was he in 1990?
22 In *True Lies* Schwarzenegger is a salesman of what?
23 What was the name of his 2014 movie, directed by David Ayer?
24 Which "Planet" restaurant chain did he back?
25 Who was Schwarzenegger's male co-star in *Stay Hungry*?
26 To which public office did Arnie win election in 2003?
27 Which country has a football stadium named in Arnold Schwarzenegger's honour?
28 Can you name the "fighting" occupation Arnie took up in 1965?
29 What competition did Arnie win for a record seventh time in 1980?
30 In which 2014 film did he return as Trench Mauser?

---

1 On which channel will you find *Britain's Got Talent*?
2 In what institution was *Scrubs* set?
3 Who was Jennifer Paterson's colleague on *Two Fat Ladies*?
4 Which drama series was set on the oil rig Osprey Explorer?
5 Which series featured Mr Clamp the greengrocer and Mr Antonio the ice cream seller?
6 Which children's author became a judge on *Britain's Got Talent* in 2012?
7 Who last role was as a supermarket manager in *Tripper's Day*?
8 In which children's series where the characters Mickey Murphy the Baker and PC McGary?
9 Which character did Ralph Waite portray in *The Waltons*?
10 Which drama features Claude Jeremiah Greengrass?
11 Who in *EastEnders* are Beppe, Bruno and Gianni?
12 What is *Jimmy's*?
13 On which children's programme did the characters Hartley Hare and Pig appear?
14 On which programme did Susan Stranks take over from Jenny Handley?
15 On which variety show was *Name That Tune* a feature?
16 Who had an elephant called Bimbo?
17 Director Tom Harper bought which family of little people to the small screen in 2011?
18 What were Rita Garnett's parents called?
19 Who is the American female commentator on BBC's coverage of Wimbledon?
20 Which showjumping commentator's first name was Dorien?
21 Which company produces *Neighbours*?
22 Which sport did Ron Pickering commentate on?
23 What was the drama series about a family in wartime Liverpool?
24 Which ITV sports programme featured Jimmy Hill?
25 Which 80s drama centred on Liverpudlian Yosser Hughes?
26 Which animals did Barbara Woodhouse usually appear with?
27 What is Charlie Fairhead's job at Holby City Hospital?
28 What was James's wife called in *All Creatures Great and Small*?
29 What is Lance Corporal Jones's occupation in *Dad's Army*?
30 Which was Britain's first pop TV show?

Answers | **Movies: Arnold Schwarzenegger** *(see Quiz 15)*

1 Austria. 2 Iron. 3 Conan. 4 The Terminator. 5 Red. 6 DeVito. 7 Total. 8 George Bush. 9 Los Angeles. 10 Her husband. 11 Conan the Barbarian. 12 Sly Stallone. 13 Maria. 14 Cameron. 15 Pregnant. 16 Austrian Oak. 17 Terminator 2. 18 True Lies. 19 "The Last". 20 1940s. 21 Kindergarten. 22 Computers. 23 Sabotage. 24 Planet Hollywood. 25 Jeff Bridges. 26 Governor of California. 27 Austria. 28 He joined the Austrian army. 29 Mr Olympia. 30 The Expendables.

1 Which team won the 2015 English Twenty20 Championship?
2 Which Durham fast bowler was dropped for the 2nd Test in New Zealand in 2008?
3 Who captained England throughout 2016?
4 Who was New Zealand's captain on their 2008 tour of England?
5 Which team won the inaugural Indian Premier League?
6 Which English wicket keeper shares his name with a breed of dog?
7 The Nursery End, the Pavilion End and St John's Road are all linked with which ground?
8 Which former England batsman Derek was known as "Rags"?
9 Which team won the County Championship in 1994 and 1995?
10 Robin Smith was an international for which country?
11 How many bails are there on a set of wickets?
12 Which county does Geoff Boycott come from?
13 What was the specialist position of Australia's Rodney Marsh?
14 Trent Bridge is in which English city?
15 How many runs are scored in a maiden over?
16 Which country was captained by Kapil Dev?
17 What were the initials of legendary Victorian cricketer Dr Grace?
18 Which country side was captained by Allan Lamb?
19 In the 1990s, which Alec opened and kept wicket for England?
20 In scoring, what does c & b stand for?
21 Was David Gower a left- or right-handed batsman?
22 Which English county did West Indies skipper Clive Lloyd play for?
23 On which day of the week were John Player's League games played?
24 How many valid deliveries are sent down in a Test cricket over?
25 Which cricket commentator on radio was known as "Johnners"?
26 What does the initial T stand for in I. T. Botham's name?
27 In which country do Sheffield Shield games take place?
28 What does the batsman score for a shot that sends the ball over the boundary without touching the ground?
29 England skippers Brearley and Gatting have both captained which county?
30 Who was known as "Lord Ted"?

Answers | **Football Pot Luck 1** *(see Quiz 18)*

1 Derby County. 2 Sheffield. 3 Arsenal. 4 United. 5 Scotland. 6 Stoke City. 7 Hungary. 8 Crystal Palace. 9 Leeds Utd. 10 Blue and white. 11 Naylor. 12 The Villains. 13 Eric Cantona. 14 Barcelona. 15 Millwall. 16 Graeme Souness. 17 Weah. 18 Denmark. 19 Jason. 20 Dele Alli. 21 Chelsea. 22 Glasgow. 23 Dalglish. 24 Bright. 25 Birmingham City. 26 Everton. 27 Italy. 28 Hampden Park. 29 Walkers. 30 Harry Kane.

1 Whose home, until May 1997, was the Baseball Ground?
2 Which city has a Wednesday and a United?
3 Rioch, Graham and Mee have all managed which club?
4 What second name is shared by Newcastle and Hartlepool?
5 Which country does diminutive striker John Spencer play for?
6 Which team are known as the Potters?
7 Which country do Ferencvaros come from?
8 With which football club did Ian Wright make his League debut?
9 Which club did Gordon Strachan join on leaving Manchester Utd?
10 What are the main colours on QPR's home shirts?
11 Which Tony was Port Vale's top League scorer in 1995–96?
12 What is Aston Villa's nickname?
13 Which overseas player was voted Footballer of the Year in 1996?
14 Bobby Robson became boss of which Spanish giants in 1996?
15 Which team does Danny Baker support?
16 Which Scotsman managed Galatasaray in 1995?
17 Which George of AC Milan was European Footballer of the Year in 1996?
18 Which country does Mikkel Beck play for?
19 What forename is shared by defenders Dodd and McAteer?
20 Which player was PFA Young Player of the Year in 2016?
21 Which club won the 2015 premier league championship?
22 Which Scottish city has had two UEFA Cup runners-up in the 21st century?
23 Which Kenny of Liverpool won the Footballer of the Year award in 1983?
24 Which Mark was Sheffield Wednesday's top League scorer in 1994–95?
25 Which team does Jasper Carrott support?
26 Fullback Gary Stevens played three FA Cup Finals for which club?
27 Which country staged the World Cup finals when "Nessun Dorma" became an anthem?
28 What is Scotland's national football stadium called?
29 What make of crisps has Gary Lineker advertised?
30 Which player won the PFA Young Player of the Year in 2015?

Answers	Cricket Pot Luck 1 *(see Quiz 17)*

1 Lancashire. 2 Steve Harmison. 3 Alastair Cook. 4 Daniel Vettori. 5 Rajasthan Royals. 6 Jack Russell. 7 Lord's. 8 Randall. 9 Warwickshire. 10 England. 11 Two. 12 Yorkshire. 13 Wicket keeper. 14 Nottingham. 15 None. 16 India. 17 W. G. 18 Northamptonshire. 19 Stewart. 20 Caught and bowled. 21 Left. 22 Lancashire. 23 Sunday. 24 Six. 25 Brian Johnson. 26 Terence. 27 Australia. 28 Six. 29 Middlesex. 30 Ted Dexter.

1 What did Bill Haley and the Comets do after Shake and Rattle?
2 What rhymes with Cupid on the title of the Connie Francis No. 1?
3 Where did Fats Domino find his thrill in 1956?
4 Which Eddie had the Summertime Blues?
5 According to the Everly Brothers in 1959 All I Have to Do is what?
6 What did Jerry Lee Lewis sing about Great Balls of in 1958?
7 What Gets in Your Eyes according to the Platters?
8 Which musical instrument did Russ Conway play?
9 What colour pink went with Apple Blossom White according to Perez Prado and Eddie Calvert in 1955?
10 Which Doris said "Whatever will be, will be" in 1956?
11 What were Guy Mitchell and Tommy Steele each singing for the first month of 1957 at the top of the charts?
12 Which Perry hit the top with "Don't Let the Stars Get in Your Eyes"?
13 How many Everly Brothers were there?
14 Which Adam hit the No. 1 spot with "What Do You Want"?
15 Which Craig was Only Sixteen in 1959?
16 Which Dickie's special day was possibly February 14?
17 Which British Frankie was behind the Green Door and in the Garden of Eden in the 50s?
18 What was the first name of the vocalist Mr Twitty?
19 In Eddie Cochran's "Three Steps to Heaven" at which step does she "fall in love with you"?
20 How was the Richard described who sang "Long Tall Sally" and "Lucille"?
21 What part of his anatomy gave Elvis Presley one of his nicknames?
22 Which Buddy was backed by the Crickets?
23 Of what was Bing Crosby dreaming in his famous hit?
24 In what sort of accident did Buddy Holly die?
25 Which Frank issued the 1958 US No. 1 album *Come Fly with Me*?
26 When was the inaugural Eurovision Song Contest held?
27 Who had a hit in 1952 with "(How Much is) That Doggie in the Window"?
28 Mitch Miller had a hit in 1955 with a recording of which American folk song?
29 What was the chart hit from the 1954 version of *The Threepenny Opera*?
30 What was Elvis Presley's first US No. 1?

Answers	Movies Pot Luck 1 *(see Quiz 20)*

1 Hollywood. 2 Shakespeare. 3 Emma. 4 Junior. 5 Humphrey Bogart. 6 Madonna. 7 1970s. 8 Anthony Hopkins. 9 Jack Nicholson. 10 1960s. 11 Demi Moore. 12 Woody Allen. 13 USSR – Latvia. 14 Sweden. 15 USSR. 16 1990s. 17 Joanne Woodward. 18 Terrestrial. 19 Barbara Bach. 20 13. 21 Hope. 22 George. 23 Dietrich. 24 Fame. 25 Cates. 26 Terminator. 27 The Were-Rabbit. 28 Danes. 29 Blondie. 30 Indecent.

Quiz 20 Movies Pot Luck 1

Answers – page 29

1 Which film centre is also known as Tinseltown?

2 Which writer "wrote" 2015's "Scottish play" starring Michael Fassbender?

3 In which movie based on a Jane Austen novel did Gwyneth Paltrow play Emma Woodhouse?

4 What follows the names of Harry Connick and Robert Downey?

5 Who played the lead role in *The African Queen* after David Niven turned it down?

6 Which singer directed 2011's *W.E*?

7 In which decade was *Star Wars* first released?

8 Who played Odin in 2011's *Thor*?

9 Who won the Best Actor Oscar for *One Flew over the Cuckoo's Nest*?

10 In which decade was *Goldfinger* released?

11 How is Demetria Guynes better known?

12 Who directed 2016's *Cafe Society*?

13 From which country did Mikhail Barishnikov defect to the USA?

14 In which country was Britt Ekland born?

15 In which eastern bloc country was the movie *Reds* set?

16 In which decade was *Mission: Impossible* released?

17 Who was Paul Newman's wife whom he directed in *Rachel, Rachel*?

18 What did T stand for in *E.T.*?

19 How is former Bond girl, Mrs Ringo Starr, Barbara Goldbach better known?

20 Which Apollo mission was the subject of a movie starring Tom Hanks?

21 Which comedian Bob has hosted the Oscars ceremony over 20 times?

22 Rupert Everett starred in "The Madness of" which king?

23 Burt Bacharach was a former accompanist for which actress Marlene?

24 Which movie did the song "Fame" come from?

25 Which Phoebe of TV mini-series *Lace* married actor Kevin Kline?

26 *The Rise of the Machines* was the subtitle of which Schwarzenegger movie series?

27 What creature's curse did Wallace and Gromit encounter in 2005?

28 Which Claire starred in 2010's *Temple Grandin*?

29 Who sang "Call Me" in *America Gigolo*?

30 Which word goes before "Proposal" in a Demi Moore movie title?

Answers | Pop: The 1950s *(see Quiz 19)*

1 Roll. 2 Stupid. 3 Blueberry Hill. 4 Cochran. 5 Dream. 6 Fire. 7 Smoke. 8 Piano. 9 Cherry. 10 Day. 11 The Blues. 12 Como. 13 Two. 14 Faith. 15 Douglas. 16 Valentine. 17 Vaughan. 18 Conway. 19 Step Two. 20 Little. 21 His pelvis. 22 Holly. 23 White Christmas. 24 Plane crash. 25 Sinatra. 26 1956. 27 Patti Page. 28 The Yellow Rose of Texas. 29 Mack the Knife. 30 Heartbreak Hotel.

1 In 2009, which TV show began, *Horrible* _____?
2 Which cable/satellite channel has the logo of a mouse's head?
3 Which cartoon character yells "Yab-a-dab-a-doo"?
4 What kind of puppet animal is *Basil Brush*?
5 Herman was the Frankenstein's monster-like father of which ghoulish family?
6 What is the real-life relationship between the children's comedy duo, *The Krankies*?
7 Which cartoon animal superhero has a pal called Spotty Man?
8 Who is Yogi Bear's smaller than the average bear pal?
9 Where would you find Ermintrude the cow and a rabbit called Dylan?
10 Which series featured International Rescue?
11 What is the name of the family *Paddington Bear* lives with?
12 What colour are Rupert Bear's checked trousers?
13 What is the symbol used by *Blue Peter*?
14 In *The Muppets*, what kind of animal is Fozzie?
15 How many human pals does *Scooby Doo* have?
16 What was the numberplate on *Postman Pat's* van?
17 Who is Rod Hull's temperamental puppet friend?
18 What is the name of Keith Harris's duck friend who wishes he could fly?
19 What programme would you have been watching if "It's Friday ... It's five o'clock ... and it's ..."?
20 In *Batman*, which villain left riddles at the scenes of his crimes?
21 Which newspaper does Superman's alter ego Clark Kent write for?
22 What was the name of the Lone Ranger's horse?
23 What was Bagpuss?
24 What letter did Zorro cut with his sword at the beginning of each episode of his series?
25 What was the name of Fred Flinstone's pet dinosaur?
26 Name the *Flowerpot Men*.
27 Who is Sooty's canine sidekick?
28 What sort of creatures were *Pinky and Perky*?
29 Gomez and Mortitia are the husband and wife of which creepy TV family?
30 What animal is Peppa?

1 What is the last word in Hamilton's team name?
2 What colour are Arsenal's home shorts?
3 Which country has John Aldridge played for?
4 Who plays at home at Old Trafford?
5 Which Anthony was Man Utds' top League scorer in 2014-15?
6 What forename is shared by Scales and Barnes who played together at Liverpool?
7 Which Billy of Celtic was Scottish Footballer of the Year in 1965?
8 With which club did Nigel Winterburn make his League debut?
9 Which club did Charlie Nicholas leave to join Arsenal?
10 Doug Ellis has been chairman of which club?
11 What is Barnet's nickname?
12 Which country has Mark Bowen played for?
13 Garry Parker and Steve Claridge scored 1996 play-off goals for which team?
14 Which manager took Manchester Utd to the 2016 FA Cup title?
15 Which Hazard was PFA Player of the Year in 2014?
16 Which country does Edgar Davids play for?
17 Which 40-year-old player manager was on show for Middlesbrough?
18 Who was Blackburn's 90s cash benefactor?
19 Sharp was on the shirts of which Premiership winners?
20 Who replaced Jack Charlton as manager of the Republic of Ireland?
21 Which club had the same manager for the first 15 seasons of the Premiership?
22 Which north Wales club was relegated from the Football League in 2008?
23 Which Portuguese club plays at the Stadium of Light?
24 What colour are Belgium's home shirts?
25 Football character "Billy the Flash" appeared in which magazine?
26 Which London club did Hans Segers play for?
27 Where do Bury play?
28 What country did Liverpool's Bjornbye play for?
29 Which Tony was West Ham's top League scorer in 1994–95?
30 Which Rodney won a championship medal with Leeds in the 1990s?

1 Who was the drummer with the Dave Clark Five?
2 Which small Mod group were all under five foot six tall?
3 Who completed the line-up of Dave Dee, Dozy, Beaky and Mick?
4 In 1965 the Kinks sang about a Dedicated Follower of what?
5 What did Marvin Gaye Hear It Through in 1969?
6 What did the Beatles Want to Hold on their first US No. 1?
7 Which Corner had Andy Fairweather-Low as lead singer?
8 Which Little girl sang "The Locomotion" in 1962?
9 Which head of the Diddymen shed Tears in 1965?
10 What is Over according to the Seekers in 1965?
11 Which Engelbert Humperdinck song's second line is "Let me go"?
12 Which 60s dance was popularized by Chubby Checker?
13 Which country were the Bachelors from?
14 What sort of Vibrations did the Beach Boys have in 1966?
15 Which Moody Blues member later joined Wings?
16 What follows "Ob-La-Di" in the Marmalade No. 1?
17 Which lover of Romeo was a hit for the Four Pennies?
18 In 1960 what was the profession of Lonnie Donegan's dad?
19 Which Pretty pink bird was a No. 1 for Manfred Mann?
20 How old was the Sweet person Neil Sedaka wished Happy Birthday to in 1961?
21 Who came between Peter and Mary in the trio?
22 With what song did Sandie Shaw win the 1967 Eurovision Song Contest?
23 Where should you wear a flower if going to San Francisco?
24 Why did Jimi Hendrix play his Fender Stratocaster upside down?
25 Which Des sang about Careless Hands in 1967?
26 Who had a hit in 1960 with "Itsy Bitsy Teenie Weenie Yellow Polka Dot Bikini"?
27 Which 1967 chart hit became the signature song of Aretha Franklin?
28 Which fictional characters had a chart hit in 1969 with "Sugar Sugar"?
29 Which Beatles chart hit was created by Paul McCartney as a "song for Ringo"?
30 Who sang lead vocals on "Baby Love"?

Answers | Movies Pot Luck 2 *(see Quiz 24)*

1 India. 2 Thompson. 3 3 hours. 4 Mike Newell. 5 The Boxer. 6 Marlon Brando. 7 1930s. 8 Cage. 9 Boxing. 10 Julia Roberts. 11 The Godfather. 12 Oldman. 13 Quentin. 14 Brad Pitt. 15 Sister. 16 Curtis. 17 Mitty. 18 Jaws. 19 Winona. 20 Reynolds. 21 Stone. 22 1980s. 23 Harlow. 24 Green. 25 Elton John. 26 2007. 27 Mr Freeze. 28 Cliffhanger. 29 Robin Williams. 30 331/2

1 Which Asian country is home to 'Bollywood'?
2 Which Emma starred in 2013's *Saving Mr Banks?*
3 To the nearest hour, how long does *Titanic* last?
4 Who directed *Four Weddings and a Funeral?*
5 In which 1997 movie did Daniel Day Lewis play a boxer?
6 Who won the Best Actor Oscar for *On the Waterfront?*
7 In which decade of the 20th century was Joan Collins born?
8 Which Nicolas starred in *2010's Kick Ass?*
9 Is *Raging Bull* about American football, boxing or bull-fighting?
10 *My Best Friend's Wedding* and *Sleeping with the Enemy* featured which actress?
11 The character Sonny Corleone was in which sequence of movies?
12 *Air Force One* starred which Gary?
13 What is the first name of the *Pulp Fiction* director?
14 Which actor links *Se7en, Sleepers* and *Thelma and Louise?*
15 What relation is Shirley MacLaine to Warren Beatty?
16 Which Tony starred in *Some Like It Hot?*
17 'The Secret Life of' which Walter formed a movie title?
18 Which early Spielberg blockbuster featured a shark?
19 Which Ms Ryder had her big break in *Beetlejuice?*
20 Which 70s actor Burt was *Cosmopolitan's* first male nude centrefold?
21 Which Oliver won the Best Director Oscar for *Born on the Fourth of July?*
22 In which decade was *Batman* with Michael Keaton released?
23 Which famous Jean tested for the role of Scarlett O'Hara?
24 Which colour completes the film title, *How ____ Was My Valley?*
25 Which pop singer wrote the music for Disney's *The Lion King?*
26 In which year was *The Simpsons Movie* released?
27 Which villain did Arnold Schwarzenegger play in *Batman & Robin?*
28 What name is given to a situation in film where a suspense scene is temporarily left unresolved?
29 Which *Patch Adams* actor died in 2014?
30 What number completes the title, Naked Gun...: The Final Insult?

---

1 Which newsreader left BBC Breakfast in 2016 after 15 years?
2 Which *Newsnight* interviewer later asked the questions on *University Challenge*?
3 Who presented *TV Eye*?
4 What time does *BBC's Breakfast Show* start?
5 Which ex-newsreader presented *The Clothes Show*?
6 Which Wright presented ITV's 2014 Football World Cup Final?
7 What nationality is Clive James?
8 Who presented *Crime Beat*?
9 What is BBC2's evening news programme called?
10 Which late presenter hosted *Whicker's World*?
11 Which Kate was an international correspondent for BBC television?
12 Which Dimbleby presented *Question Time*?
13 Which Brian had a Sunday-lunchtime political programme?
14 In the US, which Jimmy is the presenter of *The Tonight Show*?
15 Who swore while being interviewed by Bill Grundy?
16 Which is *The Shopping Channel*?
17 Who was the Chief Executive of the newly created *TV-AM*?
18 On which sport is John McCrillick most famously known?
19 Which royal event in 1953 had the largest television audience?
20 Which organization researched ITV's viewing figures?
21 What was the subject of *Triumph of The Nerds*?
22 What was C4's series on addictive pleasures?
23 Who presented BBC2's *Vintner's Tales*?
24 Who presented *Quest for the Lost Civilisation*?
25 What was the subject of the documentary series *Absolute Truth*?
26 Who was the subject of the documentary *A Very Singular Man*?
27 Which Docu-soap featured yachtswoman Tracy Edwards?
28 Who circumnavigated the globe in 79 days and 7 hours?
29 What was the first global TV programme?
30 What was the first British fly-on-the-wall documentary series?

1 Who plays at home at Portman Road?

2 What colour are Brazil's home shorts?

3 Little, Atkinson and Taylor have all managed which club?

4 What second name is shared by Oldham and Charlton?

5 Which country did Graeme Le Saux play for?

6 Which colour goes with claret in Bradford's home shirts?

7 Which country do Sampdoria come from?

8 With which club did Gary Flitcroft make his League debut?

9 Which club did Julian Dicks join on leaving Liverpool?

10 What colour are the stripes on Sheffield Utd's home shirts?

11 Which Daniel was QPR's top League scorer in 1995–96?

12 Which club has the nicknames Tykes, Reds and Colliers?

13 Which player won the Footballer of the Year award in 2015?

14 Which team does US comedian Will Ferrell support?

15 Tony Parkes has been caretaker manager of which club?

16 Which country has Carlos Valderrama played for?

17 Who became known as "El Tel" when he went abroad as a manager?

18 Which club did Gianfranco Zola leave to join Chelsea?

19 Which David danced magically on Dancing on Ice in 2008?

20 Which Kevin of Ipswich was PFA Young Player of the Year in 1974?

21 Who was Chelsea manager when they lost the 2008 Champions League Final?

22 Who scored a hat-trick for Northern Ireland when they beat Spain 3–2 in 2006?

23 What is the colour of Italy's home shirts?

24 Which team does June Whitfield support?

25 Which Ian of Liverpool won the Footballer of the Year award in 1984?

26 Jeremy Goss and Ruel Fox were teammates at which club?

27 In which decade did Blackburn first play European soccer?

28 Which Scottish United does Lorraine Kelly support?

29 Which country does Branco play for?

30 Who brought a libel case against a paper involving his ex-wife Danielle?

1 Which People were with the "YMCA" in 1979?
2 Who was the lead singer with Wings?
3 Which seasonal Nights did John Travolta and Olivia Newton-John sing about?
4 Which country did the Eurovision winner Dana come from?
5 Who had a single called "Killer Queen"?
6 Who were Stayin' Alive?
7 Which birds of prey stayed at the Hotel California?
8 Which glam group had an album called *Sweet Fanny Adams*?
9 Who had hits with "Close to You" and "We've Only Just Begun"?
10 What colour ribbons did Dawn tie round the Old Oak Tree?
11 Which Ms Knight was backed by the Pips?
12 Which Roberta was "Killing Me Softly with His Song"?
13 Which Gary was "Leader of the Gang"?
14 Whose single and album *Bridge Over Troubled Water* went to No. 1?
15 Which former Supreme was Still Waiting in 1971?
16 What did the New Seekers say They'd Like to Teach the World to do in 1972?
17 What did Tyrannosaurus Rex change their name to?
18 Which Tubular sounds were a hit for Mike Oldfield?
19 What type of Loaf had a Bat Out of Hell?
20 Which Zeppelin had a string of No. 1 albums during the 70s?
21 What Big Yellow thing did Joni Mitchell sing about in 1970?
22 Which 1970s TV comedy trio had hits with "Wild Thing" and "Funky Gibbon"?
23 Benny Andersson was a Eurovision Song Contest winner with which group?
24 How many times is Annie named in John Denver's 1974 hit "Annie's Song"?
25 In which year did Jim Morrison die?
26 Who had a hit in 1976 with "Play That Funky Music"?
27 To whom did Don McLean dedicate his 1971 hit "American Pie"?
28 Who had a hit with "Rhinestone Cowboy" in 1975?
29 Who asked "Da Ya Think I'm Sexy" in 1978?
30 Who duetted with Elton John on "Don't Go Breaking My Heart"?

Answers | Movies Pot Luck 3 *(see Quiz 28)*

1 Meg Ryan. 2 Pulp Fiction. 3 Sarandon. 4 Demi Moore. 5 1990s. 6 Leonardo DiCaprio. 7 1950s. 8 Orson Welles. 9 Dillon. 10 Sea. 11 Mia Farrow. 12 80s. 13 Sigourney Weaver. 14 Claude Rains. 15 Jodie Foster. 16 Batman. 17 Mel Gibson. 18 Tony Curtis. 19 Grapes. 20 Lee Curtis. 21 140 minutes. 22 James Cameron. 23 1980s. 24 Berlin. 25 1930s. 26 Chicago. 27 Wall-E. 28 Titanic. 29 Macaulay Culkin. 30 Brie Larson.

1 *Proof of Life* and *City of Angels* featured which actress?

2 The character Vincent Vega appeared in which movie?

3 Which Susan starred in 2015's *The Meddler*?

4 In 2011, which Moore starred in *Margin Call*?

5 In 2014, *Godzilla* got a movie reboot. But when did the one before it come out?

6 Who played Hugh Glass in 2015's *The Revenant*?

7 In which decade does *The Talented Mr Ripley* take place?

8 Who played the title role in *Citizen Kane*?

9 Which Matt starred in *Wild Things*?

10 Which word links a "Hawk" and a "Wolf" to give two film titles?

11 Who played Rosemary in *Rosemary's Baby*?

12 Was *Beverley Hills Cop* first released in the 1960s, 70s or 80s?

13 *Ghostbusters* and *Avatar* featured which actress?

14 Who played the police captain in *Casablanca*?

15 Which actress links *The Silence of the Lambs* and *Taxi Driver*?

16 Which superhero gets involved with Cat Woman?

17 Who starred in the *Lethal Weapon* series of films?

18 What is the name of Jamie Lee Curtis's actor father?

19 Which fruit would complete this title, *The ____ of Wrath*?

20 Which Jamie starred in *Halloween*?

21 Does *Mary Poppins* last for 140, 200 or 240 minutes?

22 Who won the Best Director Oscar for *Titanic*?

23 In which decade was *Rain Man* released?

24 Which group had a giant hit with the movie-linked song "Take My Breath Away"?

25 In which decade of the 20th century was Sean Connery born?

26 Which American city was the title of the 2002 Best Picture Oscar winner?

27 Ben Burtt voiced over which summer 2008 hit movie?

28 Which film earned James Cameron a 1997 Oscar?

29 *Home Alone* made which child into a worldwide star?

30 Who won the 2015 Best Actress Oscar?

Answers	Pop: The 1970s *(see Quiz 27)*

1 Village. 2 Paul McCartney. 3 Summer. 4 Ireland. 5 Queen. 6 Bee Gees. 7 Eagles. 8 Sweet. 9 Carpenters. 10 Yellow. 11 Gladys. 12 Flack. 13 Glitter. 14 Simon and Garfunkel. 15 Diana Ross. 16 Sing. 17 T. Rex. 18 Bells. 19 Meat. 20 Led. 21 Taxi. 22 The Goodies. 23 Abba. 24 None. 25 1971. 26 Wild Cherry. 27 Buddy Holly. 28 Glen Campbell. 29 Rod Stewart. 30 Kiki Dee.

1 In America, Simon Cowell is the most feared judge on which reality show?
2 Which "Apprentice" star became the host of *Countdown* in 2012?
3 Which BBC programme presented the pop charts?
4 Chart toppers Berlin sang the theme music to which film starring Tom Cruise?
5 On which channel was the *Saturday Chart Show* broadcast?
6 Which two of the Osmonds hosted their own TV series?
7 On which night is ____ *Night at the Palladium* screened?
8 Former *Generation Game* hostess Rosemarie Ford introduced which evening dance series on BBC1?
9 The Royal Variety Performance raises money for which charity?
10 What nationality is TV entertainer Barry Humphries?
11 David Nixon was famed for what kind of TV act?
12 Who presented *This is your Life* from 2007?
13 Matthew Kelly, Sarah Kennedy, Henry Kelly and Jeremy Beadle formed the quartet which presented which madcap weekend show?
14 Which 1990s BBC2 series showcased famous ballets?
15 Which former DJ presented his chat show three times a week?
16 Which former BBC impressionist has the initials M.Y.?
17 Who hosted *TFI Friday's comeback* in 2015?
18 How many Monkees were there?
19 Which singer won the Eurovision Song Contest with "Puppet On A String"?
20 What colour was the *Whistle Test*?
21 In 1994 who sang the theme tune "Crocodile Shoes"?
22 Who was the British lead singer of *The Monkees*?
23 Which singer was televised singing in the Wimbledon rain in 1996?
24 Channel 4's *The Tube* was presented by which Paula?
25 Who hosted ITV's *Stars in Their Eyes*?
26 *It'll Be Alright on the Night* is hosted by who?
27 Which televised pop concert raised money for famine relief in Ethiopia?
28 Which TV duo topped the charts with "Unchained Melody"?
29 What was the title of Mr Blobby's first No 1 single?
30 Which Ukraine singer won the 2016 Eurovision Song Contest with "1944"?

Answers | **Football Pot Luck 4** *(see Quiz 30)*

1 Midlothian. 2 England. 3 Blue and white. 4 St James' Park. 5 Lee. 6 Manchester City. 7 Everton. 8 Leeds Utd. 9 Manchester Utd. 10 Griffiths. 11 The Blues. 12 N. Ireland. 13 Southampton. 14 John Aldridge. 15 Cantona. 16 Tim. 17 Wycombe Wanderers. 18 Wolves. 19 Wimbledon. 20 Kenny Dalglish. 21 World Cup 2006. 22 Sam Allardyce. 23 Tottenham Hotspur. 24 Leeds Utd. 25 Yes. 26 Mark Hateley. 27 Keegan. 28 Red. 29 Aston Villa. 30 Liverpool.

1 What is the third word in the full name of Hearts?
2 Which country has Mick Mills played for?
3 What colour are the stripes on Brighton's home shirts?
4 Which ground do Newcastle Utd play at?
5 Which Jason was Forest's joint top League scorer in 1995–96?
6 Francis Lee has been chairman of which club?
7 Which was Daniel Amokachi's first English club?
8 With which club did John Lukic make his league debut?
9 Which club did Paul McGrath leave to join Aston Villa?
10 Which Leigh of Celtic was Scottish Footballer of the Year in 2016?
11 What is Birmingham's nickname?
12 Which country has Jimmy Quinn played for?
13 Dave Merrington was manager of which Premiership team for 1995–96?
14 Which veteran striker was known as "Aldo"?
15 Which Eric was PFA Player of the Year in 1994?
16 What name is shared by 1990s teammates Flowers and Sherwood?
17 Martin O'Neill took which club into the Football League?
18 The Hayward family put 90s money into which Midlands club?
19 Holdsworth and Ekoku have played together for which team?
20 Who was Blackburn boss for the 1994–95 Premiership triumph?
21 During which competition did Graham Poll show three yellow cards to a player?
22 Who took over from Roy Hodgson to manage England in 2016?
23 Barmby and Anderton played together at which club?
24 Phil Masinga started in England with which club?
25 Can a goal be scored directly from a corner kick?
26 Which veteran striker moved from Rangers in Scotland to Rangers in London for £1.5 million at the end of 1995?
27 Which Kevin of Southampton was PFA Player of the Year in 1982?
28 What colour are Wales's home shirts?
29 Andy Townsend and John Fashanu were teammates at which club?
30 Ronnie Whelan made over 350 appearances for which club?

Answers | **TV: Music & Variety** *(see Quiz 29)*

1 American Idol. 2 Nick Hewer. 3 Top of the Pops. 4 Top Gun. 5 ITV. 6 Donny and Marie. 7 Sunday. 8 Come Dancing. 9 Royaly Variety Charity. 10 Australian. 11 A magic act. 12 Trevor McDonald. 13 Game for a Laugh. 14 Summer Dance. 15 Terry Wogan. 16 Mike Yarwood. 17 Chris Evans. 18 Four. 19 Sandie Shaw. 20 Grey (it was old, too). 21 Jimmy Nail. 22 Davy Jones. 23 Cliff Richard. 24 Paula Yates. 25 Matthew Kelly. 26 Denis Norden. 27 Live Aid. 28 Robson and Jerome. 29 Mr Blobby. 30 Jamala.

Quiz 31 | Pop: The 1980s

Answers – page 42

1 Which Olivia got "Physical" in 1981?
2 How many Tribes were a big hit for Frankie Goes to Hollywood?
3 Which Boy was a "Karma Chameleon"?
4 Which ex-Supreme joined Lionel Richie on "Endless Love"?
5 Which Careless sound was a hit for George Michael?
6 Which Kenny and Dolly recorded "Islands in the Stream"?
7 Who had a Celebration with Kool?
8 What were the USA for on "We are the World"?
9 Noddy Holder was the lead singer with which band?
10 What did Wham! say to do Before You Go Go?
11 Which Sultans of Swing took the Walk of Life?
12 Which Irish group's name is made up of one letter and a number?
13 Which Boys had a No. 1 with "West End Girls"?
14 Which Simon sang with Duran Duran?
15 Which highwayman demand did Adam and the Ants give in 1981?
16 Which House provided Madness with their first No. 1?
17 Who had huge album success with *Thriller*?
18 Which Bruce was "Born in the USA"?
19 What was Whitney Houston's first album called?
20 Which Purple weather was a film soundtrack album for Prince?
21 The theme to which 1984 comedy movie was a No. 1 hit for Ray Parker Jr?
22 "When I Think of You" was which female artist's first US No. 1?
23 What did the Pretenders have in pocket in 1980?
24 What accompanied Ebony on the Stevie Wonder/Paul McCartney collaboration?
25 Which *Neighbours* actor had a hit with "Sealed with a Kiss" in 1989?
26 Who had a chart hit with "Flashdance … What a Feeling" in 1983?
27 Who took "Hello" to No. 1 in 1984?
28 Who had a 1987 hit with "I Just Wanna Dance with Somebody (Who Loves Me)"?
29 What was on the B-side of "Do They Know It's Christmas?"
30 What was in the pocket of The Pretenders according to their No. 1 hit of January 1980?

Answers	Movies Pot Luck 4 *(see Quiz 32)*

1 Sherlock Holmes. 2 Buster. 3 McGregor. 4 Nicole Kidman. 5 Macaulay Culkin. 6 Ewan McGregor. 7 Quinn. 8 Whitney Houston. 9 Mack Sennett. 10 Lightyear. 11 Attenborough. 12 Stewart. 13 Ross. 14 Brigitte Bardot. 15 Dolls. 16 Dallas. 17 1980s. 18 Yul Brynner. 19 The Doors. 20 Williams. 21 Tom Cruise. 22 The X-Files. 23 Jackson. 24 1950s. 25 "A View to a Kill". 26 High School Musical. 27 John Williams. 28 Jack Nicholson. 29 Marilyn Monroe. 30 Carrey.

1 Which detective has been portrayed on screen over 200 times?
2 Which 1988 film did rock star Phil Collins star in?
3 Which Ewan stars in *Trainspotting 2,* released in 2017?
4 Which actress starred in 2012's *The Paperboy* alongside Zac Efron?
5 Which *Home Alone* star was the 20th century's highest-paid child in the movies?
6 Who played the young Obi Wan Kenobi in *Star Wars Episode I: The Phantom Menace*?
7 Which Anthony played *Zorba the Greek*?
8 Who sang "I Will Always Love You" in her film, *The Bodyguard*?
9 Which film legend Mack inspired the musical *Mack and Mabel*?
10 Which Buzz appears in *Toy Story 4*?
11 Which veteran actor Richard was Dr Hammond in *Jurassic Park*?
12 Which James starred in the original *Harvey*?
13 Which singer Diana starred in *Lady Sings the Blues*?
14 Which French sex symbol became an animal rights campaigner?
15 Which children's toys are linked with "Guys" in the title of a film based on a musical?
16 In which TV soap did Larry Hagman find fame after appearing on the big screen?
17 In which decade was *Return of the Jedi* released?
18 Which actor links *The Magnificent Seven* and *The King and I*?
19 Val Kilmer played Jim Morrison in the movie about which rock band?
20 Which Robin starred in *2014's Night at the Museum*?
21 Which actor links *Mission: Impossible, A Few Good Men* and *Days of Thunder*?
22 What was the name of the movie based on TV's *The X-Files*?
23 Which Glenda won the Best Actress Oscar for *Women in Love*?
24 In which decade of the 20th century was Jamie Lee Curtis born?
25 What was the Bond theme for *A View to a Kill* called?
26 Which 2006 made-for-TV romantic musical movie became a global hit?
27 Which guitar legend won the BAFTA music award for *Memoirs of a Geisha*?
28 Which star actor was in *As Good As it Gets* and *The Shining*?
29 The original "Candle in the Wind" was about which movie icon?
30 Which Jim starred in *2013's Kick Ass* sequel?

Answers	Pop: The 1980s *(see Quiz 31)*

1 Newton-John. 2 Two. 3 George. 4 Diana Ross. 5 Whisper. 6 Rogers, Parton. 7 The Gang. 8 Africa. 9 Slade. 10 Wake Me Up. 11 Dire Straits. 12 U2. 13 Pet Shop. 14 Le Bon. 15 Stand and Deliver. 16 House of Fun. 17 Michael Jackson. 18 Springsteen. 19 Whitney Houston. 20 Rain. 21 Ghostbusters. 22 Janet Jackson. 23 Brass. 24 Ivory. 25 Jason Donovan. 26 Irene Cara. 27 Lionel Richie. 28 Whitney Houston. 29 Feed the World. 30 Brass.

1 Which bald-headed comedian hosts *You've Been Framed*?
2 Which stand-up comedienne was a psychiatric nurse before finding fame?
3 Who is Gary's best friend in *Men Behaving Badly*?
4 Who is Wayne's wife in *Harry Enfield and Chums*?
5 Who is Gareth Hale's comedy partner?
6 Who was the comic with the "short fat hairy legs"?
7 Who are Monica, Rachel, Phoebe, Chandler, Joey and Ross?
8 What is *Frasier*'s surname?
9 Who was the cafe owner, played by Gordon Kaye, in *'Allo, 'Allo*?
10 What was Del Boy's surname in *Only Fools and Horses*?
11 Who was the star of *Sez Les*?
12 In which cartoon series do Itchy and Scratchy appear?
13 What is the English version of *All in the Family*?
14 Which comedy series is set in a Torquay hotel?
15 In which series is the character Sally Smedley?
16 Who played the role of Louis Canning on The Good Wife, since 2010?
17 Who was the last barman in *Cheers*?
18 Who was Ronnie Barker's comedy partner in *The Two Ronnies*?
19 In *Porridge* who was Lennie Godber's cellmate?
20 Which actor played Ernie Bilko?
21 Who played Eric Sykes's twin sister in *Sykes*?
22 Who was Stan's sister in *On the Buses*?
23 In *Absolutely Fabulous* who was Edina's best friend?
24 Who created Gizzard Puke?
25 Who played Barbara in *The Good Life*?
26 In which series was the character Frank Spencer?
27 Who portrays *Ellen*?
28 Who was Ritchie's flatmate in *Bottom*?
29 In *Goodnight Sweetheart* what is Nicholas Lyndhurst's character?
30 In which series is Dorian the next-door neighbour?

| **Answers** | **Formula One Pot Luck** *(see Quiz 34)* |

1 Donington Park. 2 Silverstone (1950). 3 Stirling Moss. 4 Graham Hill. 5 Lotus. 6 Brands Hatch. 7 Le Mans Bugatti Circuit. 8 Lewis Hamilton. 9 March. 10 Interlagos. 11 Hesketh. 12 Nurburgring. 13 Jenson Button. 14 Austrian GP. 15 Nelson Piquet. 16 McLaren. 17 Ayrton Senna. 18 McLaren. 19 Riccardo Patrese. 20 Magny-Cours. 21 Spa-Francorchamps. 22 Alain Prost. 23 Jos Verstappen. 24 Portugal. 25 Damon Hill. 26 Heinz-Harald Frentzen. 27 Jordan. 28 Stowe. 29 McLaren-Honda. 30 Italy.

1 A grand prix was held in Britain in 1935. At which circuit?

2 Where was the first-ever World Championship grand prix held?

3 Who was Fangio's British teammate with Mercedes in 1955?

4 Who crashed when leading the 1960 British Grand Prix?

5 What car was Jim Clark driving when he won the 1962 British Grand Prix at Aintree?

6 In 1964, the British Grand Prix moved to which circuit for the first time?

7 At which circuit was the French Grand Prix held in 1967, for the one and only time?

8 Which British driver won the 2015 F1 World Championship?

9 Which new marque arrived in force for the opening grand prix of the 1970 season in South Africa?

10 Emerson Fittipaldi won his home race in 1973 at which circuit?

11 James Hunt's success in the 1975 Dutch Grand Prix gave which British marque its first win?

12 In 1976, Niki Lauda nearly met his end in a bad crash at which circuit?

13 Who won the F1 World Championship in 2009?

14 At which grand prix did Nigel Mansell make his debut?

15 The 1983 World Championship went to the final round at Kyalami. Who came away as champion?

16 Alain Prost quit Renault to join which team for 1984?

17 Who scored the first of his six wins at Monaco in 1987?

18 Which team won 15 of the 16 grands prix held in 1988?

19 Which Williams driver won the 1990 San Marino Grand Prix?

20 The French Grand Prix moved to which new venue in 1991?

21 Michael Schumacher scored his first grand prix win at which circuit in 1992?

22 Who replaced Nigel Mansell at Williams for 1993?

23 Which Dutch driver was enveloped by flames during the 1994 German Grand Prix?

24 In 1995, David Coulthard scored his first grand prix win in which country?

25 Who won the final race of the 1996 season to win the World Championship?

26 Which Williams driver won the 1997 San Marino Grand Prix?

27 Which team scored its first win at the 1998 Belgian Grand Prix?

28 At which corner did Michael Schumacher break a leg in the 1999 British Grand Prix?

29 For which team did Fernando Alonso drive for in 2016?

30 In which country is the Scuderia Toro Rosso team based?

Answers | TV: Comedy 1 *(see Quiz 33)*

1 Harry Hill. 2 Jo Brand. 3 Tony. 4 Waynetta. 5 Norman Pace. 6 Ernie Wise. 7 The Friends. 8 Crane. 9 René. 10 Trotter. 11 Les Dawson. 12 The Simpsons. 13 Till Death Us Do Part. 14 Fawlty Towers. 15 Drop the Dead Donkey. 16 Michael J. Fox. 17 Woody Boyd. 18 Ronnie Corbett. 19 Fletch. 20 Phil Silvers. 21 Hattie Jacques. 22 Olive. 23 Patsy. 24 Kenny Everett. 25 Felicity Kendal. 26 Some Mothers Do 'Ave 'Em. 27 Ellen Degeneres. 28 Eddie. 29 Gary Sparrow. 30 Birds of a Feather.

1 John Sissons played in an FA Cup Final for which team?
2 Which country did Eusebio play for?
3 Which country did Jimmy Greaves move to before joining Tottenham Hotspur?
4 Alf Ramsey guided which club to the Championship?
5 Who became the first active footballer to be knighted?
6 Who was boss of Liverpool throughout the 60s?
7 At which club did Jimmy Dickinson clock up his 700th League game?
8 Which team featured Auld, Gemmell and Murdoch?
9 Which team was thrashed 9–3 by England at Wembley in 1961?
10 Which team featured Kidd, Aston and Foulkes?
11 Who was Leeds's manager from 1961 onwards?
12 Which bearded former Fulham player became PFA Chairman?
13 Joe Mercer guided which club to the Championship?
14 Which country did Gary Sprake play for?
15 England's Moore, Hurst and Peters came from which club side until 1969?
16 Which Rodney scored a Wembley wonder goal for QPR?
17 In which position did Ron Springett play?
18 Which country did Mike England play for?
19 Roger Hunt was scoring goals for which club side?
20 Jock Stein was manager of which great Glasgow club side?
21 The USSR won which inaugural competition in 1960?
22 What was Denis Law doing when England won the World Cup?
23 Which England World Cup winner became an undertaker when he retired?
24 Which club, formerly Headington United, joined the Football League in 1962?
25 In which city did Celtic win the 1967 European Cup Final?
26 Who hosted the 1962 World Cup finals?
27 Who won the FA Cup in 1966?
28 Who scored two goals in extra time for Swindon Town in the final of the 1969 League Cup?
29 Who were the first British winners of the European Cup?
30 Who was the tournament's top goal scorer in the 1966 World Cup?

Answers	Pop Pot Luck 5 (see Quiz 36)

1 "Hymn for the Weekend". 2 Gallagher. 3 10. 4 Scarborough. 5 Video. 6 Iceland. 7 "Return to Sender". 8 In a Bottle. 9 Electric Light. 10 Dylan. 11 Clarinet. 12 Beach Boys. 13 Gilbert O'Sullivan. 14 Three. 15 Stevens. 16 Dolly Parton. 17 Joan Armatrading. 18 Bob Dylan. 19 Mike Rutherford. 20 Yellow Brick Road. 21 Take That. 22 Scottish. 23 Nash. 24 k. d. lang. 25 42. 26 The Bluenotes. 27 Closer. 28 Flea. 29 21 April. 30 O'Donnell.

1 In 2016, which song was a hit for Beyoncé and Coldplay?
2 Which Noel formed the High Flying Birds?
3 How many c.c. were in the group which sang "I'm Not in Love"?
4 Which Yorkshire town's Fair was the subject of a Simon and Garfunkel song?
5 What Killed the Radio Star according to the Buggles?
6 What is the home country of Björk?
7 Which Elvis song has the line "I gave a letter to the postman, he put it in his sack"?
8 Where did the Police find a Message in 1979?
9 Which Orchestra joined Olivia Newton-John on "Xanadu"?
10 Which Bob wrote "Knockin' on Heaven's Door"?
11 Which instrument does Acker Bilk play?
12 Which band was the subject of the 2014 film, *Love and Mercy*?
13 Who was Alone Again (Naturally) in 1972?
14 How many members of the Thompson Twins were there?
15 Which surname is shared by Cat and Shakin'?
16 Which country star pleaded for Jolene not to take her man in 1976?
17 Whose first hit was "Love and Affection"?
18 Who released the album Fallen Angels in 2016?
19 Who was lead singer with the Mechanics?
20 Which thoroughfare did Elton John say Goodbye to in 1973?
21 Mark Owen took lead vocals on which boy band's 2007 hit "Shine"?
22 What nationality are the Proclaimers?
23 Who makes up the trio with Crosby and Stills?
24 Which Canadian sang "Miss Chatelaine" in 1993?
25 Which Level had "Lessons in Love" in 1986?
26 What was Harold Melvin's backing group?
27 Where did Phyliss Nelson invite us to Move in the 80s and 90s?
28 Which Spanish insect was a hit for Herb Alpert?
29 Which day and month, in 2016, died Prince die?
30 Which Daniel pondered Whatever Happened to Old Fashioned Love in 1993?

| **Answers** | **Football: The 1960s** *(see Quiz 35)* |

1 West Ham Utd. 2 Portugal. 3 Italy. 4 Ipswich. 5 Stanley Matthews. 6 Bill Shankly. 7 Portsmouth. 8 Celtic. 9 Scotland. 10 Manchester Utd. 11 Don Revie. 12 Jimmy Hill. 13 Manchester City. 14 Wales. 15 West Ham. 16 Marsh. 17 Goalkeeper. 18 Wales. 19 Liverpool. 20 Celtic. 21 European Championship. 22 Playing golf. 23 Ray Wilson. 24 Oxford United. 25 Lisbon. 26 Chile. 27 Everton. 28 Don Rogers. 29 Celtic. 30 Eusebio.

1 Who directed 2011's *Thor*?
2 Who, according to the movie, fathered *Rosemary's Baby*?
3 In which Dracula movie did Anthony Hopkins play Professor van Helsing?
4 What was the sequel to *Scream* called?
5 Who wrote the screenplay of William Peter Blatty's *The Exorcist*?
6 What was the first name of Dracula actor Lugosi?
7 What sort of "Man" was Claude Rains in 1933?
8 Which Stephen's first novel *Carrie* was a successful 70s movie?
9 Who was Transylvania's most famous vampire?
10 Which Tom starred in 2015's *Rogue Nation*?
11 Which creepy-crawlies are the subject of *Arachnophobia*?
12 Which Stanley made *The Shining* with Jack Nicholson?
13 What part did Boris Karloff play in the pre-World War II *Frankenstein*?
14 Which 1978 movie shares its name with the spooky 31st October?
15 Which Sissy played the title role in *Carrie*?
16 On which street was the "Nightmare" in the 80s movie series?
17 In which decade was *The Exorcist* first released?
18 Who was the female star of *Rosemary's Baby*?
19 What was Frankenstein's first name in the Kenneth Branagh version?
20 Where was the "American Werewolf" in the 1981 movie with David Naughton?
21 Which Hitchcock movie featured feathered attackers?
22 Who directed and starred in *Psycho 3* in 1986?
23 Which British actor won an Oscar for *The Silence of the Lambs*?
24 Which Michelle co-starred with Jack Nicholson in *Wolf*?
25 Which British studios were famous for their horror movies?
26 Who did Aliens meet in 2004?
27 Who played the wicked character Deadshot in 2016's *Suicide Squad*?
28 Who directed the 2005 British horror film *The Descent*?
29 Which 2004 British zombie comedy starred Simon Pegg and Nick Frost?
30 Which 2006 American horror film had the tagline "They're Hungry ... You're Dinner"?

1 Which Doctor returned to the BBC in 2005 after almost 16 years away?
2 Who starred as the villain in 2016's *The Night Manager*?
3 What was the farmer's name in *Bod*?
4 How did Alan Bradley die in *Coronation Street*?
5 Who has a cameo as Bail Organa in 2016's Star Wars: Rogue One?
6 What profession do the characters Mark Greene and Kerry Weaver follow?
7 Which series featured the lawyer Theodore Hoffman?
8 What is Captain Janeway's Christian name in *Voyager*?
9 Who is Greg Medavoy's partner in *NYPD Blue*?
10 Which channel shows *The Sky at Night*?
11 Where is *The Last Night of the Proms* broadcast from?
12 What was the original title for *The Bill*?
13 Which rodent was the star of *Good Morning Britain*?
14 Which BBC2 series features aviation topics?
15 What is the series featuring viewers' amusing home video clips?
16 Where was *Magnum P. I.* set?
17 Who was Maude Grimes's daughter in *Coronation Street*?
18 Which series starred a black Pontiac TransAm as a hero?
19 Which series featured the character Jessica Fletcher?
20 Who was the star of *Gulliver's Travels*?
21 Who played Woodrow in *Streets of Laredo*?
22 What was the name of the drama documentary about a football stadium disaster?
23 What was the nickname of mountain man James Adams?
24 Which character does Graham Cole portray in *The Bill*?
25 Who was the author of *Tinker Taylor Soldier Spy*?
26 Which series featured the character Hannibal Hayes?
27 Which Paul directed Jason Bourne in 2016?
28 Who played Assumpta Fitzgerald in *Ballykissangel*?
29 What is Geena Lee Nolin's character in *Baywatch*?
30 Which series starred Susan Dey as Grace Van Owen?

Answers	Movies: Horror *(see Quiz 37)*

1 Kenneth Branagh. 2 The Devil. 3 Bram Stoker's Dracula. 4 Scream 2. 5 William Peter Blatty. 6 Bela. 7 Invisible. 8 King. 9 Dracula. 10 Cruise. 11 Spiders. 12 Kubrick. 13 The creature. 14 Halloween. 15 Spacek. 16 Elm Street. 17 1970s. 18 Mia Farrow. 19 Victor. 20 In London. 21 The Birds. 22 Anthony Perkins. 23 Anthony Hopkins. 24 Pfeiffer. 25 Hammer. 26 Predator. 27 Will Smith. 28 Neil Marshall. 29 Shaun of the Dead. 30 Feast.

1 Which club did Kenny Dalglish leave to join Liverpool?
2 Which country did Ron Yeats come from?
3 Who was manager of Everton's 80s championship winning sides?
4 What position did Gordon West play?
5 Who went to Hamburg from Liverpool in 1977?
6 Which Dave skippered Everton's 1995 FA Cup-winning team?
7 What name was shared by Thompson and Boersma?
8 Which Gary presents the BBC's "Match of the Day" in 2016?
9 Which country did Kevin Ratcliffe play for?
10 Which star of the 60s and 70s set a Liverpool appearance record?
11 Which Mersey team plays at Prenton Park?
12 Which Liverpool player was referred to as "The Great Dane"?
13 Who took over as Everton manager from Mike Walker?
14 Bob Paisley took over from which manager?
15 Which club did John Barnes join Liverpool from?
16 Which midfielder Steve played for both Everton and Liverpool in the 80s?
17 Which Alan Bleasdale TV drama featured players Souness and Lee?
18 Which fellow Liverpool forward was an Ian Rush lookalike?
19 Who was player-manager in Liverpool's 1986 double-winning team?
20 Along with Giggsy, who opened a football hotel in 2016?
21 For which team did Everton's Tim Cahill play in an FA Cup Final?
22 Whose own goal equalised for Chelsea in the 2008 Champions League semi-final?
23 How old was Wayne Rooney in years when he made his Everton debut in 2002?
24 Which legendary Liverpool goal scorer returned to play for the club in 2005–06?
25 Which Birkenhead-born ex-Red Jason retired as a Tranmere player in 2007?
26 At which club did Joey Barton begin his football career?
27 What is the title of Jamie Carragher's autobiography?
28 Who was made a Freeman of the Borough of Knowsley in 2007?
29 Which Merseysider moved to LA Galaxy in 2015?
30 With which club did Alan Stubbs end his playing career in 2008?

Answers | **Pop Pot Luck 6** *(see Quiz 40)*

1 USA. 2 Mick Jagger. 3 Sue. 4 Young. 5 South America. 6 Trumpet. 7 Gore.
8 Cardiff. 9 Donny. 10 Three Degrees. 11 The Dock of the Bay. 12 George Martin.
13 The Faces. 14 Parton. 15 Margaret Thatcher. 16 Michael Ball. 17 M People.
18 The Vandellas. 19 Sting. 20 Warwick. 21 Janet. 22 Leeds. 23 Red. 24 Lions.
25 Cash. 26 Bruce Springsteen. 27 Tamla Motown. 28 David Bowie. 29 Enya. 30
Cleo Laine.

1 What is the home country of Michael Bolton?
2 Which Rolling Stone, in 2016, became a father at the age 72?
3 Which Peggy was a classic 50s hit for Buddy Holly?
4 Which surname is shared by Neil and Paul?
5 Which continent is famous for its pan pipes?
6 Which brass instrument did Louis Armstrong play?
7 Which Lesley had the original hit with "It's My Party"?
8 Which Welsh city was Shirley Bassey born in?
9 Which Osmond had a hit with "Young Love"?
10 Which trio was made up of Sheila Ferguson, Valerie Thompson and Fayette Pickney?
11 What was Otis Redding Sittin' On in 1968?
12 Which record producer was known as the Fifth Beatle?
13 Which group was formed when the Small Faces disbanded?
14 What name is shared by Dolly and Stella?
15 Which politician did the Spice Girls say was an original Spice Girl?
16 Whose first hit was "Love Changes Everything"?
17 Which People was Heather Small lead singer of?
18 Who were Martha Reeves's backing group?
19 Which ex-Police man sang "Fields of Gold" in 1993?
20 Which Dionne was a Heartbreaker in 1982?
21 Which Jackson married Wissam Al Mana in 2012?
22 From which English city do the Kaiser Chiefs originate?
23 What colour Box did Simply Red Open Up in 1986?
24 Matt Munro is famous for singing "Born Free", a film about which animals?
25 What is the surname of the country stars Johnny and Roseanne?
26 Which singer is nicknamed the Boss?
27 Which record label was founded in Detroit?
28 Whose first hit was "Space Oddity" in 1969?
29 Whose first solo hit was "Orinoco Flow" in 1988?
30 How is the jazz singer Clementine Campbell better known?

Answers | Football: Merseysiders *(see Quiz 39)*

1 Celtic. 2 Scotland. 3 Howard Kendall. 4 Goalkeeper. 5 Kevin Keegan. 6 Watson. 7 Phil. 8 Gary Lineker. 9 Wales. 10 Ian Callaghan. 11 Tranmere Rovers. 12 Jan Molby. 13 Joe Royle. 14 Bill Shankly. 15 Watford. 16 McMahon. 17 Boys from the Black Stuff. 18 John Aldridge. 19 Kenny Dalglish. 20 Gary Neville. 21 Millwall. 22 John Arne Riise. 23 16. 24 Robbie Fowler. 25 McAteer. 26 Manchester City. 27 Carra. 28 Steven Gerrard. 29 Kevin Nolan. 30 Derby County.

1 Which pop superstar did Sean Penn marry in 1985?
2 Which ex-Mrs Sonny Bono played Loretta Castorini in *Moonstruck*?
3 When Billy Crystal was Harry, who was Meg Ryan?
4 Which 24-year-old Michael played teenager Marty in *Back to the Future*?
5 Which husband of Demi Moore played John McLane in *Die Hard*?
6 Which Kirstie appeared in *Star Trek II*?
7 Which tough guy actor has the nickname Sly?
8 Which Melanie was a "Working Girl" for Harrison Ford?
9 Who played Tom Cruise's autistic brother in *Rain Man*?
10 Which Patrick practised "Dirty Dancing" with Jennifer Grey?
11 Which Glenn's "Attraction" looked "Fatal" to Michael Douglas in 1987?
12 Which successful US talk show hostess appeared in *The Color Purple*?
13 Who changed her name from Susan Weaver before appearing in movies such as *Ghostbusters*?
14 In *Born on the Fourth of July*, Tom Cruise played a veteran from which war?
15 Which Canadian Leslie found big-screen fame as Lieutenant Frank Drebin?
16 Which Richard was the *American Gigolo*?
17 Which Mel played the title role in *Mad Max II*?
18 Which Kevin played opposite Meryl Streep in *Sophie's Choice*?
19 Which animal was a star with Clint Eastwood in *Any Which Way You Can*?
20 What did Elliott call his pet alien in the 80s Spielberg movie?
21 What sort of busters were Dan Aykroyd and Bill Murray?
22 Which Michael was in *Romancing the Stone* in 1984?
23 What was the name of the cartoon rabbit in the title of the movie with Bob Hoskins?
24 Michael Keaton starred as which caped crusader in 1989?
25 Which 007 joined Harrison Ford in *Indiana Jones and the Last Crusade*?
26 Which Tom played a cop who adopted the slobbering dog Hooch?
27 Whose demonic grin was on the movie posters for *The Shining*?
28 Who played opposite Billy Crystal in *When Harry Met Sally*?
29 Who plays Dale McKussic in *Tequila Sunrise*?
30 Which actress voiced the *femme fatale* in *Who Framed Roger Rabbit*?

Answers | TV Pot Luck 6 *(see Quiz 42)*

1 E20 6PQ. 2 Tony. 3 Zimmerman. 4 Bomber. 5 Blackadder. 6 This Morning. 7 Happy Days. 8 The Young Ones. 9 Waldorf. 10 Wendy Craig. 11 D.I. Burnside. 12 Detective Chris Cagney. 13 Anthony Edwards. 14 David Addison. 15 Mind Your Language. 16 Dr Who. 17 Potman. 18 The Dagmar. 19 Pam Willis. 20 Brookside. 21 Dudley Moore. 22 Sir John Harvey-Jones. 23 Blankety-Blank. 24 Merton. 25 The Bill. 26 Poldark. 27 David Starkey. 28 Postman Pat. 29 Sinbad. 30 Inspector Frost.

Quiz 42 TV Pot Luck 6 Answers – page 51 LEVEL 1

1 In 2011, the postcode of Albert Square was revealed as_____?
2 Who was the head of the Soprano family?
3 What is the name of the holographic doctor in *Voyager*?
4 Which of the lads in *Auf Weidersehen Pet* came from Bristol?
5 In which series was the character Mrs Miggins?
6 On which show did Caron Keating stand in for Judy Finnegan?
7 Which series featured Howard Cunningham?
8 Which program featured Neil the hippy?
9 Which other grump did Statler star opposite in 2014's *The Muppets Most Wanted*?
10 Who conceived and starred in *The Nanny*?
11 Who does Christopher Ellison portray in *The Bill*?
12 Which character was first played by Loretta Swit in a pilot episode?
13 Who portrays Dr Mark Greene in *ER*?
14 What was the name of Bruce Willis's character in *Moonlighting*?
15 Which series starred Barry Evans as an English teacher?
16 In which series was The Master an enemy?
17 What was Jack Duckworth's first job at the Rover's Return?
18 In which other bar in Walford did Lofty work apart from the Queen Vic?
19 Who was Doug's wife in *Neighbours*?
20 Which soap featured a special video episode entitled *The Lost Weekend*?
21 Who was Peter Cook's partner in *Not Only but Also*?
22 Who presented the *Trouble-shooter* series on TV?
23 Which game show has been presented by both Lily Savage and Les Dawson?
24 Which *Mrs* presented her own chat show?
25 Which cop show featured an Arsenal footballer in a 1998 Christmas special?
26 What TV drama series was based on the novels set in Cornwall by Winston Graham?
27 Which TV historian fronted *Henry VIII: Mind of a Tyrant*?
28 Which delivery man had a cat named Jess?
29 Which character does Michael Starke portray in *Brookside*?
30 Which TV detective was created by R. D. Wingfield?

Answers	Movies: Stars of the 1980s (see Quiz 41)

1 Madonna. 2 Cher. 3 Sally. 4 J. Fox. 5 Bruce Willis. 6 Alley. 7 Sylvester Stallone. 8 Griffith. 9 Dustin Hoffman. 10 Swayze. 11 Close. 12 Oprah Winfrey. 13 Sigourney Weaver. 4 Vietnam. 15 Nielsen. 16 Gere. 17 Gibson. 18 Kline. 19 Orang Utan. 20 E.T. 21 Ghostbusters. 22 Douglas. 23 Roger. 24 Batman. 25 Sean Connery. 26 Hanks. 27 Jack Nicholson. 28 Meg Ryan. 29 Mel Gibson. 30 Kathleen Turner.

1 Who scored Manchester Utd's winner in the '96 final against Liverpool?
2 Gazza played in the 1991 final with which London club?
3 Gordon Durie hit a hat-trick in which club's 5–1 demolition of Hearts?
4 In a 70s triumph, Jim Montgomery inspired underdogs Sunderland. Which position did he play?
5 Duxbury, Albiston and McQueen played together for which Cup-winning club in the 80s?
6 Which English team did Bobby Robson lead to Cup Final success?
7 They sound like a London team, but who were the side to win the first Scottish Cup?
8 Who was in goal for Wimbledon when they beat Liverpool in 1988?
9 What part of his anatomy did Trevor Brooking use to score West Ham's winner against Arsenal?
10 Jim Leighton played in a final for which English club?
11 Before joining Liverpool, John Barnes was a losing finalist for which club?
12 Dave Webb scored a winning goal for which club?
13 Which club won its first ever Scottish Cup in 1994?
14 Which Norman scored a Manchester Utd winner against Everton?
15 Howard Kendall became the youngest FA Cup finalist when playing for which club?
16 Which star from Argentina hit a memorable goal for Tottenham Hotspur against Manchester City in a replay?
17 With which team was George Burley an FA Cup winner?
18 Sanchez hit a Wembley winner for which club?
19 Who was Manchester Utd boss when they won the 1990 Final?
20 Which Bobby scored a final winner for Southampton?
21 Who won the 2010 FIFA World Cup?
22 Which continent provided the goal scorers of the 2007 and 2008 FA Cup Finals?
23 Who won the first League Cup Final played at refurbished Wembley Stadium?
24 Who scored twice in the last eight minutes to deny Arsenal the 2001 FA Cup?
25 Which team lost 3–0 to Manchester United in the 2004 FA Cup Final?
26 Which Manchester United player missed a penalty in the 2008 Champions League final shoot-out?
27 Who came second in Euro 2016?
28 Who won the final of the 2008 African Cup of Nations?
29 Who did Hearts beat in the final of the 2006 Scottish Cup?
30 Who did Zinedine Zidane head butt in the final of the 2006 World Cup?

Answers	**Movies Pot Luck 5** *(see Quiz 44)*

1 Danny Boyle. 2 1950s. 3 Kitty. 4 85 minutes. 5 Ingrid Bergman. 6 Winona Ryder. 7 Diamonds. 8 Madness. 9 A Return to Oz. 10 Tina Turner. 11 Gone with the Wind. 12 Oldman. 13 Nazis. 14 The Full Monty. 15 Dolly Parton. 16 Audrey Hepburn. 17 Michelle Pfeiffer. 18 Sophie's Choice. 19 Stockholm. 20 Michael Jackson. 21 Diane Keaton. 22 Whoopi Goldberg. 23 1960s. 24 Peter Sellers. 25 1930s. 26 A cave. 27 Zombies. 28 John Travolta. 29 Paltrow. 30 Fatal.

1 Which Danny directed the 2012 Olympic Opening Ceremony?
2 In which decade of the 20th century was Kevin Costner born?
3 Which girl's first name completes the film title, ____ *Foyle*?
4 Did *Ace Ventura, Pet Detective* run for 65, 85 or 155 minutes?
5 Who got the lead in *Casablanca* after Hedy Lamarr turned it down?
6 Which actress stars as Spock's mother in the 2009 Star Trek reboot?
7 What, according to Monroe's song, are "a girl's best friend"?
8 Which ailment is mentioned in the title of a movie about King George III?
9 What was the sequel to *The Wizard of Oz* called?
10 Which female pop star featured in *Mad Max Beyond Thunderdome*?
11 Scarlett O'Hara was heroine of which epic film?
12 Which Gary starred 2014's *Dawn of the Planet of the Apes*?
13 Which political group is central to the plot of *The Sound of Music*?
14 Which 90s movie told of a group of stripping Sheffield steelworkers?
15 Which blonde country star had a cameo role in *The Beverly Hillbillies*?
16 Which Audrey starred in *My Fair Lady*?
17 Who played the female lead in *Grease 2*?
18 In which movie did Meryl Streep play a Polish holocaust survivor?
19 Greta Garbo was born in which European capital city?
20 Martin Scorsese directed the video *Bad* for which pop superstar?
21 Which Diane was in *The First Wives' Club*?
22 *The Color Purple* and *Sister Act 2* featured which actress?
23 In which decade was *The Graduate* released?
24 Which Peter played *Inspector Clouseau*?
25 Did Shirley Temple first win an Oscar in the 1930s, 50s or 70s?
26 In what are the characters in *The Descent* trapped?
27 What type of creatures provide the horror in *2013's World War Z*?
28 Which star actor was in *Pulp Fiction* and *Look Who's Talking*?
29 Which Gwyneth starred in *Iron Man 3*?
30 Which word goes before "Attraction" in a Michael Douglas movie title?

Answers | **Football: Cup Finals** *(see Quiz 43)*

1 Eric Cantona. 2 Tottenham Hotspur. 3 Rangers. 4 Goalkeeper. 5 Manchester Utd.
6 Ipswich Town. 7 Queens Park. 8 Dave Beasant. 9 His head. 10 Manchester Utd.
11 Watford. 12 Chelsea. 13 Dundee Utd. 14 Whiteside. 15 Preston North End.
16 Ricky Villa. 17 Ipswich Town. 18 Wimbledon. 19 Alex Ferguson. 20 Stokes.
21 Spain. 22 Africa. 23 Tottenham Hotspur. 24 Michael Owen. 25 Millwall. 26 Cristiano Ronaldo. 27 France. 28 Egypt. 29 Gretna. 30 Marco Materazzi.

1 Which James co-stars in *New Tricks*?
2 Which City was a spin-off of *Casualty*?
3 Where did the Robinson family become lost?
4 On which channel is *NYPD Blue* transmitted?
5 What rank is Mitch Buchanan in *Baywatch*?
6 Which series featured WDC Viv Martella?
7 Where was *Harry's Game* set?
8 Which Superhero is portrayed on TV by Tyler Hoechlin?
9 What is the house in Netflix's *House of Cards*?
10 Which character was the butler in *Upstairs Downstairs*?
11 Which country was the location for *Jewel in the Crown*?
12 Who played Paris in *Mission Impossible*?
13 In which series does Robbie Coltrane portray Fitz?
14 Who plays the character of *Maisie Raine*?
15 Which 19th-century hero does Sean Bean play?
16 What was the sequel to *Band of Gold*?
17 Who was Dr Finlay's partner in practice?
18 Which character is played by George Clooney in *ER*?
19 What is Seigfried Farnon's occupation?
20 Which *Charlie's Angel* played Mrs King?
21 Who was Dempsey's sidekick?
22 Which series featured the character Pug Henry?
23 Who played Jesus of Nazareth?
24 Who played Barlow?
25 Which western series featured Big John and Blue?
26 What was *Lou Grant*'s occupation?
27 Which detective did Angie Dickenson portray?
28 Which of *Randall and Hopkirk* was not a ghost?
29 Who played Rowdy Yates in *Rawhide*?
30 Who presented *Tales of the Unexpected*?

Answers | **Football Pot Luck 5** *(see Quiz 46)*

1 Aston Villa. 2 City. 3 Blackburn Rovers. 4 City. 5 The Republic of Ireland. 6 Blackburn Rovers. 7 France. 8 Middlesbrough. 9 Sheffield Utd. 10 Blue and white. 11 Quinn. 12 The Tangerines or Seasiders. 13 Kinnear. 14 Denmark. 15 Shearer. 16 Tottenham Hotspur. 17 QPR. 18 Green. 19 Norwich. 20 Day. 21 Spanish. 22 The losers' ribbons. 23 Ian Botham. 24 Abide with Me. 25 Stoke City. 26 Yellow. 27 Southall. 28 No. 29 Sheffield Utd. 30 Newcastle Utd.

Quiz 46   Football Pot Luck 5

1 Who were runners-up of the FA Cup in 2015?
2 Which Bristol team plays in red shirts at home?
3 Dalglish and Harford have both managed which club?
4 What second name is shared by Cardiff and Bradford?
5 Which country has Andy Townsend played for?
6 Mike Newell and Chris Sutton have both played for which team?
7 Which country do Nantes come from?
8 With which club did Stuart Ripley make his League debut?
9 Which club did Vinnie Jones join on leaving Leeds?
10 What two colours are on Sheffield Wednesday's home shirts?
11 Which Jimmy was Reading's top League scorer in 1995–96?
12 What is Blackpool's nickname?
13 Which Joe became Wimbledon boss in January 1992?
14 Which country did Allan Nielsen play for?
15 Which Alan won the Footballer of the Year award in 1994?
16 Erik Thorstvedt played for which London club?
17 Which club were the first in England to have an artificial pitch?
18 What colour are the home shirts of Northern Ireland?
19 Which team does Delia Smith support?
20 Which Mervyn of West Ham was PFA Young Player of the Year in 1975?
21 What nationality was the manager who replaced Martin Jol at Tottenham?
22 What is taken to the FA Cup final every year but never used?
23 Which England cricketer played for Scunthorpe?
24 Which hymn has been traditionally sung before the FA Cup Final?
25 Which team does Nick Hancock support?
26 What colour are the home shirts of Brazil?
27 Which Neville won the Footballer of the Year award in 1985?
28 Can a player be offside in his team's own half of the pitch when the ball is played?
29 Dave Bassett was manager at which Yorkshire club for eight years?
30 Darren Huckerby left which club to join Coventry City?

Answers   **TV: Drama** *(see Quiz 45)*

1 Bolam. 2 Holby. 3 Space. 4 Channel 4. 5 Captain. 6 The Bill. 7 Northern Ireland. 8 Superman. 9 The White House. 10 Hudson. 11 India. 12 Leonard Nimoy. 13 Cracker. 14 Pauline Quirke. 15 Richard Sharpe. 16 Gold. 17 Dr Cameron. 18 Doug Ross. 19 Vet. 20 Kate Jackson. 21 Makepiece. 22 The Winds of War. 23 Robert Powell. 24 Stratford Johns. 25 The High Chaparral. 26 Newspaper Editor. 27 Pepper Anderson. 28 Randall. 29 Clint Eastwood. 30 Roald Dahl.

1 Which Melody took Robson and Jerome to No. 1?
2 How long were Take That Back for in 1995?
3 Which Paradise was a hit for Coolio Featuring LV?
4 Which Night was special for Whigfield?
5 What is the nationality of chart-topper Alanis Morissette?
6 Whose *Immaculate Collection* was a 1991 bestseller?
7 What was Oasis's first album called?
8 Which opera singer had a hit with "Nessun Dorma" in 1990?
9 Which Ms O'Connor had a No. 1 with "Nothing Compares 2 U"?
10 What was the title of the Spice Girls' debut single?
11 Which superstar's first solo No. 1 was "Sacrifice" in 1990 after more than 50 hit singles?
12 Which Jimmy was famous for his Crocodile Shoes?
13 Which Tasmin reached No. 1 with her first single "Sleeping Satellite" in 1992?
14 Which group named themselves after the hit record "Boys to Men"?
15 Which Mariah had a hit with "Without You" in 1994?
16 What is All Around according to Wet Wet Wet in 1994?
17 Where was Celine Dion Falling into in 1996?
18 Which country do Boyzone come from?
19 Which former Wham! member released an album called *Older*?
20 Which Peter chose the right Flava to get to No. 1?
21 Which Australian soap actress released the album *Love and Kisses* in 1991?
22 Who had a UK chart hit with "Doin' the Do" in 1990?
23 How are actors and No. 1 recording artists Greene and Flynn better known?
24 Which two *Fantasy Football* fans were No. 1 during football's Euro 96?
25 Who had the last UK No. 1 of the 1990s?
26 Who had a hit in 1990 with a cover version of "Nothing Compares 2 U"?
27 What hit single was originally recorded for the soundtrack of *The Bodyguard*?
28 What was Britney Spears's debut single?
29 Who performed "The Power of the Dream" at the 1996 Atlanta Olympic Games?
30 Who had a US No. 1 with "Gonna Make You Sweat (Everybody Dance Now)"?

1 Which Warwick had a cameo in 2015's The Force Awakens?

2 In which country was Leslie Nielsen born?

3 Which Helen was the only American nominated for Best Actress Oscar in 1998?

4 Which actor links *Batman*, *A Few Good Men* and *Wolf*?

5 Steven Spielberg made "Close Encounters of" which kind?

6 Which much-quoted actress wrote an autobiography called *Goodness Had Nothing to Do with It*?

7 Which whale was played by Keiko in a 90s movie?

8 *Top Gun* was about which of the armed services?

9 Was *Bambi* first released in the 1920s, 40s or 60s?

10 Which Frank starred in the 50s movie *From Here to Eternity*?

11 What is Nicolas Cage's real surname?

12 Real-life character Lee Harvey Oswald appears in which Oliver Stone movie?

13 Which word completes the film title, *I am a ____ from a Chain Gang*?

14 Which character was voiced by Robin Williams in *Aladdin*?

15 Which James Bond has an actor son called Jason?

16 *Total Recall* and *Casino* both featured which actress?

17 Who played opposite Ginger Rogers 10 times?

18 Which pop star Tina did Angela Bassett play in the 1993 biopic?

19 In which decade was *Batman Forever* released?

20 Who won the Best Actor Oscar for *The Godfather*?

21 Which actress Natalie did Robert Wagner marry twice?

22 In which decade of the 20th century was Michelle Pfeiffer born?

23 Which mode of transport completes the film title, *Night ____ To Munich*?

24 Which Kevin played Bottom in the 1990s *A Midsummer Night's Dream*?

25 Which Mark starred in 2015's *The Force Awakens*?

26 Which Miss Winters passed away in January 2006?

27 What was the subject of the 2015 movie, *Southpaw*?

28 Reporters Woodward and Bernstein featured in which movie?

29 Which Anthony starred in *The Elephant Man*?

30 In which decade was *Room at the Top* released?

Answers	Pop: The 1990s *(see Quiz 47)*

1 Unchained. 2 Good. 3 Gangsta's. 4 Saturday. 5 Canadian. 6 Madonna. 7 Oasis. 8 Pavarotti. 9 Sinead. 10 Wannabe. 11 Elton John. 12 Nail. 13 Archer. 14 Boyz II Men. 15 Carey. 16 Love. 17 You. 18 Ireland. 19 George Michael. 20 Andre. 21 Danii Minogue. 22 Betty Boo. 23 Robson & Jerome. 24 David Baddiel and Frank Skinner. 25 Westlife. 26 Sinead O'Connor. 27 I Will Always Love You. 28 … Baby One More Time. 29 Celine Dion. 30 C+C Music Factory.

1 In 2012, what major event happened to Ian Beale?
2 Kent Riley plays which Zak in *Hollyoaks*?
3 What animal appears on the opening credits of *Coronation Street*?
4 What was Trevor Jordache buried under in *Brookside*?
5 In the 1960s series *Compact*, what was Compact?
6 What was Emmerdale previously called?
7 In which US soap did Joan Collins star?
8 In which Landing did some of the Ewings settle after *Dallas*?
9 Which ITV soap featured actress Noelle Gordon and the character Amy Turtle?
10 Which is the Australian spoof medical soap?
11 Alf Roberts was mayor of Wetherfield in which ITV soap?
12 Which soap was set in a Birmingham motel?
13 Which comedy spoof series finished its weekly introductory plot summary with the words "Confused? You will be after the next exciting episode of…"?
14 *Emmerdale* is set in which UK county?
15 What is the name of the pub in *Emmerdale*?
16 Who left *EastEnders* for France with two of her children?
17 Who is the metal-headed character in *Brookside*?
18 In *Coronation Street*, who is Ken Barlow married to?
19 Did the TV astrologer Russel Grant appear in *Brookside* or *EastEnders*?
20 Who was Frank Tate's murdered wife in *Emmerdale*?
21 Which pub sells Newton & Ridley beer?
22 June Brown plays which dotty character in *EastEnders*?
23 Which bespectacled comedian plays a major character in *EastEnders*?
24 Which Mike once owned the factory in *Coronation Street*?
25 Which Fred was a butcher in *Coronation Street*?
26 Which TV company produces *Emmerdale*?
27 The Carringtons featured in which US soap?
28 Bill Tarmey plays which character in *Coronation Street*?
29 In which soap was JR shot?
30 Which Place was an early TV soap?

Answers	Formula One Drivers *(see Quiz 50)*

1 Tyrrell. 2 Caesar's Palace, Las Vegas. 3 Ferrari. 4 1985. 5 Minardi. 6 French. 7 Italian. 8 Tyrrell. 9 The 1995 Canadian Grand Prix. 10 Ferrari. 11 Sauber. 12 Larrousse. 13 Mercedes AMG Petronas. 14 Jacques Laffite. 15 McLaren. 16 England. 17 Ferrari. 18 He'd broken an arm. 19 New Zealander. 20 A puncture. 21 Hungary. 22 Robert Kubica. 23 Mercedes-McLaren. 24 German. 25 Timo Glock. 26 Felipe Massa. 27 Fernando Alonso. 28 Sir Stirling Moss. 29 1976. 30 Stevenage.

1 Michele Alboreto broke into Formula One with which team?

2 Where did he score his first grand prix win in 1982?

3 For which Italian team did he drive between 1984 and 1988?

4 In which season did he finish second in the World Championship?

5 What was the final team Michele Alboreto drove for before quitting Formula One?

6 What nationality is Jean Alesi?

7 What nationality are Jean Alesi's parents?

8 What was his first Formula One team?

9 Which was his one and only grand prix win?

10 For which team did he score this win?

11 Which team did he quit in 1999?

12 With which team did Philippe Alliot spend the majority of his Formula One career?

13 With which team did Hamilton win the 2015 Championship?

14 He joined Ligier midway through 1986 as a substitute for which injured driver?

15 For which British team did he have a one-off outing in 1994?

16 From which country does Cliff Allison originate?

17 For which team did he finish second in the 1960 Argentinian Grand Prix?

18 Why did he not start the following race at Monaco?

19 What nationality is Chris Amon?

20 What deprived him of victory in the 1972 French Grand Prix?

21 In which country did Jenson Button win his first Formula 1 Grand Prix?

22 Who became the first Pole to drive in Formula 1?

23 For which team did Lewis Hamilton drive in 2007?

24 What is the nationality of Sebastian Vettel?

25 Who did Lewis Hamilton pass late on the last lap of the last race to become 2008 World Champion?

26 Which driver was born in Sao Paulo in 1981?

27 Who retained the Drivers' Championship in 2006?

28 Who is the narrator of kids TV show "Roary the Racing Car"?

29 Which year did James Hunt win the Drivers' Championship?

30 Which Hertfordshire town is the birthplace of Lewis Hamilton?

Answers | **TV: Soaps** *(see Quiz 49)*

1 Homeless. 2 Ramsey. 3 A cat. 4 The patio. 5 A magazine. 6 Emmerdale Farm. 7 Dynasty. 8 Knott's Landing. 9 Crossroads. 10 Let the Blood Run Free. 11 Alf Roberts. 12 Crossroads. 13 Soap. 14 Yorkshire. 15 The Woolpack. 16 Cindy Beale. 17 Tinhead. 18 He isn't married. 19 Brookside. 20 Kim. 21 The Rover's Return. 22 Dot Cotton. 23 Mike Read. 24 Mike Baldwin. 25 Fred Elliott. 26 Yorkshire TV. 27 Dynasty. 28 Jack Duckworth. 29 Dallas. 30 Peyton Place.

1 Which two brothers were in the England World Cup-winning team?
2 At which club were father and son Clough connected?
3 What are the first names of the 90s Neville brothers?
4 With which club did they make their debuts?
5 What's the last name of strikers Justin and John?
6 Father Frank and son Andy Gray have both played for which club?
7 Who is goalkeeper Ian Walker's manager father?
8 What is the name of midfielder Scott Gemmill's father?
9 Did Bobby Charlton ever play at club level in the same side as his brother?
10 Which Manchester Utd manager sold his son Darren?
11 Which country did the Allchurch brothers play for?
12 What's the surname of Clive and Bradley, both former QPR strikers?
13 Which club had Bobby Gould as boss and son Jonathan in goal?
14 What is Nicky Summerbee's father called?
15 What's the last name of dad Tony and son Mark, both tall centre forwards?
16 Which legendary striker was Bobby Charlton's uncle?
17 Which West Ham boss had a son playing for Liverpool and England?
18 Which Alan was boss at York while brother Brian was boss at Villa?
19 What's the name of David Holdsworth's striking brother?
20 Which Cruyff played for Manchester Utd?
21 Which Neville brother was the first to leave Manchester United?
22 The son of which legendary Midlands manager took charge of Burton Albion?
23 Which extended family includes Les, Rio and Anton?
24 Leroy and his son Liam Rosenior both played for which London club?
25 The son of which legendary Danish goalkeeper played for Manchester City in 2007?
26 Who played for Wales alongside brother Neil in the 1950s?
27 Who captained AC Milan to victory in European Cup final 40 years after his father had achieved the same feat?
28 Who played for Wales alongside brother Mel in the 1950s?
29 The son of which Scottish international was a mainstay of the Nottingham Forest team of the 1990s?
30 Which twins Willy and René played for Holland in the 1970s?

Answers | **Pop Pot Luck 7** (see Quiz 52)

1 Berry. 2 Robin. 3 Doll. 4 Lloyd-Webber. 5 Petula. 6 Pale. 7 Jerry. 8 East 17. 9 Oasis. 10 The Beach Boys. 11 P. J. 12 Teenage. 13 Stardust. 14 Sister. 15 Manilow. 16 Phil Collins. 17 In the Street. 18 Rod. 19 Palmer. 20 Wales. 21 Eminem. 22 One Dance. 23 John Lennon. 24 Jackie (he's one of the brothers). 25 Liverpool. 26 Gloria. 27 40. 28 The Coconuts. 29 Scotland. 30 Twice.

1 Which surname is shared by Chuck, Dave and Nick?

2 Which Bee Gee died in 2012?

3 Which Livin' object was Cliff Richard's first No. 1?

4 Which Andrew wrote the music for *Jesus Christ Superstar*?

5 Which Miss Clark had a 60s hit with "Downtown"?

6 Procul Harum sang about a Whiter Shade of what?

7 Which Mungo sang "In the Summertime" in 1970?

8 Which part of East London had the 1994 Christmas No. 1 "Stay Another Day"?

9 Which 90s band sounds like a fertile part of a desert?

10 Whose first hit was "Surfin' USA"?

11 Which initials went with Duncan on "Let's Get Ready to Rhumble" in 1994?

12 What sort of Rampage did Sweet go on in 1974?

13 Take That sang the closing tune to which 2007 film?

14 Which relative was seen to Swing Out with "Breakout" and "Surrender" in the 80s?

15 "Mandy" gave which Barry his first UK hit?

16 Who was lead singer with Genesis in the 80s?

17 Martha Reeves, David Bowie and Mick Jagger have all been Dancing where?

18 Which Stewart sang "You're in My Heart" in 1977?

19 Who makes up the trio with Emerson and Lake?

20 What is the home country of Tom Jones?

21 Who had a hit with "Like Toy Soldiers" in 2005?

22 What was Drake's big hit in 2016?

23 Which Beatle's younger son is called Sean?

24 Who is not one of the Jackson sisters – Janet, LaToya, Jackie?

25 Which northern city is Sonia from?

26 Which first name is shared by Estefan and Gaynor?

27 What fallows UB in the name of the band?

28 Who was Kid Creole's backing group?

29 Which part of the UK is Barbara Dickson from?

30 How many times did Celine Dion Think on her best-selling 1995 single?

Quiz 53 | Movies: Late Greats | Answers – page 64

1 In what type of crash did James Dean meet his death?
2 Which Lillian was dubbed the First Lady of the Silent Screen?
3 Which Lee turned down George C. Scott's role in *Patton*?
4 Who won the Best Actor Oscar for *My Fair Lady*?
5 Which Clark's last movie was *The Misfits*?
6 Which David's autobiography was called *The Moon's a Balloon*?
7 Where was Jessica Tandy born?
8 In what type of building did Oliver Reed die?
9 Which British David, who once played Tesla, died in January 2016?
10 Who won the Best Actress Oscar for *Gone with the Wind*?
11 Which Welsh actor directed and starred in *Dr Faustus* in 1968?
12 Which husband and wife starred in *The Great Dictator* in 1940?
13 Who was Bogart talking to when he said, "You look very soft for a rock"?
14 Which British actor won an Oscar for *Hamlet* in 1948?
15 Which Ava was Oscar-nominated for *Mogambo*?
16 Which Bette tested for the role of Scarlett O'Hara?
17 Which Sammy starred in *Sweet Charity*?
18 How was William Claude Fields known to cinema goers?
19 Jennifer Grant is the only daughter of which great from the heyday of Hollywood?
20 Which part of him did Jimmy Durante insure for $100,000?
21 How was John Gleason known in movies?
22 Which James died in 1997 aged 89?
23 What was Orson Welles's first film, in 1941?
24 Which doomed James starred in *Rebel without a Cause*?
25 How was Elizabeth Ruth Grable better known?
26 Which Ledger died in 2008?
27 Which Jane, the first wife of Ronald Reagan, died in 2007?
28 Whose last screen role was in the 2002 film *Road to Perdition*?
29 Which star of Hollywood Biblical epics died in 2008?
30 Which acclaimed Alan, star of *Eye in the Sky*, died in 2016?

| **Answers** | **TV Pot Luck 7** *(see Quiz 54)* |

1 Nadiya Hussain. 2 Horse Racing. 3 Jason King. 4 Pop Music. 5 Ayres. 6 Radio Times. 7 Alan Bleasdale. 8 Deals on Wheels. 9 Bobbie Charlton. 10 Blake Harrison. 11 Kenny Beale. 12 Kenny. 13 The Landlord of the Nag's Head. 14 Ground Force. 15 The Golden Shot. 16 Trevor MacDonald. 17 Spain. 18 Roy Dotrice. 19 Itt. 20 Nicole. 21 Are You being Served? 22 Dr Peter Benton. 23 Pot Black. 24 Bobby Simone. 25 Bakersfield PD. 26 Give Us a Clue. 27 Pigs. 28 Don Estelle and Windsor Davies. 29 Vulcan. 30 Desmond's.

1 Who won Season 6 (2015) of *Great British Bake Off*?
2 On which sport was John Rickman a commentator?
3 Which screen hero was a thriller writer in *Department S*?
4 What was the subject of the children's programme *Lift-Off*?
5 Which Pam won *Opportunity Knocks* in the 1970s?
6 What is the name of Britain's best loved TV's listings magazine?
7 Who wrote the series *GBH*?
8 Which consumer programme was presented by Mike Brewer and Richard Sutton?
9 Who had a *Football Scrapbook* television programme?
10 Who played Pike in the 2016 film version of *Dad's Army*?
11 Which *EastEnders* character emigrated following an extra-marital affair?
12 Who gets killed in every *South Park* episode?
13 Who was Mike in *Only Fools and Horses*?
14 Which garden-revamping program starred Alan Titchmarsh?
15 On which game show did Anne Aston keep the scores?
16 Who do the magazine *Private Eye* refer to as Trevor Barbados?
17 In which country was *El Dorado* set?
18 Who played Vincent's father in *Beauty and the Beast*?
19 Who is Gomez & Morticia's super-hairy cousin in the *Addams Family*?
20 Which Renault advertising character frequently met her father in compromising situations?
21 Which series featured the character Young Mr Grace?
22 Who is Eriq La Salle's character in *ER*?
23 Which game show is based on snooker?
24 Who is Andy's partner in *NYPD Blue*?
25 Which surreal US cop show only lasted one series in the early 1990s?
26 In which show were Una Stubbs and Lionel Blair team captains?
27 What animals are Peppa's family?
28 Which actors had a hit with "Whispering Grass"?
29 What race is Dr Spock?
30 Which programme is set in a Brixton barbers?

1 Who followed Van Gaal as Man Utd manager in 2016?
2 Who has managed Watford and England?
3 Which club side did Don Revie manage in the 60s and early 70s?
4 In 1996 Trevor Francis became manager of which Midlands club?
5 Which manager's CV reads Wimbledon, Watford, Sheffield Utd and Crystal Palace?
6 Who is known as "The Bald Eagle"?
7 Which club did Joe Royle steer to an FA Cup Final victory over Manchester Utd?
8 Who was in charge of Manchester City when they were relegated in 1996?
9 Which club did Terry Venables manage before taking over the England team?
10 Which Mike has twice become manager of Norwich?
11 Brian Little followed Ron Atkinson at which club?
12 Which Scottish side was managed by Liam Brady?
13 Who returned from Turkey to become boss of Southampton?
14 Which club links Bobby Gould, Phil Neal and Ron Atkinson as managers?
15 Who took Bolton to the Premiership then left for Arsenal?
16 Who took over from Brian Clough at Nottingham Forest?
17 The 50s and 60s at Old Trafford were the years of which manager?
18 Which club made a statement saying that, "Mr Graham did not act in the best interests of the club"?
19 Which Herbert steered Arsenal to three Championships?
20 Terry Butcher took over at which Midlands team in 1990?
21 Which former coach of Finland took over at Fulham in spring 2008?
22 Who left as Sheffield United's manager when they were relegated in 2007?
23 Who was the last Englishman to be manager of Chelsea?
24 Which two London clubs effectively swapped Alan managers in late 2006?
25 Which Dutch club hired former England coach Steve McClaren in 2008?
26 Which manager guided Hull City to the Premiership in 2008?
27 Who was appointed as head coach of the Argentina national team in 2008?
28 Which manager is nicknamed Big Phil?
29 Who succeeded Harry Redknapp as manager of Portsmouth?
30 Who won the 2001 Premier League Manager of the Year despite not winning the title?

1 How is Cherilyn Sarkasian LaPier better known?

2 Which Kylie became engaged to actor Joshua Sasse in 2016?

3 The Colour of what was Celine Dion's top-selling album of 1995?

4 Which instrument did Suzi Quatro play?

5 Which singer called David played Che in the original stage production of *Evita*?

6 What did the painter paint along with Matchstalk Men?

7 Who were Gerry's backing group?

8 Which quartet's only UK No. 1 was "Reach Out I'll be There"?

9 Which country does Demis Roussos come from?

10 Whose first hit was "Love Me Do"?

11 What is the home country of Lulu?

12 Who was Cher's husband when she recorded her first singles?

13 In 1985 Tears for Fears said Everyone Wants to Rule what?

14 Which record label shares its name with an ocean?

15 Which country were the Three Degrees from?

16 Which Bonnie had a 1984 hit with Shakin' Stevens?

17 Which surname is shared by Rod and Dave, formerly of the Eurythmics?

18 Which temptress provided Tom Jones with a 60s hit?

19 Who was lead singer with the Boomtown Rats?

20 Which fruity Fields were the Beatles in in 1967?

21 Whose album was called *Confessions on a Dance Floor*?

22 In which year did Justin Timberlake have a hit with "Sexyback"?

23 Which country singer's autobiography is called *Stand by Your Man*?

24 Who was once backed by the Revolution?

25 Whose Ding-A-Ling took him to No. 1 in 1972?

26 What do the letters r.p.m. stand for?

27 Which family had a hit with "Love Me for a Reason" in 1974?

28 Which Simon and Garfunkel classic has the lines "When tears are in your eyes, I will dry them all?"

29 Which painter is Don McLean's hit "Vincent" about?

30 How may members of the Mamas and Papas were there?

Answers | Football: Managers (see Quiz 55)

1 Jose Mourinho. 2 Graham Taylor. 3 Leeds Utd. 4 Birmingham City. 5 Dave Bassett. 6 Jim Smith. 7 Everton. 8 Alan Ball. 9 Tottenham Hotspur. 10 Walker. 11 Aston Villa. 12 Celtic. 13 Graeme Souness. 14 Coventry City. 15 Bruce Rioch. 16 Frank Clark. 17 Sir Matt Busby. 18 Arsenal. 19 Chapman. 20 Coventry City. 21 Roy Hodgson. 22 Neil Warnock. 23 Glenn Hoddle. 24 West Ham and Charlton (Pardew and Curbishley). 25 Twente Enschede. 26 Phil Brown. 27 Diego Maradona. 28 Felipe Scolari. 29 Tony Adams. 30 George Burley.

1 Which musical set in New York won 10 awards in 1961?

2 "Dances with" what was the first winner of the 1990s?

3 The chauffeur was "Driving Miss" whom in 1989?

4 Who was "in Love" in 1998 to take Best Film honours?

5 *Chariots of Fire* was about events at which 1924 sporting event?

6 What was "Confidential" in the movie with Kim Basinger?

7 Which musical Mary had 13 nominations and five awards in 1964?

8 Judi Dench played which queen in *Shakespeare in Love*?

9 Which "List" won in 1993?

10 *The English Patient* tells of a desert explorer during which war?

11 Which continent was in the title of an 80s winner with Meryl Streep?

12 Which pacifist leader of India was the subject of a 1982 biopic?

13 What was the name of the sequel to *The Godfather* which won two years after the original?

14 Which "Hunter" was the 1979 winner?

15 What was the name of the musical based on a Dickens novel about the boy who asked for more?

16 In which country was *Gigi* set?

17 Who was the 1984 winner *Amadeus* about?

18 Which 80s film is about the Dragon Throne?

19 Which "Connection" was Best Picture of 1971?

20 *Platoon* was set during which Asian conflict?

21 *The Greatest Show on Earth* was about what type of entertainment?

22 *The Sting* won Best Picture during which decade?

23 The most successful winner of the 90s had the shortest name: what?

24 Who was "versus Kramer" in 1979?

25 In which European country was *Cabaret* set during the 1930s?

26 In which year did *Crash* win the Best Picture Oscar?

27 Who wrote the *Lord of the Rings* books, turned into Oscar-winning movies?

28 Which crime thriller won the Best Picture award for 2007?

29 Which Ridley Scott movie won Best Picture for 2000?

30 Who directed 2016's *Sully*?

Answers | TV Pot Luck 8 (see Quiz 58)

1 Juliet Bravo. 2 Newport. 3 Only Fools and Horses. 4 Around the World in 80 Days. 5 The Muppet Show. 6 Lt Fancy. 7 The X-Files. 8 Howe. 9 Crossroads. 10 Robert Lindsay. 11 Mears. 12 Mary Tyler Moore. 13 Lisa. 14 Alexis. 15 Michael Praed. 16 Jan. 17 Sheila. 18 Fantasy Football League. 19 Celebrity Squares. 20 Adrian Chiles. 21 In a windmill. 22 Lottery draw machines. 23 Anita Dobson. 24 You've Been Framed. 25 The Waterhole. 26 Carla Lane. 27 American Football. 28 Lonely. 29 Officer Crabtree. 30 Rose Leslie.

1 Which police drama could be thought as the phonetic alphabet's JB?

2 On which California Beach is *The OC* set?

3 Which series features Denzil and Trigger?

4 Which title by Jules Verne was re-enacted by Michael Palin?

5 Which show featured Animal and Gonzo?

6 Who is in charge of the 15th squad of detectives in *NYPD Blue*?

7 Which programme featured the character Deep Throat?

8 What was Rebecca's surname in *Cheers*?

9 Which soap featured Malcolm McDowell in a guest role?

10 Who played Michael Murray in *GBH*?

11 Which Ray presents his World of Survival on BBC2?

12 Who played Laura in *The Dick Van Dyke Show*?

13 Who is Bart Simpson's older sister?

14 Which character did Joan Collins play in *Dynasty*?

15 Who first played *Robin of Sherwood*?

16 Who was Tom Howard's wife in *Howard's Way*?

17 Who was Barry Grant's mother in *Brookside*?

18 On which programme did Statto and Jeff Astle appear?

19 What was the name of the quiz where the guests sat in boxes?

20 Who hosts *The Apprentice: You're Fired!*?

21 In *Jonathon Creek* where does Jonathon live?

22 What are Lancelot, Guinevere and Arthur?

23 Who recorded "Anyone Can Fall In Love"?

24 Which show features video clips sent in by members of the public?

25 What is the pub in *Neighbours*?

26 Who wrote *Butterflies*?

27 What does Gary Imlach introduce?

28 Who was Callan's informer?

29 What was the policeman's name in *'Allo, 'Allo*?

30 Which actress first said the famous *Game of Thrones* line, "You know nothing, Jon Snow."

Answers	Movies: Oscars – Best Films *(see Quiz 57)*

1 West Side Story. 2 Wolves. 3 Daisy. 4 Shakespeare. 5 Olympic Games. 6 LA. 7 Mary Poppins. 8 Elizabeth I. 9 Schindler's List. 10 World War II. 11 (Out of) Africa. 12 Gandhi. 13 The Godfather Part II. 14 The Deer Hunter. 15 Oliver! 16 France. 17 Mozart. 18 The Last Emperor. 19 The French Connection. 20 The Vietnam War. 21 Circus. 22 1970s. 23 Titanic. 24 Kramer. 25 Germany. 26 2006. 27 J. R. R. Tolkien. 28 The Departed. 29 Gladiator. 30 Clint Eastwood.

1 Which Steve has played 400 plus times for Coventry?
2 Who was Blackburn's regular keeper when they won the Premiership in 1994–95?
3 Which country did Dino Zoff play for?
4 In 2016, which team does Joe Hart play for?
5 Jim Leighton and Les Sealey have both played for which club?
6 Which Liverpool keeper modelled clothes for Giorgio Armani?
7 John Lukic won a Championship medal with Leeds and also with which other club?
8 Casey Keller plays for which country?
9 Who was England's No. 1 in Euro 2016?
10 Who was in trouble for a Nazi-style salute made at Tottenham Hotspur in 1996?
11 Which first name is shared by keepers Dibble and Goram?
12 Joe Corrigan was a great servant for which club?
13 Which Liverpool keeper was dubbed "Jungle Man" by his teammates?
14 For which club has Ludek Miklosko played 300 plus games?
15 Which country does Shay Given play for?
16 Who was England's keeper when they won the World Cup Final?
17 Which Premiership club could boast keepers with Christian names of Pavel and Shaka?
18 Alex Stepney and Gary Bailey have played for which club?
19 Which country does Eike Immel come from?
20 Pressman and Woods have played for which club?
21 Which goalkeeper started wearing a leather helmet in 2007?
22 Who was Arsenal's No. 2 but Germany's No. 1 at Euro 2008?
23 Which Paul was dropped by both Steve McClaren and Juande Ramos in 2007–08?
24 Who collected a 1996 FA Cup runners-up medal and a winner's one in 2008?
25 Which Australian goalkeeper played in the 2005–06 UEFA Cup Final?
26 Who played in goal for Italy in the finals of World Cup 2006?
27 Who won the Yashin Award for best goalkeeper at the 1998 World Cup?
28 How many England caps did Peter Shilton win in his international career?
29 Which Chelsea goalkeeper was nicknamed "The Cat"?
30 Who replaced Jim Leighton for Manchester United in the replay of the 1990 FA Cup final?

Answers | Pop Pot Luck 9 *(see Quiz 60)*

1 Brooks. 2 Elvis. 3 Smile. 4 Five. 5 Ireland. 6 Carlisle. 7 Sensible. 8 That Doggie. 9 Oliver!. 10 Blues. 11 Carroll. 12 Shout. 13 King. 14 70s. 15 The Who. 16 Lauper. 17 Caroline. 18 White Riot. 19 Streets. 20 Something. 21 Amy Winehouse. 22 Fat. 23 Carpenter. 24 Georgie Fame, Alan Price. 25 Alexis. 26 Cleo Laine. 27 k. d. lang. 28 They did not perform on any of their hit records. 29 Greece. 30 She died.

1 Which surname is shared by Elkie and Garth?
2 According to Kirsty MacColl, "There's a Guy Works Down the Chipshop Swears he's" who?
3 What Can't Barry Manilow do Without You according to his 1978 hit?
4 How many members of 1D were there before Zayn Malik left in 2015?
5 What is the home country of Clannad?
6 Which Belinda sang "Heaven is a Place on Earth" in 1987?
7 Which Captain took "Happy Talk" to No. 1 in 1982?
8 What was In the Window when the 50s star Lita Roza asked How Much it was?
9 In which musical, revived in the West End in the 90s, does Fagin appear?
10 Which Moody group sang "Nights in White Satin"?
11 Which Dina pleaded "Don't be a Stranger" in 1993?
12 What did Chaka Demus and Pliers do as well as Twist at No. 1 in 1993?
13 What was the nickname of Natalie Cole's father Nat?
14 In which decade did Hot Chocolate first make the charts?
15 Roger Daltrey was lead singer of which 60s wild group?
16 Which Cyndi proved Girls Just Want to Have Fun in 1984?
17 Which Sweet girl was a 1971 hit for Neil Diamond?
18 What was The Clash's debut single?
19 In which London thoroughfares was Ralph McTell in 1974?
20 What's Gotten Hold of My Heart according to Gene Pitney in 1967?
21 Which singer released the appropriately titled single "Rehab"?
22 Which adjective describes Les, the band who had a hit with "Vindaloo"?
23 Which surname is shared by Karen and Mary-Chapin?
24 Who were Fame and Price together?
25 What was the first name of the Blues guitarist Korner?
26 Which UK jazz singer is married to John Dankworth?
27 Whose first names are Kathryn Dawn although she does not use them in full as a stage name?
28 What was odd about the two members of Milli Vanilli's performance on their hit records?
29 Which country is Vangelis from?
30 What happened to Bobby Goldsboro's Honey in 1968?

| **Answers** | Football: Goalkeepers *(see Quiz 59)* |

1 Ogrizovic. 2 Tim Flowers. 3 Italy. 4 Manchester City. 5 Manchester Utd. 6 David James. 7 Arsenal. 8 USA. 9 Joe Hart. 10 Mark Bosnich. 11 Andy. 12 Manchester City. 13 Bruce Grobbelaar. 14 West Ham Utd. 15 The Republic of Ireland. 16 Gordon Banks. 17 Newcastle Utd. 18 Manchester Utd. 19 Germany. 20 Sheffield Wednesday. 21 Peter Cech. 22 Jens Lehmann. 23 Robinson. 24 David James. 25 Mark Schwarzer. 26 Gianluigi Buffon. 27 Fabien Barthez. 28 125. 29 Peter Bonetti. 30 Les Sealey.

1 *Rebecca* was the first Hollywood movie for which director Alfred?
2 Which Disney movie featured a wooden puppet?
3 Which 1943 movie was outlawed for six years because of Jane Russell's attributes?
4 The 1944 Judy Garland movie says "Meet Me in" which town?
5 What went with "Arsenic" in the comedy with Cary Grant?
6 *National Velvet* centred on what type of animals?
7 *It's a Wonderful Life* is set at which festive time of year?
8 Which Rita played the title role in *Gilda*?
9 At what time of year was the "Parade" which starred Fred Astaire and Judy Garland?
10 Which "Magnificent" family was the subject of a 40s movie directed by Orson Welles?
11 What sort of animal was Dumbo?
12 Which "Story" with Cary Grant and Katharine Hepburn had the name of a US state in its title?
13 Which colour completes the title of 1941 Oscar winner, *How ____ was My Valley*?
14 What was the nationality of the "Falcon" in the 1941 movie with Humphrey Bogart and Peter Lorre?
15 Which "Citizen" was a debut for Orson Welles?
16 On which street was there a "Miracle" in a 1947 film?
17 What colour were the dancing shoes in the movie with Moira Shearer?
18 Which movie has the line, "Here's lookin' at you kid"?
19 In which Austrian city is *The Third Man* set?
20 What type of servicemen were on leave in *On the Town*?
21 Which private detective Marlowe is the subject of *The Big Sleep*?
22 Which dictator did Chaplin play and mock in *The Great Dictator*?
23 Which Disney movie was the tale of a young fawn?
24 Who was the most famous director of *Fantasia*?
25 What went with "Kind Hearts" in the movie with Alec Guinness?
26 Which Daphne Du Maurier novel was turned into a 1940 blockbuster?
27 *The Pride of* which baseball team received Oscar nominations in 1942?
28 Who played the disillusioned nightclub owner in *Casablanca*?
29 Which actress starred in *The Life and Death of Colonel Blimp*?
30 Who directed *Arsenic and Old Lace* in 1944?

Answers | **TV Pot Luck 9** *(see Quiz 62)*

1 Julianna Margulies. 2 Warrior. 3 The Sullivans. 4 Paul Henry. 5 Sylvia Costas. 6 Anita Harris. 7 Bless This House. 8 Local Heroes. 9 Michael Newman. 10 Arnie Thomas. 11 Weather presenters. 12 Camelot. 13 625. 14 Astra. 15 Esther Rantzen. 16 Les Dawson. 17 Kermit the Frog. 18 Five. 19 A chat show host. 20 Oprah. 21 Basil Brush. 22 Magpie. 23 Derek Nimmo. 24 Wilma. 25 Gordon Kaye. 26 Barcelona. 27 Mel Smith. 28 Mrs Slocombe. 29 Peter Sellers. 30 Wilson.

1 Which actress is *The Good Wife*?
2 What type of Princess was Xena?
3 What was the first Australian soap shown in the UK?
4 Who recorded *Benny's Theme*?
5 Who is Andy Sipowicz married to in *NYPD Blue*?
6 Who starred in *Anita in Jumbleland*?
7 In which series did Robin Stewart play Sally Geeson's brother?
8 Which series is presented by Adam Hart-Davis?
9 Which character on *Baywatch* plays himself?
10 What was Tom Arnold's character in *Roseanne*?
11 What are Suzanne Charlton and John Kettley?
12 Who runs *The National Lottery*?
13 How many lines are transmitted in terrestrial television?
14 What satellites beam BSkyB programmes?
15 Who presented *That's Life*?
16 Who appeared with Roy Barraclough as Cissie and Ada?
17 Which Muppet is adored by Miss Piggy?
18 How many channels are available on analogue terrestrial television?
19 What is David Letterman?
20 What is chat show host Ms Winfrey's first name?
21 Which fox is a puppet?
22 Which programme did Mick Robertson and Douglas Rae present?
23 Who played Noote in *All Gas and Gaiters*?
24 Who is Fred Flintstone's wife?
25 Who plays Rene Artois in *'Allo, 'Allo*?
26 Where does Manuel come from in *Fawlty Towers*?
27 Who is Griff Rhys-Jones's comedy partner?
28 Who was worried about her pussy in *Are You being Served*?
29 Which of *The Goons* was an international film star?
30 Which character is a sergeant in *Dad's Army*?

1 Which club is known as the Gunners?

2 "Psycho" is the nickname of which fullback?

3 Which club are called the Trotters?

4 Which Midlands team have a name to be sheepish about?

5 Which London club are known as the Blues?

6 What is the animal link with Hull?

7 SLOW is an anagram of which club's nickname?

8 Which creatures could sting you at Brentford?

9 Which England player is known as Rodney?

10 At which club can you shout Cobblers to show your appreciation?

11 Management men Ron and Jack are usually described by what word?

12 Which Scottish team is known as the Dons?

13 And which English team is known as the Dons?

14 Who are The Blades?

15 Who is known as "Sparky"?

16 Which ground are you at if the Foxes are at home?

17 Which nickname dogs Huddersfield?

18 Who are the Toffees?

19 The Bhoys is the nickname of which team?

20 Which Liverpool player was nicknamed "Digger"?

21 Who was self-dubbed "The Special One"?

22 Which Royals spent two seasons in the Premiership?

23 Who was dubbed "Braveheart" during his spell with Rangers?

24 Initially, how was the Chelsea captain in 2007–08 known?

25 What colour felines might be spotted at the Stadium of Light?

26 Who are the Saints of Paisley?

27 Who were once nicknamed the Biscuitmen?

28 Which Italian football club is known as the Old Lady?

29 Which African national team is nicknamed the Elephants?

30 Who was nicknamed "The Sultan of the Stepover"?

---

1 Sasha Baron Cohen almost portrayed which singer in a 2016 biopic?

2 Which Little girl did the Everly Brothers tell to Wake Up in 1957?

3 Which Hank was part of the Shadows and has had solo success?

4 Which surname is shared by the singer/drummer Phil and singer Judy?

5 Which military duo were the top-selling album artists of 1995?

6 What is the home country of Men at Work, who had a No. 1 with "Down Under"?

7 In which band does Francis Rossi play guitar and take lead vocals?

8 Which Bette is known as "The Divine Miss M"?

9 How is Ultravox's James Ure better known?

10 Which Irish group had a hit with the Osmonds' "Love Me for a Reason" in 1994?

11 What goes before Order and Model Army in the names of groups of the 80s and 90s?

12 Which Gary took "Cars" to the top in 1979?

13 Which 90s Disney film was Peter Andre's "Kiss the Girl" taken from?

14 Which animal links the performer Roland and the subject of the song "Ben"?

15 How many Degrees were in the group that sang "When Will I See You Again"?

16 How is Thomas Woodward better known?

17 Which sporting event shot the Lightning Seeds to fame?

18 Elvis sang about what kind of Heart in 1961?

19 What is the home country of Mariah Carey?

20 Which Hollies hit begins "The road is long, with many a winding turn"?

21 What nationality is Nelly Furtado?

22 Tom Fletcher is the lead singer of which band?

23 Which part of the UK is Aled Jones from?

24 Who was Zag's puppet partner on "Them Girls Them Girls" in 1994?

25 Which word goes before Affair and Unlimited in the names of groups?

26 Which band was originally called Curiosity Killed the Cat?

27 Which singer was nicknamed the King?

28 Which glam group went on a "Teenage Rampage"?

29 How is David Robert Jones better known?

30 How many members of Meat Loaf are there?

Answers | Football: Nicknames *(see Quiz 63)*

1 Arsenal. 2 Stuart Pearce. 3 Bolton. 4 Derby County (the Rams). 5 Chelsea. 6 Tigers. 7 Sheffield Wednesday (Owls). 8 Bees. 9 Tony Adams. 10 Northampton. 11 Big. 12 Aberdeen. 13 Wimbledon. 14 Sheffield Utd. 15 Mark Hughes. 16 Filbert Street. 17 Terriers. 18 Everton. 19 Celtic. 20 John Barnes. 21 Jose Mourinho. 22 Reading. 23 Gennaro Gattuso. 24 J. T. 25 Black. 26 St Mirren. 27 Reading. 28 Juventus. 29 Ivory Coast. 30 Cristiano Ronaldo.

1 What colour were Paul Newman's eyes?
2 Which Elizabeth was his co-star in *Cat on a Hot Tin Roof*?
3 In which decade was he Oscar-nominated for *The Hustler*?
4 Which Martin directed him in *The Color of Money*?
5 Who was his co-star in *Butch Cassidy and the Sundance Kid*?
6 In which 70s disaster movie did he play the architect of a skyscraper?
7 In which city is *The Sting* set?
8 In which decade was *Butch Cassidy* first released?
9 Which actor Sidney is co-partner in his production company First Artists?
10 He founded the Scott Newman Foundation in memory of his son who died from what?
11 Which actress Joanne did Paul Newman marry in 1958?
12 What "Menagerie" did he direct in 1987?
13 Which singer Julie was his co-star in *Torn Curtain* in 1966?
14 Which speed sport was he involved in, which he used in 1969 in *Winning*?
15 Which western hero Billy did he play in *The Left-Handed Gun*?
16 In 1978 which Democratic US President appointed him a US delegate to the UN Conference on Nuclear Disarmament?
17 In *Butch Cassidy and the Sundance Kid*, which part did he play?
18 Which "Long Hot" season was the title of a 1958 movie?
19 In which movie did he play conman Henry Gondorff?
20 How was his character Eddie Felson described?
21 Which "Cool Hand" character did he play in 1967?
22 What type of salad product did he market for charity?
23 He and his wife played "Mr and Mrs" who in 1990?
24 Which Oscar did he win for *The Color of Money*?
25 In which decade did he team up again with Redford for *The Sting*?
26 In which film did Newman depict the career the boxer Rocky Graziano?
27 For which 2005 TV mini-series did Newman win an Emmy and a Golden Globe?
28 Which actress became Newman's second wife?
29 Which presidential candidate did Newman prominently support in 1968?
30 What was the original product of Newman's Own?

1 Philip Fry is the hero in which long-running cartoon series?
2 Which host of *QI* got married in 2015?
3 Who did Karl Howman play in *Brushstrokes*?
4 What is the clown's name in *The Simpsons*?
5 What type of programme was *Dungeons & Dragons*?
6 Who is the headmaster in *Home and Away*?
7 Who is Madge's husband in *Neighbours*?
8 Who stars as Sheldon Cooper in B*ig Bang Theory*?
9 What is Superman's earthly name?
10 Who is Sooty's female friend?
11 Which private detective was portrayed by Buddy Ebsen?
12 Which character had three sons, Adam, Hoss and Little Joe?
13 Which *Doctor Who* starred in the very first *Carry On* film?
14 Which satellite channel is famous for re-running old programmes?
15 What was *The Fugitive*'s profession?
16 Who did James Arness portray in *Gunsmoke*?
17 Who played Jonathan in *Highway to Heaven*?
18 Who played Paladin in *Have Gun Will Travel*?
19 Which post did Michael Hayes hold?
20 Which character was the D.J. in *Midnight Caller*?
21 Who created *Neighbours*?
22 Which James was "in the pits" for ITV's Formula One coverage in 1998?
23 Who was the first British winner of *The World's Strongest Man*?
24 What was *Catweazle*?
25 Who played Jack in *On the Buses*?
26 On which show would you hear the catchphrase "Cheque, please"?
27 In which series is the character Dave Hedgehog?
28 Who played Booker in *Roseanne*?
29 Who in *Drop the Dead Donkey* is Henry's co-presenter?
30 Which landlady, in *Coronation Street*, was mugged on her way home from The Rover's Return?

Answers | **Movies: Paul Newman** *(see Quiz 65)*

1 Blue. 2 Taylor. 3 1960s. 4 Scorsese. 5 Robert Redford. 6 Towering Inferno.
7 Chicago. 8 1960s. 9 Poitier. 10 Drug overdose. 11 Woodward. 12 The Glass
Menagerie. 13 Andrews. 14 Motor racing. 15 Billy the Kid. 16 Jimmy Carter. 17
Butch Cassidy. 18 Summer. 19 The Sting. 20 Fast. 21 Luke. 22 Salad dressing. 23
Bridge. 24 Best Actor. 25 1970s. 26 Somebody up There Likes Me. 27 Empire Falls.
28 Joanne Woodward. 29 Eugene McCarthy. 30 Salad dressing.

1 Which jockey rode the winning horse at the 2016 Grand National?
2 Which horse was first to win the Grand National three times?
3 Where is the William Hill Lincoln Handicap held?
4 Trainers Lynda and John Ramsden won a libel case against which paper?
5 In which country was Shergar captured?
6 In which month is the Melbourne Cup held?
7 Who was National Hunt champion jockey from 1986 to 1992?
8 Which horse won the 2016 Grand National?
9 Which English classic is held at Doncaster?
10 Which 100-1 shot won the 2009 Grand National?
11 Which horse race was abandoned in 1997 after a bomb scare?
12 The Prix du Jockey-Club is held at which race course?
13 Which horse had the nickname Corky?
14 Which Gordon, a trainer of over 2000 winners, died in September 1998?
15 Which country hosts the Belmont and Preakness Stakes?
16 Which race meeting is described as Glorious?
17 The 12th Earl of where gave his name to a famous race?
18 The Curragh is in which Irish County?
19 Where did Frankie Dettori have his record-breaking seven wins?
20 In which country is Flemington Park race course?
21 The Velka Pardubice is the top steeplechase race in which European country?
22 Which jockey was retired because of his injuries in the 2008 Grand National?
23 In which Irish county is Aidan O'Brien's yard situated?
24 In which Middle East country is the world's richest race held?
25 On which famous race course do horses cross The Chair and Melling Road?
26 Which horse won the Cheltenham Gold Cup in 2007?
27 Which American thoroughbred was the subject of a major film in 2003?
28 Which Southampton footballer went on to become a successful racehorse trainer?
29 How much would you be wagering if you put a "Monkey" on a horse?
30 On which French race course is the Prix de l'Arc de Triomphe run?

| **Answers** | **Football Pot Luck 6** (see Quiz 68) |

1 Thistle. 2 Blue. 3 Scotland. 4 Liverpool. 5 Agent. 6 Greig. 7 Francis. 8 Chester City. 9 Nottingham Forest. 10 The Cherries. 11 Grobbelaar. 12 The Republic of Ireland. 13 Mabbutt. 14 Joe Royle. 15 McGrath. 16 Wimbledon. 17 France. 18 Ian Wright. 19 Switzerland. 20 Eric Cantona. 21 23. 22 Middlesbrough. 23 Norwich City. 24 Edinburgh. 25 John Barnes. 26 Pale blue and white stripes. 27 Wark. 28 Eric Cantona. 29 Nottingham Forest. 30 Liverpool.

1 What is the last word in Partick's name?
2 What is the main colour in Cardiff's home strip?
3 Which country has Pat Nevin played for?
4 Philippe Coutinho was 2015's Player of the year for which club?
5 What is the job of Rune Hauge?
6 Which John of Rangers was Scottish Footballer of the Year in 1966?
7 Which Gerry became Tottenham Hotspur's boss in November 1994?
8 With which club did Ian Rush make his League debut?
9 Which club did Lars Bohinen leave to join Blackburn?
10 What is Bournemouth's nickname?
11 Which keeper Bruce was charged with match-fixing in 1995?
12 Which country has Mark Lawrenson played for?
13 Which Gary has played 450 plus games in defence for Tottenham Hotspur?
14 Which manager won the 1995 FA Cup with Everton?
15 Which Paul was PFA Player of the Year in 1993?
16 Which team became known as "The Crazy Gang"?
17 Which country did Zinedine Zidane play for?
18 Who had "I Love The Lads" written on his T-shirt?
19 Artur Jorge was whose national coach during Euro 96 ?
20 Who returned after an eight-month suspension in October 1995?
21 What number shirt did David Beckham wear at Real Madrid?
22 At which Premiership club was Steve McClaren boss before replacing Eriksson?
23 Which East Anglian side did John Bond manage?
24 Which Tottenham Hotspur defender shares his surname with a Scottish city?
25 Which England player is the son of a Jamaican international?
26 What colour are Argentina's home shirts?
27 Which John of Ipswich was PFA Player of the Year in 1981?
28 Who was the first player to win the League with different teams in consecutive seasons?
29 Des Walker and Roy Keane were teammates at which club?
30 Which club did Ray Clemence leave to join Tottenham Hotspur?

Answers	Horse Racing (see Quiz 67)

1 David Mullins. 2 Red Rum. 3 Doncaster. 4 The Sporting Life. 5 Ireland. 6 November. 7 Peter Scudamore. 8 Rule the World. 9 St Leger. 10 Mon Mome. 11 National. 12 Chantilly. 13 Corbiere. 14 Richards. 15 United States. 16 Goodwood. 17 Derby. 18 Kildare. 19 Ascot. 20 Australia. 21 Czech Republic. 22 Mick Fitzgerald. 23 Tipperary. 24 Dubai. 25 Aintree. 26 Kauto Star. 27 Seabiscuit. 28 Mick Channon. 29 £500. 30 Longchamp.

1 Which Girls reunited as a trio in 2016 to celebrate 21st anniversary of debut album?
2 Which Irish sisters were In the Mood for Dancin' in the 70s?
3 Which group's debut album was *Always and Forever* – like their name?
4 Which group were once called the Bangs?
5 How many people made up Bananarama?
6 Name this popular girl : _____ Harmony
7 How many Degrees said Take Good Care of Yourself in 1975?
8 Which Phil Spector group had Ronnie Bennett on lead vocals?
9 Which Motown group consisted of Diana Ross, Mary Wilson and Florence Ballard?
10 In Wilson Phillips, do the Wilsons outnumber the Phillipses or vice versa?
11 What goes before "Ron Ron" on the title of the Crystals' first major hit?
12 The Chapel of what became a million-seller for the Dixie Cups?
13 What was the surname of Martha who was often backed by the Vandellas?
14 Were the Pointer Sisters really sisters?
15 Who was Pepa's partner in the 80s rap group?
16 Which Leader provided a once-banned hit for the Shangri-Las?
17 Which Sister group had a No. 1 with "Frankie"?
18 Which mother-and-daughter country group consisted of Wynonna and Naomi?
19 Who switched on the London Christmas lights in December 1996?
20 Whose first hit was "Be My Baby" in 1963?
21 Which girl group announced a reunion tour in 2007 after seven years apart?
22 Lisa Lopes of TLC was known for which particular facial feature?
23 From which country do the Dixie Chicks come?
24 What type of Dolls are also known as PCD?
25 Beyonce Knowles, Kelly Rowland and Michelle Williams are Destiny's what?
26 What was the name of Martha Reeves' backing group?
27 Who had a hit in 1982 with "I'm So Excited"?
28 Which Bananarama song got to No. 1 in the United States?
29 Who had a breakthrough hit in the UK with "Freak Like Me"?
30 Which girl band was "Out of Control" in 2008?

1 Which actor of *Mrs Doubtfire* and *Jumanji* died in 2016?

2 Which Danny starred in *LA Confidential*?

3 *Gregory's Two Girls* was the sequel to which film?

4 Which Michael played Marty in *Back to the Future*?

5 Which musical set in gangland New York won 11 Oscars in the 60s?

6 Which Henry wrote the score for *The Pink Panther*?

7 Peter Lawford was the brother-in-law of which late US president?

8 In the film's title, which word describes Clint Eastwood's character Harry?

9 Who wrote the musical score for *Star Wars*?

10 Who was billed in his first movie as Arnold Strong?

11 Forties movie *The Outlaw* featured which Jane?

12 Which actress links *Ghost* and *The Juror*?

13 Which musical about Danny and Sandy was re-released in the 90s?

14 Which Nicolas starred in *Leaving Las Vegas*?

15 Who was Vincente Minnelli's famous daughter?

16 Which word completes the film title, *A Room with a ____*?

17 *Land Girls* starred which Anna?

18 Which Meg starred in *When Harry Met Sally*?

19 Madonna bought a burial plot next to where which blonde icon is buried?

20 In which decade of the 20th century was Al Pacino born?

21 Which Ralph starred in the film version of *The Avengers*?

22 According to the film title, what should you do to your wagon?

23 Which Annette was Warren Beatty's first wife?

24 In which decade was *Some Like It Hot* released?

25 Did *Babe* run for 52, 92 or 182 minutes?

26 Which Peter, a British actor with a Russian surname, died in 2004?

27 In which city is 2006's Best Movie *The Departed* set?

28 Who directed *The BFG in 2016*?

29 Which Kristen starred in *The Horse Whisperer*?

30 In which decade was *Moonraker* released?

Answers | **Pop: All-Girl Groups** *(see Quiz 69)*

1 Spice. 2 Nolans. 3 Eternal. 4 The Bangles. 5 Three. 6 Fifth.
7 Three. 8 Ronettes. 9 The Supremes. 10 2 Wilsons, 1 Phillips. 11 "Da Doo". 12 Love. 13 Reeves. 14 Yes. 15 Salt. 16 Of The Pack. 17 Sledge. 18 The Judds. 19 Spice Girls. 20 The Ronettes. 21 Spice Girls. 22 Her left eye. 23 United States. 24 Pussycat Dolls. 25 Child. 26 The Vandellas. 27 The Pointer Sisters. 28 Venus. 29 Sugarbabes. 30 Girls Aloud.

1 Who is Ardal O'Hanlon's superhero in *My Hero*?
2 What is *The Third Rock from the Sun*?
3 What was Harry in *Harry and the Hendersons*?
4 Who was Lurcio in *Up Pompeii!*?
5 Who was the punk in *The Young Ones*?
6 Which comedy series featured the *River Police*?
7 Which Nick is the chairman of *They Think It's All Over*?
8 Who divorced Dawn French?
9 Which character was the *Man About the House*?
10 Who does Tony fancy in *Men Behaving Badly*?
11 Who are TV's rag and bone men?
12 In *The Good Life* who is Margo's husband?
13 In *Only Fools and Horses* who is Del's brother?
14 Who plays *Roseanne*'s husband?
15 In *Friends* who is Monica's brother?
16 What is *Seinfeld*'s christian name?
17 Which series featured Maplins Holiday Camp?
18 Who was "The One with the Glasses"?
19 Where is *Spin City* set?
20 Who plays Victor Meldrew?
21 Where does *Ellen* work?
22 Who plays Larry Sanders?
23 Who was the female star of *Moonlighting*?
24 Who played Jeeves to Hugh Laurie's Bertie Wooster?
25 What is *Seinfeld*'s job?
26 Which family feature in *Till Death Us Do Part*?
27 Which comedy show is the TV version of radio's *News Quiz*?
28 Who plays Mrs Slocombe in *Are You Being Served*?
29 What is Homer Simpson's middle initial?
30 What is Basil Fawlty's wife's name?

Answers | **Football Pot Luck 7** *(see Quiz 72)*

1 Norwich City. 2 Red. 3 Everton. 4 Rovers. 5 Holland. 6 Macari. 7 Arsenal.
8 Rangers. 9 Wimbledon. 10 Red and white. 11 Blake. 12 Bradford City. 13
Southampton. 14 Portugal. 15 Manchester City. 16 Waddle. 17 QPR. 18 Newell.
19 Goalkeeper. 20 Barnes. 21 Ashley Cole. 22 Fabio Capello. 23 Allen. 24
Blackburn Rovers. 25 Tottenham Hotspur. 26 Liberia. 27 Celtic. 28 Manchester Utd
and Carlisle Utd. 29 Arsenal. 30 Neville Neville.

1 Who plays at home at Carrow Road?
2 What is the main colour of Charlton's home shirts?
3 Kendall and Royle have both managed which club?
4 What second name is shared by Blackburn and Doncaster?
5 Which country did Ruud Gullit play for?
6 Which Lou became Stoke boss in 1994?
7 Alan Smith knocked in 23 goals when which side were champions?
8 Which British club did Oleg Salenko join in 1995?
9 Which club did Andy Thorn join on leaving Crystal Palace?
10 What colours are Southampton's home shirts?
11 Which Nathan was Sheffield Utd's top League scorer in 1995–96?
12 Which club have the nickname the Bantams?
13 Ian Branfoot was sacked in 1994 by which Premiership side?
14 Which country has Paulo Sousa played for?
15 Which team does Eddie Large support?
16 Which Chris won the Footballer of the Year award in 1993?
17 Which London club did Jan Stesjkal play for?
18 Which Mike has hit a European Cup hat-trick for Blackburn?
19 Which position does Rene Higuita play?
20 Which Peter of Manchester City was PFA Young Player of the Year in 1976?
21 Which Arsenal defender joined Chelsea in 2006?
22 Which Italian managed Real Madrid to the Spanish League title in 2007?
23 Which Clive of Tottenham Hotspur won the Footballer of the Year award in 1987?
24 Which team lost both the 1994 and 1995 Charity Shield games?
25 Which team does Bruce Forsyth support?
26 Which country does George Weah play for?
27 Which Scottish team won the Championship nine times in a row starting in 1966?
28 Martin Edwards has been chairman of which clubs?
29 Which London club has had a long-time sponsorship with JVC?
30 What is the Neville brothers' father called?

1 How many members made up the Rolling Stones when they first charted?

2 Which musical instrument does Charlie Watts play?

3 Which former Rolling Stone's real name is William Perks?

4 Which words go in brackets before the 1965 No. 1 "Satisfaction"?

5 Which two words describe the Rooster in the Stones' No. 1 in November 1964?

6 Which Merseysiders, later seen as the Stones' rivals, wrote the Stones' first top 20 hit "I Wanna be Your Man"?

7 The Stones' first album was called *The Rolling Stones*. What was the second one called?

8 Which Nervous Breakdown features in the title of the 1966 hit?

9 In which part of his home was Brian Jones found dead in July 1969?

10 Which controversial song was on the B-side of "Ruby Tuesday"?

11 Who did Bianca Rose Perez Moreno de Macias marry in 1970?

12 Complete the title of the 70s album *Goat's Head____*.

13 Which record label signed the Stones in the early 1990s?

14 Who was Jagger Dancin' in the Street with at the Live Aid concert?

15 Who quit the Stones in 1992?

16 Which Stones guitarist sang with the X-pensive Winos?

17 What colour did the Rolling Stones Paint It in 1966?

18 What was Tumbling for the Stones in their top five hit in 1972?

19 Which record label did the Stones record on throughout the 60s?

20 What was the Stones' own record label called?

21 What type of establishment is the Bill Wyman-owned Sticky Fingers?

22 What was the Stones' 2005–07 world tour called?

23 Which label did the Stones leave in 2008?

24 What cinema video for IMAX presentations was released in 2008?

25 How old was Mick Jagger at the end of the 2007 tour?

26 Name any two of the three founder members of the group.

27 What appropriately was the name of the Rolling Stones' first album?

28 Can you name their fourth British No. 1 and perhaps their best known?

29 Which Stones concert album was released in 1970?

30 What Park did the Stones play a free concert in two days after Brian Jones died?

---

1 Which Robert starred in 2015's *A Walk in the Woods*?
2 Who won the Best Actor Oscar for *Rain Man*?
3 Which pop group starred in *Spiceworld*?
4 Whose "World" was a 1992 film with Mike Myers and Dana Carvey?
5 *Shine* is about a musician playing which instrument?
6 Which actor stars as the titular hero in 2016's *Sully*?
7 Which colour goes before "Narcissus" and "mail" to form film titles?
8 Johnny Weissmuller portrayed which jungle hero?
9 Who are the two main characters in *The X-Files*?
10 Which Bo Derek film had a number as the title?
11 Who starred opposite Jennifer Gray in *Dirty Dancing*?
12 Which Donald played Hawkeye in the film *M*A*S*H*?
13 Who starred in and directed *Monsieur Hulot's Holiday*?
14 Which movie used the song "Everything I Do (I Do It for You)"?
15 In which decade of the 20th century was Jack Nicholson born?
16 Which colour links "Shoes" and "Dust" in film titles?
17 Which sergeant created by Phil Silvers featured in a 90s movie?
18 Which actress links *Fatal Attraction* and *101 Dalmatians*?
19 What is the name of Tatum O'Neal's actor father?
20 Which creatures dominated 2015's *Jurassic World*?
21 *The First Wives' Club*, *Ruthless People* and *Hocus Pocus* all feature which actress?
22 A werewolf in London and a man in Paris were both of what nationality?
23 In which decade was *The Godfather* released?
24 What was the Bond theme for *The Living Daylights* called?
25 Who played opposite Patrick Swayze in *Ghost*?
26 No what *for Old Men* won the Academy Award for Best Picture in 2007?
27 Whose adventure was *The Order of the Phoenix*?
28 Which former partner of Mick Jagger appeared in *Batman*?
29 Which John starred in *Face/Off*?
30 Which word completes the film title, *Monty Python's The ____ of Life*?

Answers | Pop: The Rolling Stones *(see Quiz 73)*

1 Five. 2 Drums. 3 Bill Wyman. 4 I Can't Get No. 5 Little Red. 6 Lennon and McCartney. 7 The Rolling Stones No. 2. 8 19th. 9 Swimming Pool. 10 "Let's Spend the Night Together". 11 Mick Jagger. 12 Soup. 13 Virgin. 14 David Bowie. 15 Bill Wyman. 16 Keith Richards. 17 Black. 18 Dice. 19 Decca. 20 Rolling Stones. 21 A restaurant. 22 Bigger Bang Tour. 23 EMI. 24 Shine a Light. 25 64. 26 Brian Jones, Ian Stewart & Mick Jagger. 27 The Rolling Stones. 28 (I Can't Get No) Satisfaction. 29 Get Yer Ya-Ya's Out!. 30 Hyde Park, London.

1 Which Peter became Doctor Who in 2013?
2 Which Beau plays the lead in *Stargate SG-1*?
3 Who was the female communications officer aboard the first USS *Enterprise*?
4 What exalted position was attained by Sheridan on *Babylon 5*?
5 Which Fox show starring Scully and Mulder got a new series in 2016?
6 Which series featured Moonbase Alpha?
7 What race is Lt Worf in *Star Trek: The Next Generation*?
8 Who were *Captain Scarlet*'s enemies?
9 Who is the captain of the USS *Voyager*?
10 Who was Sapphire's partner?
11 On which show did you find Lori Singer travelling in cyberspace?
12 "Only David Vincent knows" – about whom?
13 Who is "faster than a speeding bullet"?
14 Who is Batman's assistant?
15 Which Flash fought the evil Emperor Ming?
16 *The Hitch-Hiker's Guide* was a guide to what?
17 Who was assisted by robots called Tweaky and Theo?
18 According to the series title how many were in Blake's crew?
19 Who are flung from one dimension to the next at the end of each show?
20 Which spaceship did Lorne Green command?
21 Which space opera series was created by writers Morgan and Wong of X-files fame?
22 How many characters form the crew of *Red Dwarf*?
23 Which show about invading aliens had a one-letter title?
24 In which programme would you find an intelligent computer called KITT?
25 How was Number Six known?
26 Which alien plants invaded following a comet's blinding appearance?
27 "Anything can happen in the next half-hour" on which show?
28 What type of vehicle was *Streethawk*?
29 What colour was the *Incredible Hulk*?
30 Which Lamborghini-driving crime-fighter was generated by a computer?

Answers	**Football Pot Luck 8** *(see Quiz 76)*

1 Rovers. 2 Crystal Palace. 3 Wales. 4 Swansea City. 5 Durie. 6 Yugoslavia.
7 Liverpool. 8 Manchester Utd. 9 Derby County. 10 McStay. 11 The Bees. 12 The Republic of Ireland. 13 Sheffield Weds. 14 Holland. 15 Pallister. 16 Blue.
17 Chelsea. 18 Steve Howey. 19 Arsenal. 20 Liverpool. 21 Mark Hughes. 22 Republic of Ireland. 23 Arsenal. 24 Armfield. 25 Manchester Utd. 26 Sweden. 27 McDermott. 28 Tottenham Hotspur. 29 Quinn. 30 Liverpool.

1 What is the last word in Raith's team name?
2 Which London team wear red and blue striped shirts at home ?
3 Which country has Barry Horne played for?
4 Who plays at home at the Vetch Field?
5 Which Gordon was Rangers' top League scorer in 1995–96?
6 Which national team has Savo Milosevic played for?
7 Martin Škrtel was Player of the Year 2011-12 for whom?
8 With which club did Keith Gillespie make his League debut?
9 Which club did Mark Wright leave to join Liverpool?
10 Which Paul of Celtic was Scottish Footballer of the Year in 1988?
11 What is Brentford's nickname?
12 Which country has Terry Phelan played for?
13 David Pleat followed Trevor Francis as boss at which club?
14 Which country does Patrick Kluivert play for?
15 Which Gary of Manchester Utd was PFA Player of the Year in 1992?
16 What colour are Scotland's home shirts?
17 Durie and Dixon formed a striking duo at which London club?
18 Which Newcastle centre half had to pull out of England's Euro 96 squad?
19 Which club was dubbed as being "Lucky"?
20 Scales and Collymore were teammates for which losing FA Cup Finalists?
21 Which Welshman managed Blackburn Rovers and Manchester City in 2008?
22 Which country played internationals at Croke Park in 2007 and 2008?
23 David Rocastle played over 200 games for which London club?
24 Which Jimmy helped the FA to find a new England coach in 1996?
25 Which team does Mick Hucknell support?
26 What country has Thomas Ravelli played for?
27 Which Terry of Liverpool was PFA Player of the Year in 1980?
28 Irving Scholar was chairman of which London club?
29 Which Mick knocked in over **30** League goals for Newcastle in 1989–90?
30 In 2015-16 Philippe Coutinho played for which squad?

Answers	TV: Sci Fi 1 *(see Quiz 75)*

1 Capaldi. 2 Bridges. 3 Lt Uhura. 4 President. 5 The X Files. 6 Space 1999. 7 Klingon. 8 The Mysterons. 9 Captain Janeway. 10 Steel. 11 VR5. 12 The Invaders. 13 Superman. 14 Robin. 15 Flash Gordon. 16 The Galaxy. 17 Buck Rogers. 18 Seven. 19 The Sliders. 20 Battlestar Galactica. 21 Space – Above and Beyond. 22 Four. 23 V. 24 Knight Rider. 25 The Prisoner. 26 The Triffids. 27 Stingray. 28 A motorcycle. 29 Green. 30 Automan.

1 Which 2012 movie theme song begins "This is the end, Hold your breath and count to ten?

2 Which Will Young song begins "I'm here just like I said"?

3 Which Tony's 2005 re-release of a 1971 hit begins, "Sha la la lala lalala"?

4 How is the positive way James Blunt's "You're Beautiful" begins?

5 "Closed off from love, I didn't need the pain" opens which Leona Lewis hit?

6 Which karaoke classic begins "First I was afraid, I was petrified"?

7 Which song starts "And now the end is near"?

8 What are the first three words of "Unchained Melody"?

9 Which Rhapsody begins "Is this the real life? Is this just fantasy?"?

10 Which Boyzone hit begins "Smile an everlasting smile"?

11 How many times is "Yeah" sung in the chorus of the Beatles' "She Loves You"?

12 Which soccer anthem begins "When you walk through a storm"?

13 Which words follow "Wake up Maggie" in Rod Stewart's "Maggie May"?

14 Which words from the Abba hit go before "It's a rich man's world"?

15 What five words does Stevie Wonder sing after "I just called…"?

16 How many times are the words "We are the champions" sung in the chorus of the song?

17 Which line follows "If I said you had a beautiful body"?

18 Which Cliff Richard classic begins, "When I was young my father said"?

19 Which Slade Christmas hit includes the line "Does your grandma always tell ya, That the old songs are the best?"?

20 What did Carly Simon sing before "I bet you think this song is about you"?

21 Which Robson and Jerome hit included the lines "for every drop of rain that falls, A flower grows"?

22 Which Wet Wet Wet hit begins "I feel it in my fingers, I feel it in my toes"?

23 Which Cher No. 1 includes the lines "If you want to know if he loves you so, It's in his kiss"?

23 Which Don McLean song asks "Do you believe in rock 'n' roll?"?

25 Which song begins "Never seen you looking so gorgeous as you did tonight"?

26 "It's easy if you try" is the second line of what famous John Lennon song?

27 This Gloria Gaynor hit is one of the most played karaoke songs of all time. Name it.

28 What did Queen's Freddie Mercury admit to in the No.1 hit "Bohemian Rhapsody"?

29 This Christmas No.1 hit of 1984 begins "It's Christmas Time." Name the song.

30 Name either one of the main two singers on "You're the One That I Want".

Answers | **Movies Pot Luck 9** (see Quiz 78)

1 Harrelson. 2 Pierce Brosnan. 3 Clarice. 4 Belgium. 5 Dynasty. 6 90 minutes. 7 Keaton. 8 John Travolta. 9 Christie. 10 1990s. 11 Ryan O'Neal. 12 The Third Man. 13 Australia. 14 Matthau. 15 Wayne. 16 1960s. 17 Raiders. 18 Gwyneth Paltrow. 19 Basinger. 20 Gulf War. 21 1950s. 22 Rocky. 23 Crackers. 24 Young. 25 Irene Cara. 26 Silence. 27 Richard Pryor. 28 Bancroft. 29 Michelle Pfeiffer. 30 Temple.

1 Which Woody starred in *2016 's Now You See Me 2*?

2 Which 007 starred in *2015's November Man*?

3 What is the first name of FBI agent Starling in *The Silence of the Lambs*?

4 In which country was Jean-Claude Van Damme born?

5 In which TV soap did Joan Collins and John Forsythe find fame after appearing on the big screen?

6 Did *Aladdin* run for 60, 90 or 130 minutes?

7 Which Diane played Steve Martin's wife in *Father of the Bride*?

8 Which *Grease* star danced with Princess Diana at the White House?

9 Which Julie links *Darling* in the 1960s and *Afterglow* in the 90s?

10 In which decade of the 20th century did James Stewart die?

11 Which actor was tennis star John McEnroe's first father in law?

12 The character Harry Lime appears in which spy thriller?

13 What was Crocodile Dundee's homeland?

14 *The Sunshine Boys* starred which Walter?

15 Which western star John first acted as "Duke Morrison"?

16 In which decade was *Psycho* released?

17 In a movie title, which word goes before "of the Lost Ark"?

18 Which actress links *Se7en* and *Sliding Doors*?

19 Which Kim likened Hollywood to the Mafia?

20 *Three Kings*, with George Clooney, takes place during which war?

21 In which decade of the 20th century was Liam Neeson born?

22 In which 1976 movie did Sylvester Stallone play a boxer?

23 What type of snack completes the film title *Animal ____*?

24 Which famous Loretta tested for the role of Scarlett O'Hara?

25 Who sang "Fame" in *Fame*?

26 What was *Dead* in James Wan's 2007 movie?

27 Which comedian and star of *Brewster's Millions* and *Stir Crazy* died in 2005?

28 Which Anne starred in the 1998 *Great Expectations*?

29 *The Witches of Eastwick* and *Up Close and Personal* both feature which actress?

30 Which Shirley won an Oscar at the age of five?

Answers	Pop: Karaoke *(see Quiz 77)*

1 Skyfall. 2 (I Think I) Better Leave Right Now. 3 Christie. 4 "My life is brilliant". 5 Bleeding Love. 6 "I Will Survive". 7 "My Way". 8 "Oh my love". 9 Bohemian. 10 "Words". 11 Ten. 12 "You'll Never Walk Alone". 13 "I think I got somethin' to say to you". 14 "Money Money Money". 15 "...to say I love you". 16 Four. 17 "Would you hold it against me". 18 "Bachelor Boy". 19 "Merry Xmas Everybody". 20 "You're so vain". 21 "I Believe". 22 "Love is All Around". 23 "The Shoop Shoop Song". 24 "American Pie". 25 "Lady in Red". 26 Imagine. 27 I Will Survive. 28 Murder. 29 Do They Know It's Christmas? 30 John Travolta & Olivia Newton-John.

1 Which cult 1960s children's show was made into a 2005 movie?
2 In which year was *Grange Hill*'s final series first broadcast?
3 Who are the stars of 2014's *Most Wanted*, alongside Ricky Gervais?
4 Which country did the star of 2015's *The Paddington Movie* come from?
5 Which programme began with the words "Here is a house. Here is a door. Windows: one, two, three, four"?
6 In *Sesame Street*, what was the name of the grumpy creature who lived in a trash can?
7 What sort of animal was Skippy?
8 Who is Wile E Coyote always trying to catch?
9 Which Superhero does Princess Diana of Paradise Island become?
10 Which show featured the tallest, fastest, biggest and other outstanding achievements?
11 What did *Top Cat* sleep in?
12 Which programme featured Parsley the Lion and Lady Rosemary?
13 Which Gerry and Sylvia pioneered Supermarionation?
14 What was the name of Mork's Earthling girlfriend?
15 What was the surname of *The Beverley Hillbillies*?
16 Who was the Caped Crusader?
17 *Animal Magic* was presented by who?
18 How was Granny Smith better known?
19 On *The Magic Roundabout*, what kind of creature is Brian?
20 What was *Worzel Gummidge*?
21 Which Mike drove the *Supercar*?
22 Which cartoon cat yells "I hate those meeces to pieces!"?
23 Which programme has been presented by John Noakes, Peter Purves, Janet Ellis, Simon Groom and Lesley Judd as well as many others?
24 *Pebbles and Bam Bam* was a spin-off from which other cartoon series?
25 Which former *Minder* played *Just William*?
26 The Fat Controller, Gordon, Bertie the Bus are all characters in which series?
27 Tucker, Zammo, Stu Pot and Roly all went to which school?
28 Musky and Vince were pals of which law-enforcing cartoon dog?
29 Who was Shari Lewis's famous puppet?
30 ITV's 80s kids' interest programme was named after which acquisitive bird?

Answers | Football Pot Luck 9 (see Quiz 80)

1 Everton. 2 Norwich City. 3 Rangers. 4 City. 5 Czech Republic. 6 Chelsea. 7 Germany. 8 Aberdeen. 9 QPR. 10 Red. 11 Woan. 12 The Seagulls. 13 Wolves. 14 FA Charity Shield. 15 Nottingham Forest. 16 Holland. 17 Scotland. 18 Lineker. 19 Portugal. 20 Gray. 21 David De Gea. 22 Portugal. 23 Southampton. 24 Aston Villa. 25 Fulham. 26 Bulgaria. 27 Burns. 28 John Lyall. 29 Trinidad & Tobago. 30 QPR.

1 Who plays at home at Goodison Park?
2 Ian Crook has played over 300 games for which club?
3 Graeme Souness and Walter Smith have both managed which club?
4 What is the last word in Birmingham's name?
5 Which country has Patrik Berger played for?
6 Which team does Jeremy Vine support?
7 Which country do Cologne come from?
8 With which club did goalkeeper Bryan Gunn make his debut?
9 Which club did Ray Wilkins join on leaving Rangers?
10 What colour goes with white on Sunderland's home shirts?
11 Which Ian was Nottingham Forest's joint top League scorer in 1995–96?
12 What is Brighton's nickname?
13 Mark McGhee followed Graham Taylor as boss at which club?
14 League champions play FA Cup winners for which trophy?
15 Keeper Mark Crossley has played over 200 games for which club?
16 Which country do Ajax come from?
17 Which country did Graeme Sharp play for?
18 Which Gary won the Footballer of the Year award in 1992?
19 Which country does Rui Costa play for?
20 Which Andy of Villa was PFA Young Player of the Year in 1977?
21 Who was Manchester United's Player of the Year in 2015–16?
22 Which country won Euro 2016?
23 Tim Flowers and Neil Ruddock were in the same team at which club?
24 Dr Josef Venglos was manager of which English team?
25 Which team does Hugh Grant support?
26 Which country does Hristo Stoichkov play for?
27 Which Kenny of Forest won the Footballer of the Year award in 1978?
28 Who was West Ham manager from 1974–89?
29 Dwight Yorke plays international soccer for which team?
30 Ray Wilkins and Andy Sinton were at which club together?

Answers   TV: Children's TV 2 *(see Quiz 79)*

1 Magic Roundabout. 2 2008. 3 Muppets. 4 Peru. 5 Play School. 6 Grover. 7 A kangaroo. 8 Roadrunner. 9 Wonder Woman. 10 Record Breakers. 11 A trash can. 12 The Herbs. 13 Anderson. 14 Mindy. 15 The Clampetts. 16 Superman. 17 Johnny Morris. 18 Supergran. 19 A snail. 20 A scarecrow. 21 Mike Mercury. 22 Mr Jinks. 23 Blue Peter. 24 The Flintstones. 25 Dennis Waterman. 26 Thomas the Tank Engine. 27 Grange Hill. 28 Deputy Dawg. 29 Lamb Chop. 30 Magpie.

1 Which group includes the two Gallagher brothers?
2 Which group did Jason Orange leave in 2014?
3 Frankie Goes to where in the name of the 80s group?
4 Which Boys were famous for their surfing sound in the 60s and 70s?
5 Which City Rollers were teen idols in the 70s?
6 Which Club was fronted by Boy George?
7 What was the ELO's full name?
8 Which group shares its name with the first book of the Bible?
9 Who were the other half of the Mamas?
10 Which band's three-word name describes the British weather?
11 Which group is made up of the Gibb brothers?
12 Which ex-Beatle formed Wings?
13 Which group had albums called *The Wall* and *Dark Side of the Moon*?
14 Which group were 5 until they lost Michael?
15 What follows Earth and Wind in the group of the 70s?
16 Which point of the compass is Beautiful?
17 Which group was Sweden's biggest export?
18 Which group did Diana Ross leave to go solo?
19 Which 90s group shares its name with a district of London?
20 Which band with Mark Knopfler had the album *Brothers in Arms*?
21 Which group did Bryan McFadden leave in 2004?
22 Which group comprised Keisha Buchanan, Heidi Range and Amelle Berrabah?
23 Which band's first single was "Five Colours in Her Hair"?
24 Which Sheffield group sound like anthropoids from the North Pole?
25 Which group's first UK No. 1 single was "Viva La Vida"?
26 "The Power of Love" was the third and last UK No. 1 for this group. Name them.
27 Who enjoyed their first UK No. 1 with "Country House" in 1995?
28 What was the name of the Spice Girls' first UK No. 1 single?
29 "Never Forget" was the seventh UK No. 1 for this group. Name them.
30 In 1981, "Jealous Guy" was this band's first and only UK No. 1 hit.

Answers	Movies Pot Luck 10 *(see Quiz 82)*

1 Austin Powers. 2 Robert Zemeckis. 3 "Moon River". 4 Jungle. 5 Fonda. 6 Chariots of Fire. 7 Scar. 8 Thompson. 9 Muhammad Ali. 10 Elvis Presley. 11 Arnold Schwarzenegger. 12 39 (The Thirty-Nine Steps). 13 Barbra Streisand. 14 Gorillas. 15 1980s. 16 Vinnie Jones. 17 1950s. 18 Emma Thompson. 19 James Bond. 20 Key. 21 Jessica Lange. 22 Cruise. 23 Rowan Atkinson. 24 Hanks. 25 1960s. 26 Casino Royale. 27 Batman. 28 Arnold Schwarzenegger. 29 The Muppets. 30 Foster.

1 Who, in the movie title, is the "International Man of Mystery"?
2 Who directed 2015's The Walk?
3 Which song won Best Song Oscar for Breakfast at Tiffany's?
4 What word links a "Book" and "Asphalt" to form two film titles?
5 Which Jane starred in Barbarella?
6 Which British movie is about the 1924 Olympics?
7 What's the name of the chief villain of The Lion King?
8 Which Emma wrote the screenplay for Sense and Sensibility?
9 Which boxer appeared in The Greatest?
10 Love Me Tender was the first film for which rock 'n' roll star?
11 Which actor links True Lies, Total Recall and Escape Plan?
12 The character Richard Hannay appears in a film about how many steps?
13 Who played Dolly in the 60s movie Hello Dolly?
14 Which creatures were "in the Mist" in the title of the Sigourney Weaver movie?
15 Was Ghostbusters first released in the 1960s, 70s or 80s?
16 Which hard man English football player appeared in 2014's Galavant?
17 In which decade of the 20th century was Dennis Quaid born?
18 Which wife of Kenneth Branagh has also been Oscar nominated?
19 Who did Timothy Dalton play in Licence to Kill?
20 Which word completes the film title, ____ Largo?
21 Who played the Fay Wray role in the remake of King Kong?
22 Which Tom starred in A Few Good Men?
23 Who created the accident-prone Mr Bean?
24 Which Tom starred in 2016's Hologram for the King?
25 In which decade was You Only Live Twice released?
26 Which was the first James Bond movie to be remade, opening in 2006?
27 Which superhero was the hero of The Dark Knight?
28 Eraser, The Terminator and Last Action Hero all feature which actor?
29 Which band of puppets featured in their own Christmas Carol?
30 Which Jodie directed 2016's The Money Monster?

Answers	Pop: Groups (see Quiz 81)

1 Oasis. 2 Take That. 3 Hollywood. 4 Beach Boys. 5 Bay. 6 Culture. 7 Electric Light Orchestra. 8 Genesis. 9 Papas. 10 Wet Wet Wet. 11 Bee Gees. 12 Paul McCartney. 13 Pink Floyd. 14 Jacksons. 15 Fire. 16 South. 17 Abba. 18 Supremes. 19 East 17. 20 Dire Straits. 21 Westlife. 22 Sugababes. 23 McFly. 24 Arctic Monkeys. 25 Coldplay. 26 Frankie Goes to Hollywood. 27 Blur. 28 Wannabe. 29 Take That. 30 Roxy Music.

1 Tom Harper directed which 2015 epic BBC drama?
2 Aidensfield is the setting for which ITV drama?
3 Complete the title of this TV show: _____ Blinders?
4 What was Glenda Jackson's royal role?
5 Which series featured Colt Seevers?
6 Which TV cop is played by Paul Michael Glaser?
7 Which mystery series stars Angela Lansbury?
8 Who played Boon?
9 Who was The Prisoner?
10 Who played Mrs Peel in The Avengers?
11 Which series featured women in a Japanese prison camp?
12 What was Horace Rumpole's profession?
13 Who plays Lovejoy?
14 Which series starred Nick Berry as a policeman?
15 Which ex-Coronation Street star appeared in Where the Heart is?
16 What is the Australian series about a women's detention centre?
17 Who played The Sculptress?
18 In which series was the character Elliot Ness?
19 In which series are Peter Benton and Carol Hathaway?
20 Which series features Baz, Megan and Charlie?
21 Which drama series, set in the Edwardian era, featured the wealthy Bellamy family?
22 Which actress links House of Cards to Ultraviolet?
23 In which series did Robson and Jerome first appear together?
24 Who plays Jonathan Creek?
25 Who starred as The Equaliser?
26 Which ex-Neighbours actor starred in Bugs?
27 Who played Jonathan in Hart to Hart?
28 Who were Bodie and Doyle?
29 Who played Crockett in Miami Vice?
30 In Cagney and Lacey who was the sergeant?

Answers	**Football Pot Luck 10** *(see Quiz 84)*

1 Albion. 2 Arsenal. 3 Chelsea. 4 England. 5 Tottenham Hotspur. 6 32. 7 Murdoch. 8 West Ham Utd. 9 Leeds Utd. 10 Craig Brown. 11 The Robins. 12 Scotland. 13 Orange. 14 Liverpool. 15 Hughes. 16 Southampton. 17 Argentina. 18 George Graham. 19 McNeill. 20 Croatia. 21 Luton Town. 22 Southampton. 23 Oldham Athletic. 24 Barry Fry. 25 Red. 26 Coventry City. 27 Brady. 28 Liverpool. 29 Brazil. 30 Coppell.

1 What is the last word in Stirling's name?
2 Which London club wear red and white hooped socks?
3 With which club did Ray Wilkins make his League debut?
4 Which country has Terry Butcher played for?
5 Who plays at home at White Hart Lane?
6 How many goals did Sergio Agüero score for Man City in 2014–2015?
7 Which Bobby of Celtic was Scottish Footballer of the Year in 1969?
8 Redknapp followed Bonds as boss at which club?
9 Which club did Eric Cantona leave to join Manchester Utd?
10 Who was the Scotland manager for Euro 96?
11 What is the nickname of Bristol City?
12 Which country has Willie Miller played for?
13 What colour are the home shirts of Holland?
14 "You'll Never Walk Alone" is the anthem of which team?
15 Which Mark was PFA Player of the Year in 1991?
16 Dave Merrington was coach for 11 years before becoming boss of which club?
17 River Plate play in which country?
18 Who was boss of Arsenal's 1990–91 championship-winning side?
19 Which Billy became the first Celtic player also to manage the club?
20 Which country has Igor Stimac played for?
21 Which Coca-Cola League Two team were deducted 30 points for 2008–09?
22 Who left the Dell for St Mary's in 2001?
23 Gunnar Halle first played in England for which club?
24 Who put his money into Peterborough in 1996?
25 What colour are Middlesbrough's home shirts?
26 Kevin Richardson and John Salako were together at which club?
27 Which Liam was PFA Player of the Year in 1979?
28 Which club did Mark Walters leave to join Southampton?
29 Which country did Socrates play for?
30 Which Steve has been Technical Director for Crystal Palace?

---

1 Which international teams contest the Ashes?
2 In which city is the ground Old Trafford?
3 In LBW what does the B stand for?
4 In 2016, which Stuart was ranked the fourth best bowler in the world?
5 Which county was captained by Graham Gooch?
6 The fans of which county cricket club have Mustard and Onions to savour?
7 The Vauxhall End, the Laker Stand and the Harleyford Road are all linked to which ground?
8 Which team won the County Championship in 2003, 2006 and 2007?
9 Which England player is nicknamed "Freddie"?
10 Which Test team does Chris Gayle play for?
11 What is the distance in yards between the two sets of stumps on a cricket pitch?
12 Which county does Monty Panesar play for?
13 What was the specialist fielding position of Australia's Mark Waugh?
14 Edgbaston is in which English city?
15 How many wickets fall in a hat-trick?
16 What are the initials of Alan Knott?
17 Which country was captained by Stephen Fleming?
18 In the 1930s, which Les was a wicketkeeper-batsman for England?
19 In scoring, what does LBW stand for?
20 Which county side was captained by Jack Bond?
21 Who succeeded Michael Vaughan as captain after he resigned in August 2008?
22 Which England coach took ten wickets in an innings for Durham in 2007?
23 Whose Test wicket record did Muttiah Muralitharan pass in 2007?
24 What is the nickname of the 2008 IPL Champions from Rajasthan?
25 Who played for Ireland in the 2007 World Cup qualifiers and England in the finals?
26 Name the Andre who was voted the Irish Cricketer of the Year for 2008.
27 Can you name the coach of England at the 2007 Cricket World Cup?
28 After what cartoon character does Andrew Flintoff get the nickname "Freddie"?
29 Name the Mickey who was appointed the coach of South Africa in 2005.
30 This Pakistan fast bowler was detained in Dubai in 2008 for possessing opium.

1 Which Pistols rotter advertised butter in 2010?
2 Which Olivia had a 70s hit with "Sam"?
3 Which Christie featured on a 90s "Walk Like a Panther"?
4 How many members of Bucks Fizz were there?
5 What is the home country of Chris de Burgh?
6 What was Justin Bieber's second single from *Purpose* in 2015?
7 Which country does Bonnie Tyler come from?
8 Which birthday did Shirley Bassey celebrate in January 1997?
9 Which US state had a hit with "White on Blonde"?
10 Which hostel did the Village People stay at?
11 How does the country singer Whitman describe his physique?
12 How many times did Dawn say to knock on the ceiling in their 1971 hit?
13 Who was the shortest Beatle?
14 Which Roy was lead singer with Wizzard?
15 Which record label shares its name with a fruit?
16 Which Deep colour is the name of a band who first found fame in the 70s?
17 What goes with Parsley and Sage in the Simon and Garfunkel song?
18 What do the letters R and B stand for?
19 Who is Tom Jones singing about when he sings "My, my, my" then "Why why why"?
20 Which soul singer Heard It Through the Grapevine?
21 Which Preachers charted with "The Masses Against the Classes"?
22 In which decade was Britney Spears born?
23 Which film star's eyes were a hit for Kim Carnes?
24 What was Bruce Springsteen Born to do in 1987?
25 Which wine was Elkie Brooks singing about in 1978?
26 What went with Gypsies and Tramps on Cher's 1971 single?
27 Which Crisis had an 80s hit with "Arizona Sky"?
28 The Bangles were heard to Walk Like who in 1986?
29 Which Lynn had an international hit with "Rose Garden"?
30 Whose remix of "Downtown" re-entered the charts in 1988?

Answers | **Cricket Pot Luck 2** (see *Quiz 85*)

1 Australia and England. 2 Manchester. 3 Before. 4 Broad. 5 Essex. 6 Durham. 7 The Oval. 8 Sussex. 9 Andrew Flintoff. 10 West Indies. 11 22. 12 Northamptonshire. 13 The slips. 14 Birmingham. 15 Three. 16 A.P.E. 17 New Zealand. 18 Ames. 19 Leg Before Wicket. 20 Lancashire. 21 Kevin Pietersen. 22 Ottis Gibson. 23 Shane Warne. 24 Royals. 25 Ed Joyce. 26 Andre Botha. 27 Duncan Fletcher. 28 Fred Flintstone. 29 Mickey Arthur. 30 Mohammad Asif.

1 Which "World" was a blockbuster in 2015?
2 Who played Jordan in 2013's *Wolf of Wall Street*?
3 What was the nationality of Oskar Schindler in Spielberg's movie?
4 Which shark-infested movie was the first to take $100 million at the box office?
5 In which movie was someone told to "phone home"?
6 What sort of "Menace" was Episode I in the *Star Wars* movies?
7 What mythical sea creature did Daryl Hannah play in *Splash!*?
8 Who played Schindler in *Schindler's List*?
9 Which song was used for the hugely successful *The Full Monty*?
10 What was the most expensive film made in the 20th century?
11 What was the name of the 24th Bond film, released in 2015?
12 Who played Dan Gallagher in *Fatal Attraction*?
13 Which musical was made about Eva Peron?
14 How was the "Mission" described in the 1996 release with Tom Cruise?
15 For which role was Faye Dunaway Oscar-nominated in *Bonnie and Clyde*?
16 Mel Gibson's movie *Gallipoli* was set during which war?
17 Which "King" grossed the fourth highest sum in the US in the 1990s?
18 What did E stand for in *E.T.*?
19 Which singer played Rachel Marron in *The Bodyguard*?
20 Who won the Best Director Oscar for *Schindler's List*?
21 Which "Day" was released just before the 4th of July in the US?
22 "Tomorrow is another day" is the last line of which movie?
23 In which movie did Warren Beatty say, "We rob banks"?
24 *The Empire Strikes Back* was the sequel to which blockbusting film?
25 Which David won the Best Director Oscar for *The Bridge over the River Kwai*?
26 What was the title of Sylvester Stallone's 2006 reprise of his boxer hero?
27 Who had an adventure in the Chocolate Factory in 2005?
28 Can you name the "*Citizen*" Orson Welles portrayed in a 1941 blockbuster?
29 This 1942 masterpiece is set in a western city of Morocco staring Humphrey Bogart.
30 Marilyn Monroe, Tony Curtis and Jack Lemmon star in this 1959 sizzler.

Answers   **TV Pot Luck 11** *(see Quiz 88)*

1 Everybody. 2 Have I Got Old News for You. 3 Karl Malden. 4 Hamish Macbeth. 5 The Naked City. 6 Jack Klugman. 7 A spoof soap. 8 Ben Murphy. 9 Ballykissangel. 10 Teri Hatcher. 11 Mission: Impossible. 12 Northern Exposure. 13 Marian. 14 Sam Malone. 15 Auf Wiedersehen Pet. 16 The Dick Van Dyke Show. 17 Darren. 18 Seattle. 19 Two. 20 Blanche Deveraux. 21 Gary. 22 Mrs Doyle. 23 Candice Bergen. 24 Ritchie Cunningham. 25 Michael Crichton. 26 The Trotters. 27 Sarah. 28 Coronation Street. 29 Baywatch. 30 Face to Face.

1 Who hates Chris in the American sitcom?
2 How are repeat editions of *Have I Got News for You* billed?
3 Who co-starred with Michael Douglas in *The Streets of San Francisco*?
4 Which series starred Robert Carlyle as a Scottish policeman?
5 Which crime series of the 60s featured tales of the 65th Precinct of New York?
6 Who plays *Quincy*?
7 What kind of programme was *Mary Hartman, Mary Hartman*?
8 Who played Kid Curry in *Alias Smith and Jones*?
9 Which series featured the character Father Peter Clifford?
10 Who portrays Lois Lane in *The New Adventures of Superman*?
11 Which series featured the IMF team?
12 Which series centred around the inhabitants of Cicely, Alaska?
13 Which character did Judi Trott portray in *Robin of Sherwood*?
14 Which ex-baseball star ran the *Cheers* bar?
15 Which series featured Tim Healy, Kevin Whately and Jimmy Nail as site workers in Germany?
16 Which series featured Rob and Laura Petrie?
17 Who was Samantha's husband in *Bewitched*?
18 Where is Frasier's radio station?
19 How many sons does Rab C. Nesbit have?
20 Which of the *Golden Girls* was a southern belle?
21 Who is Dorothy's boyfriend in *Men Behaving Badly*?
22 Who is *Father Ted*'s housekeeper?
23 Who starred as *Murphy Brown*?
24 What was Ron Howard's character in *Happy Days*?
25 Who is the creator of *ER*?
26 Who lived at Nelson Mandela House, Peckham?
27 Who is Tony Hill's sister in *EastEnders*?
28 Which soap is set in Weatherfield?
29 In which series did Erika Eleniak play a lifeguard?
30 Which series of interviews was introduced by John Freeman?

Answers | **Movies: Blockbusters** *(see Quiz 87)*

1 Jurassic Park. 2 Leonardo DiCaprio. 3 German. 4 Jaws. 5 E. T. 6 The Phantom Menace. 7 Mermaid. 8 Liam Neeson. 9 You Sexy Thing. 10 Spectre. 11 The World is Not Enough. 12 Michael Douglas. 13 Evita. 14 Impossible. 15 Bonnie. 16 World War I. 17 The Lion King. 18 Extra. 19 Whitney Houston. 20 Steven Spielberg. 21 Independence Day. 22 Gone with the Wind. 23 Bonnie and Clyde. 24 Star Wars. 25 Lean. 26 Rocky Balboa. 27 Charlie. 28 Citizen Kane. 29 Casablanca. 30 Some Like It Hot.

1 Charlie George helped which side to the double?
2 Which Derek was elected chairman of the PFA?
3 1971 witnessed over 60 deaths at which Scottish ground?
4 Giles, Lorimer and Clarke were stars of which club side?
5 League soccer was played on which day for the first time?
6 The 11-year reign of which England boss ended in 1974?
7 Which country won the 1970 World Cup?
8 Which Manchester Utd boss was sacked for an affair?
9 Which West Brom player was suspected of having a hole in the heart?
10 Which manager was known as "Big Mal"?
11 Which country was credited with developing total football?
12 Gordon Banks and George Eastham played together for which club?
13 Which manager led both Derby and Forest to the championship?
14 Which German club won the European Cup three years in a row?
15 Elton John was elected chairman of which club?
16 McGuinness and O'Farrell were managers at which club?
17 Which Brazilian player scored his 1,000th goal?
18 Which red and yellow items were introduced in the Football League in 1976?
19 Which London team were elected into the League?
20 Which England boss was banned for 10 years for bringing the game into disrepute?
21 Who did Newcastle lose to when Ronnie Radford scored a special FA Cup goal?
22 Who was sent off with Billy Bremner in the 1974 Charity Shield?
23 Who needed replays to win the FA Cup in 1970 and Cup Winners Cup in 1971?
24 Who won the Scottish League every year from 1970 to 1974?
25 How many games did England lose in the 1970 World Cup finals?
26 Stan Bowles was a star at which London club?
27 Which country attracted Pele and Bobby Moore to end their careers?
28 Who did Ipswich Town beat to win the FA Cup for the first time?
29 David Needham and Kenny Burns were together at which club?
30 Which club did Steve Heighway play for?

Answers	**Pop Pot Luck 12** *(see Quiz 90)*

1 The Aces. 2 Gibb. 3 Cyndi Lauper. 4 Tamla Motown. 5 Of Man. 6 SOS. 7 Boy George. 8 Pat. 9 USA. 10 Jim Reeves. 11 Prison. 12 Simply Red. 13 King. 14 Relax. 15 The Monkees. 16 Australia. 17 "Vogue". 18 The Roof. 19 Jack Flash. 20 Bono. 21 7. 22 Durst. 23 Roy Orbison. 24 Isley. 25 Janet. 26 Scotland. 27 Roberts. 28 Manhattan Transfer. 29 Paul Nicholas. 30 David Jones.

1 Who were Desmond Dekker's backing group?
2 Which surname is shared by the brothers Barry, Maurice and Robin?
3 Who had an album called *Seven Deadly Cyns ... And Then Some*?
4 Which record label did the Four Tops record their 60s hits on?
5 Which Brotherhood won the Eurovision Song Contest for the UK in 1976?
6 Which Abba single is a distress signal?
7 Who was Culture Club's singer?
8 What is the first name of the US vocalist Ms Benatar?
9 Which country do R.E.M. come from?
10 Which late country singer recorded "I Love You Because"?
11 What type of institution is Johnny Cash performing in on *Johnny Cash at San Quentin*?
12 Whose albums have been Simply called *Stars* and *Life*?
13 Which Carole had a best-selling 70s album called *Tapestry*?
14 How did Frankie Goes to Hollywood tell us to unwind in 1984?
15 Which animal-sounding US group had a British vocalist, Davy Jones?
16 What is the home country of Jason Donovan?
17 Which 90s Madonna hit shares its name with a glossy magazine?
18 Robson and Jerome were Up on what part of the house in 1995?
19 Which Jumpin' character was a hit for the Rolling Stones and Aretha Franklin?
20 Who is U2's lead singer?
21 What number completed the group S Club?
22 Which Fred was lead singer for Limp Bizkit?
23 Which singer was nicknamed the Big "O"?
24 Which Motown Brothers sang "Behind a Painted Smile" in 1969?
25 Which girl is the youngest of the singing Jackson family?
26 Which part of the UK is Annie Lennox from?
27 Which actress Julia was Lyle Lovett married to?
28 Which area of New York was transferred to the name of a vocal quartet?
29 Which actor/singer had an album called *Just Good Friends* after the sitcom in which he starred?
30 Which Monkee had the same name as David Bowie's real name?

Answers | Football: The 1970s *(see Quiz 89)*

1 Arsenal. 2 Dougan. 3 Ibrox. 4 Leeds Utd. 5 Sunday. 6 Sir Alf Ramsey. 7 Brazil.
8 Tommy Docherty. 9 Asa Hartford. 10 Malcolm Allison. 11 Holland. 12 Stoke City.
13 Brian Clough. 14 Bayern Munich. 15 Watford. 16 Manchester Utd. 17 Pele.
18 Cards. 19 Wimbledon. 20 Don Revie. 21 Hereford United. 22 Kevin Keegan.
23 Chelsea. 24 Celtic. 25 Two. 26 Queens Park Rangers. 27 USA. 28 Arsenal. 29 Nottingham Forest. 30 Liverpool.

1 What was the first talkie?
2 In the first *Toy Story*, which child owns the toys?
3 Which film company opened the first ever theme park?
4 Where in Italy did the first film festival take place?
5 Which monster lizard, first seen in 1955, was in a 1997 blockbuster?
6 What was the first movie in which Eastwood was Harry Callahan?
7 Which Fay was the first scream queen, in *King Kong*?
8 What was Disney's first feature film – with eight people in the title?
9 Which oriental detective Charlie first appeared on screen in 1926?
10 Where were India's first studios, giving rise to the name "Bollywood"?
11 What was the first two-colour system used in movie making?
12 *The Robe* was the first movie with what type of screen?
13 *The Scent of Mystery* was the first movie with sight, sound and what?
14 Which 1995 "Story" was the first computer-animated film?
15 What was the first major movie about the Vietnam War?
16 Which 1946 Oscar-winning Dickens film gave Alec Guinness his major movie debut?
17 Which movie with an all-child cast was Alan Parker's directorial debut?
18 Which Ralph played Steed in the first Avengers movie to hit the big screen?
19 In which decade were the Oscars first presented?
20 Which Christmas classic was first heard in *Holiday Inn*?
21 Who was Oscar-nominated for his directorial debut in *Ordinary People*?
22 Which Brothers made the first talkie?
23 In which movie did Al Jolson say, "You ain't heard nothin' yet"?
24 Which Katharine won the first BAFTA Best Actress award?
25 In which French city was the first movie in Europe shown?
26 Which Jack played the Joker in the first Tim Burton Batman movie?
27 Which was Walt Disney's first cartoon character?
28 Which was the first X-rated cartoon to be released?
29 This famous awards ceremony first took place in 1929. Name it.
30 Can you name the US city where commercial movies were first screened in 1923?

Answers | **TV Pot Luck 12** *(see Quiz 92)*

1 Bolton. 2 Channel 5. 3 Sooty. 4 The Wedding of the Prince of Wales and Lady Diana Spencer. 5 Blue Peter. 6 Bill Owen. 7 Else. 8 Paul Daniels. 9 Norway. 10 The Two Rons. 11 Emma Willis. 12 Jane Tennison. 13 Castor. 14 Jim Henson. 15 Barry Grant. 16 Bod. 17 John Major. 18 Charades. 19 Captain Mainwaring. 20 It ain't Half Hot Mum. 21 David Jacobs. 22 Lurcio. 23 Athletics. 24 Richard Cole. 25 Blackstock. 26 Mr Burns. 27 Mechanic. 28 BBC1. 29 Mr Humphries. 30 George Cole.

1 In which Lancashire town is the Phoenix Club in *Phoenix Nights*?
2 Which channel began broadcasting *Big Brother* in 2011?
3 Which puppet has been presented by father Harry and son Matthew?
4 Which Royal Event was televised on 29 July 1981?
5 Which children's programme featured Patch and Petra?
6 Who plays Compo in *Last of the Summer Wine*?
7 What was Alf's wife's name in *Till Death Us Do Part*?
8 Who was the host of *Odd One Out*?
9 Which country failed to score in the 1978 *Eurovision Song Contest*?
10 Who are referred to as "The Management"?
11 Who started presenting *Big Brother* in 2013?
12 Which character does Helen Mirren play in *Prime Suspect*?
13 What was the name of Olive Oyl's brother?
14 Which puppeteer created a muppet for *Sam and Friends*?
15 Who is the last remaining original character in *Brookside*?
16 Which cartoon featured Mr Copper?
17 Which character in *Spitting Image* commented on the peas?
18 Which party game was *Give Us a Clue* based on?
19 Who called Pike 'You stupid boy' in *Dad's Army*?
20 What was the comedy series about a concert party in India?
21 Who presented *Juke Box Jury*?
22 Who was Ludicrus Sextus's servant in *Up Pompeii*?
23 Which sport does Stuart Storey commentate on?
24 Who in *EastEnders* was known as Tricky Dicky?
25 In *Chef* what is Gareth's surname?
26 Who is Homer Simpson's boss?
27 What was Sid Hooper's occupation in *Crossroads*?
28 On which channel was *Mastermind* broadcast?
29 Whose catchphrase is "I'm free" on *Are You being Served*?
30 Who played Arthur Dailey in *Minder*?

Answers	**Movies: Famous Firsts** *(see Quiz 91)*

1 The Jazz Singer. 2 Andy. 3 Disney. 4 Venice. 5 Godzilla. 6 Dirty Harry. 7 Wray.
8 Snow White and the Seven Dwarfs. 9 Chan. 10 Bombay. 11 Technicolor. 12
Widescreen (Cinemascope). 13 Smell. 14 Toy Story. 15 The Deer Hunter. 16 Great
Expectations. 17 Bugsy Malone. 18 Fiennes. 19 1920s. 20 "White Christmas".
21 Robert Redford. 22 Warner. 23 The Jazz Singer. 24 Hepburn. 25 Paris. 26
Nicholson. 27 Mickey Mouse. 28 Fritz the Cat. 29 Academy Awards. 30 New York
City.

1 Who plays at home at Griffin Park?
2 Which London club did Anders Limpar play for?
3 Who beat Fulham to win the 70s all-London FA Cup Final?
4 John Spencer left which London club to join QPR?
5 Graham Roberts played for Chelsea and which other London club?
6 Barry Hearn became chairman of which East London club?
7 At which stadium do MK Dons play their home games?
8 Which London club did Stan Bowles play for?
9 Have Charlton ever won an FA Cup Final?
10 Which club plays nearest to the River Thames?
11 Which London club did Peter Osgood play for?
12 Which Billy has made a record number of League appearances for West Ham?
13 George Graham and John Docherty have both managed which London club?
14 Which side did manager Steve Coppell take to an FA Cup Final?
15 Jimmy Hill has been chairman of which London team?
16 Who won 108 England caps playing for one club?
17 For which London side did Peter Shilton make his 1,000th League appearance?
18 Who are nicknamed the Hornets?
19 Which London club did Gary Lineker play for?
20 Which London side finished highest in the Premiership in season 1995–96?
21 Which London club sacked Martin Jol in autumn 2007?
22 Which London club entered the Football League for the 2007–08 season?
23 Which London club was relegated from the Premiership in May 2007?
24 Who took over as Queens Park Rangers' manager in the summer of 2008?
25 Which London club moved into the Emirates Stadium in 2006?
26 Can you name the London club which celebrated its Centenary Year in 2005?
27 In 1901, this London club became the only non-League side to win the FA Cup.
28 Name the most recent London club to win the Premier League.
29 This London club's ground is also known as the Boleyn Ground.
30 What was the name of the Chelsea song which reached No. 5 in the charts in 1972?

Answers | Pop Pot Luck 13 *(see Quiz 94)*

1 Five. 2 Bowie. 3 Green and Flynn. 4 The Magic Whip. 5 They were both called Seal. 6 Charming. 7 Moyet. 8 Afternoon. 9 Piano. 10 Graceland. 11 Cliff Richard. 12 Mickie. 13 Goss. 14 Take That. 15 Spain. 16 Wet Wet Wet. 17 Guitar. 18 Harris. 19 Barbara Ann. 20 Marc Bolan. 21 Italy. 22 Shirley. 23 Smoke. 24 Play. 25 Iron Maiden. 26 Simon Smith. 27 Right Said Fred. 28 Great Expectations. 29 Kylie Minogue. 30 Quatro.

1 How many members were there in Dave Clark's group altogether?
2 Which David celebrated his 50th birthday on 8 January 1997?
3 What are the surnames of Robson and Jerome?
4 Name Blur's 2015 album.
5 What did Seal call his first two albums?
6 Which Prince were Adam and the Ants in 1981?
7 Which Alison's nickname is Alf?
8 In which part of the day did Starland Vocal Band experience Delight in 1976?
9 Which musical instrument does Richard Clayderman play?
10 Which Elvis Presley home gave Paul Simon an album title?
11 Who had albums in 1988 called *Mistletoe and Wine* and *Private Collection*?
12 What was the first name of the record producer called Most?
13 What was the surname of the Bros twins, Matt and Luke?
14 Which 90s group was made up of Howard, Gary, Jason, Robbie and Mark?
15 What is the home country of Julio Iglesias?
16 Marti Pellow is lead vocalist with which group?
17 Which musical instrument does the veteran musician Bert Weedon play?
18 What is singer Emmylou's surname?
19 Which Barbara was a 60s hit for the Beach Boys?
20 Who was lead singer with T. Rex?
21 Which country did Luciano Pavarotti originate from?
22 Who was Pepsi's singing partner?
23 What Gets in Your Eyes according to the Platters?
24 What did Pink Floyd See Emily do on the 1967 single?
25 Which Maiden took "Bring Your Daughter to the Slaughter" to No. 1?
26 Who had an Amazing Dancing Bear according to Alan Price?
27 Which Fred said "I'm Too Sexy" in 1991?
28 Which Great book by Charles Dickens is the title of the debut album by Tasmin Archer?
29 Whose first hit was "I Should be So Lucky" in 1988?
30 Which Suzi's first No. 1 was "Can the Can"?

Answers | Football: London Clubs *(see Quiz 93)*

1 Brentford. 2 Arsenal. 3 West Ham. 4 Chelsea. 5 Tottenham Hotspur. 6 Leyton Orient. 7 stadium:mk. 8 QPR. 9 Yes (1947). 10 Fulham. 11 Chelsea. 12 Bonds. 13 Millwall. 14 Crystal Palace. 15 Fulham. 16 Bobby Moore. 17 Leyton Orient. 18 Watford. 19 Tottenham Hotspur. 20 Arsenal. 21 Tottenham. 22 Dagenham & Redbridge. 23 Charlton. 24 Iain Dowie. 25 Arsenal. 26 Chelsea. 27 Tottenham Hotspur. 28 Chelsea. 29 West Ham United. 30 Blue is the Colour.

1 What sort of films did the Keystone Company make?
2 Samuel Goldfish changed his name to what after founding a film company?
3 In which state did William Fox found his film production company in 1912?
4 Which "Little Lord" was played by Mary Pickford, who also played his mother?
5 Which movie about the little boy who asked for more starred Jackie Coogan?
6 In which decade did Chaplin make *The Kid*?
7 How many "Horsemen of the Apocalypse" were there in the Valentino movie?
8 In which decade of the 20th century was Keystone founded?
9 Which Gloria found fame in *The Danger Girl* in 1916?
10 "The Taming of" what was the only movie to star Douglas Fairbanks and Mary Pickford together?
11 Ford Sterling led which Kops?
12 What was the first name of Langdon of *Tramp Tramp Tramp* fame?
13 Which regal first name did director/producer/writer Vidor have?
14 Which Fred's tours to the US brought Chaplin from England?
15 Pathe Weekly showed what on their reels?
16 Which Brothers released their first major feature in 1915?
17 Which Rudolph shot to stardom in *The Sheik*?
18 Who was forced out of Goldwyn Pictures in 1922?
19 Cecil B. de Mille's *King of Kings* was about whom?
20 *Birth of a Nation* was the first movie screened at which presidential home?
21 Which Cecil made the spectacular *Ten Commandments*?
22 Who made *The Gold Rush*?
23 Lon Chaney starred as which Phantom in 1925?
24 Which D. W. made *Birth of a Nation*?
25 Which "Singer" marked the end of the silent era?
26 What building feature did Harold Lloyd memorably hang from in *Safety Last*?
27 What type of hat did Charlie Chaplin wear in *City Lights*?
28 Name the Mel Brooks movie which is a parody of the silent movie era.
29 How many seconds did the first ever silent movie made in 1888 last for?
30 Can you name the 1923 movie which starred Theodore Roberts as *Moses*?

---

1 What anniversary did *Hollyoaks* celebrate in October 2015?

2 What US sports event was shown live on BBC TV for the first time in 2008?

3 Which comedy series featured the Clampetts?

4 Who presents *The Sky at Night*?

5 Who was Krystle Carrington's husband in *Dynasty*?

6 In *Steptoe and Son* what is the father's name?

7 What was *Quincy*?

8 Which series featured BA Baracus?

9 Who played the title role in *Faith in the Future*?

10 Which Irishman took over from Terry Wogan as the BBC presenter of *The Eurovision Song Contest*?

11 Which TV comedy star recorded *Splish-Splash*?

12 To which singing group do Donny, Marie and Jimmy belong?

13 Who was Dick Grayson's alter-ego?

14 What is the name of *Rab C. Nesbitt*'s youngest son?

15 What was the name of Granada's weekly review of the press?

16 What was the prequel of *The Fenn Street Gang*?

17 Which series starred Paula Wilcox and Richard Beckinsale?

18 Who was the quizmaster on *The Sky's the Limit*?

19 What was the name of ITV's Saturday sports programme?

20 Name the two high-voiced puppet pigs.

21 Where is *Coronation Street*?

22 In which city are the *Neighbours*?

23 Who presents *This Morning* with Richard Madeley?

24 What is the name of Hank Hill's wife?

25 What is the name of the "big" kid in *South Park*?

26 Which soap is set in Summer Bay?

27 Who plays Guinan in *Star Trek: The Next Generation*?

28 What is *Dr Who*'s time machine called?

29 What did Jeremy Clarkson and Quentin Willson present?

30 Who plays CJ in *Baywatch*?

Football: Champions League

Answers – page 108

1 Alan Shearer first played in the competition with which club?
2 Which Scottish side represented its country in the 1996–97 tournament?
3 Which side won the Champions League in 2016?
4 Which team were the first British side to win the trophy?
5 Which team did Bayern Munich beat on penalties in the 2001 UEFA Champions League Final?
6 Which Italian side topped Manchester Utd's group in the same season?
7 Trevor Francis scored a final goal for which club?
8 Who was Manchester Utd's manager when they won the trophy in the 60s?
9 In which decade did Liverpool first win the competition?
10 Liverpool had won the trophy how many times before the 90s?
11 Which famous Spanish side won the first five finals?
12 And which striker scored in all five of those finals?
13 Which side became known as "The Lions of Lisbon"?
14 Which were the first team from Portugal to win the tournament?
15 Who was Liverpool's manager when they first won the trophy?
16 A Ronald Koeman final goal gave which side the trophy?
17 Who were Liverpool playing in the 1985 final overshadowed by crowd trouble?
18 Who scored in the '96 final and started 1996–97 in English soccer?
19 Which Dutch team won the title three times in succession in the 70s?
20 Who was Nottingham Forest's goalkeeper when they first won the trophy?
21 Which was the first London club to play in a Champions League Final?
22 Which English club played in two finals against AC Milan in three seasons?
23 Who was Manchester United's goalkeeper when they won the cup in 2008?
24 Who was sent off in the 2008 final?
25 Which great Italian defender Paolo scored in the first minute of the 2005 final?
26 Including the 2008 final, how many teams have successfully defended the trophy?
27 From what famous cup competition did the UEFA Champions League evolve?
28 Name the Real Madrid striker who is the competition's all-time leading scorer.
29 Can you name the car manufacturer who is the competition's main sponsor?
30 Which Italian city hosted the 2009 UEFA Champions League Final?

Answers	Pop Pot Luck 14 *(see Quiz 98)*

1 Jackson. 2 Eurythmics. 3 Walk. 4 Dance. 5 Julio Iglesias. 6 Ultra Nate. 7 USA.
8 Cocker, Warnes. 9 Natalie Cole. 10 Mary. 11 The Ants. 12 "Amazing Grace". 13
Diana Ross. 14 Karma. 15 Kershaw. 16 Germany. 17 Laine. 18 Julian. 19 Mary
20 Jim Morrison. 21 Will Young. 22 Sugababes. 23 The Last Dance for Me. 24
Gardiner. 25 19. 26 France. 27 Frankie Goes to Hollywood. 28 Cheep Cheep. 29
Nilsson. 30 Cliff Richard.

1 Which Leon won The X Factor in 2007?

2 What was the name of the duet which the soloist who compiled the 1992 album *Diva* left and rejoined at the start and finish of the 90s?

3 Which word goes before "In the Black Forest" and "On the Wild Side" in song titles?

4 What did Eddy Grant Not Wanna do in 1982?

5 Which singer took "Begin the Beguine" into the charts?

6 "Free" was a top ten hit in 1997 for which singer?

7 What is the home country of New Kids on the Block?

8 Which Joe and Jennifer were Up Where We Belong in 1983?

9 What is the singing daughter of Nat King Cole called?

10 Who makes up the trio with Peter and Paul?

11 Who was Adam's backing group?

12 Which Judy Collins record entered the charts an Amazing eight times in the 70s?

13 Which ex-Supreme had a hit every year for 33 years?

14 Which Chameleon hit the top for Culture Club in 1983?

15 Which Nik was a Wide Boy in 1985?

16 What was the home country of Kraftwerk, who had a 1981 No. 1 with "Computer Love"?

17 Which surname is shared by the jazz singer Cleo and the 50s vocalist Frankie?

18 Which son Lennon recorded the album *Valotte*?

19 Who were the Sutherland Brothers in the Arms of in 1976?

20 Who was lead singer with the Doors?

21 Which singer released *85% Proof* in 2015?

22 Which female band had a hit with "Hole in the Head"?

23 What did the Drifters say to Save on their best-selling hit?

24 Which Boris sang "I Want to Wake Up with You" in 1986?

25 Which number was important for Paul Hardcastle in 1985?

26 Which country did 60s vocalist Francoise Hardy come from?

27 Which Frankie said "Welcome to the Pleasure Dome" in 1985?

28 Which two words followed Chirpy Chirpy on Middle of the Road's 70s No. 1?

29 Who recorded the album with his own name and "Schmilsson" in the title?

30 Whose first hit was "Move It" in 1958?

Answers | Football: Champions League *(see Quiz 97)*

1 Blackburn Rovers. 2 Rangers. 3 Real Madrid. 4 Celtic. 5 Valencia. 6 Juventus. 7 Nottingham Forest. 8 Matt Busby. 9 The 70s. 10 Four. 11 Real Madrid. 12 Alfredo di Stefano. 13 Celtic. 14 Benfica. 15 Bob Paisley. 16 Barcelona. 17 Juventus. 18 Fabrizio Ravanelli. 19 Ajax. 20 Peter Shilton. 21 Arsenal. 22 Liverpool. 23 Edwin van der Sar. 24 Didier Drogba. 25 Maldini. 26 None. 27 European Cup. 28 Raul. 29 Ford. 30 Rome.

1 In which country was Elizabeth Taylor born?
2 Which horse race was her movie *National Velvet* about?
3 Which Egyptian queen did she play in the 1960s?
4 Which singer Eddie did she marry after her third husband was killed?
5 Which Shakespeare play, with Taylor as the volatile Katherine, did Taylor and Burton bring to the big screen?
6 Who wrote the whodunnit on which her 1980 movie *The Mirror Crack'd* was based?
7 Which number followed "Butterfield" in her first Oscar-winning movie?
8 Which husband did she fall in love with on the set of *Cleopatra*?
9 Which Fred's mother-in-law was she when she played Pearl Slaghoople in 1994?
10 In 1993 she received an award at the Oscars ceremony for her work with sufferers from what?
11 On which pop star Michael's estate did she marry for the eighth time?
12 What was the nationality of her parents?
13 "Who's Afraid of" whom was the title of her second Oscar-winner?
14 What type of beauty product did she launch towards the end of the 20th century?
15 What colour are her famous eyes?
16 She was the voice of Baby Maggie in which cartoon series?
17 Which star of *Star Wars* was her one-time step-daughter?
18 Which Mickey was her co-star in *National Velvet*?
19 In which movie based on a Tennessee Williams play was she the "cat" Maggie?
20 Which actor did Elizabeth Taylor marry twice?
21 Which "Little" film was based on the classic by Louisa May Alcott?
22 In which decade did she make her very first movie?
23 In which movie about Charlotte Bronte's most famous heroine did she appear in 1944?
24 Which Spencer played the title role in *Father of the Bride*?
25 In *A Little Night Music* she sang "Send in the" what?
26 Which "round-number" birthday did Elizabeth celebrate in 2002?
27 What was the first name of her husband Mr Fortensky?
28 How many times did Elizabeth win an Academy Award for best actress?
29 In which wealthy north-west district of London was Elizabeth born?
30 What part did she play in *Doctor Faustus* in 1967?

Answers	**TV Pot Luck 14 (see Quiz 100)**

1 Pauline Fowler. 2 2008. 3 The Worthington Cup. 4 Astro. 5 Miss Boathook.
6 Game for a Laugh. 7 The Great Sorprendo. 8 Delia Smith. 9 Heathrow. 10
Emmerdale. 11 Reverend Jim. 12 Fred Savage. 13 Channel 4. 14 Voyager. 15
Gary Coleman. 16 This Life. 17 100 acre wood. 18 15. 19 Liverpool Docks. 20
Dennis Potter. 21 Fly on the wall documentary. 22 Denise Van Outen. 23 David
Attenborough. 24 Jean-Paul Gaultier. 25 Live TV. 26 Swithinbank. 27 Chris Tarrant.
28 Geoff Hamilton. 29 Ainsley Harriott. 30 Jeremy Spake.

1 Which *EastEnders* character died in the Christmas Day 2006 edition?
2 In which year, in the 2000s, did the BBC last broadcast the FA Cup Final live?
3 What did the Coca-Cola Cup change its name to in 1998?
4 What was the name of The Jetsons' dog?
5 Who was Colonel K's secretary in *Dangermouse*?
6 Rusty Lee and Jeremy Beadle co-presented which programme?
7 Which magician was married to Victoria Wood?
8 Which TV cook's first series was *Family Fare*?
9 What was the setting for *Airport*?
10 In which series is the fictional village Beckingdale?
11 In *Taxi* what was Jim Ignatowski's nickname?
12 Who played Kevin Arnold in *The Wonder Years*?
13 Which channel broadcasts *Cutting Edge* documentaries?
14 Which S.F. series features the character Neelix?
15 Who played Arnold in *Diff'rent Strokes*?
16 In which programme would you find Milly and Egg?
17 Where do Winnie the Pooh and his friends live?
18 How many contestants start the quiz programme hosted by William G. Stewart?
19 From where was *This Morning* originally broadcast?
20 Which playwright created *Blackeyes*?
21 What type of programme was *Lakeside*?
22 Which breakfast-time presenter appeared in *Babes in the Wood*?
23 Which presenter and programme maker has a brother Lord Dickie?
24 Which dress designer co-presented *Eurotrash*?
25 On which channel would you find *The Weather in Norwegian*?
26 Which Anne presented *Gardens of the Caribbean*?
27 Who presented *Man-O-Man*?
28 Which late TV personality had a garden at Barnsdale?
29 Which TV Chef presented *Party of a Lifetime*?
30 Who was the Aeroflot customer care manager featured on *Airport*?

1 Mercedes AMG Petronas has which Lewis at the helm in 2016?
2 Name the founder of the Simtek team.
3 In which year did Simtek arrive in Formula One?
4 Which Australian driver was Simtek's team leader that season?
5 What colour Bull entered F1 in 2005?
6 Who was the team's driver?
7 Three-time world champion Jackie Stewart formed which team in 1997?
8 What is the first name of his son, one of the co-founders?
9 Who were their drivers in that first season?
10 In which grand prix did the team score its first points?
11 Which world champion on two wheels and four drove a Formula One car bearing his name?
12 Who was the fellow motorcycle racing ace who joined the team in 1972?
13 What company was the team's publicity-generating sponsor in 1976?
14 What nationality was the Talbot team?
15 What was the traditional colour of its cars?
16 Who financed the Theodore team?
17 Who was the first driver to race for the Theodore team in Formula One?
18 With which team did Theodore amalgamate in 1983?
19 How did Ted Toleman make the money to form his own Formula One team?
20 In which year did Toleman enter Formula One?
21 Which team did Fernando Alonso leave in 2006 and rejoin for 2008?
22 For which Italian team did Kimi Raikkonen drive in 2008?
23 Which company ran two teams in 2007, one English-named, the other Italian?
24 Which country's name is attached to the Force team?
25 With which Japanese team did Timo Glock drive in 2008?
26 Which company provided all the F1 teams with tyres in 2008?
27 What colour dominated the famous John Player Special car of the late 1970s?
28 Can you name the 2008 F1 driver whose father won the world title three times?
29 This former Ferrari Team Principal joined Honda in 2008. Name him.
30 This F1 team's fans are known as the Tifosi. Name the team.

Answers | **Football Pot Luck 11** *(see Quiz 102)*

1 Leeds Utd. 2 Sheffield Utd. 3 Man City. 4 Wanderers. 5 Wales. 6 Chapman.
7 Switzerland. 8 Wimbledon. 9 Newcastle. 10 Red. 11 Hirst. 12 Bristol Rovers.
13 Strachan. 14 Swindon Town. 15 Bjornebye. 16 Manchester Utd. 17 Paisley.
18 Andy Roxburgh. 19 Semi-finals. 20 Woodcock. 21 Juande Ramos. 22 Milan 3, Liverpool 0. 23 London. 24 Portugal. 25 Hughes. 26 White. 27 Arsenal. 28 Eric Cantona. 29 Millwall. 30 Norwich City.

1 Who plays at home at Elland Road?
2 Which team does Sean Bean support?
3 Who won the Premier League in 2011-2012?
4 What is the last word in Bolton's name?
5 Which country has Chris Coleman played for?
6 Which Lee was the Leeds target man when they won the championship in 1992?
7 Which country do Grasshoppers come from?
8 With which club did Dennis Wise make his League debut?
9 Which club did Ruel Fox join on leaving Norwich?
10 What colour are Swindon's home shirts?
11 Which David was Sheffield Wednesday's top League scorer in 1995–96?
12 Which team is known as the Pirates?
13 Which Gordon of Leeds Utd won the Footballer of the Year award in 1991?
14 Hoddle followed Ardiles as boss at which club?
15 Which Premiership player rejoiced in the real name of Stig-Inge?
16 Steve Bruce played over 300 games for which team?
17 Which Liverpool legend Bob passed away in February 1996?
18 Who was Scotland's manager before Craig Brown?
19 At which stage were France knocked out of Euro 96?
20 Which Tony of Forest was PFA Young Player of the Year in 1978?
21 Who did Harry Redknapp replace as manager of Spurs?
22 What was the half-time score in the 2005 Champions League Final?
23 Which city does David Beckham come from?
24 Which country has midfielder Luis Figo played for?
25 Which Emlyn of Liverpool won the Footballer of the Year award in 1977?
26 What colour are the home shorts of Holland?
27 Glenn Helder first played in England for which club?
28 Which Manchester Utd star had a baby girl in 2011?
29 With which club did Teddy Sheringham make his League debut?
30 Gary Megson has had two spells in charge of which East Anglian team?

Answers | **Formula One Teams** *(see Quiz 101)*

1 Hamilton. 2 Nick Wirth. 3 1994. 4 David Brabham. 5 Red. 6 Stefan Johansson. 7 Stewart. 8 Paul. 9 Rubens Barrichello and Jan Magnussen. 10 The Monaco Grand Prix. 11 John Surtees. 12 Mike Hailwood. 13 Durex. 14 French. 15 Blue. 16 Teddy Yip. 17 Keke Rosberg. 18 Ensign. 19 Car transporting. 20 1981. 21 Renault. 22 Ferrari. 23 Red Bull/Toro Rosso. 24 India. 25 Toyota. 26 Bridgestone. 27 Black. 28 Nelson Piquet Jr. 29 Ross Brawn. 30 Ferrari.

1 Which astronaut sang "Space Oddity" in space in 2013?
2 Which Alvin had a No. 1 with "Jealous Mind"?
3 Which Way were OMD Walking on in 1996?
4 Which Man did Elton John sing about in 1972?
5 Which star was in the title of the hit Elton John had with George Michael?
6 Which space puppets are Go in the FAB hit of 1990?
7 Which David sang "Space Oddity" back in 1969?
8 What was "In the Sky" according to Doctor and the Medics in 1986?
9 What Always Shines on TV according to A-Ha in 1985?
10 The Dark Side of which celestial body was a classic album for Pink Floyd?
11 Which all-girl group sang "Venus" in 1986?
12 Which Song was a 1995 No. 1 for Michael Jackson?
13 What was the Satellite doing on Tasmin Archer's No. 1?
14 What did M/A/R/R/S Pump Up in 1987?
15 Who did Sarah Brightman Lose Her Heart to in 1978?
16 What was David Essex Gonna Make You in 1974?
17 What sort of Craft were the Carpenters Calling All Occupants of in 1977?
18 Where were the Police Walking on in 1979?
19 What sort of Star did gravel-voiced Lee Marvin sing about in 1970?
20 Which intergalactic Wars theme got into the top ten in 1977?
21 What was Venus wearing in Jimmy Clanton's 1962 hit?
22 What type of Girl did McFly sing about in November 2006?
23 The Arctic Monkeys went to No. 11 in 2013 with?
24 What was the Sun doing when the Chemical Brothers sang about it in 1996?
25 In which year was *Rocket Man: The Definitive Hits* album released?
26 Who took *Spirit in the Sky* to No. 1 in 1986?
27 What planet was David Bowie singing about life on in 1973?
28 This artist had a hit with *A Spaceman Came Travelling* in 1976. Name him.
29 What was Showaddywaddy in love under in 1976 with this No. 1 hit?
30 What planet did the girl band Bananarama take into the charts in 1986?

Answers | **Movies Pot Luck 11** *(see Quiz 104)*

1 Eyes Wide Shut. 2 Hawke. 3 Grasshoppers. 4 Pierce Brosnan. 5 80 minutes.
6 Ireland. 7 Attenborough. 8 1950s. 9 Popeye. 10 Uma Thurman. 11 The Vietnam War. 12 Willis. 13 Kramer (Kramer versus Kramer). 14 Apollo 13. 15 Dog. 16 Guinness. 17 Jerry Lewis. 18 Faye Dunaway. 19 Wayne. 20 Anna. 21 Alien. 22 Michelle Pfeiffer. 23 The Reader. 24 Charlie Chaplin. 25 Gerry and the Pacemakers. 26 California. 27 King Kong. 28 A nun. 29 Francis Ford Coppola. 30 Humphrey Bogart.

1 What was the last movie made by Stanley Kubrick?
2 Which Ethan starred in 2015's *Boyhood*?
3 What type of insects were posing the greatest threat in *A Bug's Life*?
4 Who replaced Timothy Dalton as James Bond?
5 Did *Toy Story* last 45, 80 or 240 minutes?
6 Where was 1990s James Bond, Pierce Brosnan, born?
7 Which Richard won the Best Director Oscar for *Gandhi*?
8 In which decade of the 20th century was Kirstie Alley born?
9 Robin Williams played which cartoon sailor?
10 *The Avengers* and *Dangerous Liaisons* both featured which actress?
11 *The Deer Hunter* was about which war?
12 Which Bruce starred in *2012's Looper*?
13 Who did Kramer take to court?
14 Ed Harris played the mission controller in which Tom Hanks film?
15 Is Gromit a person, a dog or a sheep?
16 Which Sir Alec starred in *Star Wars*?
17 Which zany comedian often co-starred with Dean Martin in the 50s?
18 Who played a lead role in *Bonnie and Clyde* after Jane Fonda turned it down?
19 Which John won the Best Actor Oscar for *True Grit*?
20 Which woman's name links the King of Siam and Karenina?
21 "In space no one can hear you scream" was the cinema poster line for which Sigourney Weaver movie?
22 Which actress links *Batman Returns*, *One Fine Day* and *Scarface*?
23 For her performance in which film did Kate Winslett win an Oscar for Best Actress in 2009?
24 Who played the Little Tramp in *The Kid*?
25 Which Liverpool band appeared in the movie *Ferry Cross the Mersey*?
26 Which West Coast US state elected Elizabeth Taylor into its Hall of Fame in 2007?
27 Which famous monkey returned to the big screen with a new adaptation in 2005?
28 In *Sister Act* what was Whoopi Goldberg disguised as?
29 Who directed *Apocalypse Now*?
30 *Bogey's Baby* was a biography of the wife of which movie star?

Answers | Pop: Space Oddity *(see Quiz 103)*

1 Chris Hadfield. 2 Stardust. 3 Milky Way. 4 Rocket. 5 The Sun ("Don't Let the Sun Go Down on Me"). 6 Thunderbirds. 7 Bowie. 8 Spirit. 9 Sun. 10 The Moon. 11 Bananarama. 12 "Earth". 13 Sleeping. 14 The Volume. 15 A Starship Trooper. 16 A Star. 17 Interplanetary. 18 The Moon. 19 Wand'rin'. 20 "Star Wars". 21 Blue Jeans. 22 Star. 23 Do I Wanna Know. 24 Setting. 25 2007. 26 Dr & the Medics. 27 Mars (Life on Mars). 28 Chris de Burgh. 29 The Moon. 30 Venus.

1 What does Dara O'Briain Mock as host of the comedy panel show?
2 Where are *Max & Paddy on the Road to*?
3 Who is Harry Enfield's writing partner on *Harry Enfield and Chums*?
4 In which series are Julia Sawalha and June Whitfield related?
5 Which characters were *Just Good Friends*?
6 What was Mrs Boswell's Christian name in *Bread*?
7 Who played *The New Statesman*?
8 Which comedy series featured Ted Bovis?
9 Who played Sir Humphrey in *Yes, Minister*?
10 Where does BooBoo live?
11 Which TV actress was Eggsy's mum in 2015's *Kingsman*?
12 What is Agent Smart's Christian name in *Get Smart*?
13 Who plays Jeannie in *I Dream of Jeannie*?
14 Who is Barbara's husband in *The Good Life*?
15 What is Tim Taylor's programme in *Home Improvements*?
16 Who was Lucy in *I Love Lucy*?
17 From which country does *Kids in the Hall* originate?
18 What was Alan Alda's role in *M*A*S*H*?
19 Which comedy series featured the Dead Parrot Sketch?
20 Which strange family had a niece named Marilyn?
21 To which family is Lurch the butler?
22 In which country is *'Allo, 'Allo* set?
23 Which sitcom features Bill and Ben Porter?
24 Who played Edmund Blackadder?
25 Who is *Caroline in the City*?
26 Who plays Sam Malone in *Cheers*?
27 Which sitcom is about Catholic clergy on remote Craggy Island?
28 Which TV series was the forerunner of *The Naked Gun* films?
29 What is *Frasier's* profession?
30 Who is the star of *The Fresh Prince of Bel Air*?

---

1 What is the last word in Luton's name?
2 Which country has Pat Bonner played for?
3 What colour are Fulham's home shirts?
4 Who plays at home at the City Ground?
5 Who were the runners up of the Premier League 2014–15 season?
6 Alan Buckley followed Keith Burkinshaw as boss at which club?
7 Gianfranco Zola plays for which country?
8 With which club did Graeme Le Saux make his League debut?
9 Which club did Dion Dublin leave to join Coventry?
10 Which Richard of Rangers was Scottish Footballer of the Year in 1989?
11 What is Burnley's nickname?
12 Which country has John Toshack played for?
13 Which manager took Liverpool to FA Cup Final triumph over Sunderland?
14 What colour are the home shirts of Switzerland?
15 Which David was PFA Player of the Year in 1990?
16 Which club brought Juninho to play in England?
17 Which national team decided to accept "collective responsibility" for damage done on a plane in 1996?
18 Which Paul said his manager gave him "unbelievable belief"?
19 Which country has Roy Wegerle played for?
20 Which England fullback Lee has made over 300 appearances for Arsenal?
21 What colour are Bury's home shirts?
22 What is Millwall's nickname?
23 Which Kevin of Liverpool won the Footballer of the Year award in 1976?
24 What is the main colour of Bulgaria's home shirts?
25 Which team do the Gallagher brothers of Oasis support?
26 Matthew Simmons is the most famous – or infamous – of which club?
27 Which country did Luigi Riva play for?
28 Which Scottish side signed Paulo Di Canio from AC Milan?
29 Which club had Deehan, O'Neill and Megson as managers in 1995?
30 Peter Ndlovu played for which country?

Answers | **TV: Comedy 3** *(see Quiz 105)*

1 The Week. 2 Nowhere. 3 Paul Whitehouse. 4 Absolutely Fabulous. 5 Vince and Penny. 6 Nellie. 7 Rik Mayall. 8 Hi De Hi!. 9 Nigel Hawthorne. 10 Jellystone Park. 11 Samantha Janus. 12 Maxwell. 13 Barbara Eden. 14 Tom Good. 15 Tooltime. 16 Lucille Ball. 17 Canada. 18 Hawkeye Pierce. 19 Monty Python's Flying Circus. 20 The Munsters. 21 The Addams Family. 22 France. 23 2 Point 4 Children. 24 Rowan Atkinson. 25 Lea Thompson. 26 Ted Danson. 27 Father Ted. 28 Police Squad. 29 A psychiatrist. 30 Will Smith.

Quiz 107 Pop: No. 1s

Answers – page 120

1 Who sang 2016's mega number one entry, "One Dance"?

2 Which Gina sang "Ooh Aah Just a Little Bit" in May 1996?

3 Who had three consecutive No. 1s with "Knowing Me, Knowing You", "The Name of the Game" and "Take a Chance on Me"?

4 Which American solo singer has had the most No. 1 hits?

5 Who did Kylie Minogue share the top spot with in 1988?

6 How many Lions topped the charts in June 1996?

7 What did Billy Ocean say happened When the Going Gets Tough?

8 Which football side were the first to have a No. 1 in 1994 with "Come On You Reds"?

9 Which Liverpool group has had a record-breaking 17 No. 1 hits?

10 Which No. 1 artist was pink with yellow spots?

11 Which Scottish female singer had her first hit "Shout" in 1964, before any of Take That were born, but topped the charts with them in 1993?

12 Which star of *The Bodyguard* took "I Will Always Love You" to the No. 1 spot making it the bestselling CD single at that time?

13 Which cartoon group did "The Bartman" in 1991?

14 Whose first solo No. 1 was in 1990, 14 years after hitting the top spot with Kiki Dee and "Don't Go Breaking My Heart"?

15 Which New Kids had their first No. 1 in 1989?

16 Which Canadian Bryan was at No. 1 for 16 weeks in 1991?

17 Where were David Bowie and Mick Jagger Dancing in 1985?

18 According to Robson and Jerome, who have had love that's now departed?

19 In 1984 Stevie Wonder Just Called to Say what?

20 Whose Midnight Runners sang "Come On Eileen" in 1982?

21 Leon Jackson had the Christmas 2007 UK No. 1 with "When You" what?

22 Who sang "Bleeding Love", the UK's top-selling single of 2007?

23 "Bound 4 Da Reload" by Oxide & Neutrino was based on which TV theme tune?

24 Who did Peter Andre take to No. 1 in March 2004 after his jungle stint?

25 Which female artist had her 13th UK No. 1 in April 2008 with "4 Minutes"?

26 Which X Factor winner took "Against All Odds" to the UK No. 1 slot in January 2005?

27 Who claimed his 20th No. 1 and the UK's 1,000th No. 1 with "One Night" in 2005?

28 Whose "Hips" didn't lie when she reached No. 1 with Wyclef Jean in 2006?

29 Who took "Walk This Way" to the top of the UK charts in March 2007?

30 Can you name the artist who had her twelfth No. 1 with "Sorry" in 2006?

1 Where in America was Leonardo DiCaprio born?

2 Which Dan starred in *The Blues Brothers*?

3 A 90s movie title was "The Bridges of" which county?

4 The song 'Circle of Life' features in which animated movie?

5 Who voiced Bagheera in 2016's *The Jungle Book*?

6 Who played herself in *Dear Brigitte* in 1965?

7 Which actor links *Face/Off* and *Grease*?

8 The Japanese attack on where is central to *From Here to Eternity*?

9 Who played Truman in *The Truman Show*?

10 *Postcards from the Edge* was based on the life of which Carrie?

11 Which Ms Smith played the Mother Superior in Whoopi Goldberg's *Sister Act*?

12 Which 1997 movie equalled *Ben Hur*'s record haul of Oscars?

13 Who starred as the male adult lead in 2015's *Tomorrowland*?

14 Which Melanie married Antonio Banderas?

15 Robert De Niro sang about New York in which film?

16 Which Jane was one of the first movie stars to produce fitness videos?

17 Who was Kenneth Branagh's wife whom he directed in *Much Ado About Nothing* in 1993?

18 What was the Bond theme for *For Your Eyes Only* called?

19 What is Bruce Willis's profession in *The Sixth Sense*?

20 Which James was the knife thrower in *The Magnificent Seven*?

21 In which decade was *Bullitt* released?

22 Which word completes the film title, *In _____ We Serve*?

23 In which decade of the 20th century was Julie Andrews born?

24 Who directed *Evita*?

25 Which Jeff starred in 2011's *RIPD*?

26 Which singer/actress married Sean Penn in 1985?

27 Which Bruce starred in 2016's *Marauders*?

28 Who directed *The Beaver*?

29 In which decade was *My Fair Lady* released?

30 What did Demi Moore have removed to make *G.I. Jane*?

| **Answers** | Pop: Instrumentals *(see Quiz 111)* |

1 Violin. 2 Germany. 3 Eric Clapton. 4 Violin. 5 Brother. 6 Alpert. 7 Prado. 8 Buddy Holly. 9 "Don't Cry for Me Argentina". 10 Ireland. 11 Bagpipes. 12 Mike Oldfield. 13 Virgin. 14 Tony Meehan. 15 French. 16 Williams. 17 The Bad and the Ugly. 18 Miami Vice. 19 Clarinet. 20 "God Save the Queen". 21 Walk. 22 Green. 23 Magnificent. 24 Henry Mancini. 25 Portsmouth. 26 Axel F. 27 Green Onions. 28 Apache. 29 Ennio Morricone. 30 Arrival.

1 Which Vera died in *Coronation Street* in 2008?

2 Which Danny joined the *EastEnders* cast as Mick Carter in 2013?

3 Who is Toyah's sister in *Coronation Street*?

4 Who is Ricky Butcher's wife in *EastEnders*?

5 In *Neighbours*, whose daughter was Julie Martin?

6 Who is Ailsa's husband in *Home and Away*?

7 Which pub did Alan Turner run in *Emmerdale*?

8 Which TV writer created *Brookside*?

9 In which Western state of the USA is *Knots Landing* set?

10 Which 60's US soap starred Mia Farrow and Ryan O'Neal?

11 Who was famed for his allotment in *EastEnders*?

12 Which character did Michelle Gayle portray in *EastEnders*?

13 Who was Bet Gilroy's estranged husband in *Coronation Street*?

14 What is Susan Kennedy's occupation in *Neighbours*?

15 Who was Bobby Ewing's mother in *Dallas*?

16 Who is Jacqui's dad in *Brookside*?

17 Which character in *Coronation Street* was married to Samir Rashid?

18 Who owned The Meal Machine in *EastEnders*?

19 Which character does John James portray in *The Colbys*?

20 In which establishment was the office of Ozcabs in *EastEnders*?

21 Who in *Coronation Street* was Gail Platt's late husband?

22 Who is Michael Ross's wife in *Home and Away*?

23 Name Debbie Martin's younger sister in *Neighbours*.

24 Who is Pete Beale's sister in *EastEnders*?

25 Which Hartman did Kimberley Davies portray in *Neighbours*?

26 Who sold her baby to the Mallets in *Coronation Street*?

27 Who is Max's wife in *Brookside*?

28 Which BBC1 soap was created by Tony Holland and Julia Smith?

29 Which Sean owned the Bookmakers in Rosamund Street around the corner from *Coronation Street*?

30 In *Coronation Street*, where did Rita find her dead husband, Ted Sullivan?

Answers	**Football Pot Luck 13** *(see Quiz 110)*

1 Blackpool. 2 Southampton. 3 Nottingham Forest. 4 City. 5 Northern Ireland. 6 Man City. 7 Turkey. 8 Bolton Wanderers. 9 Blackburn Rovers. 10 White. 11 Matthew Le Tissier. 12 The Shakers. 13 A dog. 14 Watford. 15 Barnes. 16 Tottenham Hotspur. 17 Holland. 18 Regis. 19 White. 20 Coton. 21 The Magpies. 22 The Republic of Ireland. 23 Portsmouth. 24 Barnsley. 25 Town. 26 Everton. 27 Shilton. 28 Canada. 29 Lindisfarne. 30 Fashanu.

1 Who plays at home at Bloomfield Road?

2 Grobbelaar and Beasant were together at which club?

3 Brian Clough and Frank Clark have both managed which club?

4 What is the last word in Bradford's name?

5 Which country has Iain Dowie played for?

6 Which team came fourth in the Premier League in 2015–16?

7 Which country do Fenerbahce come from?

8 With which club did Alan Stubbs make his League debut?

9 Which club did Colin Hendry join on leaving Manchester City?

10 What colour are Tottenham Hotspur's home shirts?

11 Which player was Southampton's top League scorer in 1995–96?

12 What is Bury's nickname?

13 What kind of creature found the stolen World Cup in 1966?

14 Which team does Elton John support?

15 Which John of Liverpool won the Footballer of the Year award in 1990?

16 Venables followed Pleat as boss at which club?

17 Which country has Danny Blind played for?

18 Which Cyrille of West Brom was PFA Young Player of the Year in 1979?

19 What colour are the Republic of Ireland's home shorts?

20 Which keeper Tony had spells for both Manchester Utd and City in the 90s?

21 What is Newcastle United's nickname?

22 Which country has Ronnie Whelan played for?

23 The Chimes were traditionally heard at which club?

24 Which team did Michael Parkinson support as a boy?

25 What is the second word in Shrewsbury's name?

26 Which team does John Parrott support?

27 Which Peter of Nottingham Forest was PFA Player of the Year in 1978?

28 Which country did Craig Forrest play for?

29 Gazza recorded "Fog on the Tyne" with which group?

30 Which John was Wimbledon's top League scorer in 1989–90?

Answers | **Pop: No. 1s** *(see Quiz 107)*

1 Drake. 2 G. 3 Abba. 4 Elvis Presley. 5 Jason Donovan. 6 Three. 7 The Tough Get Going. 8 Manchester United. 9 The Beatles. 10 Mr Blobby. 11 Lulu. 12 Whitney Houston. 13 The Simpsons. 14 Elton John. 15 On the Block. 16 Adams. 17 The Street. 18 The Broken Hearted. 19 I Love You. 20 Dexy's. 21 Believe. 22 Leona Lewis. 23 Casualty. 24 Mysterious Girl. 25 Madonna. 26 Steve Brookstein. 27 Elvis Presley. 28 Shakira. 29 Sugababes vs Girls Aloud. 30 Madonna.

1 What instrument does Neil Amin-Smith play for Clean Bandit?
2 Which country does the bandleader James Last come from?
3 Which legendary slowhand announced in 2016 he can no longer play?
4 Which musical instrument does Vanessa-Mae play?
5 What relation is the cellist Julian Lloyd-Webber to the composer Andrew?
6 Which Herb had a Tijuana Brass?
7 Which Perez had chart success in 1994 with "Guaglione"?
8 In '96 Hank Marvin released an album of which late 50s star's songs?
9 Which song from *Evita* did the Shadows release in 1978?
10 The *Riverdance* album has music from which country?
11 Which musical instrument features most strongly on the Royals Scots Dragoon Guards' recording of "Amazing Grace"?
12 Who played lead guitar on *Tubular Bells*?
13 On which Richard Branson label was it first released?
14 Who left the Shadows with Jet Harris and took "Diamonds" to No. 1?
15 What is the nationality of Jean-Michel Jarre?
16 Which classical guitarist John was a member of Sky?
17 Who joined the Good on the orchestral No. 1 film theme for Ennio Morricone?
18 Which TV cop show gave Jan Hammer chart success with "Crockett's Theme"?
19 What instrument does trad jazz man Acker Bilk play?
20 Which anthem did Queen play as an instrumental?
21 What did the Ventures recommend that you do instead of running?
22 What colour was the Tune Rockers' "Mosquito"?
23 Al Caiola released what superlative "Seven"?
24 Who composed the theme for *The Pink Panther* movies?
25 Which Hampshire town was a hit for instrumentalist Mike Oldfield?
26 Can you name the electronic hit theme from the 1984 movie *Beverly Hills Cop*?
27 What colour were the onions in the 1962 hit by Booker T & the MGs?
28 The Shadows had a 1960 hit named after this famous tribe of Indians. Name it.
29 Who composed the theme for the movie *The Good, the Bad and the Ugly*?
30 This 1976 Abba instrumental track was on an album of the same name.

1 *Maverick* and *Freaky Friday* both featured which actress?
2 Which character returned to the big screen in 2016 fighting Superman?
3 Which star of *Sliding Doors* split with fiancé Chris Martin in 2014?
4 Who wrote most of the songs for *Saturday Night Fever*?
5 *Philadelphia* became the first mainstream Hollywood movie to focus on which disease?
6 Which Shirley sang the Bond song "Diamonds are Forever"?
7 In a Disney film title, which animal did Pete own?
8 Which actress links *Batman and Robin* and *Pulp Fiction*?
9 Was *King Kong* first released in the 1930s, 50s or 70s?
10 Which Bruce is the voice of Mikey in *Look Who's Talking*?
11 Which blonde French actress's real name is Camille Javal?
12 Which Disney movie was based on the life of a native American?
13 Who met husband-to-be Richard Burton on the set of *Cleopatra*?
14 The cop Popeye Doyle first appeared in which classic thriller?
15 In which decade of the 20th century was Richard Attenborough born?
16 Which Ernest starred in *The Wild Bunch*?
17 To the nearest hour, how long does *Lady and the Tramp* last?
18 According to the film title, Lawrence was "of" which country?
19 Who played the lead role in *Fatal Attraction* after Debra Winger turned it down?
20 In which decade was *E.T.* released?
21 Which actor was in *A River Runs Through It*, *Meet Joe Black* and *Legends of the Fall*?
22 What colour is Queen Victoria, according to the film title?
23 Who sang "A Groovy Kind of Love" in *Buster*?
24 Which Robert won the Best Actor Oscar for *Raging Bull*?
25 Marlene Dietrich was born in which European capital?
26 In what decade was *Home Alone* released?
27 What was Boris Karloff's role in *Frankenstein*?
28 Which Denise starred in *Wild Things*?
29 *Misery* is based on the novel by which writer?
30 Which word completes the film title, *Sense and ____*?

| **Answers** | **Football Pot Luck 14 (see Quiz 114)** |

1 Town. 2 England. 3 Blue and white. 4 Chelsea. 5 Barcelona. 6 Jason Lee. 7 Jardine. 8 Crystal Palace. 9 Manchester Utd. 10 The U's. 11 Swindon Town. 12 Northern Ireland. 13 Martin O'Neill. 14 Southampton. 15 Barnes. 16 Ian Wright. 17 Noades. 18 Croatia. 19 Leeds Utd. 20 Black. 21 Manchester City. 22 Moscow. 23 Norwich City. 24 City. 25 The Republic of Ireland. 26 Baggio. 27 Norway. 28 Arsenal. 29 Newcastle Utd. 30 Booth.

1 In December 2015 which channel bought the rights to broadcast F1?
2 Which darts game show returned on the Challenge cable/satellite station in 2006?
3 Who was a footballer for Arsenal and a cricket player and commentator?
4 Which competition pitted champions of differing sports against each other?
5 For which sport is John Spencer a commentator?
6 For which sport is Barry Venison a pundit?
7 Which television sports programme was introduced by Dickie Davies?
8 Which company sponsored Monday Night Football on Sky TV in 1998?
9 Which sport did Dan Maskell commentate on?
10 For which sport is Eric Bristow renowned?
11 Who wears pyjamas on *Fantasy Football League*?
12 Who said, "They think it's all over – it is now" in 1966?
13 Who is the chairperson of *A Question of Sport*?
14 On which sports programme does Joe Jordan appear?
15 What sport did Ted Lowe commentate on?
16 Who was Eddie the Eagle?
17 *Gladiators* was based on which US TV show?
18 In which park does the London Marathon start?
19 Which annual event features the crews of Oxford and Cambridge?
20 Where is the Grand National run?
21 Which presenter got awful reviews as F1 presenter in 2015?
22 Who presents *Auntie's Sporting Bloomers*?
23 Henry Cooper advertised which aftershave?
24 Which multi-athletic event is screened in the summer every four years?
25 Which former Arsenal goalkeeper has presented football on both the BBC and ITV?
26 What is the name of the long-running Saturday-afternoon sports programme on BBC1?
27 Which former Liverpool football club captain was also captain on *Question of Sport*?
28 Who are *Saint and Greavsie*?
29 *The Manageress* was about a female manager in which sport?
30 Name Gary Lineker's hairy comic partner from *They Think It's All Over*.

Answers | TV: Crime 1 *(see Quiz 117)*

1 The Navy. 2 Ashley Jensen. 3 Sun Hill. 4 John Thaw. 5 William Shatner. 6 Miss Marple. 7 John Watt. 8 Cornwall. 9 D. I. Frost. 10 Hill Street Blues. 11 Luther. 12 Raymond Burr. 13 Chuck Norris. 14 Mary Beth. 15 A Mountie. 16 Oscar Blaketon. 17 Between the Lines. 18 Andy. 19 California. 20 Due South. 21 Tubbs. 22 Magnum P. I. 23 A Boxer. 24 Adam Faith. 25 Hercule. 26 Wiggum. 27 Amanda Burton. 28 Columbo. 29 Kojak. 30 Cracker.

1 What is the last word in Mansfield's name?
2 Which country has defender Mark Wright played for?
3 What colour are the stripes on Huddersfield's home shirts?
4 Who plays at home at Stamford Bridge?
5 Which team walked away with the UEFA Champions League in 2015?
6 Which Nottingham Forest player was ribbed for his "pineapple" hair cut?
7 Which Sandy of Rangers was Scottish Footballer of the Year in 1975?
8 With which club did John Salako make his League debut?
9 Which club did Andrei Kanchelskis leave to join Everton?
10 What is Cambridge United's nickname?
11 Steve McMahon followed John Gorman as boss at which club?
12 Which country has Pat Rice played for?
13 Which manager was with Wycombe Wanderers when they came into the Football League?
14 Mick Channon is the leading all-time scorer for which club?
15 Which John of Liverpool was PFA Player of the Year in 1988?
16 Who was top scorer for Arsenal for five consecutive seasons in the 90s?
17 Which Ron has been chairman of Crystal Palace?
18 Which country has Davor Suker played for?
19 Howard Wilkinson managed which side to the League title?
20 What is the colour of Germany's home shorts?
21 Which club left Maine Road after the Commonwealth Games were in England?
22 In which city was the 2008 UEFA Champions League Final played?
23 Walker and O'Neill have both managed which club?
24 What is the second word in Hull's name?
25 Which country has Steve Staunton played for?
26 Which Roberto was European Footballer of the Year in 1993?
27 Which country does Rosenberg come from?
28 With which club did David O'Leary make his League debut?
29 Which club did David Beasant join on leaving Wimbledon?
30 Which Scott was Aberdeen's joint top League scorer in 1995–96?

1 Which Barry sang about the Copacabana?
2 Which David's hits include "I'm Gonna Make You a Star" and "Hold Me Close"?
3 Which Billy sang about his Uptown Girl in 1983?
4 Which ex-Police man Spread a Little Happiness in 1982?
5 Which Genesis drummer went solo to No. 1 with "You Can't Hurry Love"?
6 Which Ms Franklin commanded Respect in 1967 and had A Deeper Love in 1994?
7 Which Icelandic singer's first Top 20 hit was "Play Dead" in 1993?
8 Who starred opposite Kevin Costner in *The Bodyguard*?
9 Which Chris was Driving Home for Christmas in 1988?
10 Which Elvis was supported by the Attractions?
11 Which Barbra sang "As If We Never Said Goodbye" in 1994?
12 What did Gabrielle say to give her a Little More of in 1996?
13 What did Gina G sing immediately after "Ooh aah"?
14 In 1986 George Michael sang about a Different what?
15 Which regal-sounding soloist had his first No. 1 with "The Most Beautiful Girl in the World"?
16 Eric Clapton sang I Shot who back in 1974?
17 Which glamorous granny had a No. 1 with "What's Love Got to Do with It"?
18 Who changed his name from Robert Zimmerman and found fame?
19 Which Mr Astley was Never Gonna Give You Up in 1987?
20 Which Ocean produced "When the Going Gets Tough, the Tough Get Going"?
21 Who went back to No. 1 with "Jailhouse Rock" to celebrate his 70th birthday?
22 Which female singer topped the charts with "Smile" in 2006?
23 Before her marriage what was former Destiny's Child Beyonce's surname?
24 Which Justin released "Can't Stop the Feeling" in 2016?
25 Which McFadden had a September hit with "Real to Me"?
26 This legendary US singer was born Cherilyn Sarkisian in 1946. Name her.
27 Who took "19" to No. 1 in the UK singles charts for five weeks on 11 May 1985?
28 Whose first UK No. 1 hit was entitled "Into The Groove" and released in 1985?
29 Which English artist has enjoyed 14 British No. 1 hits?
30 Prior to embarking on his solo career what band was Robbie Williams part of?

1 Which Ben portayed Batman in 2016?
2 Who won the Best Actor Oscar for *As Good as It Gets*?
3 How is Oscar-winning actress, former Mrs Sonny Bono, better known?
4 Which actress was BAFTA nominated for *Angela's Ashes*?
5 Which Celia starred in the tearjerker *Brief Encounter*?
6 Which director Martin did Isabella Rossellini marry?
7 Who was born Maurice Micklewhite?
8 Which pop star's first film was *Purple Rain*?
9 Dustin Hoffman was in a movie about what kind of "Dogs"?
10 In which country was Arnold Schwarzenegger born?
11 Who played the title role in *The Wrestler*?
12 Which Kim did Alec Baldwin divorce?
13 Which name completes the film title, *Peggy ____ Got Married*?
14 Which British film director directed 2015's *Steve Jobs*?
15 In which TV cop series did Peter Falk find fame after appearing on the big screen?
16 Which Henry won the Best Actor Oscar for *On Golden Pond*?
17 In film titles, what sizes are foxes and a mermaid?
18 In which decade of the 20th century was Sharon Stone born?
19 Which Ursula co-starred with Elvis in *Fun in Acapulco*?
20 *Don't Look Now* is set in which Italian city?
21 Which actor directed 2016's *Hacksaw Ridge*?
22 Which animal links a canary and a tin roof in film titles?
23 Which David starred in *The X-Files*?
24 Which movie did the song 'Stand by Me' come from?
25 In which decade was *West Side Story* released?
26 Which mountain was a 2006 Oscar-winning cowboy movie?
27 Which *Mary Poppins* and *The Sound of Music* star voiced "Queen" in *Shrek 2*?
28 *A Few Good Men* and *One Flew Over the Cuckoo's Nest* featured which actor?
29 The 1990s version of *Sergeant Bilko* featured which Steve?
30 Which word follows *The Bonfire of the ____* in a Bruce Willis movie title?

Answers	**Snooker & Darts** *(see Quiz 118)*

1 Steve Davis. 2 Organisation. 3 Canada. 4 Pink. 5 Lowe. 6 20. 7 Jimmy White. 8 Pink. 9 70s. 10 Rees. 11 John Higgins. 12 Mark Selby. 13 Leyton Orient. 14 England. 15 Alex Higgins. 16 1. 17 Jimmy White. 18 36. 19 John Parrott. 20 Billiards. 21 170. 22 Phil Taylor. 23 Ronnie O'Sullivan. 24 143. 25 Las Vegas. 26 When the defending World Champion loses in the opening round. 27 Phil Taylor. 28 James Wade. 29 888. com. 30 £330,000

1 With section of the American Armed Forces has an NCIS department?
2 Who stars as Agatha Raisin in 2016's *The Quiche of Death*?
3 What is *The Bill*'s local nick?
4 Who played the role of Chief Inspector Morse?
5 Who played *TJ Hooker*?
6 Who is Agatha Christie's foremost lady sleuth?
7 Who was Charlie Barlow's sergeant in *Z Cars*?
8 Where is *Wycliffe* set?
9 Which cop does David Jason play?
10 Which police series was set on the Hill?
11 Name the BBC's gritty police drama, launched in 2010.
12 Who played Perry Mason?
13 Who plays *Walker – Texas Ranger*?
14 What are Lacey's Christian names in Cagney and Lacey?
15 What is Constable Benton Fraser?
16 Which character was Nick Rowan's sergeant in *Heartbeat*?
17 Which series featured Tony Clark and Harry Taylor?
18 What is Sipowicz's first name in *NYPD Blue*?
19 In which American state was *L.A. Law* located?
20 Which series featured Diefenbaker?
21 Who is Crockett's partner in *Miami Vice*?
22 Which series set in Hawaii stars Tom Selleck?
23 What was Terry's previous profession in *Minder*?
24 Who played *Budgie*?
25 What is Poirot's first name?
26 What is the name of the Police Chief in *The Simpsons*?
27 Who was the star of *Silent Witness*?
28 What was the name of Peter Falk's scruffy detective?
29 Whose first name was Theo?
30 In which series was there a female detective named Penhaligon?

1 Who was snooker's world champion most times in the 80s?
2 What does the letter O stand for in BDO?
3 Cliff Thorburn – "The Grinder" – came from which country?
4 Which ball is worth one point less than a black?
5 Which John scored the first nine-dart 501 in a major tournament?
6 Moving anti-clockwise on a dartboard which number is after 1?
7 Which snooker player was nicknamed "Whirlwind"?
8 Which ball is worth one point more than a blue?
9 In which decade was snooker's World Championship first staged at The Crucible?
10 Which Leighton became darts' first World Professional Champion?
11 Who took over No. 1 ranking from Stephen Hendry?
12 Which player walked away with the 2016 World Championship?
13 Which London soccer team is Barry Hearne connected with?
14 Dennis Priestley plays for which country?
15 Which snooker player was known as "Hurricane"?
16 On a dartboard which number is directly opposite the 6?
17 Which "veteran" sensationally beat Stephen Hendry in the first round of the 1998 World Championship?
18 What's the smallest three-dart score made with three trebles all in different even numbers?
19 Which player broke up Hendry's World Championship monopoly of the early 90s?
20 What does the B stand for in the WPBSA?
21 What is the highest possible check-out with three darts?
22 Which darts player is known as "The Power"?
23 Who won his third World Snooker Championship in 2008?
24 What is the break score for 15 reds, 12 blacks, 2 pinks, 1 blue and all the colours?
25 Where in Nevada is the Desert Classic darts tournament staged?
26 What is meant by the term "The Curse of the Crucible"?
27 Who claimed his first tournament win in 12 months at the 2007 Grand Slam of Darts?
28 This darts player is known as "The Machine". Can you name him?
29 Name the company which sponsored the 2008 World Snooker Championship.
30 What was the price money earnings at the 2016 World Championship?

1 Who missed a penalty kick and put a bag on his head in a pizza place?
2 Beardsley and Shearer have been on the spot for which club?
3 Andy Brehme scored a World Cup final penalty for which country?
4 Where should a goalkeeper stand for a penalty?
5 Who made the first Wembley save from an FA Cup final penalty kick?
6 Ron Flowers has been on the spot for which country?
7 Which team has participated in the most World Cup penalty shootouts?
8 Which Julian became a 1990s penalty expert for West Ham?
9 Yorke and Townsend have been on the spot for which club?
10 Robbie Rensenbrink scored four penalties in the 1978 World Cup finals for which team?
11 Which London team won the UEFA Cup final of 1984 after a shoot-out?
12 Who missed from the spot for Scotland against England in Euro 96?
13 How many penalties were scored at the 2014 World Cup finals?
14 Who scored two penalty kicks in an FA Cup final for Manchester United in the 1990s?
15 Wise and Hughes have been on the spot for which club?
16 Which country was awarded a penalty in the Euro 96 final?
17 In 1994, the final of which major tournament was decided on a penalty shoot-out for the first time ever?
18 Which Tottenham Hotspur player failed to score from the spot in the 1991 FA Cup final?
19 In a league game, can a penalty taker score from a rebound off the keeper?
20 Which Francis was a penalty-kick king for Manchester City in the 1970s?
21 Whose scored a Champions League semi-final penalty for Chelsea in April 2008?
22 Which Jerzy saved two penalties in the 2005 Champions League Final shoot-out?
23 Which country has been in two World Cup Final penalty shoot-outs?
24 Who scored a penalty in the 2006 World Cup Final and was later sent off?
25 Which team lost an FA Cup Final on penalties after drawing 3–3 in 120 minutes?
26 Which club lost the 2005 FA Cup Final to Arsenal in a penalty shoot-out?
27 Can you name the team that lost the 2008 Community Shield in a penalty shoot-out?
28 Who missed the penalty that would have won the 2007–08 UEFA Champions League for Chelsea?
29 Who was the first player to miss a penalty kick in an FA Cup Final at Wembley?
30 Which side put Chelsea out of the 2008–09 Carling Cup in a penalty shoot-out?

| **Answers** | **Movies: Unforgettables** *(see Quiz 121)* |

1 Davis. 2 High Society. 3 Paint Your Wagon. 4 Swanson. 5 Oliver Reed. 6 Richard Burton. 7 Humphrey Bogart & Lauren Bacall. 8 Mae West. 9 Henry Fonda. 10 Dietrich. 11 Elvis Presley. 12 Jeanette Macdonald. 13 Charlie Chaplin. 14 Durante. 15 John Wayne. 16 Transylvania. 17 Legs. 18 1970s. 19 Rex Harrison. 20 Joan Crawford. 21 Spencer Tracy. 22 Car. 23 Laurence Olivier. 24 First. 25 Kelly. 26 Titanic. 27 Silence of the Lambs. 28 Gone with the Wind. 29 The Quiet Man. 30 The Magnificent Seven.

1 How many members of Take That were left for 2015's tour?
2 Which Family group sang with Limmie in the 70s?
3 What is the home country of Daniel O'Donnell?
4 Which word describes the vocalists Eva and Richard?
5 What type of Love did Love Affair have in 1968?
6 Which People were "Moving On Up" in 1993?
7 Which country does Craig McLachlan come from?
8 Which blonde US singer fell off the stage at 2015's BRIT Awards?
9 Which Street Preachers had a hit with the "Theme from M*A*S*H" in 1992?
10 Which song was a No. 1 for Elvis Presley and UB40?
11 Which Donna and Barbra had chart success in 1979 with "No More Tears (Enough is Enough)"?
12 How many people made up the 80s group Tears for Fears?
13 Why was the No. 1 album called *Walthamstow* very appropriately named for East 17?
14 Which punk group had the soloist who recorded *Sid Sings* left?
15 How many Seasons were in the group that sang "Rag Doll"?
16 Which group takes its name from an Unemployment Benefit card?
17 How is the Irishman Raymond Edward O'Sullivan better known?
18 Which surname is shared by Tom and Aled?
19 Who was Clyde's co-gangster on Georgie Fame's 60s Ballad?
20 Which Johnson was lead singer with Frankie Goes to Hollywood?
21 What variety of Peas were chart-toppers in 2003?
22 Whose 2014 album was called *Rock or Bust*?
23 Which musical instrument does Herb Alpert play?
24 Which Thin group sang "Whiskey in the Jar" in 1973?
25 Which Diddyman's first hit was "Love is Like a Violin"?
26 Which Roger was Leavin' Durham Town in 1969?
27 Which Five were Glad All Over in 1963?
28 Whose first hit was "Apache" in 1960?
29 Which TV holiday programme is also the title of an album by Pink Floyd?
30 Which group reunited in 2016 as a trio?

Answers | **TV Pot Luck 15** *(see Quiz 122)*

1 New Tricks. 2 Seattle. 3 Luther. 4 Dangerfield (Havers replaced Le Vaillant). 5 Light Lunch. 6 Cider with Rosie. 7 Ray Mears. 8 David Attenborough. 9 Delia Smith. 10 This Morning. 11 Danny de Vito. 12 Oscar Blaketon. 13 Alma Baldwin. 14 Britton. 15 Nigel. 16 London's Burning. 17 Deborah. 18 David Hasselhoff. 19 Alf Garnett. 20 Cole. 21 Sue Pollard. 22 Sharon Watts. 23 Kylie Minogue. 24 Holiday. 25 Parliamentary Channel. 26 Fitz. 27 1986. 28 Tennis. 29 A Bicycle. 30 Des Lynam.

1 Which Bette said, "Until you're known in my profession as a monster, you're not a star"?

2 What was Grace Kelly's last film, with Frank Sinatra and Bing Crosby?

3 In which 1961 movie did Lee Marvin have a singing role?

4 Which Gloria played Norma Desmond in *Sunset Boulevard*?

5 Which famous hell-raising actor wrote an autobiography called *Reed All About It*?

6 Which Welshman's real name was Richard Jenkins?

7 Which husband and wife starred in *Key Largo* in 1948?

8 Which film star wrote the novel *Constant Sinner*?

9 Who played the father of real-life daughter Jane in *On Golden Pond* in 1981?

10 Which Marlene found fame with *The Blue Angel*?

11 Who played two parts in *Kissin' Cousins* in 1964?

12 Who played opposite Nelson Eddy eight times?

13 Robert Downey Jr was Oscar-nominated for playing which unforgettable star of the silent screen?

14 Which Jimmy's nickname was Schnozzle?

15 Who played the Ringo Kid in the classic western *Stagecoach*?

16 Where was Bela Lugosi born?

17 Which part of her did Cyd Charisse insure for $5 million?

18 In which decade of the 20th century was River Phoenix born?

19 Which British actor won an Oscar for *My Fair Lady*?

20 Whose autobiography was called *A Portrait of Joan*?

21 Who died 15 days after finishing *Guess Who's Coming to Dinner*?

22 In what type of crash did Jayne Mansfield meet her death?

23 Who directed and starred in *Hamlet* in 1948?

24 In which World War did Humphrey Bogart receive a facial injury which gave him his trademark sneer?

25 Which Gene discovered Leslie Caron?

26 DiCaprio and Winslet starred in which movie based on a 1912 shipping disaster?

27 Which thriller featured a cannibal called Hannibal?

28 This epic starred Clark Gable and Vivien Leigh. Can you name it?

29 Starring John Wayne and Maureen O'Hara, which masterpiece was set in Ireland?

30 Yul Brynner, Robert Vaughan, Steve McQueen and the boys starred in this classic.

Answers	**Football: Penalty Kicks** *(see Quiz 119)*

1 Gareth Southgate. **2** Newcastle United. **3** West Germany. **4** On the goal-line and between the posts. **5** Dave Beasant. **6** England. **7** Argentina. **8** Dicks. **9** Aston Villa. **10** Holland. **11** Tottenham Hotspur. **12** Gary McAllister. **13** 26. **14** Eric Cantona. **15** Chelsea. **16** Czech Republic. **17** The World Cup. **18** Gary Lineker. **19** Yes. **20** Lee. **21** Frank Lampard. **22** Dudek. **23** Italy. **24** Zinedine Zidane. **25** West Ham Utd. **26** Manchester United. **27** Portsmouth. **28** John Terry. **29** John Aldridge. **30** Burnley.

1 What do four retired policemen investigating old cases turn?
2 In which Washington State city is *Grey's Anatomy* set?
3 Which crime detective series, starting in 2010, stars Idris Elba?
4 Where did one Nigel replace another?
5 Which daytime programme became *Late Lunch*?
6 Which Laurie Lee book has been made into an ITV film version?
7 Who presented *World of Survival* on BBC2?
8 Who presented *The Private Life of Plants*?
9 Who presented *How to Cook* on BBC2?
10 Which daytime TV programme does Dr Chris Steele appear on?
11 Which actor played Louie de Palma in *Taxi*?
12 Who runs the post office in *Heartbeat*?
13 Who did Don Brennan kidnap in his taxi in *Coronation Street*?
14 Which Fern presents *Ready Steady Cook*?
15 Who plays Dr Jonathan Paige in *Dangerfield*?
16 In which drama series were Sicknote and Vaseline members of Blue Watch?
17 Who lives in the flat above Gary and Tony in *Men Behaving Badly*?
18 Which *Knight Rider* became a lifeguard?
19 Which bigoted character supported West Ham?
20 Which George portrayed Arthur Dailey in *Minder*?
21 Who played Peggy the chalet maid in *Hi De Hi*?
22 Which character in *EastEnders* was played by Letitia Dean?
23 Which former *Neighbours* actress had a hit with *The Locomotion*?
24 Which programme did Jill Dando present in the winter?
25 Which channel is dedicated to the House of Commons?
26 What is the US version of *Cracker* called?
27 In which year was *Neighbours* first broadcast in Britain?
28 On which sport did Jack Kramer commentate?
29 What is the presenter of *Local Heroes'* form of transport?
30 Who was the first male presenter of *How Do They Do That*?

1 Which Manchester City manager said, "We've got 1 point from 27 but it's not as bad as that"?

2 According to Eric Cantona what would be thrown off the trawler?

3 Which Gary said, "This is not a normal injury. Fashanu was playing without due care and attention"?

4 Whose departure from Lazio caused the president to remark, "He will only return to Rome as a tourist"?

5 Which Liverpool player was supposedly, "happier at Southend"?

6 Which company decided that, "1966 was a great year for English football. Eric was born"?

7 Which ex-Arsenal boss said, "I am as weak as the next man when it comes to temptation"?

8 Which manager suffered from the *Sun*'s turnip jibes?

9 Which Brazilian great talked of "the beautiful game"?

10 Which short-stay boss Phil said, "Watching Manchester City is probably the best laxative you can take"?

11 Which England international Peter said, "I often get called Quasimodo"?

12 Which modest 60s player said in the 90s, "I'd be worth around £14 to £15 million by today's prices"?

13 Who claimed in 1996 that he had "given up beer and guzzling"?

14 Which German said in 1994, "Me dive? Never!"?

15 What did Arrigo Sacchi say might be thrown at him after Euro 96?

16 When did Terry Venables say, "It's a football match, not a war"?

17 Which team did Alf Ramsey liken to "Animals"?

18 Who in 1996 took "the only job I would have left Chelsea for"?

19 Who said, "I've only taken one penalty before, for Crystal Palace"?

20 "As daft as a brush". Who was Bobby Robson talking about?

21 Who, in 2007, said, "I believe I am a better manager than I was 18 months ago"?

22 Who said, "I am special for my friends and for my family. As a manager, so-so"?

23 Which boss said, "You cannot say that you are happy when you don't win"?

24 Which Gordon said, "The Celtic job has to be the best job in the world. I love it"?

25 What did Jose Mourinho say Spurs left in front of the goal after a 0–0 draw?

26 Who said "I feel like Superman" after scoring against his former club Arsenal?

27 Which West Ham Utd boss said "I know I am not the most experienced manager"?

28 Who said "I'm now a dad who can't take his kids to a football game"?

29 Name the Spurs boss who said "I haven't seen my missus, Sandra all week."

30 Which Blackburn boss said "Football is not a game for women"?

---

1 Which surname is shared by Carole, Ben E. and B. B.?
2 Who has albums called *Bad* and *Dangerous*?
3 Which Caribbean island was Bob Marley from?
4 Which Neil added his name to Crosby, Stills and Nash in 1970?
5 Which Rita was married for six years to Kris Kristofferson?
6 Where were there Tears on Eric Clapton's 1990s single?
7 How are the duo Charles Hodges and Dave Peacock better known?
8 Which 70s group's name was abbreviated to AWB?
9 Which Marc once described himself as "The Acid House Aznavour"?
10 Which clothes were Swinging on the Hippy Hippy Shake in 1963?
11 Who sang with Ant on "When I Fall in Love"?
12 Which Luther duetted with Mariah Carey on "Endless Love"?
13 Which band took its name from the acronym for Rapid Eye Movement?
14 How did the soul singer Otis Redding meet his early death?
15 Who had a hit with "Strangers in the Night" in 1966?
16 How many Pet Shop Boys are there?
17 How did Madonna describe Jessie on her 1989 hit?
18 Who was lead singer with the Commodores?
19 What is the home country of Gilbert O'Sullivan?
20 How is Elaine Bikerstaff better known?
21 Who *Started Out with Nothing and Still Got Most of It Left*?
22 Which Gallager released *Chasing Yesterdays* in 2015?
23 Whose first hit was "If Not for You" in 1971?
24 Which Fern sang "Together We are Beautiful"?
25 How were the Motown Spinners later known?
26 For which country did Johnny Logan win the Eurovision Song Contest?
27 Who sang about Major Tom being stranded in space?
28 Who had a triple platinum album with Zenyatta Mondatta in the 80s?
29 Which family of brothers wrote and co-produced Barbra Streisand's No. 1 "Woman in Love"?
30 Whose first album was called *Blue Gene* in 1964?

Answers | TV Pot Luck 16 (see Quiz 126)

1 Lewis. 2 Michael Smiley. 3 Wayne. 4 Dorien. 5 The Newsroom. 6 Star Trek: Voyager. 7 Bill Maynard. 8 The Drew Carey Show. 9 Sean. 10 Fresh Fields. 11 Cinema. 12 Wacky Races. 13 A Nurse. 14 The Blue Heelers. 15 Wendy Craig. 16 Never Mind the Quality, Feel the Width. 17 Reg Cox. 18 Elsie Tanner. 19 Cuthbert. 20 Eddie Catflap. 21 The Aidensfield Arms. 22 The Sky at Night. 23 The Glums. 24 Honor Blackman. 25 Changing Rooms. 26 BBC2. 27 Mark Lamarr. 28 The Adventure Game. 29 Fallon. 30 Jock Ewing.

1 What character did Harrison kill-off in 2015's *The Force Awakens*?

2 Which 007 played his father in *Indiana Jones and the Last Crusade*?

3 Which Steven directed Ford in *Raiders of the Lost Ark*?

4 Which Kate was his co-star in *Indiana Jones and the Temple of Doom*?

5 In which sci-fi movie did he first find fame?

6 Which Melanie was a co-star in *Working Girl*?

7 In which movie did he play Richard Kimble in a film version of the TV series?

8 What sort of "Graffiti" was the title of a 1973 movie?

9 In which decade did he star in *Witness*?

10 In which decade was Ford born?

11 In which California city was *Blade Runner* set?

12 What is the occupation of Indiana Jones?

13 What was "Presumed" in the title of the 1990 movie?

14 In which decade did he star in the first *Star Wars* movie?

15 Which 1997 film was the name of a special aircraft?

16 "Clear and Present" what was the title of Ford's 1994 movie?

17 Which Annette co-starred with him in *Regarding Henry*?

18 Who directed him as Col. Lucas in *Apocalypse Now*?

19 What relation to Harrison Ford is scriptwriter Melissa Mathison?

20 In *Air Force One* he plays the role of a man in which office?

21 In what sort of "Games" did he play ex-CIA agent Jack Ryan in 1992?

22 How many "Nights" go with the "Six Days" in a movie title?

23 What was the first *Star Wars* sequel in which he starred?

24 Which Bonnie plays Ford's wife in *Presumed Innocent*?

25 Which "Solo" part did he play in the *Star Wars* movies?

26 In which Kingdom did Indiana Jones have his 2008 adventure?

27 What was the codename of the nuclear sub nicknamed the Widowmaker?

28 Who starred alongside Harrison Ford in *What Lies Beneath*?

29 Can you name the cult 1982 sci-fi movie in which he played Rick Deckard?

30 What role did he play in *Patriot Games* and *Clear and Present Danger*?

1 Which series centres on Inspector Morse's former assistant?
2 Which *Spaced* actor stars opposite Idris Elba in Luther?
3 Which character did the late Gary Holton play in *Auf Weidersehen Pet*?
4 Who is Lesley Joseph's character in *Birds of a Feather*?
5 Which Sorkin drama is set in a Newsroom?
6 Lieutenant B'Elanna Torres appears in which S.F. series?
7 Which actor played both Selwyn Froggitt and the Gaffer?
8 In which sitcom does Ryan Stiles play Lewis?
9 What is Dr Maddox's Christian name in *Casualty*?
10 What series was the prequel to *French Fields*?
11 Which programme has been presented by Mike Scott and Derek Grainger?
12 Which programme featured Dick Dastardly and Muttley?
13 What was Gladys Emmanuel in *Open All Hours*?
14 In which series are Sgt Nick Schultz and Dash McKinlay?
15 Who was the star of *And Mother Makes Five*?
16 What was the comedy series set in a tailors' shop?
17 Whose body was discovered in the first episode of *EastEnders*?
18 Who worked in Miami Modes in *Coronation Street* with Dot Greenhalgh?
19 What is Mr Rumbold's Christian name in *Are You Being Served*?
20 Who was Richie Rich's minder?
21 What is the pub in *Heartbeat*?
22 What is the name of Patrick Moore's astronomy programme?
23 Which TV series featured the characters from radio's *Take It from Here*?
24 Who played Diana Weston's mother in *The Upper Hand*?
25 On which interior design programme does Andy Kane appear?
26 Which channel broadcast *The Phil Silvers Show*?
27 Who hosted *Never Mind the Buzzcocks*?
28 Which odd series featured celebs trying to complete various trials supposedly set by the Rangdo, leader of the planet Arg, who usually appeared as an Aspidestra?
29 Which character in *Dynasty* was played by both Pamela Sue Martin and Emma Sams?
30 Which *Dallas* character died in 1982?

---

1 What position did Stanley Matthews play?
2 Which legend married a 23-year-old air hostess on his 49th birthday?
3 Which Dutch international player went on to managerial success at Barcelona in the 1990s?
4 With which London club did Jimmy Greaves begin his career?
5 Who was the first England captain of a World Cup-winning team?
6 Which country did Zbigniew Boniek play for?
7 Which League club did Billy Wright play for?
8 Who was "Wor Jackie"?
9 In which country was Ferenc Puskas born?
10 At which club did Denis Law finish his career?
11 Who was "Kaiser Franz"?
12 How many clubs did Tom Finney play for?
13 Who was known as "The Black Panther"?
14 Who was England's keeper in the 1966 World Cup-winning side?
15 How did Edson Arantes do Nascimento become better known?
16 Which goalkeeper with Christian names Patrick Anthony played over 100 times for his country?
17 Which French midfielder of the 70s and 80s became France's top scorer?
18 In which city did Billy Meredith play his soccer?
19 Which player turned out in a record **21** World Cup finals matches for Argentina?
20 At which club did Stanley Matthews begin and end his career?
21 Which flame-haired England World Cup winner died in 2007?
22 Which Matthew was known to Southampton fans as "Le God"?
23 What was Celtic and Scotland winger Jimmy Johnstone's nickname?
24 At which London club did French legend David Ginola play 100 League games?
25 Which Chelsea legend was a former teammate of Diego Maradona at Napoli?
26 Name the 1995 World Player of the Year who joined Manchester City in 2005.
27 Which England international won the inaugural European Player of the Year award?
28 Who won the European Player of the Year award in 1968?
29 Who won the championship with Leeds United and Manchester United in the 1990s?
30 Which Dutch striker won two European Cups before joining Chelsea in 1995?

Answers – page 140

1 How many members were there in Dave Dee's group altogether?

2 Which *Cabaret* star appeared in 2014's *Arrested Development*?

3 Which country did Prince die in 2016?

4 Where did Ben E. King say to Stand in 1961 and again in 1987?

5 Which Charles Aznavour hit contained just three letters?

6 What was Blondie's Heart made of on their 70s single?

7 Which Irish group includes the vocalist Ronan Keating?

8 Which musical instrument is the jazzman Buddy Rich famous for?

9 Which Reddy Australian is best remembered for "I am Woman"?

10 Which former Radio 1 DJ is nicknamed Ginger?

11 How did Neil Sedaka describe Breaking Up in 1962 and 1976?

12 Which zodiac sign first name did Gerald Hugh Sayer adopt?

13 Which Four had Frankie Valli as their lead singer?

14 Which Images sang "Happy Birthday" and "I Could be Happy"?

15 Which 60s musical creatures included Eric Burdon and Alan Price?

16 Which Midlands city does Jasper Carrott come from?

17 How did the 6' 7" tall singer John Baldry describe himself?

18 Which group did Bob Geldof and Midge Ure found to raise money to combat famine in Africa?

19 Which Tori was a "Cornflake Girl" in 1994?

20 Which Hamilton dated a Pussycat Doll?

21 By what name is Miss Gudmundsdottir better known?

22 Whose first No. 1 was in 1965 and fourth No. 1, "Believe", was in 1998?

23 Which Johnny is nicknamed the Man in Black?

24 Which member of Cilla Black's family is her manager?

25 What do the letters LP stand for?

26 Who were Bill Haley's backing group?

27 Is Vangelis the artist's first name or surname?

28 Whose first hit was "Only the Lonely" in 1960?

29 Which number follows East in the name of the band?

30 Which game of reptiles and climbing apparatus is the title of an album by Gerry Rafferty?

Answers | **TV Pot Luck 17** *(see Quiz 130)*

1 Scandal. 2 Scrubs. 3 Pink Elephant. 4 Suggs. 5 The Last Night of the Proms. 6 Fletcher. 7 Happy Days. 8 Xena – Warrior Princess. 9 4. 10 Helicopter. 11 Maggie Bolton. 12 Scrap Heap. 13 Julia Bradbury. 14 Ian Wright. 15 Jancis Robinson. 16 Mick Johnson. 17 Anthony Worrall Thompson. 18 Jeremy Isaacs. 19 Arthur C. Clarke. 20 Watching. 21 Chef. 22 The Chuckle Brothers. 23 Daily Live. 24 Upper Crust. 25 Trauma. 26 The Haunted Fishtank. 27 In Your Dreams. 28 Family Affairs. 29 Kermit the Frog. 30 Don't Wait Up.

1 Which 007 voiced *Sir Billi* in 2012?

2 Who links *Silkwood* and *The French Lieutenant's Woman*?

3 Who died shortly after finishing *On Golden Pond*?

4 Which George, a superstar of the small screen, had a big-screen flop with *The Peacemaker*?

5 Whose real first names were Norma Jean?

6 Which singer/actress's surname is Ciccone?

7 How is Sofia Scicolone better known?

8 Who was dying of cancer when he made *The Shootist* about a gunman dying of cancer?

9 Which actor won his first oscar for portraying Hugh Glass in 2015?

10 Which blonde reached superstar status after playing Sandy in *Grease*?

11 Who played opposite Joanne Woodward 11 times?

12 Whose real name is Nicholas Coppola?

13 Which husband and wife starred in *Eyes Wide Shut* in 1999?

14 What was the name of Sylvester Stallone character in 2015's *Creed*?

15 Who first starred with Spencer Tracy in *Woman of the Year*?

16 In which decade of the 20th century was Michael Douglas born?

17 Who won the Best Actress Oscar for *Mary Poppins*?

18 In which movie did Al Pacino play Carlito Brigante?

19 Where in Europe was Bruce Willis born?

20 In which "G.I." movie did Demi Moore shave her head?

21 Who played Winona Ryder's eccentric mother in *Mermaids*?

22 Brad Pitt's affair with Gwyneth Paltrow began on the set of which movie?

23 Which painter did Anthony Hopkins play on screen in 1996?

24 What was Whoopi Goldberg's first film, in 1985?

25 Which cartoon character did Warren Beatty play in a 1990 movie?

26 Who played "Dubya" in Oliver Stone's biopic of George W. Bush?

27 Which Mr Ford played Max Brogan in *Crossing Over*?

28 Name the legendary actor whose first talking movie was *The Great Dictator*.

29 Who played the maverick detective in the *Dirty Harry* series of movies?

30 Her movies include *Erin Brokovich* and *Oceans Eleven*. Name her.

Answers | Football: Soccer Legends *(see Quiz 127)*

1 Outside right. 2 George Best. 3 Johan Cruyff. 4 Chelsea. 5 Bobby Moore. 6 Poland. 7 Wolves. 8 Jackie Milburn. 9 Hungary. 10 Manchester City. 11 Franz Beckenbauer. 12 One. 13 Lev Yashin. 14 Gordon Banks. 15 Pele. 16 Jennings. 17 Michel Platini. 18 Manchester. 19 Diego Maradona. 20 Stoke City. 21 Alan Ball. 22 Le Tissier. 23 Jinky. 24 Tottenham. 25 Gianfranco Zola. 26 George Weah. 27 Stanley Matthews. 28 George Best. 29 Eric Cantona. 30 Ruud Gullit.

1 Kerry Washington stars in which US TV show about a political fixer?
2 Sacred Heart Hospital is the setting for which American comedy series?
3 In the children's series *Johnson and Friends* what animal is Johnson?
4 Who is the presenter of the Karaoke-style *Night Fever* on Channel 5?
5 Which annual event concludes with the playing of "Land of Hope And Glory"?
6 Name the Justin who is CBeebies' Mr Tumble?
7 Which US series featured the character Potsie?
8 Which fantasy series stars Lucy Lawless?
9 How many zones are there in *The Crystal Maze*?
10 How did Anneka Rice fly in *Treasure Hunt*?
11 Which character does Kazia Pelka portray in *Heartbeat*?
12 Which Channel 4 series features two teams building a project from salvaged items?
13 Who presents Channel 5's *The Movie Chart Show*?
14 Who was the traveller in *Lonely Planet*?
15 Who presented her *Wine Course*?
16 Who has a son Leo in *Brookside*?
17 Who succeeded as chef on *Food and Drink*?
18 Who took over John Freeman's role in *Face to Face*?
19 Which S.F. novelist presented his *Mysterious World*?
20 Which comedy series featured the characters Brenda and boyfriend Malcolm?
21 What is Antonio Carluccio's occupation?
22 Who are the stars of *Chucklevision*?
23 Which lifestyle guide was presented by Paul Ross?
24 Which series featured the culinary arts of the nobility?
25 Which fly-on-the-wall documentary followed the staff of Selly Oak Hospital, Birmingham?
26 Which programme presented by Ed Hall previewed the week's television?
27 Which Channel 4 series was concerned with nightmares and dreams?
28 What is the twice-daily five-times-a-week soap on Channel 5?
29 Which green creature was Frank Oz the voice of?
30 Which sitcom featured the Drs Latimer?

Answers | **Pop Pot Luck 17** *(see Quiz 128)*

1 Five. 2 Liza Minnelli. 3 USA. 4 By Me. 5 She. 6 Glass. 7 Boyzone. 8 Drums. 9 Helen Reddy. 10 Chris Evans. 11 Hard to Do. 12 Leo. 13 Seasons. 14 Altered Images. 15 The Animals. 16 Birmingham. 17 Long. 18 Band Aid. 19 Amos. 20 Lewis. 21 Bjork. 22 Cher. 23 Cash. 24 Her husband. 25 Long playing (record). 26 The Comets. 27 First name. 28 Roy Orbison. 29 17. 30 Snakes and Ladders.

1 Where did Eoin Jess move to on leaving Aberdeen?
2 In what position did Frank Haffey play?
3 Which club was Kenny Dalglish with when he was first capped?
4 Which striker played for Manchester Utd and Torino in the 60s?
5 What forename is shared by strikers Collins and Spencer?
6 With which club did fullback Tommy Gemmell spend most of his career?
7 Which defender or midfielder clocked up a record 496 league games for Rangers?
8 Who won Scottish Player of the Year in 2014–25 season?
9 Which club did Billy Liddell play for in the 40s and 50s?
10 Which Glasgow-born striker Mo notched 14 goals for his country?
11 Which club did Alex McLeish play for?
12 The chant, "Six foot two, Eyes of Blue" was about which defender?
13 Which classy Liverpool defender of the 70s and 80s landed only 26 caps?
14 Which player failed a dope test and was sent home from the 1978 World Cup in Argentina?
15 What did a certain lager claim to restore for Joe Jordan?
16 Which Arsenal goalkeeper of the 70s played for Scotland?
17 What forename is shared by defenders Donachie and Miller?
18 Which London club did Alan Gilzean play for?
19 Who moved to Monaco as a free agent in the summer of 1996?
20 Which Paul of Celtic was injured and missed Euro 96?
21 Who managed Celtic to three consecutive League titles, 2006–08?
22 Which Gary scored Scotland's winner against France at Hampden in 2006?
23 Which club did goalkeeper Craig Gordon leave to join Sunderland in 2007?
24 What is the first name of Rangers' former Kilmarnock striker Boyd?
25 At which Ayrshire club did Ally McCoist finish his club career in 2001?
26 Whose autobiography is entitled *The Real Mackay*?
27 Which 2008 UEFA Champions League winner captained Scotland the same year?
28 Which ex-international succeeded Alex McLeish as the manager of Scotland in 2008?
29 Name the Wolves striker who missed an open goal against Norway in 2008.
30 Who is the only player to win 100 or more Scottish caps?

Answers	**Movies: The 1950s** *(see Quiz 133)*

1 Eve. 2 Roman. 3 Eden. 4 Monaco. 5 Oklahoma!. 6 80 Days. 7 Queen. 8 Ben Hur. 9 St Valentine's Day Massacre. 10 The Diary of Anne Frank. 11 The River Kwai. 12 Paris. 13 Peyton Place. 14 Marilyn Monroe's. 15 Desire. 16 Limelight. 17 Stewart. 18 Peter Pan. 19 Twenty Thousand. 20 Silk. 21 Rabbit. 22 Monsieur Hulot's Holiday. 23 M. 24 Seven Brides. 25 On a Train. 26 Jose. 27 High Noon. 28 Lady and the Tramp. 29 James Dean. 30 Elvis Presley.

1 How is David Solberg better known?
2 Which surname is shared by Martha of the Vandellas and the late country star Jim?
3 Whose 1993 album was called *Bat out of Hell II*?
4 Which Midlands city does Joan Armatrading come from?
5 Which Boys included three members of the Wilson family?
6 Which musical instrument does Jeff Beck play?
7 Who had a No. 1 with "Under the Moon of Love"?
8 Who was Gloria Estefan's backing group?
9 What is the home country of Sheena Easton?
10 Who is Bon Jovi's lead vocalist?
11 Which zany TV Timmy joined Bombalurina on "Seven Little Girls Sitting in the Backseat" in 1990?
12 Which Boy's autobiography was called *Take It Like a Man*?
13 Which Emily Bronte novel inspired Kate Bush's 1978 No. 1?
14 What colour did Stevie Wonder's Woman wear in 1984?
15 What went with Powder and Paint on Shakin' Stevens's 1985 hit?
16 Pete Townshend and Keith Moon were members of which group?
17 Which 80s duo was Andrew Ridgeley part of?
18 Which part of the UK do Wet Wet Wet come from?
19 Which brothers wrote Dionne Warwick's 1982 hit "Heartbreaker"?
20 Which first name did the singer/guitarist Charles Edward Anderson Berry take?
21 Who had a No. 1 after winning *I'm a Celebrity: Get Me out of Here!* in 2004?
22 From which country did girl group B*Witched originate?
23 Which Park gave hit records for Donna Summer and Richard Harris?
24 Who hosted the Eurovision Song Contest on BBC1 in the 1990s?
25 Which country does Gina G come from?
26 Which Gilbert appeared on stage in short trousers, cropped hair and cloth cap?
27 Which Australian appeared in "The Sullivans" and "The Hendersons" before enjoying chart success?
28 Whose first hit was "Love Me for a Reason" in 1994?
29 What is George's surname and Mr Bolton's first?
30 Whose first album was called *Otis Blue* in 1966?

Answers	Football: Scottish Internationals *(see Quiz 131)*

1 Coventry City. 2 Goalkeeper. 3 Celtic. 4 Denis Law. 5 John. 6 Celtic. 7 John Greig. 8 Stefan Johansen. 9 Liverpool. 10 Johnston. 11 Aberdeen. 12 Jim Holton. 13 Alan Hansen. 14 Willie Johnston. 15 His front teeth. 16 Bob Wilson. 17 Willie. 18 Tottenham Hotspur. 19 John Collins. 20 McStay. 21 Gordon Strachan. 22 Caldwell. 23 Hearts. 24 Kris. 25 Kilmarnock. 26 Dave Mackay. 27 Darren Fletcher. 28 George Burley. 29 Chris Iwelumo. 30 Kenny Dalglish.

1 Bette Davis starred in a film "All About" whom?
2 What sort of "Holiday" was had by Gregory Peck and Audrey Hepburn?
3 James Dean was "East of" where in 1955?
4 In which principality, a favourite with millionaires, was *To Catch a Thief* with Grace Kelly set?
5 Which movie named after a US state includes "Oh What a Beautiful Morning"?
6 How long did Phileas Fogg have to go round the world in?
7 "The African" what was a 1951 movie with Bogart and Hepburn?
8 Which 1959 Charlton Heston movie is famous for its chariot races?
9 Which massacre takes place at the start of *Some Like It Hot*?
10 Which tragic diary was filmed in 1959?
11 "The Bridge on" which Asian river was a big hit of the 50s?
12 In a 1951 film, where was "An American in", as played by Gene Kelly?
13 Which "Place" was a top 50s film which later became a top soap with Ryan O'Neal and Mia Farrow?
14 Whose dress is blown up by the air from a subway grating in *The Seven Year Itch*?
15 What was "A Streetcar Named" in the Brando and Vivien Leigh movie?
16 What "light" was Chaplin's last US movie, made in 1952?
17 Which James appeared in *Vertigo* and *Rear Window*?
18 Which story set in Never Never Land was made by Disney in 1953?
19 How many "Leagues under the Sea" were in the title of the 1954 movie with Kirk Douglas?
20 What were the "Stockings" made from in the title of the 1957 movie?
21 What type of animal is Harvey in the movie of the same name?
22 What was *Les Vacances de Monsieur Hulot* called in English?
23 What did you Dial for Murder in Hitchcock's classic?
24 How many brides were there "for Seven Brothers" in 1954?
25 Where were "Strangers" in the title of a 1951 Hitchcock movie?
26 Which Ferrer won the Best Actor Oscar for his part in *Cyrano de Bergerac*?
27 What time was the title of Gary Cooper's award-winning 1952 movie?
28 Which Walt Disney film about dogs was the biggest-grossing movie of the decade?
29 Can you name the iconic American actor who died in a car accident in 1955?
30 Which superstar made his screen debut in *Love Me Tender* in 1956?

Answers	**TV Pot Luck 18** *(see Quiz 134)*

1 Independent Television. 2 Pub Landlord. 3 Michael Barrymore. 4 Selfridges. 5 South Park. 6 A Comedy Sports Quiz. 7 Australian. 8 Evergreen Terrace. 9 Madhur Jaffrey's. 10 Clampers. 11 Auntie. 12 Underworld. 13 Ricki Lake. 14 Clive Anderson. 15 Simon Mayo. 16 Gregg Wallace. 17 Chris Barrie. 18 Caroline Quentin. 19 Premier Passions. 20 Mariella Frostrup. 21 Seasiders. 22 Anita Dobson. 23 Jack Dee. 24 Smith. 25 Australia. 26 Frasier. 27 Julia Roberts. 28 Gabby Logan (daughter of Terry Yorath). 29 Hannibal. 30 Eerie.

1 What does ITV stand for?
2 What profession has Al Murray taken from his stage show to the small screen?
3 Who presented *Strike It Rich*?
4 Which store was featured in *The Shop*?
5 Which adult animation series features Kyle, Kenny and Cartman?
6 What type of programme is Channel 5's *Sick as a Parrot*?
7 What nationality are comedians Roy and H.G.?
8 In which road do *The Simpsons* live?
9 Whose culinary series was *Far Eastern Cookery*?
10 What was the fly-on-the-wall documentary about traffic wardens?
11 Which relation featured in the title of the commemoration of 75 years of the BBC?
12 Which black comedy series concerning gangland figures starred Mike Reid and James Fleet?
13 Who presents *X-Rated Ricki*?
14 Which chat show host was *All Talk*?
15 Which radio presenter hosted *Confessions*?
16 Who hosts *Masterchef* opposite John Torode?
17 Which star of *Red Dwarf* was *A Prince Among Men*?
18 Which *Men Behaving Badly* actress appeared in *Kiss Me Kate*?
19 Which fly-on-the-wall documentary featured Sunderland Football Club?
20 Who presented her Brunch on Channel 5?
21 Which behind-the-scenes documentary series featured a holiday centre?
22 Which ex-*Eastender* appeared in *Get Well Soon*?
23 Which comedian had a *Sunday Service*?
24 What was Wolfie's surname in the south London-based sitcom?
25 From which country did *The Paul Hogan Show* originate?
26 In which series does Daphne Moon look after Martin Crane?
27 Which film actress went in search of orang-utans?
28 Which footballer's daughter fronts *Inside Sport*?
29 What was John Smith's nickname in *The A-Team*?
30 Where did Marshall Teller move to in Indiana?

Answers	**Pop Pot Luck 18** *(see Quiz 132)*

1 David Soul. 2 Reeves. 3 Meat Loaf. 4 Birmingham. 5 Beach Boys. 6 Guitar. 7 Showaddywaddy. 8 The Miami Sound Machine. 9 Scotland. 10 Jon Bon Jovi. 11 Mallett. 12 Boy George. 13 Wuthering Heights. 14 Red. 15 Lipstick. 16 The Who. 17 Wham!. 18 Scotland. 19 The Gibbs. 20 Chuck. 21 Peter Andre. 22 Ireland. 23 MacArthur. 24 Terry Wogan. 25 Australia. 26 O'Sullivan. 27 Kylie Minogue. 28 Boyzone. 29 Michael. 30 Otis Redding.

1 Which tragedy is always called "the Scottish play" by superstitious actors?
2 What colour is said to be unlucky in the theatre?
3 Which musical is set in a St Tropez night club featuring drag artistes?
4 What was the Monty Python musical that might have been about sending emails?
5 On which Avenue do Muppet-like puppets play?
6 According to the comedy, There's a what in My Soup?
7 Where is the Fiddler in the musical which starred Topol?
8 Which London theatre's motto was, "We never closed"?
9 Which New York street is famous for its theatres?
10 Which musical about Professor Higgins and Eliza Doolittle is based on *Pygmalion*?
11 Who wrote the 2015 smash hit Broadway play *Hamilton*?
12 What do the initials RSC stand for?
13 Which musical is based on T. S. Eliot's poems?
14 Who first played the title role in "Evita" in the West End?
15 Who wrote the script for the musical *Mamma Mia!*?
16 Which show includes "Climb Ev'ry Mountain"?
17 Which musical is the name of a fairground ride?
18 Which musical is about a circus impresario?
19 In which musical does Fagin appear?
20 Which Boulevard is the title of a musical?
21 Which part of the Pacific is the setting for a popular musical?
22 Which class of Society is a musical based on *The Philadelphia Story*?
23 Oh which Indian city appears in the title of a controversial show?
24 The Importance of Being what is the name of an Oscar Wilde play?
25 Who are with the Guys in the show about gangsters?
26 Which girl is the lecturer Educating in the play by Willy Russell?
27 Which Miss is a musical set in Vietnam?
28 What is the full name of the show often just referred to as Les Mis?
29 What do you say to Dolly in the title of the show?
30 Aspects of what are the theme of which Lloyd Webber musical?

1 Who plays at home at Upton Park?

2 What is the main colour of Watford's home shirts?

3 Jack Charlton and Kevin Keegan have both managed which club?

4 What is the last word in Brighton & Hove's name?

5 Which country has Jamie Vardy played for?

6 Which Glenn of Tottenham Hotspur was PFA Young Player of the Year in 1980?

7 Which country do Atletico Madrid come from?

8 With which club did Andy Hinchcliffe make his League debut?

9 Which club did Tony Dorigo join on leaving Chelsea?

10 Which John was Hearts' top League scorer in 1995–96?

11 What colour are Aston Villa's home shorts?

12 What is Cardiff's nickname?

13 Which team does David Mellor support?

14 Denis Smith followed Lawrie McMenemy as boss at which club?

15 What is the main colour of Spain's home shirts?

16 Which Steve of Liverpool won the Footballer of the Year award in 1989?

17 Which country did Gerson play for?

18 With which club did Chris Sutton make his League debut?

19 Who hit 34 League goals in Newcastle's first season in the Premier League?

20 Defenders Parker and Pallister were teammates with which club?

21 Which Frenchman was Liverpool manager when they won three cups in 2001?

22 Which Scottish Premier League club went bust in early 2008?

23 Which team does Russell Brand support?

24 Which striker Frank played over 200 games for both Arsenal and Machester Utd?

25 Chris Waddle scored an FA Cup Final goal for which club in the 1990s?

26 Sasa Curcic first played in England for which club?

27 Which Andy of Villa was PFA Player of the Year in 1977?

28 What is the first name of Matteo who first played for Liverpool?

29 What is the second word in Southend's name?

30 Eric Gates played for which East Anglian club?

---

1 Which city do Oasis come from?
2 Which Gallagher brother was lead vocalist in the mid-90s?
3 With which band was there a media feud to decide on the top BritPop act?
4 What is Paul McGuigan's nickname?
5 How many people were in Oasis when they had their first No. 1 single?
6 What was the band's debut album?
7 What goes in brackets before *Morning Glory* on the album title?
8 Who is the elder of the two Gallagher brothers?
9 Which actress Patsy married Liam in the 90s?
10 Which drug was Liam charged with possession of in 1996?
11 Which football team do the Gallaghers support?
12 What is the nationality of Noel and Liam's parents?
13 What is their mother called?
14 Which musical instrument does Noel play?
15 In which country was a tour cancelled in 1996 when Liam returned home?
16 After which TV pop show did Oasis sack their drummer in 1995?
17 Which Wonder record was a 1995 hit for the band?
18 In 1996, how did Oasis say Don't Look Back?
19 At which Somerset Festival did Oasis perform in front of 30,000 fans in 1994?
20 What goes With It on the record title in 1995?
21 Which son of a Beatles drummer joined Oasis in 2004?
22 What did Oasis want you to *Dig Out* according to their 2008 album title?
23 Where did Oasis receive its Outstanding Contribution to Music award in 2007?
24 What "milestone" birthday did Noel celebrate in 2007?
25 "The Importance of Being" what was the title of the eighth British No. 1 in 2005?
26 Liam and Noel both support the same football team. Name the club.
27 What is the name of the double compilation album released by the band in 2006?
28 "Definitely ____" was the name of the band's first album. Complete the title.
29 What type of "Chemistry" did Oasis release in 2002?
30 Can you name the fast-sounding title of Oasis's first single?

Answers	**Theatre & Musicals** *(see Quiz 135)*

1 Macbeth. 2 Green. 3 La Cage aux Folles. 4 Spamalot. 5 Q. 6 Girl. 7 On the Roof. 8 The Windmill. 9 Broadway. 10 Lin-Manuel Miranda. 11 Sullivan. 12 Royal Shakespeare Company. 13 Cats. 14 Elaine Paige. 15 Catherine Johnson. 16 The Sound of Music. 17 Carousel. 18 Barnum. 19 Oliver. 20 Sunset. 21 South. 22 High. 23 Calcutta. 24 Earnest. 25 Dolls. 26 Rita. 27 Saigon. 28 Les Miserables. 29 Hello. 30 Love.

1 Was *The Ten Commandments'* running time nearer to 60, 100 or 220 minutes?

2 *Shakespeare in Love* and *Iron Man* both feature which actress?

3 According to a movie title, "Only Angels Have" what?

4 Which word follows 'Never Say Never' in a Sean Connery movie title?

5 What is the name of Michael Douglas's actor father?

6 Which star actor was in *Apollo 13*, *Sleepless in Seattle* and *Big*?

7 Who sang the theme song for *Titanic*?

8 Which word follows "Dirty Rotten" in a Steve Martin movie title?

9 War veteran Ron Kovic features in which movie?

10 Which Barbra starred with Nick Nolte in *The Prince of Tides*?

11 Who sang the title song of *Help!*?

12 Which famous Carole tested for the role of Scarlett O'Hara?

13 In which decade of the 20th century was Rowan Atkinson born?

14 Which Melanie starred in *Working Girl*?

15 According to the film title, how many "Degrees of Separation" are there?

16 Which Elliott featured in *M*A*S*H*?

17 Which director had a long custody battle for his children with Mia Farrow?

18 *The Empire Strikes Back* was a sequel to which blockbuster?

19 Which actor Martin was assigned to assassinate Brando in *Apocalypse Now*?

20 Which actress links *Pretty Woman* and *Hook*?

21 Dancer Eugene Curran Kelly became known under which name?

22 In *Mary Poppins*, what job does Mary take?

23 Which Jonathan starred in *Evita*?

24 Which spread can complete the film title, *A Taste of* ____?

25 *Lady and the Tramp* were what type of animals?

26 What computer term was the title of the 2006 Harrison Ford crime thriller?

27 Kate Hudson and Anne Hathaway co-star in which matrimonial romantic comedy?

28 Which Audrey starred in *Breakfast at Tiffany's*?

29 Which word completes the title, *The Spiral* ____?

30 Which Debra starred in *An Officer and a Gentleman*?

Answers | Football Pot Luck 15 *(see Quiz 136)*

1 West Ham Utd. 2 Yellow. 3 Newcastle Utd. 4 Albion. 5 England 6 Hoddle. 7 Spain. 8 Manchester City. 9 Leeds Utd. 10 Robertson. 11 White. 12 The Bluebirds. 13 Chelsea. 14 Sunderland. 15 Red. 16 Nicol. 17 Brazil. 18 Norwich City. 19 Andy Cole. 20 Manchester Utd. 21 Gerard Houllier. 22 Gretna. 23 West Ham Utd. 24 Stapleton. 25 Sheffield Wednesday. 26 Bolton Wanderers. 27 Gray. 28 Dominic. 29 United. 30 Ipswich Town.

1 In what state are the impressionist group Ringers?
2 Jonny from *Two Pints of Lager* was Anthony in which sitcom?
3 Who played Brenda in *Baghdad Cafe*?
4 Whose daughters were Darlene and Becky?
5 Rose Marie and Morey Amsterdam starred in which comedy series?
6 What were the names of the two families in *Soap*?
7 Which character does Christopher Ryan play in *Bottom*?
8 Who is Connie Booth's character in *Fawlty Towers*?
9 What was Kim Hartman's character in *'Allo, ' Allo*?
10 By what name was Daisy Moses better known in *The Beverley Hillbillies*?
11 Who runs a catering business in *2 Point 4 Children*?
12 Who is Saffron's brother in *Absolutely Fabulous*?
13 Which hospital comedy starred Peter Bowles, James Bolam and Christopher Strauli?
14 What is *Chef* Lenny Henry's character first name?
15 In which sitcom was the song *My Little Horse* entered for a contest?
16 Who has a brother Niles?
17 Who plays Dave Lister in *Red Dwarf*?
18 In which show would you hear the catchphrase "suits you, sir"?
19 What rank is Ernie Bilko in *The Phil Silvers Show*?
20 Who was the star of *Police Squad*?
21 Who presents *Shooting Stars*?
22 *Three's Company* was the American version of which British sitcom?
23 Who plays Charlie in *Babes in The Wood*?
24 Who is Tim Taylor's assistant in *Tool Time*?
25 What is *Caroline in the City*'s occupation?
26 Who marries Monica in *Friends*?
27 Which series features Martin and Mandy as tenants?
28 Whose neighbours are the Leadbetters?
29 Which 1960s series featured Ricky Ricardo?
30 Which series starred Larry Hagman and Barbara Eden?

---

1 What is the last word in Northampton's name?
2 Which country has Vinnie Jones played for?
3 What is the main colour of Hull's home shirts?
4 Which team has its stadium in South Africa Road, London?
5 Which player was Manchester Utd's top League scorer in 1995–96?
6 Which club traditionally selected its managers from the Boot Room?
7 Which midfielder Jason went from Ipswich to Tottenham Hotspur in the 90s?
8 With which club did John Wark make his league debut?
9 Which club did Kevin Gallacher leave to join Blackburn?
10 Which Alex of Aberdeen was Scottish Footballer of the Year in 1990?
11 Who are The Cumbrians?
12 Which country has Roy Keane played for?
13 What kind of animal was World Cup Willie?
14 Howard Kendall followed Dave Bassett as boss at which club?
15 Which Clive was PFA Player of the Year in 1987?
16 What colour are Croatia's home shirts?
17 Who was in goal when Liverpool won the 1995 Coca Cola Cup?
18 Which Terry has managed both Arsenal and Tottenham Hotspur?
19 England striker Alan Smith won a championship medal at which club?
20 Which Archie has been assistant manager to Walter Smith?
21 In 2012, Roy Hogdson replaced who as England manager?
22 Who was Reading boss when they were first promoted to the Premier League?
23 Which Guy has hit goals for Portsmouth, Aston Villa and Sheffield Wednesday?
24 Which country did Marcel Desailly play for?
25 Which team did veteran DJ John Peel support?
26 Which Chris was in goal as Sheffield Wednesday lost the 1993 FA Cup Final?
27 Teale and Townsend were together at which club?
28 What is the colour of Hungary's home shirts?
29 Alf Inge Haaland first played in England for which club?
30 How many games did Germany lose in Euro 96?

Answers | **Movies Pot Luck 16** *(see Quiz 142)*

1 Gary Shandling. 2 China. 3 Falcon Crest. 4 Myers. 5 Christie. 6 Diaz. 7 Samuel L. Jackson. 8 They dress as women. 9 Kate Winslet. 10 Kline. 11 Raging Bull. 12 Accept it. 13 Aladdin. 14 Eye patch. 15 Costner. 16 West. 17 Never. 18 Park. 19 Wayne. 20 Indiana Jones. 21 Hackman. 22 Daughter. 23 Warren Beatty. 24 1960s. 25 Reynolds. 26 Johansson. 27 Ghost. 28 River Phoenix. 29 Sarandon. 30 Chicago.

1 Which Little Jimmy wanted to be A Long Haired Lover from Liverpool?
2 Which Roses did his 14-year-old sister Marie sing about in 1973?
3 Which 10-year-old Lena took "Ma, He's Making Eyes at Me" to No. 10?
4 Where was the choirboy Aled Jones Walking in 1985?
5 Which Brenda was known as "Little Miss Dynamite"?
6 Which Helen said "Don't Treat Me Like a Child" aged 14 in 1961?
7 Which 15-year-old girl from Glasgow was heard to "Shout" in 1964?
8 Which Stevie was called Little in his early showbiz years?
9 Which late-80s teen group were revamped as NKOTB in 1993?
10 Which Michael first sang with his four brothers at the age of six?
11 Which Mary hit the No. 1 spot with "Those Were the Days" after winning *Opportunity Knocks*?
12 Which Australian teenager had a No. 1 with "I Should be So Lucky"?
13 To two years either way, how old was Cliff Richard when he had his first hit "Move It" in 1958?
14 Which dancer/singer called Bonnie won *Opportunity Knocks* aged six?
15 Which Donny sang professionally with his brothers from the age of six and had chart success with "Puppy Love" and "Too Young"?
16 Which 17-year-old Sandie had a 60s hit with "Always Something There to Remind Me"?
17 Which Neil wrote "Oh Carol" for Carole Klein, later Carole King, whom he met at high school?
18 Which Genesis drummer called Phil was a former child actor?
19 The kids from which TV dance show had chart success in the 80s?
20 Which girl, later the name of a famous princess, gave 16-year-old Paul Anka chart success in 1957?
21 What was the title of Vanessa Hudgens debut album?
22 What is the famous surname of Dream Street member Jesse?
23 Sisters Alyson and Amanda Michalka are better known as which singing duo?
24 "Baby One More Time" was the debut single and global hit for which teenager?
25 Sam Concepcion sang the theme song for which 2008 DreamWorks movie?
26 Which group's debut single was titled "Five Colours in Her Hair"?
27 Which group sang "I'm a Believer" and "All Star" in the movie *Shrek*?
28 Who sang "What's New Pussycat" for the movie *Flushed Away*?
29 Which Ben sang several songs for the 2006 movie *Over the Hedge*?
30 Elton John sang the theme song for which 1994 Walt Disney movie?

Answers | TV: Comedy 4 *(see Quiz 139)*

1 Dead. 2 The Royle Family. 3 Whoopi Goldberg. 4 Roseanne. 5. The Dick Van Dyke Show. 6 Tates & Campbells. 7 Dave Hedgehog. 8 Polly Sherman. 9 Helga. 10 Granny Clampett. 11 Bill Porter and Rona. 12 Serge. 13 Only When I Laugh. 14 Gareth. 15 Father Ted. 16 Frasier Crane. 17 Craig Charles. 18 The Fast Show. 19 Master Sergeant. 20 Leslie Neilsen. 21 Vic Reeves & Bob Mortimer. 22 Man About the House. 23 Karl Howman. 24 Al. 25 Cartoonist. 26 Chandler. 27 Game On. 28 Tom and Barbara Good. 29 I Love Lucy. 30 I Dream.

1 Which US comic star Gary featured in the 90s *Doctor Dolittle*?
2 Which country links "town" and "Syndrome" in movie titles?
3 In which TV soap did Jane Wyman find fame after appearing on the big screen?
4 Which Mike starred in *Wayne's World*?
5 Which 60s star Julie was Oscar-nominated in 1998?
6 *There's Something About Mary* featured which Cameron?
7 Which actor links *Jurassic Park* and *Coming to America*?
8 In *Some Like It Hot*, what disguise do Curtis and Lemmon adopt?
9 Which actress appeared on the cinema poster for *Titanic*?
10 Which Kevin featured in *A Fish Called Wanda*?
11 In which 1980 movie did Robert De Niro play a boxer?
12 What did George C. Scott refuse to do with his Oscar for *Patton*?
13 The song "A Whole New World" comes from which animated movie?
14 What did John Wayne wear on his face in *True Grit*?
15 Which Kevin won a Best Director Oscar for *Dances with Wolves*?
16 Which direction completes the film title *Once upon a Time in the* ____?
17 How many times did Greta Garbo marry?
18 Which Nick won an Oscar for *The Wrong Trousers*?
19 Which John starred in *Stagecoach*?
20 Which Mr Jones was a character in *Raiders of the Lost Ark*?
21 Which Gene won the Best Actor Oscar for *The French Connection*?
22 Which family member completes the film title, *Ryan's* ____?
23 Who directed *Dick Tracy*?
24 In which decade of the 20th century was Nicolas Cage born?
25 Which Debbie starred in *Singin' in the Rain*?
26 Which Scarlett played Molly in *Home Alone 3*?
27 In which weepy was Demi's Moore's boyfriend Patrick Swayze murdered?
28 Who was the late brother of Joaquin Phoenix, known in some movies as Leaf?
29 Which Susan won the Best Actres Oscar for *Dead Man Walking*?
30 *The Sting* took place in which gangster city?

1 Which Bruce presented *Strictly Come Dancing*?
2 Who hosts *Pointless* with Richard Osman?
3 Which programme did Cilla Black use for matchmaking?
4 Which cartoon character appeared in *Bullseye*?
5 Which show was famously hosted by Bob Holness?
6 How many contestants are there each day on *Countdown*?
7 Kenneth Kendall and Anneka Rice hosted which Channel 4 quiz in which contestants had to seek and answer clues?
8 Who first hosted *The Price Is Right*?
9 What colour was the famous contestant's chair on *Mastermind*?
10 Who many contestants faced the challenge of the *Krypton Factor* in each episode?
11 Which female impersonator hosted *Blankety Blank* from 1997 to 2002?
12 What were the odds of winning the Channel 4 afternoon quiz hosted by William G. Stewart?
13 Which barrister presented Channel 4's *Whose Line Is It Anyway*?
14 Who hosted *Family Fortunes* after Les Dennis?
15 What is the subject matter of *Never Mind the Buzzcocks*?
16 Who took over from Jeremy Clarkson as the host of *Robot Wars*?
17 Which channel is dedicated to gameshows?
18 Who hosted *Telly Addicts*?
19 Who succeeded Nick Hancock as the host of *They Think It's All Over*?
20 Nicholas Parsons hosted an Anglia TV gameshow called *The Sale Of… what*?
21 In which show did Robert Llewellyn makes teams build devices out of scrap?
22 Who preceded Sue Barker as the host of *A Question of Sport*?
23 Which programme featured Bernard Falk putting contestants in sticky situations?
24 Who presented *Every Second Counts*?
25 Which movie quiz did Michael Aspell host in the 1970s?
26 Which Gaby presented *Whatever You Want*?
27 Which show features a "quickie bag"?
28 Who nosed around stars homes in *Through the Keyhole*?
29 *The Great Antiques Hunt* was presented by which female wine connoisseur?
30 Complete this title: _____ *I lie to You*.

Answers	Pop: Soul & Motown *(see Quiz 145)*

1 Piano. 2 Stevie Wonder. 3 Warwick. 4 Holland. 5 The Temptations. 6 Baby Love. 7 Lionel Richie. 8 ABC. 9 Farewell. 10 Gaye. 11 Queen of Soul. 12 Tops. 13 Isley Brothers. 14 Brown. 15 Martha and the Vandellas. 16 The Miracles. 17 The Pips. 18 60s. 19 Wilson. 20 Detroit. 21 Ross. 22 Hayes. 23 Lay It Down. 24 Joss Stone. 25 Berry. 26 Gospel. 27 Motown Records. 28 Stevie Wonder. 29 Tamla Motown. 30 Marvin Gaye.

1 Who plays at home at Easter Road?

2 Which Ian of Liverpool was PFA Young Player of the Year in 1983?

3 Gerry Francis and David Pleat have both managed which club?

4 What is the second word in Cambridge's name?

5 Which country has Peter Schmeichel played for?

6 Which team did Eric Morecambe support?

7 Which country do Sturm Graz come from?

8 With which club did keeper David James make his League debut?

9 Which club did Pat Jennings join on leaving Tottenham Hotspur?

10 What pattern is on West Bromwich Albion's home shirts?

11 Which Mike was Stoke's top League scorer in 1995–96?

12 Who are the Addicks?

13 Which Terry of Liverpool won the Footballer of the Year award in 1980?

14 What is the main colour of the Romanian home strip?

15 What forename links players Parlour and Houghton?

16 Which Lou got the Celtic sack in 1994?

17 Which club was banned from the 1994–95 FA Cup then allowed back in?

18 Which country did Stefan Effenberg play for?

19 Ruel Fox and Andy Cole were teammates at which club?

20 Which energy-giving drink has John Barnes advertised?

21 Who was Portsmouth manager when they won the 2008 FA Cup Final?

22 Which Dutchman played for Arsenal for 11 seasons until 2006?

23 What colour goes with blue on Oldham's home shirts?

24 Who plays home games at Vicarage Road?

25 Who won the FA Cup in 1970?

26 Which Charlie won the championship with which club?

27 Paul Parker won the championship with which club?

28 With which club did Nigel Spink make his League debut?

29 Which club did Alan Smith leave to join Arsenal?

30 Ille Dumitrescu first played in England for which club?

Answers | Movies Pot Luck 17 *(see Quiz 146)*

1 Robin Hood. 2 Anthony Hopkins. 3 3 hours. 4 Meg Ryan. 5 1970s. 6 Tandy. 7 Reynolds. 8 Dracula. 9 The Kennedy family. 10 Oliver! 11 1990s. 12 New York. 13 Sylvester Stallone. 14 Liza Minnelli. 15 Lynn. 16 451 (Fahrenheit 451). 17 1950s. 18 Wales. 19 Lemmon. 20 Elizabeth Taylor. 21 Saturday. 22 Rudolph Valentino. 23 "Live and Let Die". 24 1980s. 25 General Hospital. 26 Harrison. 27 Sean Penn. 28 Day. 29 Lady. 30 Fisher.

1 Which musical instrument did Ray Charles play?
2 Which Motown star's real name is Steveland Judkins?
3 Which Dionne had a hit with "Walk on By" in 1964 and "Heartbreaker" 18 years later?
4 Who completed the Holland, Dozier trio who wrote many of the Motown hits of the 60s and 70s?
5 Which major all-male Tamla Motown group recorded "I'm Gonna Make You Love Me" with Diana Ross and the Supremes?
6 Which Baby gave the Supremes their first No. 1?
7 Who sang "Endless Love" with Diana Ross in 1981?
8 Which letters took the Jackson Five into the Top Ten in 1970?
9 What did Michael Jackson say to his Summer Love in 1984?
10 Which Marvin was Too Busy Thinking 'Bout his Baby in 1969?
11 Which Queen is Aretha Franklin known as?
12 Which Four were Standing in the Shadows Of Love in 1967?
13 Which Brothers charted with "This Old Heart Of Mine" in 1966 and 1968?
14 Which James was "Living in America" in 1986?
15 How were Martha Reeves and the Vandellas billed on their first Motown hits?
16 Who was Smokey Robinson's backing group?
17 How were Gladys Knight's brother Merald and cousins Edward and William known as collectively?
18 At the start of which decade did Berry Gordy set up the Tamla label?
19 Which Jackie recorded "Reet Petite" in 1957?
20 In which US city did Motown begin?
21 Which long-time Motown artist Diana left the label for the second time in 2002?
22 Which soul legend Isaac died in August 2008?
23 What was the title of Al Green's album released in 2008?
24 Whose debut album was titled *The Soul Sessions*?
25 What is the first name of the founder of the Motown label, Mr Gordy Jr?
26 Soul music is often said to have its roots in which type of Church music?
27 Can you name the famous record company founded by Berry Gordy?
28 Who had a major hit single with the soul classic "I Just Called to Say I Love You"?
29 What was Motown Records also known as?
30 Who "heard it through the grapevine" in 1968?

Answers	TV: Quiz & Game Shows *(see Quiz 143)*

1 Bruce Forsyth. 2 Alexander Armstrong. 3 Blind Date. 4 Bully. 5 Blockbusters. 6 Two. 7 Treasure Hunt. 8 Leslie Crowther. 9 Black. 10 Four. 11 Paul O'Grady. 12 Fifteen to One. 13 Clive Anderson. 14 Vernon Kay. 15 Pop music. 16 Craig Charles. 17 Challenge TV. 18 Noel Edmonds. 19 Lee Mack. 20 The Century. 21 Junkyard. 22 David Coleman. 23 Now Get Out Of That. 24 Paul Daniels. 25 Angus Deayton. 26 Gaby Roslin. 27 Ready Steady Cook. 28 Lloyd Grossman. 29 Jilly Goolden. 30 Would.

1 Who was described as the "Prince of Thieves" in the title of a 90s blockbuster?

2 Which Anthony starred in *Thor*?

3 Does *South Pacific* last nearly 1, 2 or 3 hours?

4 Which actress links *Sleepless in Seattle* and *You've Got Mail*?

5 Was *Alien* first released in the 1960s, 70s or 80s?

6 Which Jessica became the then-oldest Oscar winner for *Driving Miss Daisy*?

7 Which Burt starred in *Smokey and the Bandit*?

8 For which role is Bela Lugosi best remembered?

9 Which famous US family did Arnold Schwarzenegger marry into?

10 The song "Who Will Buy" features in which musical movie?

11 In which decade was *Forrest Gump* released?

12 Which city was Macaulay Culkin lost in, in *Home Alone 2*?

13 Who co-wrote and starred in the *Rambo* films?

14 Which singer/actress won the Best Actress Oscar for *Cabaret*?

15 Which Redgrave was nominated for an Oscar in 1999?

16 At what Fahrenheit temperature do books burn in the film title?

17 In which decade of the 20th century was Alec Baldwin born?

18 Catherine Zeta Jones comes from which country?

19 Which Jack starred in *Some Like It Hot*?

20 Which wife of Richard Burton has also been Oscar-nominated?

21 Upon which day of the week does "Night Fever" occur?

22 Which silent screen heartthrob starred in *The Sheik*?

23 What was the Bond theme for *Live and Let Die* called?

24 In which decade was *Twins* released?

25 Which soap did Hollywood actress Demi Moore star in?

26 Which Ford was Max Brogan in *Crossing Over*?

27 Who won the Best Actor Oscar for *Mystic River*?

28 Which Doris starred in romantic films with Rock Hudson?

29 Which word completes the film title, The ____ Vanishes?

30 Which Carrie featured in *When Harry Met Sally*?

Answers | **Football Pot Luck 17** *(see Quiz 144)*

1 Hibernian. 2 Rush. 3 Tottenham Hotspur. 4 United. 5 Denmark. 6 Luton Town. 7 Austria. 8 Watford. 9 Arsenal. 10 Stripes. 11 Sheron. 12 Charlton Athletic. 13 McDermott. 14 Yellow. 15 Ray. 16 Macari. 17 Tottenham Hotspur. 18 Germany. 19 Newcastle Utd. 20 Lucozade Sport. 21 Harry Redknapp. 22 Dennis Bergkamp. 23 Red. 24 Watford. 25 Chelsea. 26 Nicholas. 27 Manchester Utd. 28 Aston Villa. 29 Leicester City. 30 Tottenham Hotspur.

Answers – page 159

1 Mack Brown is the lead character in which forensic drama?
2 Who played Illya Kuryakin in the 1960s and "Ducky" Mallard in the 2000s?
3 *Bonanza* was set in which country?
4 What dangerous occupation did *The Fall Guy* have?
5 In which public service did *Juliet Bravo* serve?
6 Who stars as *Cracker* in the UK?
7 Which 1990s American crime drama featured a man who could see into the minds of criminals?
8 What was the profession of most of the characters in *This Life*?
9 Who starred as *Doctor Kildare*?
10 Pam Ferris and David Jason played Ma and Pa who in *Darling Buds of May*?
11 Which Peter starred in *The Irish RM* and with Penelope Keith in *To the Manor Born*?
12 In the series name, Reilly was Ace of what?
13 Which former *Liver Bird* played *The District Nurse*?
14 Which actor connects *The Sweeney*, *Morse* and *Kavanagh*?
15 What was the profession of Mary Fisher in *The Life and Loves Of a She Devil*?
16 The mystery drama written by Dennis Potter was called *The Singing ____*?
17 *London's Burning* follows the drama in which emergency service?
18 What kind of house was *The House of Elliot*?
19 Which Lady, based on D. H. Lawrence's classic, was first televised in 1993?
20 What kind of Practice stars Kevin Whately as a rural GP?
21 Sean Bean stars as which 19th-century British officer?
22 Which *Man From Auntie* comedian wrote *Stark*?
23 In the BBC series, John Thaw and Lindsay Duncan spent how long in Provence?
24 The BBC2 medical drama was called *Cardiac* what?
25 Who wrote the classic *Martin Chuzzlewit*, dramatised by the BBC in 1994?
26 Which Victorian female author wrote *Middlemarch*?
27 Which family of four brothers starred in the historical drama, *The Hanging Gale*, set in 19th-century Ireland?
28 The 1995 drama series *Pride and Prejudice*, was based on whose novel?
29 Which show centres around the fictional Earls Park Football Club?
30 What kind of transportation featured in *The Onedin Line*?

Answers | Pop: Novelty Songs *(see Quiz 149)*

1 "Mr Blobby". 2 The Goodies. 3 John Kettley. 4 Abbott. 5 Keith Harris. 6 Terry Wogan. 7 Harry Enfield. 8 19. 9 Julian Clary. 10 Ernie. 11 Halfway up (or Halfway down). 12 Woolpackers. 13 Billy Connolly. 14 Dudley Moore. 15 Elephant. 16 Snooker players. 17 Combine Harvester. 18 Roland Rat. 19 The Smurfs. 20 Dave Lee Travis. 21 Frog. 22 Yankovic. 23 Barbie. 24 Chanukah. 25 Dog. 26 The Streak. 27 Joe Dolce. 28 "Star Trekkin'". 29 Afroman. 30 My Ding-A-Ling.

1 What is the second word in Norwich's name?
2 Which country has Jason McAteer played for?
3 What is the main colour in Ipswich's home shirts?
4 Which London club did Wimbledon ground-share with in the 90s?
5 Which German player was Manchester City's top scorer in 1995–96?
6 Rod Wallace and Gary Speed were teammates at which club?
7 Which Danny of Celtic was Scottish Footballer of the Year in 1977?
8 With which club did Roy Keane make his League debut?
9 Which club did Chris Armstrong leave to join Tottenham Hotspur?
10 What is Chelsea's nickname?
11 What colour are Denmark's home shirts?
12 Which country did Norman Whiteside play for?
13 Which Dean was Aston Villa's top scorer in 1994–95?
14 Which Mick played a record number of games for Ipswich?
15 Which Gary was PFA Player of the Year in 1986?
16 Who was Alex Ferguson's assistant for Manchester Utd for the 1995–96 double season?
17 Jeff Kenna and Ken Monkou were teammates at which club?
18 Howard Kendall got the boot as boss of which Division 1 club in 1995?
19 Graham Rix played over 350 games with which club?
20 Alan Stubbs was a losing Coca-Cola Cup Finalist with which club?
21 Who were relegated three years after reaching the Champions League semi-final?
22 In which country were the 2006 champions relegated after a match-fixing scandal?
23 Which Jean-Pierre was European Footballer of the Year 1991?
24 Ablett and Hinchcliffe were together at which club?
25 Which team does Sebastian Coe support?
26 What colour are Wales's home shorts?
27 Which country did Jairzinho play for?
28 Charles and Wright were full backs together at which club?
29 In which city are Glentoran based?
30 Which Newcastle winger was in the tabloids in 1996 for running up gambling debts of around £60,000?

1 What was Mr Blobby's first No. 1 hit called?
2 Dr Graeme Garden was part of which comedy trio which had hits in the 1970s?
3 Which Weatherman was immortalized in song by Tribe of Toffs in '88?
4 Which Russ spread some Atmosphere in 1984?
5 Who helped Orville to sing "Orville's Song"?
6 Which Irish DJ performed a Floral Dance on disc?
7 Who had Loadsamoney in 1988?
8 Which number was important for Paul Hardcastle in 1985?
9 Who or what was the Joan Collins Fan Club, a 1988 chart entrant?
10 What was the name of Benny Hill's "Fastest Milkman in the West"?
11 Where was Robin the Frog on the stairs?
12 Which Packers danced a Hillbilly Rock in 1996?
13 Which Scots comedian filed for D.I.V.O.R.C.E. in 1975?
14 Who said "Goodbye-ee" with Peter Cook in 1965?
15 What type of animal was Nellie, who took the Toy Dolls to No. 4 in the charts in 1984?
16 Which type of sportsmen made up the Matchroom Mob with Chas and Dave in 1986?
17 Which piece of farm equipment gave the Wurzels a No. 1 to "Brand New Key" in 1976?
18 Which Superstar was Rat Rapping in 1983?
19 Which cartoon characters lost Father Abraham from the 70s and refound chart success in 1996?
20 Which bearded DJ joined Paul Burnett to become Laurie Lingo and the Dipsticks?
21 "Axel F" is associated with which Crazy creature?
22 Which Weird Al won the Best Comedy Album Award in 2004 for *Poodle Hat*?
23 Aqua celebrated which famous doll?
24 Which winter Jewish festival did Adam Sandler sing about?
25 *Come Poop With Me* was a hit for Triumph the Insult Comic what?
26 Which Ray Stevens hit from 1974 was all about taking your clothes off?
27 Who had a hit in 1981 with "Shaddap Your Face"?
28 Which 1987 single from *The Firm* boldly went where no song had gone before.
29 Who had a hit in 2000 with "Because I Got High"?
30 What was Chuck Berry singing about in 1972, a No. 1 hit in the UK and the USA?

1 What is Goldie Hawn's real name?
2 Which Linda starred in the *Terminator* movies?
3 Which 2008 docudrama portrayed a 1970s French tightrope walker's stunt of walking between the Twin Towers?
4 *Lethal Weapon, Ransom* and *The* all feature which actor?
5 In the *Die Hard* movies what is the job of the Bruce Willis character?
6 Who played the Count in *Bram Stoker's Dracula*?
7 In which TV cop series did movie actor Telly Savalas find fame?
8 Which William starred in *Star Trek: The Motion Picture*?
9 Was Disney's *Snow White* released before, after or during World War II?
10 Which Jodie starred in *Bugsy Malone*?
11 Who played C. S. Lewis in *Shadowlands*?
12 Which creature was "Called Wanda" in a movie title?
13 Which superhero battles against Lex Luther?
14 Who went on to *Hannah and Her Sisters* from TV's *Peyton Place*?
15 Lee Marvin headed a "Dirty" cast of how many in a 60s movie?
16 Who sang the title song of *The One and Only*?
17 In which decade of the 20th century was Helena Bonham-Carter born?
18 Which Carrie starred in *The Empire Strikes Back*?
19 Which Kenneth was dubbed "the new Olivier"?
20 Which actress Lucille did Desi Arnaz marry twice?
21 Frank J. Cooper took on which first name in Hollywood?
22 Which actor links *The Rock, Moonstruck* and *Leaving Las Vegas*?
23 In which decade was *Grease* released?
24 Which Jim starred in *The Mask*?
25 Which word completes the film title, *The Old Dark ___*?
26 What is the first name of Oscar-nominated Spanish director Almodovar?
27 Which actress co-wrote and starred in *Kill Bill: Vol. 1*?
28 Which Ben co-wrote and starred in *Good Will Hunting* with Matt Damon?
29 What is the nationality of Antonio Banderas?
30 Which "Show" was a big hit for Jim Carrey?

1 In which city was *Friends* set?
2 What was Ms Shepherd's 1990s comedy series called?
3 In which series did Tony Randall play Felix Unger?
4 Who is David Jason's character in *Only Fools and Horses*?
5 Who had a sister named Brenda Morgenstern?
6 Who was the _____ *Teenage Witch*?
7 Who were *The Two Ronnies*?
8 Who was George Roper's wife in *Man About the House*?
9 Who was playwright Jack Rosenthal's wife?
10 In which series did Eamonn Walker play Winston the home help?
11 Whose neighbours are Pippa and Patrick?
12 Which character in *Absolutely Fabulous* is a fashion magazine executive?
13 Who was the accident-prone deputy manager of Whitbury Leisure Centre?
14 Who played the president of the USA in *Whoops Apocalypse*?
15 What was the sequel to *No Honestly* featuring Lisa Goddard?
16 Where was Dawn French the vicar of?
17 Which comedian and star of *Jolson* played an ex-con in *Time After Time*?
18 Which *Doctor Who* appeared in *The Two of Us*?
19 Which sitcom starred Nicola MacAuliffe and Duncan Preston as surgeons?
20 Who was Julian in *Terry and Julian*?
21 What was the sitcom starring Judy Loe and Roger Rees set around a singles bar?
22 Who played the butler in *Two's Company*?
23 *Home James* was a spin-off from which sitcom starring Jim Davidson?
24 Who played Clarence the short-sighted removal man?
25 Which series was a sequel to *The Growing Pains of P.C. Penrose*?
26 Which American actress starred in *Shirley's World*?
27 Which sequel to *Are You being Served* was set in a large country house?
28 Which *Steptoe and Son* actor's last series was *Grundy*?
29 What was the sequel to *Happy Ever After* starring June Whitfield and Terry Scott?
30 Which character in *Red Dwarf* was played by both Norman Lovett and Hattie Hayridge?

Answers	**Football: Going Up** *(see Quiz 153)*

1 Blackburn Rovers. 2 Leicester City. 3 Kevin Keegan. 4 Oxford Utd. 5 West Ham Utd. 6 Swindon Town. 7 Nottingham Forest. 8 Bryan Robson. 9 Wimbledon. 10 Bolton Wanderers. 11 Wycombe. 12 Norwich City. 13 Peter Reid. 14 Kamara. 15 Barnet. 16 Collymore. 17 Leicester City. 18 Sheffield. 19 Leeds Utd. 20 John Toshack. 21 Swansea City. 22 2007. 23 MK Dons. 24 Jewell. 25 United. 26 Manchester City. 27 Norwich City. 28 Sunderland. 29 West Bromwich Albion. 30 Reading.

1 The A1-Ring was built over what Austrian circuit?

2 In which year did the A1-Ring first host a grand prix?

3 Name the South Australian city that was awarded the Australian Grand Prix in 1985.

4 Which was the last year the Formula One circus visited that city?

5 The Avus circuit can be found in which German city?

6 If one of the circuit's corner names can be translated as the South Curve, how would you translate the name of the other one?

7 Name the famous Brands Hatch corner located at the start of each lap.

8 In which year did Brands Hatch last host a grand prix?

9 Which circuit was added in 2016?

10 Which Argentinian president oversaw the construction of the Buenos Aires circuit?

11 Who won there on Formula One's last visit in 1998?

12 Outside which Spanish city is the Circuit de Catalunya located?

13 In which year was a temporary tyre chicane built after the Campsa corner?

14 Name the driver who won the grands prix there in 1998 and 1999?

15 Which British circuit hosted the European Grand Prix in 1993?

16 Who was victorious in the rain that day?

17 Which Portuguese circuit hosted a grand prix between 1984 and 1997?

18 Who won the first grand prix held there for McLaren?

19 Who overtook Michael Schumacher around the outside at the final corner in 1996?

20 Which was the final year that Estoril hosted a grand prix?

21 Which East Midlands track was announced as the British GP venue from 2010?

22 In which US state is the Brickyard, which staged the US Grand Prix 2000–07?

23 In honour of which legendary Canadian driver is the Montreal circuit named?

24 In which country is the Fuji Speedway?

25 Which track, famous for its 24-hour race, staged the French Grand Prix in 1967?

26 Which city track hosted F1's first ever night race in 2008?

27 Which German driver won the 2008 German Grand Prix at Hockenheim?

28 Which Spanish circuit hosted the 2008 European Grand Prix?

29 At which racetrack is the Turkish Grand Prix staged?

30 In which city's circuit did Lewis Hamilton clinch the 2008 World Drivers' title?

Answers | **Pop Pot Luck 19 (see Quiz 154)**

1 Australia. 2 Two. 3 Bob Geldof. 4 Braxton. 5 "Be Bop". 6 Navy. 7 Bobby Vee. 8 USA for Africa. 9 Private. 10 Two. 11 James Taylor. 12 Campbell. 13 Chapman. 14 Sonny. 15 Ireland. 16 Bosnia. 17 Flute. 18 Lipstick. 19 Minogue. 20 Clapton. 21 Blondie. 22 Rihanna. 23 Hynde. 24 The 50s. 25 Pink Floyd. 26 Pickett. 27 Bing Crosby. 28 Telly Savalas. 29 10cc. 30 Paula Yates.

1 Which team did Kenny Dalglish lead into the Premiership?
2 Which team went up to the Premiership in 1994 and again in 1996?
3 Who was manager of Newcastle when they were promoted to the Premiership in 1993?
4 Which club made it to the First Division for the first time ever in 1985?
5 Ludek Miklosko has been in two promotion campaigns with which club?
6 Steve McMahon took which team to the First Division at the first attempt?
7 Which team did Frank Clark lead back to the Premiership in the 1990s?
8 Who gained promotion for Middlesbrough in his first season as a player/manager in 1995?
9 Which club were in Division 4 in 1982 and Division 1 in 1986?
10 John McGinlay was with which club in promotions from the Second division to the Premiership?
11 Which Wanderers entered the League in 1993?
12 Steve Bruce was ever-present when which East Anglian side were Second Division champions?
13 Who was manager of Sunderland when they were promoted in 1996?
14 Which Chris took Bradford to Division 1 in 1996?
15 Which London team joined the League in 1991?
16 Which Stan was Nottingham Forest's top marksman in their '94 promotion?
17 Joachim and Walsh played in a play-off final for which team?
18 Goals by Deane and Agana took which United to the top flight?
19 Batty and Strachan helped which club to promotion?
20 Who was the boss who took Swansea to their 1980s promotions?
21 Which Welsh club returned to the Championship in 2008?
22 Which year saw Gretna promoted to the Scottish Premier League?
23 Paul Ince won promotion as manager of which League 2 club in 2008?
24 Which Paul was Wigan Athletic's boss when they went up to the Premiership?
25 Which Sheffield club went up to the Premiership in 2006 and back down in 2007?
26 Which Lancashire club won promotion to the Premiership in 2002?
27 Which City won promotion to the Premiership as Champions in 2005–06?
28 Which "Cats" won the Football League Championship in season 2006–07?
29 Which West Midlands club won promotion to the Premiership for 2004–05?
30 Which Royal sounding team won promotion to the Premiership for 2006–07?

Answers | TV: Comedy 5 *(see Quiz 151)*

1 New York. 2 Cybill. 3 The Odd Couple. 4 Derek Trotter. 5 Rhoda. 6 Sabrina. 7 Barker and Corbett. 8 Mildred. 9 Maureen Lipman. 10 In Sickness and in Health. 11 The Meldrews. 12 Edina. 13 Colin Weatherby. 14 Peter Cook. 15 Yes, Honestly. 16 Dibley. 17 Brian Conley. 18 Patrick Troughton. 19 Surgical Spirit. 20 Julian Clary. 21 Singles. 22 Donald Sinden. 23 Up the Elephant and Round the Castle. 24 Ronnie Barker. 25 Rosie. 26 Shirley Maclaine. 27 Grace and Favour. 28 Harry H. Corbett. 29 Terry and June. 30 Holly.

1 What is the home country of 5 Seconds of Summer?

2 How many members of the Eurythmics were there?

3 Who was lead singer with the Boomtown Rats?

4 Which Toni was heard to Breathe Again in 1994?

5 What goes before "A-Lula" on the Gene Vincent classic?

6 In which branch of the armed services were the Village People in 1979?

7 How did Bobby Velline reduce his surname when he had chart success in the 50s?

8 Which American band was inspired by the all-UK Band Aid?

9 What sort of Dancer is Tina Turner on her first solo album?

10 How many members made up Tyrannosaurus Rex?

11 Which 70s star recorded the classic album *Sweet Baby James*?

12 Which Glen was a Rhinestone Cowboy?

13 Which Tracy made a memorable appearance at the Nelson Mandela 70th Birthday Tribute Concert at Wembley in 1988?

14 How was Salvatore Bono better known?

15 Which country are the Chieftains from?

16 For which war children did Luciano Pavarotti perform benefit concerts in the mid-1990s ?

17 Which musical instrument does James Galway play?

18 What did Connie Francis see on Your Collar in 1959?

19 Which surname is shared by sisters Kylie and Dannii?

20 Which Eric has been part of Cream and Derek and the Dominoes?

21 After an 18-year gap Deborah Harry returned to No. 1 in 1999 with which band?

22 Who was a *Good Girl Gone Bad* according to her 2008 album?

23 Which Chrissie sang with the Pretenders?

24 In which decade did the Platters enjoy their greatest success?

25 Which 70s supergroup included Roger Waters and David Gilmour?

26 Which Wilson was "In the Midnight Hour" in the 60s and in the 80s?

27 Which late US crooner is nicknamed the Old Groaner?

28 Which TV detective star's only album was called Telly?

29 Who had a hot with "I'm Not in Love" in 1975?

30 Who was Mrs Bob Geldof at the start of the 1990s?

---

1 Whose movies included *The Great Escape* and *Bullitt*?
2 Peter O'Toole played the title role in which movie set in the sands of the Middle East?
3 Which 007 played opposite Tippi Hedren in *Marnie*?
4 Which sister of Warren Beatty starred with Jack Lemmon in *The Apartment*?
5 Who was Elizabeth Taylor's husband on and off screen in *Who's Afraid of Virginia Woolf*?
6 Which star of *Psycho* is the mother of Jamie Lee Curtis?
7 Which sometime partner of Woody Allen starred in *Rosemary's Baby*?
8 Whose real name is Ann-Margret Olsson?
9 Which star of *My Fair Lady* was born in Belgium?
10 Which singing superstar was the Funny Girl in the title of the movie?
11 Which Jack found fame in *Easy Rider*?
12 Which "Cowboy" was played by Jon Voight in 1969?
13 Which future star of *Phantom of the Opera* appeared in *Hello Dolly*?
14 Which actor father of *Fatal Attraction*'s Michael starred in *Spartacus*?
15 Which star of westerns starred in, produced and directed *The Alamo*?
16 Which *The King and I* star was 'the old Cajun' in *The Magnificent Seven*?
17 Which Jack and Walter played *The Odd Couple*?
18 George Lazenby played whom in *On Her Majesty's Secret Service*?
19 Which Ursula's first major English-language film was *Dr No*?
20 Which long-haired blonde starred in *Darling*, for which she won an Oscar?
21 Which Hayley played both twins in *The Parent Trap*?
22 Which blonde's last movie was *The Misfits*, written by Arthur Miller?
23 Which pop group starred in *A Hard Day's Night*?
24 Which Burt frolicked in the surf with Deborah Kerr in *From Here to Eternity*?
25 Who starred as Fast Eddie Felson in *The Hustler*, a role he was to reprise 25 years later in *The Color of Money*?
26 Which Miss Andrews played Mary Poppins?
27 By what name is the star of *Summer Holiday*, born Harry Webb, better known?
28 Who played the lead role in the 1961 musical *Blue Hawaii*?
29 Which queen was portrayed by Elizabeth Taylor in 1963?
30 What was the name of the secret agent in the 1962 movie *Dr No*?

Quiz 156 | TV Pot Luck 19

Answers – page 168

1 What did Billie Piper keep as the call girl Blanche in the ITV series?
2 How often has *Coronation Street*'s Emily Bishop been married?
3 Who is the bartender in *The Simpsons*?
4 Which children's detective was a Koala Bear?
5 Who is Dorothy's mother in *The Golden Girls*?
6 What is Sheriff Buck's first name in *American Gothic*?
7 Which series features twins Brittany and Cynthia Daniel?
8 In which series was Nathan Bridger the captain of a submersible?
9 Which fly-on-the-wall documentary concerned cabin crew staff?
10 In which series was Troy the family pet?
11 What was *Robin's Nest*?
12 Which character played by Bill Maynard had the Christian name Selwyn?
13 What was the occupation of the workers in *Common as Muck*?
14 Which angling programme was presented by Nick Fisher?
15 What was the BBC's longest-running observational documentary series?
16 Whose comedy series was *As Seen on TV*?
17 Which summer 98 music festival event was hosted by John Peel?
18 Which S.F. drama series featured the invasion of Scotland by UFOs?
19 Whose series of sketches and stand-up comedy was titled *Merry Go Round*?
20 Which sitcom starred Emma Wray as a nurse?
21 Which country did the game show *Endurance* come from?
22 Which quiz is presented by Bradley Walsh and Jenny Powell?
23 Who was the star of *Worzel Gummidge Down Under*?
24 What was *George and Mildred*'s surname?
25 Who hosted *That's Showbusiness*?
26 Who was Lenny in *Lenny's Big Amazon Adventure*?
27 What is *Donahue*'s first name?
28 Which Gaby was presenter of *The Real Holiday Show*?
29 Who was *The Man from Auntie*?
30 Which sitcom featured the characters Eric and Hattie?

| **Answers** | Pop Pot Luck 20 *(see Quiz 158)* |

1 Nelson. 2 Ireland. 3 Clapton. 4 Drums. 5 Marty and Kim Wilde. 6 The Supremes.
7 Manchester. 8 Three. 9 The Cranberries. 10 Max Bygraves. 11 Tony Bennett.
12 Bad. 13 Spector. 14 Virgin and V2. 15 Cat Stevens. 16 Diamond. 17 Seal 18
Piano. 19 The Shadows. 20 Captain. 21 Coldplay. 22 Glastonbury. 23 Moyet. 24
Surname. 25 Sony. 26 Bob Marley. 27 Alvin Stardust. 28 Parsley, Sage, Rosemary
and Thyme. 29 Morecambe and Wise. 30 Slade.

1 Which United manager signed Eric Cantona?
2 How old was Ryan Giggs when he made his first-team debut?
3 Who wrote the autobiography *The Good, the Bad and the Bubbly*?
4 Which player went to Newcastle as part of the deal that bought Andy Cole to Old Trafford?
5 In which country was Sir Matt Busby born?
6 Which club was Paul Ince bought from?
7 Mark Hughes has moved from Manchester Utd twice. Which clubs did he join?
8 Which team were the opponents in the Cantona Kung-Fu spectator attack in January 1995?
9 Alex Ferguson sold his son Darren to which club?
10 Who is the elder of the Neville brothers?
11 What was Denis Law's usual shirt number?
12 What infamous first went to Kevin Moran in the 1985 FA Cup Final?
13 What is the surname of 1970s brothers Brian and Jimmy?
14 Which United manager signed Bryan Robson?
15 Who was the scoring skipper in the 1996 FA Cup Final?
16 Paddy Roche was an international keeper for which country?
17 Who was dubbed "El Beatle" after a 60s European triumph?
18 Which forename links Beckham, May and Saddler?
19 Which two United players were members of England's World Cup-winning team?
20 Who was the first Manchester Utd player to hit five goals in a Premier League match?
21 From which club did United sign Michael Carrick in 2006?
22 Which teenage striker was signed from Everton in 2004?
23 What was the score in the 1999 FA Cup Final against Newcastle United?
24 Who passed Sir Bobby Charlton as United's appearances record-holder?
25 Assistant manager Carlos Queiroz became coach of which national team in 2008?
26 What is the club's nickname?
27 How many times had United won the Premier League up to the end of 2007–08?
28 Name any year in which United won the European Cup/UEFA Champions League.
29 Can you name United's talismanic French striker from 1992–97?
30 Who did Alex Ferguson replace as the manager of Manchester United?

1 Which surname is shared by Rick, Sandy and Willie?

2 What is the home country of Sinead O'Connor?

3 Which Eric was *Unplugged* in 1993?

4 Which instrument did Dave Clark play?

5 How are Reginald Smith and his daughter Kim better known?

6 Who was Diana Ross's backing group?

7 Which city are the Hollies from?

8 How many Degrees were in the group which sang "When Will I See You Again?"?

9 Which fruity band's first album was *Everybody Else is Doing It, So Why Can't We?*?

10 Which showbiz veteran recorded the Singalonga series of albums?

11 Who has won Grammy awards for "I Left My Heart in San Francisco" 32 years apart?

12 What sort of Moon was Rising for Creedence Clearwater Revival in 1969?

13 Which Phil was record producer for the Crystals?

14 Which record labels were founded by Richard Branson?

15 Which Cat's debut single was "I Love My Dog"?

16 What sort of Life was a debut album for Sade?

17 Whose real name is Sealhenry Samuel?

18 Which musical instrument does Neil Sedaka play?

19 Which group's members have included Hank Marvin and Brian Bennett?

20 Which nautical chief joined Tennille on disc?

21 Chris Martin and Jonny Buckland were the founding members of which band?

22 For which music festival is Michael Eavis famous?

23 Which Alison sang with Yazoo?

24 Is Morrissey the performer's first name or surname?

25 Which corporation did George Michael begin his lawsuit against in the 1990s?

26 Which Jamaican singer was given a state funeral in 1980?

27 Whose first hit was "My Choo-Ca-Choo" in 1973?

28 Which four herbs were the title of an album by Simon and Garfunkel?

29 On which comedy duo's show did Shirley Bassey sing wearing a hobnail boot?

30 Who had a 70s No. 1 album with Slayed?

Answers	TV Pot Luck 19 *(see Quiz 156)*

1 Secret Diary. 2 Twice. 3 Moe. 4 Archibald. 5 Sophia. 6 Lucas. 7 Sweet Valley High. 8 Seaquest DSV. 9 Airline. 10 Dangerfield. 11 A restaurant. 12 Froggitt. 13 Dustbin men. 14 Screaming Reels. 15 Doctors at Large. 16 Victoria Wood. 17 Glastonbury. 18 Invasion Earth. 19 Alexei Sayle. 20 My Wonderful Life. 21 Japan. 22 Wheel of Fortune. 23 Jon Pertwee. 24 Roper. 25 Mike Smith. 26 Henry. 27 Phil. 28 Roslin. 29 Ben Elton. 30 Sykes.

1 In which country does the action of *The Horse Whisperer* take place?
2 What disability does Al Pacino have in *Scent of a Woman*?
3 Which singer starred in and directed *The Prince of Tides*?
4 In *Terms of Endearment* Debra Winger is dying from which disease?
5 Which doomed lovers were played by Leonard Whiting and Olivia Hussey in 1968?
6 Which Lana was the star of *Imitation of Life*?
7 What was the name of Leonardo DiCaprio's character in *Titanic*?
8 What type of "Encounter" occurred between Celia Johnson and Trevor Howard in the movie classic?
9 Which Juliette nursed the "English Patient"?
10 Which Claire starred in *Little Women* and *Romeo and Juliet*?
11 Which husband of Melanie Griffith starred opposite Tom Hanks in *Philadelphia*?
12 Which Nicholas Evans novel was *The Horse Whisperer* based on?
13 Who falls for Meryl Streep in *The Bridges of Madison County*?
14 What follows "Truly, Madly" in the Anthony Minghella weepie?
15 Who played the title role in *Dr Zhivago*?
16 Which movie had the ad line, "There are three sides to this love story"?
17 The 1996 version of *Romeo and Juliet* mentioned its writer's name in the title; what was it called?
18 Which Mary, famous for her TV roles, starred opposite Donald Sutherland in *Ordinary People*?
19 Which Thomas Hardy novel was *Tess* based on?
20 Who played Mrs Kramer in the 1979 weepie?
21 Which daughter of Charlie Chaplin starred in *Dr Zhivago*?
22 In which decade was *Ghost* released?
23 Who won the Best Actor Oscar for *Kramer versus Kramer*?
24 *Ever After* was a remake of which fairy story?
25 Ryan O'Neal's affair with Ali McGraw began on the set of which movie?
26 Rose DeWitt Bukater was played by which English actress in *Titanic*?
27 *Field of Dreams* is about which sport?
28 What type of "Story" proved to be too sad for Ryan O'Neal in 1970?
29 Where did E.T. go at the end of the movie of the same name in 1982?
30 Which 1998 movie starring Bruce Willis had the audience in tears?

Answers	Football: The 1980s *(see Quiz 161)*

1 Manchester City. 2 Points for a win. 3 Crystal Palace. 4 Robert Maxwell. 5 Swansea City. 6 Italy. 7 The Milk Cup. 8 Bob Paisley. 9 Tottenham Hotspur. 10 Kevin Keegan. 11 Gary Lineker. 12 Liverpool. 13 Jock Stein. 14 France. 15 England. 16 France. 17 Terry Venables. 18 Arsenal. 19 Chelsea. 20 Play-offs. 21 Watford. 22 Wimbledon. 23 Liverpool. 24 Ruud Gullit. 25 Arsenal. 26 Bobby Robson. 27 Aston Villa. 28 West Ham United. 29 Ipswich Town. 30 Manchester United.

1 Which Ricky Gervais series had a US version which ended in 2013?
2 The Gallagher and Maguire families appear in which brass-necked series?
3 Which US series featured the lives and relationships of people on a cruise ship?
4 Who narrated *Classic Homes* on Channel 4?
5 Who presented the children's show *Get Your Own Back*?
6 Which interior design programme is presented by Mark Curry?
7 In which series is the Aidensfield Arms?
8 What was the name of the lovers in *The Glums*?
9 Which Howard in *Howard's Way* was played by Maurice Colbourne?
10 Who presented *That was the Week That Was*?
11 Who was Darwin in *Seaquest DSV*?
12 What was Gerry Anderson's 90's S.F. space series?
13 Where did *Billy Liar* work?
14 Who was the transsexual in *Coronation Street*?
15 What was Cliff Huxtable's full Christian name in *The Cosby Show*?
16 In which state was *Eerie* a weird town?
17 Which Irish comedian was famous for his cigarette and bar stool?
18 Which western series was about a cattle drive?
19 Which Saturday sports programme is presented by Steve Rider?
20 Which series chronicled the 20th century?
21 On which motorway is *Motorway Life* filmed?
22 Who was the boss of Firman's Freezers in *Coronation Street*?
23 Which series was presented by Rhona Cameron and Richard Fairbrass?
24 Who links *Blind Date* to *The Moment of Truth*?
25 Which company celebrated *30 Years of Laughter with Denis Norden*?
26 On which day was *Fully Booked* transmitted?
27 Which antiques show is presented by Jilly Goolden?
28 What is the Sunday-evening hymns programme on BBC1?
29 Which magicians presented their *Unpleasant World*?
30 In which city is The Wire set?

1 Which club did both Malcolm Allison and John Bond manage?
2 What changed from two to three in all games at the start of the 1981–82 campaign?
3 Which London team were hailed as "The Team of the Eighties"?
4 Which tycoon became Oxford chairman?
5 Which team was top of the First Division during 1981 but back in the Fourth Division by 1986?
6 Who won the 1982 World Cup?
7 What was the League Cup known as after a deal with the National Dairy Board?
8 Who retired as Liverpool boss after a season in which both the championship and League Cup were won?
9 Garth Crooks and Steve Archibald played together at which club?
10 Which former England captain ended his playing days at Newcastle Utd?
11 Which Englishman was the top scorer in the 1986 World Cup finals?
12 Who did Wimbledon beat in their first FA Cup Final victory?
13 Which manager collapsed and died seconds before the end of the Wales v Scotland World Cup qualifying game?
14 On leaving Tottenham Hotspur, Chris Waddle moved to which country?
15 UEFA banned the clubs of which country from participation in European competitions?
16 Which host nation won the 1984 European Championship?
17 Which British manager took over at Barcelona?
18 Which team won the 1988–89 championship in the last minute of the season?
19 Kerry Dixon was Division 1 top scorer in 1984–85 with which team?
20 Which extra games were introduced to decide promotion?
21 Which Hertfordshire team lost the 1984 FA Cup Final?
22 Which club were known as the "Crazy Gang"?
23 Which club completed a League and FA Cup double in the 1980s?
24 Which dreadlocked striker scored in the 1988 European Championship Final?
25 Which club won their first League Championship for 18 years in 1989?
26 Who replaced Ron Greenwood as the England manager in 1982?
27 Can you name the British club who won the European Cup in 1982?
28 Name the London club who beat Arsenal in the 1980 FA Cup Final.
29 Which Town lifted the Uefa Cup in 1981?
30 Which club lost the 1983 League Cup Final but won the 1983 FA Cup?

Answers	Movies: Weepies (see Quiz 159)

1 USA. 2 Blind. 3 Barbra Streisand. 4 Cancer. 5 Romeo and Juliet. 6 Turner.
7 Jack. 8 Brief. 9 Binoche. 10 Danes. 11 Antonio Banderas. 12 The Horse Whisperer. 13 Clint Eastwood. 14 Deeply. 15 Omar Sharif. 16 Kramer versus Kramer. 17 William Shakespeare's Romeo and Juliet. 18 Tyler Moore. 19 Tess of the d'Urbervilles. 20 Meryl Streep. 21 Geraldine. 22 1990s. 23 Dustin Hoffman. 24 Cinderella. 25 Love Story. 26 Kate Winslet. 27 Baseball. 28 Love Story. 29 Home. 30 Armageddon.

1 Which Elvis is the star of 2016's *Elvis vs Nixon*?

2 How many Seasons were there?

3 Which Helen held the record for making more than 12 radio and TV appearances before the age of 15 in 1961?

4 Which barefoot pop star's autobiography was called *The World at My Feet*?

5 What was Tina Turner's first husband called?

6 What is the home country of Daniel O'Donnell?

7 Whose second solo album was called *There Goes Rhymin' Simon*?

8 Which music paper is often abbreviated to *NME*?

9 Which football team does Simply Red's Mick Hucknall support?

10 Which Midlands town do Slade originate from?

11 Which Family group backed Sly?

12 Who makes up the trio with Stock and Aitken?

13 What is the home country of Shirley Bassey?

14 Which East End gangsters did Spandau Ballet's Kemp twins portray on film?

15 Which band were Rockin' All Over the World in 1977?

16 What was Sting's profession before he entered show business?

17 What do the letters CD stand for?

18 Who started out as the Guildford Stranglers?

19 Which Paul links the Style Council and the Jam?

20 What is Art short for in Art Garfunkel's name?

21 In which month/year did Band Aid 20 release "Do They Know It's Christmas"?

22 Which girl band had three consecutive Christmas No. 1s 1996–98?

23 David Sylvian was lead singer of which oriental-sounding group?

24 In which country was Engelbert Humperdinck brought up?

25 Which record label did Holland-Dozier-Holland leave in 1968?

26 Which hero of Cinderella gave his name to an album by Adam Ant?

27 Whose first solo hit was "Give Peace a Chance" in 1969?

28 How many members of the Righteous Brothers are there?

29 Who was Bob Marley's backing group?

30 What do the letters MW stand for on your radio?

Answers | TV Pot Luck 20 *(see Quiz 160)*

1 The Office. **2** Shameless. **3** The Love Boat. **4** John Peel. **5** Dave Benson Phillips. **6** Change That. **7** Heartbeat. **8** Ron and Eth. **9** Tom. **10** David Frost. **11** A Dolphin. **12** Space Precinct. **13** An Undertaker's. **14** Hayley Patterson. **15** Heathcliff. **16** Indiana. **17** Dave Allen. **18** Rawhide. **19** Grandstand. **20** The People's Century. **21** M6. **22** Leo Firman. **23** Gaytime TV. **24** Cilla Black. **25** London Weekend Television. **26** Sunday. **27** The Great Antiques Hunt. **28** Songs of Praise. **29** Penn and Teller. **30** Baltimore.

1 Which Sam said, "A producer shouldn't get ulcers, he should give them"?
2 In which country was Stanley Kubrick born?
3 Which English producer David was head of Columbia for two years in the 80s?
4 What was Bob Fosse's contribution to *Cabaret* and *All That Jazz*?
5 What was the first name of producer Thalberg who has given his name to a special movie award?
6 Which Winner appeared in *You Must be Joking* as well as directing?
7 Which actor directed *Star Trek V: The Final Frontier*?
8 Which letter was used to show the superior film when there was a cinema double-feature?
9 Which soft-drinks company once owned Columbia Pictures?
10 What was the name of MGM's lion?
11 *The Peacemaker* was the first release from which Spielberg stable?
12 Which man and dog were the creation of Briton Nick Park?
13 Who did Martin Scorsese direct in *Raging Bull* and *Taxi Driver*?
14 Which actor Leonard stayed behind the camera for *Three Men and a Baby*?
15 Which Mrs Minnelli, Judy, did Vincente direct in *The Pirate*?
16 What name is given to the hinged board which shows the film's details during shooting?
17 Who was Oscar-nominated for his debut as director of *Dances with Wolves*?
18 What precedes "Star" in the name of the studio which made *Men in Black*?
19 In which of his own movies did Cecil B. de Mille appear in 1950?
20 Which George links *Star Wars* and *Raiders of the Lost Ark*?
21 What is the first name of director Zemeckis of *Back to the Future*?
22 Which member of Dire Straits wrote the music for *Local Hero*?
23 Buena Vista was set up to distribute which studio's films?
24 What geographical symbol did Paramount use as its logo?
25 What is the name of Garry Marshall's sister who is also a film director?
26 Which three letters are used as shorthand for special effects?
27 Christopher Nolan was director of which 2014 movie?
28 Can you name the director who often made a cameo appearance in his own movies?
29 Who won an Academy Award for directing *Raiders of the Lost Ark* in 1981?
30 Who directed the 2015 movie *The Man from U.N.C.L.E.*?

Answers | **Football: Midfield Men** *(see Quiz 165)*

1 Blackburn Rovers. 2 Arsenal. 3 Michel Platini. 4 Osvaldo Ardiles. 5 Bremner. 6 Manchester City. 7 Graeme Souness. 8 Lothar Matthaus. 9 Parker. 10 Arsenal. 11 Scott. 12 Belgium. 13 Fulham. 14 Paul McStay. 15 Liverpool. 16 Wolfgang. 17 Bryan Robson. 18 Everton. 19 Manchester Utd. 20 Yes. 21 2007. 22 Lampard. 23 Aston Villa. 24 France. 25 David Beckham. 26 Steven Gerrard. 27 West Ham Utd. 28 Roy Keane. 29 Tim Cahill. 30 Liverpool.

1 Which 1960s soap was revived in the early 2000s?
2 What US state is Disney TV's rock star child Hannah's surname?
3 On the quiz, whose *Price is Right*?
4 Which science series was presented by Richard Vranch?
5 Of which football club is the subject of *The Alex Ferguson Story* the manager?
6 Which star of *The Color Purple* has her own talk show?
7 Who presented ITV's *What Will They Think of Next*?
8 What was *Clothes Show* presenter Franklyn's Christian name?
9 Who was Mandy to marry in *Game On*?
10 Who is Butch's father in *Emmerdale*?
11 What was the BBC's first digital channel?
12 Which channel broadcasts live League Cup football?
13 What is Pauline McLynn's character in *Father Ted*?
14 Who does Victoria Smurfit portray in *Ballykissangel*?
15 On which game show does Melanie Stace assist Jim Davidson?
16 What was Sanjay's surname in *EastEnders*?
17 From where were the 1998 Commonwealth Games televised?
18 Who was the presenter of *Still in Bed with MeDinner*?
19 Who is David Baddiel's co-presenter on *Fantasy Football League*?
20 What is Mr Bing's first name in *Friends*?
21 Which children's TV presenter took over the stage role of Joseph?
22 What does Brendan Foster commentate on?
23 What was Jason Donavon's character in *Neighbours*?
24 Who is the northern motorbike fan who co-presents *Top Gear*?
25 In which fantasy series did Granny Weatherwax appear?
26 Who is Sally Webster's youngest daughter?
27 Who is magician Penn's partner?
28 On which channel is *DOSH*?
29 Who shares a show with Ren?
30 Who originally placed the letters on *Countdown*?

| **Answers** | **Pop Pot Luck 22** *(see Quiz 166)* |

1 Madness. 2 Denver. 3 French. 4 Lonnie. 5 Ian Dury. 6 Ready Steady Go. 7 Tina Turner. 8 Harmonica. 9 Dawn. 10 Ireland. 11 "Dizzy". 12 9 to 5. 13 Royce. 14 The Shadows. 15 Enya. 16 David Essex. 17 Cuba. 18 Annie Lennox. 19 Diamond. 20 Robinson. 21 Madonna. 22 2005. 23 "It's My Party". 24 Peter Sellers. 25 A Rose. 26 Glitter. 27 Geldof. 28 Gaynor. 29 Waterloo. 30 Suzi Quatro.

1 Tim Sherwood led which club to the Premiership?
2 David Platt, Ray Parlour and Liam Brady have all played for which club?
3 Which French superstar was European Player of the Year three times in the 80s?
4 According to song, who was dreaming of Wembley with Tottenham Hotspur?
5 Which Billy was at the heart of Leeds's success in the 1960s and 70s?
6 Which English club did Kazimierz Denya join in the 70s?
7 Which former Liverpool skipper moved to Sampdoria?
8 Which midfield dynamo captained the West Germans in Italia 90?
9 Which Gary has played for Luton, Forest, Villa and Leicester?
10 Which London team did Stefan Schwartz play for?
11 What name is shared by Minto and Sellars?
12 Enzo Scifo has played for which country?
13 Which was Johnny Haynes's only English club?
14 Which-long serving Celtic and Scotland skipper first played back in 1982?
15 Michael Thomas has scored an FA Cup Final goal for which team?
16 What is the first name of West German 60s and 70s stalwart Overath?
17 Who was England's "Captain Marvel"?
18 Which club had the dream midfield of Ball, Harvey and Kendall?
19 Paul Ince was at which club when he made his England debut?
20 Has Robert Lee ever played for England?
21 In which year did Owen Hargreaves first play for Manchester United?
22 Which Frank scored in the 2008 Champions League Final?
23 Which club did Gareth Barry play for in 2007?
24 What country does Senegalese ex-Arsenal captain Patrick Vieira play for?
25 Which England midfielder won his 100th international cap in 2008?
26 Which Liverpool player was linked with a move to Chelsea in 2005?
27 At what London club did Joe Cole begin his professional career?
28 Who began his career at Nottingham Forest and ended it with Glasgow Celtic?
29 Name the attacking Australian midfielder who joined Everton in 2004.
30 Roberto Firmino joined which Premier League club in 2015?

Answers	Movies: Behind the Camera (see Quiz 163)

1 Goldwyn. 2 USA. 3 Puttnam. 4 Choreography. 5 Irving. 6 Michael. 7 William Shatner. 8 A. 9 Coca Cola. 10 Leo. 11 Dreamworks. 12 Wallace & Gromit. 13 Robert De Niro. 14 Nimoy. 15 Garland. 16 Clapperboard. 17 Kevin Costner. 18 Tri. 19 Sunset Boulevard. 20 Lucas. 21 Robert. 22 Mark Knopfler. 23 Disney. 24 Mountain. 25 Penny. 26 SFX. 27 Interstellar. 28 Alfred Hitchcock. 29 Steven Spielberg. 30 Guy Ritchie.

1 Who released the album *Oui Oui, Si Si, Ja Ja, Da Da* in 2012?

2 Which John's album chart debut was *Rocky Mountain High*?

3 In which language other than English did Celine Dion record in the 80s?

4 Which showbiz first name did Anthony James Donegan adopt?

5 Who was backed by the Blockheads?

6 Which TV pop show sounded like the start of a race?

7 How is Annie-Mae Bullock better known?

8 Which instrument does Bob Dylan play other than guitar?

9 Which group did Tony Orlando lead?

10 What is the home country of Van Morrison?

11 Which song has been a No. 1 for Tommy Roe and Vic Reeves?

12 What were Dolly Parton's working hours in 1981?

13 Which Rose shares her surname with part of the name of a car?

14 Which British group had to change its name from the Drifters because of the existence of the US group?

15 Who left Clannad and had her first solo single in 1988?

16 Which actor/singer was born David Cook in Plaistow?

17 Which Caribbean island is Gloria Estefan originally from?

18 Who was the female singer of the Eurythmics?

19 Which Neil made a Beautiful Noise in the 70s?

20 Which surname is shared by Smokey and Tom?

21 Who did Justin Timberlake duet with on the 2008 hit "Four Minutes"?

22 In which year did Kanye West release his *Late Registration* album?

23 Which song's second line is "And I'll cry if I want to"?

24 Which comic actor has a hit album *Songs for Swinging Sellers*?

25 What did Seal sing about a Kiss from in 1994?

26 Which Gary was famous for his platform soles and silver outfits?

27 Which Bob formed the company that first produced Channel 4's "The Big Breakfast"?

28 Which Gloria sang "Never Can Say Goodbye" in 1974?

29 Which battle provided Abba with the title of their first album?

30 Who played bass guitar in Suzi Quatro's group?

---

1 Who found fame when he was left *Home Alone*?
2 Which O'Connor was a child star before being a huge success in *Singin' in the Rain*?
3 In which musical movie did Karen Dotrice appear as a child with a superhuman nanny?
4 Which child star later played Maria in the musical *West Side Story*?
5 Jack Wild played which cheeky role in *Oliver!*?
6 In which decade did Shirley Temple win a Special Oscar for her outstanding contribution to movies?
7 Which star of *E.T.* wrote an autobiography called *Little Girl Lost*?
8 Eight-year-olds Azharuddin Ismail and Rubin Ali starred in which film?
9 Which Deanna was a contemporary of Judy Garland?
10 Anna Paquin won an Oscar with Holly Hunter for which movie?
11 What was the name of Henry Thomas's character in *E.T.*?
12 Who co-starred with Mickey Rooney 10 times on screen?
13 Who played Wednesday Addams in the 1991 film version of *The Addams Family*?
14 Which Mary was the "world's sweetheart" and made her first movie aged 16 in 1909?
15 Who played the gangster's moll in *Bugsy Malone* before later becoming a multiple Oscar winner?
16 Who played the father of Tatum in *Paper Moon*?
17 Which member of the Fox family, brother of Edward, was known as William when he was a child star?
18 Who was asked to "Come Home" in Elizabeth Taylor's 1943 movie?
19 In which decade of the 20th century was Drew Barrymore born?
20 Which Jackie was immortalized in Chaplin's *The Kid*?
21 How many Von Trapp children were there in *The Sound of Music*?
22 In which movie did Drew Barrymore find fame as Gertie?
23 Justin Henry was Oscar-nominated for which movie where his parents Meryl Streep and Dustin Hoffman are to divorce?
24 Which Mickey married eight times?
25 Which Ethan starred in *Explorer* before his 20th birthday?
26 The Bad News Bears played which American sport?
27 Which movie starred Linda Blair as a possessed teenager?
28 Name the iconic American tap-dancing actress of the 1930s.
29 Which American actress played Velvet Brown in the 1944 movie *National Velvet*?
30 Who played the daughter of Brad Pitt and Cate Blanchett in *Babel*?

1 From which planet do the Hoobs come?
2 Who played Patsy Stone in *Absolutely Fabulous*?
3 What kind of animal is *Babar*?
4 Which TV drama portrays a troubled Greater Manchester comprehensive school?
5 Which character in *Coronation Street* had only one leg?
6 What is HG of Roy and HG's surname?
7 Who wrote *Wyrd Sisters*?
8 Who presented *Hearts of Gold*?
9 Who presented *Smillie's People*?
10 What is *Supermarket Sweep*'s Winton's first name?
11 What is the first name of presenter DeVine?
12 What type of programme is BBC2's *Just One Chance*?
13 Who hosted *The National Lottery Dreamworld*?
14 What is Max's surname in *Brookside*?
15 Who presented *She's Gotta Have It*?
16 Who presents *The Countryside Hour*?
17 Which ex-*Coronation Street* actor appears as Jack Gates in *Family Affairs*?
18 What is the name of BBC2's short series of 10-minute films by new directors?
19 What did Ivy run in *Last of the Summer Wine*?
20 Who portrayed *Maximum Bob*?
21 Who narrated *Cold War*?
22 What was the subject of the documentary series *Glory of the Geeks*?
23 Which channel is dedicated to cookery?
24 Who is the father of presenter Samantha Norman?
25 Who created *Ballykissangel*?
26 Who is Lily Savage otherwise known as?
27 Who was Roland Rat's sidekick?
28 Which series featured Gillian Taylforth as one of a family on their way to the 1998 World Cup?
29 Which terrestrial channel first broadcast *The X-Files*?
30 What kind of a programme was Channel 5's *100 Per cent*?

Answers	**Football Pot Luck 19** *(see Quiz 170)*

1 West Bromwich Albion. 2 Chelsea. 3 QPR. 4 United. 5 Georgia. 6 Romelu. 7 Belgium. 8 Leeds Utd. 9 Newcastle Utd. 10 Claret. 11 Russell. 12 The Railwaymen. 13 Barnet. 14 Eric Cantona. 15 Blackburn Rovers. 16 Blue. 17 Thijssen. 18 Barcelona. 19 Ayr. 20 Rideout. 21 George Graham. 22 Espanyol. 23 Muller. 24 Portsmouth. 25 Twice. 26 Yellow. 27 Todd. 28 Rangers. 29 McAllister. 30 USA.

1 Which team scored 50 points in the 1999 Rugby League Challenge Cup Final?
2 What international Southern Hemisphere rugby union cup began in 1996?
3 What are the initials of champion jump jockey McCoy?
4 Which Australian golfer Ian won the British Open golf championship in 1991?
5 In which New Zealand city were the 1990 Commonwealth Games held?
6 In 1994 which rugby-playing Gavin was made an OBE?
7 Which Scottish soccer side monopolized the championship throughout the first half of the 1990s?
8 Which Phil was world darts champion in 1990 and 1992?
9 Which country returned to playing international sport in the 90s?
10 Which city hosted the 1996 Olympic Games?
11 Which steeplechase did Party Politics win in election year 1992?
12 Which rugby league team won the Challenge Cup every year for the first half of the 1990s?
13 Which Sally won Olympic gold in the 400-metre hurdles?
14 Which manager left Arsenal after taking a "bung"?
15 Why did no horse win the 1993 Grand National?
16 What is the first name of athlete Akabusi?
17 At which sport did Karen Pickering excel?
18 Which country did Sonia O'Sullivan race for?
19 Which former Villa player David became England's soccer captain?
20 What does Alberto Tomba wear on his feet when he competes?
21 Who does Mary Pierce play tennis for?
22 Which country is snooker star Stephen Hendry from?
23 Which Kenny took Blackburn to the Premiership championship?
24 What is the first name of athlete Regis?
25 Which Miss Martinez beat Martina in a Wimbledon final?
26 Who won the World Drivers' Championship in 1994–95?
27 Which English team won the European Cup Winners' Cup in 1991?
28 In which event was Jonathan Edwards world champion in 1995?
29 What does Steve Backley throw?
30 Which soccer nation were surprise winners of the 1992 European Championship?

Answers	**Movies: Child Stars** *(see Quiz 167)*

1 Macaulay Culkin. 2 Donald. 3 Mary Poppins. 4 Natalie Wood. 5 The Artful Dodger. 6 1930s. 7 Drew Barrymore. 8 Slumdog Millionaire. 9 Durbin. 10 The Piano. 11 Elliott. 12 Judy Garland. 13 Christina Ricci. 14 Pickford. 15 Jodie Foster. 16 Ryan O'Neal. 17 James. 18 Lassie. 19 1970s. 20 Coogan. 21 Seven. 22 E.T. 23 Kramer versus Kramer. 24 Rooney. 25 Hawke. 26 Baseball. 27 The Exorcist. 28 Shirley Temple. 29 Elizabeth Taylor. 30 Elle Fanning.

1 Who plays at home at the Hawthorns?
2 Gavin Peacock and Dennis Wise were teammates at which club?
3 Stewart Houston and Ray Wilkins have both managed which club?
4 What is the second word in Carlisle's name?
5 Which country has Georgiou Kinkladze played for?
6 Name the player: _____ Lukaku?
7 Which country do Standard Liege come from?
8 With which club did Gary Speed make his League debut?
9 Which club did Peter Beardsley join on leaving Everton?
10 What is the main colour of West Ham's home shirts?
11 Which Craig was Sunderland's top League scorer in 1995–96?
12 What is Crewe's nickname?
13 Stan Flashman has been connected with which club?
14 Which player is a great admirer of the 19th-century poet Rimbaud?
15 Which team does Jim Bowen support?
16 What is the main colour of France's home shirts?
17 Which Frans of Ipswich won the Footballer of the Year award in 1981?
18 Which club plays at the Nou Camp Stadium?
19 Which Scottish team are known as the Honest Men?
20 Which Paul was Everton's top scorer in 1994–95?
21 Which Scotsman managed Arsenal, Leeds United and Tottenham Hotspur?
22 What is the name of the second biggest club in Barcelona?
23 Which Gerd of Bayern was European Footballer of the Year in 1970?
24 Darren Anderton played in an FA Cup semi-final for which Second Division club?
25 How many times did Arsenal win the championship with George Graham as boss?
26 What colour are Sweden's home shirts?
27 Which Colin was PFA Player of the Year in 1975?
28 Steven and Stevens were together at which Scottish club?
29 Which Gary played in every game when Leeds Utd were champions in 1992?
30 Which country has John Harkes played for?

Answers	**TV Pot Luck 22** *(see Quiz 168)*

1 Hoobland. 2 Joanna Lumley. 3 Elephant. 4 Waterloo Road. 5 Don Brennan. 6 Nelson. 7 Terry Pratchett. 8 Esther Rantzen. 9 Carol Smillie. 10 Dale. 11 Magenta. 12 Consumer programme. 13 Ulrika Jonsson. 14 Farnham. 15 Liza Tarbuck. 16 Bob Langley. 17 Ken Farrington. 18 10x10. 19 The Cafe. 20 Beau Bridges. 21 Kenneth Branagh. 22 The Internet. 23 Carlton Food Network. 24 Barry Norman. 25 Kieron Prendiville. 26 Paul O'Grady. 27 Kevin the Gerbil. 28 Lost in France. 29 BBC2. 30 Quiz Show.

1 Who did Elvis meet in the 2016 movie *Elvis Vs _____*?
2 Which "rank" was Elvis's manager Tom Parker known by?
3 What was the first name of Elvis's wife?
4 What were Elvis's shoes made out of in his 1956 hit?
5 Elvis's gyrations on stage gave him which nickname?
6 In which European country was G.I. Elvis stationed?
7 What is the name of Elvis's mansion in Memphis?
8 What was the instruction with the letter Elvis sang about in 1962?
9 Although known as the King, which King was he in the 1958 film?
10 Which Elvis film title contained the same word three times?
11 Which relatives are Kissin' in the 1964 top ten hit?
12 What is the name of Elvis's daughter?
13 Which country of the UK is the only one Elvis visited?
14 Which Rock was a film and a No. 1 hit in 1958?
15 Where was Elvis Crying in 1965?
16 What was special about the camera work on Elvis's up-tempo songs on the USA's *Ed Sullivan Show*?
17 Which "canine" hit did Elvis have in 1956?
18 Which commemoration to Elvis was issued by the US Post Office in 1993?
19 The name of which toy was the title of an Elvis hit in 1957?
20 Who did Elvis's daughter marry in 1994?
21 In which of the US forces did Elvis serve, Navy, Army, Air Force or Marines?
22 In which US state was his famous mansion?
23 How many times did he play at the London Palladium?
24 What colour suit did he wear most often when he did his Las Vegas stage shows?
25 In which decade did he have his first No. 1 hit?
26 Which Elvis hit was the first song to go straight in at No. 1 in the UK Charts?
27 What was Elvis's middle name?
28 If you've never caught a rabbit, you ain't no what?
29 What did Elvis have a little less of with JXL in 2002?
30 In which comedy film does Nicolas Cage encounter a group of skydiving Elvis impersonators?

1 What type of dogs did Johnny Depp and Amber Heard smuggle in to Oz?

2 In which decade of the 20th century was Brooke Shields born?

3 Which star actress was in *The Pelican Brief*, *Six Days Seven Nights* and *Stepmom*?

4 Which Woody Allen film title includes a reference to a feline?

5 Which singer played the tough guy captain in *Von Ryan's Express*?

6 Which 80s film was the most profitable in Australian history?

7 Which sequel had the subtitle "Judgment Day"?

8 Who played the lead in *Casablanca* after George Raft turned it down?

9 Which actress links *Eyes Wide Shut* and *Practical Magic*?

10 What kind of fruit can you get at the Whistle Stop Café, according to the film title?

11 Where was Gary Oldman "Lost" in the 1998 hit movie?

12 Which movie veteran Katharine was the first actress to win four Oscars?

13 Which word follows "Trading" in an Eddie Murphy movie title?

14 Bing Crosby had just finished a round of what when he died?

15 Which Rick starred in *Honey, I Shrunk the Kids*?

16 Which brothers starred in *Monkey Business*?

17 *Patriot Games*, *Pulp Fiction* and *Sphere* all feature which actor?

18 Which direction completes this film title, *North by ____*?

19 In which decade was *One Flew Over the Cuckoo's Nest* released?

20 Which singer/actress won the Best Actress Oscar for *Moonstruck*?

21 Which time period completes the film title, *Saturday Night and Sunday ____*?

22 In which decade of the 20th century was Lucille Ball born?

23 To the nearest hour, how long does *The Sound of Music* last?

24 Which Dustin starred in *Tootsie*?

25 What did Nicole Kidman forecast in *To Die for*?

26 At what time does the train leave for Yuma?

27 On which Street did Johnny Depp practise as the barber Sweeney Todd?

28 In which city did Hugh Grant make the headlines for "lewd conduct"?

29 Which Julie's voice was damaged after a minor op went wrong?

30 Who died two days after finishing *Giant*?

Answers	Football Pot Luck 20 *(see Quiz 174)*

1 United. 2 England. 3 White. 4 Charlton Athletic. 5 Roberts. 6 Malpas. 7 Woods. 8 John Spencer. 9 Celtic. 10 The Eagles. 11 Bolton Wanderers. 12 Wales. 13 Green. 14 Spink. 15 The Bluebirds. 16 Platt. 17 Reid. 18 Endsleigh. 19 Palmer. 20 Manchester City. 21 Togo. 22 Newcastle United. 23 Nottingham Forest. 24 Fleck. 25 Ruud Gillit. 26 Sheffield Wednesday. 27 Jurgen Klinsmann. 28 Port Vale. 29 Shaka Hislop. 30 Sunderland.

1 Which *Antiques* were the spoof soap created by Victoria Wood?

2 *Peyton Place* was a soap opera set in which country?

3 Which Jason left *Neighbours* and has played the lead in West End musicals?

4 In which decade was *Brookside* first aired?

5 What had been the occupation of Betty Turpin's husband in *Coronation Street*?

6 In *Soap* who preceded Saunders as the Tates' butler?

7 Which character in *The Colbys* was played by Charlton Heston?

8 What was the name of Dot Cotton's husband?

9 Who is Ricky's boss at the Arches in *EastEnders*?

10 In *Neighbours* who was Daphne's husband?

11 Where in *Emmerdale* is the Woolpack located?

12 Who in *EastEnders* had two sons, David and Simon?

13 Who was Danni and Brett's mother in *Neighbours*?

14 In *Coronation Street* which of Liz McDonald's sons has been in prison?

15 Who owns a hairdressers in *Brookside*?

16 What was the name of Joe Mangel's son in *Neighbours*?

17 Who is Roy's son in *EastEnders*?

18 Which Channel 4 soap shows a map of Chester in its opening credits?

19 Who was Jim Robinson's entrepreneurial mother-in-law in *Neighbours*?

20 Which character in *Dallas* was portrayed by Priscilla Presley?

21 Which character did pop star Peter Noone play in *Coronation Street*?

22 What was Punk Mary's surname in *EastEnders*?

23 What was Don Brennan's trade in *Coronation Street*?

24 What was the name of Mavis Riley's budgie in *Coronation Street*?

25 Whose mother's name was Mo in *EastEnders*?

26 Which character does Brooke Satchwell play in *Neighbours*?

27 Who is Mark's wife in *EastEnders*?

28 Which character does Judy Nunn portray in *Home and Away*?

29 Who did Sarah Beaumont have an adulterous affair with in *Neighbours*?

30 Who was butcher Fred Elliot's nephew in *Coronation Street*?

---

1 What is the second word in Oxford's name?
2 Which country has Des Walker played for?
3 What is the main colour of Leeds's home shirts?
4 Who plays home games at the Valley?
5 Which Iwan was Leicester City's top scorer in 1995–96?
6 Which Maurice of Dundee Utd was Scottish Footballer of the Year in 1991?
7 Which Chris was Leeds's top scorer in 2015-2016?
8 Who was Chelsea's leading League goalscorer in the 1995–96 season?
9 Which club did Brian McClair leave to join Manchester Utd?
10 What is Crystal Palace's nickname?
11 Jason McAteer and John McGinlay were teammates at which club?
12 Which country has Ian Rush played for?
13 What colour are Portugal's home shorts?
14 Which goalkeeper Nigel made over 300 appearances with Aston Villa?
15 What is the club nickname of Cardiff City?
16 Which David was made England's new captain in March 1994?
17 Which Peter of Everton was PFA Player of the Year in 1985?
18 Which Gloucester-based insurance company agreed to sponsor the Football League in 1993?
19 Which Carlton has played for Sheffield Wednesday and Leeds Utd?
20 Peter Swales was chairman of which club?
21 For which country did Emmanuel Adebayor play in the 2006 World Cup Final?
22 Joey Barton left Manchester City for which club in 2007?
23 Chettle and Phillips were together at which club?
24 Which striker Robert returned to Norwich City in 1995 after an unhappy spell with Chelsea?
25 Which Dutch player with AC Milan was European Footballer of the Year in 1987?
26 Which team does politician Roy Hattersley support?
27 Which player said in 1995, "I would not have wanted to leave Spurs if Sugar had shown more ambition"?
28 John Rudge has had ten years plus as boss of which club?
29 Which goalkeeper cost Newcastle £1.5 million in August 1995?
30 Ord and Bracewell were together at which club?

Answers	Movies Pot Luck 19 *(see Quiz 172)*

1 Yorkshire terriers. 2 1960s. 3 Julia Roberts. 4 What's New Pussycat? 5 Frank Sinatra. 6 Crocodile Dundee. 7 Terminator 2. 8 Humphrey Bogart. 9 Nicole Kidman. 10 Fried green tomatoes (Fried Green Tomatoes at the Whistle Stop Café). 11 In Space. 12 Hepburn. 13 Places. 14 Golf. 15 Moranis. 16 The Marx Brothers. 17 Samuel L. Jackson. 18 Northwest. 19 1970s. 20 Cher. 21 Morning. 22 1910s. 23 3 hours. 24 Hoffman. 25 The weather. 26 3:10. 27 Fleet. 28 Los Angeles. 29 Andrews. 30 James Dean.

1 Which group was Marc Bolan associated with?
2 Which Janis died in Hollywood in 1970?
3 Who won an award for his classic hit "Pretty Woman" after his death?
4 Whose death triggered "Bohemian Rhapsody"/"These are the Days of Our Lives" entering the charts at No. 1?
5 How did Buddy Holly meet his death?
6 Which Big star died at the same time as Buddy Holly?
7 Which live recording of a Frank Sinatra classic went into the top ten for Elvis Presley in January 1978?
8 Kurt Cobain was a member of which band?
9 Which famous Liverpudlian was murdered outside his New York flat?
10 Which musical instrument did Jimi Hendrix play?
11 Which Patsy became the first female solo performer to be inducted into the Country Music Hall of Fame?
12 Whose first top ten hit, "(Sittin' On) the Dock of the Bay" charted after his death?
13 Who was without his first name Harry when he sang "Without You"?
14 Which was the most famous group Mama Cass was a member of?
15 Which Rolling Stone died in 1969?
16 Whose pioneering rock 'n' roll career came to an end in 1981 after selling more than 60 million discs Round the Clock?
17 Which soul singer Marvin was shot by his own father?
18 Which highly successful female Motown group was the late Florence Ballard a member of?
19 Which band did Sid Vicious belong to?
20 Which Small group were fronted by the late Steve Marriott?
21 Syd Barrett was lead singer for which 1960s group?
22 Which was the second member of the Beatles to die?
23 Which R&B performer Mr Diddley died in 2008?
24 James Brown, who died in 2006, was known as the "Godfather of" what?
25 How close to Tulsa was Gene Pitney?
26 Which pioneer of rock 'n' roll died in a plane crash in 1959?
27 Which famous US female artist sang "Crazy" and died in 1963 aged just 30?
28 Who was the famous "Man in Black" who died in 2003?
29 What was Robert Palmer "Addicted to" in 1986?
30 Which ex-singer is better remembered for hosting TV's "The Record Breakers"?

Answers | TV: Children's TV 3 *(see Quiz 177)*

1 A ship's flag. 2 Rugrats. 3 Gloria Hunniford. 4 Mr Tumble. 5 Saturday. 6 BBC1. 7 Pink. 8 Blue. 9 He was cross-eyed and wore glasses. 10 A tank engine. 11 Four. 12 David Hasselhoff. 13 Ulrika Jonsson. 14 Captain of the USS Enterprise. 15 Stingray. 16 Zebedee. 17 Byker Grove. 18 Mrs McClusky. 19 The Flintstones. 20 Blue Peter. 21 TC. 22 Scooby Doo. 23 Pob. 24 The Pet Detective. 25 Yogi Bear. 26 A Dolphin. 27 Adam West. 28 Postman Pat. 29 Lady Penelope. 30 Gripper.

1 Who partners Turner in a Tom Hanks movie?

2 Who played the title role in 2015's *The Gunman*?

3 How often are the Oscars presented?

4 Which star actress was in *Dangerous Minds*, *Wolf* and *One Fine Day*?

5 Which word completes the film title, *Since You Went* ____?

6 Which Bill had a cameo in 2016's *Ghostbusters* reboot?

7 What is the first name of Mr Hytner who directed *The Crucible* and *The Madness of King George*?

8 According to the movie title, what do "Gentlemen Prefer"?

9 Which British actor Jeremy was an Oscar winner with *Reversal of Fortune*?

10 In which decade was *Thelma and Louise* released?

11 Which Tom took the male lead in 2014's *Edge of Tomorrow*?

12 Which word follows "Jumpin' Jack" in a Whoopi Goldberg movie title?

13 What did Dumbo do immediately before his ears grew so big?

14 Which actress Debra served in the Israeli army?

15 In which decade of the 20th century was Clint Eastwood born?

16 Which Caped Crusader was the subject of one of the top 80s films?

17 Which actor links *Platoon*, *Donnie Brascoe* and *Nick of Time*?

18 How many gunfighters were hired in the "Magnificent" film of 1960?

19 Who was Warren Beatty's wife whom he directed in *Bugsy* in 1991?

20 Which word completes the film title, *The Rocky Horror Picture* ____?

21 "Evergreen" won an Oscar when it was used in which movie in 1976?

22 Which Tom won the Best Actor Oscar for *Forrest Gump*?

23 In which decade was *The Spy Who Loved Me* released?

24 Who directed *The Commitments*?

25 Charlie Chaplin was famous for wearing what type of hat?

26 For which role in *Brokeback Mountain* was Heath Ledger nominated in 2005?

27 What does the "L." in Samuel L. Jackson stand for?

28 Which English actress was the first woman to play M in the Bond movies?

29 Bob Hope was born in which European capital city?

30 What's the Italian food often linked with westerns?

---

1 What nautical item is a "Blue Peter"?
2 Angelica and Tommy Pickles and Phil and Lil DeVille were in which series?
3 Former *Blue Peter* presenter Caron Keating is the daughter of which Irish-born female TV host?
4 How many days each week was *Play School* broadcast?
5 Who is Justin Fletcher also known as?
6 On which channel was the *Multi-coloured Swap Shop*?
7 What colour was the *Pink Panther*'s sports car?
8 What colour are the *Smurfs*?
9 What was unusual about Clarence the lion in *Daktari*?
10 What kind of locomotive was Thomas?
11 How many *Teletubbies* are there?
12 Who played the *Knight Rider*?
13 Who is the female presenter of *The Gladiators*?
14 What was James T. Kirk?
15 In which series did the mute woman Marina appear?
16 Who said "time for bed"?
17 Which children's series featured Ant and Dec?
18 Who was *Grange Hill*'s headmistress?
19 Which cartoon series featured Fred and Barney?
20 Which series features a Christmas Appeal?
21 How was *Top Cat* known to his close friends?
22 Which cartoon series features a Great Dane?
23 Which Polish programme, shown on Channel 4, featured Toyah Wilcox and Nigel Kennedy narrating the English version, and a wooden main character?
24 What was *Ace Ventura*?
25 Who lives in Jellystone Park?
26 What was Flipper?
27 Who played *Batman* in the 1960s TV series?
28 Which postman had a black and white cat?
29 Who in *Thunderbirds* owned a pink Rolls Royce?
30 In *Grange Hill* what was Stebson's nickname?

Answers | Pop: Late Greats *(see Quiz 175)*

1 T. Rex. 2 Joplin. 3 Roy Orbison. 4 Freddie Mercury. 5 Plane crash. 6 Big Bopper. 7 "My Way". 8 Nirvana. 9 John Lennon. 10 Guitar. 11 Cline. 12 Otis Redding. 13 Nilsson. 14 The Mamas and the Papas. 15 Brian Jones. 16 Bill Haley. 17 Gaye. 18 The Supremes. 19 Sex Pistols. 20 Small Faces. 21 Pink Floyd. 22 George Harrison. 23 Bo. 24 Soul. 25 24 Hours. 26 Buddy Holly. 27 Patsy Cline. 28 Johnny Cash. 29 Love. 30 Roy Castle.

1 Who plays at home at St Marys Stadium?
2 Name Wayne Rooney's first born child, born in 2010?
3 Glenn Hoddle and Ruud Gullit have both managed which club?
4 What is the second word in Chester's name?
5 Which country has Keith Gillespie played for?
6 Which Tony of West Ham was PFA Young Player of the Year in 1986?
7 Which country do Slavia Sofia come from?
8 With which club did Michael Thomas make his League debut?
9 Which club did Tony Mowbray join on leaving Middlesbrough?
10 Which Scottish football club has maroon shirts?
11 Which Wayne was Swindon's top League scorer in 1995–96?
12 What is Darlington's nickname?
13 John Salako and Ray Houghton were teammates at which club?
14 Which country does Michael Laudrup play for?
15 Which team does Jo Brand support?
16 Which Steve of Tottenham Hotspur won the Footballer of the Year award in 1982?
17 What is the colour of Bulgaria's home shorts?
18 Which London club briefly had a "famous five" lineup of attackers in the 90s?
19 Which country does Dmitri Kharine of Chelsea come from?
20 Which Steve has scored most League goals in a career for Wolves?
21 Who played for Celtic, Barcelona and Manchester Utd in the Champions League?
22 Who preceded Jose Mourinho as Chelsea manager?
23 What colour are Northern Ireland's home shorts?
24 Fox and Calderwood were together at which club?
25 In 1996, which Ian had an on/off transfer from Norwich to Ipswich?
26 Which seaside club finished bottom of Division Three in 1996 but stayed in the League?
27 Which Norman of Leeds was PFA Player of the Year in 1974?
28 Which Ron was the oldest Premiership boss in 1996?
29 Which north London team does Tom "Lofty" Watt follow?
30 Who were the first side to hit nine goals in Premier League game?

1 Who sang "The Shoop Shoop Song" in 1990?
2 Which Bob Dylan song was featured in *Pat Garrett & Billy the Kid*?
3 Which hero was the subject of the film for which Bryan Adams sang "(Everything I Do) I Do It For You"?
4 Who sang "Ben" from the film about a rat?
5 Which Meg Ryan/Billy Crystal film's songs were sung by Harry Connick Jr?
6 Who appeared in and had hits with songs from *Grease* and *Xanadu*?
7 Which Dire Straits guitarist played "Going Home" from *Local Hero*?
8 What was or were Falling on My Head in the theme music from *Butch Cassidy and the Sundance Kid*?
9 In which Lloyd Webber film did Madonna play the title role?
10 Which 1981 film starring Dudley Moore, Liza Minnelli and John Gielgud had a theme sung by Christopher Cross?
11 Who sang "Love is All Around" from *Four Weddings and a Funeral*?
12 Whose first film was *A Hard Day's Night*?
13 Which Welsh-born female vocalist had a hit with "Goldfinger"?
14 Which film about the 1924 Paris Olympics won an Oscar for the composer Vangelis?
15 Which classic film with Humphrey Bogart and Ingrid Bergman includes the song "As Time Goes By"?
16 Which duo sang "Mrs Robinson" from *The Graduate* in 1968?
17 Who Does It Better according to Carly Simon from *The Spy Who Loved Me*?
18 Which creatures were the subject of the film *Born Free*?
19 Which film featured "Stuck in the Middle With You" by Stealer's Wheel?
20 Who was Forever in the film to which Seal sang the theme song?
21 Which Derek and the Dominos hit was featured in *Goodfellas*?
22 Hans Zimmer's "Spider" what from *The Simpsons Movie* was a UK chart hit?
23 Which song does Marty McFly play on guitar during *Back to the Future*?
24 "You Can Leave Your Hat On" was the theme for which stripping movie?
25 *Shaun of the Dead* has the theme tune of "Don't Stop Me Now" by which group?
26 Which Bee Gees album shares the same title as a 1977 disco movie?
27 Can you name Survivor's song which was the theme tune to *Rocky III*?
28 Which film featured "The End" by The Doors?
29 Which Bill Medley & Jennifer Warnes duet was the theme song to *Dirty Dancing*?
30 Which Kenny sang "Footloose" in the 1984 movie of the same name?

1 What type of "Storm" starred Sigourney Weaver and Kevin Kline in 1997?
2 Does *Pulp Fiction* last 50, 150 or 250 minutes?
3 Which famous Claudette tested for the role of Scarlett O'Hara?
4 In which decade of the 20th century was Laura Dern born?
5 Which Billy starred in *When Harry Met Sally*?
6 On what vehicle did Steve McQueen try to flee in *The Great Escape*?
7 Which actress links *Basic Instinct* and *Last Action Hero*?
8 Which water-linked film took over from *Waterworld* as the most costly to make?
9 *Yankee Doodle Dandy* starred which James?
10 Kathleen Turner was concerned with Prizzi's what?
11 Which Susan starred in *The Client*?
12 Brigitte Bardot had a theatre named after her in which French city?
13 Who created Tom and Jerry at MGM in the 40s?
14 *The Music Lovers* was about which Russian composer?
15 Which son of a *M*A*S*H* star starred in *Young Guns II*?
16 Which Richard replaced John Travolta in *American Gigolo*?
17 Where is "The Sword", according to the Disney film title?
18 Which TV cartoon character did John Goodman play in a movie?
19 Which film tells the story of a rubbish-collecting robot?
20 Which word follows "The Fisher" in a Robin Williams movie title?
21 Which star actor was in *Top Gun*, *Jerry Maguire* and *Born on the Fourth of July*?
22 Who played the lead role in *The Wizard of Oz*?
23 In which decade of the 20th century was Dame Judi Dench born?
24 Whose real name is James Baumgarner?
25 What was the Bond theme for *From Russia with Love* called?
26 Which 2005 movie had characters Brian, Zebedee, Ermintrude and Florence?
27 Who was nominated for the Best Actress Oscar for *About Schmidt* in 2003?
28 In which city does the action of Batman take place?
29 What's the name of the actor brother of Beau Bridges?
30 What was the first Bond movie with Sean Connery?

1 Which Tom won bronze at the 2016 Rio Olympics in diving?
2 At which sport was TV presenter Andrew Castle a top-ranked British player?
3 Which Michael is a former England cricket captain and Sky Sports commentator?
4 Sky Sports' Richard Keys was a director of which Bedfordshire football club?
5 Which race meeting on the BBC uses both sports and fashion commentators?
6 Ian Botham was a captain on which TV sports quiz?
7 Which British motor racing champion was BBC Sports Personality of the Year in 1994?
8 Which former England captain presents rugby on ITV?
9 At what time is Sky's *Sports Centre* normally broadcast?
10 Who retired as host of *A Question of Sport* in 1997?
11 *They Think It's All Over* is presented by who?
12 Which female champion swimmer was a Gladiator?
13 Fatima Whitbread was televised winning Olympic gold in which athletic discipline?
14 Which sport does Brendan Foster commentate on?
15 Which Desmond presents sport on BBC?
16 Which boxer became BBC Sports Personality of the Year in 1970?
17 Dan Maskell commentated on which sport?
18 On what day was *Match of the Day Extra* broadcast?
19 Which Steve presents *Grandstand*?
20 Mark Lawrenson and Alan Hansen are regulars on which football show?
21 Which late-night series shows highlights of Nationwide Football league matches?
22 On Channel 4 which impressionist, Alistair, hosted his *Football Backchat*?
23 Which channel hosts *Sports Review Of The Year*?
24 Ex-footballer Jeff Astle sang on which show hosted by Skinner and Baddiel?
25 Ski Sunday is broadcast on which channel?
26 Which channel broadcasts *Football Italia*?
27 With what form of transport is the Tour de France contested?
28 How many contestants are there in each episode of *Gladiators*?
29 Frank Bough hosted which Saturday-afternoon sports programme?
30 Which BBC football presenter played for Leicester City and Tottenham Hotspur?

1 What is the second word in Peterborough's name?
2 Which country has Frank Stapleton played for?
3 What is the main colour of Leicester's home shirts?
4 Who plays home games at Oakwell?
5 Which Robbie was Liverpool's top scorer in 1995–96?
6 Which Derek of Rangers was Scottish Footballer of the Year in 1978?
7 Campbell and Calderwood were teammates at which club?
8 With which club did Stan Collymore make his League debut?
9 Which club did Gary Stevens join on leaving Everton?
10 Which Paul first captained England in June 1993?
11 Which Terry played 800+ league games, mostly for Southampton?
12 What country has Paul Mariner played for?
13 Which Peter was Newcastle's top league scorer in 1994–95?
14 Has there ever been an England international with the surname Bastard?
15 Which team does veteran politician Michael Foot support?
16 Which Gianni was known as Italy's "Golden Boy"?
17 Which Ian of Liverpool was PFA Player of the Year in 1995?
18 Which country has Gica Popescu played for?
19 Which was the first Scottish side that Stuart McCall played for?
20 Who scored an amazing chip goal in Euro 96 for the Czech Republic against Portugal?
21 Which Chelsea captain was born on December 7, 1980?
22 Which club completed a hat-trick of Scottish Premier League titles in 2008?
23 Which Danny of Tottenham Hotspur won the Footballer of the Year award in 1961?
24 Which country's fullback was shot dead after scoring an own goal in the 1994 World Cup tournament?
25 Which team does veteran rock singer Robert Plant support?
26 Warhurst and Wilcox were together at which club?
27 Alvin Martin has made 450+ appearances for which club?
28 Which was the first Scottish side that Dean Winduss played for?
29 What colour is the Nigerian national kit?
30 What is the second word in Ayr's name?

1 What is Cliff Richard's real name?
2 In which country was he born?
3 What was the name of his backing group, which included Bruce Welch?
4 In which film did Cliff head for the continent on a London Transport bus?
5 In 1996 where did Cliff give a concert with Martina Navratilova and Virginia Wade in his backing group?
6 Cliff came second with which song in the 1968 Eurovision Song Contest?
7 Which award did Cliff receive from the Queen in 1995?
8 In which musical based on a novel by Emily Bronte did Cliff play the title role?
9 With what type of Doll did Cliff chart accompanied by the Shadows and then the Young Ones?
10 Which 60s hit began with "When I was young my father said ..."?
11 What features in the title with Wine on Cliff's Christmas No. 1 in 1988?
12 Which blonde tennis star had her name linked with Cliff in the 80s?
13 What date of Never was a hit for Cliff in 1964?
14 What did Cliff say to Samantha when he said Goodbye to Sam?
15 Which wife of Andrew Lloyd-Webber did Cliff duet with in "All I Ask of You" from *Phantom of the Opera*?
16 Which Olivia sang with Cliff on "Suddenly" and "Had to be"?
17 Whose Day was the Christmas No. 1 in 1990?
18 What was Cliff's first hit single?
19 Which part of Cliff was Lucky in the title of his 1964 hit?
20 Which Everly did Cliff duet with in "She Means Nothing to Me"?
21 Which irreverent 1980s TV sitcom took its name from a Cliff Richard film?
22 How many decades in the music industry did Cliff Richard complete in 2008?
23 Which Iberian country gave Cliff the equivalent of a knighthood in 2006?
24 In which decade did Cliff Richard last have two British No. 1s?
25 Whose "List" reached No. 5 as Cliff's Christmas single in 2003?
26 What was Cliff's first record label?
27 Which "Prayer" went to No. 1 in the Charts for Cliff at Christmas 1999?
28 Who is the only one solo artist with more weeks in the British singles charts than Cliff?
29 Which of his albums included "Devil Woman"?
30 In which decade did Cliff have a No. 1 hit with "We Don't Talk Anymore"?

Answers | TV: Comedy 6 *(see Quiz 185)*

1 Wanamaker. 2 1970s. 3 Bill Maynard. 4 George & Mildred. 5 Porridge. 6 First of the Summer Wine. 7 Anton Rodgers. 8 Yorkshire. 9 Nigel Havers. 10 Paramount Comedy. 11 Porridge. 12 One Foot in the Grave. 13 Liverpool. 14 The Piglet Files. 15 Lyndsey De Paul. 16 The Navy Lark. 17 Nelson's Column. 18 Nearest & Dearest. 19 Whatever Happened to the Likely Lads? 20 You Rang M'Lord? 21 Russ Abbot. 22 Tony Robinson. 23 Bob Mills. 24 Eddie Large. 25 Stephen & Hugh. 26 Brush Strokes. 27 Only When I Laugh. 28 Torquay. 29 Harry Secombe. 30 Three.

1 Which Juliette starred in *Natural Born Killers*?
2 Which word completes the film title *Single White* ____?
3 Which Gwyneth starred in the 2015 box office bomb, *Mortdecai*?
4 The song 'Oh What a Beautiful Morning' features in which musical movie?
5 Which actor links *Beverly Hills Cop*, *Harlem Nights* and *Boomerang*?
6 Which Gregory starred in *The Omen*?
7 Which 70s Agatha Christie movie was about a murder on a train?
8 Which number completes the film title *Slaughterhouse* ____?
9 Which Sylvester starred in 2013's *Escape Plan*?
10 Which friend of Fred Flintstone was played by Rick Moranis?
11 *City Slickers* starred which Billy?
12 Which Richard starred in *An Officer and a Gentleman*?
13 Which 2008 American fantasy drama film was inspired by an F. Scott Fitzgerald short story?
14 Which *Grease* and *Saturday Night Fever* actor is a qualified pilot?
15 Which word follows "The Age of" in a Michelle Pfeiffer movie title?
16 Which Diane starred in *The Godfather*?
17 Whose black bra made £4,600 at auction in 1997?
18 Which Annie features in a Woody Allen movie title?
19 Which Holly won the Best Actress Oscar for *The Piano*?
20 What metal are "Magnolias" made from, according to the film title?
21 In which decade of the 20th century was Richard Gere born?
22 How many Mr Olympia titles did Arnold Schwarzenegger win – five, seven or nine?
23 Which star actress was in *Mermaids*, *Little Women* and *Alien: Resurrection*?
24 How was Ruth Elizabeth Davis better known?
25 Which Kevin starred in *Wild Things*?
26 Which Oscar-winner (Gandhi) was nominated for *House of Sand and Fog* in 2003?
27 Which actress plays the role of the Bond girl in *Quantum of Solace*?
28 A cowardly lion appears in which musical movie?
29 Who played Hawkeye in the 90s movie *The Last of the Mohicans*?
30 Who went on to the Die Hard movies from TV's *Moonlighting*?

Answers	**Painters & Sculptors** *(see Quiz 186)*

1 Paris. 2 15 minutes. 3 Tracey. 4 J. M. W. 5 1890s. 6 Arms. 7 Horses. 8 Gauguin. 9 Van Gogh. 10 Andy. 11 Goya. 12 El Greco. 13 Picasso. 14 Toulouse-Lautrec. 15 Dutch. 16 Edouard Manet, Claude Monet. 17 Umbrellas. 18 Sculpture. 19 German. 20 National Gallery. 21 Michelangelo. 22 Princess of Wales. 23 David. 24 Henry VIII. 25 Bronze. 26 English. 27 Prince Charles. 28 Tate. 29 Henry. 30 L. S. Lowry.

1 Which actress Zoe is married to the character Ben Harper in *My Family*?

2 In which decade did *Last of the Summer Wine* first air?

3 Which *Heartbeat* actor was *The Gaffer*?

4 Which spin-off from *Man About the House* featured Brian Murphy and Yootha Joyce?

5 From which sitcom was *Going Straight* the sequel?

6 A sequel to *Last of the Summer Wine* featured the characters in their younger days. What was its title?

7 Who starred with Julia Mackenzie, as her husband, in *French Fields*?

8 In which county was Arkwright's corner shop?

9 Who played Tony Britton's son in *Don't Wait Up*?

10 What was the UK's first dedicated (non-terrestrial) comedy channel?

11 A pilot show entitled *Prisoner and Escort* became which sitcom?

12 The credits of which sitcom feature a tortoise?

13 Where did the Boswells live?

14 What was the series featuring Nicholas Lyndhurst and Clive Francis as inept spies?

15 Who wrote and sang the theme for *No Honestly*?

16 The nautical TV series *HMS Paradise* was based on which comedy radio show?

17 In which series did John Gordon Sinclair play a journalist?

18 Which sitcom featured Nellie and Eli Pledge?

19 What was the sequel to *The Likely Lads*?

20 What was the sitcom about servants and masters written by Jimmy Perry and David Croft?

21 Which Russ ran his *Madhouse* on TV?

22 Who starred as *Blackadder*'s sidekick Baldrick?

23 Which comic presents *In Bed with MeDinner*?

24 Who is Sid Little's comedy partner?

25 What are the first names of Fry and Laurie?

26 The painter and decorator Jacko appeared in which comedy series?

27 Which comedy's theme tune began with the words "I'm H-A-P-P-Y"?

28 In which town is *Fawlty Towers* set?

29 Which former Goon presented the religious programme *Highway*?

30 In *Only Fools and Horses* Del Boy's van had how many wheels?

---

1 In which city is the Louvre, home of the Mona Lisa?

2 For how long did pop artist Andy Warhol say everyone deserved to be famous?

3 What is the first name of artist Miss Emin, famous for *My Bed*?

4 What were the initials of the artist Mr Turner?

5 In which 19th-century decade was Henry Moore born?

6 Which parts of the Venus de Milo are missing?

7 Which animals is George Stubbs famous for painting?

8 Which Paul was famous for paintings of the South Seas?

9 Which Vincent lost an ear?

10 What was the first name of pop artist Warhol?

11 How is Francisco de Goya y Lucientes more simply known?

12 Which Greek artist's name means "The Greek"?

13 Which Spanish painter Pablo was the founder of Cubism?

14 Who was famous for his posters of French dance halls and cabarets?

15 What was the nationality of Rembrandt?

16 Edouard and Claude were Manet and Monet. Which was which?

17 Which items useful on a rainy day did Renoir paint?

18 Which branch of the arts was Barbara Hepworth famous for?

19 What was the nationality of Albrecht Durer?

20 Which art gallery is in Trafalgar Square?

21 Who painted the ceiling of the Sistine Chapel?

22 In late 1995 the painting of which Royal caused controversy?

23 What is the first name of pop artist Hockney?

24 Which Tudor king is Hans Holbein famous for painting?

25 Which metal is sculptress Elisabeth Frink famous for using?

26 What was the nationality of portrait painter Millais?

27 Which member of the royal family has had his paintings reproduced on a set of stamps?

28 Which London art gallery was founded with the financial support of a sugar merchant?

29 What is the first name of sculptor Moore?

30 Which English artist is famous for his matchstalk men pictures?

---

1 Who formed a famous double act with Jimmy Greaves?
2 Which country did Sky man Andy Gray play for?
3 Who famously called a Polish keeper a "clown" on the box in 1973?
4 To four years either way, when did BBC TV first show *Match of the Day* on Saturday evening?
5 Which team does Des Lynam support?
6 Which club did Bob Wilson mainly play for?
7 Which exuberant BBC football commentator is a Bristol City fan?
8 Who, in the season Manchester Utd won their first double, said about them, "You don't win anything with kids"?
9 True or false – Jimmy Hill is a qualified referee?
10 Which club does Brian Moore support?
11 Who commentated at a Wembley Final presentation, "How apt that a man named Buchan should climb the 39 steps"?
12 Which former Tottenham Hotspur and Stoke striker reports for BBC?
13 Which impersonator features Des Lynam and Motty in his TV shows?
14 Which former presenter David went politically green?
15 Who was involved in tabloid headlines concerning sex-change Bond girl Caroline Cossey?
16 Who in 1977 became the youngest commentator on an FA Cup Final?
17 Who was a regular golfing partner of Kenny Dalglish?
18 Which pundit has been manager of Portsmouth?
19 Which *Match of the Day* expert became George Graham's assistant at Leeds?
20 Who declared Cantona was "nothing more than a brat" after a stamping incident against Norwich?
21 Which former QPR, Man. Utd and England player is Setanta's non-League pundit?
22 Which pundit Steve played for and managed Millwall in the 2000s?
23 Which TV pundit is known as "Lawro"?
24 Which Jimmy played with Stanley Matthews and was on BBC Radio 5 in 2008?
25 Which country did Alan Hansen represent?
26 Which former Liverpool and England international co-hosts "Football on Five"?
27 Which ex-Man. Utd goalkeeper has his own football show in Denmark?
28 Who is the only player to score more goals for England than Gary Lineker?
29 Which ex-Spurs & Man. Utd striker can be found on the BBC's "Final Score"?
30 Who turned down a chance to coach Portsmouth in favour of "Football Focus"?

1 Which Brothers were known as Little Donnie and Baby Boy Phil?
2 Which Linda, Dolly and Emmylou recorded the album *Trio*?
3 What did Suzi Quatrocchio change her surname to?
4 Which Robert was Addicted to Love in 1986?
5 Which Boys had a hit with "Always on My Mind" in 1988?
6 On which soul record label was Jimmy Ruffin's version of "What Becomes of the Broken Hearted?"?
7 Who sang about a Smooth Operator in 1984?
8 Which Del was a Runaway in 1961?
9 Which Great Train Robber featured on the Sex Pistols' "No One is Innocent"/"My Way"?
10 Which Percy released "When s Man Loves a Woman" in '66 and '87?
11 Who had a minor hit with "Doggy Dogg World"?
12 Which Billie Jo put her Blanket on the Ground in 1975?
13 Which *The Tube* presenter was a member of Squeeze?
14 How did Status Quo alter the title of "Rockin' All Over the World" to promote the Race Against Time in 1988?
15 How were Shakin' Stevens and Bonnie Tyler billed on "A Rockin' Good Way"?
16 In 1975 10c.c., said Life was like which kind of soup?
17 What is the home country of k. d. lang?
18 Which Biel married Justin Timberlake in 2012?
19 How many Pennies sang "Juliet"?
20 Which surname is shared by Hank and former Take That star Robbie?
21 What was the title of R.E.M.'s chart-topping 2008 album?
22 Which thrash metal band was founded by Jeff Hanneman and Kerry King?
23 Which porky pair recorded "Reet Petite" in 1993?
24 What relation are the individual members of the Nolans to each other?
25 What did Isaiah Turner change his first name to?
26 Which supergroup was Agnetha Faltskog a member of?
27 Which summer month gave its name to an album by Eric Clapton?
28 Whose first hit was "Seven Seas of Rhye" in 1974?
29 Which Roger was King of the Road in 1965?
30 What completes the trio with Earth and Wind?

Answers | TV Pot Luck 23 *(see Quiz 190)*

1 Kirsty. 2 Dibley. 3 Lady Tara Oakwell. 4 One Man and His Dog. 5 Quincy. 6 The Magic Roundabout. 7 Match of the Day. 8 Porridge. 9 Chief Supt. Brownlow. 10 Bill Fraser. 11 David Duchovny. 12 Casualty. 13 A Grand Day Out. 14 A (talking) horse. 15 Journalist. 16 Blossom. 17 U.S.S. Voyager. 18 That was the Week That was. 19 Richard Briers. 20 Michael Barrymore. 21 Dudley Moore. 22 Michelle Collins. 23 Captain Nathan Bridger. 24 Hetty. 25 The Beatles. 26 Panorama. 27 Buster Merryfield. 28 The Outer Limits. 29 Chris Tarrant. 30 Emma Forbes.

1 Which "Raging" animal won for Robert De Niro in 1980?

2 In which movie did Anthony Hopkins play Hannibal Lecter?

3 Which street made Michael Douglas an 80s winner?

4 Who was the only actor to win two Best Actor Oscars in the 1990s?

5 Which body part is in the title of a Daniel Day-Lewis winning movie?

6 Which Gary is one of only a handful of actors to win Best Actor twice?

7 Which fields made a Best Supporting winner of Haing S. Ngor?

8 Which 007 was Best Supporting Actor in *The Untouchables*?

9 Which 70s Mafia movies both won three nominations for Best Supporting Actor?

10 Best Actor winners in 1990 and 1991 came from which kingdom?

11 Which man made Dustin Hoffman a 1988 winner?

12 Which Henry was the oldest Best Actor winner of the 20th century?

13 Which two Jacks were 70s winners in the Best Actor category?

14 What is the nationality of 1998 winner Roberto Benigni?

15 In 1992 Al Pacino won for "Scent of a" what?

16 What is the middle initial of Best Actor Scott who won for *Patton*?

17 Which simple fellow with a heart of gold won Tom Hanks a second Oscar?

18 Which Paul won for *The Color of Money*?

19 Which James was nominated for *The Godfather*?

20 Which Robin won Best Supporting Actor for *Good Will Hunting*?

21 Geoffrey Rush won for *Shine*, a biopic about what type of musician?

22 Which Kevin was Best Supporting Actor in *A Fish Called Wanda*?

23 Nicolas Cage was "Leaving" where in his 1995 winning role?

24 Who, with the name of the American capital in his name, won Best Supporting Actor for *Glory*?

25 Which Tom Hanks winning portrayal was a ping-pong star?

26 Playing which African despot earned Forrest Whittaker the award for 2006?

27 Which Jamie won the Oscar in 2004 playing Ray Charles?

28 Charlton Heston won the award for 1959 playing this character.

29 Who scooped the award in 1971 for his role in *The French Connection*?

30 Playing which fictional Doctor earned Anthony Hopkins the award for 1991?

Answers | Football: TV Pundits *(see Quiz 187)*

1 Ian St John. 2 Scotland. 3 Brian Clough. 4 1964 (1960–68 is OK). 5 Brighton. 6 Arsenal. 7 Jonathan Pearce. 8 Alan Hansen. 9 True. 10 Gillingham. 11 John Motson. 12 Garth Crooks. 13 Rory Bremner. 14 Icke. 15 Des Lynam. 16 John Motson. 17 Alan Hansen. 18 Ian St John. 19 David O'Leary. 20 Jimmy Hill. 21 Paul Parker. 22 Claridge. 23 Mark Lawrenson. 24 Armfield. 25 Scotland. 26 John Barnes. 27 Peter Schmeichel. 28 Bobby Charlton. 29 Garth Crooks. 30 Martin Keown.

1 Newsreaders Ms Young and Ms Wark share which first name?
2 In which village was Geraldine Grainger the vicar?
3 Who did Biff Fowler sleep with on her wedding night?
4 What was BBC2's sheepdog trials programme called?
5 In which series is Jack Klugman a pathologist?
6 On which children's programme did Nigel Planer succeed Eric Thompson as narrator?
7 Which was the football highlights show, *Match of the Day* or *The Big Match*?
8 Which sitcom was set behind the bars of H.M.P. Slade?
9 Who is the senior officer of Sun Hill in *The Bill*?
10 Who played Snudge in *The Army Game*?
11 Who is Tea Leone's husband?
12 In which series is Dr Sean Maddox the senior house officer?
13 What was Wallace and Gromit's first adventure?
14 What sort of animal was *Mr Ed*?
15 What job did Beth Saunders do in *Dangerfield*?
16 Who was Alan Jackson's grandmother in *EastEnders*?
17 On which ship is Lt Tom Paris an officer?
18 What was the full name of the satirical programme abbreviated to *TW3*?
19 Who narrated *Roobarb & Custard*?
20 Which entertainer's catchphrase is "Awright!"?
21 Who starred with Peter Cook in *Not Only... but Also*?
22 Which ex-*EastEnder* appeared in *Real Women*?
23 What was Roy Scheider's character in *Seaquest DSV*?
24 What is amateur detective Mrs Wainthropp's first name?
25 In 1963, which Fab Four pop group were panellists on *Juke Box Jury*?
26 Which BBC current affairs programme began broadcasting in 1953?
27 Who played Uncle in *Only Fools and Horses*?
28 Which S.F. show began by announcing "Do not adjust your set"?
29 Which ex-Tiswas host presents *Man-o-Man* on ITV?
30 Who presented *Tip Top Challenge*?

---

1 Which non-League team beat Newcastle in February 1972?
2 Which Paul scored a 90s FA Cup-winning goal for Everton?
3 Which London club won the FA Cup in 1981 and 1982?
4 Who was Des Walker playing for when he scored a final own goal?
5 Dickie Guy was a goalkeeping hero with which 1970s non-League side?
6 Which United won the Scottish FA Cup for the first time in the 80s?
7 In which decade was the first Wembley final?
8 Which Harry Redknapp team did a giant killing knocking out Manchester Utd in 1984?
9 Andy Linighan scored a last-minute final winner for which team?
10 Who beat Chelsea in the 1996 semi-finals?
11 Brian Flynn was boss as which club shocked Arsenal in 1992?
12 Cornishman Mike Trebilcock hit final goals for which team in the 60s?
13 Ray Walker hit a screamer as which Midland team dumped Tottenham Hotspur in the 80s?
14 Who was Man of the Match at 2016's FA Cup Final?
15 In 1989 Sutton United beat which First Division team 2–1?
16 Who was the first Frenchman to captain an FA Cup-winning side?
17 Ray Crawford inspired which team to the ultimate giant killing by beating Leeds 3–2 in 1971?
18 In the 1980s, which south coast side were losing finalists the year they were relegated from the First Division?
19 What accounted for the 1990 Scottish final score of Aberdeen 9 Celtic 8?
20 Geoff Thomas captained which London side in a 1990s final?
21 Which former English non-League club played in the 2006 SFA Cup Final?
22 Who scored the first FA Cup Final goal at the new Wembley?
23 In which town did 2008 Scottish Cup Final runner-up Queen of the South play?
24 With which club did Portsmouth's Nwankwo Kanu first win the FA Cup?
25 In which year did the last non-English club play in the FA Cup Final?
26 Which club has won more Scottish FA Cups than any other?
27 Who was the first post-war player to captain three FA Cup-winning sides?
28 What unique record does the Scottish FA Cup hold in world football?
29 Which manager has won the FA Cup five times?
30 Which European competition do both Cup winners qualify for?

1 Which Tina's album was *Simply the Best* in 1991?
2 Which Austrian city was a No. 1 for Ultravox in 1981?
3 Which country is Mary Hopkin from?
4 Which Suzanne was in "Tom's Diner" in 1990?
5 How did Barry White complete the song title "You're My First My Last"?
6 Which dance did Wizzard See My Baby do in 1973?
7 Who is Adam Wiles better known as?
8 What was Venus wearing according to Mark Wynter in 1962?
9 Abba are credited with being from Sweden and which other Scandinavian country?
10 How is Terry Nelhams better known?
11 Who was K.C.'s backing band?
12 What is the home country of Whitney Houston?
13 Whose debut album was called *Boomania*?
14 Which musical instrument does Harry Connick Jr play?
15 Curiosity Killed what according to the name of the 80s band?
16 Chrissie Hynde was lead singer with which group?
17 Who had the classic "Whiter Shade of Pale" in the 60s?
18 Which Jarvis sings with Pulp?
19 What qualification do Hook and Feelgood have?
20 Which surname is shared by the late Jackie and the beehive hair-do queen Mari?
21 What was the title of the album released by Keane in October 2008?
22 How are Cee-Lo (Thomas Callaway) and Danger Mouse (Brian Burton) known?
23 Which type of Singer was Neil Diamond in his 1980 film?
24 Which times of day is associated with Dexy's Runners?
25 Which singer is nicknamed the Rhinestone Cowboy?
26 Desmond Dekker was one of the first artists in which brand of Jamaican music?
27 Which Chris had a hit on both sides of the Atlantic with "Who Pays the Ferryman?"
28 Which illness did Ian Dury suffer from in childhoon?
29 Which Scottish city is Sheena Easton from?
30 Which record producer called Phil was famous for his "Wall of Sound"?

Answers   **TV Pot Luck 24** *(see Quiz 194)*

1 Better Call Saul. 2 Your Enthusiasm. 3 Edward. 4 Ronnie Corbett. 5 Yogi Bear.
6 Custard. 7 Chipmunk. 8 Business Breakfast. 9 Italy. 10 Countdown. 11 Buck
Rogers. 12 Highway to Heaven. 13 Cindy & Jim. 14 Honor Blackman. 15 Bob
Carolgees. 16 Cook Report. 17 Jo Brand. 18 Legg. 19 Poldark. 20 Graham
Chapman. 21 Mariella. 22 The Walking Dead. 23 Watchdog. 24 Top Gear. 25
Tracey Ullman. 26 Parish. 27 Hughie Green. 28 Baltimore. 29 Pete McCarthy. 30
This Life.

1 Which Pratt stars in 2016's reboot of *The Magnificent Seven*?
2 During which American war was *Dances with Wolves* set?
3 Which spaghetti western icon was "The Good" in *The Good, The Bad and The Ugly*?
4 Which animal name precedes "Ballou" in the Jane Fonda western spoof?
5 Which Gary won the Best Actor Oscar for *High Noon*?
6 Which Lee won the Best Actor Oscar playing opposite Jane Fonda?
7 Which Robert co-starred with John Wayne in *El Dorado*?
8 Which 60s folk singer had a minor role in *Pat Garrett and Billy the Kid*?
9 "I Was Born under a Wandrin' Star" comes from which western?
10 In which decade did spaghetti westerns first hit the screens?
11 Westerns were referred to as what type of operas?
12 Which Gene was dubbed the Singing Cowboy?
13 Which Lee found fame in spaghetti westerns?
14 In which "True" western did John Wayne famously wear an eye patch?
15 Who won the Best Director Oscar for *Unforgiven*?
16 Which Barbara, star of *Forty Guns*, was one of the few female members of the National Cowboy Hall of Fame?
17 Which Morgan appeared with Clint Eastwood in *Unforgiven*?
18 Which blue-eyed Paul starred in *Hud*?
19 In which decade was *High Noon* released?
20 Which Kevin won the Best Director Oscar for *Dances with Wolves*?
21 "Come back, Shane" is the last line of which movie?
22 Which Gene won an Oscar as the sheriff in *Unforgiven*?
23 Which western legend John's final movie was *The Shootist*?
24 Which movie was a remake of *Seven Samurai*?
25 Which Lee starred in *The Man Who Shot Liberty Valance*?
26 Which Mr Gyllenhaal starred in *Brokeback Mountain*?
27 John Wayne's battle for which famous Texan fort was remade in 2004?
28 What was Clint Eastwood fighting for "A Fistful of" in 1964?
29 Name the movie starring the Carry On team in 1966.
30 Which "Magnificent Seven" movie starred George Kennedy in 1969?

Answers	**Football: Grounds** *(see Quiz 195)*

1 Birmingham City. 2 42,785. 3 The Goldstone Ground. 4 Heysel. 5 Fulham. 6 Bristol City. 7 Chelsea. 8 Deepdale. 9 Huddersfield Town. 10 Aberdeen. 11 Old Trafford. 12 Oldham Athletic. 13 Blackburn Rovers. 14 Real Madrid. 15 Sunderland. 16 Wembley. 17 Bradford City. 18 Watford. 19 Hillsborough. 20 Brazil. 21 Arsenal. 22 Old Trafford. 23 Derby County. 24 Birmingham. 25 Fulham. 26 Manchester City. 27 Sunderland. 28 Reading. 29 Fratton Park. 30 Tottenham Hotspur.

1 What TV show stars Saul Goodman?

2 What were you asked to *Curb* in the sitcom?

3 Which Royal Prince appeared on *Des O'Connor Tonight* in 1998?

4 Who always told a long joke from a black chair on *The Two Ronnies*?

5 Who was "smarter than the average bear"?

6 What was Roobarb's feline companion called?

7 What kind of animated animal is Alvin?

8 What is the name of BBC1's early morning financial programme?

9 Which country's football league has a *Serie A*?

10 Which daytime show was presented by Richard Whiteley?

11 Which S.F. series featured the character Major Wilma Dearing?

12 In which series does Victor French play Mark?

13 Who were Brenda and Brandon Walsh's parents in *Beverley Hills 90210*?

14 What ex-Avenger appeared in *The Upper Hand*?

15 Which Bob assists Cilla Black in *Surprise, Surprise*?

16 Which programme became known as 'the antiques rogue show'?

17 Who presents *Through The Cake Hole*?

18 Which doctor in *Eastenders* had the christian name Harold?

19 What was the drama series set in Cornwall written by Winston Graham?

20 Which *Python* was a qualified doctor?

21 What is the christian name of the presenter of *Frostrup On Friday*?

22 Which TV show stars Rick Grimes as the lead character?

23 On which programme does Alice Beer appear?

24 On which series is Tiff Needell a presenter?

25 Which English actress played Dr Tracey Clark in *Ally McBeal*?

26 Which Sarah played the part of Katie Roden in *Mistresses*?

27 Which *Opportunity Knocks* presenter died in 1997?

28 In which city is the American drama series *The Wire* set?

29 Who was *Desperately Seeking Something* on C4?

30 In which drama series were Milly and Anna lawyers?

Answers | **Pop Pot Luck 24** *(see Quiz 192)*

1 Turner. 2 Vienna. 3 Wales. 4 Vega. 5 My Everything. 6 Jive. 7 Calvin Harris. 8 Blue Jeans. 9 Norway. 10 Adam Faith. 11 The Sunshine Band. 12 USA. 13 Betty Boo. 14 Piano. 15 The Cat. 16 The Pretenders. 17 Procul Harum. 18 Cocker. 19 Dr. 20 Wilson. 21 Perfect Symmetry. 22 Gnarls Barkley. 23 Jazz singer. 24 Midnight. 25 Glen Campbell. 26 Reggae. 27 De Burgh. 28 Polio. 29 Glasgow. 30 Spector.

1 Which team's ground is called St Andrews?
2 What is the capacity of Villa Park stadium?
3 In the 90s Brighton have been dogged by the attempted sale of which ground?
4 At which Stadium was there crowd trouble at the Liverpool v Juventus European Cup Final of 1985?
5 Which club play at Craven Cottage?
6 Which side is at home if the venue is Ashton Gate?
7 Which London team has its ground situated in the Fulham Road?
8 What is Preston's ground called?
9 Who play at home at the Alfred McAlpine Stadium?
10 Which Scottish side were the first to boast an all-seater stadium?
11 Which stadium is situated in Sir Matt Busby Way?
12 Who plays at home at Boundary Park?
13 Which club has the Walker Steel stand on its ground?
14 Which club play at the Santiago Bernabeu Stadium?
15 Roker Park was home for most of the 20th century to which team?
16 Which stadium had the Twin Towers?
17 At which Yorkshire club was there a fire tragedy in 1985?
18 Who plays at Vicarage Road?
19 The 1991 Liverpool and Nottingham Forest FA Cup semi-final was at which ground?
20 The Maracana Stadium is in which country?
21 Which club plays in a new stadium sponsored by a Middle East airline?
22 Which English club ground has a capacity of more than 75,000?
23 Who calls Pride Park home?
24 In which city is Villa Park?
25 Which club's dressing rooms are in a cottage inside the stadium?
26 Which club's former home was Maine Road?
27 Which club lights up The Stadium of Light?
28 Can you name the team who play their home games at the Madejski Stadium?
29 At what Park do Portsmouth play their home games?
30 Who calls White Hart Lane home?

| **Answers** | **Football: FA and SFA Cup** *(see Quiz 191)* |

1 Hereford Utd. 2 Rideout. 3 Tottenham Hotspur. 4 Nottingham Forest. 5 Wimbledon. 6 Dundee Utd. 7 1920s. 8 Bournemouth. 9 Arsenal. 10 Manchester Utd. 11 Wrexham. 12 Everton. 13 Port Vale. 14 Wayne Rooney. 15 Coventry City. 16 Eric Cantona. 17 Colchester Utd. 18 Brighton. 19 Game decided on penalties. 20 Crystal Palace. 21 Gretna. 22 Didier Drogba. 23 Dumfries. 24 Arsenal. 25 2008. 26 Celtic. 27 Bryan Robson. 28 The record score (Arbroath 36, Bon Accord 0). 29 Sir Alex Ferguson. 30 The UEFA Cup.

The Medium Questions

This next selection of questions is getting a little more like it. For an open entry quiz then you should have a high percentage of medium-level questions – don't try to break people's spirits with the hard ones, just make sure that people play to their ability.

Like all questions this level of question can be classed as either easy or impossible depending on whether you know the answer or not and although common knowledge is used as the basis for these questions there is a sting in the tail of quite a few. Also, if you have a serious drinking squad playing then they can more or less say goodbye to the winners' medals, but that isn't to say they will feel any worse about it.

Specialists are the people to watch out for, as those with a good knowledge of a particular subject will doubtless do well in these rounds, so a liberal sprinkling of pot-luck questions are needed to flummox them.

1 Who has scored most League goals for Celtic?
2 Which Sheffield does Steven Fletcher play for?
3 Alex Ferguson appeared in a Scottish Cup Final for which team?
4 Which team plays at Boghead Park?
5 Beating Dunfermline in the 1991 League Cup Final gave which club its first major trophy for 19 years?
6 Which side provided a great Scottish Cup shock by knocking Aberdeen out in 1995?
7 Which club broke their own transfer record to buy Paul Bernard from Oldham Athletic in 1995?
8 Which club got a 0–4 home drubbing from Juventus in the 90s?
9 Which League team comes from Perth?
10 Which club left the League in 1967?
11 What did Meadowbank Thistle change its name to?
12 Which team made their European debut in 1992?
13 Who joined the League in 1994 along with Caledonian Thistle?
14 Tommy Coyne joined which club when he left Tranmere Rovers?
15 Were Hibs founder members of the Scottish League?
16 What is the nickname of Montrose?
17 Which team holds the British record for a League victory?
18 Which Dunfermline player tragically died in the 1995–96 season?
19 Who beat Real Madrid in the 1983 European Cup Winners' Cup Final?
20 Who were the first Scottish club to play on artificial turf?
21 Which Athletic joined the Scottish League for 2008–09?
22 Which club – in the same town – replaced Airdrieonians FC in 2002?
23 Which was the last club from outside the SPL to play in the Scottish Cup Final?
24 Which team lost the Scottish Cup Final and was relegated from the SPL in 2007?
25 What is the name of Peterhead's Stadium?
26 Which Scottish club is nicknamed the Jags?
27 Can you recall the team Aberdeen beat to win the European Cup Winners' Cup?
28 Name the oldest professional football club in Scotland.
29 Which County calls Victoria Park home?
30 Which bank sponsored the 2008–09 Scottish Premier League?

Answers	**Pop Pot Luck 1** *(see Quiz 2)*

1 1940s. 2 Angie. 3 Wizzard. 4 Lulu. 5 Abba. 6 Bette Davis. 7 The Proclaimers. 8 Adam Faith. 9 Crawford. 10 Manchester. 11 Joan Armatrading. 12 "Copacabana". 13 HMV. 14 Oxford. 15 Guy Mitchell. 16 Cliff Bennett. 17 Denmark. 18 Annie Lennox. 19 Curtis Stigers. 20 1970s. 21 McFly. 22 Bryan McFadden. 23 Roger Daltrey. 24 Bill Haley. 25 Prince. 26 Level 42. 27 Earl. 28 Steve Winwood. 29 Father Mackenzie. 30 John Travolta.

1 In which decade was Bruce Springsteen born?
2 Which Baby girl did Helen Reddy sing about in 1975?
3 Who had a No. 1 with "Angel Fingers"?
4 Whose first hit was "Shout"?
5 Who had a 70s album called *Arrival*?
6 Which film star's Eyes did Kim Carnes sing about?
7 Which band was King of the Road in 1990?
8 How is Terence Nelhams better known?
9 Which surname is shared by Michael and Randy?
10 Which city did the Smiths hail from?
11 Who sang about Love and Affection in 1976?
12 Which Barry Manilow hit song became a stage show?
13 Which record label showed a dog listening to a gramophone?
14 Which university town do Supergrass come from?
15 Who had a 1953 hit with "She Wears Red Feathers"?
16 Whose backing group were the Rebel Rousers?
17 What is Whigfield's home country?
18 Who is the female half of the Eurythmics?
19 Who had a 1992 hit with "You're All That Matters to Me"?
20 In which decade did Roxy Music have their first hit?
21 Who appeared in *Just My Luck* with Lindsay Lohan and did the soundtrack album?
22 Who is the only person to have left the boy band Westlife?
23 Who played the title role in Tommy?
24 Which rocker had a kiss curl over his forehead as his trademark?
25 Who is almost naked on a bed, on the cover of his 1999 album?
26 Which group were giving "Lessons in Love" in 1986?
27 Where was Gene Chandler the Duke of?
28 Who was lead singer with the Spencer Davis Group?
29 What was the name of the priest in "Eleanor Rigby"?
30 Who appears with the Bee Gees on the *Saturday Night Fever* album cover?

1 In which movie did Errol Flynn say, "It's injustice I hate, not the Normans"?
2 What was the Marx Brothers' first film for MGM?
3 Who found fame in *Public Enemy*?
4 Which subject of the 90s movie *Gods and Monsters* directed *Frankenstein*?
5 Which movie was about Longfellow Deeds?
6 Which famous Robert Louis Stevenson personality was the subject of a 1932 movie with Fredric March?
7 The star of many Tarzan movies had been an accomplished Olympian in which sport?
8 Who played Elizabeth I in *Elizabeth and Essex* opposite Errol Flynn?
9 In which movie did Bela Lugosi say, "Listen to them, children of the night. What music they make"?
10 Who choreographed *Forty-Second Street*?
11 In which 1934 Oscar-winning movie did Clark Gable famously say, "Behold the walls of Jericho"?
12 Which movie made a star of Claude Rains, though he was only seen for a few moments?
13 Which "Bride" was Elsa Lanchester in a 1935 classic?
14 Who did Charles Laughton play in *Mutiny on the Bounty*?
15 Which studio filmed *Goodbye Mr Chips* in England?
16 Which British star of *Gone with the Wind* was "The Scarlet Pimpernel"?
17 Which city was terrorized by *King Kong*?
18 To the nearest hour, how long does *Monkey Business* last?
19 Who starred as "Camille"?
20 Who was the French star of *Love Affair* in 1939?
21 In which movie did Chaplin satirize the mechanical society?
22 Which youthful duo starred in *Babes in Arms*?
23 How was song-and-dance director William Berkeley Enos better known?
24 Which British-born director made *Sabotage*?
25 In which 1934 movie did Astaire and Rogers dance "The Continental"?
26 Adolph Marx became famous as which brother?
27 In which country was Marlene Dietrich's *The Blue Angel* filmed?
28 Where was Alice in the 1934 movie?
29 Whose thirsty daughter was the subject of the 1936 Lambert Hillyer movie?
30 Which 1939 movie shares the same title as a No. 1 song by Kate Bush?

Answers	TV Pot Luck 1 *(see Quiz 4)*

1 A doctor (GP). 2 Kirk Jones. 3 Thriller Writer. 4 Charlene. 5 Robert Powell. 6 James. 7 Bloodhound. 8 Richard Dimbleby. 9 Motorbike & sidecar. 10 Julie T. Wallace. 11 Jenji Kohan. 12 Xylophone. 13 Yorkshire. 14 Christopher Day. 15 Alexei Sayle. 16 Formula One Grands Prix. 17 Kate O'Mara. 18 Dirk Benedict. 19 Frank and Kim Tate. 20 The Thrift. 21 Russell Grant. 22 Margaery Tyrel. 23 Ian McShane. 24 Glynn Christian. 25 Kenny Everett. 26 Erica Matthews. 27 Dermot. 28 Cilla Black. 29 Hampshire. 30 David Soul.

1 What occupation is Ted Danson's character in *Becker*?

4 Who played the role of Blade in the 2006 TV series?

3 What was the ocupaton of Dorothy McNabb in *Two's Company*?

4 Who punched her future husband in *Neighbours*, the first time they met?

5 Who went from *Doomwatch* to *The Detectives*?

6 What is the first name of *Kavanagh QC*?

7 What does *The Great Antiques Hunt* have as a mascot?

8 Which BBC TV commentator described the Queen's Coronation service?

9 What transport do the Two Fat Ladies favour?

10 In *Life and Loves of a She Devil*, the central character Ruth was played by whom?

11 Who created *Orange Is the New Black*, that first aired on Netflix in 2013?

12 What instrument does astronomer Patrick Moore play?

13 *Where the Heart is* was set in which county?

14 Who portrays *Rab C. Nesbitt* in the 2016 tribute show?

15 In *Whoops Apocalypse* which comedian played Commissar Solzhenitsyn?

16 Jamiroquai's lead singer, Jay Kay, composed the theme for which sporting ITV feature?

17 Who played the leading female role in *Triangle*?

18 Which actor links *The A-Team* to *Battlestar Galactica*?

19 Which *Emmerdale* couple renewed their wedding vows in Ripon Cathedral?

20 In *Bramwell*, what is the name of the infirmary?

21 Which astrologer has worked on both the BBC's *Breakfast Time* and GMTV?

22 What character does Natalie Dormer play on *Game of Thrones*?

23 Who starred as *Lovejoy*?

24 Which descendant of the Bounty mutineer Fletcher Christian appeared as a cook on *Breakfast Time*?

25 Whose characters included Marcel Wave and Gizzard Puke?

26 In *Peak Practice*, which female doctor replaced Beth Glover?

27 Which role was played by Harry Enfield in *Men Behaving Badly*?

28 Who is the presenter of *Blind Date*?

29 In which English county was the soap *Howard's Way* set?

30 Which US actor accompanied Martin Bell on his election campaign?

---

1 Which Gray brothers were in the Leeds Utd team of the 1970s?
2 Striker Gary came back to League soccer with Barnet in the 1990s while brother Steve was scoring goals for which club?
3 What were the forenames of the Dutch Koeman brothers?
4 What were the names of QPR's Morgan twins of the 60s?
5 In which year did both Charlton brothers play their last international?
6 What was the name of Bill Shankly's brother who was also a soccer manager?
7 Who is Chris Casper's footballing father?
8 Which brothers Graham and Ray played at Chelsea in the 1970s?
9 Brothers Danny, Rodney and Ray Wallace were together at which club?
10 Who were the first brothers to be at an English double-winning club?
11 What was the name of the Futcher twins?
12 What is the name of Elton John's footballing uncle?
13 Which of the Laudrup brothers did not play when Denmark won the European Championship?
14 Player/manager Ian Bowyer was in the same side as son Gary at which club?
15 What is the name of Clive Allen's dad, also a Spurs player?
16 If dad John is the boss and son Kevin is a defender, what is the surname?
17 What was the name of Terry Hibbitt's soccer-playing brother ?
18 Which brothers Mel and John played together for Wales in the 1950s?
19 What is the surname of strikers Allan, Frank and Wayne?
20 At which club did Eric Cantona's brother Joel make his English League debut?
21 Whose stepson moved from Manchester City to Chelsea and returned in 2008?
22 Which 2000s England international is the nephew of Harry Redknapp?
23 What relation is Anton Ferdinand to Rio Ferdinand?
24 In which decade did the Schmeichels play in goal for Manchester City?
25 Which Cambridgeshire club did Sir Alex Ferguson's son Darren manage?
26 Which ex-Man. Utd player is the son of a European Cup winner three times with Ajax?
27 Which ex-Chelsea striker came on for his father in an international game in 1996?
28 Which legendary Newcastle United striker was Bobby and Jack Charlton's uncle?
29 Can you name Kolo Toure's brother who played for Barcelona in 2008?
30 Name the two Greenhoff brothers who played in the same Man. Utd team.

Answers | Pop Pot Luck 2 *(see Quiz 6)*

1 Michael Ball. 2 Baby Jane. 3 MacArthur. 4 Wayne Fontana. 5 Guitar. 6 Blondie. 7 Stevie Wonder (his name backwards!). 8 Linda McCartney. 9 "One Fine Day". 10 Brian Epstein. 11 His car hit a tree. 12 Mick Jagger, David Bowie. 13 Hatch and Trent. 14 Bryan Adams. 15 1950s. 16 1980s. 17 The Housemartins. 18 Shakin' Stevens. 19 "Summer in the City". 20 Perry Como. 21 Lily Allen. 22 Scissor Sisters. 23 1930s. 24 David Bowie. 25 West Virginia. 26 Chicory Tip. 27 Peter Gabriel. 28 Queen. 29 16. 30 57.

Quiz 6 | Pop Pot Luck 2

Answers – page 211

LEVEL 2

1 Who had a 1989 hit with "Love Changes Everything"?
2 Which Baby girl did Rod Stewart sing about in 1983?
3 Which Park was Donna Summer in in 1978?
4 Whose backing group was the Mindbenders?
5 Which musical instrument does Johnny Marr play?
6 Whose first hit was "Denis"?
7 Who has recorded under the name of Eivets Rednow?
8 Who was the female member of Wings?
9 Which Goffin and King song by the Chiffons shares its name with an aria from Puccini's *Madame Butterfly*?
10 Who was Cilla Black's first manager?
11 How did T. Rex's Marc Bolan meet his death?
12 Which duo with combined ages of over 80 topped the charts in September 1985 for four weeks?
13 Who were the first husband-and-wife team to top the charts?
14 Who had a 90s album called *Waking Up The Neighbours*?
15 In which decade was Karen Carpenter born?
16 In which decade did the Beautiful South have their first hit?
17 Who had a No. 1 with "Caravan of Love"?
18 How is Michael Barratt better known?
19 Which Summer song did Lovin' Spoonful sing in 1966?
20 Who had a 1953 hit with "Don't Let the Stars Get in Your Eyes"?
21 Whose first album was *Alright, Still*?
22 Ana Matronic is a member of which glam rock group?
23 In which decade was Dusty Springfield born?
24 Which David released *David Live* in 1974?
25 Which state is "almost heaven" for John Denver?
26 Which group had a hit with "Son of My Father"?
27 Which member of the group Genesis left in 1975?
28 Whose second No. 1 album was *A Day at the Races*?
29 How many "vestal virgins" were leaving in "Whiter Shade of Pale"?
30 How old (or young!) was Prince when he died in 2016?

| **Answers** | **Football: Famous Families** *(see Quiz 5)* |

1 Eddie and Frank. **2** Wolves. **3** Ronald and Erwin. **4** Ian and Roger. **5** 1970. **6** Bob. **7** Frank. **8** Wilkins. **9** Southampton. **10** Gary and Phil Neville. **11** Paul and Ron. **12** Roy Dwight. **13** Michael. **14** Hereford United. **15** Les. **16** Bond. **17** Kenny. **18** Charles. **19** Clarke. **20** Stockport County. **21** Ian Wright. **22** Frank Lampard. **23** Brother. **24** 2000s. **25** Peterborough Utd. **26** Jordi Cruyff. **27** Eidur Gudjohnsen. **28** Jackie Milburn. **29** Yaya. **30** Brian and Jimmy.

1 In which 1999 movie were Harvey Keitel and Jennifer Jason Leigh replaced by Tom Cruise and Nicole Kidman?
2 Who did Danny Boyle direct in both *Trainspotting* and *Shallow Grave*?
3 Which director was Geena Davis's third husband?
4 Harvey Keitel is particularly known for his work with which director?
5 How did Joanne Whalley style herself during her 1988–1996 marriage?
6 Marilyn Monroe divorced Arthur Miller a week after the premiere of which movie?
7 Who was Uma Thurman's on- and off-screen partner in *Gattaca*?
8 Fred Quimby was partly responsible for bringing which duo to the big screen?
9 Mimi Rogers was the first wife of which superstar of the 80s and 90s?
10 Which star of *Twins* married John Travolta?
11 Which wife of director James Keach was a Bond girl in *Live and Let Die*?
12 Which star of *The Horse Whisperer* married a French doctor?
13 Who married Danny DeVito during a break on *Cheers*?
14 Which tough guy played opposite Jill Ireland 12 times?
15 What was Abbot and Costello's first feature film?
16 Who played the mother of her daughter Rumer in *Striptease* in 1996?
17 Which brothers appeared in *The Fabulous Baker Boys*?
18 Which wife of Frank Sinatra was Oscar-nominated at the same time as him?
19 Which singer/actress was Mrs Bobby Brown?
20 *Dark Passage* featured which couple?
21 Who married Debbie Reynolds's daughter in 1983?
22 Which director did Rita Hayworth marry?
23 Who was Ethan Hawke's partner on-screen during the making of 2015's *Boyhood*?
24 Vanessa Redgrave's affair with Franco Nero began on the set of which musical movie?
25 What was the name of Mrs Michael Douglas who divorced him in 1995?
26 Lyricist Alan Jay Lerner worked with composer Frederick who?
27 Which family, Lloyd, Jeff and Beau, have stars on Hollywood's Walk of Fame?
28 What is the name of Sherlock Holmes's assistant?
29 Abbott and Costello were a famous double-act but what were their Christian names?
30 Which husband and wife starred in *Who's Afraid of Virginia Woolf*?

Answers	TV Pot Luck 2 *(see Quiz 8)*

1 My Family. 2 Channel Five. 3 Victoria. 4 A computer. 5 Gus. 6 CJ. 7 Jane Seymour. 8 On the bed in her "Boudoir". 9 Alan Turner. 10 Fred Streeter. 11 Paradise Gardens. 12 Jonathan Gash. 13 Gravesend. 14 1927. 15 Phyllis Calvert. 16 The River Hamble, Hampshire. 17 Boston, USA. 18 Roger Thursby. 19 Andrew Cruickshank. 20 The Eastern Insurance Company. 21 Percy Thrower. 22 Jesse Pinkman. 23 1946. 24 Arthur Negis. 25 Into the Labyrinth. 26 1923. 27 OTT. 28 Chris Tarrant. 29 Due South. 30 June Whitfield.

1 Dr Ben Harper is the lead character in which sitcom?

2 Which terrestrial channel broadcast Test cricket highlights in 2008?

3 Which Wood died on 20 April 2016?

4 Who or what was Orac?

5 In *Drop the Dead Donkey*, whose catchphrase was "I'm not here"?

6 What was Reggie Perrin's boss called?

7 Who plays *Dr Quinn, Medicine Woman*?

8 Where did Paula Yates hold interviews on *The Big Breakfast*?

9 Which character's son had an affair with Sandy Merrick in *Emmerdale*?

10 Who was the presenter of the 1940s series *Television Garden*?

11 Which Geoff Hamilton series was first shown after his death?

12 The series *Lovejoy* was based on whose novels?

13 Where was Dot living before returning to Walford in 1997?

14 When did John Logie Baird first experiment in colour TV?

15 Who played the title role in the series *Kate*?

16 Which UK river featured in *Howard's Way*?

17 Where does *Master Chef* presenter Loyd Grossman originate from?

18 In *Brothers In Law*, Richard Briers played which up-and-coming barrister?

19 Who took a break from *Dr Finlay's Casebook* to be "Mr Justice Duncannon"?

20 In *The Cheaters*, which insurance company did John Hunter work for?

21 Who first presented *Gardening Club* in 1955?

22 Who partners Walter White in *Breaking Bad*?

23 In what year was the first televised church service?

24 Which antiques expert starred in the original series of *Antiques Roadshow*?

25 In which programme were three children sent through time hunting the Nidus, with which they could free the magician Rothgo from the trap of his evil enemy, Belor?

26 In which year was the *Radio Times* first published?

27 What was the name of the adult version of *Tiswas*?

28 Who presented *Saturday Stayback*?

29 In which series would you find Benton Frazer?

30 Who is Suzy Aitchison's comedienne mother?

Answers	Movies: Partnerships *(see Quiz 7)*

1 Eyes Wide Shut. 2 Ewan McGregor. 3 Renny Harlin. 4 Martin Scorsese. 5 Joanne Whalley-Kilmer. 6 The Misfits. 7 Ethan Hawke. 8 Tom & Jerry. 9 Tom Cruise. 10 Kelly Preston. 11 Jane Seymour. 12 Kristin Scott Thomas. 13 Rhea Perlman. 14 Charles Bronson. 15 One Night in the Tropics. 16 Demi Moore. 17 Jeff & Beau Bridges. 18 Ava Gardner. 19 Whitney Houston. 20 Bogart & Bacall. 21 Paul Simon. 22 Orson Welles. 23 Rosanna Arquette. 24 Camelot. 25 Diandra. 26 Loewe. 27 The Bridges. 28 Dr Watson. 29 Bud and Lou. 30 Richard Burton and Elizabeth Taylor.

1 Charleston is the capital of which Appalachian US state, abbreviated WV?
2 Which US state, whose capital is Montgomery, has AL as its abbreviation?
3 Which city, located in the province of Ontario, is the largest in Canada?
4 Boise is the capital of which US state, abbreviated as ID?
5 The reality TV show *Jersey Shore* is about the inhabitants of which state?
6 Annapolis is the capital of which US state, abbreviated as MD?
7 New Orleans is the largest city of which southern US state?
8 What is the capital of Mexico?
9 The city of Providence is the capital of which small US state?
10 The movie industry district of Hollywood is in which Californian city?
11 In 1867, the USA purchased the state of Alaska from whom?
12 In which state of the USA would you find the Grand Canyon?
13 Seattle and Olympia are cities in which state?
14 Chicago is the largest city of which US state?
15 Which US state is home to the cities of Memphis and Nashville?
16 What is the official abbreviation of Mark Twain's home state of Missouri?
17 Which famous park contains the continent's largest active supervolcano caldera?
18 Boston is the capital of which New England state?
19 Raleigh is the capital of which US state, abbreviated as NC?
20 The inhabitants of which state are known as Hoosiers?
21 Which US state shares its name with the chief river of the USA's largest water drainage system?
22 What is the standard abbreviation for the state of North Dakota?
23 Mexico is the most populous of the countries that speak which official language?
24 Who is the monarch of Canada?
25 The US state of Montana shares a border with which other country?
26 For which industry is Las Vegas in the state of Nevada best known?
27 About 80% of Canadians live within 100 miles of what?
28 Detroit in Michigan is the former American centre of which industry?
29 SC is the standard abbreviation of which US state?
30 Burlington is the largest city of which New England state?

Answers	**Pop Pot Luck 3** *(see Quiz 10)*

1 Chrissie Hynde. 2 1960s. 3 Booker T. 4 Gilbert O'Sullivan. 5 Paul McCartney. 6 To Love. 7 Cat Stevens. 8 Laine. 9 T'Pau. 10 Saturday Night. 11 "The Power of Love". 12 Abba. 13 Major Tom ("Space Oddity"). 14 Dick Tracy. 15 Bread. 16 "Black (is Black)". 17 Australia. 18 1940s. 19 Carrie. 20 Kanye West. 21 Mika. 22 The Proclaimers. 23 The Blackhearts. 24 Roxy Music. 25 Barbra Streisand. 26 Alanis Morissette. 27 Chaka Khan. 28 PJ and Duncan. 29 England Dan and John Ford Coley. 30 "Forever Love".

1 Who was the female member of the Pretenders?
2 In which decade did Jeff Beck have his first solo hit?
3 Whose backing group was the MGs?
4 Who had a No. 1 with "Clair"?
5 Whose first No. 1 under his name alone was "Pipes of Peace" in 1984?
6 What did Tina Charles say "I Love" to do in 1976 and 1986?
7 How is Steven Demetri Georgiou better known in the charts?
8 Which surname is shared by Cleo and Frankie?
9 Who sang "Heart and Soul" in 1987?
10 When was Barry Blue Dancing in 1973?
11 Which song title links Jennifer Rush and Frankie Goes to Hollywood?
12 Which group was once called the Anni-Frid Four?
13 Which David Bowie song hero was "floating in my tin can"?
14 In which film did Madonna play the part of Breathless Mahoney?
15 Whose first hit was "Make It with You"?
16 Which colour provided a hit for Los Bravos and La Belle Epoque?
17 What was Johnny Logan's original home country?
18 In which decade was Adam Faith born?
19 Which girl who "doesn't live here any more" did Cliff Richard sing about in 1980?
20 Who released an album in 2016 called *The Life of Pablo*?
21 Under what name does Beirut-born Michael Holbrook Penniman perform?
22 With which band did Brian Potter and Andy Pipkin record a 2007 Comic Relief hit?
23 Who was Joan Jett's backing group?
24 Brian Eno was a member of which group?
25 Who has recorded with Barry Gibb, Neil Diamond and Don Johnson?
26 Who released the album *Jagged Little Pill*?
27 How is Yvette Stevens better known?
28 What were Ant and Dec previously known as?
29 Who sang "I'd Really Love to See You Tonight"?
30 What was Gary Barlow's first solo single after Take That split in the 1990s?

Answers | **North America** *(see Quiz 9)*

1 West Virginia. 2 Alabama. 3 Toronto. 4 Idaho. 5 New Jersey. 6 Maryland.
7 Louisiana. 8 Mexico City. 9 Rhode Island. 10 Los Angeles. 11 Russia.
12 Arizona. 13 Washington. 14 Illinois. 15 Tennessee. 16 MO. 17 Yellowstone.
18 Massachusetts. 19 North Carolina. 20 Indiana. 21 Mississippi. 22 ND.
23 Spanish. 24 Queen Elizabeth II. 25 Canada. 26 Gambling. 27 The US border.
28 Cars. 29 South Carolina. 30 Vermont.

1 Who or what was Andre in the film of the same name?
2 What sort of whale was Willy?
3 Which movie saw a creature threatening Amity off the Long Island coast?
4 What was the sequel to *Beethoven* called?
5 On whose novel was *101 Dalmatians* based?
6 Which creatures predominate in *Deep Blue Sea*?
7 Which actress founded the Born Free Foundation after appearing in the movie?
8 What sort of animal was the star of *Gus*?
9 In which film does Tom Hanks use the help of a dog to solve a murder?
10 Which veteran, and former child star, was one of the voices in the 80s *The Fox and the Hound*?
11 What sort of star was Rhubarb?
12 Which *X-Files* star played a villain in *Beethoven*?
13 Which animals were the stars of *Ring of Bright Water*?
14 What was Tom Mix's horse called?
15 The first dog to play which big-screen star was really called Pal?
16 What was the name of the basketball-playing golden retriever in *Air Bud* in 1997?
17 How many horses did Gene Autry have called Champion?
18 In which musical does Bill have a dog called Bullseye?
19 What type of animal was Digby in the Peter Sellers movie?
20 What breed of dog was K9 in the John Belushi movie?
21 How many dogs and cats make *The Incredible Journey*?
22 Which little girl had a dog as a nanny, called Nana?
23 What sort of animal featured in *My Friend Flicka*?
24 What was the cat called in *Breakfast at Tiffany's*?
25 What was the sequel to *The Incredible Journey* called?
26 What animal was Will Smith's only companion in *I am Legend*?
27 What creature's bite turned Peter Parker into a superhero?
28 What was the name of the pig in the *Toy Story* movies?
29 What type of animal was Skippy?
30 What was the name of King of the Jungle's chimpanzee in the *Tarzan* movies?

Answers   **TV Pot Luck 3** *(see Quiz 12)*

1 Denton. 2 Russell. 3 Fallon. 4 Ned Stark. 5 The Flintstones. 6 Francis Wilson.
7 Ruth. 8 September 1957. 9 Joanna Lumley. 10 Clarissa Dickson Wright. 11 The
Liberator. 12 Aidensfield. 13 Roland Rat. 14 An advertisement broadcast in the guise of
a genuine programme. 15 Sir Robert Winston. 16 Lawyers. 17 Napoleon. 18 1950s.
19 Late Lunch. 20 Michael Parkinson. 21 Pauline Quirke. 22 Lady Jane Felsham. 23
Don Adams. 24 Jan Harvey. 25 Glasgow. 26 Diane-Lousie Jordan. 27 The first BBC TV
broadcast from a ship at sea. 28 Pernell Roberts. 29 Telstar 1. 30 1957.

1 In which fictional town does Detective Inspector Jack Frost work?
2 Which Keri has led *The Americans* to success since 2013?
3 Which Jimmy has hosted *The Tonight Show* since 2013?
4 Which character is beheaded in the last episode of season one of *Game of Thrones*?
5 *The Simpsons* became the longest-running cartoon family in 1997, replacing whom?
6 Who was the original weatherman on BBC's *Breakfast Time*?
7 Which character in *EastEnders* is Mark's wife?
8 In which year did the BBC TV schools service begin?
9 Which actress had to survive on her own on a desert isle?
10 Who is Jennifer Paterson's cooking partner?
11 What was the name of the first space ship used by *Blake's 7*?
12 Which fictional village is *Heartbeat* set in?
13 Which rodent starred on *TVAM*?
14 What was an Admag, banned by Parliament in 1963?
15 Who presented *The Human Body*?
16 What is the profession of the major characters in *This Life*?
17 What did the ARP Warden call Captain Mainwaring?
18 In which decade was *Hi-De-Hi!* first set?
19 Which early-evening programme do Mel and Sue introduce?
20 Who is the current host of *Going for a Song*?
21 Which actress played *The Sculptress*?
22 Who was *Lovejoy*'s original love interest?
23 Which actor was Maxwell Smart?
24 Who played Tom Howard's wife in *Howard's Way*?
25 In which city was PI Daniel Pike based?
26 Who moved from *Blue Peter* in 1996 to *Songs of Praise*?
27 What TV first occurred during the 1953 Naval Review at Spithead?
28 Who played Adam Cartwright in *Bonanza*?
29 Which satellite was used for the first transatlantic broadcast?
30 In what year did *The Sky at Night* begin?

Answers | **Movies: Animals on Screen** *(see Quiz 11)*

1 Seal. 2 Orca (Killer Whale). 3 Jaws. 4 Beethoven's Second. 5 Dodie Smith. 6 Sharks. 7 Virginia McKenna. 8 Mule. 9 Turner and Hooch. 10 Mickey Rooney. 11 Cat. 12 David Duchovny. 13 Otters. 14 Tony. 15 Lassie. 16 Buddy. 17 Three. 18 Oliver!. 19 Dog. 20 German Shepherd. 21 Two dogs, one cat. 22 Wendy (Peter Pan). 23 Horse. 24 Cat. 25 Homeward Bound: The Incredible Journey. 26 A German Shepherd dog. 27 A spider. 28 Hamm. 29 A bush kangaroo. 30 Cheeta.

1 Which famous comedian and TV personality is a supporter of WBA?
2 Which team were originally known as Small Heath Alliance?
3 Who did Blackburn Rovers play in the 1994 Charity Shield match?
4 Which club did Danny Blanchflower play for before he joined Tottenham Hotspur?
5 Name the two goalkeepers in the 1983 Manchester Utd v Liverpool FA Cup Final?
6 Kemar Roofe started playing for which squad in 2016?
7 Gordon Banks won the League Cup with which different clubs?
8 Alan Hudson and Geoff Hurst both played for which Midlands team?
9 Which Midlands' star made a goal-scoring England debut against Scotland in 1989?
10 Who was manager of Stockport at the start of the 1996–97 season?
11 Who scored a hat-trick for Blackpool in the 1953 FA Cup Final?
12 Which club dropped from First to Fourth Divisions between 1984–86?
13 What was the nickname of Aston Villa's 1930s player Thomas Waring?
14 In 1960 the Blackpool v Bolton game achieved a first. What was it?
15 Which player did Real Madrid sign from WBA for £1 million in 1979?
16 Who created the first £10,000 transfer fee joining Arsenal from Bolton?
17 Which Aston Villa forward won the Young Player of the Year award in 1977?
18 Who played for Arsenal and Everton and managed Aston Villa, Manchester City and England?
19 What happened to Manchester City in 1938 after being champions in 1937?
20 Which club did Bobby Charlton manage between 1973 and '75?
21 Which club won only one Premier League game in 2007–08?
22 Who left their home ground Boothferry Park in 2002?
23 Which club chairman resigned as manager to appoint Roy Keane as boss?
24 Which Lancashire coast club entered the Football League in 2007?
25 Which West Midlands Football League club has never played in the Premiership?
26 Name the club which has won more European Cups than League championships.
27 Which manager guided two different clubs to the First Division championship?
28 Which club used to play their home games at Ayresome Park?
29 What was the last major trophy won by Newcastle United?
30 Who was the manager of Aston Villa when they won the European Cup in 1981?

1 In which decade did the Bee Gees have their first hit?
2 Whose backing group was the Blue Flames?
3 Who sang "Heart of Gold" in 1972?
4 Which colour Monday was a hit for New Order in 1983 and 1988?
5 How is Mary O'Brien better known?
6 Which Park were the Small Faces in in 1967?
7 Who had a No. 1 with "Down Under"?
8 Which greeting linked Stevie Wonder and Altered Images in 1981?
9 Who was the first member to leave Take That in 1995?
10 Who was the female member of Blondie?
11 In which decade was Neil Sedaka born?
12 Who had a No. 1 with "I Can't Give You Anything (but My Love)"?
13 What was Sting's first solo single?
14 Who had a backing group called the Steelmen?
15 Whose man was So Macho in 1986?
16 Which Summer song did Abba sing in 1978?
17 What did Shanice say "I Love" in 1991 and 1992?
18 Whose first hit was "School's Out"?
19 Who had a 90s album called *Auberge*?
20 Whose Clown were the Everly Brothers in 1960?
21 Who had a big 2008 hit with "That's Not My Name"?
22 Which is the only song to be a big hit four times, all with different performers?
23 Which musical instrument does Ravi Shankar play?
24 Who was Johnny Kidd's backing group?
25 Which "drink" was the Four Seasons' first hit?
26 In which decade was Chris Rea's first top ten hit?
27 In which decade was Lionel Richie born?
28 Who starred as Bongo Herbert in a film?
29 Who had an album called My People were *Fair and Had Sky in Their Hair but Now They're Content to Wear Stars on Their Brows*?
30 Which song title links Cars and R.E.M.?

---

1 What was his nickname?

2 In which classic western did he play the Ringo Kid?

3 Which sport did he play competitively when he was at college?

4 Which wife of Charlie Chaplin was his co-star in *Reap the Wild Wind*?

5 What was the first movie in which he starred with Maureen O'Hara?

6 Which singer was his drunken assistant in *Rio Bravo*?

7 What type of sportsman did he pay in *The Quiet Man*?

8 Which Hollywood great was his female co-star in *The Shootist*?

9 In which movie did he famously say, "Truly this man was the son of God"?

10 Which role did he play in *The Alamo*?

11 In which 1975 movie did he reprise his role from *True Grit*?

12 What was his real name?

13 He starred in and directed *The Green Berets* during which war?

14 What was the first movie for which he received an Oscar?

15 Which movie earned him his first Oscar nomination?

16 Which TV western series did he introduce the first episode of on camera?

17 Which legendary ruler did he play in *The Conqueror*?

18 What was the name of his first major movie?

19 Which director gave him the role in *She Wore a Yellow Ribbon*?

20 In which city was *Brannigan* set?

21 On what occasion was his last public appearance?

22 What was his directorial debut?

23 In which movie did he play Civil War veteran Ethan Edwards?

24 *El Dorado* was a virtual remake of which 1959 hit movie?

25 What was the name of his final movie?

26 Boxing grandnephew Tommy Morrison claimed to have beaten which condition?

27 Which eye was covered with a patch in Rooster Cogburn?

28 Which Vietnam War movie did he star in and direct in 1968?

29 What type of shop did the teenage Wayne work in?

30 Which actor played Wayne in the 2015 movie *Trumbo*?

Answers | TV Pot Luck 4 *(see Quiz 16)*

1 Jason Connery. 2 Johnnie Vaughan. 3. Sky Television and BSB. 4 Grant Show. 5 £175. 6 English Literature. 7 Chris Kelly. 8 John Fashanu. 9 Lord Reith. 10 Harper's, West One. 11 Bob Geldof. 12 Carlton. 13 Guinness. 14 Good Morning Television. 15 Ten shillings (50p). 16 Cuba Gooding Jr. 17 Alfred Lynch. 18 Billy. 19 Eamon Andrews. 20 Yorkshire. 21 Perry King. 22 Nigel Havers. 23 David Icke. 24 Paula Wilcox. 25 Ramsay MacDonald. 26 Daniel Pike. 27 Warren Clarke. 28 Bob Mills. 29 Clement Attlee. 30 Richard Burton.

1 Who played the author Ian Fleming on televsion?
2 Which breakfast presenter hosted *Moviewatch*?
3 Which TV companies merged to form BSkyB?
4 Who played Jake Hanson in *Melrose Place*?
5 In 1957 how much did a colour TV cost?
6 What is *The X Files'* David Duchovny's masters degree in?
7 Who has produced *Kavanagh QC* and presented *Food & Drink*?
8 Who was the first male presenter of *Gladiators*?
9 Who was the first Director General of the BBC?
10 Which soap revolved around a West End department store?
11 Which pop star's production company launched *The Big Breakfast*?
12 Which company replaced Thames TV in the early 90s?
13 Which drink did Rutger Hauer advertise?
14 What does GMTV stand for?
15 How much did the first TV licence cost?
16 Which actor plays OJ Simpson in *American Crime Story*, aired in 2016?
17 Who played Hereward the Wake?
18 Which Kennedy was in love with Ann Wilkinson in *Neighbours*?
19 Who was the very first presenter of *This is Your Life*?
20 Where was *Hadleigh* set?
21 Which role did Lane Smith play in *Superman*?
22 Which actor was *The Charmer*?
23 Who originally presented the sports summaries on *Breakfast Time*?
24 Which actress played Beryl in *The Loners*?
25 Who was the first Prime Minister to install a TV at home?
26 Roddy McMillan played which Scottish PI?
27 Which actor portrays Andy Dalziel?
28 Who presented *In Bed with MeDinner*?
29 Who gave the first direct TV broadcast by a Prime Minister in 1948?
30 Name the narrator of *The Valiant Years*.

---

1 What was the official time for Usain Bolt's 200m world record in the 2008 final?

2 Which two sports were dropped from the Games after 2008?

3 In which event did Shanaze Reade fall at the final bend of the final?

4 Tom Daley won silver, gold or bronze at the 2016 Olympics in Rio?

5 Which was the only year in which Great Britain exceeded its 2008 medal haul?

6 In which two successive Olympics did Daley Thompson win gold?

7 In which team game did Britain's men win gold in Seoul in 1988?

8 Which country has won most summer Olympic medals since 1896?

9 Whose long-jump record in the 1968 Olympics lasted for 24 years?

10 Which boxer won gold for Canada in Seoul in 1988?

11 Which country did athletes with FRG after their names represent?

12 Who won silver at 100 metres in '88 and gold in the same event in '92?

13 What do equestrian medallists Virginia Holgate and Virginia Leng have in common?

14 Which gymnast scored the first perfect ten in Olympic history?

15 Where were the 1964 Olympics held?

16 Who was disqualified after a drugs test in the men's 100 metres in 1988?

17 Who collided with Zola Budd in the 3000 metres in 1984?

18 Who won Britain's first men's swimming gold for 68 years in 1976?

19 At which sport was Katarina Witt an Olympic champion?

20 In which city were the Winter Olympics held when Torvill and Dean won gold in 1984?

21 What did 1964 Marathon winner Abebe Bikila wear on his feet?

22 Which swimming event was introduced to the Olympics in 1984?

23 Who won gold in the women's singles in tennis in 1988?

24 Which British skater won gold in 1980?

25 What are the five colours of the Olympic rings?

26 In 1984 who won gold in the men's 800 metres and the 1500 metres?

27 In which country were the first modern Olympics held in 1896?

28 Who won the women's 400-metre hurdles in Barcelona in 1992?

29 How many judges out of nine gave Torvill & Dean full marks for artistic impression in 1984?

30 Who was Britain's first-ever gold medallist in a throwing event in 1984?

Answers | **Football Pot Luck 1** *(see Quiz 18)*

1 1940s. 2 Red. 3 Luton Town. 4 The Netherlands. 5 Racecourse Ground.
6 Matt Le Tissier. 7 Aston Villa. 8 Nottingham Forest. 9 Walsall. 10 Real Madrid.
11 1930s. 12 Jurgen Sommer. 13 The Republic of Ireland. 14 Gianluigi Lentini.
15 Nottingham Forest. 16 Sheffield Wednesday. 17 Todd. 18 Derby County. 19
Peter. 20 Alan Ball. 21 Swansea City. 22 Marco van Basten. 23 Manchester City.
24 United. 25 Scotland. 26 Law. 27 Greece. 28 West Ham Utd. 29 Rangers.
30 White.

1 In which decade did Charlton Athletic first win the FA Cup?
2 What colour are Barnsley's home socks?
3 Which was Iain Dowie's first league club?
4 Arjen Robben is from which country?
5 What is Wrexham's ground called?
6 Which England player was born on Guernsey in 1968?
7 Cyrille Regis and Kevin Richardson were in the same team at which club?
8 Which club did Peter Shilton join on leaving Stoke City?
9 Which club's nickname is the Saddlers?
10 Julio Iglesias was reserve team goalkeeper with which club?
11 In which decade was Ron Atkinson born?
12 Who was the regular keeper in QPR's 1995–96 relegation season?
13 Which country did Terry Mancini play for?
14 Which £13 million player was involved in a 1993 car crash?
15 Bob McKinlay set a League appearance record at which club?
16 Which team were beaten 2–1 by Arsenal in the 1993 FA Cup Final?
17 Which Colin became Middlesbrough manager in 1991?
18 Craig Short joined Everton from which club?
19 What is Chris Armstrong's middle name?
20 Chairman Francis Lee flew to Marbella to sign which holidaymaker as his club manager?
21 Who were champions of Coca-Cola League 1 in 2007–08?
22 Which former AC Milan striker was Dutch coach in the 2006 World Cup finals?
23 Horton and Campbell have both managed which club?
24 What is the second word in Ayr's name?
25 Which country has Gordon Strachan played for?
26 Which Denis was European Footballer of the Year in 1964?
27 Which country do AEK Athens come from?
28 With which club did Paul Ince make his League debut?
29 Which club did Paul Gascoigne join on leaving Lazio?
30 Which veteran striker Steve was Hereford's top league scorer in 1995–96?

Answers | Olympics *(see Quiz 17)*

1 19.30 secs. 2 Baseball/Softball. 3 BMX. 4 Bronze. 5 1908. 6 1980 and 1984. 7 Hockey. 8 United States. 9 Bob Beamon's. 10 Lennox Lewis. 11 West Germany. 12 Linford Christie. 13 Same person. 14 Nadia Comaneci. 15 Tokyo. 16 Ben Johnson. 17 Mary Decker. 18 David Wilkie. 19 Ice skating. 20 Sarajevo. 21 Nothing. 22 Synchronized swimming. 23 Steffi Graf. 24 Robin Cousins. 25 Black, yellow, red, green, blue. 26 Sebastian Coe. 27 Greece. 28 Sally Gunnell. 29 Nine. 30 Tessa Sanderson.

1 Who sang with the Checkmates?
2 Which film did "The Harry Lime Theme" come from?
3 Which girl was on the other side of "All I Have to Do Is Dream" for the Everly Brothers?
4 Which first No. 1 for Adam Faith was a question?
5 What was the 50s' best-selling single?
6 Who took "Mary's Boy Child" in to the charts in the 50s?
7 Which 50s classic begins "I'm so young and you're so old"?
8 Which singer was married to Debbie Reynolds and Elizabeth Taylor?
9 Who had a Secret Love in 1954?
10 Who sang "Yes Tonight Josephine"?
11 Which singer with which group had a hit with "Livin' Doll"?
12 Whose girl was Only Sixteen at No. 1 in 1959?
13 Which instrumentalist hit the top with "Let's Have Another Party"?
14 Which Buddy Holly hit was the first after his death and went to No. 1?
15 Who told the Story of His Life in 1958?
16 Who went from the Green Door to the Garden of Eden?
17 Who had a 1955 No. 1 with "Unchained Melody"?
18 Who had a "Dreamboat" in 1955?
19 Which 50s musical provided Vic Damone with a 1958 No. 1?
20 What does Anne Shelton finally sing after "Lay Down Your Arms" in her 1956 No. 1?
21 In which American state was Buddy Holly's fatal plane crash?
22 By what name was J. P. Richardson better known?
23 Which Carole was believed to be the subject of Neil Sedaka's "Oh Carol"?
24 What did Frankie Laine want you to do in his 1953 Christmas No. 1?
25 Which Shirley had her first British No. 1 in 1959?
26 What was wrong with the "Wings" which The Stargazers took to No. 1 in 1953?
27 This Perry Como No. 1 was used by Quality Street sweets in a TV advert.
28 What was "Cupid" in Connie Francis's No. 1 hit of 1958?
29 Which popular foreign-sounding radio station broadcast a sheet music Top 20?
30 What was the last UK No. 1 hit of the decade by Emile Ford & The Checkmates?

Answers	Movies Pot Luck 1 *(see Quiz 20)*

1 Sylvester Stallone. 2 Ridley Scott. 3 Whoopi Goldberg. 4 1930s. 5 River Phoenix. 6 Roberto Benigni. 7 Stowe. 8 2 hours. 9 Shu. 10 T. S. Eliot. 11 Captain John Miller. 12 Andrew. 13 Rita Moreno. 14 Canadian. 15 Josh. 16 Jane Campion. 17 Christopher Plummer. 18 "Whatever Will be, Will be" ("Que Sera, Sera"). 19 The English Patient. 20 Jodie Foster. 21 1990s. 22 Agutter. 23 Peter Weir. 24 Helen Mirren. 25 Joe DiMaggio. 26 Joel & Ethan. 27 Thoroughbred. 28 Wall Street. 29 Charles Bronson. 30 Jared Leto.

1 Who turned down Eddie Murphy's role in *Beverly Hills Cop*?
2 Who directed *Thelma and Louise*?
3 How is Caryn Johnson better known?
4 In which decade was *Mr Smith Goes to Washington* released?
5 *Indiana Jones and the Last Crusade* and *Speakers* both feature which actor?
6 Who won the Best Actor Oscar for *La Vita e Bella* (*Life is Beautiful*)?
7 Which Madeleine starred in *The Last of the Mohicans*?
8 To the nearest hour, how long does *The Birds* last?
9 Which Elisabeth starred in *Leaving Las Vegas*?
10 Which poet's life story is told in *Tom and Viv*?
11 What was the name of Tom Hanks's character in *Saving Private Ryan*?
12 What is actress Drew Barrymore's real first name?
13 Who played Anita in *West Side Story*?
14 What nationality does Juliette Binoche play in *The English Patient*?
15 What was the name of Tom Hanks's character in *Big*?
16 Who directed *The Piano* and *The Portrait of a Lady*?
17 *International Velvet* and *Dreamscape* both featured which actor?
18 Which song won Best Song Oscar for *The Man Who Knew Too Much*?
19 Anthony Minghella won his first Best Director Oscar for which movie?
20 Who won the Best Actress Oscar for *The Accused*?
21 *Goodfellas* was released in which decade?
22 Which Jenny starred in *Logan's Run*?
23 Who directed *The Truman Show*?
24 Who played George III's consort in *The Madness of King George*?
25 Which baseball star did Marilyn Monroe marry in 1954?
26 What are the first names of the filmmakers, the Coens?
27 What breed of horse was Seabiscuit?
28 In which film did Michael Douglas declare that "Greed is good"?
29 Who played Bernardo in *The Magnificent Seven*?
30 In 2016, which Oscar winner portrayed The Joker in *Suicide Squad*?

Answers	Pop: The 1950s (see Quiz 19)

1 Emile Ford. 2 The Third Man. 3 Claudette. 4 "What Do You Want?". 5 "Rock Around the Clock". 6 Harry Belafonte. 7 Diana. 8 Eddie Fisher. 9 Doris Day. 10 Johnny Ray. 11 Cliff Richard and the Drifters. 12 Craig Douglas. 13 Winifred Atwell. 14 "It Doesn't Matter Anymore". 15 Michael Holliday. 16 Frankie Vaughan. 17 Jimmy Young. 18 Alma Cogan. 19 My Fair Lady ("On the Street Where You Live"). 20 "And surrender to mine". 21 Iowa. 22 The Big Bopper. 23 Carole King. 24 Answer Me. 25 Bassey. 26 They were Broken. 27 Magic Moments. 28 Stupid. 29 Radio Luxembourg. 30 What Do You Want to Make Those Eyes at Me for.

1 What is unusual about the blood-spatter analyst Dexter Morgan?
2 Which was the first city to have a CSI spin-off?
3 In which district of London was *The Chinese Detective* set?
4 Alice is Idris Elba's secret in which BBC crime drama?
5 What was the profession of David Gradley's partner in *Zodiac*?
6 Which actor played *Cribb*?
7 Which actor links *Dangerfield* to *Casualty*?
8 What was Dangerfield's occupation?
9 Who did Eddie Shoestring work for?
10 What was the subject of *The Defenders*?
11 Which American drama series starred, among others, Jimmy Smitz and Susan Dey?
12 Which make of car does Morse drive?
13 Micky Spillane's "Mike Hammer" was played by which actor?
14 Which detective was played by William Conrad?
15 Who portrayed Rumpole of the Bailey?
16 What was the subject of *The Knock*?
17 Which agent did Robert Stack play in *The Untouchables*?
18 Who did Paul Drake work for?
19 Who preceded Tim Piggott-Smith as *The Chief*?
20 Which TV series took its title from the cockney rhyming slang for Flying Squad?
21 Al Waxman played which character in *Cagney and Lacey*?
22 Which Frank was a DI in *The Bill*?
23 Which series starred Cybil Shepherd and Bruce Willis?
24 In which European city is *Cadfael* filmed?
25 Rupert Davies and Richard Harris both played which TV character?
26 Which series starred Daniel Benzali as a defence lawyer?
27 In *NYPD Blue*, which character's son had joined the police before being killed in a bar?
28 Edward Hardwicke and David Burke have both played which character?
29 Which court drama is an updated version of *Crown Court*?
30 Nick Ross presents which real-life crime programme?

Answers	**Football Pot Luck 2** *(see Quiz 22)*

1 Manuel. 2 Red and black. 3 Middlesbrough. 4 Ruud Gullit and Mark Hughes.
5 Springfield Park. 6 Blackburn Rovers. 7 Chesterfield. 8 Sampdoria. 9 Bristol.
10 McNeill. 11 Eike Immel. 12 1920s. 13 Manchester City. 14 Clive Allen. 15 Wolves. 16 Wales. 17 Nigel Martyn. 18 David Pleat. 19 Paul. 20 1950s. 21 Senegal. 22 Didier Drogba. 23 Blanchflower. 24 Colombia. 25 Manchester Utd. 26 Everton. 27 1890s. 28 Bari. 29 The Republic of Ireland. 30 Kevin Keegan.

1 What is Neuer's first name? Clue: he's German.
2 What are the two main colours on Bournemouth's home shirts?
3 What was Colin Cooper's first League club?
4 The gate for a Paul Elliott benefit game in July 1995 was boosted by which two new Chelsea signings?
5 What is Wigan Athletic's ground called?
6 Kevin Moran and Colin Hendry were in the same team at which club?
7 Who are nicknamed the Spireites?
8 Which club did David Platt leave to join Arsenal?
9 In which city was Gary Mabbutt born?
10 Which Billy became Aston Villa manager in 1986?
11 Who played every game in goal in Manchester City's 1995–96 relegation season?
12 In which decade did Cardiff first win the FA Cup?
13 Eddie Large was a trainee at which club?
14 Which Tottenham Hotspur player was the First Division's leading scorer in 1986–87?
15 Derek Parkin set a League appearance record at which club?
16 Which country did Tony Norman play for?
17 Who was the regular goalkeeper in Crystal Palace's 1994–95 relegation season?
18 Luton Town chairman David Kohler demanded £300,000 compensation after which manager moved?
19 What is Teddy Sheringham's middle name?
20 In which decade was Dave Beasant born?
21 Which African nation reached the 2002 World Cup quarter-finals?
22 Who was the leading goal scorer in the Premier League in 2006–07?
23 Which Danny of Tottenham Hotspur won the Footballer of the Year award in 1961?
24 Which country's fullback was shot dead after scoring an own goal in the 1994 World Cup tournament?
25 Which club has a fanzine called *United We Stand*?
26 Pat Nevin and Kevin Sheedy were in the same side at which club?
27 In which decade did Nottingham Forest first win the FA Cup?
28 Which club did David Platt join on leaving Aston Villa?
29 Which country did Chris Hughton play for?
30 Which manager said, "Newcastle supporters have, in the last few years, been thick through thick and thin"?

Answers | TV: Crime 1 *(see Quiz 21)*

1 He's a serial killer. 2 Miami. 3 Limehouse. 4 Luther. 5 An astrologer. 6 Alan Dobie. 7 Nigel le Valliant. 8 Forensic Pathologist. 9 Radio West. 10 The American legal system. 11 LA Law. 12 Jaguar. 13 Stacey Keach. 14 Frank Cannon. 15 Leo McKern. 16 Customs & Excise. 17 Elliot Ness. 18 Perry Mason. 19 Martin Shaw. 20 The Sweeney (Sweeney Todd) 21 Lt Burt Samuels. 22 Frank Burnside. 23 Moonlighting. 24 Budapest. 25 Maigret. 26 Murder One. 27 Det. Andy Sipowicz. 28 Dr Watson. 29 Verdict. 30 Crimewatch.

1 What was Engelbert Humperdinck's first single?
2 Who had a hit with "Sugar Sugar"?
3 Which 60s band started life as The Mann-Hug Blues Brothers?
4 Who took "You Really Got Me" to No. 1 in 1964?
5 Which group included Tony Hicks and Graham Nash?
6 Who recorded the album *Pet Sounds*?
7 Which group had Judith Durham as lead singer?
8 Which trio included the two Clusky brothers?
9 Who was Tommy James's backing group?
10 Who were famous for their Tottenham Sound?
11 Which satellite was a hit for the Tornados?
12 Which 60s group included Carl Wayne and Roy Wood?
13 Whose first No. 1 was "Sweets for My Sweet"?
14 Which instrumentalist in the Honeycombs was female?
15 Who had a 1965 No. 1 with "Go Now"?
16 Which Group included Steve and Muff Winwood?
17 How many people sang "Concrete and Clay"?
18 What was Wayward on Frank Ifield's 1963 No. 1?
19 Who spent the early part of her career with brother Tom plus Tim Field before going solo?
20 Who was lead singer with Amen Corner?
21 Which trio, known by their first names, were "Leaving on a Jet Plane"?
22 What was Lonnie Donegan's "Old Man"?
23 What was Del Shannon's only No. 1?
24 Ray and Dave Davies co-founded which 1960s group?
25 In what year was Jimi Hendrix's first album released in the UK?
26 Who had a No. 1 hit in the UK and the US in 1965 with "You've Lost That Lovin' Feelin'"?
27 What did the Beatles have a "Ticket to"?
28 Can you name the sexy song Jane Birkin and Serge Gainsbourg had a No. 1 hit with?
29 Which Beatles "ballad" was the Fab Four's 17th and last No. 1?
30 What did the Rolling Stones want us to "Get Off" in their November 1965 No. 1 hit?

Answers | Movies Pot Luck 2 *(see Quiz 24)*

1 Anthony Perkins. 2 William. 3 Crowe. 4 Victor Fleming. 5 Tatiana Romanova.
6 Denys Finch-Hatton. 7 Ming the Merciless. 8 1970s. 9 Bean. 10 Los Angeles.
11 Jason Gould (her real-life son). 12 139 minutes. 13 Malcolm McDowell. 14 John Lasseter. 15 Bowie. 16 The Avengers. 17 Three. 18 Howard Keel. 19 Dr Evil.
20 Tomlinson. 21 Tony Curtis. 22 Tony Scott. 23 Claudette Colbert. 24 1940s.
25 Joe Pesci. 26 Richard Pryor. 27 Sean and Alexandra Astin. 28 Kathleen Turner.
29 Some Like It Hot. 30 Chris Evans.

1 *Desire under the Elms* and *Psycho III* both feature which actor?
2 What is the first name of Brad Pitt, who uses his middle name in the movies?
3 Which Russell starred in *LA Confidential*?
4 Who won the Best Director Oscar for *Gone with the Wind*?
5 What was the name of the Bond girl in *From Russia with Love*?
6 What was the name of Robert Redford's character in *Out of Africa*?
7 What was the name of the villain in *Flash*?
8 In which decade was *Mean Streets* released?
9 Which Sean starred in *GoldenEye*?
10 Where does Rowan Atkinson's *Bean* take place?
11 Who played Barbra Streisand's son in *The Prince of Tides*?
12 Within twenty minutes, how long does *Apocalypse Now* last?
13 Who did Stanley Kubrick cast in the lead role in *A Clockwork Orange*?
14 Who directed *Toy Story*?
15 Which David starred in *Labyrinth*?
16 A character named Sir August de Wynter appeared in which film?
17 How many Oscars did Woody Allen win for *Annie Hall*?
18 Who played opposite Betty Hutton in *Annie Get Your Gun*?
19 Who is the bad character in *Austin Powers: International Man of Mystery*?
20 Which David featured in *Mary Poppins*?
21 Who played Albert DeSalvo in *The Boston Strangler*?
22 Who directed *Top Gun*?
23 Who won the Best Actress Oscar for *It Happened One Night*?
24 In which decade was Disney's *Pinocchio* released?
25 *Home Alone* and *Lethal Weapon 3* both feature which actor?
26 Which comedian, who died in 2005, was Gene Wilder's partner in *Stir Crazy*?
27 Which father and daughter starred in *The Lord of the Rings: The Return of the King*?
28 Who was the voice of Jessica Rabbit in *Who Framed Roger Rabbit*?
29 In which movie does Sugar Kane appear?
30 Who plays Captain America in 2016's *Civil War*?

Answers	Pop: The 1960s *(see Quiz 23)*

1 "Release Me". 2 The Archies. 3 Manfred Mann. 4 The Kinks. 5 The Hollies. 6 The Beach Boys. 7 The Seekers. 8 The Bachelors. 9 The Shondelles. 10 The Dave Clark Five. 11 "Telstar". 12 The Move. 13 The Searchers. 14 The drummer. 15 The Moody Blues. 16 The Spencer Davis Group. 17 Six (Unit Four Plus Two). 18 Wind. 19 Dusty Springfield. 20 Andy Fairweather-Low. 21 Peter, Paul and Mary. 22 A dustman. 23 "Runaway". 24 The Kinks. 25 1967. 26 The Righteous Brothers. 27 Ride. 28 "Je t'aime… moi non plus". 29 The Ballad of John & Yoko. 30 Their Cloud.

1 Which former teen pop star became *Doctor Who*'s assistant in 2005?
2 What was the first name of Captain Picard in *Star Trek: The Next Generation*?
3 Where was *Quatermass II* set?
4 Who was the creator of *TekWar*?
5 Which star of *The Color Purple* is a regular in *Star Trek: The Next Generation*?
6 In The *X-Files* what is Mulder's first name?
7 In *Babylon 5*, Londo Molari is the Ambassador for which race?
8 Who played Frank Bach in *Dark Skies*?
9 What was the name of Michael Knight's robot car?
10 In which series did Lori Singer play an on-line crime-buster?
11 Who on Red Dwarf is Holly?
12 Which creature did Dr David Banner become when stressed?
13 Who did Lorne Greene play in *Battlestar Galactica*?
14 Which series featured Tweaky?
15 Which series written by Ray Bradbury starred Rock Hudson?
16 Where do the *Sliders* slide to?
17 What was the sixties SF series starring James Darren?
18 What, speaking chemically, were *Sapphire and Steel* supposed to be?
19 Where would you have found Old Bailey selling Rook stew at the Floating Market?
20 Which futuristic organization featured in the science-fiction drama *UFO*?
21 Who created *Space Precinct*?
22 Which character did Sally Knyvette play in *Blake's Seven*?
23 Which hero was aided by the Destiny Angels?
24 In which series did you meet the character Duncan Macleod?
25 What number was Patrick McGoohan?
26 In which series did Roddy McDowall play a chimpanzee?
27 Which electronic hero was aided by Desi Arnaz Jr?
28 Which character did George Takei play in *Star Trek*?
29 How were Homo Superior more commonly known?
30 in 2013, Andrea Riseborough starred opposite which Tom in *Oblivion?*

Answers | **Football Pot Luck 3** *(see Quiz 26)*

1 Alan Cork. 2 Red and white. 3 Aston Villa. 4 1914. 5 Torquay Utd. 6 Neal.
7 Hamilton Academical. 8 Leeds Utd. 9 Bolton. 10 1920s. 11 Alan Wright.
12 Chelsea. 13 Man City. 14 Liverpool. 15 Manchester Utd. 16 David Ginola.
17 Southampton. 18 Ossie Ardiles. 19 Craig Forrest. 20 Germany. 21 Marcello
Lippi. 22 France. 23 Sheffield Wednesday. 24 1960s. 25 Blackburn Rovers.
26 Robert. 27 Arsenal. 28 Leicester City. 29 White. 30 England.

1 Which player with 430 games set a Wimbledon appearance record?
2 What colours are Brentford's home shirts?
3 What was Tony Daley's first League club?
4 To five years each way, when did Burnley first win the FA Cup?
5 Who plays at home at Plainmoor?
6 Which Phil became Bolton manager in 1985?
7 Which team are known as the Accies?
8 Which club did Richard Jobson join on leaving Oldham?
9 In which town was Nat Lofthouse born?
10 In which decade was Tommy Docherty born?
11 Which defender played in all Aston Villa's 1995–96 League games?
12 Dave Beasant and Andy Townsend were in the same team at which club?
13 Which league club did Sergio Agüero play for in 2015-16?
14 Stan Boardman was once on the books of which club?
15 Which team were beaten 3–2 by Arsenal in the 1979 FA Cup Final?
16 Which Newcastle player was sent off in a 1996 Coca Cola quarter-final after clashing with Arsenal's Lee Dixon?
17 Francis Benali has played 200+ games for which club?
18 Which Tottenham Hotspur manager signed Jurgen Klinsmann?
19 Who was the regular goalkeeper for Ipswich in their 1994–95 relegation season?
20 Which country has Fredi Bobic played for?
21 Who was coach of Italy in the 2006 World Cup finals?
22 Against which country did David Beckham win his 100th England cap?
23 Which club did Nigel Worthington leave to join Leeds Utd?
24 In which decade was Robert Lee born?
25 Which club has a fanzine called *Loadsamoney*?
26 What is Keith Gillespie's middle name?
27 Brian Marwood and Martin Hayes were in the same side at which club?
28 Which team were beaten 3–1 by Wolves in the 1949 FA Cup Final?
29 What colour are Portsmouth's home shorts?
30 Which country did Mike Bailey play for?

Answers | TV: Sci-Fi 1 *(see Quiz 25)*

1 Billie Piper. 2 Jean-Luc. 3 In a chemical plant. 4 William Shatner. 5 Whoopi Goldberg. 6 Fox. 7 Centauri. 8 J. T. Walsh. 9 KITT. 10 VR5. 11 Ship's computer. 12 The Incredible Hulk. 13 Adama. 14 Buck Rogers. 15 The Martian Chronicles. 16 Parallel Universes. 17 The Time Tunnel. 18 Elements. 19 Neverwhere. 20 SHADO. 21 Gerry Anderson. 22 Jenna. 23 Captain Scarlet. 24 Highlander. 25 6. 26 Planet of the Apes. 27 Automan. 28 Sulu. 29 The Tomorrow People. 30 Cruise.

1 Who had a best-selling album called *Rumours*?
2 Whose first No. 1 was "Tiger Feet"?
3 Who had Tony Orlando as their lead singer?
4 Who had a "Year of Decision" in 1974?
5 Whose first hit was "Get Down and Get with It"?
6 Which instrument did Marc Bolan play on "Ride a White Swan"?
7 Which pop sensation included Derek and Alan Longmuir?
8 Which record label were Wings' early records on?
9 Which Sweet No. 1 began with police sirens wailing?
10 Who was the original drummer with the ELO?
11 Who sang about Pretty Little Angel Eyes in 1978?
12 How many founder members of the Eagles were there?
13 Which musical instrument did Karen Carpenter play?
14 Whose debut album was *New Boots and Panties!*?
15 Which 1978 Bee Gees album was the bestseller of all time at that time?
16 Which Brotherhood of Man No. 1 shares its name with an opera?
17 Which group had Errol Brown as lead singer?
18 Which rock legend died in August 1977?
19 Which US state did Pussycat sing about?
20 How was the chart-topper Detective Ken Hutchinson better known?
21 Which Rick played keyboards for Yes?
22 Which actor had a No. 1 with "Wand'rin' Star"?
23 Who had his only No. 1 posthumously with "Voodoo Chile"?
24 What was the question asked by Telly Savalas in his only No. 1?
25 Which TV station aired with "Video Killed the Radio Star" as its first ever item?
26 Can you recall the 1970 No. 1 hit song from the England football team?
27 Sweet got their first and only UK No. 1 hit in 1973. Name their chart topper.
28 Which Lieutenant took "Mouldy Old Dough" to No. 1 in the music charts?
29 Who was "canning the can" at No. 1 in January 1973?
30 Which "Grandad" had a No. 1 hit in January 1971?

1 What is Liam Neeson's real first name?
2 At what sport did Paul Newman excel?
3 Who won the Best Actor Oscar for *Stalag 17*?
4 Who directed *Sense and Sensibility*?
5 In which decade was the epic *Samson and Delilah* released?
6 Which Ray starred in *Field of Dreams*?
7 What is Harry's surname in *When Harry Met Sally*?
8 Who played Smee in *Hook*?
9 In which state is *The Green Mile* set?
10 Which actor links *Tremors* and *Flatliners*?
11 To the nearest hour, how long does *The Blues Brothers* last?
12 Who starred as Professor X in 2016's *X Men Apocalypse*?
13 *Taps* and *We're No Angels* featured which actor?
14 In which film did a character named Robbie Hart appear?
15 Which Bernard featured in *Moonraker*?
16 Whose real name was Ethel Zimmerman?
17 Which composer did Tom Hulce play in a 1984 Milos Forman film?
18 What is the last name of Bill from *Bill and Ted's Excellent Adventure*?
19 Who directed *Shine*?
20 In which country was Bruce Willis born?
21 What was Katharine Hepburn's first film, in 1932?
22 In which decade was *Raging Bull* released?
23 Which Frances starred in *Fargo*?
24 Who won the Best Director Oscar for *Ben Hur*?
25 Which Stephen did John Hurt play in *Scandal*?
26 In which year was *Chicken Little* released in the UK?
27 Which Madeline was a regular partner in Mel Brooks's movies?
28 Which director Roger links Bardot, Deneuve and Fonda?
29 Which actress links *Hannah and Her Sisters and Beaches*?
30 Which Oscar did Kevin Costner win for *Dances with Wolves*?

Answers	Pop: The 1970s *(see Quiz 27)*

1 Fleetwood Mac. 2 Mud. 3 Dawn. 4 The Three Degrees. 5 Slade. 6 Electric Guitar. 7 The Bay City Rollers. 8 Apple. 9 Blockbuster. 10 Bev Bevan. 11 Showaddywaddy. 12 Four. 13 Drums. 14 Ian Dury and the Blockheads. 15 Saturday Night Fever. 16 "Figaro". 17 Hot Chocolate. 18 Elvis Presley. 19 Mississippi. 20 David Soul – Hutch from Starsky and Hutch. 21 Wakeman. 22 Lee Marvin. 23 Jimi Hendrix. 24 If. 25 MTV. 26 Back Home. 27 Blockbuster. 28 Lieutenant Pigeon. 29 Suzi Quatro. 30 Clive Dunn.

1 Hywel Bennett played which layabout in a series which lasted 14 years?
2 In which English county is *The Vicar of Dibley* set?
3 Which series starred Geoffrey Palmer and Dame Judy Dench as a middle-aged couple?
4 Who went from *Solo* to become *The Mistress*?
5 In *For the Love of Ada*, who were in love?
6 Who was Bilko's commanding officer, played by Paul Ford?
7 Who play the *Babes in the Wood*?
8 How old was Adrian Mole when he wrote his Secret Diary?
9 In *Sykes,* how were Eric and Hatty related?
10 Who plays a Trotter brother and Gary Sparrow?
11 Which Dame starred in *A Fine Romance*?
12 What national motoring organization was portrayed in *The Last Salute*?
13 Who in the series *Sitting Pretty* was described as "the Jackie Onassis of Bethnal Green"?
14 What was the setting for *The Brittas Empire*?
15 Which rap singer plays the title role in *The Fresh Prince of Bel-Air*?
16 In which comedy series did a giant cat terrorize London?
17 Who played the respective children of the rivals in *Never the Twain*?
18 What ministry did Jim Hacker run before becoming PM?
19 What was the name of Frankie Howerd's first TV series in 1952?
20 Who are *The Detectives*?
21 Who were "Just Good Friends"?
22 Which Likely Lad ended up a patient in *Only When I Laugh*?
23 In *Goodnight Sweetheart* which year is the hero transported back to?
24 What was the sequel to *Up Pompeii!*?
25 In *The Growing Pains of PC Penrose*, which actor played the title role?
26 What was the name of Lucille Ball's husband who starred with her in *I Love Lucy?*
27 Which army sergeant turned antiques dealer?
28 Who starred as Reginald Perrin?
29 Which *Fifteen-to-One* presenter produced *Bless This House*?
30 What are Father Ted's equally odd colleagues called?

Answers	**Football Pot Luck 4** *(see Quiz 30)*

1 LA Galaxy. 2 White. 3 Crewe Alexandra. 4 1960s. 5 Stockport County.
6 Newcastle Utd. 7 The Grecians. 8 Eintracht Frankfurt. 9 1911. 10 Little. 11 Billy Bonds. 12 Coventry City. 13 Australia. 14 David Seaman. 15 Manchester Utd.
16 WBA. 17 Doncaster Rovers. 18 Bryan Gunn. 19 England. 20 Malcolm.
21 2004. 22 South Korea. 23 Notts County. 24 1940s. 25 Hereford Utd.
26 Alexander. 27 Derby County. 28 Reading. 29 Black. 30 Windsor Park.

1 Which US team did Ashley Cole play for in 2016?
2 What colour are the home shorts of both Bristol clubs?
3 What was Bruce Grobbelaar's first league club?
4 In which decade was Tony Adams born?
5 Who plays at home at Edgeley Park?
6 Which club was Malcolm Macdonald with when he was First Divison leading scorer in 1974–75?
7 What is the nickname of Exeter City?
8 Which club did Tony Yeboah leave to join Leeds?
9 To five years either way, when did Bradford City first win the FA Cup?
10 Which player and manager Brian was born in Peterlee in November 1953?
11 Who played 663 times to set West Ham Utd's League appearance record?
12 Kevin Gallacher and Paul Furlong were in the same team at which club?
13 Ned Zelic has captained which country?
14 Who was the only ever-present league player for Arsenal in 1995–96?
15 Which team was beaten 2–0 by Bolton in the 1958 FA Cup Final?
16 Bryan Robson was at which League club when he made his England debut?
17 Which club did comedian Charlie Williams play for in the 1950s?
18 Who was the regular keeper for Norwich City in their 1994–95 relegation season?
19 San Marino hit a goal in nine seconds in 1993 against which team?
20 What is Jason Wilcox's middle name?
21 In which year was Sir Bobby Robson sacked as Newcastle United manager?
22 Which Asian country has gone furthest in the World Cup?
23 Which club did Dean Yates leave to join Derby County?
24 In which decade was Bobby Gould born?
25 Which club has a fanzine called *Talking Bull*?
26 What is Andy Cole's middle name?
27 Geraint Williams and Dean Saunders were in the same side at which club?
28 Which was Neil Webb's first League club?
29 What colour are Brentford's home shorts?
30 At which ground do Linfield play?

Answers | TV: Comedy 1 *(see Quiz 29)*

1 Shelley. 2 Oxfordshire. 3 A Fine Romance. 4 Felicity Kendall. 5 Ada Crosswell & Walter Bingly. 6. Colonel Hall. 7 Samantha Janus, Denise Van Outen, Natalie Walter. 8 13¾. 9 Brother and sister. 10 Nicholas Lyndhurst. 11 Judi Dench. 12 The AA. 13 Annie Briggs. 14 A leisure centre. 15 Will Smith. 16 The Goodies. 17 Julia Watson & Robert Kermode. 18 Administrative Affairs. 19 The Howerd Crowd. 20 Jasper Carrott & Robert Powell. 21 Vince & Penny. 22 James Bolam. 23 1943. 24 Whoops Baghdad. 25 Paul Greenwood. 26 Desi Arnaz. 27 Windsor Davies. 28 Leonard Rossiter. 29 William G. Stewart. 30 Dougal & Jack.

1 What did Dora Bryan want for Christmas in 1963?
2 In which decade did Bing Crosby's "White Christmas" first enter the UK charts?
3 What did John Lennon's "Happy Christmas" have in brackets in 1980?
4 According to Adam Faith, what was in a Christmas Shop in 1960?
5 Who said "Please Come Home for Christmas" in 1994?
6 Which Christmas Rock has been a hit for Max Bygraves and Chubby Checker with Bobby Rydell?
7 Who wished It Could be Christmas Every Day in 1973?
8 What was Johnny Mathis's 1976 Christmas hit?
9 Which group beat Bieber to the UK Xmas Number One in 2015?
10 Who said "All I Want for Christmas is You" in 1994?
11 Which comedian was "Rockin' Around the Christmas Tree" in 1987?
12 Which Snowman did the Cocteau Twins sing about in 1993?
13 Who covered the Carpenters' "Santa Claus is Comin' to Town" in 1985?
14 Where was Santa Claus according to Spitting Image in 1986?
15 Who pleaded with Santa Baby in the 1990s?
16 Who sang with the Smurfs on "Christmas in Smurfland" in 1978?
17 Whose "Christmas Alphabet" went to No. 1 in 1955?
18 Who had a Wonderful Christmas Time in 1979?
19 What is the theme song from *The Snowman*?
20 Who had "White Christmas" on the other side of "Too Risky"?
21 The winner of which show 2005–07 also had the UK Christmas No. 1?
22 "Sound of the Underground" was the first Christmas No. 1 for which group?
23 Robbie Williams and Nicole Kidman covered whose No. 1 "Something Stupid"?
24 What did Bob the Builder ask if he could "Fix" in 2000?
25 What were Mud "This Christmas" in their 1974 Christmas No. 1 hit?
26 Can you name the School Choir who topped the charts at Christmas 1980?
27 Which Johnny Mathis classic was the 1976 Christmas No. 1 hit.
28 What were the Spice Girls saying with their 1998 Christmas No. 1?
29 Name the Westlife song which was the last Christmas No. 1 of the 20th century.
30 Which Christmas No. 1 from Dave Edmunds was his only ever No. 1 hit?

Answers | Movies Pot Luck 4 *(see Quiz 32)*

1 Wes Craven. 2 Jane Seymour. 3 1950s. 4 Hamilton. 5 Kathy Bates. 6 Live and Let Die. 7 K. 8 Billy Wilder. 9 Days of Wine and Roses. 10 Gina Lollobrigida.
11 Sam Neill. 12 Cher. 13 "We May Never Love Like This Again". 14 Dirty Dancing.
15 Dudley Moore. 16 Richard Attenborough. 17 The Misfits. 18 Liam Neeson.
19 2 hours. 20 Alec Baldwin. 21 Baz Luhrmann. 22 1970s. 23 Nicolas Cage.
24 Collette. 25 Jane Seymour. 26 102. 27 Julie Kavner. 28 Vincente Minelli.
29 Vertigo. 30 Deadpool.

1 Who directed *Scream*?
2 How is Joyce Frankenberg better known?
3 In which decade was *Gigi* released?
4 Which Linda starred in *Dante's Peak*?
5 Who won the Best Actress Oscar for *Misery*?
6 In which film did Roger Moore first play 007?
7 What was the name of Tommy Lee Jones's character in *Men in Black*?
8 Who won the Best Director Oscar for *The Apartment*?
9 Used in *Breakfast at Tiffany's*, "Moon River" is the theme music from which film?
10 Who was "La Lollo"?
11 Who co-starred with Meryl Streep in *A Cry in the Dark*?
12 Who received her first Oscar nomination for *Silkwood*?
13 Which song won Best Song Oscar for *The Towering Inferno*?
14 In which film did a character named Johnny Castle appear?
15 Who replaced George Segal in Blake Edwards's comedy *10*?
16 Who directed Anthony Hopkins in *Shadowlands*?
17 What was Marilyn Monroe's last film?
18 Who plays the title role in *Michael Collins*?
19 To the nearest hour, how long does *The Bodyguard* last?
20 Which actor links the films *Alice* and *Malice*?
21 Who directed *Romeo + Juliet*?
22 In which decade was *Willy Wonka and the Chocolate Factory* released?
23 Who won the Best Actor Oscar for *Leaving Las Vegas*?
24 Which Toni starred in *Emma*?
25 Who played the Bond girl in *Live and Let Die*?
26 How many *Dalmations* were in the 2000 movie sequel starring Glenn Close?
27 Who is the voice of Marge Simpson in *The Simpsons Movie*?
28 Who won the Best Director Oscar for *Gigi*?
29 In which film did a character named Madeleine Elster appear?
30 Ryan Reynolds, in 2016, reigned supreme with which superhero?

Answers | **Pop: Christmas Records** *(see Quiz 31)*

1 A Beatle. 2 1970s. 3 "War is Over". 4 Lonely Pup. 5 Bon Jovi. 6 "Jingle Bell Rock". 7 Wizzard. 8 "When a Child is Born". 9 NHS Choir. 10 Mariah Carey. 11 Mel Smith. 12 Frosty. 13 Bruce Springsteen. 14 On the Dole. 15 Madonna. 16 Father Abraham. 17 Dickie Valentine. 18 Wings. 19 "Walking in the Air". 20 Jim Davidson. 21 X-Factor. 22 Girls Aloud. 23 Frank and Nancy Sinatra. 24 It. 25 Lonely. 26 St. Winifred's. 27 "When a Child is Born". 28 Goodbye. 29 "I Have a Dream/Seasons in the Sun". 30 "I Hear You Knockin'".

1 Who hosted the first series of Countdown after Richard Whiteley's death?
2 Who hosts *Pointless* with Alexander Armstrong?
3 Who preceded Des O'Connor as host of *Take Your Pick*?
4 Who presented *Bullseye*?
5 Who hosted *The Krypton Factor*?
6 Who co-hosted the first season of *Robot Wars* with Phillippa Forrester?
7 Who hosted *Punchlines*?
8 Who was the host of *Going for Gold*?
9 What was the children's version of *Criss Cross Quiz*?
10 How many celebrity guests appear each week on *Blankety Blank*?
11 What was the top prize on *Turner Round the World*?
12 Who originally presented *Dotto*?
13 Name the quiz featured on *Sunday Night at the London Palladium*.
14 Who was Larry Grayson's co-host on *The Generation Game*?
15 Who presented *Family Fortunes* after Bob Monkhouse?
16 Which game show has been chaired by both Robert Robinson and Bob Holness?
17 Which programme has been chaired by Max Robertson and Michael Parkinson?
18 Which trophy has been won by both an underground train driver and a cabbie?
19 Which show hosted by Bob Monkhouse required phone contestants to direct the shooting of an arrow at a target?
20 Glyn Daniel chaired which popular quiz in which an expert panel had to identify unusual objects?
21 Who had charge of the gong in the yes/no interlude on *Take Your Pick*?
22 Who was the first woman to present *Busman's Holiday*?
23 Which Channel 4 show was both presented and devised by Tim Vine?
24 Name the team captains on *Shooting Stars*.
25 What is Channel 5's gardening quiz called?
26 Who presides over the Channel 4 quiz *Fifteen-to-One*?
27 On *Countdown*, how many points are awarded for correctly solving the conundrum?
28 Who hosted *Wheel of Fortune* after Nicky Campbell and before John Leslie?
29 Who hosted *The $64,000 Question*?
30 What shape are the cells that hold the letters on the *Blockbusters* board?

Answers	Supermodels & Fashion *(see Quiz 34)*

1 Alba. **2** Donna Karan. **3** Jamie Hince. **4** Justin Timberlake. **5** Spanish. **6** Helena Christensen. **7** Magician. **8** Estee Lauder. **9** David Bailey. **10** Paula Hamilton. **11** Zandra Rhodes. **12** Pineapple. **13** Barbara Bach. **14** Edina Ronay. **15** Make-up. **16** John Frieda. **17** Kilt. **18** Kate Moss. **19** Mary Quant. **20** Versace. **24** Linda Evangelista. **22** Yves. **23** Revlon. **24** New Zealand. **25** Sandie Shaw. **26** Galliano. **27** Carnaby Street. **28** Vidal Sassoon. **29** Milan. **30** Westwood.

1 Elle MacPherson replaced which Jessica as the "Face of Revlon" in 2008?
2 Who is the DK from fashion group DKNY?
3 Kate Moss has been married to whom, since 2011?
4 Which singer/dancer became the face of Givenchy men's fragrances in 2008?
5 What is the nationality of Paco Rabanne?
6 Who was Michael Hutchence's girlfriend before Paula Yates?
7 What is the profession of Claudia Schiffer's fiance?
8 Which cosmetic house did Liz Hurley become the face of in 1995?
9 Which famous photographer was Marie Helvin married to?
10 Which model was famous for the ad in which she returned all her man's gifts but kept the car keys?
11 Which designer is well known for her pink hair?
12 Which fruit gave its name to ex-model Debbie Moore's dance studio?
13 Which former model did Ringo Starr marry?
14 Who is the designer daughter of food critic Egon Ronay?
15 In what area of fashion is Barbara Daly famous?
16 Which famous hairdresser married Lulu?
17 Which garment is Jean-Paul Gaultier famous for wearing?
18 Which supermodel's name has been linked with that of actor Johnny Depp?
19 Who said, "A woman is as young as her knees"?
20 Who designed Liz Hurley's famous "safety pin" dress?
21 Who was crowned Supermodel of the Year in 1995?
22 What is the first name of designer St Laurent?
23 Which cosmetic house did Charles Revson found?
24 Which is the home country of Mrs Rod Stewart, model Rachel Hunter?
25 Which pop singer was designer/TV presenter Jeff Banks married to?
26 What is the surname of Designer of the Year, John?
27 Which London street was famous for its 1960s boutiques?
28 Which hairdresser pioneered the geometric haircut in the 1960s?
29 Which Italian city is at the heart of the fashion industry?
30 Which Vivienne is famous for her outrageous designs?

Answers	**TV: Quiz & Game Shows** *(see Quiz 33)*

1 Des Lynam. 2 Richard Osman. 3 Michael Miles. 4 Jim Bowen. 5 Gordon Burns. 6 Jeremy Clarkson. 7 Lenny Bennet. 8 Henry Kelly. 9 Junior Criss-Cross Quiz. 10 Six. 11 Two round-the-world air tickets. 12 Robert Gladwell. 13 Beat the Clock. 14 Isla St Clair. 15 Les Dennis. 16 Call My Bluff. 17 Going for a Song. 18 The Mastermind Trophy. 19 The Golden Shot. 20 Animal, Vegetable, Mineral. 21 Alec Dane. 22 Sarah Kennedy. 23 Fluke. 24 Mark Lamarr and Ulrika Jonsson. 25 The Great Garden Game. 26 William G. Stewart. 27 Ten points. 28 Bradley Walsh. 29 Bob Monkhouse. 30 Hexagonal.

1 Which French club did Mo Johnston play for?
2 Thierry Henry played for which US club from 2010–2014?
3 What is the main stadium used for French home internationals?
4 David Ginola and George Weah have played for which French club?
5 Which team lost in the final of the 1992 European Cup Winners' Cup?
6 At what stage did France get knocked out of the 1994 World Cup?
7 Which French keeper joined Sunderland in 1996?
8 How many different clubs in France did Eric Cantona play for before coming to England?
9 At which Italian club did Michel Platini end his career?
10 At which ground do Marseille play?
11 Which team are known as the Greens – les Verts?
12 Which Arsenal and England player moved to Le Havre in the early 1990s?
13 Which Manuel holds the appearance record for France?
14 Which club won the 1996 European Cup Winners' Cup?
15 Which French club did Chris Waddle play for?
16 Which team scored within 27 seconds against France in the 1982 World Cup?
17 Which two English internationals helped Monaco to the Championship in 1988?
18 In which country did France first win the European Championship?
19 Which French Player of the Year in 1994 moved to England in 1995?
20 For which club has Eric Cantona made most appearances?
21 Which Frenchman was Rangers' manager for only eight months in 2006–07?
22 Who was the only Premiership player to score in a World Cup Final before 2010?
23 Which English club was managed by a Frenchman to win the UEFA Cup?
24 Which club did Mikael Silvestre join upon leaving Manchester United in 2008?
25 Which Frenchman has played for Fulham, Manchester United and Everton?
26 Can you name the former Premiership manager who managed France from 1998–99?
27 Which 1998 World Cup-winning defender joined Man. Utd in 2001?
28 Which ex-Premiership striker is France's leading goal scorer?
29 Which player joined Bolton Wanderers from FC Kaiserslautern in 2002?
30 Can you recall the World Cup-winning defender who signed for Chelsea in 1998?

---

1 What did T. Rex say "I Love" to do in 1976?

2 Which surname is shared by Iris and Deniece?

3 What was Abba's Anni-Frid Lyngstad's home country?

4 In which decade did Blondie have their first hit?

5 Who sang "Heart on My Sleeve" in 1976?

6 How is Christopher John Davidson better known?

7 Who had a No. 1 with "Eternal Flame"?

8 Which colour Lady provided a hit for David Soul in 1977?

9 In which decade was Lisa Stansfield born?

10 What time did Smokie say to Meet You in 1976?

11 Which song title linked Demis Roussos and Slik in 1976?

12 Which planet was a hit for Shocking Blue?

13 Whose first No. 1 was "Runaway" in 1961?

14 Who took "Ebeneezer Goode" to the top in 1992?

15 Which girl did Tyrannosaurus Rex sing about in 1968?

16 Who was the female member of the Seekers?

17 Who had a 90s album called *Our Town – Greatest Hits*?

18 Whose first hit was "Sylvia's Mother"?

19 Who had a 70s album called *Voulez-vous*?

20 Whose backing group was the Crickets?

21 What is the name of Rihanna's 2016 album?

22 What is the surname of the two sisters in All Saints?

23 Who did Elvis Presley name his private jet after?

24 What was special about the paintwork of John Lennon's 1965 Rolls-Royce?

25 Who had the best-selling 1984 album *Can't Slow Down*?

26 What was first unveiled at the Palais Royal Saloon in San Francisco in 1889?

27 In which show did Samantha Juste play the records?

28 Whose 70s instrumental album sold over two million copies in the UK?

29 Which Portuguese singing sensation was created by Steve Coogan?

30 Which Irish singer released "Don't Cry for Me Argentina" as a single in 1992?

| **Answers** | **Football: The French Connection** *(see Quiz 35)* |

1 Nantes. 2 New York Red Bulls. 3 Parc des Princes. 4 Paris St Germain. 5 Monaco. 6 They failed to qualify. 7 Lionel Perez. 8 Five. 9 Juventus. 10 Stade Velodrome. 11 St Etienne. 12 Graham Rix. 13 Amaros. 14 Paris St Germain. 15 Marseille. 16 England. 17 Mark Hateley and Glenn Hoddle. 18 France. 19 David Ginola. 20 Manchester Utd. 21 Paul Le Guen. 22 Emmanuel Petit. 23 Liverpool. 24 Arsenal. 25 Louis Saha. 26 Gerard Houllier. 27 Laurent Blanc. 28 Thierry Henry. 29 Youri Djorkaeff. 30 Marcel Desailly.

1 Who was 80 when he won for *The Sunshine Boys*?
2 What was Michael Douglas's first nomination as performer?
3 For which movie did Ralph Fiennes receive his second nomination?
4 Which film won best documentary at the 2016 Oscars?
5 Which 1999 Oscar nominee played Lord Alfred Douglas in *Wilde*?
6 What was Bing Crosby's profession in *Going My Way*?
7 Who won the first Oscar for Best Actor?
8 What was John Gielgud's profession in the movie *Arthur* for which he won an award?
9 When Brenda Fricker first won as Best Actress which winner played her son?
10 For which movie did Woody Harrelson receive his first nomination?
11 What is the total number of Oscars won by Errol Flynn, Peter Cushing and Richard Burton?
12 Who was nominated for *Cleopatra* but won a year later as Professor Higgins?
13 Jon Voight's first nomination was for which X-rated movie?
14 How many Oscars did Sean Connery win for James Bond?
15 What was Michael Douglas's first win as Actor?
16 Which King gave Nigel Hawthorne a nomination?
17 For which Spielberg movie was Anthony Hopkins nominated in 1997?
18 What was the second of Jack Nicholson's three nominations between 1973 and 1975?
19 Who was the first actor to be awarded two posthumous Oscars?
20 Which 80s winner and 90s nominee is the son of Jill Balcon and a poet laureate?
21 Whose first award was for playing Terry Malloy in a 50s classic?
22 For which movie did John Hurt receive a nomination after *Midnight Express*?
23 Who did Robert De Niro play in *The Godfather Part II*?
24 Which Spielberg movie gave Liam Neeson his first nomination?
25 Which Brit won Best Actor in a musical the same year that Julie Andrews won for *Mary Poppins*?
26 Which former star of ER was nominated for the first time in 2007?
27 Disney's *Pirates of the Caribbean* won which Johnny a nomination in 2003?
28 Who holds the record for most nominations (8) without ever winning the award?
29 Name either one of the two male actors who declined to accept the award.
30 Which Western earned Gary Cooper his Oscar in 1952?

1 Newsround. 2 22. 3 Painting. 4 Southern. 5 Nanette Newman. 6 Gerald Cock.
7 Sue Perkins. 8 Skullion. 9 Melissa Benoist. 10 Blackwall. 11 The King's Own
Fusiliers. 12 Jed Shepherd. 13 Noele Gordon. 14 Frederick Grisewood. 15 Peter
Powell. 16 Alan Titchmarsh. 17 Holly and Duncan. 18 The Learning Zone. 19 A
fuel and power crisis. 20 Julia Somerville. 21 625. 22 Orson Welles. 23 Paula Yates.
24 Seven hours. 25 Bernard Delfont. 26 Channel 4. 27 Barry Bucknall. 28 Chuck
Norris. 29 The Napoleonic War. 30 Inspector Henry Crabbe.

Quiz 38 TV Pot Luck 5

Answers – page 243

1 Which children's news programme celebrated its 35th anniversary in 2007?
2 How many suitcases are there in the British version of *Deal or No Deal*?
3 Which form of art do you associate Nancy Kaminsky?
4 Which television region produced *Houseparty*?
5 Who is Emma Forbes's actress mother?
6 Who was the BBC's first director of TV?
7 Who is Mel Giedroyc's partner on *Late Lunch*?
8 What was the name of the head porter in *Porterhouse Blue* played by David Jason?
9 Who has starred as *Supergirl* since 2015?
10 Which firestation features in *London's Burning*?
11 *Soldier, Soldier* follows the activities of the fictitious "A" Company of which infantry regiment?
12 Which budding singer-songwriter did Jimmy Nail play in *Crocodile Shoes*?
13 Who was the host of *Lunchbox*?
14 Who supplied the BBC commentary for the Coronation of King George VI?
15 Which disc jockey married Anthea Turner?
16 Which gardener leads the *Ground Force* team?
17 What are the Christian names of the Hurt twins in *Family Affairs*?
18 What is the title of BBC2's early-morning educational programmes?
19 What forced daytime shutdown of TV transmissions in Feb.–March 1947?
20 Which newsreader presents *I-Spy*?
21 How many lines are broadcast on UHF on British Television?
22 Which larger-than-life actor advertised sherry?
23 Which female television personality had a daughter named Trixie-Belle?
24 How long did the 1953 Coronation broadcast last?
25 Which impresario was the brother of Lou Grade?
26 Which channel broadcast *The Girlie Show*?
27 Who was the BBC's first DIY expert?
28 Which actor was "Walker, Texas Ranger"?
29 *Sharpe* is set during which war?
30 Who does Roger Griffith play in *Pie in the Sky*?

Answers	**Movies: Oscars – Best Actors** *(see Quiz 37)*

1 George Burns. 2 Wall Street. 3 The English Patient. 4 Amy. 5 Jude Law. 6 Priest.
7 Emil Jannings. 8 Manservant. 9 Daniel Day-Lewis. 10 The People versus Larry Flint.
11 None. 12 Rex Harrison. 13 Midnight Cowboy. 14 None. 15 Wall Street. 16
George III. 17 Amistad. 18 Chinatown. 19 James Dean. 20 Daniel Day-Lewis. 21
Marlon Brando. 22 The Elephant Man. 23 Don Corleone. 24 Schindler's List. 25 Rex
Harrison. 26 George Clooney. 27 Depp. 28 Peter O'Toole. 29 George C. Scott and
Marlon Brando. 30 High Noon.

1 Pressman and Turner were the keepers as which club went down?
2 Who went down in 1974 after 37 years in the top flight?
3 In the 1980s, which club was the first to be automatically demoted from the League?
4 In which decade were Bristol City last in the top flight in England?
5 Who was boss when Leicester City went down in 1994–95?
6 Robert Lee missed just one League game as which side went down?
7 Which team were relegated from the Scottish Premier League in 1993 and again in 1996?
8 Parris and Potts played for which relegated side?
9 Which Welsh club was finally wound up in February 1989?
10 Who was boss when Swindon Town went down in 1994–95?
11 Mark Pembridge played every 1992 game as which team went down?
12 In 1994, after going down, which boss said, "If you continually play Russian roulette eventually you're going to get the bullet"?
13 In which decade did Blackpool last play in the top division?
14 In 1990 which Sheffield team went down while the other went up?
15 Which Yorkshire team went out of the League in 1993?
16 Which team went down two seasons after winning the championship in the 60s?
17 Which seaside club went out of the League in 1978?
18 How many times were Aberdeen relegated in the 50 years following the Second World War?
19 Robins and Ekoku started the season as strikers, but left before which club went out of the Premiership?
20 Who was Portsmouth's manager when they went down from the top flight in 1988?
21 Which club were relegated to the third level for the first time in 2008?
22 Which was the last Welsh club to lose its Football League status?
23 Which club tried to get West Ham relegated in their place in 2007?
24 Which club was Steve Coppell managing when they were relegated in 2008?
25 How long was it between Leeds's Champions League semi-final and relegation?
26 Which London club was relegated from the Premier League at the end of 1992–93?
27 Which "County" which was relegated from the First Division in 1984?
28 Which 2008 Premiership London club was relegated to Division Three in 1980?
29 What was unusual about the three teams relegated from the Premiership in 2001?
30 Name the final team relegated from the Premier League 2015–16.

1   Zager and Evans sang about which year – among others – in 1969?

2   Which girl did Slade say Gudbuy T' in 1972?

3   What did Cat Stevens say "I Love" to in 1966?

4   Which duo sang "Heartache" in 1987?

5   Who was the female member of Steeleye Span?

6   Which Summer song did Hylda Baker and Arthur Mullard sing in the 80s?

7   Which colour Velvet provided a hit for Alannah Myles in 1990?

8   Who had a No. 1 with "I Want to Know What Love is"?

9   How is Sean Sherrard better known?

10 Which song title links Johnny Nash in 1975 and Kylie Minogue in 1990?

11 Whose first No. 1 was "Smile"?

12 Which TV presenter had a hit with "Close Every Door"?

13 Which national soccer side had a hit with "Ole Ola (Mulher Brasileira)"?

14 Which 70s chart-topper often performed dressed as a circus clown?

15 In which decade were the Everly Brothers born?

16 Who had a 90s album called *One Woman – The Ultimate Collection*?

17 Whose first hit was "Modern Girl"?

18 Who were in Creeque Alley in 1967?

19 In which decade did the Carpenters have their first hit?

20 Whose backing group were the Pirates?

21 Who released the album *Peachtree Road* in 2004?

22 For which movie's soundtrack and theme song did Eminem win an Oscar in 2003?

23 Who had the best-selling album *Oxygene*?

24 Which was the only group to have an album among the top ten of the decade in the 70s and the 80s?

25 How much did an LP measure across?

26 In which language was Falco's "Rock Me Amadeus" sung?

27 "Money for Nothing" and "So Far Away" featured on which album?

28 Which Boys featured on the Fat Boys' "Wipe Out" in 1987?

29 Which record label used by Daniel O'Donnell shares its name with a famous London hotel?

30 Which band took a dip in *A Moon Shaped Pool* in 2016?

Answers	**Football: Going Down** *(see Quiz 39)*

1 Sheffield Weds. 2 Manchester Utd. 3 Lincoln City. 4 1970s. 5 Mark McGhee. 6 Charlton. 7 Falkirk. 8 West Ham United. 9 Newport County. 10 John Gorman. 11 Luton Town. 12 Dave Bassett. 13 1960s. 14 Sheffield Weds. 15 Halifax Town. 16 Ipswich Town. 17 Southport. 18 Never. 19 Norwich City. 20 Alan Ball. 21 Leicester City. 22 Wrexham. 23 Sheffield Utd. 24 Reading. 25 Three years. 26 Crystal Palace. 27 Notts County 28 Fulham. 29 They were all called City – Bradford, Coventry and Manchester. 30 Hull City.

1 In which classic did Paul Heinreid play Victor Laszlo?
2 Which animal sings "We're off to see the wizard, the wonderful Wizard of Oz" with Dorothy and co.?
3 In which movie did Trevor Howard play Alec Harvey?
4 What was deemed the cinema's first epic?
5 Which 50s movie told of Moses leading the children of Israel to the Promised Land?
6 "All right, Mr de Mille, I'm ready for my close-ups now" is the last line of which movie?
7 In which movie did Debra Winger begin with, "Anyone here named Loowis?"?
8 Was Debbie Reynolds 18, 20 or 22 when she made *Singin' in the Rain*?
9 Which inventor did Michael Redgrave play in *The Dam Busters*?
10 Which of the stars of *The Philadelphia Story* donated his salary for the movie to war relief?
11 Who was Spade in *The Maltese Falcon*?
12 In *The Third Man* who had Joseph Cotten come to Vienna to meet?
13 Which movie had the ad line, "Meet Benjamin. He's a little worried about his future"?
14 *A Man for All Seasons* is about whom?
15 Which 1946 Frank Capra movie with James Stewart became a Christmas classic?
16 Who did Marlene Dietrich play in *The Blue Angel*?
17 Who does James Cagney play in *White Heat*?
18 Which movie opens with the line, "What can you say about a 25-year-old girl who died"?
19 Which member of the Corleone family did Al Pacino play in the *Godfather* trilogy?
20 In which movie did Rita Hayworth remove a glove to "Put the Blame on Mame"?
21 What was Lauren Bacall's first film, in 1943?
22 In *Genevieve* who or what was Genevieve?
23 Which movie did Elvis Presley make next after *King Creole*?
24 Who played opposite Lana Turner in the original *The Postman Always Rings Twice*?
25 In which 1954 movie did Marlon Brando play a boxer?
26 In which year was the main action of Titanic set?
27 In Philadelphia, what is central character Andrew Beckett's profession?
28 This "Queen" earned Humphrey Bogart an Oscar in 1952.
29 How many "Flew Over the Cuckoo's Nest" in 1975?
30 Name the 1988 classic which starred Dustin Hoffman and Tom Cruise.

Answers | TV Pot Luck 6 *(see Quiz 42)*

1 7 p.m. 2 The Thin Blue Line. 3 Rainbow. 4 Mr Robot. 5 Diana Moran. 6 Charlie Dimmock. 7 Michael Palin. 8 Campion. 9 Phil Collins. 10 John de Lancie. 11 Spiderman. 12 Vietnam. 13 Husband and wife. 14 Cordelia. 15 Battle of Britain Sunday. 16 David Frost. 17 Lori Singer. 18 20 million. 19 Barry Took. 20 Compact. 21 Cliff Mitchelmore. 22 Peter Snow. 23 Bellamy's Bugle. 24 Bob Monkhouse. 25 Moira Lister. 26 Kelloggs Rice Krispies. 27 Director General. 28 Peter Watkins. 29 The National Viewers and Listeners Association. 30 Ariel.

1 At what time is Channel 4's main evening news programme?
2 Constable Goody was a character in which police sit-com?
3 Where would you find Zippy, Bungle and George?
4 Rami Malek is better known as?
5 Which keep fit expert was dubbed "The Green Goddess"?
6 Who was the first female member of the *Ground Force* team?
7 Who journeyed *Around the Pacific Rim*?
8 Brian Glover played which private detective's manservant?
9 Which pop singer played a game show host in *Miami Vice*?
10 Who played Q in *Star Trek: The Next Generation*?
11 What was Peter Parker's alter ego?
12 What was the subject of *Tour of Duty*?
13 In *Emmerdale*, what's the real-life connection between Chris and Kim Tate?
14 Helen Baxendale played which character in *An Unsuitable Job for a Woman*?
15 What did the first televised church service commemorate?
16 Name the presenter of *Through the Keyhole*.
17 Who played characters in *Fame* and *VR5*?
18 What was the estimated number of UK viewers of the 1953 Coronation?
19 Who was Marty Feldman's writing partner?
20 Jean Harvey, Nicholas Selby, and Gareth Davies played editors of which fictional magazine?
21 Who ended his programme with the words "The next *Tonight* is tomorrow night"?
22 On election nights who wields his Swingometer?
23 What was David Bellamy's chat show called?
24 Who presented *Mad Movies*?
25 Which actress played *The Very Merry Widow*?
26 Which cereal is advertised as the one that goes, "Snap, Crackle and Pop"?
27 Which post did Alastair Milne hold finally at the BBC?
28 Who made the controversial *The War Game*?
29 Which organization did Mary Whitehouse represent?
30 What is the BBC's house magazine?

Answers	Movies: Classics *(see Quiz 41)*

1 Casablanca. 2 Lion. 3 Brief Encounter. 4 Birth of a Nation. 5 The Ten Commandments. 6 Sunset Boulevard. 7 Shadowlands. 8 20. 9 Barnes Wallis. 10 Cary Grant. 11 Humphrey Bogart. 12 Harry Lime. 13 The Graduate. 14 Thomas More. 15 It's a Wonderful Life. 16 Lola Lola. 17 Cody Jarrett. 18 Love Story. 19 Michael. 20 Gilda. 21 To Have and Have Not. 22 Car. 23 GI Blues. 24 John Garfield. 25 On the Waterfront. 26 1912. 27 Lawyer. 28 African. 29 One. 30 Rain Man.

1 Real Madrid play at which stadium?
2 Which Spanish club did John Aldridge play for?
3 What was the half-time score in the England v Spain Euro 96 game?
4 Which team won the Spanish league in 1991, '92, '93 and '94?
5 What was the nickname of 1980s striker Emil Butragueno?
6 Real Betis come from which city?
7 In Euro 96, David Seaman produced a penalty shoot-out save to deny which Spanish player?
8 Which Luis was the last Spanish European Footballer of the Year before the 1990s?
9 Which Scottish Steve played for Barcelona in the 80s?
10 What colour are Real Madrid's home socks?
11 At which club did Alfredo di Stefano end his playing career?
12 Which Javier was in charge of Spain for Euro 96?
13 Which club did Zubizarreta move to from Barcelona?
14 Which Welshman managed Real Madrid and Real Sociedad?
15 Which former England player died in a car crash in Madrid in July 1989?
16 Which country did Real Madrid's scoring star Hugo Sanchez play for?
17 At which club did an English and a Welsh international link up?
18 Who had a goal disallowed for offside against England in Euro 96?
19 Castilla are the nursery side of which club?
20 Which special person was enrolled as member No. 108,000 at Barcelona?
21 Against which country did David Villa score a hat-trick for Spain in Euro 2008?
22 Which club did Juande Ramos leave to take over as coach of Tottenham Hotspur?
23 Which club finished as runners-up to Real Madrid in the 2007–08 La Liga?
24 Which Spaniard finished joint-second in the Premiership goal scorers in 2007–08?
25 Who left Real Madrid for Bolton in 2002 and stayed there until 2008?
26 From which club did Liverpool sign Xabi Alonso in 2004?
27 Which club did Gerard Piquet join after leaving Man. Utd in 2008?
28 Gerard Piqué was born in which year – 1986 or 1987?
29 Which English player won the UEFA Champions League with a Spanish club?
30 What Spanish side plays their home games at the Vicente Calderon Stadium?

1 On whose book was the River Phoenix film *Stand by Me* based?
2 Who won the Best Actor Oscar for *The Color of Money*?
3 Which Linda starred in *Crocodile Dundee*?
4 Who recorded the title song of *The Good, the Bad and the Ugly*?
5 Who starred opposite Nicole Kidman in *The Peacemaker*?
6 Who won the Best Director Oscar for *On the Waterfront*?
7 *Tootsie* and *Scrooged* both feature which actor?
8 A character named Charlie Babbitt appeared in which film?
9 Which Lionel featured in *New York, New York*?
10 Who played Cosmo Brown in *Singin' in the Rain*?
11 Which actor's split from long-time partner Michelle introduced the word "palimony"?
12 *Ghostbusters* and *Parenthood* both feature which actor?
13 Who did John Cleese play in *A Fish Called Wanda*?
14 In which decade was *Bus Stop* released?
15 In which film was Laurence Olivier teamed with Marilyn Monroe?
16 Which actor links *In the Bleak Mid-Winter* and *Othello*?
17 Who directed Mel Gibson in *Hamlet*?
18 To the nearest hour, how long does *Alien* last?
19 Which Marx brother was born Julius?
20 What was the Bond theme for *The Spy Who Loved Me* called?
21 Who directed *A River Runs Through It*?
22 Who won the Best Actress Oscar for *Dangerous*?
23 Which John starred in *Con Air*?
24 Which singer appeared in *The Wall*?
25 In which decade was *Pygmalion* released?
26 Which woman US Presidential candidate did Liz Taylor endorse in 2008?
27 Which actor played Harry Potter?
28 What was the first sequel to an Oscar winner to win an Oscar?
29 Which 90s movie was a remake of *Dial M for Murder* with Grace Kelly?
30 Which Simon wrote 2016's *Star Trek Beyond*?

1 Which presenter was nearly killed on a test run during *Top Gear* in 2006?
2 What is the span of years that Richard and Judy were on Channel 4?
3 *Roving Report* was produced by which news team?
4 Which chat show host clashed with singer Grace Jones?
5 *DEF II* was produced by whom?
6 Which comic impersonates Trevor Macdonald's news reading on Channel 4?
7 Who presented *In the Footsteps of Alexander the Great*?
8 Who replaced the late Geoff Hamilton on *Gardener's World*?
9 Who is Richard Madeley's partner?
10 Which Donald was the 2016 Republican presidential nominee?
11 Who formed the original panel of experts on *Don't Ask Me*?
12 Who is the presenter of *Working Lunch*?
13 In which studios was *Tonight* produced?
14 Name the presenter of *Face to Face*.
15 Who presents *Right to Reply*?
16 Which award-winning television programme featured life on the paediatric wards?
17 Who walked out on Sir Robin Day during an interview in 1983?
18 Name the presenter of *Eye of the Storm*.
19 Who presents *The Sky at Night*?
20 Which chat show host recently returned after many years away?
21 Jon Snow presents which Channel's evening news service?
22 The documentary *A Prince for Our Time* was about which modern Royal?
23 Which singer found fame on *The Cruise*?
24 Which TV weathergirl is the daughter of a famous footballer?
25 Who presented *The Island of the Colour Blind*?
26 Which silver-haired ex-MP hosted a weekday-morning debate show?
27 What was the name of the Liverpool Hotel in the fly-on-the-wall series of the same name?
28 Who interviewed Princess Diana on *Panorama* in 1995?
29 Who was ITN's Mike in the Falklands?
30 Who travelled from *Pole to Pole*?

Answers	**Football Pot Luck 5** *(see Quiz 46)*

1 1920s. 2 Black. 3 Burnley. 4 Gary McAllister. 5 New Meadow. 6 Crystal Palace. 7 Paris Saint-Germain. 8 Wimbledon. 9 United. 10 McClair. 11 Brentford. 12 1940s. 13 Henning Berg. 14 Tony Brown. 15 Manchester City. 16 England. 17 Leeds Utd. 18 Richard Gough. 19 Colin. 20 Alan Kelly. 21 2000. 22 Dick Advocaat. 23 Manchester Utd. 24 1940s. 25 Peter. 26 Bolton Wanderers. 27 Aston Villa. 28 Arsenal. 29 Blue. 30 Northern Ireland.

1 In which decade did Bolton Wanderers first win the FA Cup?
2 What colour goes with amber on Cambridge United's home shirts?
3 Which was Trevor Steven's first League club?
4 Which Scottish captain was born in Motherwell in 1964?
5 Where do Shrewbury Town play at home?
6 Geoff Thomas and Eddie McGoldrick were in the same team at which club?
7 Which French team did Beckham join in 2013?
8 Which club did Vinnie Jones join on leaving Chelsea?
9 What is Hereford United's nickname?
10 Which Brian of Celtic was Scottish Premier Divison leading scorer in 1983–84?
11 As a teenager Rod Stewart had trials with which club?
12 In which decade was Alan Ball born?
13 Who was the only League ever-present for Blackburn Rovers in the 1995–96 season?
14 Who holds the WBA League appearance record?
15 Which team were beaten 3–1 by Newcastle United in the 1955 FA Cup Final?
16 Which country did Alfred Strange play for?
17 Which English club did Jock Stein manage?
18 Which Scottish captain was born in Stockholm?
19 What is Ray Wilkins's middle name?
20 Who was the regular keeper for Sheffield Utd in their 1993–94 relegation season?
21 When did Inverness Caley Thistle knock Celtic out of the Scottish Cup 3–1?
22 Which Dutchman was coach of South Korea in the 2006 World Cup finals?
23 Which club did Mark Robins leave to join Norwich City?
24 In which decade was Brian Kidd born?
25 What is Vinnie Jones's middle name?
26 Which club had a fanzine called *Tripe'N'Trotters*?
27 Chris Price and Nigel Callaghan were in the same side at which club?
28 Which team were beaten 1–0 by Leeds Utd in the 1972 FA Cup Final?
29 What is the main colour of Rochdale's home shirts?
30 Which country did Billy Hamilton play for?

Answers | TV: Current Affairs 1 *(see Quiz 45)*

1 Richard Hammond. 2 2001–08. 3 ITN. 4 Russell Harty. 5 Janet Street-Porter. 6 Rory Bremner. 7 Michael Wood. 8 Alan Titchmarsh. 9 Judy Finnegan. 10 Trump. 11 Magnus Pike, David Bellamy, Miriam Stoppard. 12 Adrian Childs. 13 Lime Grove. 14 John Freeman. 15 Roger Bolton. 16 Children's Hospital. 17 John Nott. 18 Richard Madeley. 19 Patrick Moore. 20 Michael Parkinson. 21 Channel 4. 22 Prince Charles. 23 Jane MacDonald. 24 Susanne Charlton. 25 Oliver Sacks. 26 Robert Kilroy-Silk. 27 The Adelphi. 28 Martin Bashir. 29 Michael Nicholson. 30 Michael Palin.

1 Who had Paul Weller as their lead singer at the beginning of the 80s?
2 Who was Roxy Music's "Jealous Guy" recorded in honour of?
3 What was the nationality of Aneka who performed "Japanese Boy" on *Top of the Pops* dressed in a kimono?
4 How was Julio Iglesias's single "Volver a Empezar" better known?
5 Who took "The Lion Sleeps Tonight" to the top of the charts?
6 Who played Coco Hernandez in *Fame* and charted with the single?
7 Who had an album called *Business as Usual*?
8 Which group took its name from the Jane Fonda film *Barbarella*?
9 Which girlfriend/supermodel did Billy Joel dedicate "Uptown Girl" to?
10 Which Radio 1 DJ refused to play Frankie Goes to Hollywood's "Relax" on his breakfast show?
11 How many Red Balloons did Nena release in 1984?
12 Who sang "All Night Long" at the closing ceremony of the Los Angeles Olympics?
13 Who was the elder of the two Wham! members?
14 Which trio produced Dead or Alive's "You Spin Me Round (Like a Record)"?
15 Which band was named after Mr Spock's Vulcan friend in *Star Trek*?
16 Which twins did Craig Logan leave when he left their band?
17 Which band was Morten Harket part of?
18 Who wrote the Ferry Aid No. 1 which charted in 1987?
19 Whose first No. 1 was "You Got It (The Right Stuff)" in 1989?
20 Who had an album called *Rattle and Hum*?
21 Kenny Rogers sang about the "Coward of the" what?
22 What was Abba's last UK No. 1?
23 Who was Frankie Goes to Hollywood's lead singer?
24 Who had a hit with "The Final Countdown"?
25 Which South American river did Enya sing about in 1988?
26 In May 1980, Dexy's Midnight Runners took this song to No. 1. Name it.
27 The Specials made this "Town" a No. 1 hit in July 1981.
28 Where did Phyllis Nelson want us to "Move" in her 1985 No.1 song?
29 Can you recall the city Simple Minds' child came from in their only No. 1 hit?
30 What was Barbra Streisand a "Woman in" with her 1980 No. 1 hit single?

Answers	Movies Pot Luck 6 (see Quiz 48)

1 Johnny Depp. 2 Lithgow. 3 87 minutes. 4 Jonathan Demme. 5 1940s. 6 Lane.
7 Brad Pitt. 8 Andrew Stanton, Angus MacLane. 9 The Deer Hunter. 10 Scream.
11 1970s. 12 Moorehead. 13 Sharon and Susan. 14 Groucho Marx. 15 Crocodile
Dundee. 16 Kelly McGillis. 17 Dan Aykroyd. 18 Mel Gibson. 19 Holly Goodhead.
20 Broderick. 21 Mrs Pearce. 22 Jack Lemmon. 23 Blind Date. 24 Katharine
Hepburn. 25 1950s. 26 Bridget Jones. 27 DeMille Award. 28 Anna and the King.
29 Indiana Jones and the Last Crusade. 30 Oliver's Story.

1 Which movie star had "Winona Forever" tattooed on his arm?

2 Which John starred in *Cliffhanger*?

3 Within fifteen minutes, how long does *The Blair Witch Project* last?

4 Who won the Best Director Oscar for *The Silence of the Lambs*?

5 In which decade of the 20th century was Chevy Chase born?

6 Which Diane featured in *Rumble Fish*?

7 Who played JD in *Thelma and Louise*?

8 Who directed 2016's *Finding Dory*?

9 Which Michael Cimino film about Vietnam won five Oscars in the 70s?

10 In which film did a character named Gale Weathers first appear?

11 In which decade was *Chinatown* released?

12 Which Agnes appeared in *Citizen Kane* and *Jane Eyre*?

13 What are the names of the twins in *The Parent Trap*?

14 Margaret Dumont was which comedian's most famous film stooge?

15 In which 80s action comedy did the character Sue Charlton appear?

16 Who was Tom Cruise's leading lady in *Top Gun*?

17 Which actor links *The Couch Trip* and *Sergeant Bilko*?

18 Which actor's middle names are Columcille Gerard?

19 What was the name of the Bond girl in *Moonraker*?

20 Which Matthew starred in *The Cable Guy*?

21 Who is Professor Higgins's housekeeper in *My Fair Lady*?

22 Who won the Best Actor Oscar for *Save the Tiger*?

23 What was Bruce Willis's first film, in 1987?

24 Who won the Best Actress Oscar for *Morning Glory*?

25 In which decade was *Around the World in Eighty Days* released?

26 Texan Renee Zellweger played which English diarist on the *Edge of Reason*?

27 Which award was won by Robin Williams at the 2005 Golden Globes?

28 Which Jodie Foster movie was a remake of a 50s music classic with Deborah Kerr?

29 Which movie announced, "The man with the hat is back. And this time he's bringing his dad"?

30 What was the follow-up to *Love Story*?

---

1 When the Trotters became millionaires at the auction, who fainted first?
2 Which character has been in control of Empire Entertainment since 2015?
3 What was *Boon* before he became a despatch rider?
4 Who starred as Edna the *Inebriate Woman*?
5 Who played the title role in *Dear John: USA*?
6 Which larger than life actor played Danny McGlone in *Tutti Frutti*?
7 Name the original title of *The Phil Silvers Show* starring the character Bilko.
8 Which female comic duo formed part of the *Comic Strip* team?
9 Honor Blackman plays whose passionate mother in *The Upper Hand*?
10 Which series told of the misadventures of young Dr Stephen Daker?
11 Which retirement home features in *Waiting for God*?
12 Who played the head porter, Scullion, in *Porterhouse Blue*?
13 Which singer/actress played Adrian Mole's mother in *The Growing Pains of Adrian Mole*?
14 Who are Elizabeth and Emmeline better known as?
15 How many arms did Zaphod Beeblebrox have in the *Hitchhiker's Guide to the Galaxy*?
16 What is the name of Martin Crane's dog in *Frasier*?
17 Which *To the Manor Born* actor starred in *Lytton's Diary*?
18 Which duo link *Blackadder* to *Jeeves and Wooster*?
19 In which district of South London was *Only Fools and Horses* set?
20 Name the DIY show in *Home Improvement*.
21 Alexei Sayle played which forger in *Selling Hitler*?
22 Which *Are you being Served* actress played Nerys Hughes's mum in the *Liver Birds*?
23 In which comedy would you find the character Bubbles?
24 Name *The Goodies*.
25 Peter Howitt played which Boswell in *Bread*?
26 Sgt Flagg was played by which actor in *The Growing Pains of PC Penrose*?
27 What were the names of Lucille Ball's neighbours in *I Love Lucy*?
28 Which *Good Life* actress went it alone in *Solo*?
29 Complete the title of this series starring Sid James: *Bless This...*?
30 Who played Barry in *Auf Wiedersehen Pet*?

1 The Spanish Grand Prix moved to which circuit in 1926 and stayed there through the 1930s?
2 Where was the English Grand Prix held in 1926 and 1927?
3 Who won it?
4 Which British driver won the Monaco Grand Prix in 1928 and 1929?
5 Maserati scored its first win in the 1930 Italian Grand Prix with who at the wheel?
6 Which Monegasque driver won his home grand prix in 1931?
7 What was unusual about three 1931 grands prix?
8 Which Italian driver won the first three grands prix of 1932?
9 What car was he driving?
10 Where was the Czech Grand Prix held in the 1930s?
11 Which driver who starred in the 1950 Formula One season won for Alfa Romeo in the 1933 Italian Grand Prix?
12 In 1934, which was the first German marque to win?
13 In which grand prix?
14 With which famous father of a famous son at the wheel?
15 Name the rival German marque that came good later in the year.
16 Where did they make their breakthrough?
17 Which politician financed the German racing programme as a whole?
18 Where was the German Grand Prix held in this era?
19 Which German driver scored four grands prix wins in 1935?
20 For which team?
21 In which English county was the first purpose-built racing circuit, Brooklands, created?
22 Which British racetrack was a grand prix venue in 1937 and 1938?
23 Which German marque ended the run of Italian success in the 1930s?
24 Under which flag did Louis Chiron drive?
25 What was the first name of multiple champion Nuvolari?
26 Can you name the country which staged the first official car race in the late 1890s?
27 At what circuit did the first grand prix take place in 1906?
28 What was the name of the Cup contested by nations from 1900 to 1905?
29 Can you name the country which dominated auto construction in the early 1900s?
30 The Vanderbilt Cup was the first major trophy for racing in which country?

---

1 In which city was the 1990 England v West Germany semi-final?
2 What date did the 2014 World Cup in Brazil end?
3 Which country knocked Germany out of the 1994 tournament?
4 Who was the goalkeeper in the controversial "Hand of God" goal?
5 Who were England's first-choice fullbacks for Italia 90?
6 Which three teams were in the Republic of Ireland's group in USA in 1994?
7 Which country hosted the World Cup in the wake of a tragic earthquake?
8 Which 1994 World Cup winner later played for Middlesbrough?
9 England and the Republic of Ireland were in which group in Italia 90?
10 Who became the first person to captain and manage World Cup-winning sides?
11 Which country did Scotland beat in the 1990 finals?
12 Which Trevor came on as an English sub in the 1990 semi-final?
13 What was the score after 90 minutes in the 1994 final?
14 Who was English boss in Spain in 1982?
15 Before the 90s when did Brazil last win the trophy?
16 Illgner was in goal for which World Cup-winning country?
17 McGrath, McCarthy, Morris – who was the fourth defender with an initial M in the Republic of Ireland's great 1990 campaign?
18 Who did England beat in the 1990 quarter-final?
19 Bertoni scored a final goal for which country?
20 In which year was the final held at the Rose Bowl?
21 Which was the second German city to stage a World Cup final?
22 Who scored and was sent off against England in the 2002 World Cup?
23 Whose departure from the Ireland 2002 squad left them a player short?
24 How many players were sent off when Portugal played Holland in 2006?
25 By what score did Germany beat Saudi Arabia in the 2002 finals?
26 What country was the first European nation to win the World Cup?
27 Can you recall the name given to the original World Cup trophy?
28 Name the football governing body which organizes the World Cup.
29 What was the name of the dog who found the World Cup after it was lost in 1966?
30 In what two years was the World Cup cancelled because of World War II?

Answers	**Pop Pot Luck 7** *(see Quiz 52)*

1 Billy J. Kramer. 2 Views. 3 Washington. 4 Trinidad. 5 Ram Jam. 6 Meat Loaf. 7 January. 8 Dionne Warwick. 9 "Woman in Love". 10 Demis Roussos. 11 Kenny Rogers. 12 1950s. 13 Harper Valley P. T. A. 14 Michelle. 15 David Essex. 16 Eloise. 17 1970s. 18 Herman's Hermits. 19 Nirvana. 20 Judy Dyble. 21 Madonna. 22 Cliff Richard. 23 Donna Summer. 24 David Bowie. 25 Glenn Medeiros. 26 Ken Dodd. 27 "Day Tripper". 28 "Mull of Kintyre". 29 Human League. 30 Jennifer Rush, Stevie Wonder.

1 Whose backing group was the Dakotas?
2 What was the name of Drake's 2016 album?
3 Which surname is shared by Dinah and Geno?
4 Where was Billy Ocean born?
5 Who sang "Black Betty" in 1977 and 1990?
6 How is Marvin Lee Aday better known?
7 Which month was a No. 1 for Pilot in 1975?
8 Who sang "Heartbreaker" in 1982?
9 Which song title links Frankie Laine in 1956 and Barbra Streisand in 1980?
10 Who was Happy to be on an Island in the Sun in 1975?
11 Who accompanied First Edition on "Ruby Don't Take Your Love to Town"?
12 In which decade was Annie Lennox born?
13 Which association was a hit for Jeannie C. Riley in 1968?
14 Which girl took the Overlanders to No. 1 in January 1966?
15 Whose first hit was "Rock On"?
16 Which girl did the Damned sing about in 1986?
17 In which decade did the Jacksons have their first hit?
18 Who had a No. 1 with "I'm into Something Good"?
19 Who had a 90s album called *In Utero*?
20 Who was the first female member of Fairport Convention?
21 Who had a *Re-Invention Tour* in 2004?
22 Who was the only living artist to have hits in the first six decades of the charts?
23 How is LaDonna Andrea Gaines better known?
24 Which pop star called his son Zowie?
25 Who had a hit with "Nothing's Gonna Change My Love for You" aged 18?
26 Which comedian had the bestselling record of 1965?
27 What was on the other side of the Beatles' "We Can Work It Out"?
28 Which single of 1977 was the first ever to sell two million in the UK?
29 Who sang "Do You Want Me?" in 1981?
30 Who were the only two Americans to have million-selling singles in the 80s in the UK?

Answers	Football: World Cup *(see Quiz 51)*

1 Turin. 2 Sunday, July 13. 3 Bulgaria. 4 Peter Shilton. 5 Paul Parker, Stuart Pearce. 6 Italy, Mexico, Norway. 7 Mexico. 8 Branco. 9 Group F. 10 Franz Beckenbauer. 11 Sweden. 12 Steven. 13 0–0. 14 Ron Greenwood. 15 1970. 16 West Germany. 17 Moran. 18 Cameroon. 19 Argentina. 20 1994. 21 Berlin. 22 Ronaldinho. 23 Roy Keane. 24 Four. 25 8–0. 26 Italy. 27 The Jules Rimet Trophy. 28 FIFA. 29 Pickles. 30 1942 and 1946.

1 In which TV series did Robin Williams find fame in the 70s/80s?
2 Who played his ex-wife in *Mrs Doubtfire*?
3 Who was his male co-star in *Awakenings*?
4 In which decade did he make his first major movie?
5 In *Good Morning, Vietnam*, which President does Cronauer alias Williams impersonate?
6 Which 007 starred in *Mrs Doubtfire*?
7 Which 80s movie saw co-star Glenn Close win an Oscar nomination?
8 Which cartoon character did he play in a 1980 Robert Altman movie?
9 Which then-husband of Emma Thompson directed *Dead Again*?
10 In which movie does he play Daniel Hilliard?
11 What is the occupation of the grown-up Peter Pan in *Hook*?
12 Which member of the Bridges family was a co-star in *The Fisher King*?
13 Whose voice did he provide in *Aladdin*?
14 Who did he play in *Hook*?
15 Who played Olive to his Popeye?
16 Where in Scotland is the "nanny" from in *Mrs Doubtfire*?
17 In which film was he "released" from a board game after 26 years?
18 What was his job in *Good Morning, Vietnam*?
19 In which early film did he play a Russian saxophonist?
20 Which former Python Terry directed him in *The Fisher King*?
21 Which movie gave him his first Oscar nomination?
22 In which movie did he play an unorthodox prep school teacher?
23 Which Barry directed him in *Good Morning, Vietnam*?
24 In which film is he a car salesman held hostage by a jealous husband?
25 The 80s *Good Morning, Vietnam* featured songs from which decade on its soundtrack?
26 Which US President did Williams play in *Night at the Museum*?
27 How many times has Williams been nominated for the Best Actor Oscar?
28 What "Dead Society" did Williams star in in 1989?
29 What "helpful" role gave him an Oscar in the 1998 movie "Good Will Hunting"?
30 On what day in 2014 did Robin Williams tragically die?

---

1 The church in *Hollyoaks*, blown up by Niall Rafferty, honoured which saint?
2 In the quiz show, what age do contestants have to prove they are *Smarter than*?
3 *This is Your Life* was first shown on which channel?
4 Who was the host of *The White Heather Club*?
5 What in TV production history was a VERA?
6 Dominic Diamond presented which computer programme?
7 Which Neighbour later appeared in *The Flying Doctors*?
8 Which product did Nanette Newman advertise?
9 Who played Frank Buck in *Dark Skies*?
10 Which star of *The Newcomers* appeared in *Manhunt*?
11 Kyle MacLachlan appeared in which unusual series in the 1990s?
12 Were Alexandra Palace TV studios in north or south London?
13 Which gardening programme came from Scotland?
14 Which fictitious TV station taught viewers to "Ski in Your Home"?
15 Who was the sixth Dr Who?
16 Which footballer and Northern Ireland manager refused to be the subject of a *This is Your Life* programme?
17 Name the annual gardening event screened from the Royal Hospital.
18 Who played "Mrs Thursday"?
19 Which former Arsenal star hosted his own Friday-night chat show?
20 Which TV chef hosted *Party of a Lifetime*?
21 In which year were the first BBC TV studios formed?
22 What was Joe Loss's signature tune?
23 Which political commentator is brother of Jonathan and the son of Richard?
24 Who is the survival expert on *Wildtracks*?
25 Who was the Royal presenter of *Crown and Country*?
26 Which former newsreader hosted the *Clothes Show*?
27 Who was the screenwriting husband of Maureen Lipman?
28 What are Dame Edna Everage's favourite blooms?
29 In the post-war magazine programme *Kaleidoscope* who was the Memory Man?
30 What is Bruce Forsythe's real name?

---

1 Which 1990s goalkeeper has played soccer and cricket for Scotland?
2 Which West Indian batsman played for Antigua in the 1978 World Cup qualifying games?
3 Which soccer striker played for the MCC against the Germans, scored a run and said, "It's always nice to score one against the Germans"?
4 Which member of England's 1966 World Cup-winning side played first-class cricket with Essex?
5 Which England batsman played in the 1950 FA Cup Final for Arsenal?
6 Which Football League club did Ian Botham play for?
7 Which county did England centre forward Ted Drake play cricket for?
8 Which Republic of Ireland defender Chris won cricket honours for Cornish schools?
9 England's cricket captain Brian Close played soccer in the 1950s for whom?
10 Apart from soccer, Kevin Moran was a star in which sport?
11 Which Phil skippered both Lincoln and Worcester CCC in the 1980s?
12 Which club did cricketer Arnold Sidebottom play for in the mid-1970s?
13 England's Mickey Stewart played for which Football League club?
14 Which Chris played for Leicestershire at cricket in the day and for Doncaster Rovers in an evening match on the same date?
15 Which Southampton and England striker turned to breeding and training racehorses?
16 In the 1960s, cricketer Jim Standen played for which London club?
17 Worcestershire CCC's Jimmy Cumbes played which position in soccer?
18 Which 1970s League Cup-winning side was Jimmy Cumbes in?
19 Boris Becker had soccer trials for which club?
20 Which David was a Yorkshire wicket keeper and Bradford City player?
21 Julian Dicks was planning to play which sport after quitting football?
22 At what other sport did football goalkeeper Andy Goram represent Scotland?
23 At which sport was Soviet footballer Sergei Baltacha's daughter Britain's No. 1?
24 Which former footballer and racehorse trainer won the 2006 *Celebrity Fit Club*?
25 Which 1950s Northampton footballer was a jockey, pop star, then a TV entertainer?
26 Which ex-England international won an edition of the *Superstars* TV series in the 1970s?
27 Which England cricket captain played in the 1902 FA Cup Final for Southampton?
28 Which Arsenal right-half from 1950 to 1955 was once capped for England and also represented his country at cricket on six occasions?
29 Which 1974 World Lacrosse Championship winner coached the USA at the World Cup finals of 2002 and 2006?
30 Which Frank joined New York City in 2015?

Answers	**Pop Pot Luck 8** *(see Quiz 56)*

1 Sunday. 2 Pet Shop Boys. 3 Marty Wilde. 4 Spencer Davis Group. 5 Love Me Love.
6 Whitney Houston. 7 Walker. 8 1940s. 9 Pet Shop Boys. 10 Gold. 11 "Long Live Love". 12 "48 Crash". 13 1999. 14 "Killer Queen". 15 Elkie Brooks. 16 "Summertime Blues". 17 The Kinks. 18 Juliet. 19 1970s. 20 Paul Revere. 21 Alicia Keys. 22 Frank Sinatra. 23 1980s. 24 Ricky Valance. 25 "When the Girl in Your Arms is the Girl in Your Heart". 26 33 1/3 27 Phil Collins. 28 Marianne Faithfull. 29 Kendrick Lamar 30 Perry Como.

1 What was a Lazy day for the Small Faces in 1968?
2 Who had a 90s album called *Very*?
3 How is Reginald Smith better known?
4 Who had a No. 1 with "Keep On Running"?
5 What did Gary Glitter follow "I Love You" with in 1973?
6 Whose first hit was "Saving All My Love for You"?
7 Which surname is shared by Scott and Junior?
8 In which decade was Gilbert O'Sullivan born?
9 Who sang "Heart" in 1988?
10 Which colour provided a hit for Spandau Ballet in 1983?
11 Which song title links Sandie Shaw and Olivia Newton-John?
12 Which Crash was a hit for Suzi Quatro?
13 Which year was a hit for Prince in 1983?
14 What was Queen's second hit?
15 Who was the female member of Vinegar Joe?
16 Which Summertime song did Eddie Cochran sing in 1958 and 1968?
17 Who were in a Dead End Street in 1966?
18 Which girl did the Four Pennies sing about in 1964?
19 In which decade did Kool and the Gang have their first hit?
20 Whose backing group were the Raiders?
21 Whose 2007 album was called *As I am*?
22 Which former No. 1 artist's death in 1998 led to the Las Vegas lights being dimmed?
23 In which decade did John Lennon's "Imagine" hit the top spot?
24 Whose "Tell Laura I Love Her" was banned in 1960?
25 Which Cliff Richard record before 1997 has the longest title?
26 How many r.p.m. did an LP have?
27 Who had the 1981 album *Face Value*?
28 What is Marianne Faithfull's real name?
29 *Untitled Unmastered* was an album by who, in 2016?
30 Which veteran had a 70s album *And I Love You So*?

Answers | Football: All Round Sportsmen *(see Quiz 55)*

1 Andy Goram. 2 Viv Richards. 3 Gary Lineker. 4 Geoff Hurst. 5 Denis Compton. 6 Scunthorpe. 7 Hampshire. 8 Morris. 9 Bradford. 10 Gaelic football. 11 Neale. 12 Manchester Utd. 13 Charlton Athletic. 14 Balderstone. 15 Mick Channon. 16 West Ham Utd. 17 Goalkeeper. 18 Aston Villa. 19 Bayern Munich. 20 Bairstow. 21 Golf. 22 Cricket. 23 Tennis. 24 Micky Quinn. 25 Des O'Connor. 26 Kevin Keegan. 27 C. B. Fry. 28 Arthur Milton. 29 Bruce Arena. 30 Lampard.

1 Who was the voice of the dragon in *Mulan*?
2 Which 2016 movie featured Rovio birds?
3 What was the first full-length animated movie to be Oscar-nominated for Best Film?
4 Whose songs feature in *Toy Story*?
5 Where do the characters live in *Who Framed Roger Rabbit?*?
6 Which 1945 Gene Kelly movie featured an animation sequence by Hanna and Barbera?
7 Which movie features Jiminy Cricket and Figaro?
8 *The Land Before Time* features an orphaned what?
9 Which 1995 movie saw Robin Williams being rescued from a board game?
10 Hakuna Matata is in which movie?
11 What are the Siamese cats called in *Lady and the Tramp*?
12 What was the name of the wicked uncle in *The Lion King*?
13 What is the name of the dinosaur in *Toy Story*?
14 *The Return of Jafar* was the sequel to which movie?
15 Which classic film has a rabbit called Thumper?
16 Which director provided a voice in *Antz*?
17 Which star of *Friends* provides a voice in *The Iron Giant*?
18 Who was the voice of John Smith in *Pocahontas*?
19 Who was the voice of Jessica in *Who Framed Roger Rabbit?*?
20 Which studio, famous for musicals, did Hanna and Barbera work for in the 40s?
21 Which 1999 movie featured the voices of Minnie Driver and Tony Goldwyn?
22 Which duo's first movie was in *Puss Gets the Boot*?
23 Lea Salonga sang on the soundtrack of *Aladdin* after making her name in which musical?
24 In *The Lion King* what sort of animal was Shenzi?
25 What is the name of "the king of the swingers" in Disney's *Jungle Book*?
26 What animal is voiced by Angelina Jolie in Kung Fu Panda?
27 The Land of Far, Far Away should be the domain of which swamp-dweller?
28 In what 1986 movie can you find Optimus Prime?
29 What Disney movies tells the story of a young prince's quest to rule the Pride Lands?
30 Which Louis provided a voice for 2016's Secret Life of Pets?

Answers | TV Pot Luck 8 *(see Quiz 58)*

1 FremantleMedia. 2 Washington DC. 3 1956. 4 Southern Television, Southampton. 5 University Challenge. 6 Geoff Hamilton. 7 Dorothy McNab's butler. 8 Wodehouse Playhouse. 9 Leonard Rossiter. 10 Bernard Braden. 11 Jeremy Isaacs. 12 Changing Rooms. 13 Eric Idle. 14 Trisha. 15 Roy "Chubby" Brown. 16 A Mickey Mouse cartoon. 17 Robbie Coltrane. 18 Max Bygraves. 19 Clarissa Dickson Wright. 20 Jack Docherty. 21 Cliff Mitchelmore. 22 Gaby Roslyn. 23 Judi Trott. 24 The Freak. 25 Trudie Styler. 26 Ball. 27 Alan Titchmarsh. 28 Wendy Craig. 29 Robert Llewelyn. 30 Walking Dead.

1 Which company produced *Neighbours* from August 2007?
2 In which American city is the NCIS department?
3 In which year did Granada TV start covering the North-West of England?
4 Which was the first truly local independent TV station?
5 On which UK TV programme did Clive James first appear?
6 Who presented the first *Gardener's World Live* show on BBC1 in 1993?
7 Which role did Robert play in *Two's Company*?
8 Which series of plays starred John Alderton and Pauline Collins in various guises?
9 Who played the lead role in *The Fall and Rise of Reginald Perrin*?
10 Name the Canadian born TV presenter and actor married to Barbara Kelly.
11 Who was the first Chief Executive of Channel 4?
12 On which show did Laurence Llewelyn-Bowen find fame?
13 Which Python created *The Rutles*?
14 Who replaced Vanessa on ITV's daytime discussion show?
15 What is Roy Vasey's stage name?
16 When TV was interrupted in 1939 by WWII what programme was on?
17 How is Anthony Robert McMillan better known?
18 Whose catchphrase is "I wanna tell you a story"?
19 Which of the *Two Fat Ladies* travels in the sidecar?
20 Who hosts a late-night chat show on Channel 5?
21 Who first presented *Holiday*?
22 Who interviewed the male members of *Friends* on Channel 4?
23 Who played Marian to Michael Praed's Robin?
24 What was Joan Ferguson's nickname in *Prisoner Cell Block H*?
25 Who is Sting's actress wife?
26 The father is Johnny, the daughter is Zoe. What is their surname?
27 Which TV gardener wrote a steamy novel called *Mr MacGregor*?
28 Who was the star of *And Mother Makes Three*?
29 Name the presenter of *I, Camcorder*.
30 Robert Kirkman is responsible for which US TV show, that first aired in 2010?

---

1 Alex Ferguson managed which two Cup Winners' Cup winners?
2 Which Borussia Dortmund player scored a record 14 goals in 1965–66?
3 Who were the first English team to win the trophy in the 1990s?
4 Kevin Sheedy played in a trophy-winning team with which club?
5 Who were the first Soviet side to win the competition?
6 Which team beat Liverpool in a 1960s final?
7 Rangers' victory in 1972 was marred by hooligan trouble. What was the Scottish team's penalty for this trouble?
8 Which Italian side were the first winners of the competition?
9 In what year was the first final played?
10 Who was coach of the Spanish team that won the 1989 final?
11 Who was in goal for that final ?
12 What was strange about the West Ham Utd v Castilla 1980 game?
13 Who lost a final to Valencia in 1980 in a penalty shoot-out?
14 Paul Furlong scored three times in the 1994–95 competition for which club?
15 But for UEFA's ban, which two sides would have represented England in 1985–86?
16 And why would it have been two clubs in the 1985–86 season?
17 Which Welsh player, rejected by Barcelona, scored the winning goal against the Spanish side in the 1991 Final?
18 1860 Munich and Anderlecht have both played which English team in finals?
19 West Ham Utd played their first final in which stadium?
20 Which Russian side did Rangers beat in the 1972 final?
21 Which club lost finals to both Chelsea and Aberdeen?
22 Who was Arsenal's match-winner in the 1994 final?
23 Which English ground was the venue for the last ever final?
24 In which country did Chelsea win the 1998 final?
25 Which was the only club to lose the final on a penalty shoot-out?
26 Who did Man. Utd beat to win the 1991 competition?
27 Name the Scottish club who lifted the trophy in 1971–72.
28 Which winners of 1963 became the first British side to win a major European trophy?
29 After penalties, who won the 2016 UEFA Champions League Final?
30 Apart from Johan Cruyff, who has managed two different winning teams?

Answers	Pop Pot Luck 9 *(see Quiz 60)*

1 "When I Fall in Love". 2 Georgie Fame. 3 "Because". 4 Cilla Black. 5 Toni Tennille. 6 Jive Bunny and the Mastermixers. 7 1960s. 8 Red. 9 "9 to 5". 10 Junior Walker. 11 Billy Preston. 12 Freda Payne. 13 Roy Orbison's. 14 Portsmouth. 15 UB40. 16 Status Quo. 17 American. 18 David Bowie. 19 1970s. 20 Layla. 21 Kylie Minogue. 22 Sia. 23 Ayatollah Khomeini. 24 Bread. 25 Phil Oakey. 26 Jimmy Cliff. 27 Dave Clark. 28 "Jack and Diane". 29 Trumpet. 30 So You Win Again.

1 Which song was a No. 2 for both Nat King Cole and Rick Astley?

2 How is Clive Powell better known?

3 What did Jim Reeves follow "I Love You" with in 1964 and 1971?

4 Who sang "Anyone Who Had a Heart" in 1964?

5 Who was the female member of the Captain and Tennille?

6 Who had a No. 1 with "Let's Party"?

7 In which decade was Little Jimmy Osmond born?

8 Which colour Corvette provided a hit for Prince in 1983 and 1985?

9 Which song title links Dolly Parton and Sheena Easton?

10 Whose backing group were the All Stars?

11 Who sang with the Beatles on their 1969 No. 1 "Get Back"?

12 Who sang "Band of Gold" in 1970?

13 Which singer/songwriter's wife was "Claudette" in the Everly Brothers' song?

14 Which port was a hit for Mike Oldfield?

15 Who sang with Robert Palmer on "I'll be Your Baby Tonight" in 1990?

16 Whose first hit was "Pictures of Matchstick Men"?

17 What was the nationality of Linda McCartney before she married?

18 Who had a 90s album called *Black Tie White Noise*?

19 In which decade did Meat Loaf have his first hit?

20 Which girl did Derek and the Dominoes sing about in 1972?

21 Who had a global hit with "Can't Get You Out of My Head" in 2001?

22 Who released *This Is Acting* in 2016?

23 Which religious political leader were the Clash referring to in "Rock the Casbah"?

24 Which group received a gold record for "Baby I'm a Want You" in 1972?

25 Who duetted with Georgio Moroder on "Together in Electric Dreams"?

26 Who sang "Wonderful World Beautiful People" in 1969?

27 Who was the manager of Dave Clark Five?

28 Which John Cougar hit has the lyric "two American kids growin' up in the heartland"?

29 What is Ringo Starr holding on the cover of the *Sgt Pepper* album?

30 What was the title of Hot Chocolate's No. 1 from 1977?

---

1 What sort of accent does Meryl Streep have in *Out of Africa*?
2 Who was described as the Buster Keaton of Hong Kong?
3 Which star of *Chariots of Fire* and *Gandhi* died of AIDS in 1990?
4 Where does Rutger Hauer hail from?
5 Which Oscar-winner from *Ordinary People* was married to Debra Winger for three years?
6 What was Diane Keaton's next Oscar nomination after *Annie Hall*?
7 Kevin Kline appeared in the movie of which Gilbert & Sullivan opera which he had starred in on Broadway?
8 What sort of musician was Sigourney Weaver in *Ghostbusters*?
9 Which outspoken talk-show hostess made her movie debut in *Hairspray*?
10 Which widow of Kurt Cobain was a star of *Sid and Nancy*?
11 In which film did Jack Nicholson say, "Here's Johnny"?
12 Which star of TV's *Cheers* is famous on the big screen for *Look Who's Talking*?
13 Who won the National Society of Film Critics award in the US for playing the ghoul in *Beetlejuice*?
14 Who was the aerobics instructor in *Perfect*?
15 Who gained notoriety for her "you like me, you really like me" Oscar acceptance speech in 1984?
16 Who had his wife as co-star in *Shanghai Surprise*?
17 Which father and son appeared in *Wall Street*?
18 Who played Loretta Lynn in *Coal Miner's Daughter*?
19 For which movie was Julie Walters Oscar-nominated on her film debut?
20 Which husband and wife starred in *DOA* in 1988?
21 Who played two parts in *Dead Ringers* in 1988?
22 In which movie did Debra Winger play an angel?
23 Who played Sid Vicious in *Sid and Nancy*?
24 Which writer did Jack Nicholson play in *Reds*?
25 Who married Melanie Griffith twice?
26 Who had his first leading role in *Splash* in 1984?
27 What was the spoof air disaster movie starring Leslie Nielsen and Lloyd Bridges?
28 What was the name of the boxer Robert De Niro portrayed in the 1980 movie *Raging Bull*?
29 Can you recall the name of Michael Douglas's character in *Wall Street*?
30 What iconic role did Ben Kingsley play in 1982 earning him an Oscar?

Answers | **Pop Pot Luck 9** *(see Quiz 62)*

1 Paul Merton. 2 Tony. 3 Anthony Newley. 4 Floyd Uncorked. 5 Carroll O'Connor. 6 Pauline Yates. 7 Cot Death Syndrome. 8 Game of Thrones. 9 Clive Anderson. 10 Barbara Feldon. 11 Ray Walston. 12 British Academy of Film and Televsion Arts. 13 Nighthawks. 14 Citroen. 15 30-line. 16 Charles Hill. 17 White City. 18 Mack McKenzie. 19 The Real Life Holiday Show. 20 Monty Don. 21 Angela Rippon. 22 World in Action. 23 Nixon. 24 Gerald Seymour. 25 The Earl of Listowel, Postmaster General. 26 Dirk, Nasty, Stig & Barry. 27 Better Call Saul. 28 Andy. 29 David Frost. 30 Points of View (Robinson).

1 Who appeared in 15 *Whose Line is It Anyway* and 300 *Have I Got News for You*?
2 Which Hutchinson was the last original *Hollyoaks* character still in the soap?
3 Which actor played Gurney Slade?
4 What was Keith Floyd's series touring vineyards called?
5 Who played Archie Bunker?
6 Reggie Perrin's wife, Elizabeth was played by which actress?
7 Which cause does Ann Diamond campaign for?
8 Who introduced *Eurotrash*?
9 Ian McShane starred in one episode of which US TV show in 2016?
10 Who played "Agent 99" in *Get Smart*?
11 Who was the star of *My Favourite Martian*?
12 What does BAFTA stand for?
13 Name the series which featured three nightwatchmen.
14 Which make of car did Bryan Brown advertise?
15 Was the original 1930's TV definition system **30**-line, 50-line or 70-line?
16 Which TV doctor became chairman of the BBC?
17 Where is BBC TV Centre?
18 Which character did Kevin Dobson play in *Knotts Landing*?
19 Which holiday programme did Gaby Roslin introduce?
20 He presented *Real Gardens*. Who is he?
21 Which female newsreader danced with Morecambe and Wise?
22 What is the name of Granada TV's weekly current affairs programme?
23 Which president spoke live to the first man on the moon?
24 Name the writer of *Harry's Game*.
25 Who formally declared TV services open after its WWII closure?
26 Who were the "pre-fab four" in *The Rutles*?
27 What was the lawyer-based spinoff series from *Breaking Bad* called?
28 Which resident DIY expert on *Changing Rooms* is "handy"?
29 Who created the company Paradine Productions?
30 Which programme has been presented by both Anne and Robert who share the same surname?

Answers	Movies: 1980s Stars *(see Quiz 61)*

1 Danish. 2 Jackie Chan. 3 Ian Charleson. 4 Holland. 5 Timothy Hutton. 6 Reds. 7 Pirates of Penzance. 8 Cellist. 9 Ricki Lake. 10 Courtney Love. 11 The Shining. 12 Kirstie Alley. 13 Michael Keaton. 14 Jamie Lee Curtis. 15 Sally Field. 16 Sean Penn. 17 Martin & Charlie Sheen. 18 Sissy Spacek. 19 Educating Rita. 20 Dennis Quaid & Meg Ryan. 21 Jeremy Irons. 22 Made in Heaven. 23 Gary Oldman. 24 Eugene O'Neill. 25 Don Johnson. 26 Tom Hanks. 27 Airplane. 28 Jake LaMotta. 29 Gordon Gekko. 30 Gandhi.

1 Miller and Roberts formed a partnership at which London club?
2 Which fullback captained England in the World Cup in Spain?
3 Shaun Teale went to which club after leaving Villa?
4 Which 17-year-old made his debut at left-back for AC Milan in 1985 and was holding the position ten years later?
5 Which club did England's Bob Crompton play for?
6 Thiago Silva defends which French team in 2016?
7 Whose clubs read: Leeds Utd, Wimbledon, Manchester City, Chelsea, Everton?
8 Which club did Phil Neal play for before he joined Liverpool?
9 To a year each way, when did Stuart Pearce first play for England?
10 Did iron man Tommy Smith ever play for England?
11 Butterworth and Culverhouse were in the same team at which club?
12 Which Scottish side did Neil Pointon move to?
13 Gary Pallister went on loan to which north-east club in his Middlesbrough days?
14 Which left-back was displaced by Graeme Le Saux at Blackburn Rovers?
15 George Cohen was with which club when he played for England?
16 Which club did Booth and Caton play for?
17 Which England full back Roger died in the Munich air disaster?
18 Which ex-Blackburn Rovers defender faced his old team in the 1994 Charity Shield?
19 Which country did Paul Breitner play for?
20 Which Kevin played for Norwich, Manchester City and Southampton?
21 Which two brothers started at West Ham and had a cousin who was a striker?
22 How many goals has Gary Neville scored for England?
23 At which club was Welsh international Chris Coleman a player and manager?
24 Which former Republic of Ireland defender was Wolves manager in autumn 2008?
25 Who was Brazil's captain in the 2002 World Cup Final?
26 Who has played for Leeds United, Newcastle United and Real Madrid?
27 Which highly successful manager played for RC Strasbourg from 1978 to 1981?
28 Can you name the former Ipswich player who managed the club and Derby?
29 What nationality is Man. Utd's Nemanja Vidic?
30 Name the former Aston Villa defender who was a Premiership manager in 2008.

Answers | **Pop Pot Luck 10** *(see Quiz 64)*

1 Geri. 2 Kenya. 3 Harrison. 4 "D. I. V. O. R. C. E". 5 Bonnie Tyler. 6 Wilcox. 7 1950s. 8 The Medicine Show. 9 New Order. 10 Midge Ure. 11 Bob Dylan. 12 Silk. 13 Sisters with Voices. 14 Eric Clapton. 15 Starland Vocal Band. 16 Chairmen of the Board. 17 Pat Boone. 18 Robert de Niro. 19 Nashville Teens. 20 Petula Clark. 21 Blackout. 22 Robbie Williams. 23 Of '69. 24 ABC. 25 Davy. 26 Barry Green. 27 Bette Midler. 28 The Pretenders. 29 The Culprits. 30 Deep Blue Something.

1 Which Spice Girl was Ginger Spice?

2 In which country was Roger Whittaker born?

3 Which surname is shared by Noel and George?

4 Which song title links Tammy Wynette and Billy Connolly?

5 How is Gaynor Hopkins better known?

6 What is Toyah's surname?

7 In which decade was Michael Bolton born?

8 Who was Dr Hook's backing group on "Sylvia's Mother"?

9 Who had UK top ten hits in 1983 and 1988 with"'Blue Monday"?

10 Who has topped the charts with Slik and Band Aid?

11 Who closed the American side of the Live Aid concert?

12 What is Steve Hurley's "middle" nickname?

13 What does SWV stand for?

14 Who had a solo album called *Journeyman*?

15 Who experienced "Afternoon Delight" in 1976?

16 Whose first hit was "Give Me Just a Little More Time"?

17 Who celebrated April Love in 1957?

18 Who's Waiting according to Bananarama?

19 Who had a 60s hit with "Tobacco Road"?

20 Who sang "Don't Sleep in the Subway"?

21 What was the title of Britney Spears's 2007 album?

22 Which British singer formed a football team in Los Angeles called LA Vale?

23 Which Summer was a 1985 hit for Bryan Adams?

24 Whose first album was *The Lexicon of Love*?

25 Who's On the Road Again according to Manfred Mann's Earth Band in 1978?

26 What is Barry Blue's real name?

27 Who is known as the Divine Miss M?

28 Whose first hit was "Stop Your Sobbing" in the 70s?

29 Who are Craig McLachlan's backing group?

30 Who had Breakfast at Tiffany's in 1996?

Answers	**Football: Defenders** *(see Quiz 63)*

1 Tottenham Hotspur. 2 Mick Mills. 3 Tranmere Rovers. 4 Paolo Maldini. 5 Blackburn Rovers. 6 Arsenal (Seamen, Adams, Bould). 7 PSG. 8 Northampton. 9 1987. 10 Yes (once in 1971). 11 Norwich City. 12 Hearts. 13 Darlington. 14 Alan Wright. 15 Fulham. 16 Manchester City. 17 Byrne. 18 David May. 19 West Germany. 20 Bond. 21 Rio & Anton Ferdinand. 22 None. 23 Fulham. 24 Mick McCarthy. 25 Cafu. 26 Jonathan Woodgate. 27 Arsene Wenger. 28 George Burley. 29 Serbian. 30 Gareth Southgate.

1 Which 70s weepie saw Meryl Streep as his co-star?

2 How many 20th-century Oscars did he win?

3 In which movie did he play a prisoner on Devils' Island?

4 What was his occupation in *All the President's Men*?

5 Which Matthew played his son in *Family Business*?

6 Which Shakespeare play did he appear in on Broadway and in London in 1989 and 1990 respectively?

7 Who was his female co-star in *Tootsie*?

8 What Panda movie stars Mr Hoffman?

9 Which Mike directed him in *The Graduate*?

10 In which western did he age from 12 to 121?

11 In which city was he born?

12 In which 1991 movie did he play gangster Dutch Schultz?

13 For which movie did he receive his first Oscar nomination?

14 Which movie saw him as a female soap star?

15 Which character did he play on stage in *Death of a Salesman*?

16 What was his character called in *Rain Man*?

17 In which movie did he play Ratso Rizzo?

18 For which 1976 role did he famously keep himself awake for seven days to look the part?

19 For which flop did he team up with Warren Beatty?

20 What was the name of his character in *All the President's Men*?

21 In which 1979 biopic did he receive mixed reviews?

22 Who did he portray in *Lenny*?

23 Which superstar played his father in *Family Business*?

24 In which Warren Beatty movie did he play Mumbles in 1990?

25 Which character was he in a 1991 film based on a children's classic?

26 Which member of the Focker family did Hoffman play in *Meet the Fockers*?

27 Which Barry directed Hoffman in 1996's *Sleepers*?

28 What was the name of Mr Magorium's shop in the movie of the same name?

29 Can you name the character Hoffman voiced for in *Kung Fu Panda*?

30 What ceremony did he say was "obscene, dirty and no better than a beauty contest"?

Answers | **TV Pot Luck 10** *(see Quiz 66)*

1 Arrow. 2 The Day Today. 3 OJ Simpson. 4 The South Bank Show. 5 As TV Announcers. 6 The Antiques Roadshow. 7 David Caruso. 8 Roy Dotrice. 9 Denise Van Outen. 10 Norman Beeton & Isabel Lucas. 11 Barry Norman. 12 Anneka Rice (Challenge Anneka). 13 Holiday: Fasten Your Seatbelt. 14 The Grove Family. 15 Lost in Space. 16 Tranquillity Base. 17 Sally Magnusson. 18 The Rutles. 19 Fred MacMurray. 20 Ally McCoist. 21 Nick Berry. 22 John Rhys Davies. 23 Chris Tarrant. 24 Vince Edwards. 25 TV hire firm. 26 Michael Parkinson. 27 Jeremy Clarkson. 28 Clive Anderson. 29 Margi Clarke. 30 Max Robertson.

1 Since 2012, who is Oliver Queen better known as?

2 What was the first TV series featuring Steve Coogan as Alan Partridge?

3 Who was Richard and Judy's first guest when their programme moved to London?

4 Which arts show replaced *Aquarius* in 1977?

5 For what were Mary Malcolm and Sylvia Peters known?

6 On which show do you hear advice from Bunny Campione and Henry Sandon?

7 Who plays Michael Hayes?

8 Which actor has actress daughters named Michelle and Karen?

9 Who left *The Big Breakfast* on New Year's Day 1999?

10 Who played Samuel and Pearl Foster in the comedy *The Fosters*?

11 Which film buff left the BBC for Sky in 1998?

12 Which celebrity chased around in a beach buggy answering challenges?

13 Which spin-off from *Holiday* features celebrities working in holiday resorts?

14 What was the first British TV soap?

15 Where did the Robinsons get lost?

16 From where on the moon did Neil Armstrong broadcast?

17 What is the name of Magnus's presenter daughter?

18 Which fictitious group sang "All You Need is Lunch" and "WC Fields Forever"?

19 Who starred in *My Three Sons*?

20 Who was the opposing team captain to John Parrott on *A Question of Sport*?

21 *Every Loser Wins* was a hit sung by which former soap star?

22 Who played the Professor in *Sliders*?

23 Who was *Man-O-Man*'s first presenter?

24 Who played Ben Casey?

25 *The Squirrels* was set in an accounts department of what kind of business?

26 Whose nickname is "Parky"?

27 Who presented *Motorworld*?

28 Who was *Our Man in Goa*?

29 Who presented *The Good Sex Guide*?

30 Name the original host of *Going for a Song*.

Answers | Movies: Dustin Hoffman (see Quiz 65)

1 Kramer versus Kramer. 2 Two. 3 Papillon. 4 Journalist. 5 Broderick. 6 The Merchant of Venice. 7 Jessica Lange. 8 Kung Fu Panda. 9 Nichols. 10 Little Big Man. 11 Los Angeles. 12 Billy Bathgate. 13 The Graduate. 14 Tootsie. 15 Willy Loman. 16 Raymond. 17 Midnight Cowboy. 18 Marathon Man. 19 Ishtar. 20 Carl Bernstein. 21 Agatha. 22 Lenny Bruce. 23 Sean Connery. 24 Dick Tracy. 25 Captain Hook in Hook. 26 Bernie. 27 Levinson. 28 Mr Magorium's Wonder Emporium. 29 Shifu. 30 The Oscars.

1 Novak Djokovic is from which country?
2 After which Wimbledon champion is the main court at the US Open named?
3 Which British player reached the 1997 US Open final?
4 Ana Ivanovic and Novak Djokovic are from which country?
5 Which Open is the second Grand Slam event on the calendar?
6 Who is the only black American to have won the men's singles at Wimbledon?
7 Who is Czech Cyril Suk's famous sister?
8 In which year did Ivan Lendl win Wimbledon?
9 Which British pair won the Wimbledon mixed doubles in 1987?
10 Who sobbed on the Duchess of Kent's shoulder when she lost her Wimbledon final to Steffi Graf?
11 Which woman French player won the Australian Open in 1995?
12 Which duo released "Rock 'n' Roll" with the Full Metal Rackets?
13 Which cup for women was contested between the US and Britain?
14 Where is the final of the US Open played?
15 Which US champion was married to British player John Lloyd?
16 Who was the first male tennis player to win 100 tournaments?
17 Which two women competed in the all-British Wimbledon final in 1961?
18 What is the international team competition for men called?
19 What are the colours of the All England Lawn Tennis Club?
20 Who was the then youngest-ever woman to receive a Women's International Tennis Association ranking in 1982?
21 What did line judge Dorothy Brown do in a 1964 Wimbledon match?
22 Whom did Virginia Wade beat in the final to win Wimbledon in 1977?
23 Which German won the Wimbledon men's singles in 1991?
24 Who won his first US Open title in 1990?
25 Between 1980 and 1995 only one French men's Open winner has won Wimbledon. Who?
26 What is the surface of the courts at Roland Garros in Paris?
27 Why did Catherine McTavish make Wimbledon history in 1979?
28 Who was stabbed on court by a fan of her chief rival?
29 What is the score in tennis when the tie break is introduced?
30 Who was once described as Garbo with ground strokes?

Answers	**Football Pot Luck 6** *(see Quiz 68)*

1 1930s. 2 Blue. 3 Sunderland. 4 Neville Southall. 5 Scunthorpe Utd. 6 Centre-back. 7 Shrewsbury Town. 8 Brondby. 9 1950s. 10 Manchester Utd. 11 Francis. 12 Steve Pears. 13 Phelan. 14 Luther Blissett. 15 Leeds United. 16 McDermott. 17 Vinnie Jones. 18 Mirandinha. 19 Iceland. 20 Robert. 21 1–0. 22 Michael Owen. 23 Gillingham. 24 Watford. 25 Two. 26 Notts County. 27 Leicester City. 28 Newcastle Utd. 29 Scotland. 30 Alf Ramsey.

1 In which decade did Arsenal first win the FA Cup?
2 What is the main colour of Carlisle Utd's home shirts?
3 What was Barry Venison's first League club?
4 Who was the only League ever-present for Everton in 1995–96?
5 Who plays at home at Glanford Park?
6 What position does Gerard Piqué play for FC Barcelona?
7 Which team are known as the Shrews?
8 Which club did Peter Schmeichael leave to join Manchester Utd?
9 In which decade was John Aldridge born?
10 Paul Parker and Clayton Blackmore were in the same team at which club?
11 Which Trevor became QPR manager in 1988?
12 Who was the regular keeper for Middlesbrough in their 1992–93 relegation season?
13 Which Mike of Manchester Utd won his only England cap in 1989?
14 With 415 games, who holds Watford's League appearance record?
15 Which team was beaten 1–0 by Sunderland in the 1973 FA Cup Final?
16 Which midfielder Terry was born in Kirby in December 1951?
17 Who was booked within five seconds of the start of the Chelsea v Sheffield Utd 1992 FA Cup tie?
18 Which Brazilian player joined Newcastle United in 1987?
19 Which country has Gudni Berggson played for?
20 What is Darren Anderton's middle name?
21 What was the score in the final when Greece won Euro 2004?
22 Who scored England's last goal in the 2002 World Cup finals?
23 Which was Steve Bruce's first League club?
24 Glenn Roeder left as boss of which club in February 1996?
25 How many Premiership games did Bolton win in the first half of the 1995–96 season?
26 Albert Ironmonger set a League appearance record for which club?
27 Brian Little followed David Pleat as a manager of which club?
28 Which club did Peter With join on leaving Nottingham Forest?
29 Which country did George Wood play for?
30 Which England boss was born in Dagenham in 1920?

1 Who sang about "Saturday Night" in 1994?
2 What was on the other side of Robson and Jerome's "I Believe"?
3 What goes after Meat Loaf's "I Would Do Anything for Love"?
4 Which soundtrack was a top-selling 1992 album in the UK and the US?
5 Which '91 chart toppers share a name with an instrument of torture?
6 Which band included Siobhan Fahey and Marcella Detroit?
7 Which 1994 chart topper was written by the Troggs' Reg Presley?
8 Who were Baby, Posh, Scary, Ginger and Sporty?
9 Who had the album *Automatic for the People*?
10 Who was Take That's usual lead vocalist?
11 Which No. 1 artist was the creation of the TV producer Mike Leggo?
12 Whose first No. 1 was "End of the Road"?
13 What was Boyzone's first chart hit?
14 Which superstar did Bobby Brown marry in 1992?
15 Who had the bestselling album *Blue is the Colour*?
16 What was the Dunblane single called?
17 Which veteran band released *Voodoo Lounge* in 1994?
18 Whose 1994 Greatest Hits album was called *End of Part One*?
19 Which band included the bass player Paul McGuigan?
20 What was reported in the press as "Cliffstock"?
21 What did Kylie Minogue have on her Pillow in 1990?
22 In which year did Freddie Mercury die?
23 "It's in His Kiss" was the subtitle to which No. 1 enjoyed by Cher in 1991?
24 Whose only chart-topper was 1997's "The Drugs Don't Work"?
25 Which was the first Spice Girl to have a No. 1 as a solo artist?
26 What was Wamdue "King of" in their November 1999 No.1 hit?
27 Who had a worldwide hit in 1999 with "Livin' La Vida Loca"?
28 Can you recall what type of "Eye" Joe had in Rednex's only ever No. 1 single?
29 Which single gave Gerri Halliwell her first solo UK No. 1?
30 What were Oasis "All Around" when they claimed their fourth UK No. 1 hit single?

Answers | **Movies Pot Luck 7** *(see Quiz 70)*

1 Cameron Poe. 2 1980s. 3 Anthony Hopkins. 4 Cary Grant. 5 Perkins. 6 Frederic March. 7 Tiffany. 8 Zeppo. 9 Austrian. 10 Nurse Ratchet. 11 To Kill a Mockingbird. 12 Spacey. 13 Joanne Woodward. 14 Ewan McGregor. 15 Kiss Me Kate. 16 1960s. 17 Sophia Loren. 18 Matt Monro. 19 Bette Davis. 20 Charley Partanna. 21 Long. 22 Anne Bancroft. 23 Dyslexia. 24 Zach Snyder. 25 Rhea Perlman. 26 Truman Capote. 27 Uganda. 28 Blanche. 29 Allen. 30 Shirley MacLaine.

1 What was the name of Nicolas Cage's character in *Con Air*?
2 In which decade was *Driving Miss Daisy* released?
3 Which movie star released a single called "A Distant Star" in 1986?
4 Which suave actor turned down Robert Preston's role in *The Music Man*?
5 Which Elizabeth starred in *Big*?
6 Who won the Best Actor Oscar for *Dr Jekyll and Mr Hyde*?
7 What is Richard Gere's middle name?
8 Who was the youngest Marx brother?
9 What is Schindler's nationality in *Schindler's List*?
10 Who did Louise Fletcher play in *One Flew Over the Cuckoo's Nest*?
11 For which film did Gregory Peck win his first Oscar?
12 Which Kevin featured in *Se7en*?
13 Who was Paul Newman's second wife?
14 Who played Renton in *Trainspotting*?
15 Which film features the song "Brush Up Your Shakespeare"?
16 In which decade was *El Dorado* released?
17 Which actress was Mrs Carlo Ponti?
18 Who sang the Bond theme "From Russia with Love"?
19 Who won the Best Actress Oscar for *Jezebel*?
20 What was the name of Jack Nicholson's character in *Prizzi's Honor*?
21 Which Shelley starred in *The Brady Bunch Movie*?
22 Who played the devious US Senator in *GI Jane*?
23 Which type of disability affects Tom Cruise and Susan Hampshire?
24 Who directed *Batman v Superman: Dawn of Justice* in 2016?
25 Who is Mrs Danny DeVito?
26 Playing which writer won Philip Seymour Hoffman the Best Actor award in 2005?
27 *The Last King of Scotland* is about the despotic leader of which country?
28 What was the name of Baby Jane's sister in *Whatever Happened to Baby Jane*?
29 Which Nancy featured in *Robocop*?
30 Who won the Best Actress Oscar for *Terms of Endearment*?

Answers   Pop: The 1990s *(see Quiz 69)*

1 Whigfield. 2 "Up on the Roof". 3 "But I Won't Do That". 4 The Bodyguard. 5 Iron Maiden. 6 Shakespear's Sister. 7 "Love is All Around". 8 The Spice Girls. 9 R. E. M. 10 Gary Barlow. 11 Mr Blobby. 12 Boyz II Men. 13 "Love Me for a Reason". 14 Whitney Houston. 15 The Beautiful South. 16 "Knockin' on Heaven's Door". 17 The Rolling Stones. 18 Wet Wet Wet. 19 Oasis. 20 Cliff Richard's impromptu singing during rain at Wimbledon tennis. 21 Tears. 22 1991. 23 The Shoop Shoop Song. 24 Verve. 25 Mel B (Scary). 26 My Castle. 27 Ricky Martin. 28 Cotton. 29 Mi Chico Latino. 30 The World.

1 Summer Bay is the setting for which Channel 5 soap?

2 Where would you buy draught Newton & Ridley beer?

3 In *EastEnders*, what was Carol Jackson's sister called?

4 In *Dallas* what relation was Cliff Barnes to Pamela Ewing?

5 Which *Coronation Street* actress achieved *Rapid Results* when she donned a leotard?

6 What kind of establishment was *Crossroads*?

7 Which *Brookside* baddie was buried under a patio?

8 How many episodes in total of *Albion Market* were recorded?

9 What is "Curly" Watts's first name?

10 The soap opera *United!* was about what?

11 Which soap was a spin-off from *Dynasty*?

12 What was the first major UK soap on Channel 5?

13 Who left *Dallas* and became *The Man from Atlantis*?

14 Who had a brief affair with Ricky Butcher in *EastEnders*?

15 Who left *EastEnders* to become a policeman in *Heartbeat*?

16 Who shot J.R.?

17 Mick Carter is played by which actor in *EastEnders* ?

18 Who was kidnapped by a UFO in the *Colbys*?

19 In *Brookside*, who did the Farnhams pay to act as a surrogate mother?

20 What was ITV's first long-running twice-weekly soap?

21 What connects *EastEnders* and *Are You being Served*?

22 Who in *Coronation Street* decided to have blue and white cladding on the front of their house?

23 Which English actress played Alexis in *Dynasty*?

24 What role did Bill Treacher play in *EastEnders*?

25 In which district of Melbourne is *Neighbours* set?

26 What kind of market stall did Pete Beale own in *EastEnders*?

27 *Home and Away* is set in which fictitious bay?

28 Who is the longest-serving member of *Coronation Street*?

29 Where did Alexis marry Cecil Colby?

30 Which actress, better known for her comic roles, plays the Mitchell brothers' mum?

Answers   **Football Pot Luck 7** *(see Quiz 72)*

1 1920s. 2 White. 3 Leeds Utd. 4 Tottenham Hotspur. 5 Scarborough. 6 Manchester City. 7 Sheffield Utd. 8 Watford. 9 The Robins. 10 1880s. 11 Edinburgh. 12 Leeds Utd. 13 Luton Town. 14 Alan Shearer. 15 Foulkes. 16 Lou Macari. 17 Everton. 18 Mark Crossley. 19 Croatia. 20 Manchester Utd. 21 Mick McCarthy. 22 One. 23 Tottenham Hotspur. 24 March. 25 Lawrence. 26 1970s. 27 Liverpool and Tottenham Hotspur. 28 Everton. 29 Arsenal. 30 Black and white.

1 In which decade was Danny Blanchflower born?
2 What colour are Charlton's home shorts?
3 Which was Scott Sellars's first League club?
4 Steve Perryman set a League appearance record at which club?
5 Who plays at home at the McCain Stadium?
6 David White and Keith Curle were in the same team at which club?
7 Martin Peters had a short stay as boss of which club in 1981?
8 Which club did Pat Rice join on leaving Arsenal?
9 What is Swindon Town's nickname?
10 In which decade did Aston Villa first win the FA Cup?
11 In which Scottish city was Dave Mackay born?
12 Which club was John Charles with when he was First Divison leading scorer in 1956–57?
13 Chamberlain and Sutton shared the goalkeeping duties in the 1991–92 relegation season for which club?
14 Who said "That's life" when asked why a new England kit was launched soon after Christmas 1996?
15 Which Bill of Manchester Utd won his only England cap in 1954?
16 Who started his second spell as Stoke City boss in September 1994?
17 Which team were beaten 3–2 by Liverpool in the 1989 FA Cup Final?
18 Who was the only League ever-present for Nottingham Forest in 1995–96?
19 Which country did Zvonimir Boban play for in Euro 96?
20 The French player Prunier played twice in 1995–96 season for which Premiership side?
21 Who was coach of the Republic of Ireland in World Cup 2002?
22 How many goals did Portsmouth concede on their way to winning the 2008 FA Cup?
23 Paxton Road goes by the ground at which club?
24 Sergio Ramos was born in what month in 1986 – March or December?
25 Which Lennie became boss of Luton Town in December 1995?
26 In which decade did Southampton first win the FA Cup?
27 Ray Clemence was an FA Cup winner with which two clubs?
28 Which team took part in the Charity Shield from 1984 to 1987?
29 What was Martin Keown's first League club?
30 What two colours are on Hereford United's home shirts?

Answers | TV: Soaps 1 *(see Quiz 71)*

1 Home & Away. 2 Rover's Return. 3 April. 4 Brother. 5 Beverly Callard. 6 A motel. 7 Trevor Jordache. 8 100. 9 Norman. 10 A football team. 11 The Colbys. 12 Family Affairs. 13 Patrick Duffy. 14 Nathalie. 15 Nick Berry. 16 Kristen Shepard. 17 Danny Dyer. 18 Fallon. 19 Jacqui Dixon. 20 Emergency-Ward 10. 21 Actress Wendy Richards. 22 The Duckworths. 23 Joan Collins. 24 Arthur Fowler. 25 Erinsborough. 26 Fruit stall. 27 Summer Bay. 28 William Roache (Ken Barlow). 29 In a hospital. 30 Barbara Windsor.

Quiz 73 | Pop: Dance & Disco | Answers – page 280

1 Which Patrick Swayze film had a top-selling soundtrack album in 1987?
2 Who took "Dr Love" into the top ten in 1976?
3 In which decade were the *Dance Mix* albums first released?
4 Who had a 1986 album called *Disco*?
5 Who sang "He's the Greatest Dancer" in 1979?
6 Who took "Yes Sir, I Can Boogie" to the top of the charts?
7 Who was "Dancing on a Saturday Night" in 1973?
8 Who sang with the Sex-O-Lettes?
9 Who was heard to Rock his Baby in 1974?
10 Who was "Happy Just to Be With You" in 1995?
11 Who had an 80s hit with "Ooh La La La (Let's Go Dancin')"?
12 Who were in a "Gangsta's Paradise" in 1995?
13 What completes the title of Chic's "Dance Dance Dance"?
14 Which word follows Dance Yourself in the song title by Liquid Gold?
15 Which Brothers went "Boom Boom Boom" in the 90s?
16 Which Donna Summer disco hit was at No. 1 when Elvis Presley died?
17 Who were a "Sight for Sore Eyes" in the 90s?
18 Which dance record was the Bee Gees' first 70s No. 1?
19 Which Bee Gees song did N Trance take to the charts nearly 20 years after the original?
20 Who had a 1974 No. 1 with "You're My First, My Last, My Everything"?
21 With which group did Bryan Adams team up to record "Don't Give Up" in 2000?
22 What type of dance gave Steps a second No. 1?
23 What nationality was DJ Otzi?
24 For which US city did Fredde Le Grand want you to "Put Your Hands Up"?
25 "Singing in the Rain" as a dance track was a hit for which band in 2008?
26 What hospital BBC TV show was Oxide & Neutrino's "Bound 4 Da Reload" from?
27 What DJ teamed up with Leo Sayer in 2006 for the No. 1 hit "Thunder in My Heart"?
28 Can you name "Jet" Spillar took to the top of the charts in August 2000?
29 These "Sisters" didn't feel like dancing despite going to No. 1 in September 2006.
30 Name the dance group who released "Cake by the Ocean" in 2016.

Answers | **Movies Pot Luck 8 (see Quiz 74)**

1 Fatal Attraction. 2 Hunt. 3 Michael Caine. 4 1960s. 5 Jennifer Jones. 6 Tiffany Case. 7 Jonathan Demme. 8 James Mason. 9 Return of the Jedi. 10 Callow. 11 Woody Allen. 12 Burt Reynolds. 13 Walter Matthau. 14 Marianne Faithfull. 15 Liar Liar. 16 "I Just Called to Say I Love You". 17 Preston. 18 Jessica Lange. 19 1970s. 20 Burt Lancaster. 21 Mayer. 22 Redgrave. 23 Lee Marvin. 24 John Schlesinger. 25 Bening. 26 Four. 27 The Year. 28 Caan. 29 Dr Abbey Yates. 30 Annie Wilkes.

1 A character named Dan Gallagher appears in which film?

2 Which Helen starred in *As Good as It Gets*?

3 How is Maurice Micklewhite better known?

4 In which decade was *Planet of the Apes* released?

5 Who won the Best Actress Oscar for *The Song of Bernadette*?

6 What was the name of the Bond girl in *Diamonds are Forever*?

7 Who directed *Philadelphia*?

8 *A Star is Born* and *The Verdict* featured which actor?

9 Jabba the Hutt is a villain in which 1983 movie sequel?

10 Which Simon featured in *Four Weddings and a Funeral*?

11 Which actor links *Hannah and Her Sisters* and *Mighty Aphrodite*?

12 Which actor's first two wives were Judy Carne and Loni Anderson?

13 Who played Oscar Madison in *The Odd Couple*?

14 Who was Alain Delon's *Girl on an Motorcycle* in 1968?

15 A character named Fletcher Reede appeared in which film?

16 Which song won Best Song Oscar for *The Woman in Red*?

17 Which Kelly featured in *Jerry Maguire*?

18 Who played opposite Dustin Hoffman in *Tootsie*?

19 In which decade was *Annie Hall* released?

20 Who won the Best Actor Oscar for *Elmer Gantry*?

21 What did the second M stand for in MGM?

22 Which Lynn featured in *Shine*?

23 *Cat Ballou* and *Paint Your Wagon* both featured which actor?

24 Who won the Best Director Oscar for *Midnight Cowboy*?

25 Which Annette starred in *The American President*?

26 How many Wallace & Gromit feature movies were released before 2009?

27 In the title, what was Robin Williams's character Tom Dobbs *Man of*?

28 Which James featured in *A Bridge Too Far*?

29 Melissa McCarthy's character name in the 2016 reboot of *Ghostbusters* is...?

30 What was the name of the lady "gaoler" in *Misery*?

Answers | Pop: Dance & Disco *(see Quiz 73)*

1 Dirty Dancing. 2 Tina Charles. 3 1980s. 4 The Pet Shop Boys. 5 Sister Sledge. 6 Baccara. 7 Barry Blue. 8 Disco Tex. 9 George McCrae. 10 Michelle Gayle. 11 Kool and the Gang. 12 Coolio Featuring L.V. 13 "(Yowsah Yowsah Yowsah)". 14 Dizzy. 15 Outhere Brothers. 16 "I Feel Love". 17 M People. 18 "Night Fever". 19 "Stayin' Alive". 20 Barry White. 21 Chicane. 22 Stomp. 23 Austrian. 24 Detroit. 25 Mint Royale. 26 Casualty. 27 Meck. 28 Groovejet. 29 Scissor. 30 DNCE.

1 Which Cass was a victim of the serial strangler in *The Bill*?
2 What is the name of William Shatner's character in *Boston Legal*?
3 Who was *The Undercover Agent*?
4 Richard Rogers played which relation to William Tell in *The Adventures of William Tell*?
5 Who played Dan Tempest in *The Buccaneers*?
6 What was the name of Maverick's English cousin?
7 Which actor starred in the TV version of *Pennies from Heaven*?
8 Who starred as *The Singing Detective*?
9 What is the longest-running police series on British TV?
10 Which 1998 vampire series starred Jack Davenport?
11 On which ranch was *The Virginian* set?
12 Who wrote the book on which the 70s mini-series *Roots* was based?
13 The series *The Adventures of Long John Silver* was based on which book?
14 Which TV series contained the line, "I am not a number, I am a free man"?
15 In which town is *The Little House on the Prairie*?
16 For whose household did Mr Hudson and Mrs Bridges work?
17 In which series did ex-investment banker Steven Crane help save a midlands car firm?
18 The 1979 mini-series *From Here to Eternity* was set in which US state at the time of Pearl Harbor?
19 Who wrote *Middlemarch*?
20 Which prison is *Prisoner Cell Block H* set in?
21 Who played the title role in *Smiley's People*?
22 Who was *The Texan*?
23 Who played the owner of *The Royalty Hotel*, Mrs Mollie Miller?
24 Which actress starred in *Tenko* and was later seen *Waiting for God*?
25 Jimmy McGill is also known as?
26 At which real-life airport was the setting for *Garry Halliday*?
27 Which Dame starred in *Jewel in the Crown*?
28 How was *Jungle Boy* orphaned?
29 Who, early in his career, played Ivanhoe and Beau Maverick?
30 Which former publican ran *The Paradise Club*?

---

1 In which decade did Blackpool first win the FA Cup?
2 What colour are the stripes on Chester's home shirts?
3 What was Peter Shilton's first League club?
4 Which Tony of WBA was First Divison leading scorer in 1970–71?
5 Who was the regular keeper for Notts County in their 1991–92 relegation season?
6 Who plays at home at the Millmoor Ground?
7 Which England attacking midfielder was born in Bootle in February 1972?
8 Which club did Andy Thorn leave to join Newcastle United?
9 What is Torquay's nickname?
10 Ian Marshall and Graeme Sharpe were in the same team at which club?
11 Steve McManaman and which other player were League ever-presents for Liverpool in 1995–96?
12 In which decade was Sir John Hall born?
13 Which team were beaten 2–0 by Everton in the 1984 FA Cup Final?
14 John Trollope set a League appearance record at which club?
15 Which Ian became Southampton manager in 1991?
16 Which John of Villa won his only England cap in 1977?
17 David Harvey played over 300 games for which club?
18 What is Nigel Clough's middle name?
19 Which country did Harry Daft play for?
20 Which ex-Liverpool star was boss at Oxford Utd for a short time in 1988?
21 What position did Ricardo, the winning penalty-taker against England at Euro 2004, play?
22 Who is the only man to play in two Champions League Finals for Manchester United?
23 Which Scot played for Torino in 1961–62?
24 With which club did Trevor Sinclair make his League debut?
25 Which Ian become boss of Northampton Town in January 1995?
26 Which club moved ground from Gay Meadow to New Meadow in 2007?
27 Vincent Jean Mpoy Kompany is from which country?
28 Ken Brown followed John Bond as boss of which club?
29 What colour are Exeter City's striped shirts?
30 Gordon Cowans was at which club when he made his international debut?

Pop: Stevie Wonder

Answers – page 284

1 Which three instruments could Stevie play by the age of seven?
2 How was Stevie known in his early days on stage?
3 What was the first record label he recorded on?
4 Which single had the subtitle "Everything's Alright"?
5 On whose *Duets II* album did he sing in 1994?
6 Which 1984 album was from a film soundtrack?
7 In which decade was Stevie Wonder born?
8 Who did he duet with on "My Love" in 1988?
9 To which monument did he sing "Happy Birthday" in Paris in 1989?
10 Who was his song "Sir Duke" dedicated to?
11 Which Miss Wright did Stevie Wonder marry in 1970?
12 Who sang with Stevie on his first No. 1?
13 To which black leader did he dedicate his Oscar?
14 Who were the other named Friends on Dionne Warwick's "That's What Friends are for"?
15 In which Key were the Songs on his 1976 album?
16 Who are Aisha Zakia and Kita Swan Di?
17 Who did he sing "Get It" with?
18 What was his first top five hit?
19 In 1984 Stevie was given the keys to which city, where he enjoyed much success?
20 For which song did he win an Oscar in 1985?
21 What is Stevie's real first name?
22 At which Olympics did Wonder play Lennon's "Imagine" to close the Games?
23 In which year did he begin his "A Wonder Summer's Night" Tour?
24 At which US Presidential candidate's acceptance did Wonder perform in 2008?
25 With which Italian classical singer did Wonder perform on the album *Amore*?
26 What "Happy" occasion was Stevie celebrating with this party song in 1981?
27 In 2010, Stevie Wonder headlined which UK festival?
28 Can you name the famous soul record label Stevie signed with when he was only 12?
29 What instrument was Stevie best known for playing in his early days?
30 Which Stevie Wonder hit from 1970 featured prominently in Barack Obama's presidential campaign?

Answers	**Movies Pot Luck 9** *(see Quiz 78)*

1 Najimy. 2 Boxing. 3 Elizabeth Mastrantonio. 4 Ingrid Bergman. 5 Steve Martin. 6 Chris Columbus. 7 Sean Archer. 8 Children of a Lesser God. 9 Rachmaninov. 10 1950s. 11 Franklin Schaffner. 12 Singin' in the Rain. 13 Air Force One. 14 Lucy Honeychurch. 15 Alfred Hitchcock. 16 Gigi. 17 Richard E. Grant. 18 Steve McQueen. 19 The Color Purple. 20 Peter Benchley. 21 Donald Pleasence. 22 Jeremy Irons. 23 Cox. 24 1980s. 25 Maximilian Schell. 26 Get Smart. 27 Paul Feig. 28 Chico. 29 Goldie Hawn. 30 Neil Simon.

1 Which Kathy featured in *Sister Act*?
2 At what sport did Robert De Niro excel?
3 Which Mary starred in *The Abyss*?
4 Who won the Best Actress Oscar for *Gaslight*?
5 *The Muppet Movie* and *The Man with Two Brains* link which actor?
6 Who directed *Mrs Doubtfire*?
7 What was the name of John Travolta's character in *Face/Off*?
8 William Hurt and Marlee Matlin's relationship began on the set of which movie?
9 Which classical composer's music features in *Brief Encounter*?
10 In which decade was *An Affair to Remember* released?
11 Who won the Best Director Oscar for *Patton*?
12 Which classic musical charts the careers of Lockwood and Lamont?
13 In which film did the character President James Marshall appear?
14 What was the name of Helena Bonham Carter's character in *A Room with a View*?
15 Who directed the 1938 version of *The Lady Vanishes*?
16 For which film was Vincente Minnelli awarded his only Oscar?
17 Who played Seward in the 90s *Bram Stoker's Dracula*?
18 *The Blob* and *Le Mans* both featured which actor?
19 Sisters named Celie and Nettie appeared in which film?
20 Who wrote the book on which *Jaws* was based?
21 Who played Heinrich Himmler in *The Eagle Has Landed*?
22 Which British actor won an Oscar for *Reversal of Fortune*?
23 Which Courtney starred in *Ace Ventura, Pet Detective*?
24 In which decade was *Airplane!* released?
25 Who won the Best Actor Oscar for *Judgment at Nuremberg*?
26 Which 1960s spoof spy TV series was released as a movie in September 2008?
27 Who directed *Ghostbusters* in 2016?
28 Who was the oldest Marx brother?
29 Which actress links *Shampoo* and *Overboard*?
30 Who wrote the play on which *The Odd Couple* was based?

Answers | **Pop: Stevie Wonder** (*see Quiz 77*)

1 Piano, drums, harmonica. 2 Little Stevie Wonder. 3 Tamla Motown. 4 "Uptight". 5 Frank Sinatra's. 6 Woman in Red. 7 1950s. 8 Julio Iglesias. 9 Eiffel Tower. 10 Duke Ellington. 11 Syreeta. 12 Paul McCartney. 13 Nelson Mandela. 14 Elton John, Gladys Knight. 15 Of Life. 16 His daughters. 17 Michael Jackson. 18 "I was Made to Love Her". 19 Detroit. 20 "I Just Called to Say I Love You". 21 Stevland. 22 Atlanta (1996). 23 2007. 24 Barack Obama. 25 Andrea Bocelli. 26 Birthday. 27 Glastonbury. 28 Motown (Tamla). 29 The harmonica. 30 Signed, Sealed, Delivered I'm Yours.

1 In which series did Ricky Gervais play Andy Millman?
2 *Third Rock from the Sun* is set in which fictional US city?
3 In *Only Fools and Horses*, who was studying computing?
4 Which former private investigator appeared as Monica's boyfriend in *Friends*?
5 Who starred as *Shelley*?
6 What was Harry Enfield's character called in *Men Behaving Badly*?
7 This Welsh singer and comedian provided voices for the telly Goons. Who is he?
8 What was the function of the army platoon to which Bilko was attached?
9 How did Mr Bean lock his car?
10 Who played the guitar on *Red Dwarf*?
11 What was the name of the store in *Are You being Served*?
12 Where was the Practice based in the series *A Very Peculiar Practice*?
13 In *Brush Strokes*, what was the name of the lead character?
14 What is the connection between *Porridge, Bloomers* and *Rising Damp*?
15 What was the occupation of *The Young Ones*?
16 In which show did Brenda and Malcolm enjoy ornithology?
17 Which late 80s sitcom starred Richard Briers as a struggling inner-city vicar?
18 Whose son-in-law was a randy Scouse git?
19 What was Marvin the Android's mental problem in the *Hitchhiker's Guide to the Galaxy*?
20 What is the name of the pub in *Only Fools and Horses*?
21 Whose first comedy series was called simply *Marty*?
22 If you heard, "So it's goodnight from me, and it's goodnight from him," which programme would you be watching?
23 Which former Beatles songwriter made a guest appearance in *Bread*?
24 How many children do Cliff and Claire Huxtable have in *The Cosby Show*?
25 Ricky Gervais is bringing back which character in 2016's *Life on the Road*?
26 In *Two Point Four Children* what is the name of Bill's husband?
27 In which city is the sitcom *Spin City* set?
28 In *The Lucy Show*, Lucille Ball worked where?
29 George Burns appeared on TV with one of his wives. Who?
30 Which duo starred in *Plaza Patrol*?

| **Answers** | **Football Pot Luck 9** *(see Quiz 80)* |

1 Ball. 2 Blue. 3 Crewe Alexandra. 4 Danny McGrain. 5 Bootham Crescent.
6 Hunt. 7 England. 8 Manchester Utd. 9 Wycombe Wanderers. 10 1880s. 11 QPR. 12 Sunderland. 13 Alan McLaren. 14 Liverpool. 15 Gray. 16 1950s. 17 Tottenham Hotspur. 18 Peter Shilton. 19 Roeder. 20 John Scales. 21 Luis Felipe Scolari. 22 11. 23 Watford. 24 Nottingham Forest. 25 Arsenal. 26 Blue and white. 27 Bayern Munich. 28 Leeds United. 29 City. 30 McGhee.

1 Which Alan became Stoke City manager in 1989?

2 What colour are Chesterfield's home shirts?

3 Which was David Platt's first League club?

4 Which Scotland captain was born in Finnieston in 1950?

5 What is the name of York City's ground?

6 Which Roger was First Divison leading scorer in 1965–66?

7 Which country did Bob McNab play for?

8 Which club did Gordon Strachan join on leaving Aberdeen?

9 Which club are nicknamed the Chairboys?

10 In which decade did Blackburn Rovers first win the FA Cup?

11 Andy Sinton and Roy Wegerle were in the same team at which club?

12 Jim Montgomery set a League appearance record at which club?

13 Who was the only League ever-present for Rangers in 1995–96?

14 In which city was Mark Hateley born?

15 Which Andy of Palace won his only England cap in 1991?

16 In which decade was Trevor Francis born?

17 Which team were beaten 3–2 by Coventry in the 1987 FA Cup Final?

18 Who was the regular keeper for Derby in their 1990–91 relegation season?

19 Which Glenn left as Watford boss in February 1996?

20 Which defender played 240 games for Wimbledon before going to Liverpool?

21 Who was coach of Brazil at the 2002 World Cup finals?

22 What number did Michael Owen wear when he was with Real Madrid?

23 Steve Harrison followed Dave Bassett as boss of which club?

24 What was Hans Segers's first English League club?

25 Which team lost 1–0 to Liverpool in the 1989 FA Charity Shield?

26 What two colours are on Hartlepool's home shirts?

27 Which club did Jurgen Klinsmann join on leaving Tottenham Hotspur?

28 Allen Clarke was at which club when he made his international debut?

29 John Stones, in 2016, is a centre back for which Manchester side?

30 Which Mark was Reading boss from 1991 to 1994?

---

1 Which song has the words "Scaramouche, will you do the fandango?"?
2 Which 2016 No. 1 started with "Hello...".
3 Which title line follows "Our thoughts to them are winging, when friends by shame are undefiled" in the Enya song?
4 Which Dire Straits hit starts "Here comes Johnny singing oldies, goldies"?
5 Which song begins "When I was young, I never needed anyone"?
6 In which song would you find the lines "Daylight. I must wait for the sunrise, I must wait for a new life. And I mustn't give in"?
7 Which Christmas classic has the lines "Man will live for evermore, because of Christmas Day"?
8 Which film song begins "From the day we arrive on the planet and, blinking, step into the sun"?
9 In the 60s who sang "We skipped the light fandango..."?
10 What is the first line of Kiki Dee's "Amoureuse"?
11 Which song has the line "Do the fairies keep him sober for a day"?
12 Which excuse for a massacre gave the Boomtown Rats a hit song?
13 What follows "The truth is I never left you" in the song from *Evita*?
14 In which song did Phil Collins sing "Wouldn't you agree, baby you and me?"
15 What follows "When I find myself in times of trouble, Mother Mary comes to me"?
16 What is the first line of the Supremes' "You Keep Me Hangin' On"?
17 Which Bee Gees hit has the line "Cause we're livin' in a world of fools"?
18 Who sang "Isn't she precious, less than one minute old?"?
19 Which song has the line "And just like the guy whose feet were too big for his bed"?
20 Which classic begins "She packed my bags last night, pre-flight"?
21 "I Will Always Love You" was written by which country star?
22 How should you "Let Your Love Flow" according to the Bellamy Brothers?
23 How old is the Dancing Queen?
24 In which American state is the Amarillo in "Is This the Way to Amarillo"?
25 Elvis Presley's "It's Now or Never" has the same tune as which Italian ballad?
26 What country was Razorlight singing the praises of in their No. 1 hit of 2006?
27 Name the line which follows "Oops!" in Britney's massive 2000 No. 1 hit?
28 What was Kylie "Spinning" in her fifth UK No.1 hit?
29 What was Nelly Furtado eating in her No. 1 hit, a popular karaoke?
30 "Buddy you're a boy make a big noise" is the opening line of which rock classic?

1 A character named Dr Sherman Klump appeared in which film?
2 Mila Kunis, Kathryn Hahn, Kristen Bell, Christina Applegate starred together in which 2016 film?
3 In which decade was *Porky's* released?
4 Which actor had siblings called Leaf, Rainbow, Summer and Liberty?
5 Who won the Best Director Oscar for *A Man for All Seasons*?
6 Which film musical features Nellie Forbush?
7 Which Denise featured in *Starship Troopers*?
8 What was the name of the Bond girl in *Octopussy*?
9 In which city does the action of *Godzilla* take place?
10 In which decade of the 20th century was Geena Davis born?
11 Which Mary featured in *Independence Day*?
12 Who won the Best Actress Oscar for *Mildred Pierce*?
13 Who played General Ben Vandervoort in *The Longest Day*?
14 To the nearest hour, how long does *Spartacus* last?
15 In which movie was Whoopi Goldberg the voice of hyena Shenzi?
16 Which writer directed *Rosencrantz and Guildenstern are Dead* in 1990?
17 The character Martin Riggs appeared in which film?
18 Which actor is the grandson of producer Michael Balcon?
19 *Local Hero* is set on the west coast of which country?
20 *Planet of the Apes* and *The Poseidon Adventure* featured which actor?
21 Which redhead sang "Bewitched, Bothered and Bewildered" in *Pal Joey*?
22 Which Sam featured in *The Hunt for Red October*?
23 In which decade was *The Bells of St Mary's* released?
24 *Top Gun* and *Cat Chaser* both feature which actress?
25 What's Arnold Schwarzenegger's job in *Total Recall*?
26 What type of creature did Robin Williams voice over in *Happy Feet*?
27 Who was the director of the 2006 movie *The Prestige*?
28 Who sings "He's a Tramp" in *Lady and the Tramp*?
29 Who played opposite Peter O'Toole in the 1960s *Goodbye Mr Chips*?
30 Who won the Best Director Oscar for *West Side Story*?

1 Who has written Luther for Idris Elba since 2010?
2 Who played Inspector Morse's faithful sergeant Det.-Sgt Robert Lewis?
3 Which role was played by both Loretta Swit and Sharon Gless?
4 Which police officer is central to the series *Heartbeat*?
5 What character did Robert Lee play in *The Chinese Detective*?
6 Which actor played Dodie and Boyle's boss?
7 In *Cribb*, name the famous elephant at London Zoo that was central to the plot in the episode called "The Lost Trumpet".
8 Who played the title role in *Jemima Shore Investigates*?
9 What department did George Carter work for?
10 Which actor played Quincy?
11 What is Skinner's FBI title in the *X-Files*?
12 Who is the creator of *Cracker*?
13 Which orchestra played the theme from *Van Der Valk*?
14 Who does *Columbo* frequently cite as his inspiration?
15 Who played Dan Tanner?
16 Name the female detective in *Cracker*.
17 Where was the setting for *Bergerac*?
18 Which two actresses originally made up the team with Jill Gascoine in *C.A.T.S Eyes*?
19 In *Knight Rider*, Michael Knight worked for the Foundation for what?
20 What was the name of Kojak's brother?
21 Jeremy Brett played which detective?
22 Name the central character in the series *Juliet Bravo*.
23 What did TV detective Jim Rockford live in?
24 Who sang the theme song from *Moonlighting*?
25 Who frequently said the words, "Evening all"?
26 Who played Elliot Ness in the TV version of *The Untouchables*?
27 Whose catchphrase was, "Book him, Danno"?
28 Name the actress who plays Sgt June Ackland in *The Bill*.
29 What was the name of the twisted tycoon played by Stanley Tucci in *Murder One*?
30 Name Perry Mason's female assistant.

1 Carlton Palmer and Paul Warhurst were in the same team at which club?
2 What colour are Port Vale's home shorts?
3 What was John Scales's first League club?
4 In which decade was Juninho born?
5 Who plays at home at Adams Park?
6 In 2016, which Giorgio was rated by The Guardian as the 50th Best Player in the World?
7 Burrows, Thomas and Wright appeared in an FA Cup Final team for which club?
8 Which club did Ray Wilkins leave to join Rangers?
9 Which Scottish club is nicknamed the Spiders?
10 To five either way, in which year did Barnsley first win the FA Cup?
11 Which England player was born on Jersey in 1968?
12 Eric Skeels set a League appearance record at which club?
13 Which club was Frank Worthington with when he was First Division leading scorer in 1978–79?
14 Which keeper can list Birmingham, Watford and Sunderland among his clubs?
15 Who was the only League ever-present for Celtic in 1995–96?
16 Which Brian of Arsenal won his only England cap in 1988?
17 Who was the regular keeper for Sunderland in their 1990–91 relegation season?
18 Which team were beaten 3–2 by West Ham Utd in the 1964 FA Cup Final?
19 What is Roy Keane's middle name?
20 Which striker – who has since played for England – was loaned to Istanbul side Besiktas in 1989?
21 Where did England draw 2–2 with Greece to qualify for the 2002 World Cup?
22 Which Frenchman won Footballer of the Year while with Tottenham Hotspur?
23 Who managed Sevilla to victory over Middlesbrough in the 2006 UEFA Cup Final?
24 Eddie Gray followed Allan Clarke as manager at which club?
25 What is the middle name of ex-Liverpool ace Mark Walters?
26 In which decade did Notts County first win the FA Cup?
27 Which 6ft 7in striker was Stockport's most expensive transfer sale when he joined Birmingham City for £800,000 in January 1995?
28 With 583 games, which keeper was Charlton's League appearance record-holder?
29 David Johnson was at which club when he made his international debut in the 1970s?
30 In their 1994–95 season, who was Everton's top League scorer?

1 Which group was Jimmy Page in before forming Led Zeppelin?
2 What was Deep Purple's first hit in the singles charts?
3 What is Ozzy Ozbourne's actual first name?
4 Which group were "Paranoid" in the charts?
5 Which group took its name from a medieval instrument of torture?
6 They were known for imaginative cover designs, but what was the title of Led Zeppelin's third album?
7 By what name is Marvin Lee Aday better known?
8 Which group founded the Bludgeon Riffola label?
9 Which city did Black Sabbath come from?
10 Ian Gillan, Graham Bonnet and David Coverdale sang for which group?
11 In which group did Angus Young wear short trousers?
12 Who recorded "Bark at the Moon"?
13 What instrument did Ian Paice play?
14 Which folk singer sang on Led Zep's "The Battle of Evermore"?
15 Which album from 1978 was reissued in 1991 and led to a 1993 sequel?
16 How were Whitesnake credited on their first recordings?
17 "Smoke on the Water" came from which album?
18 Terry Butler changed his group's name to Black Sabbath after reading a novel by which author?
19 What instrument does Iron Maiden founder Steve Harris play?
20 "Naked Thunder" was the first solo album by which singer?
21 Which band's "School's Out" was the music for a credit card advert in 2008?
22 Which Black Sabbath member has become a 2000s reality show stalwart?
23 Which member of the 2008 Van Halen line-up is not a Van Halen?
24 Which band took their name from a character in Dickens's David Copperfield?
25 Who unleashed *The Book of Souls* in September 2015?
26 Which band had a US No. 1 album in 2008 with "Death Magnetic"?
27 What card was a massive heavy metal hit for Motorhead?
28 Name the popular British band who took their name from an old Germanic tribe.
29 Name the American band formed in Los Angeles in 1981 by Lars Ulrich.
30 Whose "Back in Black" track was heard at the beginning of the hit movie *Iron Man*?

1 Whose first hit was "Rock with the Caveman"?

2 Which surname is shared by Tony and Lou?

3 In which decade was Petula Clark born?

4 Who wanted to be Bobby's Girl in 1962?

5 Who were Vic Reeves's backing group?

6 What is the home country of Paul Anka?

7 What Beach band tragically died in a bus crash in Sweden in 2016?

8 Which Beach Boys album included goats on the album cover?

9 Whose 1996 album was called *K*?

10 Dolores O'Riordan is lead singer with which band?

11 How is Vincent Furnier better known?

12 Who had Joe Strummer as lead vocalist?

13 A 1991 TV concert by Clannad was a tribute to which Irishman?

14 How are David, Stephen, Graham and Neil better known?

15 Which Gibb was not a Bee Gee?

16 Whose real surname is Gudmundsdottir?

17 Whose first chart entry was "Chantilly Lace"?

18 Who was keyboard player with the Dave Clark Five?

19 In which decade did the Faces have their first hit record?

20 Whose album *Diva* topped the charts in 1993?

21 Which band won the Mercury Music Award for Best Band in 2008?

22 Ne-Yo's 2008 album was *The Year of the* what?

23 What nickname did the DJ Steve Wright give to Prince?

24 What is Andy Summers doing on the cover of the *Synchronicity* album?

25 What did Mrs Brown have according to Herman's Hermits?

26 Which Rod Stewart album had *Blondes* in the title?

27 What was a hit for both Neil Sedaka and then the Partridge Family?

28 What was the title of Paul McCartney's first solo album?

29 Who sang "Unbreak My Heart" in 1997?

30 In which decade was Michael Bolton born?

Answers	**Heavy Metal** *(see Quiz 85)*

1 Yardbirds. 2 Black Night. 3 John. 4 Black Sabbath. 5 Iron Maiden. 6 Led Zeppelin III. 7 Meat Loaf. 8 Def Leppard. 9 Birmingham. 10 Deep Purple. 11 AC/DC. 12 Ozzy Ozbourne. 13 Drums. 14 Sandy Denny. 15 Bat out of Hell. 16 David Coverdale's Whitesnake. 17 Machine Head. 18 Dennis Wheatley. 19 Bass Guitar. 20 Ian Gillan. 21 Alice Cooper. 22 Ozzy Osbourne. 23 David Lee Roth. 24 Uriah Heep. 25 Iron Maiden. 26 Metallica. 27 The Ace of Spades. 28 Saxon. 29 Metallica. 30 AC/DC.

1 Which film has the line, "Houston, we have a problem"?

2 Who had a father called Jor-El?

3 What sport did James Caan play as Jonathan E?

4 Which sci-fi series did De Forrest Kelly star in?

5 Who did Spielberg describe as "Walt Disney's version of a mad scientist"?

6 Who replaced Alec Guinness in *The Phantom Menace*?

7 What type of creature carries the disease in *The X-Files*?

8 Who wrote the novel *Fahrenheit 451*?

9 What is the name of the robot in *Forbidden Planet*?

10 Who produced *Logan's Run*?

11 In 2014's *Interstellar* what does Murphy shout over the NASA balcony?

12 In what year is *Escape from New York* set?

13 What planet were the rebels on before Darth Vader destroyed their base in *The Empire Strikes Back*?

14 For which monument is an H-bomb intended in *Superman II*?

15 What does Mel Gibson drive in the film *Mad Max*?

16 In which British studios was *Alien* filmed?

17 In which state does the *Invasion of the Body Snatchers* take place?

18 Who produced *The Omega Man*?

19 Who created the special effects for *Star Trek: The Motion Picture*?

20 Who was the voice of Darth Vader in the *Star Wars* trilogy?

21 *2001: A Space Odyssey* is based on which Arthur C. Clarke story?

22 What is the name of Lex Luthor's henchman in *Superman*?

23 Which member of INXS appeared in *Dogs in Space* in 1986?

24 In what sort of dwelling does Ben Kenobi live?

25 What is the name of Will Smith's character in *Men in Black*?

26 Will Smith starred as Del Spooner in which 2004 movie?

27 Which animation sci-fi movie was a summer 2008 box-office smash hit?

28 Keanu Reeves played a computer hacker named Neo in which 1999 movie?

29 Name the English actor who played Theo Faron in *Children of Men*.

30 What did "V" stand for in this 2005 movie directed by James McTeigue?

| **Answers** | **TV Pot Luck 11** *(see Quiz 88)* |

1 Carl King. 2 Will Smith. 3 Geoff Hamilton. 4 Radiolympia Radio Show. 5 News 24. 6 Verity Lambert. 7 Roseanne. 8 The Interlude. 9 Richard Chamberlain. 10 Malaya. 11 Jess Yates. 12 Johnny Carson. 13 Nell Dunn. 14 Cardiac Arrest. 15 Gallifrey. 16 Vince Gilligan. 17 Jeremy Irons. 18 Michael Aspel. 19 Carmen Munroe. 20 Arkwright. 21 Eric Sykes and Hattie Jacques. 22 1954. 23 Dennis Waterman. 24 Val Doonican. 25 Sheila Steafel. 26 Shauna Lowry. 27 Antonio Carlucci. 28 Des O'Connor. 29 The A-Team. 30 Millicent Martin.

1 Who killed Tom King in *Emmerdale*?
2 Who was the eponymous *The Fresh Prince of Bel Air*?
3 Name the late presenter of *Gardener's World*.
4 During the BBCs experimental period in 1936 live transmissions were sent to which show at Olympia?
5 What was the BBC's rolling news service originally called?
6 Who founded Verity Productions?
7 Which US comedienne bought the US rights to *Absolutely Fabulous*?
8 Where were kittens playing with wool and the potter's wheel featured?
9 Which former Dr Kildare played John Blackthorne in the 80s *Shogun*?
10 Where was *Tenko* set?
11 Who first introduced *Stars on Sunday*?
12 Name the long-time host of *The Tonite Show*.
13 Who wrote *Up the Junction*?
14 In which series did Helen Baxendale play doctor?
15 Which planet does *Dr Who* come from?
16 Who created Walter White and Saul Goodman?
17 Who was the Oscar-winning actor who appeared in *Playaway*?
18 Name the *This is Your Life* former newsreader?
19 In *The Fosters*, who played their busybody neighbour, Vilma?
20 In *Open All Hours*, what was the name of the corner-shop keeper?
21 Which "brother and sister" lived at 28 Sebastopol Terrace during the 70s sitcom?
22 In which year was the soap *The Grove Family* first transmitted?
23 Who sang the theme from *Minder*?
24 Which singer do you associate with sweaters and a rocking chair?
25 Who was the regular female performer on *The Frost Report*?
26 Which Irish redhead co-presents *Animal Hospital*?
27 Who presented his *Italian Feast*?
28 Which chat show host has interviewed Tony Blair and William Hague on his TV show?
29 Which group of renegades were played by George Peppard, Dirk Benedict, Dwight Schultz and Mr T?
30 Who sang the theme to *That was the Week That was*?

Answers	Movies: Sci-Fi 2 *(see Quiz 87)*

1 Apollo 13. 2 Superman. 3 Rollerball. 4 Star Trek. 5 George Lucas. 6 Ewan McGregor. 7 Bees. 8 Ray Bradbury. 9 Robby. 10 Saul David. 11 Eureka!. 12 1997. 13 Hoth. 14 The Eiffel Tower. 15 A V-8. 16 Shepperton studios. 17 California. 18 Walter Seltzer. 19 Douglas Trumbull. 20 James Earl Jones. 21 The Sentinel. 22 Otis. 23 Michael Hutchence. 24 Cave. 25 J. 26 I, Robot. 27 Wall. E. 28 The Matrix. 29 Clive Owen. 30 Vendetta.

1 Which country finished fourth in the 1994 World Cup?
2 Which country did Nico Claesen play for?
3 Who scored England's only goal in Euro 92?
4 In which country was Richard Gough born?
5 In which stadium was the 1986 World Cup Final played?
6 Which Dutchman hit a Euro 88 hat-trick against England?
7 Who set a record by playing 96 times for Belgium?
8 How old was Dino Zoff when he was in Italy's World Cup-winning side?
9 Whose World Cup corner flag dance started the craze for dance routine celebrations?
10 Which country did Oscar Ruggeri play for?
11 Raphaël Varane was born in 1991, 1992, or 1993?
12 Which player, who died in 1990, was awarded the Order of Lenin?
13 Which Dutch outfield player was 37 when Holland won Euro 88?
14 Who, with 54 goals, was second only to Pele as a Brazilan scorer?
15 Which Australian manager got off to a winning start in January 1997?
16 Which French player went head to head with Stuart Pearce in Euro 92?
17 How old was Diego Maradona when he first played for Argentina?
18 Who was the first Croatian international to play in the English League?
19 Which Gordon scored Scotland's only World Cup goal in Mexico?
20 Which goalkeeper is Sweden's most capped player?
21 In which city did England play Andorra in September 2008?
22 Which country went out of Euro 2008 conceding two goals in stoppage time?
23 Which country won the 2008 Olympic Games men's football gold medal?
24 Who was nicknamed the "Wally with the brolly" in 2007?
25 How many matches did England lose in the Euro 2008 qualifying campaign?
26 Which England goalkeeper made a blunder against Germany in November 2008?
27 Who did the Republic of Ireland lose to for the first time under Giovanni Trapattoni?
28 These Eastern Europeans beat Northern Ireland in Belfast in November 2008.
29 Prior to England's win in 2008, who last beat Germany in Berlin back in 1973?
30 Who did Argentina beat with Diego Maradona in charge for his first game?

Answers	Pop Pot Luck 12 (see Quiz 90)

1 1970s. 2 Bobby Darin. 3 "Joanna". 4 Bill Haley and His Comets. 5 Colin Blunstone. 6 Enya. 7 None. 8 Paul Young. 9 Shane Fenton. 10 Bonzo Dog Doo-Dah Band. 11 Germany. 12 1940s. 13 Slade. 14 George Harrison. 15 Frogman. 16 Australia. 17 Cheryl Baker. 18 Hot Gossip. 19 A & M. 20 The Men in Hats. 21 Girls Aloud. 22 Louis Walsh. 23 The Blue Notes. 24 Suzi Quatro. 25 The Proclaimers. 26 Long Hot Summer. 27 Gabrielle. 28 Michael Bolton. 29 Billy. 30 Lemonade.

1 In which decade did the Smurfs have their first hit record?
2 How was Walden Robert Cassotto better known?
3 Which song title links Scott Walker and Kool and the Gang?
4 Whose first hit was "Shake, Rattle and Roll" in 1954?
5 Who was lead vocalist with the Zombies?
6 Whose album *Shepherd Moons* topped the charts in 1992?
7 How many hit singles did Frank Zappa have in the 70s?
8 Whose debut album was *No Parlez*?
9 How was Alvin Stardust previously known in the charts?
10 Which group's members included Neil Innes and Vivian Stanshall?
11 In which country were Boney M based?
12 In which decade was Dolly Parton born?
13 Whose first hit was "Get Down and Get With It"?
14 Who had an 80s hit with "Got My Mind Set on You"?
15 What is Clarence Henry's nickname?
16 What is the home country of Bjorn Again?
17 Who took part in the Eurovision Song Contest as a member of separate groups, Co-Co and Bucks Fizz?
18 Who did Sarah Brightman sing with on her first chart hit?
19 Which record label did Herb Alpert co-found?
20 What name was given to the new country stars of the 1990s?
21 Who had a UK chart hit in 2008 with "The Promise"?
22 Who put together and managed Westlife, having done the same with Boyzone?
23 What was the name of Harold Melvin's backing group?
24 Whose nickname was "Lady Leather"?
25 In the 1980s, which group's first hit was "Letter from America"?
26 What type of "Summer" was a 1980s hit for Style Council?
27 Who joined East 17 on the 1996 hit "If You Ever"?
28 Whose first album was called *Soul Provider*?
29 Who was told, "Don't be a hero" by Paper Lace in 1974?
30 What drink is the title of Beyoncé's 2016 album?

---

1 Who described himself as Mr Average Joe American?
2 Which silent star's name was an anagram of "Arab death"?
3 Who was the sister of Olivia De Havilland?
4 About whom did Elia Kazan say, "He was sad and sulky. You kept expecting him to cry"?
5 Whose biography was called *Blonde Venus*?
6 Which 30s star famous for his dislike of children said, "I am free of all prejudices, I hate everybody equally"?
7 How many times did Alan Hale play Little John in a Robin Hood movie?
8 Which director was the subject of *Gods and Monsters*, played on screen by Sir Ian McKellen?
9 Who said, "There are two reasons I'm in showbusiness and I'm standing on both of them"?
10 What colour was Danny Kaye's hair before Goldwyn made him dye it blond?
11 Who said, "Astaire represents the aristocracy when he dances. I represent the proletariat"?
12 Whose photo in a swimsuit was pinned to the atomic bomb dropped on Bikini?
13 Who did Goldwyn mean when he said, "It took longer to make one of Mary's contracts than to make one of Mary's pictures"?
14 In *Casablanca* which British actor said, "I'm only a poor corrupt official"?
15 Which Tex sang the title song from *High Noon*?
16 Which creator of *Star Trek* was executive producer on the early *Star Trek* movies?
17 Who was the mother of actress Isabella Rossellini?
18 Which French actor's body was exhumed in 1997 because of a paternity suit?
19 Who died shortly after finishing *Network*?
20 In which decade did Jean Harlow die?
21 Whose marriage to Ava Gardner lasted just seven months?
22 Anthony Perkins died during the making of which movie?
23 Who played opposite Olivia De Havilland eight times?
24 Where was Audrey Hepburn born?
25 Whose autobiography was called *Back in the Saddle Again*?
26 In which city did Heath Ledger die?
27 Which legendary Swedish film-maker died in July 2007?
28 Name the two-time Oscar-winning "Shelley" who died in 2006.
29 Name superman's adopted father, better known for his cowboy roles, who died in 2006.
30 Which *Police Academy* actor died in 2016? Clue: first name George.

Answers	TV Pot Luck 12 *(see Quiz 92)*

1 Alan Davies. 2 2005. 3 £500. 4 Grantleigh. 5 Chickens. 6 Ant and Dec. 7 International Rentals. 8 Gardener's World. 9 Up Pompeii! 10 Cold Feet. 11 Granville. 12 That's Life. 13 Ray & Allen. 14 Loyd Grossman. 15 Lord Mountbatten. 16 Jeremy Clarkson. 17 Casey Kasem. 18 Edward Evans. 19 Gary Rhodes. 20 True. 21 All have been portrayed in cartoons. 22 Carpentry. 23 A fireman. 24 Percy Thrower. 25 Annabel Croft. 26 Twin Peaks. 27 Jack Rosenthal. 28 Lalla Ward. 29 UK Living. 30 Julia Carling.

1 Which comedian, writer and actor is a *QI* regular panellist, often finishing last?

2 When did *Grey's Anatomy* first air in Britain?

3 What is the spending limit for each team on *Changing Rooms*?

4 In *To the Manor Born*, what was the name of the Manor?

5 What was Dudley Moore always searching for in the series of Tesco ads?

6 How were PJ and Duncan also known?

7 What was the name of the company in *The Squirrels*?

8 Which gardening programme developed from *Gardening Club* in 1968?

9 In which show would you meet Ludicrus Sextus and Stovus Primus?

10 Which ensemble drama, featuring Helen Baxendale, returned in 2016?

11 What was the name of the character played by David Jason in *Open All Hours*?

12 Which Esther Rantzen series was a follow-up to *Braden's Week*?

13 What are the first names of scriptwriters Galton and Simpson?

14 Who asked, "so who would live in a house like this..."?

15 Which royal relative was the subject of *This is Your Life* in jubilee year, 1977?

16 Which *Top Gear* presenter was given his own chat show in 1998?

17 Who hosted the pop programme *America's Top Ten*?

18 Who played Mr Grove in *The Grove Family*?

19 What is the name of the spiky-haired TV chef?

20 Queen Elizabeth II is the only British sovereign to have ever visited a TV studio. True or false?

21 What do the Osmonds, the Jackson Five and the Beatles have in common?

22 Dickens and Fenster had the same trade. What was it?

23 What was Boon before he was forced into retirement?

24 Name the original presenter of *Gardening Club*.

25 Which tennis star took over from Anneka Rice in *Treasure Hunt*?

26 Which series asked the question "Who killed Laura Palmer?"

27 Who wrote *Barmitzvah Boy*?

28 In *Dr Who*, who played Romana and was also married to Tom Baker?

29 Which sister channel to UK Gold used the slogan "You can't help getting involved"?

30 Whose TV career took off after the highly publicised breakdown of her marriage to a rugby player?

Answers Movies: Late Greats *(see Quiz 91)*

1 Gary Cooper. 2 Theda Bara. 3 Joan Fontaine. 4 James Dean. 5 Marlene Dietrich. 6 W. C. Fields. 7 Three. 8 James Whale. 9 Betty Grable. 10 Red. 11 Gene Kelly. 12 Betty Grable. 13 Mary Pickford. 14 Claude Rains. 15 Ritter. 16 Gene Roddenberry. 17 Ingrid Bergman. 18 Yves Montand. 19 Peter Finch. 20 1930s. 21 Artie Shaw. 22 Psycho V. 23 Errol Flynn. 24 Belgium. 25 Gene Autry. 26 New York City. 27 Ingmar Bergman. 28 Shelley Winters. 29 Glenn Ford. 30 Gaynes.

Quiz 93 | Football: Managers | Answers – page 300

1 Which Russell has been boss of Bristol City and Cardiff City?
2 Don Howe was manager of which team in 1984?
3 Bobby Gould has twice been manager of which club?
4 At which club could fans shout in 1980, "There's only one Ernie Walley"?
5 Which London club did Geoff Hurst manage?
6 Who followed Matt Busby at Manchester Utd?
7 Who was Luton's boss when they went out of the top flight in 1992?
8 How old was Joe Fagan when he became Liverpool manager?
9 With which two sides did Herbert Chapman win the championship?
10 Who was Wimbledon boss before Joe Kinnear?
11 Who was the first player/manager to win the championship?
12 John Rudge has spent more than ten years as boss of which club?
13 Who replaced Sir Alex in the Manchester Utd hot seat in 2013?
14 Which Harry was Luton manager from 1972–78?
15 Who won the championship as a player and a manager with Tottenham Hotspur?
16 Who was caretaker manager of Sunderland when he took them to the 1992 FA Cup Final?
17 Brian Clough won his first championship as a manager at which club?
18 Who was manager of the year in 1976, 1977, 1979, 1980, 1982 and 1983?
19 Which was Mike Walker's first club as a manager?
20 Who followed David Hay as Celtic manager?
21 Which Irish international won promotion in 2007, his first season as a manager?
22 Bernd Schuster took over as manager of which championship-winner in 2007?
23 Kevin Blackwell was boss of Leeds and which other relegated club in 2006–07?
24 Who was Watford's manager in their first Premiership season, 1999–2000?
25 How many times did Bill Shankly win the FA Cup Final as Liverpool manager?
26 Which Aston Villa manager resigned just weeks before they won the European Cup?
27 Who was the Arsenal manager when they won the double in 1970–71?
28 Can you name the man who took charge of England after Ramsey and before Revie?
29 Which manager famously led Sunderland to FA Cup glory in 1973?
30 Can you name the Serie A team Roy Hodgson managed in 1998?

1 Who died, at the age of 69, in January 2016?
2 Who sang "Billy Don't be a Hero" in 1974?
3 How is Ernest Evans better known?
4 Which record label shares its name with a nautical aid?
5 Who were All Out of Love in 1980?
6 Whose album *High On the Happy Side* topped the charts in 1992?
7 Who took "Charmaine", "Diane" and "Ramona" into the top ten?
8 Who did Kate Bush duet with on "Don't Give Up"?
9 Which song was a hit for Elvis Presley and Andy Williams?
10 Who had the "Bell Bottom Blues" in 1954?
11 In which decade was Frankie Valli born?
12 Which song title links the Three Degrees and Barbra Streisand?
13 Whose first hit was "Hong Kong Garden"?
14 What was Midge Ure's first solo No. 1?
15 What is the home country of Berlin?
16 What was Cilla Black's first single?
17 Which surname is shared by Ronnie and Dina?
18 Whose singles include "Call Up the Groups" and "Pop Go the Workers"?
19 Who had their second No. 1 with "Spirit in the Sky"?
20 In which decade did Genesis have their first hit record?
21 Which repetitive band did a charity remake of "With a Little Help from My Friends"?
22 Who had a 1999 hit with Mambo No. 5?
23 Who was the subject of the hits for Julie Covington and Madonna "Don't Cry for Me Argentina"?
24 What is it according to her hit that Petula Clark "Can't Live without"?
25 Who is "a star in the face of the sky" in an Elton John it?
26 Which group had a 1985 No. 1 with "I Wanna Know What Love is"?
27 Which Police album cover had coloured stripes superimposed with photos?
28 Who had a 1987 hit with "Never Can Say Goodbye"?
29 Who joined Joe Cocker on the 1983 version of "Up Where We Belong"?
30 Which group went *Atomic* in 1980?

Answers	Football: Managers *(see Quiz 93)*

1 Osman. 2 Arsenal. 3 Coventry City. 4 Crystal Palace. 5 Chelsea. 6 Wilf McGuinness. 7 David Pleat. 8 62. 9 Huddersfield & Arsenal. 10 Peter Withe. 11 Kenny Dalglish. 12 Port Vale. 13 Louis Van Gaal. 14 Haslam. 15 Bill Nicholson. 16 Malcolm Crosby. 17 Derby County. 18 Bob Paisley. 19 Colchester United. 20 Billy McNeill. 21 Roy Keane. 22 Real Madrid. 23 Luton Town. 24 Graham Taylor. 25 Twice. 26 Ron Saunders. 27 Bertie Mee. 28 Joe Mercer. 29 Bob Stokoe. 30 Inter Milan.

1 Which Merry Man did Alan Hale play in *The Adventures of Robin Hood*?

2 Which redhead played Virginia Brush in *Strawberry Blonde*?

3 Which sister did June Allyson play in *Little Women*?

4 Which blonde replaced Alice Faye in *Down Argentina Way*?

5 Which author of *Brave New World* wrote screenplays for *Pride and Prejudice* and *Jane Eyre*?

6 In which movie did Henry Travers play an angel?

7 Who played Al Jolson in *The Jolson Story*?

8 What was the first musical hit in 1947 of Lerner and Loewe, which became a movie hit seven years later?

9 In which classic movie did Edward Gwenn play Kris Kringle?

10 Who did Laurence Olivier play in *Rebecca*?

11 Who played George M. Cohan in *Yankee Doodle Dandy*?

12 Which cowboy was high up in the money-making lists in 1940?

13 Which movie had the line, "We'll always have Paris"?

14 What were Citizen Kane's first names?

15 Which garment did Howard Hughes develop for Jane Russell in *The Outlaw*?

16 Which Paul was one of Bette Davis's co-stars in *Now Voyager*?

17 Who played two parts in *Dr Jekyll and Mr Hyde* in 1941?

18 Who was the star of the 40s version of *Million Dollar Legs*?

19 Who was Father O'Malley to Ingrid Bergman's Sister Benedict in 1945?

20 What was the Leslie Howard version of *The Scarlet Pimpernel* called?

21 Which Dickens novel was successfully adapted for the big screen by David Lean in 1946?

22 *Sergeant York* was about a hero from which conflict?

23 Which Orson Welles movie was given its final edit without his approval?

24 Who was Fred Astaire's co-star in *Easter Parade*?

25 Which real-life Jennifer starred in *Portrait of Jennie*?

26 Which future politician played George Gipp in *Knute Rockne: All American*?

27 Which German legend was top-billed in the 1942 movie *The Spoilers*?

28 Name the quintessential 1940s movie starring Bogart and Bergman.

29 *Mrs ____* was a film about the perseverance of a British middle-class family during the Blitz?

30 *The Best Years of* what was a multi-Oscar-winning movie in 1946?

Answers	**TV Pot Luck 12** *(see Quiz 96)*

1 Law & Order. **2** Basil Brush. **3** 77. **4** Eileen Atkins. **5** Prof. Heinz Wolff. **6** Dara Ó Briain. **7** Sir Bernard Miles. **8** Iain Cuthbertson. **9** Monday & Wednesday. **10** Pam Shriver. **11** Miranda Richardson. **12** Watercolour Challenge. **13** Harpo. **14** Roger Lloyd Pack. **15** Soccer player. **16** Michael Palin. **17** Mel and Sue. **18** Babs. **19** The Last Resort. **20** Sugar. **21** Steve Naïve and the Playboys. **22** Elaine Stritch & Donald Sinden. **23** Cyril Fletcher. **24** Stars & Garters. **25** Undertaker's. **26** Anthony Sher. **27** Triangle Line Ferry Co. **28** Christopher Biggins. **29** 1924. **30** Danny Kaye.

1 *Special Victims Unit* is a spin-off from which long-running US series?
2 Which famous puppet fox returned to the screens in 2002 after **22** years away?
3 How old was Terry Wogan when he died in 2016?
4 Which actress won a BAFTA award in 2008 for her performance in *Cranford*?
5 Who presented *The Great Egg Race*?
6 Name the presenter of the 2016 re-ignition of *Robot Wars*.
7 Which Knight advertised eggs?
8 Who played Charlie Endell in *Budgie*?
9 On what days of the week was the soap *Triangle* broadcast?
10 Which five-times Wimbledon doubles title winner with Martina Navratilova commentates for the BBC at the championships?
11 Who played Elizabeth in *Blackadder II*?
12 Which Channel 4 artistic competition is associated with Hannah Gordon?
13 What is the name of Oprah Winfrey's production company?
14 Who is the actor father of Emily Lloyd?
15 What was the occupation of Bradley Walsh before he became a TV star?
16 Who undertook the task to circumnavigate the world 115 years after Phileas Fogg?
17 Which duo present *Late Lunch* on Channel 4?
18 Which Pan's People dancer married Robert Powell?
19 Which late-night Channel 4 chat show was hosted by Jonathan Ross?
20 What ingredient did Gary Rhodes advertise on TV?
21 What was the name of the regular band on *The Last Resort*?
22 Which two actors played the lead roles in *Two's Company*?
23 Which person on TV was famous for his Odd odes?
24 Which show first screened in 1963 featured resident singer Kathy Kirby?
25 Where did *Billy Liar* work?
26 Which actor played *The History Man*?
27 What company featured in the BBC soap, *Triangle*?
28 Who was Cilla Black's male accomplice in the early episodes of *Surprise, Surprise*?
29 In which year did John Logie Baird commence experiments in TV?
30 Which film and TV star was born Daniel Kaminski?

Answers | Movies: The 1940s *(see Quiz 95)*

1 Little John. 2 Rita Hayworth. 3 Jo. 4 Betty Grable. 5 Aldous Huxley. 6 It's a Wonderful Life. 7 Larry Parks. 8 Brigadoon. 9 Miracle on 34th Street. 10 Maxim De Winter. 11 James Cagney. 12 Gene Autry. 13 Casablanca. 14 Charles Foster. 15 Bra. 16 Henreid. 17 Spencer Tracy. 18 Betty Grable. 19 Bing Crosby. 20 Pimpernel Smith. 21 Great Expectations. 22 World War I. 23 The Magnificent Ambersons. 24 Judy Garland. 25 Jennifer Jones. 26 Ronald Reagan. 27 Marlene Dietrich. 28 Casablanca. 29 Miniver. 30 Our Lives.

1 Which Dutch team were the first to win a major European trophy?
2 As a player which club did Johan Cruyff move to when he left Ajax?
3 With 83 games who set an appearance record for Holland?
4 In which city was Ruud Gullit born?
5 Who was the top scorer in Euro 88?
6 Who were Dutch champions in 1994, 1995 and 1996?
7 Who was the Dutch coach for Euro 88?
8 Which English club did Dennis Bergkamp support as a child?
9 Which Dutch player scored against England in Euro 96?
10 Ruud Gullit became the world's most expensive player when he moved from which club to AC Milan in 1987?
11 Which English manager won two consecutive titles with PSV Eindhoven in the 1990s?
12 Who was top scorer for the Dutch in both 1974 and 1978 World Cups?
13 What are the colours of Ajax?
14 At which club did Ronald Koeman start his League career?
15 Who was the first Dutch skipper to lift a major international trophy for his country?
16 Which team knocked Holland out of the 1994 World Cup?
17 Which Dutch club did the Brazilian Romario play for?
18 In which city is the club Feyenoord?
19 Which was the first World Cup tournament that Holland qualified for after the Second World War?
20 Gullit, Van Basten and Rijkaard lined up at which Italian club?
21 Who won a Dutch, two English and a Spanish champions medal 2002–08?
22 Which Dutch international was allowed to wear goggles because of glaucoma?
23 At Euro 2000, Eindhoven, Amsterdam, Rotterdam and where staged matches?
24 Which English club did record international goal scorer Patrick Kluivert play for?
25 Which club has won the most Dutch league championships?
26 Which ex-Celtic boss played against them in the 1970 European Cup final?
27 Which striker went on strike at Nottingham Forest in 1998?
28 Who was the first Dutch player to score in the FA Cup Final?
29 Can you name the Italian side Edwin van der Sar played for?
30 Which famous Dutch player died on March 24 2016?

Answers | **Pop Pot Luck 14 (see Quiz 98)**

1 Spain. 2 Adam Ant. 3 Bruce Willis. 4 Jackie Trent. 5 Queen. 6 Blue Mink. 7 Bonnie Tyler. 8 1950s. 9 "Mr Tambourine Man". 10 "Pink Cadillac". 11 Two. 12 Spain and Germany. 13 Donovan. 14 East 17. 15 Julie Driscoll, Brian Auger and The Trinity. 16 1960s. 17 America. 18 "Better the Devil You Know". 19 Friday. 20 "1–2–3". 21 Three. 22 Make You Happy. 23 Chuck E. 24 Billy Joel. 25 The Bunnymen. 26 1960s. 27 Laurie Anderson. 28 Status Quo. 29 The Real Thing. 30 Sir George Martin.

1 Which country did Baccara come from?
2 How is Stuart Goddard better known?
3 Which actor was Under the Boardwalk in 1987?
4 Who had a 60s No. 1 with "Where are You Now (My Love)"?
5 Whose album *Innuendo* topped the charts in 1991?
6 Who had a 1969 hit with "Melting Pot"?
7 Who had a Total Eclipse of the Heart in 1983?
8 In which decade did Neil Sedaka have his first hit record?
9 What was the Byrds' debut No. 1?
10 Which car was Natalie Cole's first hit record?
11 How many members of D:Ream are there?
12 What are the home countries of the members of Los Bravos?
13 Who was a Sunshine Superman in 1966?
14 Whose first hit was "House of Love"?
15 Who had a hit in the UK in 1968 with "This Wheel's on Fire"?
16 In which decade was Enya born?
17 Who had a Horse with No Name in 1971?
18 Which song title links Kylie Minogue and Sonia?
19 Which day of the week did the Easybeats have on their mind in 1966?
20 Which numbers were a 60s hit for Len Barry?
21 How many Elvis tracks reached UK No. 1 in 2005?
22 What, in 1999, did Britney Spears claim she was "Born" to do?
23 Who, according to Rickie Lee Jones in 1979, was "in Love"?
24 Whose first Top 10 album was *52nd Street*?
25 Who was the backing group for Echo?
26 In which decade was Jon Bon Jovi born?
27 Who had a 1981 hit with "Oh Superman"?
28 Who went up to No. 1 with "Down Down" in 1974?
29 Whose first hit was "You to Me are Everything" in the 1970s?
30 Which Beatles producer sadly passed away in March 2008?

---

1 Which actress was Oscar-nominated for *The End of the Affair*?
2 What nationality are Jennifer Lopez's parents?
3 Who was Valerie Edmond's male co-star in *One More Kiss*?
4 Which actress voices Jessie in *Toy Story 2*?
5 Which actor links *Sleepy Hollow* and *Starship Troopers*?
6 Who links the films *Now and Then* and *American Beauty*?
7 Who does Virginie Ledoyden play in *The Beach*?
8 Who starred opposite Johnny Depp in *Devil's Advocate*?
9 Who played the law officer in *Double Jeopardy*?
10 Who plays Toni Collette's son in *The Sixth Sense*?
11 Which actress links *Romeo + Juliet* and *Little Women*?
12 What name links *Stigmata* and *Scream 3*?
13 Who has been Oscar-nominated for *Being John Malkovich*?
14 Who was "the next best thing" for Madonna in the movie of the same name?
15 Which actor links *The Beach* and *Angela's Ashes*?
16 Which actress links *Elizabeth* and *The Talented Mr Ripley*?
17 Who voices the Rooster in *Chicken Run*?
18 Which actress links *Pleasantville* and *Dangerous Liaisons*?
19 Who links *Trainspotting* and *Star Wars: The Phantom Menace*?
20 Which actress links *Leon* and *Star Wars: The Phantom Menace*?
21 Who played the young temptress in *American Beauty*?
22 Who links *Picture Perfect* and *The Iron Giant*?
23 What was the name of DiCaprio's character in *The Beach*?
24 Who was Oscar-nominated for *The Talented Mr Ripley*?
25 Which actress links *The Ice Storm* and *The Opposite of Sex*?
26 Which famous children's author did Renee Zellweger play in 2006?
27 Johnny Depp reprised Gene Wilder's role as which Willie?
28 What actress was "The Million Dollar Baby"?
29 Who played the lead role in *The Royal Tenenbaums*?
30 Can you name the actor who played Sergeant Sean Dignam in *The Departed*?

Answers	**TV Pot Luck 14** *(see Quiz 100)*

1 86. **2** Sansa. **3** Paul. **4** Jean Alexander. **5** Sophie Grigson. **6** The Creatives. **7** A Yorkshire police station. **8** Clive Anderson. **9** Daniella Nardini. **10** Kate Adie. **11** The A-Team. **12** Peter Davison. **13** Wilkins. **14** Ally. **15** A Question of Sport. **16** Chris Hammond. **17** Liam Cunningham. **18** Clive James. **19** John Humphries. **20** Kim Basinger. **21** Billy Cotton. **22** Korea. **23** Lee McQueen. **24** Richard Dimbleby. **25** What's My Line. **26** Phillip Schofield. **27** Snoopy Return. **28** DJ. **29** The Rover's Return. **30** Grange Hill.

1 How old was Joan Hickson when her last portrayal of *Miss Marple* was first aired?
2 Since 2011, Sophie Turner has become famous for playing which Stark?
3 What was *Dangerfield*'s Christian name?
4 Who played Auntie Wainwright in *Last of the Summer Wine*?
5 Which cook presented a series on herbs?
6 Which sitcom starred and was written by Jack Docherty and Moray Hunter?
7 Where was the series *Out of the Blue* located?
8 Which interviewing barrister was *All Talk*?
9 Which actress from *This Life* appeared in *Undercover Heart*?
10 Which journalist reported for the BBC from Tripoli in 1986 on the American bombing?
11 Which Team helped those in trouble in the 1980s?
12 Who played Tristan Farnon in *All Creatures Great and Small*?
13 What was the name of *The Family*?
14 What was the first name of McCoist in *McCoist and McCauley*?
15 Which sporting gameshow features a "what happens next" board?
16 Who replaced Nick as Station Officer in *London's Burning*?
17 Who played Mossie Sheehan in *Falling for a Dancer*?
18 Which Australian presenter met *The Supermodels*?
19 Who presented *On the Record*?
20 Which American film actress appeared in Peugeot commercials?
21 Which bandleader had a son with the same name who became a BBC executive?
22 Where did *M*A*S*H* take place?
23 Who won series four of *The Apprentice* in 2008?
24 What was the name of broadcasters David and Jonathan's father?
25 Which quiz, hosted by Eamonn Andrews, featured Gilbert Harding as a panellist?
26 Which Joseph worked with a gopher?
27 Who is Spike's brother in *Peanuts*?
28 What was the name of *Roseanne*'s son?
29 Where did Vera and Jack Duckworth live in 1998?
30 In which children's series was there a rival school named Brookdale?

Answers | Movies: Stars of the 21st Century *(see Quiz 99)*

1 Julianne Moore. 2 Puerto Rican. 3 Gerry Butler. 4 Joan Cusack. 5 Casper Van Dien. 6 Thora Birch. 7 Francoise. 8 Charlize Theron. 9 Tommy Lee Jones. 10 Haley Joel Osment. 11 Claire Danes. 12 Arquette (Patricia and David). 13 Spike Jonze. 14 Rupert Everett. 15 Robert Carlyle. 16 Cate Blanchett. 17 Mel Gibson. 18 Reese Witherspoon. 19 Ewan McGregor. 20 Natalie Portman. 21 Mena Suvari. 22 Jennifer Aniston. 23 Richard. 24 Jude Law. 25 Christina Ricci. 26 Beatrix Potter. 27 Wonka. 28 Hilary Swank. 29 Gene Hackman. 30 Mark Wahlberg.

1 Which team shocked the others when it entered what was described as a "fan car" in the 1978 Swedish Grand Prix?
2 Why was this thought to be illegal?
3 What did its designer say the fan was for?
4 The chairman of which team was arrested in 1979 on charges of trying to defraud the De Lorean Motor Company?
5 In 2016, what did Lewis Hamilton allegedly destroy in anger after a European Grand Prix qualifying crash?
6 Which grand prix was pulled from the championship in 1980 after political division?
7 Which parties were at war?
8 Name the Lotus sponsor from Essex petroleum who was arrested in 1981 for financial malpractice.
9 Which team had a mechanic killed in the cramped Zolder pit lane in 1981?
10 Which team had a mechanic hit on the grid at the same race?
11 Whose car was he attending?
12 Why did the FIA refuse to allow Lotus to enter its 88B chassis for the 1981 British Grand Prix?
13 Which teams boycotted the 1982 San Marino Grand Prix?
14 Who broke an alleged pre-race agreement to win that race?
15 With whom did he fall out as a result of this?
16 Why was Renault embarrassed after Alain Prost lost out in the 1983 finale in South Africa?
17 Who refused to let Lotus sign Derek Warwick for 1986?
18 Which team boss was paralysed in a car crash before the 1986 season?
19 Which Brabham driver died when testing at Paul Ricard in 1986?
20 Which Swiss driver ended his Formula One career after crashing in a rally, killing his co-driver?
21 Which team's secrets were handed to a McLaren engineer in a dossier in 2007?
22 At which GP did Fernando Alonso deny Lewis Hamilton the chance to qualify?
23 Which team left the Constructors Cup in 2008 after 39 pointless races?
24 Which former F1 driver Alessandro lost both legs in an IndyCar crash in 2001?
25 In which year did Minardi run its final grand prix?
26 At which grand prix did Lewis Hamilton receive racial abuse in 2008?
27 Who is alleged to have ordered MPs to exempt F1 from tobacco advertising?
28 Who was at the centre of an S&M sex scandal in 2008?
29 Can you name the driver whose world title hopes were ended by a flat tyre in 1986?
30 Who broke his leg in a crash at the start of the 1999 British Grand Prix?

| **Answers** | Football Pot Luck 11 *(see Quiz 102)* |

1 Aston Villa. 2 The Republic of Ireland. 3 Stoke City. 4 1930s. 5 Dunfermline Athletic. 6 Claudia. 7 Aston Villa. 8 Southampton. 9 Charlton Athletic. 10 Celtic. 11 Bruce Grobbelaar. 12 Carl Tiler. 13 Red. 14 1970s. 15 Phil Babb. 16 Heath. 17 Leyton Orient. 18 Roy Keane. 19 Croker. 20 Leeds Utd. 21 Aime Jacquet. 22 Sunderland. 23 Black. 24 Allen. 25 Bristol Rovers. 26 Tony Adams. 27 Coventry City. 28 Ipswich Town. 29 England. 30 Bryan Robson.

1 Tony Barton followed Ron Saunders as boss of which club?
2 Which country did Tony Galvin play for?
3 Which was Steve Bould's first League club?
2 In which decade was Duncan Edwards born?
5 Who plays at home at East End Park?
6 Philipp Lahm's wife is called _____ Lahm?
7 Charlie Aitken set a League appearance record at which club?
8 Which club did Dave Beasant join on leaving Chelsea?
9 Which team were beaten 4–1 in the first post-World War Two FA Cup Final?
10 Tommy Coyne was at which club when he made his international debut?
11 Which 38-year-old goalkeeper was released by Southampton in May 1996?
12 Who moved from Barnsley to Nottingham Forest in 1991 to set a club record for transfer fee received?
13 What colour are Aberdeen's home shorts?
14 In which decade did Chelsea first win the FA Cup?
15 Which Republic of Ireland defender was born in Lambeth, London in 1970?
16 Which Adrian became manager of Burnley in March 1996?
17 Which club did Mervyn Day leave to join Aston Villa?
18 Who was stripped of the captaincy of the Republic of Ireland in 1996 for holidaying without informing his boss?
19 Which Ted became secretary of the FA in September 1973?
20 Mel Sterland and Tony Dorigo were in the same team at which club?
21 Who was coach of France when they won the 1998 World Cup?
22 Playing for which club did Kevin Phillips top the Premiership goal-scoring charts?
23 What colour are Sheffield Utd's home shorts?
24 Which Martin became boss of Brentford in March 2004?
25 Which team were once known as Eastville Rovers?
26 Which player's book *Addicted* appeared in 1998?
27 George Curtis followed Don Mackay as manager at which club?
28 Which club did Steve Sedgley join on leaving Tottenham Hotspur?
29 Which country did Mark Chamberlain play for?
30 Which England skipper was born in Chester-le-Street in 1957?

Answers | **Formula One: Scandals & Disasters** *(see Quiz 101)*

1 Brabham. 2 Because it was thought to keep the car on the track by suction. 3 Cooling the engine. 4 Lotus. 5 A hospitality suite. 6 Spanish. 7 FOCA versus FISA. 8 David Thieme. 9 Osella. 10 Arrows. 11 Riccardo Patrese's. 12 It effectively had one chassis piggy-backing on top of the other and thus breached the rules. 13 The FOCA teams. 14 Didier Pironi. 15 Gilles Villeneuve. 16 It had flown out hordes of journalists to watch him win the world championship. 17 Ayrton Senna. 18 Frank Williams. 19 Elio de Angelis. 20 Marc Surer. 21 Ferrari. 22 Hungary. 23 Super Aguri. 24 Zanardi. 25 2005. 26 The Spanish. 27 Tony Blair. 28 Max Moseley. 29 Nigel Mansell. 30 Michael Schumacher.

1 Which group included Agnetha and Anni-Frid?
2 Who released *Nine Track Mlnd* in 2016?
3 What was on the other side of Boney M's "Rivers of Babylon"?
4 What was the Monkees' first and bestselling single?
5 Who was percussionist with the Police?
6 Who was vocalist with the News?
7 Which Irish group's name means "family"?
8 In which decade did Simple Minds have their first No. 1?
9 Who had a 1988 album called *Introspective*?
10 Which group's 1991 bestselling album was *Stars*?
11 Who had an *Appetite for Destruction* in 1987?
12 Which band's line-up included "Chrissie Boy" Foreman and Lee "Kix" Thompson?
13 Which band were *All the Way from Memphis* in 1973?
14 Who were Eric Clapton, Jack Bruce and Ginger Baker?
15 Which singer/guitarist published his autobiography *X-Ray* in 1995?
16 Which word follows Mad in the song title by Tears for Fears?
17 Paul Heaton formed which group after the Housemartins?
18 Which Gibb brother is the eldest Bee Gee?
19 Whose first No. 1 was "In the Summertime" in 1970?
20 Which two Tamla groups combined on "I'm Gonna Make You Love Me" in 1969?
21 Who is the only male member of the Corrs?
22 Damon Albarn was lead singer for which group until 2003?
23 Myleene Klass was a member of which group in 2002?
24 In which city did the Arctic Monkeys come together?
25 Which Boston group will celebrate 40 years together in 2010?
26 Name the girl band formed in 1999 by OMD's Andy McCluskey.
27 Which alternative rock band were formed in England in 1988 by singer/ guitarist Sice?
28 Which Indie rock band from Southport were winners of the 1998 Mercury Prize?
29 Which band formed in 2001 took their name from The Magic Band guitarist Bill Harkleroad.
30 Which theatrical-sounding band was formed by John Power (La's) and Peter Wilkinson of Shack?

| **Answers** | Movies Pot Luck 11 *(see Quiz 104)* |

1 Pugsley. 2 Milos Forman. 3 O'Hara. 4 Paul Henreid. 5 1980s. 6 Moonstruck. 7 Biehn. 8 Nancy Sinatra. 9 Kevin Costner. 10 Charles Russell. 11 Herself. 12 Switzerland. 13 Vivien Leigh. 14 Robert Loggia. 15 Bruce Lee. 16 1960s. 17 Saturday (Night Fever). 18 Videodrome. 19 Breakfast at Tiffany's. 20 Sophia Loren. 21 Cape Fear. 22 William Hurt. 23 Rob Bowman. 24 Dark City. 25 Daniel Day-Lewis. 26 Peter Pan. 27 Four (IV). 28 Kiss Me Kate. 29 T.J. 30 Keanu Reeves.

1 What was the name of Jimmy Workman's character in *The Addams Family*?

2 Who won the Best Director Oscar for *Amadeus*?

3 Which Catherine featured in *Home Alone*?

4 Who played Victor Laszlo in *Casablanca*?

5 In which decade was *Blade Runner* released?

6 Cher won her first Oscar for which film?

7 Which Michael featured in *The Terminator*?

8 Who sang the Bond theme from "You Only Live Twice"?

9 Who starred as Eliot Ness in *The Untouchables* in 1987?

10 Who directed *The Mask*?

11 Who did Julie Christie play in the 1975 film *Nashville*?

12 In which country did Charlie Chaplin spend the final years of his life?

13 Who won the Best Actress Oscar for *A Streetcar Named Desire*?

14 *An Officer and a Gentleman* and *Big* both feature which actor?

15 How is Lee Yuen Kam better known in western movies?

16 In which decade was *The Longest Day* released?

17 Tony Manero was a character in a movie about which day?

18 Which 1982 film did rock star Debbie Harry star in?

19 In which film did a character named Paul Varjak appear?

20 *El Cid* and *The Millionairess* both featured which actress?

21 In which film did a character named Max Cody appear?

22 Who won the Best Actor Oscar for *Kiss of the Spider Woman*?

23 Who directed *The X-Files*?

24 What was Charlton Heston's first film, in 1950?

25 Which actor is the son of a British Poet Laureate?

26 *Finding Neverland* was about J. M. Barrie, the creator of which hero?

27 Which episode of *Star Wars* (retitled *A New Hope*) was the first to be released?

28 Which musical movie is based on Shakespeare's *The Taming of the Shrew*?

29 Which Miller shined in 2016's *Deadpool*?

30 Which actor appeared in both *River's Edge* and *The Night Before*?

---

1 What sea creature fatally struck crocodile hunter Steve Irwin?
2 Which member of the Attenborough family presents wildlife series?
3 What did the series of *Creature Comforts* animations advertise?
4 What product is associated with labrador puppies?
5 What was the name of the Downing Street cat that lived with David Cameron throughout his 2010–2016 tenure?
6 Which children's show was presented by Terry Nutkin and Chris Packham?
7 Asta the dog featured in which series?
8 Who presented *Animal Magic*?
9 Vet David Grant appears in which RSPCA-based series?
10 Who produced a television series named *Zoo Quest* in the 1950s?
11 In which series does Anton Rodgers play a vet?
12 Which breed of dog was Tricky Woo in *All Creatures Great and Small*?
13 Henry is a cartoon what?
14 What type of terrain is the land surrounding the Skeleton Coast?
15 What was the name of the Harts' dog in *Hart to Hart*?
16 Which city zoo sponsored the 1950's wildlife series *Zoo Quest*?
17 Which naturalist presented *Look* and *Faraway Look* in the 1950s and 1960s?
18 What is unusual about the Sundew?
19 Who was the posthumous presenter of *Paradise Gardens*?
20 What is the name of the cartoon dog in *Garfield & Friends*?
21 Where do you find the Giant Tortoise?
22 What type of creature does Rex Hunt work most closely with?
23 *Life in the Freezer* featured the natural history of which place?
24 Author and presenter Gerald Durrell had a zoo where?
25 In the title of the show, what was ... *Flicka*?
26 Who presented *Gardener's World* in 1998?
27 What was the name of David Bellamy's first TV series in1972?
28 Do penguins live at the North or South pole?
29 The naturalist Aubrey Buxton was the original presenter of which long-running ITV nature series?
30 What word commonly describes people who follow tornados?

| **Answers** | **Football Pot Luck 12** *(see Quiz 106)* |

1 Swansea City. 2 1940s. 3 Tottenham Hotspur. 4 Manager of Wales. 5 David Batty.
6 Creaney. 7 Gold. 8 Birmingham City. 9 Leyton Orient. 10 David O'Leary. 11
Wales. 12 1980s. 13 Arsenal. 14 Bristol City. 15 Everton. 16 Fry. 17 Liverpool.
18 Leeds United. 19 Ipswich Town. 20 Rune Hauge. 21 Romania. 22 Bertie Vogts.
23 Wolves. 24 Fourth. 25 Graeme Le Saux. 26 1930s. 27 £85.3 million. 28
Carlisle United. 29 Everton. 30 John Barnes.

1 Who was keeper Roger Freestone playing for when he scored two penalty goals in 1995–96?

2 In which decade was commentator Barry Davies born?

3 Which was Mark Bowen's first League club?

4 Atkinson, Kendall and Walker were in contention for which management job in August 1995?

5 Who moved from Blackburn Rovers in 1996 for £3,750,000 to set a club record for transfer fee received?

6 Which Gerry went from Portsmouth to Manchester City in 1995?

7 What colour are Dumbarton's home shirts?

8 Which club did David Seaman leave to join QPR?

9 Who plays at home at Brisbane Road?

10 Who holds the Arsenal league appearance record?

11 Which country did George Berry play for?

12 In which decade did Coventry City first win the FA Cup?

13 Don Howe followed Terry Neill as boss of which club?

14 Which club did Rob Newman leave to join Norwich City?

15 Which team were beaten 1–0 by Manchester Utd in the 1985 FA Cup Final?

16 Which Barry became manager of Birmingham City in 1993?

17 In which city was John Aldridge born?

18 Terry Yorath was at which club when he made his international debut?

19 Frank Yallop and Neil Thompson were fullbacks at which club?

20 Who was the Norwegian agent in the George Graham "bung" case?

21 Which country knocked England out of Euro 2000 with a 3–2 win in Charleroi?

22 Who was the first non-Scotsman to manage the country?

23 Which was Tim Flowers's first League club?

24 What was Leeds United's lowest First Division finishing position 1965–74?

25 Which future England international was born in October 1968 in Jersey?

26 In which decade did Portsmouth first win the FA Cup?

27 How much was Gareth Bale's record transfer fee for in 2013?

28 At which club was Michael Knighton simultaneously manager and chairman?

29 Paul Bracewell was at which club when he made his international debut?

30 Which former England international was dismissed as coach by Celtic in 2000?

Answers	TV: Animals & Nature 1 (see Quiz 105)

1 Stingray. 2 David. 3 Electricity. 4 Andrex Toilet Tissue. 5 Larry. 6 The Really Wild Show. 7 The Thin Man. 8 Johnny Morris. 9 Animal Hospital. 10 David Attenborough. 11 Noah's Ark. 12 Pekinese. 13 Cat. 14 Desert. 15 Freeway. 16 London Zoo. 17 Peter Scott. 18 Carnivorous plant. 19 Geoff Hamilton. 20 Odie. 21 The Galapagos Islands. 22 Fish. 23 Antarctica. 24 Isle of Wight. 25 My Friend. . . 26 Alan Titchmarsh. 27 Bellamy on Botany. 28 South. 29 Survival. 30 Chasers.

1 In which city was George Michael brought up?
2 What was his debut solo album called?
3 Who did he duet with on "I Knew You were Waiting (for Me)"?
4 On whose version of "Nikita" did George sing backing vocals?
5 Where did George first meet Wham!'s Andrew Ridgeley?
6 What is George Michael's real first name?
7 In which decade was he born?
8 With which band did he record the *Five Live EP*?
9 Which female vocalist was on the same record?
10 From which newspaper did he receive damages in 1989 after accusations about gatecrashing a party?
11 What is the name of his autobiography?
12 Which item of his clothing is burned on his "Freedom 90" video?
13 What was his second solo album called?
14 Which Elton John song did he sing at the Live Aid concert?
15 Which 1990/91 conflict helped the fortunes of "Praying for Time" because of its lyric?
16 What was his 1996 comeback ballad?
17 Which album was released the same year?
18 Which corporation became parent company of Epic Records, which caused a legal battle with George?
19 What was his first solo No. 1?
20 Which film soundtrack contained the controversial, sometimes banned single "I Want Your Sex"?
21 What was the title of his 2004 album?
22 In 2007, whose £1.5 million piano did he use on his tour of North America?
23 In which year was George Michael banned from driving for two years?
24 George's 2006 compilation album celebrated how many years of recording?
25 When George started touring again in 2006, how long had he been off the road?
26 How many times has George scooped a Grammy Award?
27 What type of business did George's father own?
28 Can you name the 1985 David Cassidy single George contributed backing vocals to?
29 In which famous stadium did he play his last ever concert as a member of Wham!?
30 Including his Wham! career how many British No. 1 singles has George enjoyed?

Answers	Movies Pot Luck 12 *(see Quiz 108)*

1 3 hours. 2 1980s. 3 Julie Andrews. 4 Judd. 5 Paul Robeson. 6 Warren Beatty. 7 Tom Mullen. 8 Julia Roberts. 9 Honor Blackman. 10 Emily Lloyd. 11 1920s. 12 One Flew Over the Cuckoo's Nest. 13 Robertson. 14 Margot Robbie. 15 Moore. 16 The Rock. 17 Colin Firth. 18 Tippi Hedren. 19 Jon Voight. 20 1950s. 21 Alan Rickman. 22 Arthur Hiller. 23 Modine. 24 Audrey Hepburn. 25 Christopher Lloyd. 26 Helen Mirren. 27 M*A*S*H. 28 Daniel Hillard. 29 1960s. 30 Gladys Knight.

Quiz 108 | Movies Pot Luck 12

Answers – page 313

1 To the nearest hour, how long does *Braveheart* last?
2 In which decade was *Trading Places* released?
3 How is Julia Wells better known?
4 Which Ashley featured in *Heat*?
5 In the 1930s who sang "Old Man River" in *Showboat*?
6 Who won the Best Director Oscar for *Reds*?
7 What was the name of Mel Gibson's character in *Ransom*?
8 Who married Lyle Lovett instead of Kiefer Sutherland?
9 Who played the Bond girl in *Goldfinger*?
10 *Wish You were Here* and *The Real Thing* featured which actress?
11 Was *The Untouchables* with Kevin Costner set in the 1920s, 40s or 60s?
12 In which film did a character named Randie P. McMurphy appear?
13 Which Cliff featured in *Three Days of the Condor*?
14 Who plays Jane in the 2016 re-imaginging of *The Legend of Tarzan*?
15 Which Julianne starred in *The Lost World: Jurassic Park*?
16 A character named John Mason appeared in which film?
17 Who played Kristin Scott Thomas's husband in *The English Patient*?
18 Who was the blonde female star in *Marnie* and *The Birds*?
19 Who won the Best Actor Oscar for *Coming Home*?
20 In which decade was *The Greatest Show on Earth* released?
21 Who played the villain in *Robin Hood: Prince of Thieves*?
22 Who directed *Love Story*?
23 Which Matthew starred in *Married to the Mob*?
24 Who won the Best Actress Oscar for *Roman Holiday*?
25 *Who Framed Roger Rabbit?* and *Back to the Future III* featured which actor?
26 Which British actress won an Oscar for her role as Queen Elizabeth II?
27 Which Korean War medical drama/black comedy did Robert Altman direct?
28 What was the name of Robin Williams's character in *Mrs Doubtfire*?
29 In which decade was the biker classic *Easy Rider* released?
30 Who sang the Bond theme from *A Licence to Kill*?

Answers | **Pop: George Michael** *(see Quiz 107)*

1 London. 2 Faith. 3 Aretha Franklin. 4 Elton John's. 5 At school. 6 Georgios. 7 1960s. 8 Queen. 9 Lisa Stansfield. 10 The Sun. 11 Bare. 12 Biker jacket. 13 Listen without Prejudice Vol 1. 14 "Don't Let the Sun Go Down on Me". 15 The Gulf War. 16 "Jesus to a Child". 17 Older. 18 Sony. 19 "Careless Whisper". 20 Beverley Hills Cop II. 21 Patience. 22 John Lennon. 23 2007. 24 Twenty Five. 25 15 years. 26 Two. 27 A Greek restaurant. 28 The Last Kiss. 29 Wembley Stadium (the Old). 30 Twelve.

1 Before Ashton Kutcher took the role in 2011, who was the headline star of *Two and a Half Men*?
2 What was the first spin-off show from *Friends* called?
3 Who plays Dr Dick Solomon, the alien professor in *Third Rock from the Sun*?
4 Who played Queen Elizabeth I in the second series of *Blackadder*?
5 Who in real life is Cherie's dad and, on TV, was Alf's son-in-law?
6 Which *Prime Minister* appeared in *The Good Life*?
7 Why did Dermot leave *Men Behaving Badly*?
8 Which brothers link *Drop the Dead Donkey* and *Keeping Up Appearances*?
9 What rank was Ernie Bilko in *The Phil Silvers Show*?
10 Who is Gary's wartime wife in *Goodnight Sweetheart*?
11 Who played Hancock's sidekick Sid?
12 What is *The Vicar of Dibley* called?
13 What was the name of Adrian Mole's girlfriend?
14 Who employed Bubbles as an incompetent PA?
15 Which sitcom was set in Lord Meldrum's stately home?
16 Which actress played Daker's Polish distraction Grete Grotowska in *A Very Peculiar Practice*?
17 Which comedy show in the 80s was named after a Little Richard hit?
18 Who was the main "Smeg-Head"?
19 Neil from *The Young Ones* had a chart-topper with which song?
20 What was the cab firm called in *Taxi*?
21 The comedy *Whack-O!* starred who as the headmaster?
22 What was the name of the charlady in *Acorn Antiques*?
23 In which city did the Boswell family reside in *Bread*?
24 Which comedy featured Dr Sheila Sabatini?
25 What was the name of the horse owned by the Steptoes?
26 The ex-wrestler Pat Roach played which *Auf Wiedersehen Pet* character?
27 In *Two Point Four Children* what are the names of the children?
28 What was Private Bisley's nickname in *The Army Game*?
29 Who played Sir Humphrey Appleby in *Yes, Minister*?
30 How old was Ronnie Corbett when he died in March 2016?

Answers	**Football Pot Luck 13** *(see Quiz 110)*

1 Brighton. 2 1940s. 3 Notts County. 4 Ayr Utd. 5 Oxford Utd. 6 1.89 m. 7 Liam Daish. 8 AC Milan. 9 Liverpool. 10 The Republic of Ireland. 11 Amber. 12 1960s. 13 Blackburn Rovers. 14 England. 15 Crystal Palace. 16 McFarland. 17 Romford. 18 Birmingham City. 19 Norwich City. 20 Graeme Le Saux. 21 Ryan Giggs. 22 Rudi Voller. 23 Walsall. 24 Kendall. 25 None. 26 Billy Bremner. 27 Glenn Hoddle. 8 Cambridge Utd. 29 England. 30 Mexico.

1 Who was Jimmy Case playing for when he knocked his old club Liverpool out of the FA Cup in a 1980s shock result?

2 In which decade did Derby County first win the FA Cup?

3 Which was Mark Draper's first League club?

4 Who plays at home at Somerset Park?

5 John Aldridge was at which club when he made his international debut?

6 How tall is Brazilian footballer David Luiz – 1.89m or 1.79m?

7 Who moved from Birmingham City in February 1996 for £1,100,000 to set a club record for transfer fee received?

8 Which club did Ray Wilkins join on leaving Manchester Utd?

9 Which team were beaten 2–1 by Manchester Utd in the 1977 FA Cup Final?

10 Which country did Ashley Grimes play for?

11 What colour goes with black on Barnet's home shirts?

12 In which decade was Faustino Asprilla born?

13 Derek Fazackerley set a League appearance record at which club?

14 Shearer and Ferdinand first formed a strike-force for which team?

15 Gareth Southgate and Chris Coleman were in the same team at which club?

16 Which Roy became manager of Bolton Wanderers in 1995?

17 Where was Tony Adams born?

18 Terry Cooper followed Lou Macari as boss of which club?

19 Which club did Mike Phelan leave to join Manchester Utd?

20 Which Blackburn Rovers and England defender suffered a long-term injury against Middlesbrough in December 1995?

21 Which Welsh international retired in 2007 after winning 64 caps?

22 Which former striker was Germany's coach at the 2002 World Cup finals?

23 Which was David Kelly's first League club?

24 Which Howard became boss of Notts County in 1995?

25 How many goals did Peter Osgood score for England?

26 A statue of which former player stands outside the stadium at Elland Road?

27 Who was the last Englishman to be appointed Chelsea manager?

28 Which club played in the Football League between 1970 and 2005?

29 Which country did Colin Viljoen play for?

30 Which country appointed Sam Allardyce national coach in 2016?

Answers | **Football Pot Luck 14** (see Quiz 114)

1 Paul Gascoigne. 2 60. 3 Carlisle United. 4 1906. 5 Swansea. 6 Blackburn Rovers. 7 Jimmy Armfield. 8 Crystal Palace. 9 Alloa. 10 Kevin Richardson. 11 Arsenal. 12 Case. 13 Scotland. 14 Laurent Koscielny. 15 1940s. 16 Chelsea. 17 Manchester City. 18 Nottm Forest. 19 Chester. 20 Trevor Sinclair. 21 Phil Thompson. 22 Crystal Palace. 23 Ipswich Town. 24 Deehan. 25 Chris Sutton. 26 1960s. 27 Joey Beauchamp. 28 Cardiff City. 29 West Ham United. 30 Crewe Alexandra.

1 Which No. 1 includes vocals by Captain Tobias Wilcock?
2 Who had a 1974 No. 1 with "Rock Your Baby"?
3 Which 70s No. 1 was about a nudist?
4 Who teamed up Under Pressure in 1981?
5 What was Brotherhood of Man's Mexican shepherd boy called?
6 Who had a 70s No. 1 with "Show You the Way to Go"?
7 What was on the other side of the Detroit Spinners' "Forgive Me Girl"?
8 Who wore a Pierrot costume for his "Ashes to Ashes" video?
9 Who had three No. 1's in the first two months of 1981?
10 Who had their first No. 1 with "This Ole House"?
11 Which No. 1 was based on the Zulu folk tune "Wimoweh"?
12 Who was the first German band to have a UK No. 1 in 1982?
13 Why did Stevie Wonder not receive full billing on his No. 1 with Paul McCartney?
14 Which 80s No. 1 was a song from the musical *South Pacific*?
15 Who had a 70s No. 1 album called *Horizon*?
16 Who had a 60s hit with "Fire"?
17 Which 60s group were named after an American Civil War battle and wore period army uniforms?
18 Who was the oldest ever artist at the time to have a No. 1 record in 1968?
19 Who was lead singer on the 1968 No. 1 "Mighty Quinn"?
20 Which 70s No. 1 had a French title?
21 Who got to No. 1 in 2001 with "Because I Got High"?
22 Who went to No. 1 with a track from the soundtrack of the Thunderbirds movie?
23 Which *X-Factor* winner had the bestselling single of 2007 with "Bleeding Love"?
24 What did Rihanna invite you to do with her spring 2008 chart-topper?
25 In which country was Daniel Bedingfield born?
26 Whose "Rock DJ" was a No. 1 hit in August 2000?
27 "Breathless" is this band's only ever UK No. 1 hit. Name them.
28 What duo took an old Beatles song to No. 1 in October 2002?
29 *I Like It When You Sleep, for You Are So Beautiful yet So Unaware of It is* the title of which band's No.1 album?
30 What was Nelly featuring Kelly Rowland posing in this No. 1 hit single?

1 In which film does a character named Rod Tidwell appear?
2 The song "Unchained Melody" was revived by featuring in which movie?
3 Which Alan featured in the 1991 movie *Hamlet*?
4 Who won the Best Director Oscar for *Forrest Gump*?
5 Who played Susie Diamond in *The Fabulous Baker Boys*?
6 Who won the Best Actress Oscar for *The Three Faces of Eve*?
7 Who played Cruella De Vil's sidekick Jasper in *101 Dalmatians*?
8 Which veteran starred with Burt Lancaster in *Tough Guys* in 1986?
9 What was the name of the Keir Dullea character in *2001: A Space Odyssey*?
10 In which decade was *Romancing the Stone* released?
11 Who directed *Lethal Weapon*?
12 Which early screen comedian's real name was Louis Cristillo?
13 Which soap did Hollywood star Alec Baldwin star in?
14 In which film did Clint Eastwood first play "The man with no name"?
15 Who was the US teacher in *To Sir with Love*?
16 In which decade was *Fahrenheit 451* released?
17 Who played King Arthur in the film musical *Camelot*?
18 *Dracula* and *The Man with the Golden Gun* both featured which actor?
19 In 2016, Jeff Goldblum returned to fight a Resurgence...on which Day?
20 *Dances with Wolves* concerns a soldier from which war?
21 Who played Doug Roberts in *The Towering Inferno*?
22 *2010* and *Memphis Belle* both feature which actor?
23 Who won the Best Actor Oscar for *The Private Life of Henry VIII*?
24 What was the Bond girl's name in *The Man with the Golden Gun*?
25 Which Burt appeared in *Bean –The Ultimate Disaster Movie*?
26 Daniel Day-Lewis won an Oscar as Daniel Plainview in *There Will be* what?
27 Which *X Files* star plays a doctor's wife in *Last King of Scotland*?
28 Which Tim featured in *Reservoir Dogs*?
29 Which writer directed the 1973 movie *Westworld*?
30 Which actor was twice married to the actress Natalie Wood?

Answers Pop: No. 1s *(see Quiz 111)*

1 "Barbados". 2 George McCrae. 3 "The Streak". 4 Queen and David Bowie. 5 Angelo. 6 Jacksons. 7 "I'm Working My Way Back to You". 8 David Bowie. 9 John Lennon. 10 Rosemary Clooney. 11 "The Lion Sleeps Tonight". 12 Kraftwerk. 13 His record label Motown would not allow it. 14 "Happy Talk". 15 Billy Bragg. 16 The Crazy World of Arthur Brown. 17 Union Gap. 18 Louis Armstrong. 19 Mike D'Abo. 20 "Chanson d'Amour". 21 Afroman. 22 Busted. 23 Leona Lewis. 24 Take a Bow. 25 New Zealand. 26 Robbie Williams. 27 The Corrs. 28 Gareth Gates & Will Young (The Long and Winding Road). 29 The 1975. 30 Dilemma.

1 Which children's soap broadcast its last episode in September 2008?
2 What new technical device did the makers of *Neighbours* introduce in 2007?
3 At the British Soap Awards 2016, which show won Best British Soap?
4 In *Crossroads*, whose fiancee died on their wedding day?
5 Which tennis player's former father-in-law appeared in *Peyton Place*?
6 What was the name of the cook in *Dynasty*?
7 What was Tracy Corkhill's occupation in *Brookside*?
8 In *Crossroads*, who shot David Hunter?
9 Which actor played the market superintendent Derek in *Albion Market*?
10 Who are the feuding families in *Dallas*?
11 What is the name of the local football club in *EastEnders*?
12 What was Gail's maiden name in *Coronation Street*?
13 What was Lorna Cartwright's addiction in *EastEnders*?
14 Which soap role had Barbara Bel Geddes and Donna Reed shared?
15 Who was the Sheriff in *Flamingo Road*?
16 What domestic situation is Ken Barlow's claim to fame in *Coronation Street*?
17 After his character died in *Coronation Street*, actor Alan Rothwell appeared as a drug addict in which other soap?
18 Who played Constance McKenzie in *Peyton Place*?
19 What was the name of Jimmy Corkhill's son in *Brookside*?
20 Which Dallas star was in *I Dream of Jeannie* in the 1960s?
21 What was the name of the hospital that featured in *Emergency-Ward* 10?
22 How is Spider Nugent related to Emily Bishop in *Coronation Street*?
23 In *Coronation Street*, what does Mike Baldwin's company Underworld produce?
24 Which comedian lost his sense of humour as Frank in *EastEnders*?
25 What placed Kylie Corkhill's life in danger while she was in Sinbad's shop?
26 Which *Coronation Street* star went on to become a district nurse?
27 What role did Bill Treacher play in *EastEnders*?
28 Who ran the Kool for Kutz hairdressers in *EastEnders*?
29 What is the name of Grant and Tiffany's daughter in *EastEnders*?
30 In *Brookside*, whom did the Farnhams pay to act as a surrogate mother?

Answers | Pop: Instrumentals *(see Quiz 115)*

1 Van der Valk. 2 B. Bumble and the Stingers. 3 Tchaikovsky's Nutcracker Suite. 4 Licorice. 5 "Cherry Pink and Apple Blossom White". 6 Lord Rockingham's XI. 7 "Mouldy Old Dough". 8 Richard Clayderman. 9 "Telstar". 10 "Man of Mystery". 11 Brian Bennett. 12 "March of the Mods". 13 "Doop". 14 The Pipes and Drums and Military Band of the Royal Scots Dragoon Guards. 15 Drums. 16 Brighouse and Rastrick Brass Band. 17 Mason Williams. 18 Acker Bilk. 19 Liberace. 20 None. 21 Mr. 22 Apache. 23 Spaghetti Western. 24 Hot Butter. 25 The MGs. 26 Hawaii Five-O. 27 The Magnificent Seven. 28 Thin Lizzy. 29 Monty Norman. 30 Kaleidoscope.

1 Who in December 1995 got booked for "showing" the referee a yellow card after it fell from his pocket?

2 To one year each way, how old was Jack Charlton when he stood down as manager of the Republic of Ireland?

3 With which club did Peter Beardsley make his League debut?

4 To five years each way, when did Everton first win the FA Cup?

5 In which city was Ivor Allchurch born?

6 Kenny Dalglish followed Don Mackay as boss of which club?

7 Who holds the league appearance record for Blackpool?

8 Which club did Iain Dowie leave to join Southampton?

9 Which Scottish side plays at home at Recreation Park?

10 Who, in December 1995, got sent off playing for Coventry City on his return to his former club Aston Villa?

11 Paul Davis and Anders Limpar were in the same team at which club?

12 Which Jimmy became manager of Brighton in November 1995?

13 Which country did Adam Blacklaw play for?

14 What Frenchmen Laurent defended Arsenal in 2015-16 season?

15 In which decade was Roy Evans born?

16 Which team were beaten 2–1 by Tottenham Hotspur in the 1967 FA Cup Final?

17 Colin Bell was at which club when he made his international debut?

18 Which club did Lee Chapman leave to join Leeds Utd the first time?

19 Which Sir Norman produced the 1980s report "The State of Football"?

20 Who moved from Blackpool in August 1993 for £750,000 to set a club record for transfer fee received?

21 Who stood in as Liverpool manager when Gerard Houllier had heart surgery?

22 Which is the only London club Steve Bruce has managed?

23 What was Titus Bramble's first League club?

24 Which ex-player John became boss of Norwich City in 1994?

25 In 1994 which player was transferred from Norwich to Blackburn for £5.5 million?

26 In which decade did Dunfermline first win the Scottish FA Cup?

27 Which player, at £800,000 from West Ham United in 1994, was Swindon's record transfer fee paid?

28 Phil Dwyer set a League appearance record at which club?

29 Paul Goddard was at which club when he made his international debut?

30 Dario Gradi became manager for which club in 1983?

Answers   Golf Pot Luck *(see Quiz 118)*

1 Mexico. 2 Rocco Mediate. 3 Sergio Garcia. 4 Kentucky. 5 Alexander. 6 Dutch Open. 7 South Africa. 8 Daniel. 9 Trap. 10 14. 11 Howard Clark. 12 Bernhard Langer. 13 St Andrews. 14 Ben Crenshaw. 15 Spain. 16 Two strokes. 17 Professional Golfers' Association. 18 Walker Cup. 19 Sandwich. 20 Jack Nicklaus. 21 Royal Blackheath, Kent, founded 1608. 22 50 years. 23 Seve Ballesteros. 24 Cotton. 25 Fijian. 26 Tony Jacklin. 27 Arnold Palmer. 28 US Masters. 29 Tony Jacklin. 30 Bruce Forsyth.

1 "Eye Level" was the theme music for which detective series?
2 Who had a 1962 No. 1 with "Nut Rocker"?
3 Which music by which composer was it based on?
4 What was the nickname of the Shadows' Brian Locking?
5 Which music was a No. 1 twice for Eddie Calvert and Perez Prado?
6 Who had a 50s hit with "Hoots Mon"?
7 What was Lieutenant Pigeon's only hit?
8 How is the instrumentalist Philippe Pages better known?
9 Which 60s instrumental is said to be a favourite of Lady Thatcher?
10 Which Shadows hit was a theme for a series of Edgar Wallace stories?
11 Who became the Shadows' drummer after Tony Meehan left?
12 Which 60s March became a minor hit for Joe Loss and His Orchestra?
13 Which No. 1 was accompanied by 1920s flappers?
14 Who had the longest name of any group to have a No. 1?
15 Which instrument did Fleetwood Mac's Mick Fleetwood play?
16 Who had a 1977 instrumental hit with "The Floral Dance"?
17 Who had a 1968 hit with "Classical Gas"?
18 Who was the soloist on the 1976 hit "Aria"?
19 Which pianist had a 50s hit with "Unchained Melody"?
20 To the nearest five, how many instrumental No. 1s were there between 1974 and 1994?
21 What title did instrumentalist Acker Bilk have?
22 Which Native American tribe gave its name to an instrumental No. 1?
23 What movie genre was *The Good, the Bad and the Ugly*, whose theme was a hit?
24 Who had a hit with "Popcorn"?
25 Who backed Booker T?
26 Name the 60s US cop show for which the Ventures provided the theme.
27 What western movie theme did the John Barry Seven have a chart hit with?
28 Can you name the rock band whose "Yellow Pearl" used to open *Top of the Pops*?
29 Which "Monty" has been credited with writing the James Bond theme?
30 Coldplay's *A Head Full Of Dreams* (2016) featured a Barack Obama led instrumental. What was its name?

Answers | TV: Children's TV 2 *(see Quiz 117)*

1 Tucker Jenkins. 2 Sir Stirling Moss. 3 Jackanory. 4 Snowy. 5 The Teletubbies. 6 Wimpey. 7 Brown. 8 Michael Rodd. 9 Peter Glaze. 10 Chihuahua. 11 Woodstock. 12 The Children's Television Workshop. 13 Rag Dolly Anna. 14 Huey, Louie & Dewey. 15 Burt Ward. 16 Basil Brush. 17 Leila Williams. 18 Anna Sewell. 19 Daktari. 20 Emma Forbes. 21 Angelo. 22 The Penguin. 23 Mrs Goggins. 24 Neil Morrissey. 25 Bamm-Bamm & Pebbles. 26 Mr Benn. 27 Bug Juice. 28 Peter Sallis. 29 Hanna-Barbera. 30 John Gorman.

1 *King Kong* and *Cape Fear* both featured which actress?
2 Who played the journalist loosely based on Carl Bernstein in *Heartburn*?
3 Which Ben featured in *The Truth about Cats and Dogs*?
4 In which decade was *Oklahoma!* first released?
5 What was the name of Will Smith's character in *Independence Day*?
6 Who won the Best Actress Oscar for *Darling*?
7 Which poet's name was the middle name of James Dean?
8 Which Kevin featured in *A Few Good Men*?
9 Who played Jack Lemmon's daughter in *Grumpy Old Men*?
10 In which decade of the 20th century was Sally Field born?
11 A character named John Doherty appeared in which film?
12 Who played Susan Sarandon's husband in *Lorenzo's Oil*?
13 Who won the Best Director Oscar for *The Sound of Music*?
14 Who played Rudyard Kipling in *The Man Who Would be King*?
15 Who beat Meryl Streep for the lead role in *The Horse Whisperer*?
16 Which animals feature in *Oliver and Company*?
17 *The Killers* and *Field of Dreams* both feature which actor?
18 Who directed *LA Confidential*?
19 How were producers Harry, Albert, Sam and Jack known collectively?
20 In which category did Joel Gray win an Oscar for *Cabaret*?
21 Which Michelle featured in *Tomorrow Never Dies*?
22 Who directed *Labyrinth*?
23 Who played the wistful widowed father in *Sleepless in Seattle*?
24 In which decade was *Witness* released?
25 Who won the Best Actor Oscar for *The Lost Weekend*?
26 Which city is depicted in Terence Davies's *Of Time and the City*?
27 Which *Spiderman* star made her debut with Brad Pitt in *Interview with a Vampire*?
28 Who won the Best Actress Oscar for *Annie Hall*?
29 *Bull Durham* and *Bob Roberts* featured which actor?
30 What career did Mark Rylance's character pursue in 2015's *Bridge of Spies*?

---

1 Which former Grange Hill pupil returned as the uncle of "Togger" Johnson?
2 Which racing legend voices Roary the Racing Car?
3 Which storytelling programme had guest narrators?
4 What was the name of TinTin's dog?
5 Who lives in Home Hill?
6 Who was Popeye's hamburger-eating friend?
7 What was the surname of Just William?
8 Who presented *Screen Test*?
9 In *Crackerjack*, who played the comic stooge?
10 What type of dog is Ren?
11 What is the name of Snoopy's feathered friend?
12 Who produces *Sesame Street*?
13 Pat Coombs appeared with which doll?
14 Name Donald Duck's nephews.
15 Who played Robin in *Batman*?
16 With which puppet did Rodney Bewes appear?
17 Name the first female presenter of *Blue Peter*.
18 Who was the author of *Black Beauty*?
19 Which animal series starred Marshall Thompson?
20 Who co-presented the first series of *Live & Kicking* with Andi Peters?
21 What was the alien that Mike discovered in a wardrobe called?
22 Burgess Meredith played which character in *Batman*?
23 Who is the postmistress in Greendale?
24 Who voices Bob the Builder?
25 Name the children in *The Flintstones*.
26 Who visited a costume shop before embarking on various adventures?
27 What is the daytime series about American children at summer camp called?
28 Who is the voice of Wallace from the duo Wallace and Gromit?
29 Which company produced *Huckleberry Hound* and *Yogi Bear*?
30 Which member of *Scaffold* appeared in *Tiswas*?

1 Women's 2008 World No. 1 Lorena Ochoa is from which country?
2 Who lost out in a play-off against Tiger Woods in the 2008 US Open?
3 Which Spaniard finished second in the 2007 British Open?
4 In which US State was the 2008 Ryder Cup staged?
5 What is Jordan Spieth's middle name?
6 Which European Open gave Seve Ballesteros his first-ever European win back in 1976?
7 Where does Ernie Els hail from?
8 What does the D stand for in Arnold D. Palmer?
9 What is a bunker known as in the United States?
10 What is the maximum number of clubs permitted in a golf bag?
11 Which English player scored a hole in one on the final day of the 1995 Ryder Cup?
12 Who was the first German to win the German Open?
13 Where is the "home of golf"?
14 Name the veteran golfer who won the 1995 US Masters tournament?
15 Which country hosted the 1997 Ryder Cup?
16 In stroke play, what is the penalty for playing the wrong ball?
17 What do the initials PGA stand for?
18 What is the amateur's equivalent of the Ryder Cup?
19 At which "appetizing" course did Sandy Lyle win the 1985 British Open?
20 Who is "The Golden Bear"?
21 Which is the oldest golf club in England?
22 At what age can a player join the Seniors' Tour?
23 Name Europe's 1997 Ryder Cup captain.
24 Which Henry won his first British Open in 1934?
25 What nationality is golfer Vijay Singh?
26 Which British golfer won the British Open in 1969?
27 Which famous American played his last British Open in 1995?
28 In which tournament does a player win a green jacket?
29 Which golfer was non-playing captain of the 1985 Ryder Cup team?
30 Which showbiz golfer says, "I'm in charge"?

1 Which Italian got an early bath against Nigeria in the 1994 World Cup?
2 Darren Peacock was sent off as which London club knocked Newcastle Utd out of the 1995–96 FA Cup?
3 Which Scottish winger Willie of the 1960s to the 1980s was sent off 15 times?
4 Which Everton player was fouled when Kevin Moran got his 1985 FA Cup Final marching orders?
5 Who was the first Welsh player to be sent off in an international?
6 Which Manchester Utd player was sent off in the 1994 League Cup Final?
7 Who, ex-Arsenal, saw red in a Sweden v Romania World Cup quarter-final?
8 Woods and Butcher were at which club when they were off in the same game?
9 In 1996–97 which Coventry City player was dismissed in successive League games?
10 Which Igor was the only Croatian to see red in Euro 96?
11 Which keeper was sent off in the quarter-finals of the 1994 FA Cup?
12 At which club was Paul Warhurst sent off in a European Cup game?
13 Jonas Thern was playing for which country when he got sent off in a 1994 World Cup semi-final?
14 Which Brian of Everton got an early bath in a 1980 FA Cup semi-final?
15 Which Rangers player saw red in the 1996 European Cup game against Borussia Dortmund in Germany?
16 Which Bulgarian striker was banned for life after a brawl in 1985, to be reinstated six months later?
17 Which Wimbledon player walked in 1995 after tangling with Ruud Gullit?
18 Which striker was sent off on his on-loan return to Leeds Utd in 1996?
19 Which ex-West Ham player at Celtic was sent off with Butcher and Woods?
20 Which Manchester Utd player got a red card after the final whistle in 1993?
21 Which former England international was sent off in the 2008 UEFA Super Cup?
22 Who was sent off in the 2006 World Cup after tangling with Ricardo Carvalho?
23 Which country had three players dismissed in seven World Cup 98 matches?
24 How many players received red cards in the 2008 Carling Cup Final?
25 Which English team had its goalkeeper sent off in a Champions League Final?
26 What is the fewest touches of the ball made by a player before being dismissed?
27 Who in 1985 became the first player to be sent off in the FA Cup Final?
28 Name the Chelsea midfielder who said his red card against Roma was "crazy".
29 Which Man. City player was sent off against Liverpool in October 2008?
30 In 2005, who had a fight with Kieren Dyer that result in the Ref seeing red?

1 In which decade did Shakin' Stevens have his first hit record?

2 Which villain was a 70s hit for Boney M?

3 Who took "Ma He's Making Eyes at Me" into the top ten in 1974?

4 Whose first chart hit was "Wild Thing"?

5 Whose album *Sleeping With The Past* topped the charts in 1990?

6 Who said "Please Mr Postman" in 1975?

7 Which comedian sang "Don't Laugh at Me" in 1954?

8 Who pleaded to Honey to Come Back in 1970?

9 Who was Terry Dactyl's backing group?

10 Who spent "Seven Drunken Nights" in 1967?

11 In which decade was Suzi Quatro born?

12 What was Simon Dupree's backing group?

13 Whose first hit was "Planet Earth"?

14 Who made a hit Easy in 1977?

15 Who had a 60s hit with "Rescue Me"?

16 What is the home country of the Cranberries?

17 Who sang "Come and Get It" in 1970?

18 What was Tori Amos's first top ten hit?

19 Which word completes the song title by Public Image Ltd, "This is Not a ___ Song"?

20 Who was John Fred's backing group?

21 Which Irish boy band re-formed in 2007, having split in 2000?

22 Claire Richards and Faye Tozer were two members of which five-strong group?

23 Which song was highest in the charts for the Spice Girls at the beginning of 1997?

24 In which month was Pat Boone in love, in a 1957 song title?

25 What is on the cover of the *Brothers in Arms* album?

26 Which female was Shakin' Stevens singing about in his 1982 No. 1?

27 What sort of wind did Frank Ifield and Jimmy Young sing about?

28 The 2015 album Magic Whip was released by which Britpoppers?

29 Which Small Faces song asks "What did you do there?"?

30 What did Guy Mitchell have "by the number" in his final hit in 1959?

---

1 What is Macaulay Culkin's brother called who starred in *Father of the Bride*?

2 Which former child star became Mrs Andre Agassi?

3 Who played the Artful Dodger in *Oliver!*?

4 In which movie, remade in 1998, did Hayley Mills sing "Let's Get Together"?

5 Whose autobiography was called *Little Girl Lost*?

6 Who played the possessed child in *The Exorcist*?

7 Which Oscar winner from *As Good as It Gets* was a child star on US TV?

8 In which Bruce Willis movie did Haley Joe Osment star?

9 Mark Lester played the title role in which 60s musical?

10 How many movies had Macaulay Culkin made before *Home Alone*?

11 Was Judy Garland 13, 15 or 17 when she played Dorothy in *The Wizard of Oz*?

12 In which 1993 dinosaur film did Joseph Mazello star?

13 Lisa Jakub ended up having her father disguised as a nanny in which movie?

14 Rumer Willis appeared with Mum in *Striptease*; who is she?

15 Which child star appeared in *Mermaids*, aged 10, and moved on to *The Ice Storm*?

16 Was Jodie Foster 12, 14 or 16 when she starred in *Taxi Driver*?

17 Who was Macaulay Culkin's first wife?

18 Who said, "I was a 16-year-old boy for 30 years"?

19 Former child star Richard Beymer starred in which 60s musical opposite Natalie Wood?

20 In which country was Deanna Durbin born?

21 Which star of *Chasing Amy* started acting at the age of eight?

22 What was Hayley Mills's first film, in 1959?

23 How many times did Judy Garland marry?

24 Who played two parts in *The Prince and the Pauper* in 1977?

25 Who played opposite Judy Garland 10 times?

26 When was the 21st-century remake of the 1970s *Bad News Bears* released?

27 How old was Elijah Wood when *Deep Impact* was released?

28 What "Wrecks" from Woody Allen did Kirsten Dunst make her movie debut in?

29 What famous American actress played an underage prostitute in *Taxi Driver*?

30 As Alton Meyer, Jaeden Lieberher is the child star of which 2016 film?

Answers | Football: Red Cards *(see Quiz 119)*

1 Gianfranco Zola. 2 Chelsea. 3 Johnston. 4 Peter Reid. 5 Trevor Hockey. 6 Andrei Kanchelskis. 7 Stefan Schwartz. 8 Rangers. 9 Dion Dublin. 10 Stimac. 11 Peter Schmeichel. 12 Blackburn Rovers. 13 Sweden. 14 Kidd. 15 Paul Gascoigne. 16 Hristo Stoichkov. 17 Vinnie Jones. 18 Lee Chapman. 19 Frank McAvennie. 20 Eric Cantona. 21 Paul Scholes. 22 Wayne Rooney. 23 France. 24 Three. 25 Arsenal. 26 None. 27 Kevin Moran. 28 Deco. 29 Pablo Zabaleta. 30 Lee Bowyer.

1 Which 2008 comedy series co-stars Ralf Little and Carl Rice?

2 How is Wiktoria Dankowska commonly known in *Coronation Street*?

3 Which star of *The Rock Follies* had a No. I . hit with "Don't Cry for Me Argentina"?

4 Which Pamela appeared on *Not the Nine O'clock News*?

5 Which demobbed RAF serviceman was played in a series by Kenneth Cranham?

6 Who was Christopher Timothy's character in *All Creatures Great and Small*?

7 Which northern lass famous for *She Knows You Know* starred in *Not on Your Nellie*?

8 In which series did Timothy West play Arkwright, a mill owner?

9 Who was Natasha's twin sister in *Grange Hill*?

10 Which TV cop recorded "Don't Give Up On Us Baby"?

11 Who was *Roseanne*'s real-life husband who appeared in the series?

12 In *Home Improvements* what was Tim's job?

13 Which collie had her own TV series?

14 What was Lister's first name in *Red Dwarf*?

15 How many *Goodies* were there?

16 What was Dirty Den's surname in *EastEnders*?

17 Which weekly series was often televised from the Hammersmith Palais or the Lyceum?

18 Which talent show was presented by Hughie Green?

19 What was Jeff's surname in *Dynasty*?

20 What is OITNB?

21 What was Richard Beckinsale's character in *Rising Damp*?

22 Which programme linked Cyril Fletcher to Esther Rantzen?

23 Whose Half Hour featured "the lad himself"?

24 What was chat show host Harty's first name?

25 Which Australian had a puppet named Kojee Bear?

26 Which Kennedy was *Game for a Laugh*?

27 Where does ITV get its revenue from?

28 What was the subject of the variety show *The Good Old Days*?

29 *Antiques Roadshow* is broadcast on which day of the week?

30 Whose boyfriend Liam was killed in *Grange Hill* while cycling to a school fight?

Answers | **Pop Pot Luck 15** *(see Quiz 120)*

1 1980s. 2 Rasputin. 3 Lena Zavaroni. 4 The Troggs. 5 Elton John. 6 The Carpenters. 7 Norman Wisdom. 8 Glen Campbell. 9 The Dinosaurs. 10 The Dubliners. 11 1950s. 12 The Big Sound. 13 Duran Duran. 14 The Commodores. 15 Fontella Bass. 16 Ireland. 17 Badfinger. 18 Cornflake Girl. 19 Love. 20 The Playboy Band. 21 Boyzone. 22 Steps. 23 2 Become 1. 24 April. 25 A steel guitar. 26 Oh Julie. 27 A wayward wind. 28 Blur. 29 "Itchycoo Park". 30 Heartaches.

1 Which team won the FA Cup and then found their single at No. 1?
2 How many years of hurt were there in "Three Lions"?
3 Which footballer was "sitting in a sleazy snack bar, sucking sickly sausage rolls"?
4 Which football song was No. 1 for three weeks in May 1970?
5 Who sang with the Scotland squad on "Ole, Ola (Mulher Brasileira)"?
6 In which year did the originally titled "Leeds United" by Leeds United hit the charts?
7 Which Rodgers and Hammerstein song became the Anfield anthem?
8 Which squad charted in 1982 with "We Have a Dream"?
9 What was the England squad's song for Spain in 1982 called?
10 "Ferry Across the Mersey" was a charity song following which soccer disaster?
11 The Bradford City fire disaster led to a June 1985 No. 1 for various performers under which name?
12 Who had the original 1960s hit with the song?
13 Who was Cyril, the subject of "Nice One Cyril"?
14 Which Liverpool record reached No. 3 in the charts in 1988?
15 What was the England squad's song for the 1986 World Cup?
16 Which production team handled the charity version of "Ferry Across the Mersey"?
17 Which team recorded with Paper Lace?
18 "Pure" was the first hit for which soccer-connected group?
19 Who recorded the song that topped the charts for three weeks in May 1970?
20 Which group helped Manchester Utd for their 1994 chart success?
21 In 2016, who wrote and sang the Welsh pop anthem?
22 What Eastern dish became a football anthem in 1998?
23 Which of the three tenors passed away in 2007?
24 Who recorded "We're on the Ball" for the 2002 World Cup?
25 "Don't Come Home Too Soon" was Scotland's request for which World Cup?
26 What is the name of the Rod Stewart hit in which he mentions "Celtic" and "United"?
27 Which lower division club is supported by Robbie Williams and Phil Taylor?
28 Name the rockers who teamed up with Man. Utd players for "Come On You Reds."
29 Whose most famous hit is unquestionably "You'll Never Walk Alone"?
30 What cockney duo was responsible for "Ossie's Dream" in 1981?

---

1 What was Joan Baez's first top ten hit?

2 Which song was a hit for Shirley Bassey and Harry Belafonte in 1957?

3 Whose album *But Seriously* topped the charts in 1990?

4 Fife Dawg died in 2016. What group did he rap for?

5 Who sang "The Sun ain't Gonna Shine Any More" in 1966?

6 Which conservationists' "Minuetto Allegretto" charted in 1974?

7 Who was lead singer with the Troggs?

8 Which two 80s Wimbledon tennis champions had a top 100 hit in 1991?

9 Who took "Hallelujah" to No. 1 at Christmas in 2008?

10 According to Edison Lighthouse, what happens Where My Rosemary Goes?

11 In which decade was Donny Osmond born?

12 Which fellow-Western actor was on the flip side of Lee Marvin's "Wandrin' Star"?

13 Who had Magic Moments in 1958?

14 Whose first hit was "One of These Nights"?

15 Who was a Yesterday Man back in 1965?

16 Which day of the week was Beautiful to Daniel Boone in 1972?

17 How is Arnold Dorsey better known?

18 Which song title links Don Partridge and Elton John?

19 In which decade did Jackie Wilson have his first hit record?

20 What is the home country of Jimmy Cliff?

21 Which band's last album, released in 2005, was called *Home*?

22 How old was LeAnn Rimes when *Sittin' on Top of the World* was released in the US?

23 Which name links Freedom with Vanessa?

24 What was the Christians' first UK top ten hit?

25 Who had a 60s hit with "Come and Stay with Me"?

26 Andy Fairweather-Low was "Wide-Eyed" and what in his 1975 hit?

27 Which surname is shared by Rickie Lee and Quincy?

28 Which Queen was a 1970 hit for the Kinks?

29 What is the main colour on the album cover of Blur's *The Great Escape*?

30 Which word follows "Love and" in the song title by Cher?

Answers	**TV Pot Luck 16** *(see Quiz 126)*

1 Nickelodeon. 2 John-Jules. 3 Julie Kramer. 4 Fairly Secret Army. 5 William Hartnell. 6 David Essex. 7 The Gnomes of Dulwich. 8 Man About the House. 9 Caresse. 10 Billions. 11 Bebe Daniels. 12 Jeff Rawle. 13 Judy Loe. 14 Jaguar. 15 Auf Wiedersehen Pet. 16 Priscilla White. 17 Juke Box Jury. 18 Liverpool. 19 Roger Moore. 20 Dudley Moore and Peter Cook. 21 Fairclough. 22 Amsterdam. 23 Glenda Jackson. 24 Farrah Fawcett. 25 Jack Duckworth. 26 Lady Jane Felsham. 27 BBC2. 28 Titchmarsh. 29 Charlie Dimmock. 30 Wine.

1 Where does Renny Harlin hail from?
2 About which producer/director did his brother say, "Cecil always bites off more than he can chew, then chews it"?
3 Who directed and starred in *Antony and Cleopatra* in 1973?
4 Which director did Jamie Lee Curtis marry?
5 Which movie did Richard Attenborough direct about a journalist's escape from South Africa?
6 Which flop was Michael Cimino's next film after *The Deer Hunter*?
7 In which of his own movies did Quentin Tarantino appear in 1994?
8 Which British director's autobiography was called *In the Beginning*?
9 Who directed *Angela's Ashes*?
10 Which movie star is Blake Edwards married to?
11 John Ford was from a family which originally came from which country?
12 What did the B stand for in Cecil B. de Mille's name?
13 Who was Renny Harlin's wife when he directed her in *The Long Kiss Goodnight*?
14 Which Boulting brother was the director?
15 Director Tomas Gutierrez Alea hails from which island?
16 Which Douglas made his directorial debut in *Posse*?
17 Who directed his then mother-in-law in *Much Ado About Nothing* in 1993?
18 Which director, whose mother perished in Auschwitz, subsequently fled the USA on an assault charge?
19 What was John Singleton's follow-up to *Boyz N the Hood*?
20 Which movie was Spielberg editing by satellite while filming *Schindler's List*?
21 Whose directorial debut was *Crazy in Alabama*?
22 Who replaced William Wyler as director of *The Sound of Music*?
23 What was Robert Redford's first attempt at directing himself?
24 Which singer/actor's only foray behind the camera was in *None but the Brave*?
25 What was Shirley MacLaine's first film in full charge as director?
26 In which country was 2002 Oscar-winning director Roman Polanski born?
27 In which decade were the Coen brothers born?
28 Alejandro González Iñárritu won 2016's Best Director oscar. For what?
29 Name the famous director who shot "Shine a Light" for the Rolling Stones.
30 Whose epics included "The Ten Commandments" and "Samson and Deliah."

1 What is the offshoot of *Nickelodeon* aimed at very young viewers?
2 Which Danny played the Cat in seven series of *Red Dwarf*?
3 Who is the voice of Marge Simpson?
4 In which series was Major Harry Truscott played by Geoffrey Palmer?
5 Who introduced *The Clothes Show*?
6 Which pop star starred in *The River*?
7 Where did Terry Scott and Hugh Lloyd portray garden ornaments?
8 Which series featured a trainee chef sharing a flat with two girls?
9 Who was writing a book about Alexis in *Dynasty*?
10 Paul Giamatti and Damian Lewis star in which 2016 Showtime series.
11 Who was Ben Lyons's wife?
12 Which actor from *Drop the Dead Donkey* played *Billy Liar*?
13 Who was the late Richard Beckinsale's actress wife?
14 What car did Joey drive in *Bread*?
15 Which series about building workers in Germany was written by Dick Clement and Ian La Frenais?
16 What is Cilla Black's real name?
17 On which pop show did a "hooter" signify a miss?
18 With which English football team did Alan Hanson win cup honours?
19 Who first played Simon Templar on TV?
20 Who were Dud and Pete?
21 What was Rita Sullivan's former surname?
22 Where was *Van Der Valk* set?
23 Which MP played *Elizabeth R*?
24 Which Charlie's Angel married Lee Majors?
25 Who kept pigeons in *Coronation Street*?
26 What was Phyllis Logan's character in *Lovejoy*?
27 On which channel was *Not the Nine o'Clock News* shown?
28 Who is Alan presenter of *Gardener's World*?
29 Who is the redhead in *Ground Force*?
30 What is Jilly Goolden an expert on?

Answers | **Pop Pot Luck 16** *(see Quiz 124)*

1 "There but for Fortune". 2 "Banana Boat Song". 3 Phil Collins. 4 Tribe Called Quest. 5 The Walker Brothers. 6 The Wombles. 7 Reg Presley. 8 John McEnroe, Pat Cash. 9 Alexandra Burke. 10 Love Grows. 11 1950s. 12 Clint Eastwood. 13 Perry Como. 14 The Eagles. 15 Chris Andrews. 16 Sunday. 17 Engelbert Humperdinck. 18 "Blue Eyes". 19 1950s. 20 Jamaica. 21 The Corrs. 22 15. 23 Williams. 24 "Harvest for the World". 25 Marianne Faithfull. 26 Legless. 27 Jones. 28 Victoria. 29 Blue. 30 Understanding.

1 Who is the most capped German player?
2 What colour are the socks of the German team?
3 Who was in charge of the Euro 96 team?
4 Where in Germany was Jurgen Klinsmann born?
5 Mesut Özil's adult international career started in what year?
6 Who was West German manager from 1963–78?
7 In which decade did the Germans first win the World Cup?
8 In 1996 how many teams were there in the German Bundesliga?
9 Which club did Uwe Seeler play for?
10 Who was Germany's top scorer in Euro 96 and with how many goals?
11 Who was skipper of the 1990 World Cup-winning team?
12 Which club were German champions in 1995–96?
13 What two colours are in Hamburg's strip?
14 Who was the Tottenham Hotspur boss when Klinsmann left the club?
15 Which group were the Germans in at the start of Euro 96?
16 Which city do the club team with 1860 in their name come from?
17 To three either way, how many goals did Gerd Muller score for Germany?
18 Which striker had played for Magdeburg, Dynamo Dresden and Nuremberg before coming to play in England?
19 Who took the final spot kick in the England v Germany Euro 96 game?
20 Which German club did England striker Tony Woodcock play for?
21 Who won the Golden Ball – best player – award at the 2002 World Cup finals?
22 In which city is the Allianz Arena?
23 In how many World Cup finals matches did Lothar Matthaus play?
24 Which Chelsea defender was one of two overseas-based players at World Cup 2008?
25 Who was the last German player to score a World Cup finals hat-trick?
26 Name the international who scored the last ever goal at the old Wembley Stadium.
27 Can you name the club Blackburn Rovers signed Roque Santa Cruz from in 2007?
28 Who in 1970 became the first German to win the coveted Ballon d'Or?
29 Who is the only German to score in two different World Cup Finals?
30 Who scored for Germany in their 2–1 defeat to England in November 2008?

Answers | **Movies: Musicals** *(see Quiz 129)*

1 "You Must Love Me" 2 Umbrella. 3 Cyd Charisse. 4 Dirty Dancing. 5 Lina Lamont. 6 "Chim Chim Cheree". 7 Jimmy Nail. 8 Grease. 9 Martin Scorsese. 10 Annie. 11 Forbush (South Pacific). 12 Gary Brooker. 13 Donald O' Connor. 14 Sweet Charity. 15 "Feed Me". 16 My Fair Lady. 17 High Society. 18 10. 19 "Climb Every Mountain". 20 Richard E. Grant. 21 Royal Wedding. 22 La La Land. 23 Freddie Eynsford-Hill. 24 Bing Crosby & Frank Sinatra. 25 Meet Me in St Louis. 26 Sweeney Todd. 27 Nicole Kidman. 28 Carousel. 29 My Fair Lady. 30 All Shook Up.

1 Meghan Trainor released what album in 2016?
2 What is the home country of Doop?
3 Whose album *Take Two* topped the charts in 1996?
4 In which decade did Sonia have her first hit record?
5 Whose first hit was "In the Midnight Hour"?
6 Who had a No. 1 in 1967 with "Let the Heartaches Begin"?
7 Who sang "The Letter" in 1967?
8 What was Clifford T. Ward's only top ten hit?
9 What did "Paloma Blanca" become – Wurzels style?
10 Who was in "Nutbush City Limits" in 1973?
11 Who were "On the Road Again" in 1968?
12 Which James Bond married the 1950s singer Dorothy Squires?
13 Who was the most long-haired of the Eurythmics?
14 Which Shakespeare play was the title of a David Essex hit?
15 Who took the "Legend of Xanadu" to No. 1 in 1968?
16 Who had "A Little Love and Understanding" in 1975?
17 Who was vocalist with Aphrodite's Child?
18 In which decade was Chuck Berry born?
19 Who were Reparata's backing group?
20 Who were singing about "Lady Lynda" in 1979?
21 *This Is What the Truth Feels Like* was released in 2016. By whom?
22 Whose first hit was "Genie in a Bottle"?
23 In which year was the first UK record chart published: 1952, 1953 or 1954?
24 What, on the cover of *Tubular Bells*, is set against the sky?
25 Who was the tallest member of the Police?
26 Who had "A Scottish Soldier" in the charts for nine months in 1961?
27 What do the Beach Boys get from "the way the sunlight plays upon her hair"?
28 Which Elton John album cover shows him sitting in a white suit at a piano?
29 Who was the lead singer of Herman's Hermits?
30 Who had a 1996 album called *Travelling without Moving*?

| **Answers** | **TV Pot Luck 17** *(see Quiz 130)* |

1 Emmerdale. 2 Eight Out of Ten Cats. 3 The Test Card. 4 Masterchef. 5 Opportunity Knocks. 6 Boys from the Blackstuff. 7 Clive Anderson. 8 Guinness. 9 Mike. 10 Geoffrey Hughes. 11 Brian. 12 Billy. 13 Upstairs, Downstairs. 14 Pop music. 15 Leo. 16 Sophie. 17 Ever Decreasing Circles. 18 Richard. 19 Butterflies. 20 Alf Garnett. 21 The Forsyte Saga. 22 Agatha Christie. 23 Monty Python's Flying Circus. 24 Wexford. 25 Cadfael. 26 Percy Sugden. 27 Rawhide. 28 Seafood. 29 Henry Winkler. 30 Connor McIntyre.

Quiz 129 | Movies: Musicals

1 Which song won an Oscar for *Evita*, although it did not feature in the original stage show?

2 When Mary Poppins lands to take over the Banks household, what does she carry in her right hand?

3 Who was Fred Astaire's partner in *The Band Wagon*?

4 Which 80s movie has the song "I Had the Time of My Life"?

5 Which fading movie star is played by Jean Hagen in *Singin' in the Rain*?

6 Which *Mary Poppins* song won the Academy Award?

7 Who played Eva's lover Magaldi in *Evita*?

8 Which musical featured the song "Hopelessly Devoted to You"?

9 Who directed the musical *New York, New York*?

10 In which musical did Albert Finney play Daddy Warbucks?

11 Which Nellie sang "I'm Gonna Wash That Man Right Out of My Hair"?

12 Which member of Procul Harum sang about the "Rainbow Tour" in *Evita*?

13 Who climbed the walls singing "Make 'em Laugh" in *Singin' in the Rain*?

14 "The Rhythm of Life" came from which musical?

15 What is the plant's catchphrase in *Little Shop of Horrors*?

16 Which musical ends with the line, "Where the devil are my slippers"?

17 Which musical was a remake of *The Philadelphia Story*?

18 How many Oscars did *West Side Story* win?

19 What is the song played at the end of *The Sound of Music*?

20 Who was the Famous Five's manager in *Spiceworld*?

21 In which 50s musical did Fred Astaire dance on the walls and ceiling of a hotel?

22 Who won an Oscar for his role as Master of Ceremonies in *Cabaret*?

23 In 2016, Emma Stone and Ryan Gosling shine in which musical?

24 Who sang "Did You Ever" in *High Society*?

25 In which musical did Judy Garland sing "Have Yourself a Merry Little Christmas"?

26 Who was the lead character in Tim Burton's musical about a murdering barber?

27 Who played the lead role in *Moulin Rouge*?

28 Which Rodgers and Hammerstein movie was adapted from a 1909 Ferenc Molnar play?

29 Which *Flight of the Conchords* character wrote 2011's *Muppet Movie* songs?

30 Name the Elvis musical based on the plot in Shakespeare's *Twelfth Night*.

---

1 Where in "Soapland" would you find the Woolpack?

2 Which comedy panel series pokes fun at opinion poll surveys?

3 Where did a sum on a blackboard recur often on television screens?

4 Which cookery competition is hosted by Lloyd Grossman?

5 On which talent show was Pam Ayres a winner?

6 In which series did Yosser Hughes first appear?

7 Which chat show host did the Bee Gees walk out on?

8 What liquid refreshment was advertised by Pete and Dud?

9 Who was Bernie Winters's brother?

10 Who plays Onslow in *Keeping Up Appearances*?

11 Who was the snail on *The Magic Roundabout*?

12 Who was the youngest Boswell boy in *Bread*?

13 In which series were Mrs Bridges and Mr Hudson?

14 What was featured in *Thank Your Lucky Stars*?

15 What is the Christian name of actor McKern of *Rumpole* fame?

16 What is TV cook Grigson's first name?

17 In which comedy series was Penelope Wilton married to Richard Briers?

18 What was Hyacinth's husband's name in *Keeping Up Appearances*?

19 In which series was Geoffrey Palmer a collector of a variety of flying creature?

20 Who was Rita's father in *Till Death Do Us Part*?

21 Which saga was the last to be broadcast in black and white on the BBC?

22 Who created Hercule Poirot?

23 The Ministry of Funny Walks appeared in which series?

24 Which Ruth Rendell character is played by George Baker?

25 Which medieval monk is a crime solver?

26 Who ran the Neighbourhood Watch Scheme in *Coronation Street*?

27 Which 1960s western series was about a cattle drive and the drovers?

28 What is Rick Stein's gastronomic speciality?

29 Which actor in *Happy Days*, apart from Ron Howard, has directed feature films?

30 At the British Soap Awards 2016, which actor won Villain of the Year?

1 Which two Italian sides contested the final in 1995?
2 Which side won the 2015 UEFA Europa League?
3 Which Belgian side lost to a London club in the 1970 final?
4 Trevor Whymark scored four goals in a Euro game for which club?
5 Which Dutch team beat Red Boys a record 14–0 in 1984?
6 Who won the trophy the first time it was decided on penalties?
7 Wilf Rostron scored in the competition for which club?
8 Which Spanish side lost the 1988 final after being three up from the first leg?
9 In 1996, which team became the second from France to reach a final?
10 Which country did Ujpest Dozsa represent?
11 In which decade did Liverpool win the trophy for the first time?
12 Which winners did Diego Maradona play for?
13 In which decade did Real Madrid win the trophy in successive seasons?
14 Alan Brazil has scored UEFA Cup goals for Ipswich Town and who else?
15 Bobby Moncur led which team to win the trophy?
16 Which country did Red Boys represent?
17 Which Swedish side have won the competition twice?
18 Before 1996–97, which country has provided most winners?
19 The side beaten by Ipswich Town in a final was prefixed by which two letters?
20 Which Scottish side did Paul Hegarty play for in a final?
21 Which Dutchman coached Zenit St Petersburg to win the 2007–08 UEFA Cup?
22 What was the score when Liverpool beat Alaves to win the UEFA Cup in 2001?
23 Which club beat Middlesbrough 4–0 in the 2007 final?
24 In which city was the 2008 final staged?
25 Which English club lost a UEFA Cup Final to Galatasaray on penalties?
26 In what season did the UEFA Cup include the domestic cup winners for the first time?
27 What Turkish club's stadium was chosen to host the 2009 UEFA Cup Final?
28 Who were the last club to lose the UEFA Cup Final in their own stadium?
29 What competition did it replace in season 1971–72?
30 Name either one of the two English sides who contested the inaugural final in 1972.

Answers | Movies: Marlon Brando *(see Quiz 133)*

1 Motorcycles. 2 A Streetcar Named Desire. 3 Mexico. 4 Cannes. 5 1920s. 6 Vito Corleone. 7 On the Waterfront. 8 Manslaughter. 9 The Wild One. 10 Brando: Songs My Mother Never Taught Me. 11 Frank Sinatra. 12 Guys and Dolls. 13 A Dry White Season. 14 The Men. 15 Last Tango in Paris. 16 One Eyed Jacks. 17 Tahiti. 18 Vivien Leigh. 19 On the Waterfront. 20 A Countess from Hong Kong. 21 Francis Ford Coppola. 22 A Streetcar Named Desire. 23 The Teahouse of the August Moon. 24 The Godfather. 25 Mark Antony. 26 Corleone. 27 Superman. 28 2004. 29 The Godfather. 30 Sayonara.

1 Whose album *Live at the BBC* topped the charts in 1994?
2 Whose first hit was "Uptight"?
3 In which decade did Squeeze have their first hit record?
4 What year was the Bee Gees' "New York Mining Disaster"?
5 How is Pauline Matthews better known?
6 What was on the other side of Rick Astley's "My Arms Keep Missing You"?
7 Who was Belle's backing group?
8 Who took A Picture Of You in 1962?
9 With which song did Cilla Black beat Dionne Warwick to the top spot?
10 Who said "Tell Laura I Love Her" in 1960?
11 In which decade was Robin Gibb born?
12 Which two Tina Turner singles are also the names of albums?
13 What was on the other side of David Cassidy's "Cherish"?
14 Who had the original No. 1 with "Don't Cry for Me, Argentina"?
15 Which city links Spinners and Emeralds?
16 What is the home country of Falco, who had a No. 1 with "Rock Me Amadeus"?
17 Which song title links Patsy Cline and Mud?
18 Which day of the week is included in a Rolling Stones song title in 1967 and again in 1991?
19 In 1961 where was Kenny Ball and at what time?
20 What is the link between Evita and Charlie Chaplin?
21 Whose debut solo single was "When You Say Nothing at All"?
22 In which year was U2's induction ceremony into the Rock & Roll Hall of Fame?
23 Who took "Bye Bye Baby" to the top in 1975?
24 What instrument is on the back cover of Stevie Wonder's *Hotter than July* album?
25 Who was singing about "My Guy" in 1964?
26 Time of My Life was a 2016 return for which Boyzone singer?
27 Who narrated Jeff Wayne's *War of the Worlds* album?
28 What sort of entertainment were Simply Red enjoying in 1995?
29 Which group made No. 5 with "De Do Do Do, De Da Da Da?
30 Who told us he was *An Innocent Man*?

1 Karate. 2 Five. 3 Steve McFadden. 4 Jim Bergerac. 5 Gladiators. 6 Red. 7 Rumpole of the Bailey. 8 Tesco. 9 Agnes Moorehead. 10 Cheryl Baker. 11 Simon Dee. 12 Cilla Black. 13 Mars. 14 FilmFour. 15 The Green Cross Code Man. 16 Mystic. 17 John Logie Baird. 18 Carlton TV. 19 Sir Richard Attenborough. 20 Gardening. 21 The Green Goddess. 22 Harry Secombe. 23 Anneka Rice. 24 Cilla Black. 25 Channel 4. 26 Barry Norman. 27 British Broadcasting Corporation. 28 All Creatures Great and Small. 29 Antiques Roadshow. 30 BBC.

1 What modes of transport dominate *The Wild One*?
2 Which Oscar-nominated movie had Brando previously done as a play on Broadway?
3 Where was *Viva Zapata* set?
4 At which European film festival did he win with *On the Waterfront*?
5 In which decade was he born?
6 Which character did he play in *The Godfather*?
7 For which movie did he receive his first Oscar?
8 His son Christian was jailed on what charge?
9 Which movie had the ad line, "That streetcar man has a new desire"?
10 What was his autobiography called?
11 Which singer was earmarked for Brando's role in *On the Waterfront*?
12 In which musical did he play Sky Masterson?
13 For which 1989 movie did he receive an Oscar nomination?
14 In which movie did he make his screen debut?
15 For which 70s Bernardo Bertolucci film was he Oscar-nominated?
16 Which movie saw his directorial debut?
17 Near which South Sea island is his home Tetiaroa?
18 Who played Blanche opposite Brando in *A Streetcar Named Desire*?
19 In which movie did he famously say, "I coulda had class. I coulda been a contender"?
20 Which Chaplin movie did he make in 1967?
21 Who directed Brando in *The Godfather*?
22 For which movie did he receive his first Oscar nomination?
23 In which 1956 movie did he play a Japanese interpreter?
24 He sent a native American Indian to pick up his Oscar for which film?
25 Which role earned him a 1953 Oscar nomination in *Julius Caesar*?
26 What was the family name of the Mafia mob boss he portrayed in two movies?
27 In which movie series did he play Jor-El?
28 In which year did Marlon Brando die?
29 What movie did he refuse the Best Actor Oscar award for in 1972?
30 In which movie does Brando play the part of an American fighter pilot from the Korean War?

---

1 What martial art is also the name of Batfink's partner in the children's TV series?

2 How many series of *Ab Fab* were there, before the 2016 film?

3 Who won Outstanding Achievement Award (On-Screen) at the British Soap Awards 2016?

4 Who was Charlie Hungerford's son-in-law?

5 What were Cobra and Hunter? Hint: Nineties TV show on ITV.

6 What colour costumes do the lifeguards in Baywatch wear?

7 Who is John Mortimer's legal hero?

8 In which advert do Prunella Scales and Jane Horrocks appear?

9 Who played Endora in *Bewitched*?

10 Which member of Bucks Fizz became a TV presenter?

11 Which Simon left a 1960s pop group to present his own chat show?

12 Who presented *Surprise, Surprise,* before her death in 2015?

13 Which chocolate bar promised to help you "work, rest and play"?

14 What was Channel 4's film channel called, launched in November 1998?

15 Which Superheroic figure helped children to cross the road?

16 Which Meg appeared on *National Lottery Live*?

17 Who is credited with inventing TV?

18 Which independent TV company covers the London area?

19 Who is Sir David Attenborough's famous film director brother?

20 What kind of programmes did the late Geoff Hamilton present on BBC TV?

21 The TV fitness instructor Diana Moran is known as "The Green ____"?

22 The Sunday evening programme *Highway* was hosted by which former Goon and singer?

23 Who hosted *Challenge Anneka*?

24 Who hosts *Blind Date*?

25 *The Big Breakfast* is broadcast on which channel?

26 Who presented *Film 97*?

27 What does BBC stand for?

28 Christopher Timothy starred in which acclaimed BBC vet drama?

29 Which BBC antiques series hosts weekly shows in venues around the country?

30 Is *Songs of Praise* broadcast on BBC or ITV?

Answers | **Pop Pot Luck 18** *(see Quiz 132)*

1 The Beatles. 2 Stevie Wonder. 3 1970s. 4 1941. 5 Kiki Dee. 6 "When I Fall in Love". 7 The Devotions. 8 Joe Brown. 9 "Anyone Who Had a Heart". 10 Ricky Valance. 11 1940s. 12 "Private Dancer", "What's Love Got to Do with It?". 13 "Could It be Forever?". 14 Julie Covington. 15 Detroit. 16 Austria. 17 "Crazy". 18 (Ruby) Tuesday. 19 Midnight iSn Moscow. 20 Their bodies were stolen after their deaths. 21 Ronan Keating. 22 2005. 23 Bay City Rollers. 24 A piano. 25 Mary Wells. 26 Ronan Keating. 27 Richard Burton. 28 A fairground. 29 The Police. 30 Billy Joel.

1 In what vessel was Andrew Flintoff rescued during the 2007 World Cup?
2 Who retired from cricket after watching himself drop a catch on TV highlights?
3 Who beat Muttiah Muralitharan to 700 Test wickets?
4 Which English county won the right to play in the Stanford Super Twenty20?
5 Which Root plays for Yorkshire County Cricket Club and England?
6 Which county won the championship in 1990 and 1991?
7 What was remarkable about the 16 overs that South Africa's Hugh Tayfield bowled against England at Durban in 1957?
8 Who was England's youngest and later oldest post-war Test player?
9 Which player broke a leg in a Test series against New Zealand in 1992?
10 In 1995, Jack Russell took how many catches in a Test to create a new world record?
11 Which three counties did Ian Botham play for?
12 Which county have won the championship most times?
13 Where is Kent's cricket ground headquarters?
14 Edmonds and Emburey were the spinning duo for which county?
15 Which all-rounder took 100 wickets and scored 1000 runs in 16 seasons between 1903 and 1926?
16 What are the Christian names of Australia's Waugh brothers?
17 Where do Middlesex play home matches?
18 On which West Indian island is Sabina Park?
19 What was the result of the 1995–96 Test series between South Africa and England?
20 Which English county has Brian Lara played for?
21 Who was the "bodyline" bowler?
22 Gloucestershire cricketers of the 1870s W. G. and E. M. had what surname?
23 Who are the only father and son to captain England?
24 Which Englishman took 19 wickets in a 1956 Test against Australia?
25 Who was bowling for Glamorgan when Sobers hit six sixes in an over?
26 How many Test centuries did Geoff Boycott score for England?
27 What is the umpire's signal for a no-ball?
28 Who was selected for all World Cups from 1975 to 1995?
29 Which was the first new county to join the championship in the 1990s?
30 Who was West Indian captain before Richie Richardson?

Answers | Pop: Solo Singers *(see Quiz 137)*

1 Norman Greenbaum. 2 "I Pretend". 3 Tony Di Bart. 4 Mariah Carey. 5 Gary Barlow. 6 Mr Blobby. 7 Gabrielle. 8 Chesney Hawkes. 9 "Deck of Cards". 10 21. 11 Peter Sarstedt. 12 Dusty Springfield. 13 Roger Miller. 14 Tom Jones. 15 Carole King. 16 Whigfield. 17 Al Martino. 18 Lulu. 19 Billy Paul. 20 Bette Midler. 21 Eminem. 22 England. 23 George Harrison. 24 Amy Winehouse. 25 Maneater. 26 Gabrielle. 27 Mariah Carey. 28 LeAnn Rimes. 29 Watch Me DO. 30 Melanie C.

1 Kevin Sheedy was at which club when he made his international debut?
2 Where was John Barnes born?
3 Which was Colin Hendry's first League club?
4 In which decade was Garrincha born?
5 Which team were beaten 4–2 by Manchester Utd in the 1948 FA Cup Final?
6 Which Joe became manager of Bristol City in November 1994?
7 Which 46-year-old physiotherapist became Arsenal manager?
8 Which club did Peter Beardsley join on leaving Liverpool?
9 Airdrieonians and Clyde have shared which ground?
10 Who moved from Bolton to Celtic in 1994 to set a club record for transfer fee received?
11 Which country did Ralph Coates play for?
12 In which decade did Huddersfield Town first win the FA Cup?
13 What colour are Barcelona's home shorts?
14 Howard Wilkinson followed Billy Bremner as boss of which club?
15 Complete the name of this Arsenal player: Jack Andrew Garry _____
16 Eddie Hopkinson set a League appearance record at which club?
17 Regis and Atkinson were the strike force at which club?
18 Who won his 100th Scottish cap in March 1986?
19 Which club did Mike Milligan leave to join Everton?
20 At which club did former England boss Bobby Robson begin his playing career?
21 Which veteran coach was in charge of China's team at the 2002 World Cup finals?
22 Which Yorkshire League 1 club moved into the Keepmoat Stadium in 2007?
23 Which was Ray Clemence's first League club?
24 Which 1980s–90s striker scored 111 League goals for Everton?
25 Ian Pearce first played in an FA Charity Shield for which club?
26 Which ex-player George became boss of Ipswich Town in December 1994?
27 Jesper Olsen won an FA Cup winner's medal with which club?
28 Which club did Mark Kennedy join on leaving Millwall?
29 Which country did Gerry Peyton play for?
30 Which team play at home in front of the Cobbold Stand?

1 Which solo singer had a hit with "Spirit in the Sky"?
2 What was Des O'Connor's first No. 1 hit?
3 Who had a 90s No. 1 with "The Real Thing"?
4 Which singer was named after the Wind in "Paint Your Wagon"?
5 Who wrote Take That's "Babe" before pursuing a solo career?
6 Who was the first soloist to have a No. 1 hit with the same name as himself?
7 How is Londoner Ms Bobb better known?
8 Whose first single "The One and Only" went to No. 1 in 1991?
9 What is Wink Martindale's most famous hit?
10 What was the name of Adele's second album?
11 Who had a 60s hit with "Where Do You Go to My Lovely?"?
12 Who has recorded with Richard Carpenter and the Pet Shop Boys?
13 Which singer's songs ranged from "Little Green Apples" to "You Can't Roller Skate in a Buffalo Herd"?
14 Who was famous for having a rabbit's foot swinging from his belt?
15 Who had a best-selling album called *Tapestry*?
16 Who went to No. 1 in her first-ever week in the charts in 1994?
17 Who had the first-ever No. 1 in the UK?
18 Which female soloist has recorded on at least nine different record labels in a 30-year career?
19 Who sang about "Me and Mrs Jones" in 1973?
20 Which American had a 1989 hit with "The Wind Beneath My Wings"?
21 Under what name has Marshall Mathers made millions as a recording artist?
22 In what country was Craig David born?
23 Which ex-Beatle returned to No. 1 following his death in 2001?
24 Which British singer won five Grammy awards in 2008?
25 What was the title of Nelly Furtado's summer 2006 hit?
26 Who had her second and last No. 1 hit with "Rise"?
27 Westlife teamed-up with this artist for the No. 1 hit "Against All Odds."
28 Which female artist's only UK No. 1 hit was "Can't Fight the Moonlight"?
29 What is the first track of Meghan Trainor's *Thank You*?
30 Whose first No. 1 hit was "Never be the Same Again"?

Answers | **Cricket Pot Luck** *(see Quiz 135)*

1 Pedalo. **2** Adam Gilchrist. **3** Shane Warne. **4** Middlesex. **5** Joe. **6** Essex. **7** All maidens – no runs conceded. **8** Brian Close. Played at 18 and finally at 45. **9** David Lawrence. **10** 11. **11** Somerset, Worcestershire and Durham. **12** Yorkshire. **13** Canterbury. **14** Middlesex. **15** Wilfred Rhodes. **16** Mark and Steve. **17** Lord's. **18** Jamaica. **19** South Africa won 1–0. **20** Warwickshire. **21** Harold Larwood. **22** Grace. **23** Colin and Christopher Cowdrey. **21** Jim Laker. **25** Malcolm Nash. **26** 22. **27** Right arm raised in horizontal position. **28** Javed Miandad of Pakistan. **29** Durham. **30** Viv Richards.

1 What was the name of Peter Mayhew's character in *Star Wars*?
2 Who turned down Al Pacino's role in *The Godfather*?
3 At what sport did Kirk Douglas excel?
4 In which decade was *Field of Dreams* released?
5 Mickey Mouse's gloves are what colour?
6 Who won the Best Director Oscar for *The Grapes of Wrath*?
7 Which Barbara featured in *Far and Away*?
8 Who won an Oscar as Blanche in *A Streetcar Named Desire*?
9 *Subway* and *Highlander* both featured which actor?
10 A character named President Whitmore appears in which film?
11 Which song from *Philadelphia* won an Oscar?
12 Which writer directed *Sleepless in Seattle*?
13 Who played Dustin Hoffman's wife in *Straw Dogs*?
14 Who directed *Jerry Maguire*?
15 In the 1940s who was shunned by Hollywood when she left her husband for Roberto Rossellini?
16 Who won the Best Actor Oscar for *Scent of a Woman*?
17 Who was the most famous member of the Gumm Sisters Kiddie Act?
18 In which decade was *Song of the South* released?
19 What was Warren Beatty's first film, in 1961?
20 *Testimony* and *Schindler's List* both featured which actor?
21 Who played Jerry Lee Lewis in *Great Balls of Fire*?
22 For which film did Robert Redford win his first Oscar nomination?
23 Who played Fletcher Christian in *The Bounty* in 1984?
24 Who won the Best Actress Oscar for *The Miracle Worker*?
25 Which James featured in *Westworld*?
26 Who played identical twins in 1998's *The Parent Trap*?
27 Richard Kelly directed which movie about a troubled teenager and a giant rabbit?
28 2016's *10 Cloverfield Lane* is a sequel to what film?
29 Elka Wardega won what award at the 2016 Oscars?
30 Who directed the 1988 version of *Coming to America*?

| **Answers** | **Football Pot Luck 15** *(see Quiz 136)* |

1 Everton. 2 Kingston, Jamaica. 3 Dundee. 4 1930s. 5 Blackpool. 6 Jordan. 7 Bertie Mee. 8 Everton. 9 Broadwood Stadium. 10 Andy Walker. 11 England. 12 1920s. 13 Blue. 14 Leeds Utd. 15 Wilshere. 16 Bolton Wanderers. 17 Aston Villa. 18 Kenny Dalglish. 19 Oldham Athletic. 20 Fulham. 21 Bora Milutinovic. 22 Doncaster Rovers. 23 Scunthope. 24 Graeme Sharp. 25 Blackburn. 26 Burley. 27 Manchester Utd. 28 Liverpool. 29 Republic of Ireland. 30 Ipswich Town.

1 What was the name of the Drag Queen created by Paul O'Grady?
2 Which rugby league club does Johnny Vegas follow?
3 Which US character has children called Becky, Darlene and DJ?
4 Who plays the titular female character in *Gavin & Stacey*?
5 What is the name of Dorien's husband in *Birds of a Feather*?
6 What is the name of *Drop the Dead Donkey's* TV news company?
7 When Granada revived *Bootsie and Snudge* in 1974, who had become a millionnaire?
8 Since 2014, Will Arnett has voiced what cartoon horse?
9 Who played Bilko's accomplices Corporals Barbarella and Henshaw?
10 Which actor played Adrian Mole?
11 In *The River*, the part played by David Essex was originally intended for which other well-known singer?
12 Which comedienne presented *Can We Talk*?
13 At the end of which series of *Hancock's Half Hour* did Sid James leave the show?
14 In *A Very Peculiar Practice*, which doctor, played by David Troughton, didn't like his patients?
15 Which famous ancient site did Edina rearrange for a fashion show in *Ab Fab*?
16 Who played Blanco in *Porridge*?
17 Who was the American Python?
18 Which character does Thora Hird play in *Last of the Summer Wine*?
19 Who was the presenter of *Zoo Time*?
20 Whose catchphrase is "It's the way I tell 'em"?
21 Who played the 'dragon' in *George and the Dragon*?
22 Which comedy duo have the first names Tommy and Bobby?
23 Which Channel 4 sitcom led to the spin-off *Frasier*?
24 What is the name of Father Ted's doting housekeeper?
25 What was the name of the central character in *Solo*?
26 What was the name of Sir Humphrey's over-zealous assistant in *Yes, Minister*?
27 What was Lady Lavender's pet, "Captain", in *You Rang M'Lord*?
28 Who had a landlord called Jerzy Balowski?
29 In *Bread*, which actor played Grandad?
30 Which actress played the dreaded mother in *Sorry!*?

Answers	**Pop: Bob Dylan** (see Quiz 141)

1 "Blowin' in the Wind". 2 "The Times They are A-Changin'". 3 "Hey Mr Tambourine Man". 4 Blonde on Blonde. 5 Playing electric guitar. 6 Mighty Quinn. 7 Nashville Skyline. 8 £35,000. 9 Tarantula. 10 Blood on the Tracks. 11 "Lay Lady Lay". 12 Pat Garrett and Billy the Kid. 13 The Bible. 14 Accomplice Records. 15 Mark Knopfler. 16 Christianity. 17 "All Along the Watchtower". 18 Midnight Cowboy. 19 Traveling Wilburys. 20 Bob Willis. 21 Shadows in the Night. 22 2006. 23 Chronicles. 24 The Band. 25 "Someday Baby". 26 Robert Allen Zimmerman. 27 2008. 28 Guthrie. 29 The Ed Sullivan Show. 30 "Like a Rolling Stone".

1 Craig Johnston scored an FA Cup Final goal for which club?
2 The top goalscorer in 2015–16's Premier League was Harry Kane. How many goals did he score?
3 What was Steve Hodge's first League club?
4 What colour are Benfica's home shirts?
5 To ten years either way, when did Bury first win the FA Cup?
6 Who moved from Bristol Rovers in November 1989 to set a club record for transfer fee received?
7 Who plays at home at Boothferry Park?
8 Which club did Joey Jones leave to join Liverpool?
9 In which city was David Batty born?
10 Andy Goram was at which club when he made his international debut?
11 Who was Terry Venables's assistant at Barcelona?
12 Which team were beaten 1–0 by Ipswich in the 1978 FA Cup Final?
13 In which decade was Geoff Hurst born?
14 Alan Wright and Scott Sellars were in the same team at which club?
15 Which club did Wimbledon buy John Fashanu from?
16 Who holds the League appearance record at Celtic?
17 Which John became manager of Chelsea in March 1985?
18 Which country did Mick Robinson play for?
19 Ron Atkinson followed Dave Sexton as boss of which club?
20 Which club did Gary McAllister leave to join Leeds Utd?
21 Which club beat Arsenal 2–1 to win the last Football League Cup Final in Cardiff?
22 Which club won seven consecutive French League titles in the 21st century?
23 Which was Marcus Bent's first League club?
24 When did the USA first take part in the World Cup?
25 What is the first name of Joachim, formerly of Leicester City and Aston Villa?
26 In which decade did Hearts first win the Scottish FA Cup?
27 Whose 1992 £3,300,000 transfer to Blackburn from Southampton was a club record for a transfer fee received?
28 Cec Podd set an appearance record at which club?
29 Jim Baxter was at which club when he made his international debut?
30 Which England manager was born in London on 6 January 1943?

Answers | **Movies Pot Luck 16** *(see Quiz 142)*

1 1980s. 2 Tony Curtis. 3 David Mills. 4 James Stewart. 5 Roland Emmerich.
6 Binoche. 7 "You Must Love Me". 8 Gene Hackman. 9 Joseph L. Mankiewicz. 10 Michael Keaton. 11 To Have and Have Not. 12 Brenda Fricker. 13 Simone Signoret. 14 Eddie Fisher. 15 Quentin Tarantino. 16 William. 17 Bugsy Malone. 18 Ernst Stavro Blofeld. 19 1950s. 20 Stephen King. 21 Richard Dreyfuss. 22 Raul Julia. 23 Sidney Poitier. 24 Vincent Price. 25 Mars. 26 Wales. 27 Ex Machina. 28 1930s. 29 Jurassic Park. 30 Pussy Galore.

1 Which Bob Dylan composition was a US hit for Peter, Paul and Mary and Stevie Wonder?
2 What was his first UK hit single?
3 What was the first chart-topping composition by Dylan?
4 Which album includes the lengthy "Sad-Eyed Lady of the Lowlands"?
5 Why was Dylan booed off stage in 1965 and 1966?
6 Which Dylan song was a hit for Manfred Mann in 1968?
7 Which album did he record with the help of Johnny Cash?
8 To the nearest £1,000 how much did Dylan receive for a one-hour session at the Isle of Wight Festival in 1969?
9 What was the title of the novel he published in 1970?
10 Which album was said to have been due to the end of his marriage?
11 Which Dylan song was a hit for Eric Clapton and Guns N' Roses?
12 Which film did he act in and provide the music for in Mexico?
13 When asked what were the most overrated and underrated books of the last 75 years, what did he reply?
14 What was the name of his own record label?
15 Which UK guitarist co-produced *Infidels*?
16 Which religion did he embrace in the late 70s?
17 Which Dylan song was a hit for Jimi Hendrix in 1968?
18 For which film did he write "Lay Lady Lay" – though it was not chosen?
19 Which Dylan band also included George Harrison and Roy Orbison?
20 Which cricketer added Dylan to his first names?
21 2015 was the year Bob released what album?
22 In which year was *Modern Times* released?
23 What is the title of Dylan's memoirs, the first part of which was published in 2004?
24 Which of Dylan's former groups issued a 2005 compilation *A Musical History*?
25 Which single from *Modern Times* made the US Hot 100?
26 What is the real name of Bob Dylan?
27 In what year was Dylan awarded a Pulitzer Prize Special Citation?
28 Which "Woody" was the young Dylan's hero?
29 What famous American television talk show did he walk out of in protest in 1963?
30 Can you name his six minutes long 1965 US No. 2 and UK No. 4 hit?

---

1 In which decade was *The Shining* released?
2 How is Bernard Schwarz better known?
3 What was the name of Brad Pitt's character in *Se7en*?
4 Who played the man in the wheelchair in Hitchcock's *Rear Window*?
5 Who directed *Independence Day*?
6 Which Juliette featured in *The English Patient*?
7 Which song won Best Song Oscar for *Evita*?
8 Who played the sadistic sheriff in Eastwood's *Unforgiven*?
9 Who won the Best Director Oscar for *All About Eve*?
10 *Clean and Sober* and *Batman Returns* both featured which actor?
11 The Bogart and Bacall relationship began on the set of which movie?
12 Who played Christy Brown's mother in *My Left Foot*?
13 Who won the Best Actress Oscar for *Room at the Top*?
14 Who was married to Debbie Reynolds and Elizabeth Taylor?
15 Who directed *Jackie Brown*?
16 What did the W stand for in W. C. Fields's name?
17 Which musical gangster movie features "bullets" of whipped cream?
18 What was the name of the villain in *Diamonds Are Forever*?
19 In which decade was Disney's *Peter Pan* released?
20 Which horror writer directed the film *Maximum Overdrive*?
21 Who won the Best Actor Oscar for *The Goodbye Girl*?
22 *Kiss of the Spider Woman* and *The Addams Family* both feature which actor?
23 Who played the surprise guest in *Guess Who's Coming to Dinner*?
24 Which Yale graduate was known as the King of the Horror Movie?
25 Which Kenneth featured in *What's Up, Doc?*?
26 In which country was *Empire of the Sun* star Christian Bale born?
27 At the 2016 Oscars, what film won Best Visual Effects?
28 In which decade was *Monkey Business* first released?
29 A character named Dr Ellie Sattler appeared in which film?
30 What was the name of the Bond girl in *Goldfinger*?

1 Which Soprano joined the cast of Lucifer in 2016?
2 What is the first name of Inspector Gold in *The Bill*?
3 Who was the creator of *ER*?
4 In the 1950's, Conrad Philips was famous for playing which role?
5 Who played Bart in *Maverick*?
6 In which city was *Gunsmoke* set?
7 Keith Michell starred as which King Henry?
8 What was Zoe's job in *May to December*?
9 In *Blade on the Feather*, who starred as the retired Soviet spy?
10 Who sang the theme from *Rawhide*?
11 What was McCallum?
12 In which year was Dixon promoted from Police Constable to Sergeant in *Dixon of Dock Green*?
13 Jon Finch played which Australian outlaw?
14 In the serial *Cathy Come Home* which actor played Cathy's husband?
15 What was Tinker's surname in *Lovejoy*?
16 Who played the sheriff in *American Gothic*?
17 Which Canadian actor later seen in *Bonanza* starred in *Sailor of Fortune*?
18 What happens to the message tape in *Mission: Impossible*?
19 Who took over from David Caruso in *NYPD Blue*?
20 What did Yozzer famously want?
21 What was the name of the evil organization in *The Man from UNCLE*?
22 Which actress played the fiercely critical character Maud in *Flickers*?
23 Who was promoter Frank Stubbs?
24 What was the name of the cook in *Rawhide*?
25 Who played *The Virginian*?
26 What was the name of Big John's brother-in-law in *The High Chapparal*?
27 Margaret Lockwood played which character in *The Flying Swan*?
28 Hari Kumar in *Jewel in the Crown* was played by which actor?
29 In which city is *Hill Street Blues* set?
30 Who starred as an obnoxious gossip columnist named Lytton?

Answers	Pop: Soap Rock *(see Quiz 145)*

1 Letitia Dean. 2 Malandra Burrows. 3 Hattie Tavernier. 4 Mike and Alma Baldwin.
5 Jack Duckworth of Coronation Street. 6 "Anyone Can Fall in Love". 7 Ruby
O'Donnell. 8 The Woolpackers. 9 Liz Dawn (Vera Duckworth). 10 "Come Outside".
11 Mike Sarne. 12 Ian Kelsey (Dave Glover of Emmerdale). 13 Aidan Brosnan.
14 "The Ugly Duckling". 15 Rita. 16 Peter Noone. 17 Ena Sharples. 18 "Every
Loser Wins". 19 Mari Wilson. 20 Michael Ball. 21 Ant & Dec. 22 Brookside. 23
Neighbours. 24 Shaun Williamson. 25 Kylie. 26 Anita Dobson (Angie) 27 Dannii
Minogue. 28 Bill Tarney (Jack Duckworth). 29 Keith Duffy. 30 Craig McLachlan.

1 Jock Stein followed Jimmy Armfield as boss of which club?
2 In which decade did Leeds United first win the FA Cup?
3 Which was Tony Dorigo's first League club?
4 Which country did Paul Bodin play for?
5 Petr Cech was awarded Best Goalkeeper in 2015–16's Premier League season. How many clean sheets?
6 Kevin Wilson and Clive Allen were in the same team at which club?
7 In which decade was Des Lynam born?
8 Which club did Gary Taggart join on leaving Barnsley?
9 Who plays at home at Twerton Park?
10 Peter Barnes was at which club when he made his international debut?
11 Which Terry became manager of Coventry City in 1990?
12 What was the score in the drawn Manchester Utd v Brighton FA Cup Final of 1983?
13 What colour are Hearts' home shirts?
14 Brondby knocked which English team out of the UEFA Cup in 1995?
15 Tony Blair is a fan of which team?
16 Which club did Stephen Pears leave to join Middlesbrough?
17 Willie Miller set a League appearance record at which club?
18 Where was Raich Carter born?
19 Who moved from Bradford in 1995 to Wolves to set a club record for transfer fee received?
20 Kevin Campbell and Chris Bart-Williams both moved on the same day to which club?
21 Norwich City, Aston Villa and _____ were relegated in 2015-16 season.
22 In which French town did both England and Scotland go out of the 1998 World Cup?
23 At which club were the unrelated Marcus and Darren Bent first teammates?
24 Which 21st-century Scottish Cup finalists played in the FA Cup in the 20th century?
25 In which decade did Wolverhampton Wanderers first win the FA Cup?
26 At which club did Peter Taylor succeed Martin O'Neill as manager?
27 Who set an English transfer record in 1981, leaving West Brom for £1.5 million?
28 What colour are West Ham United's home shorts?
29 Which Brian was Wrexham manager 1989–2001?
30 At which stadium do fans sit in the Bob Lord Stand?

1 Who sang "Something Outa Nothing" with Paul Medford in 1986?
2 Who was Just This Side of Love in 1990?
3 How was Michelle Gayle known in *EastEnders*?
4 Which "Street" couple sang "Somethin' Stupid"?
5 How is Bill Tarmey better known?
6 What was the title of the song based on the *EastEnders* theme tune?
7 Which actress won Best Young Performance at the British Soap Awards 2016?
8 Who had an album called *Emmerdance*?
9 Who sang "Passing Strangers" with Joe Longthorne in 1994?
10 Wendy Richard, a.k.a. Pauline Fowler, was heard on which 1962 No. 1?
11 Who was the male vocalist on the record?
12 Who replaced Shane Richie in *Grease* in 1997?
13 How was Sean Maguire better known in Albert Square?
14 Which song did Mike Reid, alias Frank Butcher, take into the charts?
15 Which *Coronation Street* character was originally a singer in the soap's storyline?
16 Which 60s singer played Len Fairclough's son Stanley?
17 Whose grandson in *Coronation Street* was played by the future Monkee Davy Jones?
18 What was the title of Nick Berry's 1986 chart topper?
19 Cindy from *EastEnders* was formerly a backing singer for which artist?
20 Which musical star once played Kevin Webster's rival Malcolm Nuttall?
21 Which former *Byker Grove* actors hosted the first series of *Pop Idol*?
22 Claire Sweeney appeared in which soap before releasing an album?
23 Natalie Imbruglia appeared in which soap?
24 Which ex-EastEnders star was third in 2007's *Comic Relief Does Fame Academy*?
25 Which former *Neighbours* star had to cancel a tour because of breast cancer?
26 Name the *EastEnders* actress who reached No. 4 in the UK charts in 1986.
27 Who played Emma Jackson in *Home & Away* and has had several UK hits?
28 Which *Coronation Street* star reached No. 16 in the charts with "One Voice" in 1993?
29 Which memer of Boyzone played the part of Ciaran McCarthy in *Coronation Street*.
30 Which *Neighbours* star had a 1990 No. 2 hit entitled "Mona" with his Check 1-2 band?

1 Which star of *Look Who's Talking Too* was a TV regular on *Cheers*?
2 Who sang the Bond theme from *GoldenEye*?
3 *Mermaids* and *Hook* featured which actor?
4 Who won the Best Director Oscar for *Lawrence of Arabia*?
5 Which Dianne featured in *Edward Scissorhands*?
6 A character named Sister Helen Prejean appeared in which film?
7 Which Jon featured in *Mission: Impossible*?
8 Who directed *The Ice Storm*?
9 Who played the title role in *Goldfinger*?
10 In which decade was *From Here to Eternity* released?
11 Which British actor won an Oscar for *My Left Foot*?
12 In which film did a character named Farmer Hoggett appear?
13 How was Hollywood's Joan de Beauvoir de Havilland better known?
14 Who won Best Supporting Actor Oscar for *Ryan's Daughter*?
15 Who was the first Jane to Johnny Weissmuller's *Tarzan*?
16 Who achieved notoriety by directing *Women in Love* in 1969?
17 Dietrich appeared in the German *The Blue Angel*, but who starred in the US version?
18 Who won the Best Actress Oscar for *I Want to Live*?
19 In 2016, Dr. Stephen Strange is played by which Brit actor?
20 *The Third Man* and *My Fair Lady* featured which British actor?
21 Which star of *The Godfather* bought an island called Tetiaroa?
22 In which film did a character named Oliver Barrett IV first appear?
23 In which film did Reynolds, Kelly and O'Connor sing "Good Morning"?
24 *Lovesick* and *Santa Claus* featured which actor?
25 In which decade was *Dead Poets Society* released?
26 In which year did screen legend Marlon Brando die?
27 Who plays Sam in *The Lord of the Rings: The Return of the King*?
28 Which Julie appeared in *Shampoo*?
29 By what name was Natasha Gurdin better known?
30 Who founded the Sundance Festival for independent film makers?

Answers	**Football Pot Luck 17** *(see Quiz 144)*

1 Leeds Utd. 2 1970s. 3 Aston Villa. 4 Wales. 5 25. 6 Chelsea. 7 1940s. 8 Bolton Wanderers. 9 Bristol Rovers. 10 Manchester City. 11 Butcher. 12 2–2. 13 Maroon. 14 Liverpool. 15 Newcastle Utd. 16 Manchester Utd. 17 Aberdeen. 18 Sunderland. 19 Dean Richards. 20 Nottingham Forest. 21 Newcastle Utd. 22 St Etienne. 23 Ipswich Town. 24 Gretna. 25 1890s. 26 Leicester City. 27 Bryan Robson. 28 White. 29 Flynn. 30 Turf Moor (Burnley).

1 Who or what was Trevor Eve trying to Wake in the BBC series?
2 How many District Attorneys were there in *Law & Order* before Jack McCoy?
3 Who played the female surveillance expert in the first series of *Bugs*?
4 Brooklyn Nine Nine stars who as Jake Peralta?
5 The 1939 dramatization *The Anatomist* was about which pair of bodysnatchers?
6 The series *Jemima Shore Investigates* was based on whose novels?
7 Which newspaper critic adapted the stories for the first British Sherlock Holmes series in 1951?
8 What is 'Pie in the Sky' in the name of the series?
9 The crime series *Dragnet* was set in which US city?
10 In which European city was much of *Cadfael* filmed?
11 Which detective's "love interest" was Agatha Troy?
12 *A Touch of Frost* is based on the books by which author?
13 Which series was a spin-off from *Canned Carrott*?
14 What was Fitz's wife, played by Barbara Flynn, called in *Cracker*?
15 Which series was inspired by Nicholas Rhea's "Constable" novels?
16 In *The Beiderbecke Affair*, what was the name of the amateur detective?
17 In *Boyd QC*, who played Boyd's clerk and narrator?
18 Who played Bodie and Doyle in *The Professionals*?
19 In which fictional area of London is *The Bill* set?
20 In which series did Neil Pearson star as ambitious Tony Clark?
21 Where was the police drama *Highway Patrol* set?
22 Which police detective is famous for his old mac?
23 In which series about a Geordie investigator did Denise Welch play Jimmy Nail's wife?
24 Which writer created *Prime Suspect*?
25 *How to Get Away With Murder* stars who as Annalise Keating?
26 Which Geordie actor plays Spender?
27 Which actor played Barry Chan in *The New Adventures of Charlie Chan*?
28 The character Wycliffe first appeared in which 1993 TV film?
29 Which comic crime show was Dawn French 's first major solo series?
30 *Dial 999* starred which Canadian as Det. Insp. Mike Maguire?

Answers | **Pop: Ready to Rap** *(see Quiz 149)*

1 "U Can't Touch This". 2 "Gazza Rap". 3 Betty Boo. 4 Andy Samberg. 5 The Beastie Boys. 6 David Bowie and Queen. 7 Keep Rhythm Your Motivating Energy. 8 "Turtle Power". 9 Salt 'N' Pepa. 10 UK. 11 De La Soul. 12 "Hold On". 13 Hammer doll. 14 "Holiday Rap". 15 The Majors. 16 Jazzy Jeff and the Fresh Prince. 17 Public Enemy. 18 "Rapture". 19 Vanilla Ice. 20 "Anfield Rap". 21 2002. 22 Lil Wayne. 23 $3.2 Billion. 24 N.W.A. 25 Dead. 26 Hip Hop. 27 Dr Dre. 28 Country Grammar. 29 N.W.A.'s Straight Outta Compton. 30 The Bronx.

1 Sam Bartram set a League appearance record at which club?
2 Which ground do Chesterfield play at?
3 What was Ray Houghton's first League club?
4 In which decade was Sam Hammam born?
5 Which country did Jimmy Crapnell play for?
6 Mick McCarthy followed Bruce Rioch as boss of which club?
7 Who resigned as coach of France in July 1992?
8 Which club did David Platt leave to join Aston Villa?
9 What is the main colour of Hibernians' home shirts?
10 Who moved from Brighton to Liverpool in 1981 to set a club record for transfer fee received?
11 Which club withdrew from a £3 million bid for Geoff Thomas in 1992?
12 Which team were beaten 2–0 by West Ham Utd in the 1975 FA Cup Final?
13 In which city was Liam Brady born?
14 Terry Phelan was at which club when he made his international debut?
15 Tony Cottee and Peter Beardsley were in the same team at which club?
16 Which Alan became manager of Crystal Palace in March 1993?
17 In which decade did Leicester City win the FA Cup before the 1990s?
18 Which club did Kenny Sansom leave to join Arsenal?
19 How many matches were played in total during the 2015–16 Premier League season?
20 On July 26, 1992 the move of which player to Blackburn Rovers broke the British transfer record?
21 Which former West Ham United footballer was knighted in 2004?
22 Which club won consecutive UEFA Cups in the 2000s?
23 What was Darren Anderton's first League club?
24 How many different clubs appeared in FA Charity/Community Shield 1997–2007?
25 Howard Wilkinson followed Billy Bremner as boss of which club?
26 In which decade did Preston North End first win the FA Cup?
27 For whom did Nottingham Forest pay Celtic a club record £3.5 million transfer fee in 1997?
28 Which club did Peter Shilton join as player/manager in 1992?
29 Trevor Francis was at which club when he made his international debut?
30 Who was captain of Brazil for the 1982 and 1986 World Cups?

Answers | Movies Pot Luck 18 *(see Quiz 150)*

1 Nutcracker Suite. 2 Chris Columbus. 3 Meg Ryan. 4 Sutherland. 5 Cop. 6 (Sir) Anthony Hopkins. 7 John Carpenter. 8 Braveheart. 9 Peter Finch. 10 Popeye. 11 1960s. 12 Twiggy. 13 Coco. 14 Gordon Macrae. 15 Sir Anthony Hopkins. 16 James Garner. 17 Barry Levinson. 18 The Seven Year Itch. 19 Margaret Rutherford. 20 Dirty Harry. 21 John Malkovich. 22 Diana Rigg. 23 Jane Fonda. 24 Macchio. 25 1940s. 26 The Score. 27 Edith Piaf. 28 Busey. 29 American Gigolo. 30 13 Hours.

1 What was M.C. Hammer's debut single?

2 How was the 1990 "Geordie Boys" subtitled?

3 How is Alison Moira Clarkson better known?

4 In which city did rap originate?

5 Who said "(You Gotta) Fight for Your Right (to Party)" in 1987?

6 Which singer's and band's bass-line music features on "Ice Ice Baby"?

7 What does KRYME stand for in Partners in Kryme?

8 What was their first No. 1?

9 Which duo had a hit with "Whatta Man" in 1994?

10 What is the home country of the Rapper Derek B?

11 Who backed Queen Latifah on "Mama Gave Birth to the Soul Children"?

12 What was En Vogue's first chart success?

13 Which Mattel product did M.C. Hammer help launch in 1991?

14 Which Rap was an 80s hit for MC Miker "G" and Deejay Sven?

15 Who backed Morris Minor on "Stutter Rap"?

16 Who had a 1993 No. 1 with "Boom! Shake the Room"?

17 Who had a Top Ten album called *Fear of a Black Planet*?

18 Which Blondie single features the name of Grandmaster Flash?

19 Which blond rapper's real name was Robert Van Winkle?

20 What was Liverpool F.C.'s 1988 Rap single?

21 In which year did *Billboard* issue its first Hot Rap Tracks?

22 By what name is top rapper Dwayne Michael Carter Jr better known?

23 How much did Dr Dre allegedly make from the sale of Beats Electronic?

24 What L.A. based rap group got their own movie in 2016?

25 Nas's 2006 album said Hip Hop is what?

26 What is Rap music also often referred to as?

27 Which Dr's album *The Chronic* reached No. 1 on the US R&B Hip Hop Chart?

28 What was the name of Nelly's debut album?

29 In 1988, what was the first Gangsta Rap album to sell more than 2.5 million copies?

30 In which part of New York City did Rap music originate?

Answers | TV: Crime 3 *(see Quiz 147)*

1 The Dead. 2 Three. 3 Jaye Griffiths. 4 The Way Through the Woods. 5 Burke & Hare. 6. Lady Antonia Fraser. 7 C.A. Lejeune (The Observer). 8 A restaurant. 9 Los Angeles. 10 Budapest. 11 Inspector Alleyn. 12 R.D. Wingfield. 13 The Detectives. 14 Judith. 15 Heartbeat. 16 Trevor Chapman. 17 Charles Leno. 18 Lewis Collins & Martin Shaw. 19 Sun Hill. 20 Between the Lines. 21 California. 22 Columbo. 23 Spender. 24 Lynda la Plante. 25 Viola Davies. 26 Jimmy Nail. 27 James Hong. 28 Wycliffe & the Cycle of Death. 29 Murder Most Horrid. 30 Robert Beatty.

1 Which Tchaikovsky ballet piece features in Disney's *Fantasia*?
2 Who directed *Home Alone*?
3 Which actress played Jim Morrison's girlfriend in *The Doors*?
4 Which Donald featured in *Disclosure*?
5 What was Michael Douglas's profession in *Basic Instinct*?
6 *Magic* and *Desperate Hours* both feature which actor?
7 Who directed the 70s movie *Halloween*?
8 Which 90s film was about William Wallace?
9 Who won the Best Actor Oscar for *Network*?
10 What was Robin Williams's first film, in 1980?
11 In which decade was *Sink the Bismarck* released?
12 Who played the female lead role in *The Boyfriend* in 1971?
13 What was the name of Irene Cara's character in *Fame*?
14 Who played Curly in the 1955 musical *Oklahoma!*?
15 Which knighted Welsh actor was born on New Year's Eve?
16 Which star of *Maverick* played Brett Maverick in the TV series?
17 Who won the Best Director Oscar for *Rain Man*?
18 The character Richard Sherman is in which time-linked film?
19 Which Dame played Agatha Christie's Miss Marple in four 60s whodunnits?
20 A serial killer named Scorpio appears in which film?
21 Who played the Vicomte de Valmont in *Dangerous Liaisons*?
22 Who played the first Mrs James Bond?
23 Who won the Best Actress Oscar for *Coming Home* in 1978?
24 Which Ralph featured in *My Cousin Vinny*?
25 In which decade was *Bambi* released?
26 In which 2001 movie did Marlon Brando appear with Robert De Niro?
27 *La Mome* or *La Vie en Rose* is a musical biopic of which screen legend?
28 Which Gary featured in *Lethal Weapon*?
29 Which movie did the song "Call Me" come from?
30 Complete the 2016 movie title: _____ :*The Secret Soldiers of Benghazi.*

---

1 What temperature gauge is used on the BBC weather forecasts?
2 In 2015, what *Top Gear* presenter punched his producer?
3 Who interviewed J. Paul Getty and the Sultan of Brunei?
4 The ceiling of the Sistine Chapel features in which programme titles?
5 Who was the author and presenter of *Pebble Mill at One*?
6 From the top of which US building was *Roving Report* first broadcast?
7 Who famously "counted them all out, and counted them all back"?
8 What do Fyfe Robinson, Alan Wicker and Trevor Philpot have in common?
9 Who interviewed Prince Charles on the programme which marked the 25th anniversary of his investiture as Prince of Wales?
10 What was the name of the David Attenborough's series about Antarctica?
11 Which two Peters were among the first presenters of *Newsnight*?
12 Jeremy Spake found fame working for which airline?
13 What was Britain's first breakfast TV programme called?
14 What was the year in which *Picture Page* was finally broadcast?
15 Who hosted a satellite talk show called *Surviving Life*?
16 In which year was the BBC TV *Newsreel* introduced?
17 Who is Donald Trump's running mate?
18 Which French explorer presented *Under the Sea*?
19 What is the longest-running TV current affairs programme?
20 Who first presented *Panorama*?
21 Where was *Jimmy's* set?
22 Who was the BBC's royal correspondent at the time of Princess Diana's death?
23 In which year was *BBC TV News* first broadcast?
24 Which co-founder of TV am was married to a future Leader of the House of Lords?
25 Whose reporting of the Ethiopian famine in 1984 inspired Bob Geldof's Band Aid?
26 Who launched a singing career after telling her story on *Lakesiders*?
27 Which science show was first transmitted six months before the first satellite launch?
28 What was the follow-up series to *Diving to Adventure*?
29 Who was the original producer of *Frontiers of Science*?
30 Who first introduced *This Week* in 1956?

1 Name the director of the 1960s film *Grand Prix*.
2 What is the full version of Jackie Stewart's name?
3 What was the nickname the March team gave Jean-Pierre Jarier?
4 Which Doll was Lewis Hamilton's biggest fan?
5 Which world champion left the sport and built up an airline before returning to Formula One racing?
6 What was the nickname coined for him at the 1977 Belgian Grand Prix by David Purley?
7 What did he call Purley for getting in his way?
8 What became the symbol of the Brabham team?
9 What was the emblem of the Hesketh team in the mid-1970s?
10 Which Italian driver was known as the Monza Gorilla?
11 Why?
12 Which Surtees team sponsor raised a few eyebrows in 1976?
13 Which world champion became World Superstars Champion on TV in 1981?
14 What was Ayrton Senna's full name?
15 Name the fever that gripped British fans in the late 1980s and early 1990s.
16 Which driver entered the 1991 Japanese Grand Prix thanks to hundreds of enthusiasts who paid to have their names on his Coloni's sidepods?
17 Name the American author who wrote a handful of novels based on Formula One.
18 Name the world champion who was foil to Murray Walker in BBC's commentary box.
19 Which British driver was the first to replace him?
20 Which former world champion had Dannii Minogue as his girlfriend in 1999?
21 Who was the BBC Radio 5 Live pit-lane reporter in 2007–08?
22 Which "Iceman" was World Champion in 2007?
23 Which F1 track of the 2000s is named after the Ferrari brothers, Enzo and Dino?
24 Which DC announced his retirement at the end of the 2008 F1 season?
25 How did German fans know their seven-time world champion?
26 By what popular Italian name is the Ferrari Team known as?
27 Can you recall the British driver nicknamed "Il Leone"?
28 Which Miss Great Britain was installed as the official face of the British GP in 2008?
29 Which F1 team put the faces of their fans on their chassis for charity?
30 What television station won the UK rights to screen F1 races live from 2009?

Answers | Pop Pot Luck 19 *(see Quiz 154)*

1 17.. 2 Mariah Carey. 3 1960s. 4 Peabo Bryson. 5 Roger Whittaker. 6 Franki Valli.
7 Kim Wilde. 8 Twiggy. 9 1980s. 10 Christians. 11 Bing Crosby. 12 "I Believe".
13 Marianne Faithfull. 14 Andy Fairweather-Low. 15 Ireland. 16 Jones. 17 The
Kinks. 18 The Sex-O-Lettes. 19 Fun Boy Three. 20 Bad. 21 Geri Halliwell. 22 Paul
Cattermole. 23 Tune In, Cop Out. 24 Annie's Song. 25 Can't Get Used to Losing You.
26 Jane Asher. 27 Big Dee Irwin. 28 Daryl Hall. 29 Whisky and rye. 30 Neville.

1 Which Dutch team won the European Cup in 1988?
2 "Hand in Hand" is the unofficial anthem of which club?
3 Who was transferred from Feyenoord to Arsenal for £2.75 million in 2004?
4 Which coach led South Korea to a fourth place finish at the 2006 World Cup?
5 Which Dutch city does the football club Willem II come from?
6 Which Aston Villa defender represented Holland at Euro 2008?
7 Who is the all-time top goalscorer for Holland?
8 Which Dutch coach led FC Zenit Saint Petersburg to victory in the final of the 2008 UEFA Cup over his former side Rangers?
9 Which Dutch striker joined Celtic from PSV in 2006?
10 What are the colours of Vitesse Arnhem's home shirts?
11 Which club play their home games at Parkstad Limburg Stadion in Kerkrade?
12 Which Dutch coach took over from Jacques Santini at Tottenham Hotspur in 2004?
13 Which Newcastle player scored against Manchester United to end Edwin van der Sar's record-breaking run of clean sheets in 2009?
14 Who was named PFA Player of the Year in England for 2001–02?
15 Which Dutch team did Steve McClaren join as coach in 2007?
16 Who wrote *Brilliant Orange: The Neurotic Genius of Dutch Football*?
17 What is the nickname of the Dutch national football team?
18 Which Dutch striker was named in the Team of the Tournament at Euro 2008?
19 Who was transferred from Chelsea to Real Madrid for £24 million in 2007?
20 Which coach led Feyenoord to victory in the European Cup final in 1970?
21 How many Dutch international forwards were in Liverpool's 2007–08 squad?
22 Jan Vennegoor of Hesselink left PSV Eindhoven for which club in 2006?
23 Which was the last Dutch club before 2009 to win a European club competition?
24 Which was Edwin van der Sar's first English club?
25 Which Dutchman coached Russia in 2008?
26 In what Dutch club's stadium did Man. Utd win a European trophy in 1991?
27 In 2016, Johan Cruyff died at the age of _____?
28 Name the prolific Dutch striker who managed the Ajax Reserve Team from 2003–04.
29 What is the official name of the most senior Dutch Football Championship?
30 Name the legendary footballer who nutmegged Johann Cruyff twice in a game.

1 What number album did Bonnie Raitt release in 2016?
2 Whose album *Daydream* topped the charts in 1995?
3 In which decade was Noel Gallagher born?
4 Who duetted with Celine Dion on "Beauty and the Beast"?
5 Who was leaving Durham Town in 1969?
6 Who joined John Travolta and Olivia Newton-John on "Grease – The Dream Mix" in 1991?
7 Whose first hit was "Kids in America"?
8 Which former model hit the charts with "Here I Go Again"?
9 In which decade did Lisa Stansfield have her first hit record?
10 Who charted with "Harvest for the World" in 1988?
11 Who has duetted with Princess Grace of Monaco and David Bowie?
12 Which song title links Marcella Detroit with Robson and Jerome?
13 Who had a 60s hit with "This Little Bird"?
14 Who was "Wide-Eyed and Legless" in 1975?
15 What is the home country of Foster and Allen?
16 Which surname is shared by Howard and Paul?
17 Who sang about Victoria in 1970?
18 Who were Disco Tex's backing group?
19 Who joined Bananarama on their first two hits?
20 How is George Benson nicknamed on his first hit single?
21 "My Chico Latino" was a big hit for which singer in 1999?
22 Which S Club 7 member departed in 2002, forcing their rebranding as S Club?
23 What did Freak Power do after "Turn On" in 1995?
24 What was John Denver's only solo No. 1 single in the UK?
25 What was a No. 2 hit for Andy Williams and a No. 3 for the Beat?
26 Who was Paul McCartney's girlfriend from 1963 to 1966?
27 Who sang with the uncredited Little Eva on "Swinging on a Star"?
28 Who partnered John Oates on "Maneater"?
29 What were them "good ole boys drinkin" in "American Pie"?
30 What is the real first name of Noddy Holder of Slade?

Answers | **Formula One: Fan Culture** *(see Quiz 152)*

1 John Frankenheimer. 2 John Young Stewart. 3 Jumper. 4 Nicole Sherzinger. 5 Niki Lauda. 6 The Rat. 7 The Rabbit. 8 A scorpion. 9 A teddybear. 10 Vittorio Brambilla. 11 Because many felt that he drove with all the finesse of one. 12 Durex. 13 Jody Scheckter. 14 Ayrton Senna da Silva. 15 Mansellmania. 16 Naoki Hattori. 17 Bob Judd. 18 James Hunt. 19 Jonathan Palmer. 20 Jacques Villeneuve. 21 Holly Samos. 22 Kimi Raikkonen. 23 Imola. 24 David Coulthard. 25 Schumi. 26 Scuderia. 27 Nigel Mansell. 28 Gemma Garrett. 29 Red Bull. 30 BBC.

1 In which movie did Robert Duvall say, "I love the smell of napalm in the morning"?
2 In *Tomorrow Never Dies*, who played M?
3 Which singer appeared in *Mad Max Beyond Thunderdome*?
4 What was the third *Die Hard* movie called?
5 Which French city was the location for *French Connection II*?
6 What was the name of Sean Connery's villain in *The Avengers*?
7 Who was Harrison Ford's male co-star in *The Devil's Own*?
8 Which tunnel is the location for a helicopter pursuit in *Mission: Impossible*?
9 What was Serpico's first name, as played by Al Pacino?
10 Ian Fleming's Jamaican home gave its name to which Bond movie?
11 Which actor plays the head of the crew in *Armageddon*?
12 Which 007 starred in *Dante's Peak*?
13 What came number three in Oliver Stone's Vietnam trilogy?
14 Who directed 2016's *Central Intelligence*?
15 In *Day of the Jackal* who was the leader who was to be assassinated?
16 What was the name of Eddie Murphy's character in *48 Hours*?
17 *Courage under Fire* was about which conflict?
18 Who was the star of *Last Action Hero*?
19 Who sang the Bond theme from *For Your Eyes Only*?
20 What was Leonardo Di Caprio's first film after *Titanic*?
21 Where was *Apocalypse Now* filmed?
22 Who played the pregnant police chief in *Fargo*?
23 Which movie had the ad line, "They came too late and stayed too long"?
24 *Patriot Games* was the sequel to which movie?
25 Who played Danny Velinski in *The Great Escape*?
26 Which James Bond movie was released in 2006?
27 How many Oscars did *Lord of the Rings: The Return of the King* win?
28 Which 2000 movie stars Hugh Jackman, Patrick Stewart and Ian McKellen?
29 What are Cameron Diaz, Drew Barrymore and Lucy Liu better known as?
30 Who played "The Hulk" in the 2003 movie of the same name?

Answers | **Football: Golden Goals** *(see Quiz 157)*

1 Bastin. 2 Ajax. 3 Fabrizio Ravanelli. 4 Bobby Tambling. 5 Karel Poborsky. 6 Southampton. 7 Gerd Muller. 8 Derby County. 9 Jurgen Klinsmann. 10 349. 11 Crystal Palace and Arsenal. 12 Stockport County. 13 Arsenal. 14 Peter Schmeichel. 15 Mark Hughes. 16 Romario. 17 Arsenal. 18 Dundee Utd. 19 Ally McCoist. 20 Geoff Hurst. 21 Abel Xavier. 22 Paraguay. 23 David Trezeguet. 24 Silver goal. 25 2001. 26 1993. 27 Euro 1996. 28 Laurent Blanc. 29 FIFA Beach World Cup 30 Oliver Bierhoff.

1 What was the name of the 2008 BBC series about amphibians and reptiles?

2 What condition forced Michael J. Fox to leave *Spin City*?

3 Who was Anne Diamond's co-presenter in the daytime show *Anne and Nick*?

4 What was the surname of the husband and wife TV cooks, Fanny and Johnny?

5 Which Delia is a TV cook?

6 Which channel first broadcast *Game of Thrones* in the UK?

7 Which Alan is a TV gardener?

8 Which former England football captain advertises crisps?

9 Which TV inventor had the middle name Logie?

10 Which Gaby presented *The Big Breakfast*?

11 *The Midweek Lottery* was first presented by which Carol?

12 What was advertised on TV as "your flexible friend"?

13 *Laramie* and *Maverick* were what sort of programmes?

14 What is the name of BBC I's Sunday-evening religious service programme?

15 Which programme took place in a POW castle?

16 Which TV channel was involved in the making of the hit film *Four Weddings and a Funeral*?

17 In which show did people try to guess others' occupations?

18 Which Irish presenter hosted *This is Your Life*?

19 Which pop singer starred as *Budgie*?

20 In which month of 1997 did Channel 5 start broadcasting?

21 Which TV company serves the Midlands?

22 Which channel was the UK's third terrestrial channel?

23 When will it be Alright with Dennis Norden or Griff Rhys Jones?

24 Which show featured Richie Cunningham?

25 Who was Miles's boss in *This Life*?

26 The TV presenter Annie Rice is better known as who?

27 George Cole starred with Denis Waterman in which TV series?

28 Which Bruce starred in *Moonlighting*?

29 Who presented *Through the Keyhole*?

30 The documentary *Jimmy's* was about what kind of establishment?

---

1 Which Cliff set a career goals record at Arsenal?
2 Dennis Bergkamp's goals led which team to Euro success in 1992?
3 Who is credited – or blamed – for bringing the shirt-over-the-head-after-scoring routine to English soccer?
4 Which player of the 1950s and 60s set up Chelsea's record for most League goals for the club?
5 Whose amazing Euro 96 lob knocked out Portugal?
6 Neil Shipperley's goals kept which side in the Premiership in 1995–96?
7 Which German striker was known as "Der Bomber"?
8 Steve Bloomer notched 292 League goals for which club?
9 Who dived full-length on the pitch after his first goal for Tottenham Hotspur in the Premiership?
10 To 20 each way, what was Dixie Dean's Everton League goals total?
11 Which two clubs has Ian Wright scored for in FA Cup Finals?
12 A Brett Angell goal took which team to the Coca-Cola Cup semi-final in 1997?
13 A Charlie George goal won the FA Cup for which team?
14 A fine Davor Suker shot bamboozled which Danish keeper in Euro 96?
15 Who scored a last-gasp equalizer for Manchester Utd v Oldham in a 1990s semi-final?
16 Who was the Brazilian top scorer in the 1994 World Cup tournament?
17 Andy Linighan scored a last-minute FA Cup Final winner for which team?
18 Craig Brewster scored the only goal to win the Scottish League Cup for which club in 1993–94?
19 Which Scot was Europe's top league scorer in 1991–92?
20 Who scored England's first in the 1966 World Cup Final?
21 Whose handball gave France a golden goal penalty at the Euro 2000 semi-final?
22 Which country conceded the first World Cup finals golden goal?
23 Who scored the golden goal winner of the Euro 2000 final?
24 What replaced the golden goal at Euro 2004?
25 In which year did the UEFA Cup Final end 5–4 on a golden goal?
26 In what year did FIFA first introduce the golden goal system?
27 What was the first major tournament played using the golden goal rule?
28 Which French defender scored the first ever golden goal in the World Cup?
29 Which 2008 FIFA-recognized tournament still uses the golden goal rule?
30 Who scored the golden goal decider in the final of Euro 1996?

1 In which decade did Stevie Wonder have his first hit record?
2 How is Concetta Rosemarie Franconero better known?
3 How did Charles Aznavour Dance in the 70s?
4 Who were Acker Bilk's backing band?
5 Whose first hit was "Year of Decision"?
6 Which musical instrument does Larry Adler play?
7 Whose album *Nobody Else* topped the charts in 1995?
8 What was the Who's first chart hit?
9 Who was like a Rubber Ball in 1961?
10 Who thought Elenore was swell in 1968?
11 Who sang "Nice One Cyril" in 1973?
12 Who was Out of Time in 1966?
13 What is the home country of Boris Gardiner?
14 Which song title links Len Barry and Gloria Estefan?
15 Whose first hit was "Love is Like a Violin"?
16 Who was on the Marrakesh Express in 1969?
17 Released in 2016, *Good Times!* is the twelfth album by _____
18 In which decade was Sade born?
19 Which animals are on the cover of the Beach Boys album *Pet Sounds*?
20 Which creature links song titles by Elton John and Jimmy Nail?
21 "Bootie Call" was a hit for which girl group?
22 Who released a 2008 album *Let It be Me*?
23 What is the logo of the British record label Parlophone?
24 Who had the first instrumental No. 1 hit in 1953?
25 Who resigned as a Radio 1 DJ when he couldn't have Fridays off?
26 In which decade was Roberta Flack born?
27 Who was "Dancing on the Ceiling" according to his 1986 hit?
28 Who was a "junkie" according to David Bowie's "Ashes to Ashes"?
29 About which London Underground station did the New Vaudeville Band sing in 1967?
30 Which Mary Poppins song won an Oscar in 1964?

---

1 Who received her first Best Actress nomination for *The English Patient*?
2 Who was the female singer on "Hopelessly Devoted (to You)" from a winning soundtrack?
3 Which screenwriter was nominated for *Four Weddings and a Funeral*?
4 Who was Oscar-nominated for the music for *Angela's Ashes*?
5 What nationality is director Ang Lee?
6 In which movie did Al Pacino play Frank Slade?
7 For which Cher/Meryl Streep movie did Nora Ephron receive her first nomination?
8 How many nominations had Helen Hunt received before winning for *As Good as It Gets*?
9 Who first sang "The Way We were" in the movie of the same name?
10 In 1981 who shouted 'The British are coming' at the Oscars ceremony?
11 Who has sung two 1990s Oscar-winning songs?
12 Which Brit made the animated Oscar-winner in 1993 and 1995?
13 Who shared a best screenplay Oscar for *Pygmalion*?
14 What was the nationality of the actor who won for *Life is Beautiful*?
15 Who directed Gary Cooper to an Oscar in *Sergeant York*?
16 Who earned a nomination for the theme song from *9 to 5*?
17 Who, in addition to Cher, won an Oscar for *Moonstruck*?
18 Who designed the Oscar?
19 Which actress criticized the US government over Haiti before announcing the nominees at the 1992 Oscar ceremony?
20 Who has hosted the Oscars ceremony most often?
21 Which two British stars were nominated for *Gods and Monsters*?
22 Who was Oscar-nominated for *Twelve Monkeys*?
23 Who was 80 when she won an Oscar?
24 Who received a Special Award for *Pollyanna* aged 13?
25 Which Italian director received an honorary award in 1995?
26 *Spotlight* is a 2015 film directed by _____
27 How many Oscars has Clint Eastwood won for his acting?
28 What occupation did Clint have in the movie *Play Misty for Me*?
29 Clint played a thief in *Absolute Power*, but who played the President of the USA?
30 What name was given to Clint in Sergio Leone's trilogy of westerns?

1 Who played PC Gabriel Kent in *The Bill*?
2 Which Jon is the main presenter of *Channel 4 News*?
3 What is *Dangermouse*'s nemesis called?
4 On which channel is the National Lottery televised live?
5 C. J. Parker was a character in which US series?
6 To which magician is Debbie McGee married?
7 Which BBC1 antiques show is broadcast on Sunday evenings?
8 In which series would you meet the Lone Gunmen?
9 Who is Richard Madeley's co-presenter on *This Morning*?
10 Which Shane advertises washing powder?
11 Leonard and Sheldon work at which institute?
12 Clive Owen starred as which 1980s risk-taking businessman?
13 Which series showing compilations of TV clips is presented by Chris Tarrant?
14 Julia Louis-Dreyfus has won countless Emmy's for what Government role?
15 What kind of shows do Penn and Teller present?
16 BBC1's *The Rankin Challenge* is what kind of series?
17 Who presented *Television's Greatest Hits* on BBC1?
18 What was the name of Esther Rantzen's long-running chat show?
19 Dorinda Hafner presented *The Tastes of* which country on Channel 4?
20 Which cheese are Wallace and Gromit forever in search of?
21 Which Zone is BBC2's educational service?
22 Who hosted *Schofield's Quest* on ITV?
23 On what mountain do *The Waltons* live?
24 Hilary Jones had what role on TV?
25 Terry Christian co-presented which Channel 4 youth magazine programme?
26 Denise Van Outen and Johnny Vaughan co-presented which morning programme?
27 Name BBC1's long-running nature series, presented by Sir David Attenborough.
28 The BBC2 series *The Beechgrove Garden* concerns which subject?
29 BBC2's *Watch This or the Dog Dies* was subtitled *The History of...* what type of TV?
30 Tony Hale became famous for which *Arrested Development* role?

Answers | **Pop Pot Luck 21** *(see Quiz 162)*

1 The sky. **2** Mick Taylor. **3** "Love Me for a Reason". **4** Paul Young. **5** "My-Ding-A-Ling". **6** 42. **7** Japan. **8** Massachusetts. **9** Natasha Khan. **10** David Bowie. **11** Watership Down. **12** Adam Wiles. **13** The Vagabonds. **14** 1940s. **15** Suede **16** "Don't be Cruel". **17** Victoria. **18** Nick Cave. **19** Björk. **20** Elvis Costello. **21** 7 August 2001. **22** Roger Daltrey and Pete Townshend. **23** Mary Hopkin. **24** Diana. **25** A Painted Smile. **26** Dave Edmunds. **27** "I'm Still Waiting". **28** Yellow Submarine. **29** Apache. **30** Charlie Drake.

1 Who scored five Premiership hat-tricks in 1995–96?
2 Who finished Southampton's joint top scorer in 1995–96 with seven goals, having hit a hat-trick in the first game?
3 Which Leeds Utd midfielder hit a 1995 hat-trick against Coventry City?
4 Which Stan hit an FA Cup Final hat-trick in the 1950s?
5 Geoff Hurst hit his first England hat-trick against which team?
6 Who was Andy Gray playing for when he hit a mid-1980s European Cup Winners' Cup treble?
7 Which Ipswich player hit two hat-tricks in 1980–81 UEFA Cup games?
8 Which England player got four against San Marino in November 1993?
9 Who was Dion Dublin playing for when he hit three against Sheffield Wednesday in 1995 and still ended up on the losing side?
10 Robert Fleck has hit three in a Euro game for which club?
11 Argentina vs Panama. Saturday 11 June 2016. Who scored a hat trick?
12 Bryan Robson got his only England hat-trick in an 8–0 rout of which country in 1984?
13 Who hit Blackburn Rovers' hat-trick in the 1995–96 European Cup?
14 Who hit three-plus as Manchester Utd beat Ipswich Town 9–0 in 1995?
15 Which England player hit hat-tricks against Turkey in 1985 and 1987?
16 Adcock, Stewart and White each hit three for which team in the same game in 1987?
17 Who hit a Scottish FA Cup Final hat-trick in 1996?
18 Which player hit his first Newcastle Utd hat-trick against Wimbledon in October 1995?
19 Which player hit six England hat-tricks from 1960 to 1966?
20 Who hit a Charity Shield hat-trick for Leeds Utd in 1992?
21 Who scored the only hat-trick of the Euro 2008 finals?
22 Which 21st-century player scored a hat-trick for England in his second start?
23 Which post-war player has scored the most hat-tricks for Arsenal with 11?
24 Who scored a hat-trick of penalties for Brazil against Argentina in 2004?
25 In which city did Michael Owen score his first England hat-trick?
26 Which Man. Utd player scored a hat-trick on his debut for the club in 2004?
27 Who scored a hat-trick for Real Madrid in a 4–3 defeat to Man. Utd in 2003?
28 In 2008, he scored consecutive home hat-tricks for his Premiership club. Who is he?
29 Who scored a hat-trick for England against Jamaica in 2006?
30 Which Spurs player scored a hat-trick in their 4–0 win over Dinamo Zagreb in 2008?

1 Where was Pat Boone's gold mine in 1957?
2 Who replaced Brian Jones when he left the Rolling Stones?
3 What was the Osmonds' only No. 1 UK hit?
4 Who released an album titled *No Parlez*?
5 What novelty song was the only UK No. 1 single for Chuck Berry?
6 How old was Elvis Presley when he died? 41, 42 or 43?
7 Where are Aria electric guitars produced?
8 Which US State did the Bee Gees sing about?
9 Which singer is pseudonymously known as Bat for Lashes?
10 Who released a million-selling album in 1983 titled *Let's Dance*?
11 Which film featured the song "Bright Eyes"?
12 How is Calvin Harris better known?
13 Who was Jimmy James's backing group?
14 In which decade was David Essex born?
15 Which Britpoppers released their seventh album in January 2016?
16 Which song title links Elvis Presley and Bobby Brown?
17 Which Spice Girl is Posh Spice?
18 Which singer tragically lost his son in Eastbourne in 2015?
19 Who was lead singer with the Sugarcubes?
20 Who released the album *Goodbye Cruel World* in 1984?
21 On which day did Usher release his album *8701* in the US?
22 Which two founding members of the Who were still with the band in 2008?
23 Which Welsh singer stipulated that two songs on her albums were recorded in Welsh?
24 Who does Paul Anka ask "Oh, please, stay with me"?
25 What were the Isley Brothers behind in the title of a hit from 1969?
26 Who had a 1970 hit with a cover version of "I Hear You Knocking"?
27 What was the first UK No. 1 hit for Diana Ross as a solo artist?
28 Which Beatles LP includes "Only a Northern Song" and "Hey Bulldog"?
29 Which single gave the Shadows their first hit without Cliff Richard?
30 Which comedian had a hit with "Splish Splash" in 1958?

---

1 In *An American in Paris* who said, "That's quite a dress you almost have on"?

2 Which unknown was chosen by Chaplin to star with him in *Limelight*?

3 In *Singin' in the Rain*, who said, "We feel all our hard work ain't been in vain for nothin'!"?

4 How was Alfredo Cocozza who starred in *The Great Caruso* better known?

5 Who was the monster in *The Curse of Frankenstein*?

6 Which lady with a massive voice was the star of *Call Me Madam*?

7 Who was the blonde James Stewart had to follow in *Vertigo*?

8 Who died while filming *Giant* in 1955?

9 Which blonde starred in *Will Success Spoil Rock Hunter*??

10 In which movie did Rita Hayworth sing "Bewitched, Bothered and Bewildered"?

11 Who played Scrooge in the classic movie, with George Cole as his younger self?

12 "The Trouble with" whom was a movie debut for Shirley MacLaine?

13 Which dancer did Danny Kaye replace in *White Christmas*, a remake of *Holiday Inn*?

14 *The African Queen* is about events in which war?

15 Which Hitchcock/Cary Grant film has its climax on Mount Rushmore?

16 Who was described as France's most ogled export in 1956?

17 Which Russian-born star played the Pharaoh in *The Ten Commandments*?

18 Which husband and wife first appeared together in *The Long Hot Summer*?

19 Which Welsh actor wins Jesus' robe in a dice game in *The Robe*?

20 Whose autobiography was called *The Raw Pearl*?

21 For what was Audrey Hepburn Oscar-nominated on her film debut?

22 Who played Glenn Miller in *The Glenn Miller Story*?

23 In which movie did Tyrone Power have his final completed role?

24 Who played Big Daddy in *Cat on a Hot Tin Roof*?

25 Which dancer discovered Leslie Caron?

26 Who was the leading lady in *Pillow Talk*?

27 Which star was born Roy Harold Scherer Jr?

28 Who directed the classic Japanese movie from 1954 *Seven Samurai*?

29 Which actress played the leading role in the 1956 classic *The Girl Can't Help It*?

30 Which "Cowboy" was the first film star to appear in a sponsored TV series?

Answers | **Football: Golden Oldies** *(see Quiz 165)*

1 Stanley Matthews. 2 Preston North End. 3 Leicester City. 4 West Ham Utd. 5 Billy Wright. 6 Dixie Dean. 7 Huddersfield Town. 8 Ted Drake. 9 Joe Mercer. 10 Nat Lofthouse. 11 33 years. 12 Alex James. 13 Mackay. 14 Newcastle Utd. 15 Middlesbrough. 16 Manchester Utd. 17 Scotland. 18 Hungary. 19 Pat Jennings. 20 Yes. (He played once for Scotland.) 21 Fatty. 22 David Jack. 23 Johnny Carey. 24 Len Shackleton. 25 Alf Ramsey. 26 Stanley Matthews. 27 Ivor Broadis. 28 Danny Blanchflower. 29 Joe Mercer. 30 Bert Trautmann.

1 In which children's series did Sally James appear?
2 Where did Fred Flintstone work?
3 Who made *Worzel Gummidge*?
4 Geoffrey Bayldon played which children's character?
5 What is the number plate on the postman's van in Greendale?
6 Who was the first *Blue Peter* presenter to be sacked, for taking cocaine?
7 Name the snail in *The Magic Roundabout*.
8 Who was the star of *Dick Turpin*?
9 Which series was a role reversal version of *Robin Hood*?
10 Where do the *Munsters* live?
11 What colour are the Smurfs?
12 Who was Superted's friend?
13 Which series featured a pantomime horse?
14 Spike the Dog features in which cartoon?
15 Who first played Long John Silver in a television series?
16 What was the name of the lion in *The Lion, the Witch and the Wardrobe*?
17 Who hosted *Runaround*?
18 What is the name of Kermit the Frog's nephew?
19 Which ventriloquist worked with Lenny the Lion?
20 Who was Ray Alan's inebriated dummy?
21 Which green duck wore a nappy?
22 Who "rode" an ostrich?
23 What was the name of the cow in *The Magic Roundabout*?
24 When was *Crackerjack* first produced?
25 Which E. Nesbit dramatization featured a legendary bird?
26 What was Lamb Chop?
27 Where did the *Teenage Mutant Ninja Turtles* live?
28 From which century did *Catweazle* come?
29 For which character is Jay Silverheels remembered?
30 Whose language included the word "Flobalob"?

Answers | **Pop Pot Luck 22** *(see Quiz 166)*

1 Paul McCartney. 2 "She Loves You". 3 Midge Ure and Bob Geldof. 4 1959. 5 Janis Joplin. 6 1950s. 7 Kissing. 8 Def Leppard. 9 Bob Marley. 10 Dakota. 11 Chuck Berry. 12 David Bowie. 13 Wet Wet Wet. 14 John Kettley (is a Weatherman). 15 French Kissing. 16 Roger Whittaker. 17 "Summerlove Sensation". 18 Italian. 19 Mel B. 20 Charles. 21 Invincible. 22 Aqua. 23 Crying in the Chapel. 24 Jerry Lee Lewis. 25 Goodbye Yellow Brick Road. 26 Charles Aznavour. 27 USA. 28 Tin Soldier. 29 1930s. 30 Father Mackenzie.

1 Who was born on Feb. 1, 1915, in Hanley, Stoke on Trent?
2 Bobby Charlton came out of retirement to play for which League club?
3 Which club had goalkeepers Banks and Shilton on their books in the 1960s?
4 What was the third London side that Jimmy Greaves played for?
5 Who was travelling on a bus when he learnt that he had been made England skipper?
6 Who fractured his skull in a motorbike accident in the 1920s?
7 With which League club did Denis Law make his debut?
8 Who hit 42 goals in a season for Arsenal in the 1930s?
9 Who was aged 60 when he became England's caretaker manager?
10 Who bagged 255 League goals for Bolton in the 1940s and 1950s?
11 To two each way, how many years did Stanley Matthews play League soccer in England?
12 Who became Britain's most expensive player when he moved from Preston North End to Arsenal in 1929?
13 Which Dave of Tottenham Hotspur broke his left leg twice in a year in the 1960s?
14 Hughie Gallacher hit 36 League goals in a season for which club?
15 Where was Wilf Mannion born?
16 At which club did Brian Kidd begin his career?
17 Liverpool's legendary striker Billy Liddell came from which country?
18 Which country developed the deep-lying centre forward role just after World War II?
19 Which great goalkeeper was born in Newry on June 12, 1945?
20 Did Matt Busby ever play international soccer?
21 By what non-PC nickname was England goalkeeper Willie Foulke known?
22 Who was England's first £10,000 footballer?
23 Who was Manchester United's captain when they won the FA Cup in 1948?
24 Which 1940s and 1950s star was known as "The Clown Prince of Football"?
25 Which future England manager won a League title with Spurs in 1951?
26 Who won the inaugural FWA Player of the Year Award in 1948?
27 Who scored England's only goal when they lost 7–1 away to Hungary in 1954?
28 Name the player who captained Spurs to the League and Cup double in 1960–61.
29 Name the Arsenal star of the 1940s who went on to manage Man. City and England.
30 Which German international broke his neck in the 1956 FA Cup Final?

| **Answers** | Movies: Stars of the 1950s *(see Quiz 163)* |

1 Gene Kelly. 2 Claire Bloom. 3 Jean Hagen (as Lina Lamont). 4 Mario Lanza. 5 Christopher Lee. 6 Ethel Merman. 7 Kim Novak. 8 James Dean. 9 Jayne Mansfield. 10 Pal Joey. 11 Alistair Sim. 12 Harry. 13 Fred Astaire. 14 World War I. 15 North by Northwest. 16 Brigitte Bardot. 17 Yul Brynner. 18 Paul Newman & Joanne Woodward. 19 Richard Burton. 20 Pearl Bailey. 21 Roman Holiday. 22 James Stewart. 23 Witness for the Prosecution. 24 Burl Ives. 25 Gene Kelly. 26 Doris Day. 27 Rock Hudson. 28 Akira Kurosawa. 29 Marilyn Monroe. 30 Gene Autry.

1 "FourFive Seconds" was a 2015 song by Kanye West, Rihanna and _____?
2 What Beatles song begins "You think you've lost your love ... "?
3 Who co-produced "Do They Know It's Christmas?"?
4 In which year was Cliff Richard's first album released?
5 Who had the nickname Pearl?
6 In which decade was the Grammy award introduced?
7 What are John Lennon and Yoko Ono doing on the cover of the *Milk and Honey* album?
8 Who recorded the Heavy-Metal album *Hysteria*?
9 Who was commemorated on Jamaican stamps in 1982?
10 Where were Doris Day's Black Hills?
11 Who was the subject of the film tribute *Hail! Hail! Rock 'N' Roll*?
12 Who formed the rock band Tin Machine in 1989?
13 Who was Wishing He was Lucky in 1987?
14 Which TV personality did Tribe of Toffs celebrate in song in 1988?
15 What was Deborah Harry doing In the USA in 1986?
16 Who sang "The Last Farewell" in 1975?
17 Which Summer song was a 1974 hit for the Bay City Rollers?
18 What is the nationality of the "Do It Again" singer Raffaella Carra?
19 Which Spice Girl is Scary Spice?
20 What was Buddy Holly's real first name?
21 What was the title of Michael Jackson's 2001 album?
22 "Doctor Jones" was a 1998 hit for which European band?
23 Which religious ballad was a No. 1 for Elvis in 1965?
24 Who was doing "A Whole Lotta Shakin" in 1957?
25 From which album did "Candle in the Wind" come?
26 Whose only UK No. 1 was "She"?
27 What is Herb Alpert's home country?
28 What type of soldier was a hit for the Small Faces?
29 In which decade was Marvin Gaye born?
30 Who else is mentioned by name in "Eleanor Rigby"?

1 In which state does the action of *The Woods (2016)* take place?
2 How old was Regan MacNeil when she was possessed in *The Exorcist*?
3 What is the name of the film in *Scream 2* based on the murders in *Scream*?
4 Who plays Sergeant Neil Howie in *The Wicker Man*?
5 What is John Cassavetes's occupation in *Rosemary's Baby*?
6 What type of bird is the first to attack Melanie in *The Birds*?
7 Who played Dr Seward in *Bram Stoker's Dracula*?
8 Who wrote the score for *Psycho*?
9 What does Mike throw into the river in *The Blair Witch Project*?
10 What is the name of the lead character in *Night of the Living Dead*?
11 Who plays "Leatherface" in the film *The Texas Chainsaw Massacre*?
12 Who produced *Poltergeist*?
13 Who was the star of *The House of Wax*?
14 Who directed *Psycho III*?
15 In which horror movie did Johnny Depp make his debut?
16 What is the name of Danny's imaginary friend in *The Shining*?
17 In which movie does Anjelica Houston say, "Don't torture yourself, Gomez. That's my job"?
18 Which Mrs Charles Laughton played the title role in *The Bride of Frankenstein*?
19 Who directed *The Evil Dead*?
20 In which state is *Halloween* set?
21 Brad Pitt stayed in Peter Cushing's house while making which movie?
22 Who has the double role in *Mary Reilly*, based on *Dr Jekyll and Mr Hyde*?
23 Upon whose novel is *Carrie* based?
24 What was the first Sherlock Holmes Hammer horror movie in colour?
25 What was the name of Richard Dreyfuss's character in *Jaws*?
26 Who wrote and starred in *Shaun of the Dead*?
27 In which Will Smith movie is he a scientist trying to cure plague victims?
28 Who played *The Phantom of the Opera* in the 1925 silent classic?
29 The first vampire-themed feature movie was produced in 1925. Name it.
30 Which 1973 shocker was written by William Blatty and produced by William Friedkin?

---

1 In *Martin Kane, Private Investigator*, which actor played the title role?
2 In *Heartbeat*, what was Nick's first wife called?
3 Which character does Helen Mirren play in *Prime Suspect*?
4 What rank was *Cribb* in the programme of the same name?
5 In which series did Alan Cade replace John Stafford in the top job?
6 Which actor plays the title role in *Dangerfield*?
7 Which city was *Petrocelli* set?
8 In which series did Jimmy Smits play Bobby Simone?
9 In which series did Det. Sgt John Ho appear in the early 80s?
10 Which character had a partner called Penfold?
11 Who played Det. Chief Insp. Nick Lewis in *The Enigma Files*?
12 What disability is Columbo actor Peter Falk afflicted with?
13 Which actor plays D.I. Frost?
14 Which actor from *The Bill* died shortly after being sacked from the show because of drinking?
15 Who did Jill Dando replace on *Crimewatch UK*?
16 What is *Cadfael*'s profession?
17 What did C.A.T.S. stand for in the series *CATS Eyes*?
18 Who created *Hazell*?
19 Name the lead character in *Highway Patrol*.
20 Which Glasgow-based series developed from a three-part thriller called *Killers*?
21 *Wolf to the Slaughter* was the first programme to feature which famous Ruth Rendel detective?
22 Which former Doctor Who played private detective Albert Campion?
23 In which police station was *Juliet Bravo* set?
24 Who partnered *Crime Traveller* Chloe Annett?
25 Which actor played Charlie Chan?
26 After leaving *EastEnders* which crime series did Paul Nicholls star in?
27 Who introduced the series *Lady Killers*?
28 Name the author of *Inspector Morse*.
29 Which Eurovision Song Contest entrant starred in *Liverpool One*?
30 Since 2015, Matt Murdock is famous for which crime-fighting Netflix superhero?

Answers | **Football Pot Luck 19** *(see Quiz 170)*

1 None. 2 Princess Alexandra. 3 Leeds Utd. 4 1970s. 5 Newcastle Utd. 6 The Republic of Ireland. 7 Bradford City. 8 Juventus. 9 Leyton Orient. 10 6–1. 11 Red. 12 Bolton Wanderers. 13 1920s. 14 Crystal Palace. 15 Roy McFarland. 16 Norwich City. 17 Harvey. 18 London. 19 Manchester Utd. 20 Leeds Utd. 21 Tim Howard. 22 Guus Hiddink. 23 1960s. 24 Molby. 25 Blackburn Rovers. 26 Wales. 27 Leeds United. 28 Hibernian. 29 Champions League Final. 30 Liverpool.

1 What does MLS mean?

2 When was the MLS founded?

3 Who replaced Winston as headline sponsors of NASCAR's main championship?

4 Which Canadian province had runners-up in the Stanley Cup twice in the 2000s?

5 Which Chicago baseball team won the World Series in 2005?

6 In which sport is the Stanley Cup awarded?

7 Where are the Astros baseball team from?

8 Which city do the Redskins American football team come from?

9 What were "Babe" Ruth's real first names?

10 Which two countries other than the United States have won Olympic gold medals at basketball?

11 Which US soccer player was with Blackburn and Coventry?

12 The First Budweiser Bowl in the UK in 1986 was won by which team?

13 The Princetown College rules drawn up in 1867 affect which sport?

14 Which US soccer team plays at Anaheim Stadium?

15 In American football in which year did the AFL and the NFL merge?

16 How many people are there in an ice hockey team?

17 What game is played by the Detroit Pistons?

18 What was the nickname of baseball's Lawrence Peter Berra?

19 Giants and Jets have triumphed in the Super Bowl for which city?

20 The invention of which sport is credited to Dr J. A. Naismith?

21 In baseball, which team bats first?

22 Which year were American professionals first allowed to enter the World Basketball Championships?

23 Which sport do the Miami Dolphins play?

24 In which country were the rules for modern ice hockey formulated?

25 Which two American men won ice skating Olympic gold in the 1980s?

26 Which trophy do teams from AFC and NFC players contest?

27 Which two US women skaters had a battle on and off the rink in 1994?

28 Which team won the first Super Bowl?

29 Which sport do the Atlanta Braves play?

30 How many players are there in a baseball team?

Answers	**Movies: Horror** *(see Quiz 167)*

1 Maryland. 2 12. 3 Stab. 4 Edward Woodward. 5 Actor. 6 Seagull. 7 Richard E. Grant. 8 Bernard Herrmann. 9 The map. 10 Barbara. 11 Gunner Hansen. 12 Steven Spielberg. 13 Vincent Price. 14 Anthony Perkins. 15 A Nightmare on Elm Street. 16 Tony. 17 The Addams Family. 18 Elsa Lanchester. 19 Sam Raimi. 20 Illinois. 21 Interview with the Vampire. 22 John Malkovich. 23 Stephen King. 24 The Hound of the Baskervilles. 25 Hooper. 26 Simon Pegg. 27 I am Legend. 28 Lon Chaney. 29 Nosferatu. 30 The Exorcist.

1 How many home League games did Manchester United lose in 1995–96?
2 Where does the Alexandra come from in Crewe's name?
3 Which was Denis Irwin's first League club?
4 In which decade did Ipswich Town first win the FA Cup?
5 Ossie Ardiles followed Jim Smith as boss of which club?
6 Which country did Gary Waddock play for?
7 Who plays at home at the Pulse Stadium?
8 Which club did Ian Rush join on leaving Liverpool for the first time?
9 Which club was Roger Stanislaus with when he failed a random drug test?
10 Manchester City beat Newcastle United in 2015. It was the biggest home win of the season. What was the score?
11 What is the main colour of Walsall's home shirts?
12 Which team were beaten 4–3 by Blackpool in the 1953 FA Cup Final?
13 In which decade was Ron Greenwood born?
14 Jim Cannon set a League appearance record at which club?
15 Which Bolton Wanderers boss got the sack on 2nd January 1996?
16 Which club did David Phillips leave to join Nottingham Forest?
17 Which Colin became manager of Everton in 1987?
18 In which city was Les Ferdinand born?
19 Kevin Moran was at which club when he made his international debut?
20 Eric Cantona and Steve Hodge were in the same team at which club?
21 Which American international goalkeeper played for Manchester United and Everton?
22 Who was coach of the Australian team at the 2006 World Cup finals?
23 In which decade did Liverpool first win the FA Cup?
24 Which Jan became manager of Swansea City in February 1996?
25 Which club's ground is alongside the River Darwen?
26 Which country did Peter Nicholas play for?
27 Which team lost 2–1 after extra time to Chelsea in the 1970 FA Cup Final?
28 Which club did Tony Mowbray leave to became manager of West Brom?
29 In which 2008 match did Ryan Giggs pass Bobby Charlton to become Manchester Utd's all-time appearance leader?
30 David James was with which club when he made his full international debut?

Answers | TV Crime 4 *(see Quiz 168)*

1 William Gargan. 2 Kate. 3 Jane Tennison. 4 Detective Sergeant. 5 The Chief. 6 Nigel le Valliant. 7 Tucson, Arizona. 8 NYPD Blue. 9 The Chinese Detective. 10 Dangermouse. 11 Tom Adams. 12 He only has one eye. 13 David Jason. 14 Kevin Lloyd. 15 Sue Cook. 16 Monk. 11 Covert Activities, Thames Section. 18 Terry Venables. 19 Chief Dan Matthews. 20 Taggart. 21 Reg Wexford. 22 Peter Davison. 23 Hartley Section Police Station. 24 Michael French. 25 Carrol Naith. 26 City Central. 27 Robert Morley. 28 Colin Dexter. 29 Samantha Janus. 30 Daredevil.

Answers – page 379

1 Which charities benefited from the Five Live EP in 1993?

2 Which comedienne featured on the B side of "The Stonk" for Comic Relief?

3 Which disaster prompted the release of "Ferry 'Cross the Mersey"?

4 Which newspaper created Ferry Aid?

5 Which album was a reinterpretation of songs from *Sgt Pepper*?

6 Who sang "With a Little Help from My Friends" for Childline?

7 Which male artist sang "She's Leaving Home" for the same charity?

8 Where was the fire which prompted the release by the Crowd?

9 Which two Motown stars wrote "We are the World" for USA For Africa?

10 What did Rod Stewart release in aid of the Zeebrugge ferry disaster?

11 The NHS Choir sang which song to get to No.1 in 2015?

12 Who was lead vocalist with the Crowd?

13 Which charity record reached No. 1 twice?

14 Who released "Ben" as a charity single?

15 Who have produced three charity singles?

16 Which Dionne Warwick single raised money for AIDS research?

17 What was the Dunblane single called?

18 Which charity benefited from "Live Like Horses"?

19 Who wrote "With a Little Help from My Friends"/"She's Leaving Home"?

20 Which Cliff Richard single helped famine relief?

21 Which group recorded the official song for Red Nose Day 2005?

22 In which year was the Live 8 single released?

23 Where did Elton John first sing "Candle in the Wind 1997"?

24 Which of the the Proclaimers' hits was covered for Comic Relief in 2007?

25 How high in the charts did Westlife's 2001 Comic Relief cover "Uptown Girl" go?

26 Which Motown artist's "Shelter in the Rain" helped victims of Hurricane Katrina?

27 Who was waiting for Peter Kay in "Is This the Way to Amarillo"?

28 What type of charity did The Proclaimers help with "I'm Gonna be (500 Miles)"?

29 Who sang "Walk This Way" for Red Nose Day 2007?

30 Who along with Michael Jackson wrote "We are the World" for USA for Africa?

Answers | TV: Comedy 6 *(see Quiz 173)*

1 Mike Judge. 2 Tom Baker. 3 Alf Garnett. 4 Les Dawson. 5 Manchester City.
6 Ronnie Barker. 7 The Prince Regent. 8 Knowing Me Knowing You. . . with Alan Partridge. 9 Blue. 10 How's Your Father. 11 Albert! 12 Paul Eddington. 13 The Korean War. 14 Michael Elphick and Angela Thorn. 15 Basil. 16 2. 17 Sally Geeson. 18 A Very Polish Practice. 19 Above the Cunninghams' Garage. 20 Scott Biao. 21 Burt Reynolds. 22 Christopher Lloyd. 23 Ronnie Corbett. 24 Rhoda's. 25 American. 26 Nurse Gladys Emmanuel. 27 Mini. 28 13. 29 Bebe Neuwirth. 30 Fosters Lagers.

1 In which film did King Jaffe Joffer appear?
2 Which Alan featured in *Die Hard*?
3 In which decade was *Rebecca* released?
4 In which movie did Winona Ryder play Cher's daughter?
5 Who won the Best Director Oscar for *One Flew over the Cuckoo's Nest*?
6 Complete this 2016 film title: _____: *Election Year.*
7 Which character did Anthony Hopkins play in *Legends of the Fall*?
8 To the nearest hour, how long does *Dances with Wolves* last?
9 "King of the Cowboys" Leonard Slye was better known as whom?
10 Who directed *Goodfellas*?
11 A character named Rooster Cogburn first appeared in which film?
12 Who played Dolly in the 60s *Hello Dolly*?
13 In which decade was *A Streetcar Named Desire* released?
14 Which James was Professor Lindenbrook in *Journey to the Centre of the Earth*?
15 Who won the Best Actress Oscar for *Children of a Lesser God*?
16 *Anna and the King of Siam* and *Cleopatra* featured which Rex?
17 Who played Blofeld in *On Her Majesty's Secret Service*?
18 In which decade of the 20th century was Danny Glover born?
19 Which pop veteran featured in *The Man Who Fell to Earth*?
20 Who was Roger Moore's first Bond girl?
21 At what sport did Warren Beatty excel?
22 Who won the Best Actor Oscar for *Captains Courageous*?
23 Which conductor was Woody Allen's father-in-law?
24 Who directed *The Full Monty*?
25 Who played Lieutenant Schaffer in *Where Eagles Dare*?
26 Which 2008 action movie stars Nicolas Cage as an assassin in the Far East?
27 Which *Happy Days* actor has become a multi-Oscar-winning director?
28 What were the names of the Blues Brothers
29 Which Jeff featured in *The Big Chill*?
30 Which musician presided over the 1987 wedding of Bruce Willis and Demi Moore?

Answers | **Football Pot Luck 20** *(see Quiz 174)*

1 Arsenal. 2 Aberdeen. 3 Bradford City. 4 Blackburn Rovers. 5 Plymouth. 6 Colchester United. 7 Manchester City. 8 Barnsley. 9 San Marino. 10 Celtic. 11 White. 12 1960s. 13 Manchester Utd. 14 Bolton Wanderers and Sheffield United. 15 QPR. 16 Wales. 17 Adams. 18 1920s. 19 Norwich City. 20 Dion Dublin. 21 Jordi (Cruyff). 22 Aston Villa 0–6 Liverpool. 23 Sheffield Wednesday. 24 Leeds United. 25 Newcastle United. 26 New Zealand. 27 1890s. 28 Ashley Young. 29 Ten. 30 Black.

1 In 2014, who created *Silicon Valley* for HBO?
2 Who is the narrator of *Little Britain*?
3 Who first said "bloody" 78 times in half an hour in a sitcom?
4 Which comedian is quoted as saying, "The mother in law thinks I'm effeminate; not that I mind that because beside her, I am"?
5 Which football team did Eddie Large play for before becoming a comedian?
6 Who played Fletcher in *Porridge*?
7 E. Blackadder Esq. was butler to whom?
8 Which series had words from an Abba song in its title?
9 What was the colour of *Monty Python's* Big Red Book?
10 Harry Worth played the father in which comedy?
11 Which sitcom, starring Rodney Bewes, was the sequel to *Dear Mother... Love Albert*?
12 Who played Jim Hacker in *Yes Minister*?
13 In which war is *M*A*S*H* set?
14 Which actors played the bickering grandparents in *Three Up, Two Down*?
15 What was the name of Manuel's Andalucian hamster?
16 How many children does *Absolutely Fabulous* character Edina have?
17 Who played the daughter in *Bless This House*?
18 What was the name of the sequel to *A Very Peculiar Practice* which was set in Poland in 1992?
19 Where did Fonzie live?
20 Who played Chachie in *Joanie Loves Chachie*?
21 Who was the male star of *Evening Shade*?
22 Who played Rev. Jim in *Taxi*?
23 Who was the diminutive star of *Sorry!*?
24 Carleton was whose doorman?
25 What nationality were the men of *The Airbase*?
26 Who was the object of Ronnie Barker's affections in *Open All Hours*?
27 What kind of car did Mr Bean drive?
28 How many episodes were in the first series of *Auf Wiedersehen Pet*?
29 She played Frasier's wife in *Cheers*. Who is she?
30 Which brew did Paul Hogan advertise?

Answers | **Pop: Charity Songs** *(see Quiz 171)*

1 AIDS charities. 2 Victoria Wood. 3 Hillsborough. 4 The Sun. 5 Sergeant Pepper Knew My Father. 6 Wet Wet Wet. 7 Billy Bragg. 8 Bradford City Football Club. 9 Michael Jackson, Lionel Richie. 10 Sailing. 11 A Bridge Ove You. 12 Gerry Marsden. 13 "Do They Know It's Christmas?". 14 Marti Webb. 15 Stock, Aitken and Waterman. 16 "That's What Friends are for". 17 "Knockin' on Heaven's Door". 18 War Child. 19 Lennon and McCartney. 20 "Livin' Doll". 21 McFly. 22 2005. 23 Westminster Abbey. 24 "(I'm Gonna be) 500 Miles". 25 No. 1. 26 Stevie Wonder. 27 Maria. 28 Terry Fox Run for Cancer. 29 Girls Aloud and the Sugababes. 30 Lionel Richie.

1 Which London club has a fanzine called *The Gooner*?
2 Alphabetically, which is the first Scottish League team?
3 What was Phil Babb's first League club?
4 Which team were beaten 3–0 by Wolves in the 1960 FA Cup Final?
5 In which city was Trevor Francis born?
6 Who plays at home at Layer Road?
7 Alan Oakes set a League appearance record at which club?
8 Which club did Gary Taggart join on leaving Manchester City?
9 Which team did Wales beat 5–0 in their first game in the 1998 World Cup campaign?
10 Chris Morris was at which club when he made his international debut?
11 What colour goes with black stripes on Swansea's home shirts?
12 In which decade did Liverpool first win the FA Cup?
13 Mal Donaghy and Denis Irwin were in the same team at which club?
14 Nathan Blake and Mark Patterson swapped over between which clubs?
15 Which club did Paul Parker leave to join Fulham?
16 Which country did Kenny Jackett play for?
17 Which Micky became manager of Fulham in February 1996?
18 In which decade was Jimmy Hill born?
19 Dave Stringer followed Ken Brown as boss of which club?
20 Who moved from Cambridge in 1992 to Manchester Utd to set a club record for transfer fee received?
21 Which ex-Manchester Utd player scored against Liverpool in the 2001 UEA Cup Final?
22 What was the Biggest Away Win of the 2015–16 Premier League season?
23 Which team lost 3–2 to Everton in the 1966 FA Cup Final?
24 David Batty was with which club when he made his international debut?
25 Which club's stadium has the Milburn Stand?
26 Which country does Ryan Nelson play for?
27 In which decade did Sheffield United first win the FA Cup?
28 Which player's transfer to Aston Villa brought Watford a club record fee of £9.6 million in 2007?
29 How many Scottish League championships did Ally McCoist win with Rangers?
30 What colour are Fulham's home shorts?

Answers	**Movies Pot Luck 19** *(see Quiz 172)*

1 Coming to America. 2 Rickman. 3 1940s. 4 Moonstruck. 5 Milos Forman. 6 The Purge. 7 Colonel Ludlow. 8 3 hours. 9 Roy Rogers. 10 Martin Scorsese. 11 True Grit. 12 Barbra Streisand. 13 1950s. 14 Mason. 15 Marlee Matlin. 16 Harrison. 17 Telly Savalas. 18 1940s. 19 David Bowie. 20 Jane Seymour. 21 American Football. 22 Spencer Tracy. 23 Andre Previn. 24 Peter Cattaneo. 25 Clint Eastwood. 26 Bangkok Dangerous. 27 Ron Howard. 28 Jake and Elwood. 29 Goldblum. 30 Little Richard.

1 What was Elvis's job before he shot to fame?
2 What was Elvis's middle name?
3 Which Elvis hit was based on the Italian song "O Sole Mio" and also used to advertise Cornetto ice cream?
4 What follows "I'm Left, You're Right" in the song title?
5 Which No. 1 is Elvis singing at a live show when he dissolves into giggles in a section that is spoken?
6 In which movie does he sing "Wooden Heart"?
7 Which Nashville quartet backed Elvis on many records starting with "Don't be Cruel" in 1956?
8 Which Beatle, critical of Elvis's post-G.I. music, said that Elvis died the day he joined the Army?
9 Which two US states are named on album titles in the 60s?
10 Which part of Elvis was removed in an operation in 1960?
11 Which Tom Jones No. 1 was a top thirty hit for Elvis in 1975?
12 What follows "Don't Cry" in the 1970 hit?
13 What Official Elvis organization was launched in 1957?
14 In which film does Elvis play Vince Everett, a man accused of manslaughter, who becomes a rock star?
15 What were the first names of Elvis's parents?
16 Which up-tempo song went to No. 1 on Elvis's death?
17 Who was in Disguise in the 1963 No. 1?
18 Why did saying he went to L.C. Humes High School convince sceptical listeners that Elvis was white, not black?
19 What was Priscilla Presley's surname before her marriage?
20 Who did Elvis say Lawdy to in 1957?
21 Where was Elvis born?
22 What was everybody in the whole cell block doing?
23 In which year was Elvis's last concert before opening in Las Vegas in 1969?
24 "As the snow flies on a cold and gray Chicago mornin'" begins which Elvis hit?
25 Who was based at 706 Union Avenue, Memphis, Tennessee 38103?
26 What rank was Elvis when he left the US Army in 1958?
27 Which Hollywood legend beat Elvis to the lead role in *The Rainmaker* in 1956?
28 What crime-sounding name was given to Elvis's closest group of friends?
29 The Memphis Draft Board granted Presley a deferment to finish this movie in 1957.
30 In 2016's *Elvis vs Nixon*, what gun did Elvis give the president?

Answers | TV: Soaps 3 *(see Quiz 177)*

1 15 years. 2 2005. 3 Bill Kenright. 4 Oz-Cabs. 5 Wellard. 6 Take the High Road. 7 Brookside. 8 Linda. 9 Sandra Gough. 10 Frank. 11 Manchester. 12 Julia Smith. 13 David Scarborough. 14 Gary Ewing. 15 Susannah. 16 Eldorado. 17 E20. 18 In Kylie's teddy-bear. 19 She was pushed from some scaffolding. 20 Danny. 21 Cracker. 22 Tessa Diamond. 23 10. 24 Dallas (Priscilla Presley, Mary Crosby). 25 Bevron. 26 Pizza Parlour. 27 Tin-Head. 28 The Bill. 29 Suffocated with a pillow. 30 The Mobey.

1 Which Jessica featured in *Play Misty for Me*?

2 How is Margaret Hyra better known?

3 In which decade was *All Quiet on the Western Front* released?

4 Who won the Best Actor Oscar for *Goodbye Mr Chips*?

5 What is Charlie Sheen's real name?

6 Omar Sharif is an expert at which card game?

7 Which Aidan featured in *Desperately Seeking Susan*?

8 Who played Scrooge in the 1951 *A Christmas Carol*?

9 A character named Harry Tasker appeared in which film?

10 Who won the Best Director Oscar for *Mr Deeds Goes to Town*?

11 Which actress links *High Noon* and *Rear Window*?

12 What was the name of Indiana Jones's sidekick in *The Temple of Doom*?

13 Who was Isabella Rossellini's mother?

14 Which song won Best Song Oscar for *The Sandpiper*?

15 The character named Charlie Croker is in which comedy/thriller film?

16 Which veteran actress said, "I acted vulgar, Madonna *is* vulgar"?

17 Which surname was shared by John, Lionel, Ethel and Drew?

18 To the nearest hour, how long does *Doctor Zhivago* last?

19 Which actor's films include *Big Jim McLain*, *McLintock* and *McQ*?

20 Who directed *A Few Good Men*?

21 Which actress links *Love on the Dole* and *An Affair to Remember*?

22 In which decade was *The Driver* released?

23 What was the name of the villain in *Moonraker*?

24 Who won the Best Actress Oscar for *Guess Who's Coming to Dinner*?

25 In which film did a character named Horace Vendergelder appear?

26 Complete this 2016 movie title: Ice Age:_____.

27 In what format was *Night of the Living Dead* remade in 2006?

28 How is Mary Cathleen Collins better known?

29 For which comedy genre was Michael Balcon responsible?

30 Who directed *Blade Runner*?

Answers	**Football Pot Luck 21** *(see Quiz 178)*

1 Portsmouth. 2 Blackburn Rovers. 3 Coventry City. 4 The Republic of Ireland. 5 Manchester City. 6 1970s. 7 Fulham. 8 Sunderland. 9 Gould. 10 Norwich City. 11 James. 12 Brighton. 13 Fox. 14 1900s. 15 Leeds Utd. 16 Liverpool. 17 Manchester. 18 Lincoln City. 19 Mick Mills. 20 Moynihan. 21 Leeds United. 22 Zico. 23 Norwich City. 24 Tranmere Rovers. 25 Newcastle United. 26 Everton. 27 Norwich City 4–5 Liverpool. 28 Paul Ince. 29 1950s. 30 Hearts.

1 How long was Tracy Barlow's sentence for killing Charlie Stubbs in *Corrie*?
2 In which year did Stan Richards (*Emmerdale*'s Seth Armstrong) die?
3 Which impresario played Betty Turpin's Gordon in *Coronation Street*?
4 What was the name of the first minicab company in *EastEnders*?
5 What was the name of Robbie's dog in *EastEnders*?
6 Which soap was set on the Scottish Glendarroch Estate?
7 In which soap did Amanda Burton play Heather Huntington?
8 What was the name of Elsie Tanner's daughter?
9 Who played Hilda Ogden's daughter in *Coronation Street*?
10 What was the Christian name of Ken Barlow's father?
11 In which city was *Albion Market* set?
12 Which late producer was dubbed "The Godmother of Soap"?
13 Who originally played Mark Fowler before Todd Carty?
14 Which Ewing moved to *Knotts Landing*?
15 What was the name of Max Farnham's first wife?
16 Which soap was launched in 1992 with the promise of "sun, sand, sangria and sex"?
17 What is the postcode of the London Borough of Walford?
18 Where did Gary Stanlow hide drugs when Lindsey, Kylie and Mike left the country?
19 How did Sue, Terry Sullivan's wife, die?
20 What was the name of Sue and Terry's son?
21 What was the name of Jimmy Corkhill's dog?
22 Who was the creator of *Emergency-Ward 10*?
23 What number house did the Jordache family live at?
24 Which US soap starred the widow of a rock star and the daughter of an American singing and acting legend?
25 What was the name of Ron Dixon and Bev's house?
26 What was Mick Johnson's first shop in *Brookside* called?
27 What is the nickname of Carmel's son in *Brookside*?
28 What ITV soap called it a day on 31 August 2010?
29 How did Gladys Charlton die?
30 What was Ron Dixon's lorry called?

1 Who won the last FA Cup Final before the Second World War?
2 Bobby Saxton followed Howard Kendall as manager of which club?
3 Which was Stuart Pearce's first League club?
4 Which country did David Langan play for?
5 Which team plays at home in front of the Kippax Stand?
6 In which decade was Daniel Amokachi born?
7 Gordon Davies set a most League goals in total record at which club?
8 Which club did Niall Quinn join on leaving Manchester City?
9 Which Bobby became Wimbledon manager in 1987?
10 Ashley Ward joined Derby County from which club?
11 What is Ian Rush's middle name?
12 Which club has a fanzine called *Gulls Eye*?
13 Which keeper Peter was with Stoke City throughout the entire 1980s?
14 In what decade did Manchester Utd first win the FA Cup?
15 Which club did Mel Sterland leave to join Rangers?
16 Peter Cormack was an FA Cup winner with which club?
17 In which city was Andy Hinchcliffe born?
18 Who plays at home at Sincil Bank?
19 Which England player set a League appearance record for Ipswich Town?
20 Which Colin was Minister for Sport in the 1980s?
21 Which club were relegated to England's third tier for the first time in spring 2007?
22 Who legendary Brazilian was coach of Japan at the 2006 World Cup finals?
23 Which club's ground is by the River Wensum?
24 Which was Steve Coppell's first club as a player?
25 David Batty and Warren Barton were teammates at which club?
26 Which club lost the 1985 FA Cup Final 1–0 after extra time?
27 What game was the most highest scoring of the 2015–16 Premier League season?
28 Which manager left Macclesfield Town to take over at MK Dons in 2007?
29 In which decade was George Burley born?
30 To which club did Sunderland pay a club record transfer fee of £9 million for Craig Gordon in 2007?

1 Which Roy Orbison single peaked at No. 3 after his death?
2 Which Eddie Cochran hit was re-released in 1988?
3 Who had the quickest hat trick of No. 1's in 1981?
4 Which soul singer died in 1964 during a shooting incident at a motel?
5 Who was the subject of *Lady Sings the Blues*?
6 Which contemporary of Marty Wilde and Tommy Steele died aged 41 in 1983?
7 Which member of Free died in 1976?
8 Who was bass guitarist with Thin Lizzy?
9 Which late Motown great was married to Berry Gordy's sister?
10 Who was famous for a banned single in French at first intended for Brigitte Bardot?
11 Which late great's songs were the subject of Jeff Beck's *Crazy Legs* album?
12 Who was the subject of the 80s biopic *La Bamba*?
13 Whose first No. 1 was "It's Only Make Believe"?
14 In which Parisian cemetery is Jim Morrison buried?
15 Who had a UK hit with "Mack the Knife"?
16 Who wrote and sang "I Guess the Lord Must be in New York City"?
17 Which former Animal and Jimi Hendrix manager died in 1996?
18 What type of car was Marc Bolan in when he met his death?
19 *Hellooo Baby* was a Greatest Hits album of which late great?
20 Whose "Winter Dance Party" tour ended in tragedy?
21 Which former partner of Tina Turner passed away in 2007?
22 In which country was Gene Pitney touring when he died in April 2006?
23 Who was "Soul Brother No. 1", "The Godfather of Soul" and "Mr Dynamite"?
24 Which Luther died in 2005 aged 54?
25 With which group did Lisa "Left Eye" Lopes enjoy most success?
26 Can you name the Italian-American crooner and television star who died in 2001?
27 This "Splish-Splash" American idol in the 1950s and 60s died in 1973.
28 At what age did Sir George Martin pass away?
29 He was born John Simon Ritchie in 1957 and died in New York in 1979. Who was he?
30 In 2016, Maurice White died. What group did he form?

Answers | TV: Music & Variety 1 *(see Quiz 181)*

1 Hughie Green. 2 Tyne Tees. 3 All have presented Come Dancing. 4 Perfect Day. 5 1953. 6 Janet Jackson. 7 Russ Conway. 8 Dancers on Top of the Pops. 9 "All", sung by Patricia Brendin. 10 Rocky Horror Picture Show. 11 They Sold a Million. 12 Norman Vaughn. 13 Joe Brown. 14 The Riverside Studios, London. 15 Mr Blobby. 16 Jools Holland. 17 Dani Behr. 18 Leslie Ash. 19 The Tiller Girls. 20 Tommy Trinder. 21 Carol Vorderman. 22 Peter Cook and Dudley Moore. 23 Leslie Garrett. 24 Susan Stranks. 25 Magyar Melody. 26 The Sound of Music. 27 ITV. 28 The Black and White Minstrel Show. 29 The Good Old Days. 30 Dolly Parton.

Answers – page 388

1 A character named Frank Farmer appeared in which film?

2 In which decade was *Father of the Bride* first released?

3 Which Christopher featured in *The Deer Hunter*?

4 Who won an Oscar as Maggio in *From Here to Eternity*?

5 "I never knew the old Vienna" is the first line of which movie?

6 Which film was about Danish author Karen Blixen?

7 Which actress links the 1950s *Carrie* and *Towering Inferno*?

8 Which movie gave Steven Spielberg his first Oscar?

9 Who was voted No. 1 pin-up by US soldiers in World War II?

10 Which English actress played an elderly Wendy in *Hook*?

11 Which Mike featured in *Pumping Iron*?

12 To the nearest hour, how long does *Dumbo* last?

13 *Saving Private Ryan* dealt with events in which part of France?

14 The relationship between Warren Beatty and Madonna began on the set of which movie?

15 Who played the title role in *Oliver!*?

16 Who directed *The Elephant Man*?

17 In *The Bridge on the River Kwai*, Alec Guinness was which Colonel?

18 Who sang the title song of *La Bamba*?

19 What is the subtitle of *Star Trek III*?

20 Who directed *The Birdcage*?

21 Before entering films which sport did Mickey Rourke practise?

22 In which decade was *If...* released?

23 Which author appeared in *The Old Man and the Sea*?

24 In which film did a character named Reggie Love appear?

25 Which Lily featured in *Nashville*?

26 In which year was the sixth *Star Wars* movie, *Revenge of the Sith* released?

27 Conrad Vernon, Greg Tiernan direct Seth Rogen in which 2016 film?

28 Which British actor's autobiography was called *The Moon's a Balloon*?

29 Which James Bond played Heathcliff in the 1970 version of *Wuthering Heights*?

30 "Up Where We Belong" won an Oscar for which movie's theme song?

Answers	**Football Pot Luck 22** *(see Quiz 182)*

1 Leicester City. 2 1940s. 3 Wimbledon. 4 Watford. 5 Coventry City. 6 Ipswich Town. 7 Jimmy Case. 8 Birmingham City. 9 1900s. 10 Norwich City. 11 White. 12 Liverpool. 13 Leeds United. 14 The club flag. 15 Mills. 16 Birmingham City. 17 Andrew. 18 Scotland. 19 King. 20 Hereford United. 21 Vienna. 22 Tottenham Hotspurs. 23 Fourth Division. 24 One. 25 Newcastle United. 26 Norwich City. 27 Fry. 28 1920s. 29 Goodison Park (Everton). 30 1880s.

1 Who used to say, "We thank you – we really do"?
2 The entrance to the studios of which TV company gave *The Tube* its name?
3 What is the connection between Peter Dimmock, Sylvia Peters, Brian Johnston, Terry Wogan, Angela Rippon and Rosemarie Ford?
4 Which song did the BBC release for *Children in Need* in 1997?
5 In which year was *The Good Old Days* first televised?
6 Which member of a famous singing family appeared in *Fame*?
7 Which pianist who had a hit with *"Side Saddle"* was a regular on *Billy Cotton's Band Show*?
8 Who were Legs and Co?
9 What was Britain's first *Eurovision Song Contest* entry?
10 Michael White found fame on what musical?
11 Vince Hill presented which popular music series?
12 Which TV host sang "Swinging in the Rain"?
13 Who starred in *Set 'Em Up Joe*?
14 Where is *TFI Friday* broadcast from?
15 Which large pink spotty character was introduced on *Noel's House Party*?
16 Whose name appeared "Later" in the music shows of the early 1990s?
17 Which girlfriend of soccer's Ryan Giggs presented *The Word*?
18 Which *Men Behaving Badly* star briefly presented *The Tube*?
19 Which dancers appeared on *Sunday Night at the London Palladium*?
20 Whose catchphrase was "You lucky people"?
21 In the first *Celebrity Stars in Their Eyes*, who said "Tonight Matthew I'm going to be Cher"?
22 Which comedy duo's theme song, composed by one of them, was 'Goodbye-ee'?
23 Which opera star hosted a Saturday Night show in the autumn of 1998?
24 Which *Magpie* presenter was a regular *Juke Box Jury* panellist as "a typical teenager"?
25 What was the first full-length musical play shown on TV in 1939?
26 *How Do You Solve a Problem Like Maria?* was a contest to appear in which musical?
27 On which channel is *Britain's Got Talent*?
28 Name the popular British television stage show which ran from 1958 to 1978.
29 In which show did the performers wear old Victorian/Early Edwardian costumes?
30 Name the country & western singer who had her own show on ABC during the late 1980s.

Answers | **Pop: Dead Famous** *(see Quiz 179)*

1 "You Got It". 2 "C'mon Everybody". 3 John Lennon. 4 Sam Cooke. 5 Billie Holiday. 6 Billy Fury. 7 Paul Kossoff. 8 Phil Lynott. 9 Marvin Gaye. 10 Serge Gainsbourg. 11 Gene Vincent. 12 Ritchie Valens. 13 Conway Twitty. 14 Pere Lachaise. 15 Bobby Darin. 16 Nilsson. 17 Chas Chandler. 18 Mini. 19 The Big Bopper. 20 Buddy Holly's. 21 Ike Turner. 22 Wales. 23 James Brown. 24 Vandross. 25 TLC. 26 Perry Como. 27 Bobby Darin. 28 90. 29 Sid Vicious. 30 Earth, Wind & Fire.

1 Which team were beaten 1–0 by Man City in the 1969 FA Cup Final?
2 In which decade was Pat Jennings born?
3 What was Alan Cork's first League club?
4 Graham Taylor followed Glenn Roeder as manager of which club?
5 Swan Lane and Thackhall Street lead to which club's ground?
6 Which club was Kevin Beattie with when he first played international soccer?
7 Which 41-year-old hung up his boots in November 1995 after a serious neck injury in a reserve team game?
8 Which club did Paul Furlong join on leaving Chelsea?
9 In what decade did Manchester City first win the FA Cup?
10 Which club has a fanzine called *I Can Drive a Tractor*?
11 What is the main colour of Stockport County's home shirts?
12 In which city was Michael Branch born?
13 Which club did Mervyn Day leave to join Aston Villa?
14 What did Souness place in the centre of the pitch after his team won the Turkish Cup Final?
15 Which Mick became Stoke City manager in 1985?
16 Steve Claridge joined Leicester City from which club?
17 What is Peter Beardsley's middle name?
18 Which country did Arthur Albiston play for?
19 Which John went upstairs at Tranmere Rovers when John Aldridge took over team affairs?
20 Which club plays at home at Edgar Street?
21 In which city was the final of Euro 2008 played?
22 Longest winning run of the 2015–16 Premier League was 6 games. Who was the lucky team?
23 What was formed in 1958 to transform the Football League?
24 How many goals did Nobby Stiles score for England?
25 Which team lost 3–0 to Liverpool in the 1974 FA Cup Final?
26 For which club did Craig Bellamy make his Premiership debut?
27 Which Barry became manager of Peterborough United in 1996?
28 In which decade was Nat Lofthouse born?
29 At which ground is there the Gwladys Street End?
30 In which decade did Hibernian first win the Scottish Cup?

1 Which film title provided a hit for Ray Parker Jr?
2 Which film other than *The Bodyguard* featured "I Will Always Love You"?
3 "The Shoop Shoop Song" was heard at the end of which Cher film?
4 In which film did Kylie Minogue play Lola Lovell and sing on the soundtrack?
5 In which film did Phil Collins revive the 60s hit "Groovy Kind of Love"?
6 Which River Phoenix film sent Ben E. King to the top of the charts?
7 Which film does "The John Dunbar Theme" come from?
8 For which film did Van Morrison sing "Brown-Eyed Girl"?
9 Which Woody Allen film starring Peter Sellers had Tom Jones singing the theme song?
10 Who sang the title song from *Grease* in 1978?
11 Who sang "Raindrops Keep Falling on My Head" in the film?
12 Which film had the theme "Take My Breath Away"?
13 Who sang "Be Prepared" in *The Lion King*?
14 Who played Madonna's night-club-singer lover in *Evita*?
15 "You'll Never Walk Alone" appears in which film musical?
16 Which song is the most famous on the *Woman in Red* soundtrack?
17 Who won an Oscar for "Flashdance – What a Feeling"?
18 What is the link between Barbra Streisand and the film *M*A*S*H*?
19 In which movie did Madonna sing "Into the Groove"?
20 Which Dionne Warwick hit is featured in *My Best Friend's Wedding*?
21 In 2016, a pig and a mouse are the musical pals of which animated film?
22 Christina Aguilera sang "Lady" what on the soundtrack to *Moulin Rouge*?
23 "Down to Earth" from Wall.E was performed by which former Genesis member?
24 Who took "Lose Yourself" from *8 Mile* to No. 1 in 2002?
25 How far up the UK charts did Will Smith take "Men in Black" in 1997?
26 In what James Bond movie did Carly Simon sing "Nobody Does It Better"?
27 "As Time Goes By" was a major hit from what wartime love triangle movie?
28 Which song from "Holiday Inn" went to No. 1 in the US charts in 1942 for 11 weeks?
29 What was the biggest-selling single from the 1977 movie *Saturday Night Fever*?
30 What was the name of the movie featuring Bryan Adams's "Everything I Do"?

Answers TV: Comedy 7 *(see Quiz 185)*

1 Chris Rock. 2 Caroline Ahern. 3 Sid. 4 Lee Whitlock. 5 Vienna. 6 Gizzard Puke. 7 Benny Hill. 8 Anna Karen. 9 Helen Atkinson Wood. 10 Fred MacMurray. 11 Robert Webb. 12 Shelley Long. 13 Hannah Gordon. 14 Whoops Baghdad. 15 Saturday Night Armistice. 16 3. 17 TV repair man. 18 Mathilda Ziegler. 19 Valerie Harper. 20 BJ Hunnicut. 21 Nora Batty. 22 Timothy Spall. 23 Edina. 24 4. 25 Hyacinth. 26 Ever Decreasing Circles. 27 Outside Edge. 28 Catastrophe. 29 Pulling. 30 Lenny Godber.

1 What was Mel Gibson's job in the 1997 thriller *Conspiracy Theory*?
2 Which George turned down Bogart's role in *The Maltese Falcon*?
3 The character Catherine Tramell appeared in which movie?
4 Who won the Best Actor Oscar for *Patton*?
5 Which Arsenio featured in *Coming to America*?
6 Who starred opposite Mickey Rooney in *National Velvet* in 1944?
7 Which Karen featured in *Raiders of the Lost Ark*?
8 Who directed *Dead Man Walking*?
9 Who played the title role in *The Bachelor*?
10 Pearl Slaghoople is mother-in-law to which fictional character?
11 Which comedian played opposite Jane Russell in *The Paleface*?
12 Who played the Bond girl in *Never Say Never Again*?
13 Who is Pongo's mate in *101 Dalmatians*?
14 Which former child star became ambassador to Ghana and Czechoslovakia?
15 Which actress links *A Streetcar Named Desire* and *Planet of the Apes*?
16 Who won the Best Actress Oscar for *Mrs Miniver*?
17 What was the first Monty Python film for the cinema?
18 In which movie did Gregory Peck play James McKay?
19 To the nearest fifteen minutes, how long does *Fantasia* last?
20 A character named Rachel Marron appeared in which film?
21 In which decade was Disney's *Sleeping Beauty* released?
22 Which brothers starred in *Young Guns*?
23 *The Sting* and *Sneakers* both featured which actor?
24 Which Henry turned down Peter Finch's role in *Network*?
25 What was the name of Tommy Lee Jones's character in *The Fugitive*?
26 Which character murders Bruce Wayne's parents in *Batman Begins*?
27 The 2016 animated movie *Storks* stars which *Saturday Night Live* actor?
28 Which actor starred in *Hot Shots!* and *Honey, I Blew Up the Kids*?
29 Which Bond girl later starred with Elvis Presley in *Fun in Acapulco*?
30 In which decade was Disney's *Lady and the Tramp* released?

---

1 Which real-life actor/comedian was the base for *Everyone Hates Chris*?
2 Which Royle Family actress/writer died, tragically, in 2016?
3 What is the name of Ivy's husband in *Last of the Summer Wine*?
4 Who played Harvey Moon's son?
5 In *Rising Damp*, Rigsby's cat shares its name with a capital city. What is it?
6 What was the name of Kenny Everett's punk caricature?
7 Fred Scuttle was an comic charcter created by which comedian?
8 Which actress played Reg Varney's sister, Olive, in *On the Buses*?
9 In *Blackadder the Third*, Mrs Miggins was played by which comic actress?
10 Who starrred in *My Three Sons*?
11 Who plays the wannabe musician Jeremy Usborne in *Peep Show*?
12 Which *The Money Pit* actress played Diane Chambers in *Cheers*?
13 Who played *My Wife Next Door*?
14 What was the follow up to *Up Pompeii!*?
15 Which 1995 Saturday Night series was presented by Armando Iannucci?
16 How many sons does Tim have in *Home Improvement*?
17 What was Gary's job in the first series of *Goodnight Sweetheart*?
18 Who played Mr Bean's long-suffering girlfriend?
19 Who starred as Rhoda?
20 Who was Trapper John's replacement in *M*A*S*H*?
21 Who was Wally's wife in *Last of the Summer Wine*?
22 Who played Frank Stubbs?
23 Who is Saffron's mother in *Absolutely Fabulous*?
24 How many sons did Mrs Boswell have in *Bread*?
25 What was Mrs Bucket's first name in *Keeping Up Appearances*?
26 Penelope Wilton and Peter Egan appeared together as neighbours in which sitcom?
27 Which sitcom about a local cricket club starred Timothy Spall and Josie Lawrence as married couple?
28 Who were Dorien's neighbours in *Birds of a Feather*?
29 Sharon Horgan stars with Rob Delaney in which calamatious sitcom?
30 Who was Fletcher's cellmate in *Porridge*?

---

1 What did Eddie Jones become in 2016?
2 Which club won four Guinness Premierships without finishing as League leaders?
3 Who replaced Clive Woodward as coach of England?
4 Which Irish Province did Brian O'Driscoll captain in 2008?
5 What is the nickname of the Super 14 team from Auckland?
6 Which League side play at Bury FC's ground, Gig Lane?
7 Who was the first Welshman to be sent off playing for his country at Twickenham?
8 Who played League between 1946 and 1964 and created a record for most tries in a career?
9 Where are you if you are at "Billy Williams's cabbage patch"?
10 Who captained Australia in their World Cup win in 1991?
11 Which nephew of Barry John became a Wigan player?
12 Who played for both England and New Zealand in the 1980s?
13 Which League club is nicknamed "The Chemics"?
14 Who captained England in the 1995 World Cup Final?
15 Who scored on his debut for Wales against England in 1996?
16 Who play at Thrum Hall?
17 Who kicked the winning goal in extra time in the 1995 World Cup Final for South Africa?
18 What was the previous name of London Broncos?
19 Who plays at the Stoop Memorial Ground?
20 To whom is the Lance B. Todd Memorial Trophy awarded?
21 In what year did Scotland first win at Parc des Princes?
22 Who in 1883 picked the ball up and ran with it to "discover" rugby?
23 Which two clubs play at home at Craven Park?
24 Who played for Wales in 53 consecutive games from 1967 to 1978?
25 In Union, which international team name was first used in 1924?
26 Who could win the Five Nations but not the Triple Crown?
27 Who scored most tries for Ireland in the 1991 World Cup?
28 Apart from Wigan name four teams beginning with a W who have been League champions?
29 In League, what is awarded for the BBC TV try of the season?
30 What was the Regal Trophy previously called?

---

1 What was Paolo Maldini's first club?
2 Which club have won the League most times?
3 Who was Italy's top scorer in the 1994 World Cup in the USA?
4 How old was Paolo Rossi when he retired from playing?
5 Which club did Graeme Souness join in Italy?
6 Leonardo Bonucci plays for which Serie A club?
7 Which team are known as the Zebras?
8 Dino Zoff became coach and later president of which club?
9 Which team knocked Italy out of Italia 90?
10 The import of what was banned in 1964, only to be lifted in the 1980s?
11 Who were the opponents for Cesare Maldini's first match as coach?
12 Who was Italy's top scorer in the 1982 World Cup tournament?
13 Michel Platini inspired Juventus to European Cup Final victory over which English side?
14 Gianfranco Zola took over the number 10 shirt at Napoli from which superstar?
15 In which decade did the Italians first win the World Cup?
16 Who were champions of Serie A in 1995–96?
17 Thomas Brolin joined Leeds United from which Italian club?
18 Who missed the final penalty for Italy in the 1994 World Cup Final?
19 Lazio play in which Italian city?
20 Who was in charge of Italy for Euro 96?
21 In which city is the Stadio Delle Alpi?
22 Who is Italy's all-time leader in international appearances?
23 Who knocked Italy out of the 2002 World Cup?
24 Which Italian international had Allan Border as his favourite sportsman?
25 Which Fabio scored the decisive penalty in the 2006 World Cup Final?
26 Who aged 40 became the oldest winner of the World Cup in 1982?
27 Name the former Middlesbrough player nicknamed "The White Feather".
28 Which player's mother refused a lucrative offer from AC Milan before he joined Roma in 1989?
29 Name the ex-Juventus and FC Barcelona defender who joined AC Milan in 2008.
30 Who played for Modena in 1994 and made Bayern Munich his 10th club in 2007?

Answers	Movies: Heroes & Villains *(see Quiz 189)*

1 Alan Rickman. 2 Arnold Schwarzenegger. 3 The Shining. 4 Gary Oldman. 5 Bela Lugosi. 6 Joe Pesci. 7 The Rat Pack. 8 On Her Majesty's Secret Service. 9 O. J. Simpson. 10 Quentin Tarantino. 11 Two. 12 Liam Neeson. 13 Roman Polanski. 14 (Tea with) Mussolini. 15 Jon Voight. 16 The Gladiator. 17 Jean Claude van Damme. 18 Christopher Walken. 19 Norman Bates (Psycho). 20 Alec Guinness. 21 Sigourney Weaver. 22 Luther. 23 Peter Lawford. 24 Rommel. 25 Erich von Stroheim. 26 Le Chiffre. 27 Fogler. 28 Ellen Ripley. 29 James Earl Jones. 30 Kirk Douglas.

1 Who had a highly successful album titled *Never Forever*?
2 Which Spice Girl is Sporty Spice?
3 Who pleaded "Hold Me Close" in 1975?
4 Which artist originated the rock classic "Tutti Frutti"?
5 Who has recorded under the name Kris Carson?
6 Which group included Mick Avory and Pete Quaife?
7 Which Eddie Cochran hit did the Sex Pistols do a cover version of in 1979?
8 Which Boney M single sold over 2 million copies on the UK?
9 Which pop band "took a break" in 2016, vowing to come back?
10 Which song title links Petula Clark and S.W.V.?
11 Who was going to Dress You Up in 1985?
12 Which TV show opened to Manfred Mann's "5-4-3-2-1"?
13 Which Wild West hero features on a Cher single?
14 Who had a late-80s album called *Viva Hate*?
15 Who rightly sang "We are Family" in 1979?
16 Who had a 1996 album called *Everything Must Go*?
17 Who in 1997 said drug taking was as normal as having a cup of tea?
18 What was on the other side of Boney M's "Oh My Lord"?
19 Which two Fleetwood Mac albums are two of the bestsellers of all time?
20 Which band leader is the one with the most chart albums in the UK?
21 Which band released their "White Album" in 2016?
22 Pearl Aday, lead singer of Mother Pearl, is the daughter of which rock legend?
23 What was "your love" according to Sade?
24 Who was the lead singer with the Union Gap on "Young Girl"?
25 What Human League hit was the only single to sell over a million in the UK in 1981?
26 In which decade was k. d. lang born?
27 What colour ribbons was Harry Belafonte singing about in 1957?
28 Which Barbra Streisand hit starts "Memories light the corners of my mind"?
29 What colour suit is Michael Jackson wearing on the cover of the *Thriller* album?
30 Which song begins "What would you do if I sang out of tune"?

Answers | TV Drama 3 *(see Quiz 190)*

1 Lynda la Plante. 2 Peter Gilmore. 3 Brimstone and Treacle. 4 Gemma Jones. 5 Landburgher Gessler. 6 Alexandra Bastedo. 7 Ballers. 8 Lord Bellamy. 9 The Peak District. 10 Lady Chatterley. 11 McCallum. 12 Castle Howard. 13 Linus Roach. 14 Gareth Hunt. 15 Jim Phelps. 16 Nevada. 17 Fred Dryer. 18 Early British cinema. 19 Gessler. 20 The Jewel in the Crown. 21 Rupert Davies & Jack MacGowan. 22 Pauline Collins. 23 Connie. 24 Lee Horsley. 25 Edge of Darkness. 26 18th century. 27 Barry Morse. 28 Kookie. 29 Warner Brothers. 30 Gill Favor.

1 Who was the villainous Sheriff in *Robin Hood: Prince of Thieves*?
2 Which tough guy directed *Christmas in Connecticut*?
3 Which movie featured Jack Torrance?
4 Which actor kidnapped Harrison Ford in *Air Force One*?
5 Which horror star did Martin Landau play in *Ed Wood*?
6 Which star of *Goodfellas* was a child star on radio?
7 *The Clan*, with Sinatra, Martin & Co. was also known as what?
8 In which movie did Diana Rigg play Mrs 007?
9 Which sportsman-turned-actor whose journey in a white truck was real-life drama had the nickname "The Juice"?
10 Whose first major movie as director was *Reservoir Dogs*?
11 How many Batman films did Michael Keaton appear in?
12 Who played outlaw Rob Roy in the 90s film of the same name?
13 Who was Sharon Tate married to at the time of her murder?
14 Which villain's name appeared in the title of a 1999 film with Cher and Maggie Smith?
15 Who won an Oscar for *Coming Home* after missing out for *Midnight Cowboy*?
16 Oliver Reed died during the making of which movie?
17 Who was nicknamed "The Muscles from Brussels"?
18 Who was in *Batman Returns* 14 years after playing the crazed POW in *The Deer Hunter*?
19 Which Hitchcock villain said, "A boy's best friend is his mother"?
20 Who played Colonel Nicholson in *Bridge on the River Kwai* after Bogart and Olivier rejected it?
21 Who is associated with the role of Ripley in *Aliens*?
22 Which Lex pitted Batman and Superman together in 2016?
23 Which member of the Rat Pack was a Kennedy brother-in-law?
24 Who did James Mason play in *The Desert Fox*?
25 Which screen villain was born Hans Erich Maria Stroheim von Nordenwall?
26 What was the name of Mads Mikkelsen's character in *Casino Royale*?
27 Which Dan played Randy Daytona in *Balls of Fire*?
28 What was the name of Sigourney Weaver's character in *Aliens*?
29 Who voiced the part of Darth Vader in *The Empire Strikes Back*?
30 Which actor played Spartacus in the movie of the same name?

1 Who wrote *Widows*?
2 Who starred in the role of James Onedin?
3 Which Dennis Potter drama was banned in 1976 and shown in 1987?
4 She played *The Duchess of Duke Street*. Who was she?
5 Name the main protagonist in *The Adventures of William Tell*.
6 Who was the female star of *The Champions*?
7 Dwayne Johnson is the star of which HBO football-agent show?
8 Which character did David Longton play in *Upstairs Downstairs*?
9 Where is the series that starred Kevin Whately and Sam Shepherd set?
10 In which steamy serial did Sean Bean star alongside Joely Richardson?
11 Which series used "Cry Me a River" as the theme?
12 Which Estate was the subject for the filming of *Brideshead Revisited*?
13 Which son of a famous soap star starred in *Seaforth*?
14 Which Avenger appeared in *Upstairs Downstairs*?
15 What was Peter Graves's character called in *Mission: Impossible*?
16 In which American state was the Ponderosa?
17 Who played the title role in *Hunter*?
18 What was the subject of the series *Flickers*?
19 Who was William Tell's enemy?
20 In which series did Geraldine James play Sarah Layton?
21 Who played Cpt Grant Mitchell's shipmates Alfonso and Sean?
22 Who was Sarah in *Thomas and Sarah*?
23 Which rag-trade series featured Stephanie Beacham?
24 Which actor was Matt Houston?
25 Which drama series starred Bob Peck and Joe Don Baker?
26 In which century was *The Buccaneers* set?
27 Which actor pursued Dr Richard Kimble?
28 Who did Ed Byrnes play in *77 Sunset Strip*?
29 Which company made *Cheyenne, Bronco and Tenderfoot*?
30 Who was the ramrod in *Rawhide*?

Answers | **Pop Pot Luck 23** *(see Quiz 188)*

1 Kate Bush. 2 Mel C. 3 David Essex. 4 Little Richard. 5 Kris Kristofferson. 6 The Kinks. 7 "C'mon Everybody". 8 "Rivers of Babylon". 9 1D. 10 "Downtown". 11 Madonna. 12 "Ready Steady Go". 13 (Just Like) Jesse James. 14 Morrissey. 15 Sister Sledge. 16 Manic Street Preachers. 17 Noel Gallagher. 18 "Mary's Boy Child". 19 Rumours, Tango in the Night. 20 James Last. 21 Weezer. 22 Meat Loaf. 23 King. 24 Gary Puckett. 25 "Don't You Want Me". 26 1960s. 27 Scarlet. 28 The Way We Were. 29 White. 30 "With a Little Help from My Friends".

1 Who is the oldest player to turn out for Wales?
2 In which decade did Wales first beat England at Wembley?
3 Who became manager of Northern Ireland in 1994?
4 Which ex-Liverpool player has managed Wales?
5 At which ground do the Republic of Ireland play home matches?
6 Which Peter scored twice for Northern Ireland in their magnificent draw with West Germany in the 1958 World Cup?
7 Who was Tony Cascarino playing for when he won his first cap?
8 When did the Republic of Ireland first qualify for the World Cup finals?
9 Which country has Vinnie Jones played for?
10 Which Welsh player was the most capped before Neville Southall?
11 Which Christian names link Northern Ireland's McIlroy and Quinn?
12 Which Northern Ireland skipper said, "Our tactics are to equalize before the other side scores"?
13 Which Republic of Ireland player was nicknamed "Chippy"?
14 In 1992 Michael Hughes made his debut for which country?
15 Which Republic of Ireland player appeared in five FA Cup Finals between 1963 and 1973?
16 In which year did Raheem Shaquille Sterling begin his England career?
17 Which home international countries were present in the 1982 World Cup finals?
18 Which Arsenal and Tottenham Hotspur manager was also team boss of Northern Ireland?
19 Which London-based striker captained Northern Ireland in 1996?
20 When did Wales last qualify for the World Cup?
21 In which city did England inflict a first competitive home loss for Croatia in 2008?
22 Which country moved to the top of the FIFA World Rankings in July 2008?
23 Which club did Craig Burley leave to take over as Scotland's manager?
24 Where was Croatia's Josip Simunic, who received three yellow cards against Australia in 2006, born?
25 Who was the first England manager to make David Beckham captain?
26 Which former West Ham player guided Croatia to two famous wins over England?
27 Who is the only player to score 100 League goals in England and Scotland?
28 Which ex-member of Chelsea's foreign brigade was awarded an OBE in 2004?
29 Name the Italian who broke Irish hearts at the 1990 World Cup finals.
30 Which ex-Premiership star played for Russia, Ukraine and the CIS?

1 Where does Susie fall asleep in the hit "Wake Up Little Susie"?

2 Which artist had a No. 3 hit in 1972 with "You're a Lady"?

3 What Killed the Radio Star according to the Buggles?

4 On which Neil Diamond album is the track "Play Me"?

5 What was Golden for the Tremeloes?

6 Which rock guitarist first set a guitar ablaze at the '67 Monterey Pop Festival?

7 In which West End musical did David Essex play the role of Jesus?

8 Who sang "Papa's Got a Brand New Bag"?

9 Where did Supertramp have Breakfast?

10 Which German phrase did Ian Dury rhyme with "Rhythm Stick"?

11 Which group included Al Jardine and Mike Love?

12 Which Sheryl Crow song was Grammy Record of the Year in 1994?

13 Who sang "How am I Supposed to Live without You?" in 1989?

14 Who had an instrumental version of "Don't Cry for Me Argentina"?

15 Which comedy actor appeared on Annie Lennox's *Walking on Broken Glass* video?

16 Which "group" was founded by Ian Broudie?

17 Who was Frankie Lymon's backing group?

18 Which song with Love in the title was a hit for the Beatles and Ella Fitzgerald?

19 What was the home city of Bob Marley's father?

20 How many Vandellas were there?

21 Which songwriter released his 13th solo album in 2016?

22 At which US political party's Presidential convention did Stevie Wonder play in 2008?

23 Who had the original hit with "Matthew and Son"?

24 Who is on the cover of the *Guilty* album with Barbra Streisand?

25 What was Tommy Steele's first No. 1 single?

26 Who was "Twistin' the Night Away"in 1962?

27 What Connie Francis hit says: "Yours was red, mine was baby pink"?

28 What group's first No. 1 single was "True"?

29 What is a beguine in the classic "Begin the Beguine"?

30 How many tears did the Goombay Dance Band sing about in 1982?

Answers | **TV Comedy 8** *(see Quiz 194)*

1 The Mary Whitehouse Experience. 2 Gregor Fisher. 3 Fawlty Towers. 4 Dustin Gee.
5 Yetta Feldman. 6 Betty Spencer. 7 Rising Damp. 8 Julia McKenzie. 9 Police Squad.
10 Paul Calf. 11 Rowan & Martin's Laugh-In. 12 Magpie's Jenny Handley is daughter
to Don't Wait Up's Dinah Sheridan. 13 Captain. 14 Dervla Kirwan. 15 Lance Percival.
16 Dermot. 17 Johnny Speight. 18 Gunther. 19 Latimer. 20 Dick & the Duchess.
21 Blamire. 22 Reece Dinsdale. 23 She has never been seen. 24 Roadsweeper. 25
Unbreakable Kimmy Schmidt. 26 "Radar" O'Reilly. 27 F Troop. 28 Sgt Bilko. 29
Lanford. 30 Grace Brothers (Are You being Served?).

1 Who was her co-star in *The Bridges of Madison County*?

2 Which of her films was about a nuclear nightmare?

3 Who was her English co-star in *The French Lieutenant's Woman*?

4 What was the name of her character in *The Deer Hunter*?

5 Which Danish author did she play in *Out of Africa*?

6 In *A Cry in the Dark* how did she say her baby had died in the Australian outback?

7 In which 90s movie did she master an Irish accent?

8 *Ricki and the Flash*. 2015. Meryl Streep's character surname is....?

9 What was the nationality of her character in *A Cry in the Dark*?

10 Which *M*A*S*H* star was her co-star in *The Seduction of Joe Tynan*?

11 Her role in *Postcards from the Edge* was based on the life of which actress who wrote the book?

12 What was her first action film in 1994?

13 In which film did she play an actress and the Victorian character she plays?

14 Which musical role eluded her in the mid-90s after she had impressed with her singing in *Postcards from the Edge*?

15 *The Deer Hunter* was the last film for which actor who was her then partner?

16 Who was her male co-star in *Death Becomes Her*?

17 In which Woody Allen film did she appear in 1979?

18 Which 70s movie about Vietnam won her her first Oscar nomination?

19 Who was her co-star in *Ironweed*?

20 In which movie did she win an Oscar for her portrayal of a Polish holocaust victim?

21 Who played her mother in *Postcards from the Edge*?

22 In which movie did she play a factory worker opposite Cher?

23 Which divorce drama won her her first Oscar?

24 Who was her co-star in the unsuccessful *Falling in Love* in 1984?

25 Which blonde actress was her co-star in *Death Becomes Her*?

26 What was *The Devil* wearing when Streep was Oscar nominated in 2007?

27 Which group's music was the backdrop for Streep's role in *Mama Mia*?

28 What is Meryl's real Christian name?

29 In which 2007 movie did she play Janine Roth alongside Tom Cruise?

30 In which 2001 Steven Spielberg movie did she voice the role of "Blue Mecha"?

---

1 Which Radio 1 comedy show spawned *Newman and Baddiel in Pieces*?
2 Who created the character Rab C. Nesbit?
3 In classic comedy do Polly and the Major both appear?
4 Who was Les Dennis's late comedy partner?
5 Whose was the female ghost in *So Haunt Me*?
6 Who was married to Frank in *Some Mothers Do 'Ave 'Em*?
7 In which series did Richard Beckinsale and Frances de la Tour play harassed lodgers?
8 Who played Hester in *Fresh Fields*?
9 Which spoof cop series featured Leslie Neilsen?
10 Which offensive drunk was created by Steve Coogan on Channel 4's *Saturday Zoo*?
11 Which comedy show did Dick and Dan compere?
12 What is the link between *Magpie* and the comedy *Don't Wait Up*?
13 In *Blackadder Goes Forth*, what rank was Blackadder?
14 Who was the star of both *Goodnight Sweetheart* and *Ballykissangel*?
15 Who created calypsos on *That was the Week That Was*?
16 Which character was played by Harry Enfield in *Men Behaving Badly*?
17 Who wrote *Till Death Us Do Part*?
18 In *Friends*, who in Central Perk is a secret admirer of Rachel?
19 What is the surname of father and son in *Don't Wait Up*?
20 The character Dick Starrett was a troubled American insurance investigator in which 50's comedy?
21 Who did Michael Bates play in *Last of the Summer Wine*?
22 Who played John Thaw's son in *Home to Roost*?
23 From the viewer's point of view, what is unusual about Niles's wife Maris in *Frasier*?
24 What was the occupation of Mr Boswell in *Bread*?
25 Tina Fey and Robert Carlock created which 2015 US comedy smash?
26 What was the nickname of Gary Burghoff's character in *M*A*S*H*?
27 What was the name of the US comedy about the cavalry?
28 Colonel Hall was which Master Sergeant's superior officer?
29 In which town does Roseanne live?
30 In which store did the actors Larry Martin and Arthur English appear?

Quiz 195 | Football: London Clubs | Answers – page 399

1 The title for Longest unbeaten run in the 2015–16 Premier League season goes to....?
2 Which Northern Ireland star is QPR's most capped player?
3 What nationality is West Ham United's Slaven Bilic?
4 If you were walking down South Africa Road, which London club's ground would you be nearest?
5 Have Millwall ever won the FA Cup?
6 Which London side did Johnny Haynes play for?
7 Who holds Chelsea's record for the most League appearances?
8 Goalie Pat Jennings played for which three London area sides?
9 Which London side defeated Wales in a friendly in May 1996?
10 Who play in red and white vertical striped shirts?
11 Chelsea's Dennis Wise was transferred from which other London club?
12 Who was Trevor Brooking's "minder" on the pitch at West Ham?
13 Who scored the final goal to win Arsenal the title in 1989?
14 Who moved from West Ham United to Celtic for £1.5 million in 1992?
15 At which club did John Barnes make his League debut?
16 Who became the chairman of Leyton Orient in 1996?
17 Which Wimbledon player joined them from Brentford in 1992?
18 Name the London team whose address is 748 High Road?
19 Who did Crystal Palace beat in the 1990 FA Cup semi-final?
20 Frank Clark managed which London side?
21 Which London club ground has the largest capacity?
22 Which club successively had Italian, Portuguese, Israeli and Brazilian managers?
23 Brentford and which other London club are nicknamed "The Bees"?
24 Which London club sacked Peter Taylor as manager in 2007?
25 Which London club plays home games close to South Bermondsey rail station?
26 How many professional teams can London boast?
27 By what name was Arsenal originally known when it was first founded?
28 Which London club was the first to win the FA Cup?
29 Name the London club which has had almost 20 home grounds.
30 Which London club calls Griffin Park home?

Answers | Football: Internationals *(see Quiz 191)*

1 Billy Meredith. 2 1970s. 3 Bryan Hamilton. 4 John Toshack. 5 Lansdowne Road. 6 McParland. 7 Gillingham. 8 1990. 9 Wales. 10 Ivor Allchurch. 11 Jimmy. 12 Danny Blanchflower. 13 Liam Brady. 14 Northern Ireland. 15 Johnny Giles. 16 2012. 17 Northern Ireland, England and Scotland. 18 Terry Neill. 19 Iain Dowie. 20 1958. 21 Zagreb. 22 Spain. 23 Southampton. 24 Australia. 25 Peter Taylor. 26 Slaven Bilic. 27 Kenny Dalglish. 28 Gianfranco Zola. 29 Toto Scilacci. 30 Andrei Kanchelskis.

The Hard Questions

If you thought that this section of this book would prove to be little or no problem, or that the majority of the questions could be answered and a scant few would test you then you are sorely mistaken. These questions are the *hardest* questions *ever*! So difficult are they that any attempt to answer them all in one sitting will addle your mind and mess with your senses. You'll end up leaving the pub via the window while ordering a pint from the horse brasses on the wall. Don't do it! For a kick off there are almost 6,500 of them, so at 20 seconds a question it will take you close on a day and a half, and that's just the time it takes to read them. What you should do instead is set them for others – addle your friends' minds.

Note the dangerous nature of these questions though. These are your secret weapons. Use them accordingly unless, of course, someone or some team is getting your back up. In which case you should hit them hard and only let up when you have them cowering under the bench whimpering "Arsenal".

These questions work best against league teams, they are genuinely tough and should be used against those people who take their pub quizzes seriously. NEVER use these questions against your in-laws.

1 Liam Brady finished his playing career at which club?
2 Steve Williams and Brian Talbot were together at which club?
3 To two each way, how many caps did Alan Ball win?
4 Which Manchester Utd player scored on his English League debut v Watford in August, 1984?
5 Who was born on September 29, 1939 at Hill o'Beath, Fife?
6 Which club did Billy Bremner move to after Leeds Utd's glory days?
7 Nick Holmes was a long-serving player with which club?
8 Which English team did Roy Keane support as a boy?
9 What was Johan Cruyff's first family link with Ajax?
10 Which heavy-smoking midfielder scored Brazil's second goal in the 1970 World Cup Final?
11 Liverpool's Lallana has a first name. What is it?
12 Johnny Metgod came from Real Madrid to which English side?
13 Micky Horswill played for which team in an FA Cup Final?
14 How old was Ray Wilkins when he was made captain at Chelsea?
15 Graeme Souness was at which club for three years without playing in the first team?
16 Bryan Robson's last England game was against which country?
17 Mills, Wigley and Walsh featured for which top-flight 80s team?
18 Cockerill and Case formed a formidable partnership at which club?
19 What number did Johan Cruyff wear for most of his Ajax career?
20 Bobby Robson was with which club when he first played for England?
21 Which long-throwing midfielder went down with Sunderland and Southampton?
22 Who left Leicester City for Celtic in 2000 and retired in 2008?
23 Who preceded Cesc Fabregas in wearing Arsenal's No. 4 shirt?
24 Which Midlands non-League club did Paul Gascoigne manage in autumn 2005?
25 The captain of which team scored twice in the 2006 FA Cup final?
26 Name the Italian midfield general who played for Glasgow Rangers from 1997 to 1998.
27 Which ex-England player walked out of Birmingham City while on loan in 2006?
28 Which Swedish international played for Everton and West Ham United?
29 Name the player who scored seven goals for the England youth team versus Spain.
30 Which future England captain went on loan to Preston North End in 1995?

Answers | **Pop Pot Luck 1** (see Quiz 2)

1 Mark McManus (Taggart). 2 Love Me Tender. 3 Sting. 4 "Roulette". 5 Lennon and McCartney. 6 Ian Dury. 7 Ritchie Valens. 8 Cher. 9 Joe Dolce. 10 Pat Boone. 11 John Lennon. 12 Southport. 13 The Rumour. 14 Not Me. 15 Charged with stealing cigarettes and chocolates from a cinema. 16 Boxing. 17 Biffy Clyro. 18 Kraftwerk. 19 Jason Donovan. 20 Jefferson Starship, Jefferson Airplane. 21 Mark McClelland. 22 Pet Shop Boys. 23 Orange. 24 Phil Collins. 25 The Smiths. 26 Marilyn Monroe, Brigitte Bardot & Jayne Mansfield. 27 Deep Purple. 28 God. 29 Roberta Flack. 30 Eric Clapton.

1 In the 1990s Sweet's Brian Connolly discovered which TV detective was his natural brother?
2 In which film did Elvis play the role of Clint Reno?
3 Who released an album entitled *The Dream of the Blue Turtles*?
4 What was Russ Conway's second No. 1?
5 Who wrote "World without Love" for Peter and Gordon?
6 Who was Capital Radio's choice as Best London Artist from 1978–80?
7 Who is the biopic *La Bamba* about?
9 Which 90s chart-topper had a fitness video called *A New Attitude*?
9 Who had a hit in 1981 with "Shaddap you face"?
10 Who wrote the lyric to the theme from *Exodus*?
11 Who said, "If music be the food of love, let's have a Beethoven butty"?
12 In which town was Marc Almond born?
13 Who backed Graham Parker?
14 What was Glenn Medeiros's debut album called?
15 Why did Donovan spend two weeks in Strangeways Prison in Manchester in the early 60s?
16 In which sport did Billy Joel excel when at school?
17 Which band was once called the Ravens?
18 Which group's name is the German for "power plant"?
19 Who won the Logie Award for Best New Talent in Australia in 1987?
20 Which two bands have President Bill Clinton's middle name in their names?
21 Who was the first regular member of Snow Patrol to leave the band?
22 Which Scottish band released *Ellipsis* in 2016?
23 What colour is the title on Neil Young's *Harvest* album?
24 Who won Grammys in 1986 for Best Album, Producer and Male Vocalist?
25 Who did Sandie Shaw record "Hand in Glove" with?
26 Which blondes are on the cover of the Rolling Stones' *Some Girls* album?
27 What links Nino Tempo & April Stevens with Donny & Marie Osmond?
28 Who does Prince give thanks to on the inner sleeve of *1999*?
29 Whose first album was *First Take* in 1970?
30 Which former Cream star backed Roger Waters on a 1984 tour?

| **Answers** | **Football: Midfield Men** *(see Quiz 1)* |

1 West Ham Utd. 2 Arsenal. 3 72. 4 Gordon Strachan. 5 Jim Baxter. 6 Hull City. 7 Southampton. 8 Tottenham Hotspur. 9 His mother was a cleaner in the offices. 10 Gerson. 11 Adam. 12 Nottingham Forest. 13 Sunderland. 14 18. 15 Tottenham Hotspur. 16 Turkey. 17 Nottingham Forest. 18 Southampton. 19 14. 20 WBA. 21 Rory Delap. 22 Neil Lennon. 23 Patrick Vieira. 24 Kettering. 25 Liverpool. 26 Gennaro Gattuso. 27 Nicky Butt. 28 Niclas Alexandersson. 29 Joe Cole. 30 David Beckham.

1 Who said, "You can't get spoiled if you do your own ironing"?
2 How is Edna Gilhooley better known?
3 What was the name of the band Johnny Depp played in before turning to acting?
4 At which university did Richard E. Grant study?
5 In which city was Edward G. Robinson born?
6 Who said he would prefer "animal" on his passport to "actor"?
7 Who said, 'I look like a quarry someone has dynamited'?
8 How is Francoise Sorya Dreyfus better known?
9 Who was dubbed the "80s Errol Flynn" by *Vanity Fair* magazine?
10 Ron Howard's daughter, star of 2016's *Pete's Dragon*, is who?
11 Who said, 'I stopped making pictures because I don't like taking my clothes off'?
12 Who played Woody Guthrie in *Bound for Glory*?
13 Which director did Theresa Russell marry?
14 Whose marriage to Michelle Phillips lasted just eight days?
15 Which film star wrote the novel *Adieu Volidia*?
16 About which of his co-stars did Anthony Hopkins say, "She's serious about her work but doesn't take herself seriously"?
17 What is Michael J. Fox's middle name?
18 Who starred in *Prom Night* and *Terror Train*?
19 Whom did Harrison Ford replace as Indiana Jones in *Raiders of the Lost Ark*?
20 Which actress's father was one of the Dalai Lama's first American Buddhist monks?
21 Which actor played drums in a band called Scarlet Pride?
22 Which actor is Sissy Spacek's cousin?
23 What does Tim Roth have tattooed on his arm?
24 What is Shirley MacLaine's real name?
25 Who played Francis Bacon in *Love Is the Devil*?
26 Maurice Micklewhite was Alfred in *Batman Begins*, but what is his stage name?
27 Paul Newman, who died in 2008, co-owned a motor racing team with whom?
28 Who played "Max Payne" in the 2008 movie of the same name?
29 Name the American actress whose career spanned 75 years, 1912–87.
30 Who was paid $50,000,000 for starring in *What Happens In Vegas*?

1 Who did Burnside replace in the CID?

2 Who played Carl Kochak in *The Night Stalker*?

3 What rank was Spikings in *Dempsey and Makepiece*?

4 Which character did Robson Green play in *Touching Evil*?

5 Which character did Trevor Eve play in *Heat of the Sun*?

6 Who played the bisexual British attorney in *LA Law*?

7 Which Mississippi town was *In the Heat of the Night* set?

8 Where were the outdoor scenes of *Hill Street Blues* filmed?

9 Who is Beck?

10 In which US crime series did Phil Collins make a guest appearance as a criminal?

11 Who is Angie Tribeca?

12 In *Hawaii Five O* where was the seat of the Hawaiian government?

13 Who starred as Gordon Cole in *Twin Peaks*?

14 Broderick Crawford appeared in which 1960s crime series?

15 Who played Jack Taylor in *Chiller*?

16 Judith Fitzgerald was a character in which crime series?

17 Which English actor was *The Girl from UNCLE*'s sidekick?

18 Who was the public defender in *NYPD Blue* before she married Andy Sipowics?

19 Whose novels were *Gideon's Way* based on?

20 What was above George Dixon's head outside the station?

21 Which 90s *EastEnders* star played Jake Barratt in *The Gentle Touch*?

22 Which detective did Anton Rodgers play in *Murder Most English*?

23 In which series did Pizza Man appear?

24 Which *Dragnet* actor appeared in *M*A*S*H*?

25 In Juliet Bravo, where was the police station?

26 Which western spoof did James Garner star in before he became investigator Jim Rockford?

27 Who played *Shoestring*'s boss?

28 In *Cat's Eyes*, who starred as Fred?

29 Who plays Charlie Scott in *ThiefTakers*?

30 What did *Matlock* do for a living?

---

1 Which Scottish side hit a record 132 Division One goals in 1957–58?
2 Which team had Manchester United played before the Munich crash?
3 After the 1952 FA Cup Final which Newcastle Utd skipper said, "Joe Mercer is the greatest player I have ever met"?
4 On February 22, 1956, Newcastle Utd visited which club for the first English League game to be played under floodlights?
5 Which Chelsea star finished as the League's top scorer in 1959?
6 Which Tranmere Rovers centre-half made a record 401 consecutive League appearances in the 1950s?
7 Which side narrowly failed to win the double in the 1951–52 season?
8 Which father and son duo played in the same Stockport County side?
9 Who beat England in a Group Two 1950 World Cup match in Belo Horizonte?
10 Who was affectionately known as "Big Ead" by the Arsenal fans?
11 Which French player finished as top scorer in the 1958 World Cup?
12 In 1958 which team were relegated for the first time in 68 years?
13 Who won their first trophy in 50 years when they beat Celtic 3–1 to claim the 1950 Scottish FA Cup?
14 Which Motherwell forward hit three goals in three minutes in 1959?
15 Who took over as England skipper from Billy Wright?
16 Which Division Two side were losing 5–1 to Huddersfield, but fought back to win 7–6 in 1957?
17 Who was manager of West Ham Utd's promotion winning side of 1958?
18 Bill Riding was boss of which team from 1951?
19 Which team was the Anderlecht captain referring to when he said, "Why don't they pick the whole side for England"?
20 What was remarkable about the Home International Championship of 1955–56?
21 Which Scotsman was Liverpool's leading goal scorer in the 1950s?
22 What was the first name of Williams, the England keeper against the US in 1950?
23 In which West Midlands town was Busby Babe Duncan Edwards born?
24 The Football League ordered which club not to enter the inaugural European Cup?
25 Which Middlesbrough striker won two England caps in 1959?
26 Name the Liverpool winger who scored 63 goals for the club 1953–64.
27 Which country inflicted England's heaviest ever defeat on them in 1954?
28 Which Preston player of the 1950s served in Montgomery's Eighth Army in Egypt in 1942?
29 Who captained England at three World Cup Finals in the 1950s?
30 Name the 1952 championship winner whose son followed him in the Man. Utd team.

---

1 Who won the 1973 Grammy for Best New Artist?

2 Who *got Weird* in 2015?

3 What was Bryan Adams's debut album called?

4 Who wrote "Blackberry Way"?

5 What colour was the MGM label in the 60s?

6 David Gest died in 2016. Who was his Pop Royalty wife, albeit briefly?

7 How is David Grundy better known?

8 Which group released an album titled *Outlandos d'Amour*?

9 Whose only UK top ten hit was "Tell Me When"?

10 Which song by the Coasters recommends "Calomine Lotion"?

11 Who starred as Ulysses S. Grant in *Hair* in Los Angeles in 1969?

12 Which singer, known only by her first name, has the surname Safka?

13 How were Berry and Torrence better known?

14 Which actress married Jean-Michel Jarre?

15 In which city was Paul Anka born?

16 Who backed Mitch Ryder?

17 Who wrote under the pseudonym of Bernard Webb?

18 Which record label did Charles Aznavour have his hit records on?

19 What was "Doc" Shuman's real first name?

20 Which group included the Batt brothers?

21 When did Simon Tong leave the Verve?

22 Which American singer was born Natalie Renee McIntyre in 1967?

23 Where is Elton John standing on the album cover of *A Single Man*?

24 What was Adam Faith's autobiography called?

25 Whose debut album was called *The Psychomodo*?

26 Why were the Nice banned from the Royal Albert Hall?

27 Who was Bubblerock on "(I Can't Get No) Satisfaction" in 1974?

28 What was Lord Rockingham XI's follow up to "Hoots Mon"?

29 How did Jim Croce die?

30 How is Cristopher Geppert better known?

Answers	**Football: The 1950s** *(see Quiz 5)*

1 Hearts. 2 Red Star Belgrade. 3 Joe Harvey. 4 Portsmouth. 5 Jimmy Greaves. 6 Harold "Bunny" Bell. 7 Arsenal. 8 Alec and David Herd. 9 USA. 10 Leslie Compton. 11 Just Fontaine. 12 Sunderland. 13 Hearts. 14 Ian St John. 15 Ronnie Clayton. 16 Charlton Athletic. 17 Ted Fenton. 18 Bolton Wanderers. 19 Manchester Utd. 20 It finished as a four-way tie. 21 Billy Liddell. 22 Bert. 23 Dudley. 24 Chelsea. 25 Brian Clough. 26 Alan A'Court. 27 Hungary (7–1). 28 Tom Finney. 29 Billy Wright. 30 John Aston Snr.

1 What was his middle name?
2 What was the occupation of his father?
3 On which ship was he serving in World War I when he injured his lip, giving him his characteristic tough look?
4 In which short did he make his screen debut?
5 Which reviewer described his acting as "what is usually and mercifully described as inadequate"?
6 How many feature films did he make between 1936 and 1940?
7 Who did he marry after Helen Menken?
8 For which character was he Oscar-nominated in *The Caine Mutiny*?
9 Which studio was he working for at the outbreak of World War II?
10 What was the name of the killer he played in *The Petrified Forest*?
11 Who collaborated with W. R. Burnett to write the hit *High Sierra*?
12 In which Errol Flynn western did he play a Mexican bandit?
13 Who turned down the Sam Spade role in *The Maltese Falcon*?
14 Who insisted he get the screen role in *The Petrified Forest* which he had played on Broadway?
15 In which movie did he play Fred C. Dobbs?
16 In which movie did he say, "I stick my neck out for nobody"?
17 Whose daughter is Philip Marlowe hired to protect in *The Big Sleep*?
18 *The Breaking Point* was a remake of which Bogart movie?
19 Which film starred Bogart in John Huston's directorial debut?
20 Which company did he form in 1947?
21 In which movie did he play Mad Dog Earle?
22 Which of his co-stars said, "There was no bunkum with Bogart"?
23 What was the name of the film released shortly before his death?
24 What role did Mrs Bogart play in *The Big Sleep*?
25 In which movie did he say, "I don't mind if you don't like my manners. I don't like them myself"?
26 How old was Bogart when he died?
27 Who was Bogart's leading lady in T*he Barefoot Contessa*?
28 In which movie does Bogart play a gang leader named Rocks Valentine?
29 In which 1947 film noir does Bogart star with Barbara Stanwyck and Alexis Smith?
30 In which film did he win his only Academy Award for Best Actor?

Answers	TV Pot Luck 1 *(see Quiz 8)*

1 Heartbeat. 2 Julie Walters. 3 Dermot Murnaghan. 4 Dunphy. 5 Eileen Downey. 6 Giedroyc & Perkins. 7 £175. 8 New Girl. 9 Desire. 10 1950's. 11 Oliver Sacks. 12 BBC2. 13 Eamonn Holmes. 14 Jess Yates. 15 Gardener's World. 16 Rebecca Stephens. 17 John Stapleton & Lynne Faulds Wood. 18 Barbara Edwards. 19 Steve Berry. 20 Armand & Michaela Denis. 21 Whoops Apocalypse. 22 Miriam Stoppard & Rob Buckman. 23 Topol. 24 Weatherman. 25 Changing Rooms. 26 Pritchett. 27 Eric Morley. 28 Joan. 29 Lulu. 30 The Golden Oldie Picture Show.

1 Ashfordly Police Station is the setting for which drama series?
2 In *Dinnerladies*, who played Petunia Gardeno?
3 Who investigates *The Big Story*?
4 What is Phil, Claire, Hailey, Alex and Luke's Family surname?
5 Who was the manager who caused a stir in the doc soap *Hotel*?
6 What are the surnames of Mel & Sue?
7 In 1957 how much did a colour TV cost?
8 Elizabeth Meriwether created which New US comedy?
9 Sophie Anderton hosted which fashion magazine show?
10 The results of which General Election were the first to be televised?
11 Who was *The Mind Traveller*?
12 Which was the first British channel transmitted exclusively on the 625 line system?
13 Who spoke the first words on GMTV?
14 Which TV presenter was Bob Geldof's father-in-law?
15 Which gardening programme developed from *Gardening Club* in 1968?
16 Which conqueror of Everest has presented *Tomorrow's World*?
17 Which husband and wife team have presented *Watchdog*?
18 Who was the first woman weather presenter on BBC TV?
19 Who is *Top Gear*'s primary motorbike correspondent?
20 Which husband and wife team went *On Safari*?
21 Alexei Sayle played the part of Commissar Solzhenitsyn in which 1982 series?
22 Which doctors hosted *Where There's Life*?
23 Which musical star played Berel Jastrow in *The Winds of War*?
24 What was Francis William's role on *Breakfast Time*?
25 On which show do Anna Ryder Richardson, Graham Wynn and Carol Smillie appear?
26 Jay, Gloria, Manny and Joe. What is their Family surname?
27 Who organized the annual *Miss World* event?
28 In *Coronation Street* what was Annie Walker's daughter's name?
29 Who was the female in *Three of a Kind* when Mike Yarwood was one of the three?
30 What was the film programme presented by Dave Lee Travis?

Answers | Movies: Humphrey Bogart *(see Quiz 7)*

1 DeForest. 2 Surgeon. 3 Leviathan. 4 Broadway's Like That. 5 Alexander Woollcott. 6 28. 7 Mary Philips. 8 Captain Queeg. 9 Warner Brothers. 10 Duke Mantee. 11 John Huston. 12 Virginia City. 13 George Raft. 14 Leslie Howard. 15 The Treasure of the Sierra Madre. 16 Casablanca. 17 General Sternwood (Charles Waldron). 18 To Have And Have Not. 19 The Maltese Falcon. 20 Santana Pictures. 21 High Sierra. 22 Katharine Hepburn. 23 The Harder They Fall. 24 Vivian Sherwood Rutledge. 25 The Big Sleep. 26 57. 27 Ava Gardner. 28 The Amazing Dr Clitterhouse. 29 The Two Mrs Carrolls. 30 The African Queen.

1 Allan Clarke became the first £150,000 man when he moved to Leicester City from which club?
2 Which player was involved the only time that the British transfer ceiling has been doubled in one move?
3 In the first £5,000 transfer Syd Puddefoot moved to which Scottish club?
4 Alberto Tarantini came from Argentina to which British club?
5 Kevin Moran left Manchester Utd in 1988 for which club?
6 Who was the first player to move for £20,000?
7 Who were Nottingham Forest's main rivals for the signature of Birmingham City's Trevor Francis?
8 Trevor Francis was Britain's most expensive player until who moved?
9 How old was Charles Buchan when he went to Arsenal?
10 Who was the £1 million pound player to leave Norwich City?
11 Ayr's record fee received was £300,000 in 1981 when which player moved to Liverpool?
12 Hughie Gallacher joined Newcastle Utd from which club?
13 Who became the first British player to move in a £500,000 transfer?
14 Who played for Leeds Utd in the first leg of a Fairs Cup Final but was transferred before the second?
15 Where did Charlie George go when he left Arsenal?
16 Partick Thistle's record fee received was £200,000 in 1981 when which player moved to Watford?
17 Arriving in 1972 from Nottingham Forest, who was Manchester Utd's first ever £200,000 signing?
18 Who was Norwich City manager when Chris Sutton left for £5 million?
19 What was the last French club that Eric Cantona played for?
20 Where did Danny Wallace go when he left Manchester Utd?
21 Who went from Ajax to Inter Milan to Arsenal to West Brom to Portsmouth?
22 In 2016, Gonzalo Higuaín cost Juventus how much?
23 Which Frenchman played in the French, English, Spanish and Turkish capitals?
24 Which Steve had two spells at both Liverpool and Aston Villa?
25 Including loan deals for how many clubs did Andy Cole play 1989–2008?
26 Who in 2001 set the world record fee for a transfer of £46 million?
27 Name the player who joined Lazio from Valencia in 2001 for £29 million.
28 Who cost a British record transfer fee of £18m in the summer of 2000?
29 In 2016, Paul Pogba cost Man Utd how much?
30 Which Parma player cost SS Lazio a world transfer record £35m in 2000?

Answers | **Pop Pot Luck 3** *(see Quiz 10)*

1 Suzie Rutollo. 2 The Playboys. 3 Joni Mitchell's. 4 Love to Love You Baby. 5 The New Musical Express. 6 Little Earthquakes. 7 "Portrait of My Love". 8 Jimi Hendrix. 9 Glen Matlock. 10 Herman's Hermits. 11 Warrington. 12 Delaney and Bonnie. 13 "Nel Blu Dipinto Di Blu" (Volare). 14 Moonlighting. 15 Flute. 16 Melle Mel and the Furious Five. 17 Carole King, Don McLean. 18 Cyndi Lauper. 19 Gibraltar. 20 Tears for Fears. 21 Nick Baines. 22 Seal. 23 John Entwistle. 24 The Carpenters. 25 Alice Cooper. 26 Sri Lanka. 27 A pool table. 28 Johnny Ray. 29 "Nikita". 30 Bernard Bresslaw.

1 Who is Bob Dylan arm in arm with on the cover of *The Freewheelin' Bob Dylan*?

2 Who backed Gary Lewis?

3 At whose party did Rod Stewart meet Britt Ekland?

4 On what single and album did Marc Almond join Bronski Beat?

5 Which music paper published Britain's first-ever record chart?

6 What was Tori Amos's debut album called?

7 What was Matt Monro's first UK hit?

8 Which guitarist formed a group called the Band of Gypsies?

9 Who did Sid Vicious replace in the Sex Pistols in 1977?

10 Which group included Derek Leckenby and Keith Hopwood?

11 In which town was Rick Astley born?

12 How are the Bramlett family duo better known?

13 Which song won the first Grammy Record of the Year in 1958?

14 Which TV show did Al Jarreau's "Since I Fell for You" feature in?

15 Which musical instrument did Jethro Tull's Ian Anderson play?

16 Who complete Grandmaster Flash's group?

17 Which two artists have recorded albums called *Tapestry*?

18 Who left home to hitch-hike through Canada with her dog Sparkle?

19 Where did John Lennon marry Yoko Ono?

20 Which group previously called themselves History of Headaches?

21 Which member of Kaizer Chiefs has the nickname "Peanut"?

22 Who released the 2007 album *System*?

23 Who drew the album cover for *The Who by Numbers*?

24 Who won a Grammy in 1970 for Best New Artist?

25 Whose pet boa constrictor died in 1977, stopping his plans for his first tour in two years?

26 Where was Duran Duran's video for "Hungry Like the Wolf" shot?

27 What is on the cover of Huey Lewis and the News' *Sports* album?

28 Which 1950s pop star used to wear a hearing aid?

29 Which 1985 song won an Ivor Novello award for Elton John and Bernie Taupin?

30 Who was at No. 6 in 1958 with "Mad Passionate Love"?

Answers	**Football: Transfer Trail** *(see Quiz 9)*

1 Fulham. 2 Trevor Francis. 3 Falkirk. 4 Birmingham City. 5 Sporting Gijon. 6 Tommy Lawton. 7 Coventry City. 8 Steve Daley. 9 33. 10 Kevin Reeves. 11 Steve Nicol. 12 Airdrie. 13 David Mills. 14 Jimmy Greenhoff. 15 Derby County. 16 Mo Johnston. 17 Ian Storey Moore. 18 John Deehan. 19 Nimes. 20 Birmingham City. 21 Nwankwo Kanu. 22 £75.3 million.. 23 Nicolas Anelka. 24 Staunton. 25 12. 26 Zinedine Zidane. 27 Gaizka Mendieta. 28 Rio Ferdinand. 29 £92.25 million. 30 Herman Crespo.

1 Which actor was known professionally for a time as Ariztid Olt?

2 What is the name of the island that *The Wicker Man* is set upon?

3 Who played Sam in *The Lost Boys*?

4 What is Peter Vincent's occupation in *Fright Night*?

5 Where does Mitch live in *The Birds*?

6 What was the name of the 1959 sequel to *The Fly*?

7 Where is the action set in 50s classic *The Thing*?

8 Which actor was originally chosen to play Bela Lugosi's role in the 1931 film *Dracula*?

9 Where does Mia Farrow live in *Rosemary's Baby*?

10 Who directed *Night of the Living Dead*?

11 What is the father's occupation in *Poltergeist*?

12 Who directed *A Nightmare on Elm Street 5: The Dream Child*?

13 How is Jason brought back to life in *Friday the Thirteenth Part VI – Jason Lives*?

14 Who receives Gizmo as a gift in *Gremlins*?

15 Which low-budget horror movie did Oliver Stone direct in 1974?

16 Which star of *The Exorcist* is also known by the name Edna Rae?

17 Who starred in *The Final Terror* with then flat-mate Rachel Ward?

18 Who wrote the score for *Jaws*?

19 Within fifteen minutes, how long does *Scream* last?

20 On which day in America did *Bram Stoker's Dracula* open?

21 Who or what plays Thing in *The Addams Family*?

22 What is unusual about Christopher Lee's role in *Dracula – Prince of Darkness*?

23 What creatures were the stars of *Them!*?

24 Who made *The Damned* for Hammer?

25 Who directed *Interview with the Vampire: The Vampire Chronicles*?

26 Who played the vengeful Dr Anton Phibes in two movies?

27 How many Freddy Kruger "Nightmare" movies were there before *Freddy vs. Jason*?

28 James Wan directs Patrick Wilson in which 2016 sequel?

29 Who in the 1920s became the first American horror movie star?

30 Name the film studio which produced *Dracula* (1931) and *The Mummy* (1932).

---

1 Jeff Stewart played which long-time constable in *The Bill*?
2 What is the surname of unrelated stand-up comedians Alan and Jimmy?
3 What was the hit record in 1956 recorded by Eamonn Andrews?
4 Which JB was allegedly called "The Thinking Man's Crumpet"?
5 Who co-presented *Notes and Queries* With Clive Anderson?
6 Who should have been *This is Your Life's* first victim, but he found out?
7 Which award did *That's Life* bestow on shoddy goods?
8 Which afternoon series was presented by Mrs Leigh Lawson?
9 On which television programme did Victoria Wood make her debut?
10 What dance series was presented by Wayne Sleep?
11 Which song did Marti Webb record to help a child shown on *That's Life* with liver disease?
12 Which two companies merged to create Thames TV?
13 Amy Schumer's comedy show, from 2013, was called what?
14 Which former Butlin's redcoat was born Michael Parker?
15 Which programme was presented by Peter McCann and Kate Bellingham?
16 Who kept the scores on *Bullseye*?
17 Who played Laura la Plaz, a trick shot artiste, in *Dad's Army*?
18 Who did Renee Bradshaw marry in *Coronation Street*?
19 Which Australian was "Late" and is now *On TV*?
20 Which variety show was hosted by Kenneth Williams?
21 In which year did *EastEnders* begin on British television?
22 Which satirist and broadcaster was co-founder of *TV-AM*?
23 Which former Ambassador to Washington presented *A Week in Politics*?
24 What did Teletext Ltd replace in 1993?
25 What was the name of the clothes shop that Emily Nugent ran in *Coronation Street*?
26 Where was Ricardo Montalban the host?
27 Which crime-solving show presenter hosted the quiz show *Dotto* in the 50s?
28 In 1979, who performed St Mark's Gospel on TV?
29 Which former presenter of *World in Action* was made a lord in 1998?
30 Which actor links *M*A*S*H* to *House Calls*?

Answers	Movies: Horror *(see Quiz 11)*

1 Bela Lugosi. **2** Summer Isle. **3** Corey Haim. **4** TV horror film host. **5** Bodega Bay. **6** Return of the Fly. **7** The Arctic. **8** Lon Chaney. **9** Manhattan. **10** George A. Romero. **11** Property developer. **12** Stephen Hopkins. **13** His body is struck by lightning. **14** Billy. **15** Seizure. **16** Ellen Burstyn. **17** Daryl Hannah. **18** John Williams. **19** 110 minutes. **20** Friday the 13th. **21** The right hand of Christopher Hart. **22** He did not speak. **23** Ants. **24** Joseph Losey. **25** Neil Jordan. **26** Vincent Price. **27** Seven. **28** The Conjuring 2. **29** Lon Chaney. **30** Universal Pictures Co. Inc.

1 How many goals did Stanley Matthews score for England?
2 Bobby Charlton's first international goal was against which country?
3 Which player was outjumped by Pele before Banks made his save in Mexico 1970?
4 Which Brighton forward came on as a substitute for eight minutes in his only England appearance?
5 How many internationals did Jimmy Greaves play after the 1966 World Cup?
6 Who was the first player to score 30 goals for England?
7 Gary Lineker missed a penalty against which team in 1992?
8 To two each way, how many caps did Glenn Hoddle win?
9 In how many games was Bobby Moore skipper of England?
10 Rodney Marsh was capped while playing for which two clubs?
11 Who scored for both sides in the friendly v Holland in 1988?
12 How many games did Billy Wright miss between his first and last appearance for England?
13 Who was capped for England while playing for Werder Bremen in 1980?
14 Kenny Sansom played his last England game in which tournament?
15 Who, in a 1962 World Cup match, picked up a dog which urinated on him?
16 To five each way, how many minutes was Kevin Hector on the field for his two England appearances?
17 How many caps did Gordon Banks win?
18 Timed at 17 seconds in 1947, who scored England's fastest goal?
19 In what year did Peter Shilton first play for England?
20 Who is the first striker whose career lasted at least six games but never scored for England?
21 Who was the last player to be sent off while Sven-Goran Eriksson was manager?
22 Who is the only England player to score in three consecutive World Cup finals?
23 What was Michael Owen's number at France 98?
24 Who, at 31, was the old man of England's World Cup 2006 squad?
25 Who scored the last England goal while Steve McClaren was coach?
26 Who scored on his debut against Andorra on 28 March 2007?
27 Whose own goal gave England a 1–0 win over Paraguay in 2006?
28 Which country did England meet for only the third time in 2007?
29 What was the plane called which flew the England team to the 2006 World Cup?
30 Daniel Sturridge. Is his middle name Andre or Andrew?

Answers | **Pop Pot Luck 4** *(see Quiz 14)*

1 Innervisions. 2 The Tremeloes. 3 The Spectres. 4 Denny Laine. 5 Bruce Springsteen. 6 T. Rex. 7 Not Satisfied. 8 Cyndi Lauper. 9 Mike Oldfield. 10 Absolute Beginners. 11 Iraq. 12 Ella Fitzgerald. 13 The Temptations. 14 Phil Lynott. 15 Jim Capaldi. 16 JFK Stadium, Philadelphia. 17 Jessie Glynne. 18 Loving You. 19 Cher. 20 The Turtles. 21 Grimes. 22 Sheryl Crow. 23 A cigarette. 24 "Wings of a Dove". 25 View to a Kill. 26 Paul Simon. 27 "Woman in Love". 28 Wild. 29 "Blackberry Way". 30 "The Shadow of Your Smile".

1 Which Stevie Wonder LP won a 1973 Grammy for Album of the Year?

2 Who had a million-seller in 1967 with "Here Comes My Baby"?

3 What were Status Quo originally called prior to 1968?

4 Which other musical personality, apart from Paul and Linda McCartney, is on the cover of the *Band on the Run* album?

5 Who married Julianne Phillips in Oregon in May 1985?

6 Who had hit albums called *The Slider* and *Futuristic Dragon*?

7 What was Aswad's debut album called?

8 Who beat Madonna to take the 1985 Best New Artist Grammy award?

9 Who recorded under the name Sallyangie?

10 What soundtrack album from 1986 showed a black-and-white photo of David Bowie?

11 Other than the USA, in which country was Joan Baez brought up?

12 Who won four out of the first five Grammy awards for Best Pop Female Vocal Performance?

13 Who were originally known as the Elgins?

14 Whose book of poems was called *Songs for While I'm Away*?

15 Who was drummer/vocalist with Traffic?

16 Where did the US part of the Live Aid concert take place?

17 *I Cry When I laugh* was a 2015 pop album by which artist?

18 In which film did Elvis play the role of Deke Rivers?

19 Who said, "The trouble with some women is they get all excited about nothing – then they marry him"?

20 Howard Kaylan was lead vocalist with which group?

21 *Art Angels* was a 2015 pop album by which artist?

22 Who released the 2005 album *Wildflower*?

23 What is Paul McCartney holding in his right hand on the cover of *Abbey Road*?

24 Which Madness video featured a van dropping out of a plane?

25 Which James Bond theme did Duran Duran sing?

26 Who was singing "If you'll be my bodyguard" in 1986?

27 What song title was a No. 1 hit for Frankie Laine and Barbra Streisand?

28 What word begins song titles that end with "Cherry" and "Horses"?

29 What was the Move's only No. 1?

30 Which song won the Oscar for the 1965 film *The Sandpiper*?

Answers | Football: Three Lions *(see Quiz 13)*

1 11. 2 Scotland. 3 Alan Mullery. 4 Peter Ward. 5 3. 6 Tom Finney. 7 Brazil.
8 53. 9 90. 10 QPR & Manchester City. 11 Tony Adams. 12 3. 13 Dave Watson.
14 European Championship 1988. 15 Jimmy Greaves. 16 18 minutes. 17 73. 18
Tommy Lawton. 19 1970. 20 Tony Cottee. 21 Wayne Rooney. 22 David Beckham.
23 20. 24 Sol Campbell. 25 Peter Crouch. 26 David Nugent. 27 Carlos Gamarra.
28 Israel. 29 Pride of the Nation. 30 Andre.

1 Which movie was advertised as "Garbo laughs"?
2 What was Johnny Weissmuller's first Tarzan movie called?
3 Which Russian-born choreographer worked on *The Goldwyn Follies*?
4 Who famously had a grapefruit squashed in her face by Cagney in *Public Enemy*?
5 In which movie did Marlene Dietrich sing "See What the Boys in the Back Room Will Have"?
6 Who played Catherine the Great in *The Scarlet Empress*?
7 In which movie did Claudette Colbert say, "The moment I saw you, I had an idea you had an idea"?
8 In which movie did Errol Flynn make his screen debut?
9 *The Country Doctor* was a movie about whose birth?
10 Which actress who appeared in *Anna Christie* wrote an autobiography called *The Life Story of an Ugly Duckling*?
11 Who played Sherlock Holmes in *The Sleeping Cardinal*?
12 Who was Janet Gaynor's most frequent partner of the 20s and 30s?
13 What was advertised as "Garbo talks"?
14 If Leslie Howard is Professor Higgins, who is Eliza Doolittle?
15 In which of his own movies did King Vidor appear in 1934?
16 Which husband and wife were Oscar-nominated together in 1931?
17 Which movie had the ad line, "He treated her rough and she loved it"?
18 Who played David Garrick to Anna Neagle's Peg Woffington in *Peg of Old Drury Lane* in 1935?
19 What was the first of Spencer Tracy's three Oscar nominations between 1936 and 1938?
20 Who played the title role in *Rembrandt* in 1936?
21 Which brother of Harold Lloyd was injured making *Scarface* in 1932?
22 Who played Captain Ahab in *Moby Dick*?
23 What were Mae West's two hits of 1933?
24 What did Miscah Auer impersonate in *My Man Godfrey*?
25 By what name did John Carradine star in movies between 1930 and 1935?
26 What was Virginia Cherrill's role in *City Lights*?
27 Who directed *Mr Smith Goes to Washington*?
28 Who made her screen debut in *The Sin of Madelon Claudet* and won an Oscar?
29 Which trio made the first of their 190 slapstick comedies in the 1930s?
30 Who won two Best Actors for his roles in *Captain Courageous* and *Boys Town*?

1 With what weapon did Chrissie kill Den Watts in *EastEnders*?
2 In the children's TV series, *My* what sea creature *Is Evil*?
3 What was Tony Palmer's series on pop music called?
4 *Hollyoaks Later* began in 2008. But when did it stop?
5 Who was the chairman of *My Music*?
6 What was the Anglian series on Victoriana?
7 What was Clement's cookery series called?
8 Which entertainer had a "Magic Box"?
9 Which *Coronation Street* star starred in the sitcom *Girls About Town*?
10 Who presented *Toolbox*?
11 Which soap actress presented *Songs That Matter*?
12 In which series did Roy from *EastEnders* appear with Diana Dors?
13 Which character's father did Rock Hudson play in *Dynasty*?
14 In which comedy series revival did Gillian Taylforth appear before *EastEnders*?
15 Who played Kelly in *Charlie's Angels*?
16 Whose role was Corkie in *Sykes*?
17 Max Bygraves, Bob Monkhouse and Les Dennis all hosted which game show?
18 Which character's middle name was Lolanthe?
19 Who played the widow next door in *The Bounder*?
20 Which company in Japan established the VHS video format?
21 Which family appeared in the fly-on-the-wall *Sylvania Waters*?
22 On which game show did Bruce Forsyth succeed Leslie Crowther?
23 Who hosted Searchline on *Surprise Surprise* for five years?
24 Which SF character has the first name Geordi?
25 What is Moe's occupation in *The Simpsons*?
26 What are the real names of the stars of *Chucklevision*?
27 Was Timothy West in *Bread*?
28 What was the name of Chandler's annoying roommate in *Friends*?
29 Who had to look on *The Bright Side*?
30 Which series featured the ex-agent McGill?

Answers	Movies: The 1930s *(see Quiz 15)*

1 Ninotchka. 2 Tarzan the Ape Man. 3 George Balanchine. 4 Mae Clarke. 5 Destry Rides Again. 6 Marlene Dietrich. 7 Midnight. 8 In the Wake of the Bounty. 9 The Dionne Quins. 10 Marie Dressler. 11 Arthur Wortner. 12 Charles Farrell. 13 Anna Christie. 14 Wendy Hiller. 15 Our Daily Bread. 16 Alfred Lunt & Lynne Fontaine. 17 Red Dust. 18 Cedric Hardwicke. 19 San Francisco. 20 Charles Laughton. 21 Gaylord. 22 John Barrymore. 23 She Done Him Wrong, I'm No Angel. 24 Gorilla. 25 John Peter Richmond. 26 A blind girl. 27 Frank Capra. 28 Helen Hayes. 29 The Three Stooges. 30 Spencer Tracy.

1 Michael Phelps won his ____ and ____ Olympic gold medal in Rio 2016.
2 Who won Great Britain's first medal of the Atlanta Games?
3 Who last won the 100m gold for Canada before Donovan Bailey?
4 In which sport did Andre Agassi's dad Mike compete in 1948 and 1952?
5 In which event did Great Britain's Henry Taylor land eight golds?
6 Women's 200-meter freestyle swimmer _____ won her first gold medal at Rio 2016.
7 Who won silver when Tessa Sanderson won gold in the javelin?
8 Which was the first city to host the Summer Olympics twice?
9 In which event did Michelle Smith win bronze in 1996?
10 What did Paavo Nurmi always carry with him during his gold-medal-winning races?
11 Who won the 400m hurdles gold sandwiched between Ed Moses's two triumphs?
12 Which country did 70s star Lasse Virren come from?
13 Who wore a T shirt saying "Thank You America for a Wonderful Games"?
14 Why was Finn Volmari Iso-Hollo's 1932 steeplechase win exceptional?
15 How many gold medals did Great Britain win in 1996?
16 In 1956 Australia hosted the games except for equestrian events, which were held in which country?
17 In which event did an individual first won four successive golds?
18 At which venue did Steve Redgrave first win gold?
19 Britain and which other country have won gold in every Summer Games?
20 In what year did baseball become a medal sport?
21 Which is double swimming gold medallist Rebecca Adlington's home town?
22 On which day was London awarded the 2012 Olympic Games?
23 Which Jason swam the last leg of Michael Phelps's two gold-medal relay events at Beijing?
24 Which cyclist won Britain's first gold medal at Beijing?
25 At what weight did James DeGale win his boxing gold medal at Beijing?
26 What was the national stadium in Beijing popularly called?
27 Which Olympian was named BBC Sports Personality of the Year in 2008?
28 Where was double gold medallist Rebecca Adlington born?
29 Which Olympian appeared nude on her bicycle for the cover of the *Observer* Sport magazine?
30 How many gold medals did Michael Phelps win at the Beijing Olympics?

Answers | **Football Pot Luck 1** *(see Quiz 18)*

1 Lennie Lawrence. 2 David Harvey. 3 Peter. 4 Burnley. 5 1930s. 6 Patrick Berger. 7 Crystal Palace. 8 Joe Parkinson. 9 Arsenal. 10 2. 11 Aston Villa. 12 Appleton. 13 Everton. 14 Entered the first FA Cup competition. 15 Sheffield Wednesday. 16 Belgium. 17 York City. 18 Wigan Athletic. 19 England. 20 13. 21 75,415. 22 Estonia. 23 RSC Anderlecht. 24 Clyde. 25 1890s. 26 Brentford. 27 Stockport. 28 Danny McGrain. 29 Watford. 30 13.

Quiz 18 | Football Pot Luck 1

Answers – page 419

LEVEL 3

1 Who played for Croydon, Carshalton Athletic and Sutton and became a Premier League manager?
2 Who was in goal when Leeds Utd won the FA Cup in the 1970s?
3 What is Jimmy Greaves's middle name?
4 At which club did Lee Dixon make his League debut?
5 In what decade did Arsenal first win the championship?
6 Who scored for the Czech Republic in the final of Euro 96?
7 Alan Mullery followed Steve Kember as manager of which club?
8 Who moved from Bournemouth to Everton in 1994 to set a club record for a transfer fee received?
9 Which club was once known as Dial Square?
10 To one each way, how many international goals did Viv Anderson score?
11 Kevin Gage and Steve Sims were in the same team at which club?
12 Which Colin became boss of Hull City in 1989?
13 John Bailey first played in an FA Cup Final for which team?
14 What is the historic link between Harrow Chequers, Hitchin Town and Reigate Priory?
15 On the day of the 1995 FA Cup Final which Premiership club announced that their manager was leaving?
16 Which European team did World Cup newcomers Saudi Arabia beat in the first round of Euro 96?
17 Which club used to play at Fullfordgate?
18 Kevin Langley set a League appearance record at which club?
19 Which country did Mike O'Grady play for?
20 How many years was Bruce Grobbelaar at Liverpool?
21 Highest stadium capacity during the 2015–16 Premier League season. Guess the figure.
22 In which country would you watch FC Levadia take on Narva JK Trans?
23 Who lost to Arsenal in the 1970 UEFA Cup Final?
24 At which club did Pat Nevin make his Scottish League debut?
25 In what decade did Sunderland first win the championship?
26 Which club had a fanzine called *Beesotted*?
27 Danny Bergara followed Asa Hartford as manager of which club?
28 Which Celtic player fractured his skull against Falkirk in 1972?
29 Which club was once known as West Herts?
30 To two each way, how many international goals did Martin Chivers score?

Answers | The Olympics *(see Quiz 17)*

1 20 and 21. 2 Paul Palmer. 3 Percy Williams. 4 Boxing. 5 Swimming. 6 Katie Ledecky. 7 Tiina Lillak. 8 Paris. 9 200m butterfly. 10 Stopwatch. 11 Volker Beck. 12 Finland. 13 Daley Thompson. 14 He ran an extra lap by mistake. 15 One. 16 Sweden. 17 Discus. 18 Los Angeles. 19 France. 20 1992. 21 Mansfield. 22 6 July 2005 23 Lezak 24 Nicole Cooke. 25 Middleweight. 26 The Bird's Nest. 27 Chris Hoy. 28 Mansfield. 29 Victoria Pendleton. 30 Eight.

1 Where was Emile Ford born?
2 Which chart-topper appeared on BBC TV's *Drumbeat*?
3 Who had a 50s No. 1 with "Here Comes Summer"?
4 Who played the piano on Bobby Darin's "Dream Lover"?
5 How was Terence Perkins better known?
6 What was Marty Wilde's highest chart hit?
7 Which female singer starred in *It's Trad Dad*?
8 What was Cliff Richard's middle name when he was Harry Webb?
9 Who was the first solo instrumentalist to have consecutive No. 1 hits?
10 Which female had four top ten hits in 1952?
11 Who sang the English version of "Le Jour Ou La Pluie Viendra"?
12 Who was the resident band on "Oh Boy"?
13 Who had the 50s hit with "It's All in the Game"?
14 Which brothers replaced which brothers at No. 1 in 1958?
15 Which Cherokee Indian was in the charts in 1958?
16 Which 1950s artist had a TV show *Relax with Mike*?
17 Who was the first British female singer to have a No. 1 in the 50s and what was it called?
18 What was Conway Twitty's real name?
19 How many records made up the charts in 1952 and 1953?
20 Which song was recorded by Al Hibbler, Les Baxter, Liberace and Jimmy Young?
21 By what name did Fats Domino impressionist Ernest Evans become famous?
22 "On the Street Where You Live" was the only No. 1 for which American singer?
23 How old was Frankie Lymon when he asked "Why Do Fools Fall in Love"?
24 How many UK No. 1s did Elvis Presley have in the 1950s?
25 Which Welsh-born singer first topped the charts with "As I Love You"?
26 Which US tenor was "Outside of Heaven" for his first UK No. 1 in 1953?
27 Which American state did Ernie Ford place befoe his name?
28 What "Alphabet" did Dickie Valentine to take to the No. 1 slot in December 1953?
29 Name the US movie idol who had a UK No. 1 hit with "Young Love" in 1957.
30 Who enjoyed his second and last UK No. 1 with "Mack the Knife" in 1959?

Answers	Movies Pot Luck 1 *(see Quiz 20)*

1 Room 1. 2 Psychologist. 3 Eddie Murphy. 4 Robert Benton. 5 Hearn. 6 135 minutes. 7 Harry Stamper. 8 1892. 9 Robert Duvall. 10 Clint Eastwood. 11 Red. 12 75. 13 George Axelrod. 14 Two Lane Blacktop. 15 Tom Hardy. 16 King Kong. 17 Wright. 18 Jill St John. 19 98 mins. 20 The Misfits. 21 Emil Jannings. 22 Tom Selleck. 23 Mike Nichols. 24 Seven. 25 Biehn. 26 Wellington (NZ). 27 Ford. 28 John Huston. 29 Steve Guttenberg. 30 Two hours.

1 What room number does Norman Bates put Janet Leigh in?

2 What is the profession of Nicole Kidman's father?

3 Which movie star released an album called *Love's Alright* in 1993?

4 Who won the Best Director Oscar for *Kramer versus Kramer*?

5 Which Ann featured in *The Accused*?

6 Within five minutes, how long does *Zulu* last?

7 What was the name of Bruce Willis's character in *Armageddon*?

8 In what year did Tom Cruise and Nicole Kidman supposedly land in Oklahoma in the film *Far and Away*?

9 Which actor links *The Paper* and *The Scarlet Letter*?

10 Who said, "Universal signed me as a contract player – which is a little lower than working in the mail room"?

11 What colour scarf is Scrooge given in *The Muppets' Christmas Carol*?

12 How old was David Lean when he made *A Passage to India*?

13 Who wrote the screenplay for *The Seven Year Itch* with Billy Wilder?

14 Which 1971 film did pop star James Taylor star in?

15 Who played Max in 2015's *Mad Max* Furious reboot?

16 Which movie gave Carlo Rambaldi a Special Award in 1976 for visual effects?

17 Which Amy featured in *The Accidental Tourist*?

18 Who played the Bond girl in *Diamonds are Forever*?

19 Within ten minutes, how long does the 1970s version of *Carrie* last?

20 In which movie did Clark Gable play Gay Langland?

21 Who won the Best Actor Oscar for *The Way of All Flesh*?

22 Who was originally set to play Indiana Jones before Harrison Ford?

23 Who directed *Wolf*?

24 How many *Road* films did Crosby, Hope and Lamour make?

25 Which Michael starred in *The Abyss*?

26 In which city was Russell Crowe born?

27 Which Glenn died, aged 90, in August 2006?

28 Who said, "I never killed an actor. Nearly lost a few"?

29 Which actor starred in *High Spirits* and *Diner*?

30 To the nearest hour, how long does *LA Confidential* last?

1 Which "English musical theatre boy band" won the eighth series of *Britain's Got Talent* in 2014?

2 Who replaced Sharon Osbourne as a judge on *X-Factor* in 2008?

3 Who was the entertainment committee chairman at *The Wheeltappers and Shunters Social Club*?

4 What was Clannad's first TV theme hit?

5 Who sang *Nappy Love*?

6 On which show did the Rolling Stones make their national TV debut?

7 Which TV group sang the song *OK*?

8 With which all-female group did *Hi-De-Hi!*'s Su Pollard start her entertainment career?

9 Who sang the theme song of the comedy *Going Straight*?

10 Jackie Lee sang the theme tune for which children's favourite?

11 *The Maigret Theme* brought success for which band leader?

12 Which duo were the stars of the musical drama *Ain't Misbehavin'*?

13 The BBC record charts are compiled by who?

14 In *Tutti Frutti*, who was bass player with The Majestics?

15 On which show did pianist Bobby Crush make his TV debut?

16 *Thank You for being a Friend* was whose theme?

17 Who was the choreographer of Pan's People?

18 How were the singing brothers Tony, Mike and Denis better known?

19 Who accompanied Lesley Garret in a memorable "Three Little Maids from School" in her 1998 TV show?

20 Who sang the *Auf Wiedersehen Pet* theme song?

21 What was the name of the Salvation Army group which regularly sang on TV?

22 Which record producer changed his name from Michael Haues?

23 Why was the Byrds song *Eight Miles High* banned by BBC TV?

24 Which soap theme was composed by Eric Spear?

25 Why did *Rock Follies'* Charlotte Cornwell sue the *Sunday People*?

26 The series *Off The Record* concerned what?

27 Which type of instruments did Bruno play in *Fame*?

28 What type of music was played on *Honky Tonk Heroes*?

29 Name the *Opportunity Knocks* winner who went on to star in *Gypsy*.

30 What was the name of the 60's heavy rock programme broadcast on BBC1?

Answers | **Football Pot Luck 2** *(see Quiz 22)*

1 West Ham Utd. 2 Everton. 3 Wycombe Wanderers. 4 Wallace. 5 Luton Town. 6 Hereford Utd. 7 Chewing Gum (Dentyne). 8 Tow Law Town. 9 Partick Thistle. 10 Ambrose. 11 Manchester Utd. 12 13,851,698. 13 Manchester City. 14 Leeds Utd. 15 1950s. 16 Everton. 17 Nottingham Forest. 18 Steve Sedgley. 19 Bristol City. 20 10. 21 CFR Cluj. 22 Billy Davies. 23 Coventry City. 24 Liverpool. 25 Hull City. 26 David & Ian. 27 Oldham Athletic. 28 John Bond & Ken Brown. 29 Leeds Utd. 30 Real Madrid.

Quiz 22 | Football Pot Luck 2 | Answers – page 423

1 At which club did Jimmy Greaves finish his League career?
2 In June 1994 Swedish player Martin Dahlin turned down a transfer to which English club?
3 Which club used to play at Loakes Park?
4 Which Danny played his only England game in 1986 against Egypt?
5 Before meeting up at West Ham Utd, where had Tim Breaker and Les Sealey been in the same side?
6 What was the first club that John Sillett managed?
7 What type of product was advertised on Southampton's open top bus as it paraded the FA Cup in the 70s?
8 Which non-League side did Chris Waddle use to play for?
9 Alan Rough set a League appearance record at which club?
10 What was Billy Wright's middle name?
11 Mal Donaghy and Mark Robins were in the same team at which club?
12 In millions, what was the overall fan attendance during the 2015–16 Premier League season?
13 Ray Ranson first played in an FA Cup Final for which team?
14 At which club did Terry Phelan make his League debut?
15 In what decade did Aberdeen first win the championship?
16 Which club had a fanzine called *When Skies are Grey*?
17 Dave Mackay followed Matt Gillies as manager of which club?
18 Who was bought by Ipswich Town in 1994 at a club record fee?
19 Which club was once known as Bristol South End?
20 To two each way, how many international goals did Billy Bingham score?
21 Which club was 2007–08 League champions in Romania?
22 Who was Derby manager when they went into the Premiership in 2007?
23 With 171 goals Clarrie Bourton became all-time top League scorer at which club?
24 Hodgson and Neal scored Euro goals in the same game for which club?
25 Which club did Raich Carter and Don Revie play for in the 1950s?
26 What are the first names of the soccer-playing Brightwell brothers?
27 Stuart Barlow, Earle Barrett and Frank Bunn played for which League Cup finalists?
28 Which two ex-West Ham Utd players have managed Norwich City in the post-war period?
29 With which team did John Lukic make his League debut?
30 Who lost 5–3 to Benfica in the final of the 1962 European Cup?

Answers	TV: Music & Variety 1 *(see Quiz 21)*

1 Collabro. 2 Cheryl Cole. 3 Colin Crompton. 4 Harry's Game. 5 The Goodies. 6 Thank Your Lucky Stars. 7 The Little Ladies. 8 Midnight News. 9 Ronnie Barker. 10 Rupert Bear. 11 Joe Loss. 12 Robson Green & Jerome Flynn. 13 Gallup. 14 Fud O'Donnell. 15 Opportunity Knocks. 16 The Golden Girls. 17 Flick Colby. 18 The King Brothers. 19 Patricia Hodge & Lily Savage. 20 Joe Fagin. 21 Joy Strings. 22 Mickie Most. 23 It was thought to be about drugs. 24 Coronation Street's. 25 The paper accused her of having a big bottom. 26 The recording industry. 27 Keyboards. 28 Country & Western. 29 Bonnie Langford. 30 Colour Me Pop.

1 Who had a 1961 album called *21 Today*?
2 Which major world event took place when Gerry and the Pacemakers were at No. 1 with "You'll Never Walk Alone"?
3 Which was the most successful Mersey group not managed by Brian Epstein?
4 Whose 1969 album was called *Goodbye*?
5 What did the J. stand for in Billy J. Kramer's name?
6 Which film did the Dave Clark Five make?
7 Who were originally called the Harmonichords?
8 Which Stones album was No. 1 in the album charts in 1966?
9 Which 60s chart-topper went on to manage James Taylor and Linda Ronstadt?
10 Which town did the Four Pennies come from?
11 What was the drummer Ann Lantree's group?
12 Who was originally offered "It's Not Unusual" before Tom Jones?
13 How old was Sonny when he had his first No. 1 record with Cher?
14 Who were Messrs Engel, Maus and Leeds?
15 Who had a 1968 album, *...Rocks but Gently*?
16 Which group did Steve Marriott leave to form which band in 1969?
17 How many different bands had a No. 1 album in 1964?
18 Which single topped the charts when England won the World Cup?
19 Which song was subtitled "Exordium and Terminus"?
20 Which group sold more singles than the Beatles in the US in 1968?
21 Who had already taken his "Three Steps to Heaven" when it went to No. 1?
22 Which was the first instrumental to go to UK No. 1 in the 1960s?
23 What were the first names of Mr & Mrs Ofarim who sang "Cinderella Rockefella"?
24 Who was the "non-Mac" member of the Scaffold?
25 Thomas John Woodward achieved great fame as whom?
26 Which Johnny enjoyed his only UK No. 1 hit with "Running Bear" in 1960?
27 What could Ray Charles not stop doing in his only ever UK No. 1 hit of 1962?
28 Who cashed in on the kinky boots fashion with a 1966 No. 1 hit?
29 What did the Seekers claim they would never find another of in their first UK No. 1?
30 What was the name of Sandie Shaw's first UK No. 1 in October 1964?

Answers | Movies Pot Luck 2 *(see Quiz 24)*

1 Michael Caine (14.3.33). 2 As Good as It Gets. 3 Balsam. 4 85 minutes. 5 Rupert Everett. 6 Tim Burton. 7 The Martian. 8 LeMat. 9 Kauai. 10 Adolph Hitler. 11 Little Big Man. 12 Christopher Hart. 13 Linda Larkin. 14 1939. 15 Woody Allen. 16 Bridge on the River Kwai. 17 Robert Davi. 18 157 minutes. 19 Jim Cannon. 20 Janet Gaynor. 21 Kiss of the Spider Woman. 22 Ryan's Hope. 23 Duke. 24 Jessica Lange. 25 Fred Zinnemann. 26 Sin City. 27 Doug Liman. 28 "It Might as Well be Spring". 29 Dickey. 30 Aria.

1 Which movie star was born on the same day as Quincy Jones?

2 A character named Melvin Udall appeared in which film?

3 Which Martin featured in *All the President's Men*?

4 Within five minutes, how long does *Yellow Submarine* last?

5 Which actor links *Another Country* and *Dance with a Stranger*?

6 Who directed *Batman*?

7 Which 2015's "comedy" (set on Mars) starred Matt Damon?

8 Which Paul featured in *American Graffiti*?

9 On which Hawaiian island was *Jurassic Park* filmed?

10 After "Best Boy" appears on the end credits of *Airplane II: The Sequel*, who appears as "Worst Boy"?

11 A character named Jack Crabb appeared in which film?

12 Who played Thing in *The Addams Family*?

13 Who voiced Jasmine in the film *Aladdin*?

14 In which year was *Destry Rides Again* released?

15 Who was quoted as saying, "Great talent is an accident of birth"?

16 Which movie is shown in the film *I Love You to Death*?

17 Who played Tony Moretti in the film *Action Jackson*?

18 Within ten minutes how long does *Sophie's Choice* last?

19 Who was Jim Carrey's make-up man for *The Mask*?

20 Who won the Best Actress Oscar for *Seventh Heaven*?

21 A character named Luis Molina appears in which film?

22 Which soap did Hollywood star Christian Slater star in?

23 Which Bill featured in *American Gigolo*?

24 Who was first choice for Sigourney Weaver's *Gorillas in the Mist* role?

25 Who won the Best Director Oscar for *From Here to Eternity*?

26 Which 2005 movie was co-directed by Frank Miller and Robert Rodriguez?

27 Who directed the first of the *Bourne* movies trilogy?

28 Which song from *State Fair* won an Oscar?

29 Which James wrote the novel, the screenplay and featured in *Deliverance*?

30 In which movie did Bridget Fonda make her debut?

Answers Pop: The 1960s *(see Quiz 23)*

1 Cliff Richard. 2 John F. Kennedy was assassinated. 3 The Searchers. 4 Cream. 5 Nothing. 6 Catch Us if You Can. 7 The Bachelors. 8 Aftermath. 9 Peter Asher. 10 Blackburn. 11 The Honeycombs. 12 Sandie Shaw. 13 30. 14 The Walker Brothers. 15 Val Doonican. 16 From the Small Faces to Humble Pie. 17 Two – the Beatles and Rolling Stones. 18 "Out of Time" – Chris Farlowe. 19 "In the Year 2525". 20 Union Gap. 21 Eddie Cochran. 22 Apache. 23 Abi & Esther. 24 John Gorman. 25 Tom Jones. 26 Preston. 27 (I Can't Stop) Loving You. 28 Nancy Sinatra (These Boots are Made for Walking). 29 Another You. 30 (There's) Always Something There to Remind Me.

1 Norman Lovett and Hattie Hayridge shared which role in *Red Dwarf*?
2 Which spaceship did ex-*Quantum Leap* star Scott Bakula captain for 98 episodes?
3 Who organized the murder of Door's family in *Neverwhere*?
4 What alien discovery was made in *Quatermass and the Pit*?
5 What is the correct name of *Xena: Warrior Princess*'s "round killing thing"?
6 According to Sapphire & Steel, which "Heavy Elements may not be used where there is life"?
7 Who plays Autolycus, King of Thieves, in *Hercules: The Legendary Journeys*?
8 Which actor accompanies Sam Beckett on his *Quantum Leaps*?
9 Which actress was named Doctor Who's new companion in 2016?
10 What firm did Ernest Borgnine run in *Airwolf*?
11 Who was the Sandman an evil enemy of?
12 *Automan* created solid objects out of thin air with the aid of what/who?
13 *Manimal* had two preferred non-human shapes, a hawk and which other?
14 Which race is Lt Tuvak a representative of in *Star Trek: Voyager*?
15 Who played Jake Cardigan in *TekWar*?
16 What rank was Don West in *Lost In Space*?
17 In VR5, Lori Singer starred as which computer expert?
18 In which city was *Space Precinct* set?
19 Which group opposed the Fathers in *Wild Palms*?
20 Which race is led by the Great Nagus in *Deep Space Nine*?
21 What colour is Klingon blood?
22 Which of *Dr Who*'s enemies posed as shop dummies, sofas and other artificial items?
23 After the Treaty of Algeron which zone was created in *Star Trek: Next Generation*?
24 How did *The Tomorrow People* refer to teleportation?
25 What was the name of the device looking like a weather balloon that guarded the Village?
26 What are the janitorial robot "helping hands" on the *Red Dwarf* called?
27 Which star of *Alien* played a trailer park owner in *Twin Peaks*?
28 In *Babylon 5*, who gave up his life so that Ivanova could live?
29 Which sci-fi writer served as creative consultant to the 80s *Twilight Zone*?
30 Which Switzerland-based group was the goal of the young heroes fighting *The Tripods*?

Answers	**Football Pot Luck 3** *(see Quiz 26)*

1 Willie Bell. 2 Alexander. 3 Wrexham. 4 David Seaman. 5 1900s. 6 Bournemouth. 7 Crystal Palace. 8 Dean Holdsworth. 9 Barnet. 10 9. 11 Arsenal. 12 Bremner. 13 Manchester United. 14 73. 15 Portsmouth. 16 Harry Cripps. 17 White and blue. 18 Bristol City. 19 St Mirren. 20 John Osborne. 21 Greece. 22 Dennis Wise. 23 Watford. 24 Coventry City. 25 1920s. 26 Bristol Rovers. 27 QPR. 28 36,451. 29 Tranmere Rovers. 30 Nine.

1 In 1966, which Leeds Utd defender won his only Scottish cap?

2 What is Tony Adams's middle name?

3 Which Welsh club used to play at Acton Park?

4 Which England keeper was featured in *Hello* magazine in February 1997?

5 In what decade did Liverpool first win the championship?

6 Which club had a fanzine called *Not the 8502*?

7 Dario Gradi followed Malcolm Allison as manager of which club?

8 Who moved from Brentford to Wimbledon in 1992 to set a club record for a transfer fee received?

9 Which London club once had Alston as part of its name?

10 To one each way, how many international goals did Alan Ball score?

11 Perry Groves and Brian Marwood were in the same team at which club?

12 Which Billy became boss of Leeds Utd in 1985?

13 Ray Wilkins played in an FA Cup Final for which team?

14 To three each way, how many goals did Phil Neal score in his 20-year-long League career?

15 What was the first club that Alan Ball managed?

16 Which Millwall defender scored over 40 goals in the 1960s and early 70s?

17 What are the main colours of IFK Gothenburg's home shirts?

18 Who was keeper Ray Cashley playing for when he scored against Hull City in 1973?

19 Tony Fitzpatrick set a Scottish League appearance record at which club?

20 Who was in goal when WBA won the FA Cup in the 1960s?

21 In which country would you watch Larissa take on PAOK?

22 Who was made Newcastle United's Director of Football in January 2008?

23 Wilf Rostron and Jimmy Gilligan scored Euro goals in the same game for which club?

24 At which club did Les Sealey make his League debut?

25 In what decade did WBA first win the championship?

26 Which club had a fanzine called *On the 2nd May*?

27 Dave Sexton followed Gordon Jago's first spell as manager of which club?

28 What was the average attendance of a game in 2015-16 Premier League Season – 36,451 or 28,765?

29 Which club was once known as Belmont AFC?

30 To one each way, how many international goals did Colin Bell score?

Answers	TV: Sci-Fi 1 *(see Quiz 25)*

1 Holly. 2 USS Enterprise. 3 The Angel Islington. 4 A 5 million-year-old Martian spacecraft. 5 Chakram. 6 Transuranic. 7 Bruce Campbell. 8 Dean Stockwell. 9 Pearl Mackie. 10 Santini Air. 11 Batman and Robin. 12 Cursor. 13 Black Panther. 14 Vulcan. 15 Greg Evigan. 16 Major. 17 Sydney Bloom. 18 Demeter City. 19 The Friends. 20 Ferengi. 21 Purple. 22 Autons. 23 The Neutral Zone. 24 Jaunting. 25 Rover. 26 Scutters. 27 Harry Dean Stanton. 28 Marcus Cole. 29 Harlan Ellison. 30 The Free Men.

1 Which duo had the first reggae No. 1 in 1971?

2 Which ex-Hoochie Coochie Men vocalist went on to have great success in the 70s and beyond?

3 Which 1972 single was the first major hit to feature a synthesizer?

4 Which singer/songwriter was "Killing Me Softly" written about?

5 Which song was about babysitting for the singer's manager?

6 Which hit featured Rob and Hilda Woodward?

7 Which 70s group leader died on February 10, 1997?

8 What was the first No. 1 for Jonathan King's UK record label?

9 Who accompanied Nottingham Forest FC on "We've Got the Whole World in Our Hands" in 1978?

10 Which group was famous for its white berets in 1974?

11 Who was the "Queen of the Blues" in the 1971 hit by Ray Stevens?

12 Who was mentioned in a 1974 song title but not in the song itself?

13 Which part did David Essex play in *That'll be the Day*?

14 Which was the third of Mud's three 70s No. 1s?

15 Which group were Jeffrey Calvert, Max West plus session musicians?

16 Whose version of "No Charge" was called "No Chance"?

17 Who was the heaviest individual chart-topper in the 70s?

18 What was Elton John's first release on Rocket?

19 What nationality were Pussycat?

20 What was Deniece Williams's profession before singing?

21 Who had a chart hit with the theme of the 1976 film *Car Wash*?

22 What was 1970 Eurovision winner Dana's occupation from 1999 to 2004?

23 In which month did Marc Bolan die?

24 Which was Brotherhood of Man's last UK No. 1?

25 Which Thames TV Today presenter was sworn at by the Sex Pistols in late 1976?

26 Who enjoyed his second and last UK No. 1 with "Baby Jump" in March 1971?

27 Name the US group which first charted in 1963 but made No. 1 with "Ms Grace."

28 Name the Paul Anka song that Donny Osmond turned into a worldwide No. 1 hit.

29 Who made "No Charge" for his countless acts in June 1976?

30 Who took "Clair" to the No. 1 slot in November 1972 for two weeks?

Answers	**Movies Pot Luck 3** *(see Quiz 28)*

1 Book editor. 2 Barry McGuigan. 3 John Ford. 4 Jessica Lange. 5 Crewson. 6 Godzilla. 7 83 mins. 8 Dabney Coleman. 9 Sicario. 10 Eddie Murphy. 11 Seven. 12 "The Power of Love". 13 New Jersey. 14 Baseball. 15 Hedaya. 16 Howard Zieff. 17 138. 18 Ralph Fiennes. 19 Frank Coraci. 20 Patsy Kensit. 21 Johnny Rico. 22 Sound effects on Robocop. 23 101 minutes. 24 Ron Howard. 25 Callow. 26 Dustin Hoffman. 27 Tobe Hooper. 28 Claude. 29 Bud Fox. 30 River Phoenix.

1 What is the job of the Jack Nicholson character in *Wolf*?

2 Who coached Daniel Day-Lewis for his role in *The Boxer*?

3 Who won the Best Director Oscar for *The Informer*?

4 Who won the Best Actress Oscar for *Blue Sky*?

5 Which Wendy featured in *Air Force One*?

6 In which film did a character named Dr Niko Tatopoulos appear?

7 To the nearest five minutes, how long does *Snow White and the Seven Dwarfs* last?

8 Which actor played the womanizing boss in *9 to 5*?

9 John Krasinki's wife starred in which 2015 crime-thriller drama film directed by Denis Villeneuve?

10 Which actor said, "I've got a filthy mouth but it's my only sin"?

11 In how many films did Roger Moore play 007 altogether?

12 What was the theme tune to *Back to the Future*?

13 In which state was John Travolta born?

14 At what sport did William Baldwin excel?

15 Which Dan featured in *Alien: Resurrection*?

16 From whom did Penny Marshall take over the direction of *Jumpin' Jack Flash*?

17 Within 20, how many actors are named on the credits for the film *Gandhi*?

18 Which actor links *Wuthering Heights* and *Quiz Show*?

19 Who directed *The Wedding Singer*?

20 Which ex-pop wife appeared in *The Great Gatsby* aged four?

21 What was the name of Casper Van Dien's character in *Starship Troopers*?

22 For what did Stephen Flick win a Special Award in 1987?

23 Within five minutes, how long does *The Wizard of Oz* last?

24 Who directed *Backdraft*?

25 Which Simon featured in *Ace Ventura: When Nature Calls*?

26 Who was the voice of Shifu in *Kung Fu Panda*?

27 Which horror film master director did 2003's *Toolbox Murders*?

28 What does the C stand for in W. C. Fields's name?

29 What was the name of Charlie Sheen's character in *Wall Street*?

30 Which actor died on the same day (31 October 1993) as director Federico Fellini?

Answers | Pop: The 1970s *(see Quiz 27)*

1 Dave and Ansil Collins. 2 Rod Stewart. 3 "Son of My Father" – Chicory Tip. 4 Don McLean. 5 "Clair". 6 "Mouldy Old Dough" – Lieutenant Pigeon. 7 Brian Connolly of Sweet. 8 "Rubber Bullets" – 10c.c. 9 Paper Lace. 10 The Rubettes. 11 Bridget the Midget. 12 Annie ("Annie's Song"). 13 Jim McClain. 14 "Oh Boy". 15 Typically Tropical. 16 Billy Connolly. 17 Demis Roussos. 18 "Don't Go Breaking My Heart". 19 Dutch. 20 Nurse. 21 Rose Royce. 22 MEP. 23 September 1977. 24 "Figaro". 25 Bill Grundy. 26 Mungo Jerry. 27 Tymes. 28 Puppy Love. 29 J. J. Barrie. 30 Gilbert O'Sullivan.

1 Who succeeded Sir Peter O'Sullevan as the BBC's main horse racing commentator?

2 Kevin Cadle, the host of Sky Sports' NFL show, was a coach in which sport?

3 Who replaced Peter Dimmock as presenter of the pioneering *Sportsview*?

4 Which boxing commentator won the American Sportscasters' Association International Award in 1989?

5 Who was the first BBC Sports Personality of the Year of the 1990s?

6 Which TV broadcaster holds the rights to broadcast the 2016 Rio Olympics?

7 Who became LWT's Deputy Controller after a career in football management?

8 On which channel is *Sunday Grandstand* broadcast?

9 Jack Solomon's *Scrapbook* concerned which sport?

10 Who aspires to become a professional boxer in the comedy *Taxi*?

11 Which programme covered the International Sheepdog Trials?

12 What BBC sport competition was first won by Ray Reardon?

13 Which sportsman recorded *We Shall Not be Moved*?

14 On which sport does Dorian Williams commentate?

15 Which sport was featured in *Cudmore's Call*?

16 Which Royal organized the *Grand Knockout Tournament*?

17 Who was the UK's very first American football commentator?

18 Who replaced Bob Wilson as presenter of *Football Focus*?

19 Which pop star featured in the closing ceremony of the 1984 Summer Olympics?

20 Who went from editor of the Cheshire County Press to TV sports reporter?

21 Who did Stuart Hall replace as host of *It's a Knockout*?

22 *The Sporting Triangles* teams wore what colours?

23 Who presented *Pro Celebrity Golf*?

24 For how many years did Dickie Davis present *World of Sport*?

25 The theme from *Chariots Of Fire* was used by the BBC for which Olympics?

26 Why in 1975 did Michael Angelow receive big publicity after visiting Lord's?

27 For the coverage of which sporting event did the BBC launch its colour service?

28 What sport featured in *The Winning Streak*?

29 Who refereed the TV football match between the Rover's Return and Maurice Jones Building on *Coronation Street*?

30 Which breakfast food was advertised by Ian Botham and Henry and George Cooper?

Answers	Football Pot Luck 4 *(see Quiz 30)*

1 Hearts. 2 Ron Greenwood. 3 Wolves. 4 Bournemouth. 5 2 (Steve Daley and Andy Gray). 6 Smith. 7 Elland Road. 8 Cambridge Utd. 9 Harvey. 10 William. 11 Middlesbrough. 12 Machin. 13 Brighton. 14 Chesterfield. 15 1890s. 16 Huddersfield Town. 17 Burnley. 18 Gordon Durie. 19 Cambridge Utd. 20 12. 21 Howard Webb. 22 Linfield. 23 Nottingham Forest. 24 Helmut Haller. 25 Southampton. 26 San Siro, Milan. 27 Leeds Utd. 28 John Barnes. 29 Hamburg. 30 Arsenal.

Quiz 30 | Football Pot Luck 4 | Answers – page 431

1 Comedian Ronnie Corbett had a trial at which Scottish club?
2 Which England manager was born in Burnley in 1921?
3 Which side from the Midlands used to play at Goldthorn Hill?
4 Sean O'Driscoll set a League appearance record at which club?
5 The first £1 million British move was in February 1979. How many more players moved for a million in the same year?
6 Which Alan went on from non-League Alvechurch to play for England?
7 The first home England international since 1966 to be played away from Wembley was in 1995 v Sweden. Where was it played?
8 What was the first League club that Ron Atkinson managed?
9 Which Colin played his only England game in 1971 against Malta?
10 What is John Aldridge's middle name?
11 Peter Davenport and Gary Pallister were in the same team at which club?
12 Which Mel became boss of Manchester City in 1987?
13 Mick Robinson first played in an FA Cup Final for which team?
14 At which club did Steve Ogrizovic make his League debut?
15 In what decade did Hearts first win the championship?
16 Which club had a fanzine called *A Slice of Kilner Pie*?
17 Jimmy Mullen followed Frank Casper as manager of which club?
18 Who moved from Chelsea to Tottenham Hotspur for £2,200,000 in 1991 to set a club record for a transfer fee received?
19 Which club was once known as Abbey United?
20 To one each way, how many international goals has Tony Cascarino scored?
21 Which English referee officiated at Euro 2008?
22 Which club was 2007–08 League champions in Northern Ireland?
23 Charles, Chettle and Glover played for which 1980s FA Cup finalists?
24 Who scored first for West Germany in the 1966 World Cup Final?
25 Fullback David Peach scored for which club in a League Cup Final?
26 The 2016 UEFA Champions League Final was played at which stadium?
27 Strachan and Shutt scored Euro goals in the same game for which club?
28 Which England player once played for Sudbury Court?
29 Who lost 1–0 to Nottingham Forest in the final of the 1980 European Cup?
30 Which club had a fanzine called *One Nil Down ... Two One Up*?

Answers | TV: Sport 1 *(see Quiz 29)*

1 Jim McGrath. 2 Basketball. 3 Brian Johnston. 4 Harry Carpenter. 5 Liz McColgan. 6 BBC. 7 Jimmy Hill. 8 BBC2. 9 Boxing. 10 Tony. 11 One Man and His Dog. 12 Pot Black. 13 Big Daddy. 14 Showjumping. 15 Sailing. 16 Prince Edward. 17 Nicky Horne. 18 Sam Leitch. 19 Lionel Richie. 20 David Coleman. 21 David Vine. 22 Yellow, green, red. 23 Peter Allis. 24 16 years. 25 The 1984 Olympics. 26 He streaked on the pitch. 27 Wimbledon. 28 Rally driving. 29 Derek Wilton. 30 Shredded Wheat.

1 Which was the largest group to have a chart-topper in 1981?
2 Who played the Fairy Godmother on Adam and the Ants' "Prince Charming" video?
3 In which decade was Julio Iglesias's first solo hit written?
4 Which band included Philip Oakey and Susanne Sulley?
5 How did Demis Roussos hit the headlines in 1985?
6 Which 80s hit was based on a Zulu folk tune?
7 Which double-sided No. 1 replaced which double-sided No. 1 in 1982?
8 How did Mark Chapman find notoriety in the 1980s?
9 Which video by which band featured Ian McKellen as Dracula?
10 Which band's name means "black" in Arabic?
11 How is the American Ms Darwisch better known?
12 Which album was T'Pau's "China in Your Hand" from?
13 What was the Bee Gees' first 80s No. 1?
14 Which country are Europe from?
15 How was Ray Burns known as an 80s soloist?
16 What did the Real Thing's Chris Amoo win in 1987?
17 Which country were the Goombay Dance Band based in?
18 Who, in which song, sang "I've been undressed by kings and I've seen some things a woman ain't supposed to see"?
19 Which city are Berlin from?
20 Which Radio 1 DJ first refused to play Frankie Goes to Hollywood's "Relax"?
21 "Suicide is Painless" was the theme song from which hit movie and TV series?
22 How many UK No. 1s did Abba have?
23 Whose wrote the UK 1981 No. 1 that ends, "And the world will live as one"?
24 Which was Madonna's first UK No. 1?
25 For how long had Jackie Wilson been dead when "Reet Petite" was No. 1 in 1987?
26 Name the US singer who had a one-hit wonder with "Together We Are Beautiful".
27 What was the name of Midge Ure's only ever solo No. 1 single in the UK?
28 What was the name of the Jam's first UK No. 1 hit single?
29 Who took "He ain't Heavy, He's My Brother" to No. 1 in 1988?
30 Which "Dance Band" took "Seven Tears" to the top of the UK music charts in 1982?

1 The ghostly sisters seen by Danny wear what colour dresses in *The Shining*?

2 Who played the villain in *Return of the Jedi*?

3 Which movie star released a single called "Pure Imagination" in 1970?

4 Which singer featured in *Annie Hall*?

5 Who directed *Wayne's World*?

6 Within five minutes, how long does *Where Eagles Dare* last?

7 Who won the Best Actor Oscar for *In Old Arizona*?

8 What was Michael Keaton's first film, in 1982?

9 Which actor links *Regarding Henry* and *Heroes*?

10 What does Helen think husband Harry does for a living in *True Lies*?

11 A character named Mark Sheridan appeared in which film?

12 What was Timothy Dalton's last film as James Bond?

13 Who won the Best Director Oscar for *Terms of Endearment*?

14 In which country was the whole of *Full Metal Jacket* filmed?

15 Who played Sam Francisco in the film *Alien Nation*?

16 Which Ed featured in *Apollo 13*?

17 What was Marlene Dietrich's last movie?

18 What was the name of Robert Mitchum's character in *Ryan's Daughter*?

19 Who said, "I love British cinema like a doctor loves his dying patient"?

20 Which actor links *Street Smart* and *Glory*?

21 Which character did Paul McGann play in the film *Alien³*?

22 Within fifteen minutes, how long does *Apollo 13* last?

23 Which James starred in *The Amityville Horror*?

24 Who won the Best Actress Oscar for *Coquette*?

25 What was the name of Michael Douglas's character in *Romancing the Stone*?

26 In which country was Cate Blanchett born?

27 Why didn't Peter Finch accept his Best Actor Oscar award in 1976?

28 Who directed *Flashdance*?

29 Which actor appeared in both *Bonnie and Clyde* and *Young Frankenstein*?

30 2015's *The Big Short* was directed by whom?

Answers	Pop: The 1980s *(see Quiz 31)*

1 St Winifred's School Choir. 2 Diana Dors. 3 1930s. 4 Human League. 5 On a hijacked plane in Beirut. 6 "The Lion Sleeps Tonight". 7 "A Town Called Malice"/ "Precious" replaced "The Model"/"Computer Love". 8 Shot John Lennon. 9 "Heart" – Pet Shop Boys. 10 Aswad. 11 Tiffany. 12 Bridge of Spies. 13 "You Win Again". 14 Sweden. 15 Captain Sensible. 16 Cruft's – at least his Afghan hound did. 17 Germany. 18 Charlene, "I've Never been to Me". 19 Los Angeles. 20 Mike Read. 21 M*A*S*H. 22 Nine. 23 John Lennon. 24 "Into the Groove". 25 Three years. 26 Fern Kinney. 27 "If I was". 28 "Going Underground". 29 The Hollies. 30 Goombay Dance Band.

1 On which day did Channel 4 begin broadcasting?
2 What was the title of 1974's first reality TV documentary following the Wilkins?
3 In which year did BBC2 commence broadcasting?
4 In which year was the *Radio Times* first published?
5 In which year was the *TV Times* first published?
6 In which year was the first BBC TV broadcast service commenced?
7 From where did the BBC TV service transmit?
8 Who was famous for his 50s cookery shows, *Cookery Lesson* and *What's Cooking?*
9 The first programme broadcast from France featured which town?
10 Who was the first Prime Minister to install TV in his home in the 1930s?
11 In which year were the first BBC TV studios founded?
12 Who chaired the first broadcasts of *What's My Line?*
13 Who was the BBC's first Director of TV?
14 Who was the BBC's first TV announcer?
15 Who presented *The Good Old Days* before Leonard Sachs?
16 In 1939 an estimated how many TVs were in regular use – 15,000, 13,000 or 11,000?
17 Which Dr Who was the first TV Robin Hood for children?
18 Which character played by Bruce Seton was one of the first TV detectives?
19 Who supplied the BBC commentary for the Coronation of King George VI?
20 What was the name of the quiz show on *Crackerjack?*
21 On which part of *Double Your Money* could you win the £1,000?
22 Who won *Celebrity Big Brother 2015?*
23 Which comedienne was the neighbour of Fred and Ethel Mertz in a popular 50s sitcom?
24 What did the first ever TV church service celebrate?
25 Who was the presenter of the 1940s series *Television Garden?*
26 What forced the daytime shutdown of transmissions in Feb.–March 1947?
27 Which Royal wedding was televised during November 1947?
28 Who gave the first direct TV broadcast by a Prime Minister?
29 In the post-war magazine programme *Kaleidoscope*, who was the "Memory Man"?
30 In which year did the BBC TV schools service begin?

Answers	**Speed Kings** *(see Quiz 34)*

1 Arrows. 2 Mercedes Formula One. 3 Nine. 4 One. 5 2004. 6 Giacomo Agostini. 7 Graham Hill. 8 Emerson Fittipaldi. 9 American. 10 Jochen Rindt. 11 Denny Hulme. 12 Brazilian. 13 Five. 14 Jacky Ickx. 15 Alain Prost. 16 Jackie Stewart. 17 Three. 18 Speedway. 19 Mike Hailwood. 20 Richard Noble. 21 Finnish. 22 John Surtees. 23 Mike Hawthorn. 24 Stirling Moss. 25 James Hunt. 26 Mansell, Hill. 27 Bruce McLaren himself. 28 Canada. 29 Roland Ratzenberger. 30 British.

1 Which team did Damon Hill join after leaving Williams?
2 Nico Rosberg drives for which F1 team in 2016?
3 In how many consecutive races was Lewis Hamilton on the podium in 2007?
4 By how many points did Kimi Raikkonen win the 2007 World Championship?
5 In which year did Michael Schumacher win his last World Drivers Championship?
6 Which motorcyclist won 122 world championships?
7 Which driver was runner-up in the world championship in '63, '64 and '65?
8 Which Brazilian was world champion driver in 1972 and 1974?
9 What was the nationality of Mario Andretti?
10 Which driver won the world championship posthumously in 1970?
11 Which New Zealander won the motor racing championship in 1967?
12 What is the nationality of Nelson Piquet?
13 How many times did Graham Hill win the Monaco Grand Prix?
14 Which Belgian won Le Mans six times between 1969 and 1982?
15 Who was driving for Ferrari when they became the first manufacturer to have 100 grand prix wins?
16 Who was the British driver with most Grand Prix wins before Nigel Mansell?
17 How many times was Ayrton Senna world champion?
18 At which sport did Ivan Maugher win six world titles?
19 Which British motorcyclist won 14 Isle of Man Tourist Trophy titles?
20 Which Briton broke the world land speed record in the US in 1983?
21 What is the nationality of Keke Kosberg?
22 Who was world championship driver in 1964 and motorcycling champion seven times?
23 Who was the first Briton to win the world motor racing championship?
24 Who had 16 grand prix wins between 1955 and 1961?
25 Which Briton was world champion in 1976 and retired three years later?
26 Which two Britons had six grand prix wins in a season and still failed to win the world championships?
27 Who drove the McLaren to its first grand prix win in 1968?
28 What is Gilles Villeneuve's home country?
29 Which driver apart from Senna lost his life in the 1994 Formula 1 season?
30 Which grand prix did Damon Hill win for the first time in 1994?

Answers | **TV: TV History** *(see Quiz 33)*

1 2 November 1982. 2 The Family. 3 1964. 4 1923. 5 1955. 6 1936. 7 Alexandra Palace. 8 Philip Harben. 9 Calais. 10 Ramsay MacDonald. 11 1932. 12 Eamonn Andrews. 13 Gerald Cock. 14 Jasmin Bligh. 15 Don Gemmell. 16 11,000. 17 Patrick Troughton. 18 Inspector Fabian. 19 Frederick Grisewood. 20 Double or Drop. 21 Treasure Trail. 22 James Hill. 23 Lucille Ball. 24 Battle of Britain Sunday. 25 Fred Streeter. 26 A national fuel and power crisis. 27 Marriage of Princess Elizabeth to Lt Philip Mountbatten. 28 Clement Attlee. 29 Leslie Welch. 30 1957 (September).

1 With which club did Gordon Banks make his League debut?
2 Who was the first Scottish player to be European Footballer of the Year?
3 Who said that he was "supremely grateful" to have played against the great Hungarian side of the 1950s?
4 Who was Footballer of the Year in 1948 and 1963?
5 Against which country did Jimmy Greaves make his scoring debut?
6 How many championships did Bobby Charlton win with Manchester Utd?
7 At which club did Wilf Mannion end his career?
8 In the season he set a new scoring record how many goals did Dixie Dean get in his last three games?
9 At which Italian club did Dino Zoff begin his career?
10 To two each way, how many caps did Alex James get for Scotland?
11 In which country was Alfredo Di Stefano born?
12 Which county did Raich Carter play cricket for?
13 Which NASL team did George Best play for?
14 What was the job of Stanley Matthew's father?
15 Which team name was one of Bobby Moore's names?
16 Who hit a record 59 goals in a season for Middlesbrough?
17 To three each way, how many goals did Ferenc Puskas score for Hungary?
18 Which free-scoring England forward moved to Germany in 1914 to be interned during World War I?
19 Danny Blanchflower started out with which Irish club?
20 How many Scottish League clubs did Denis Law play for?
21 Which 1994 World Cup finalist was still playing for his only club in 2008?
22 Which club did Ruud Gullit coach in 2007–08?
23 Wayne Rooney, from 2003 to the end of the Euro 2016 campaign, had earned how many international caps – 110 or 115?
24 Who was the last England player before David Beckham to win 100 caps?
25 Which Real Madrid legend was released by Atletico Madrid at 17 in 1992?
26 Name the World Cup winner trained by the Olympic drug-cheat Ben Johnson.
27 Who captained Brazil to World Cup glory in 1958?
28 Name the 2008 Coca-Cola Championship manager who played in the 1974 World Cup Final.
29 Name either one of the co-winners of the 1994 World Cup Golden Boot.
30 Who left River Plate after the 1982 World Cup finals to join Valencia?

Answers | Pop Pot Luck 5 *(see Quiz 36)*

1 Douglas, IOM. 2 Cigarette. 3 Paul McCartney. 4 Morris 1000. 5 Ronnie Carroll. 6 One Direction. 7 Help! 8 Beach Boys. 9 The Magic Band. 10 Octagonal. 11 Ali Campbell. 12 "Higher Love". 13 Ultravox. 14 Harry Belafonte. 15 Aunty Entity. 16 Michael Jackson. 17 The Big Bopper. 18 Deep Sea Skiving. 19 The Troglodytes. 20 David Evans. 21 "Swear It Again". 22 "Perfect Day". 23 Baked beans. 24 "Sultans of Swing". 25 Appetite for Destruction. 26 Elton John. 27 In a crossfire hurricane. 28 Buddy Holly. 29 Amazulu. 30 The Shirelles.

1 In which town was Barry Gibb born?
2 What is in the baby's mouth on the cover of Van Halen's 1984 album?
3 Who organizes Buddy Holly Week each year?
4 What type of car was used by Madness in their video for "Driving in My Car"?
5 Which fifties singer married Millicent Martin?
6 What label did the Police record all their hit albums on?
7 *Made in the A.M.* is the fifth studio album by which band?
8 Which California group toured with Maharishi Mahesh Yogi?
9 Who backed Captain Beefheart?
10 What shape is the sleeve of the Rolling Stones' *Through the Past Darkly* album?
11 Who is lead singer with UB40?
12 Which Steve Winwood song was Grammy Record of the Year in 1986?
13 Who were first formed as Tiger Lily in 1973?
14 Which veteran was behind the US fundraiser by USA for Africa?
15 Which role did Tina Turner play in *Mad Max: Beyond Thunderdome*?
16 Who was President Reagan writing to when he said, "Your deep faith in God and adherence to traditional values is an inspiration to us all"?
17 How is Jiles Perry Richardson better known?
18 What was Bananarama's debut album called?
19 What were the Troggs initially called?
20 What is U2's the Edge's real name?
21 Which was Westlife's first No. 1 in the UK?
22 Which Lou Reed single was re-released for *Children in Need* in 1997?
23 What is Roger Daltrey covered in on *The Who Sell Out* album?
24 Which song says "Check out Guitar George – he knows all the chords"?
25 What was Guns N' Roses' bestselling album of the 1980s?
26 Who swapped autographs and football chat with Lech Walesa in 1984?
27 Where was Jumpin' Jack Flash born according to the Rolling Stones?
28 Who proposed to Maria Elena Santiago on their first date?
29 Who were going to Montego Bay in 1986?
30 Who had the first UK hit with "Will You Still Love Me Tomorrow?"?

1 Spielberg said he accepted for *Schindler's List* on whose behalf?
2 Which honorary winner's autobiography was called *When the Smoke Hits the Fan*?
3 Which composer was nominated for *The Man with the Golden Arm*?
4 Which nominee has been a member of Carp and a drummer with the Rubber Band?
5 Who was a nominee for costume for *Days of Wine and Roses*?
6 Who won an honorary award in 1979 for "advancing the art of screen acting"?
7 Who did Amy Irving marry shortly after being nominated for *Yentl*?
8 Who won Best Supporting Actor the year Josephine Hull won Best Supporting Actress for *Harvey*?
9 Who did James Woods lose out to as Best Supporting Actor for *Ghosts from the Past*?
10 Who was nominated for music for *The Red Violin*?
11 What was Ben Kingsley's next nomination after his first win?
12 Who was the husband of the 1959 Best Supporting Actress?
13 The composer of the only nominated song from *Grease* was a member of which pop band?
14 The first black actress to win was honoured for which role?
15 Who won when Gloria Swanson was nominated for *Sunset Boulevard*?
16 Who supposedly named the Oscar, saying it looked like her uncle?
17 Who is the second most frequent host of the Oscars ceremony?
18 Who was the first performer to win an Oscar for a performance entirely in a foreign language?
19 Who was the Oscar winner in *Rosemary's Baby*?
20 Who in 1932 was the first director to see his film win Best Picture but not have a nomination himself?
21 What film won Best Animation at the 2015 Oscars ceremony?
22 Who was nominated for Best Actress and Best Supporting Actress in 1993?
23 What was the second of Gary Cooper's three nominations between 1941 and 1943?
24 Who won a Special Award for *The Search* aged nine?
25 Who won a Special Achievement Award for *Who Framed Roger Rabbit?*?
26 Kate Winslet and which other British actress lost to Helen Mirren in 2006?
27 Who was nominated for an Oscar playing J. M. Barrie?
28 Which actress is the only female star to win four Academy Awards for Best Actress?
29 Who won the Best Actor Oscar for playing Wladyslaw Szpilman in *The Pianist*?
30 Who is the only Australian to win the Academy Awards for Best Actress?

Answers | **TV Pot Luck 4** *(see Quiz 38)*

1 Art Attack. 2 2005. 3 Game On. 4 Geoff Hamilton. 5 Martin Tupper. 6 Jeannie. 7 Sarah Chalke. 8 Henry Cooper. 9 Robert Popper. 10 Detective sergeant. 11 Watchdog. 12 Patricia Routledge. 13 Rachel Kempson. 14 One for the Road. 15 Percy Sugden. 16 Peter Jeffrey. 17 Kenneth Baker. 18 Top of the Form. 19 Thames TV. 20 Julian Clary. 21 Royal correspondent. 22 At the Castle Gate by Sibelius. 23 Grampian. 24 Nicholas Donnelly. 25 Nurse Christine Chapel. 26 TV critic. 27 Sarah Lancashire (Raquel). 28 Debbie. 29 Ellen. 30 Gloria.

1 Which long-running CITV show might be a Cockney falling ill?

2 In which year did the final series of *Absolutely Fabulous* air?

3 In which sitcom is Miss Wilkins a lodger?

4 Which presenter of *Gardener's World* died in 1996?

5 What was the name of Brian Benben's character in *Dream On*?

6 What was the name of Larry Sanders's wife?

7 Who alternated with Lecy Goranson the role of Becky in *Roseanne*?

8 Who was the first person to win the BBC *Sports Personality of the Year* twice?

9 Which actor links Jed Stone to Marty Hopkirk?

10 In 1998 what rank had Jacqui Reed achieved in *Taggart*?

11 Jonathan Maitland is an investigator on which Weekend programme?

12 Who played Miss Fozzard in *Talking Heads II*?

13 Who is the mother of actresses Vanessa and Lynn Redgrave?

14 In which series did Alan Davies travel Europe with a video camera?

15 Since 2011, *Friday Night Dinner* has been written by which British television writer?

16 Who played Mr Peabody in *The Jewel in the Crown*?

17 On *Spitting Image* who was portrayed as a slug?

18 Which quiz show were Paddy Feeny and Geoffrey Wheeeler question masters on?

19 Euston Films was an offshoot of which TV company?

20 Who hosted *Trick or Treat* with Mike Smith?

21 What type of correspondent for the BBC was Michael Cole before he went to work for Mohammed Al-Fayed?

22 What was the first theme music to *The Sky at Night* called?

23 Which ITV region is the largest in terms of area?

24 Which actor appeared in *Dixon of Dock Green* and *Grange Hill*?

25 Which part did Mrs Gene Roddenberry play in *Star Trek: The Next Generation*?

26 What was Anne Robinson's job on *Breakfast Time*?

27 Which former *Coronation Street* star played Liz in *Bloomin' Marvellous*?

28 What was the name of Brenda's daughter in *Bagdad Cafe*?

29 Which show was originally called *These Friends of Mine* before taking on its star's name?

30 In *All In the Family* what was Archie's daughter's name?

| **Answers** | Movies: Oscars – Who's Who? *(see Quiz 37)* |

1 Poldek Pfefferberg (who told his story to Thomas Keneally). 2 Ralph Bellamy. 3 Elmer Bernstein. 4 Gary Busey. 5 Donfeld. 6 Alec Guinness. 7 Steven Spielberg. 8 George Sanders (All About Eve). 9 Cuba Gooding Jr (Jerry Maguire). 10 John Corigliano. 11 Bugsy. 12 Yves Montand (Simone Signoret). 13 The Shadows (John Farrar). 14 Mammy in Gone with the Wind (Hattie McDaniel). 15 Judy Holliday. 16 Margaret Herrick. 17 Johnny Carson. 18 Sophia Loren. 19 Ruth Gordon. 20 Edmund Goulding. 21 Inside Out. 22 Holly Hunter. 23 The Pride of the Yankees. 24 Ivan Jandl. 25 Richard Williams. 26 Judi Dench. 27 Johnny Depp. 28 Katharine Hepburn. 29 Adrien Brody. 30 Nicole Kidman.

1 Who was Everton's skipper in the 1985 European Cup Winners' Cup?
2 Who holds Liverpool's record for most League appearances?
3 Which Liverpool player appeared three times at Wembley in 1977–78, his first season in England?
4 Which Yorkshire team did Bill Shankly manage between 1956 and 1959?
5 At the start of 1996–97, which theatre impresario was listed as one of Everton's directors?
6 To two each way, in what year were Everton first relegated?
7 Which Liverpool outfield player was the only one not to score in the 11–0 rout of Stromsgodset in 1974?
8 Which Irish club did Ronnie Whelan come from?
9 Which non-League side did Everton beat in 1985 in the FA Cup?
10 Which famous player died at Goodison at the 1980 Merseyside derby?
11 Under the two points for a win system how many points did Liverpool gain to create a record in 1979?
12 Which side inflicted a 10–4 thrashing on Everton in season 1958–59?
13 Which two internationals – one Welsh, one English – did Graeme Souness sign in July 1992?
14 Which ex-Liverpool star played only 27 minutes in the final stages of a World Cup to earn the last of his 63 caps?
15 Who was skipper of Everton's 1966 FA Cup-winning side?
16 In 1990, Liverpool beat which club 9–0 in the League and lost to them in an FA Cup semi-final?
17 Which Liverpool player scored his first international goal in Rio?
18 At which ground did Everton gain their first FA Cup win in 1906?
19 Who retired in 1961 to become a lay preacher and a JP?
20 Which year in the 1980s did neither club contest the Charity Shield?
21 Which Everton player was sent off in both 2005–06 and 2007–08?
22 Finch Farm is Everton's training ground, but what is Liverpool's called?
23 From 1 January 2000 to 31 December 2008, how many derby wins did Everton have?
24 Who converted two penalties in an October 2007 derby?
25 Who was the last Englishman to manage in a derby match (not as a caretaker)?
26 Which England international played for Everton, Liverpool, Man. City and Man. Utd?
27 Which Nathaniel joined the Reds in 2015?
28 Name the former Mark who played for Liverpool whose middle name was Everton.
29 Who was the last player to captain both clubs?
30 Who moved from Everton to Liverpool in 2000 for £6 million?

1 What shape was the Small Faces' *Ogden's Nut Gone Flake* album cover?
2 Who backed Country Joe?
3 _____ is the fourth studio album by Justin Bieber.
4 Who wrote the first two No. 1 songs for Gerry and the Pacemakers?
5 Who backed Lloyd Cole?
6 What group was Steve Winwood a member of before joining Traffic?
7 What is Michael Jackson leaning on, on the cover of *Thriller*?
8 Who was the first artist to have three consecutive UK No. 1 singles?
9 Who did Lennon and McCartney write "Goodbye" for?
10 Which city saw the most Elvis performances?
11 What is Bjork's surname?
12 What type of waitress was Debbie Harry?
13 In which part of London was Damon Albarn born?
14 What was Bette Midler's 1989 Grammy Record of the Year for?
15 What is the real name of Bono of U2?
16 What is a Fender Stratocaster?
17 Who did Buddy Holly's guitarist Tommy Allsup give up his seat for on the ill-fated last flight?
18 How is Evangelos Papathanassiou better known?
19 How did the Velvet Underground get their name?
20 What was Pat Benatar's debut album called?
21 "Brimful of Asha" was the biggest hit for which duo?
22 What was the first album Jamiroquai released in the 21st century?
23 What have Genesis on their heads on the *Foxtrot* album cover?
24 What was Bobby Vinton's first million-seller?
25 Who co-wrote the songs for Disney's *The Lady and The Tramp*?
26 Who launched his chart career with the instrumental "Rebel Rouser"?
27 Which Coasters hit opens with "Fee-fee fi-fi fo-fo fum"?
28 Which Rolling Stones album cover has holes in it with movable pictures?
29 Which group did Peter Noone join in 1980?
30 What did Jimmy Page play until Jeff Beck left the Yardbirds?

---

1 Who composed the score for the 1995 movie *August*?
2 Who wrote the title song for *When the Wind Blows*?
3 Who sang the theme song for *North to Alaska*?
4 Who was Oscar-nominated for music for *The Cider House Rules*?
5 The Oscar-nominated "Save Me" came from which movie?
6 Which three people successively sang the title song in *Someone to Watch Over Me*?
7 In which movie did jazz saxophonist Charlie Barnet play his hit recording of "Cherokee"?
8 For which movie did Bernard Herrmann receive his first Oscar?
9 Who wrote the music for *Lawrence of Arabia*?
10 Which Shostakovich piece was used in *Eyes Wide Shut*?
11 Whose recording of "Why Do Fools Fall in Love" featured on the soundtrack of *American Graffiti*?
12 Who wrote the score for *The Asphalt Jungle*?
13 Who provided the score for *Never on Sunday*?
14 Which music plays in the background in *10*?
15 Whose songs were on the soundtrack of *Philadelphia*?
16 Who wrote the songs for *Lady and the Tramp*?
17 Who was Oscar-nominated for the original score for *The Talented Mr Ripley*?
18 Who contributed a song for his 1957 film *Fire Down Below*?
19 "It Might be You" comes from which movie?
20 Who wrote the songs for *Shanghai Surprise*?
21 Which famous son appeared as Michael Jackson's friend in *Moonwalker*?
22 *Don't Look Back* is an account of whose tour of Britain?
23 Whose zither music is haunting part of *The Third Man*?
24 Who wrote the score for *Double Indemnity*?
25 Which piece of music accompanies the prehistoric section of *Fantasia*?
26 Which member of Abba had a small role in *Mamma Mia!*?
27 Which city's Philharmonic Orchestra performed the *Lord of the Rings* soundtrack?
28 Which Hans scored 2013's *Man of Steel*?
29 Can you name the Alfred who has won nine Academy Awards for his music?
30 Who composed the soundtrack for *Casablanca* and *Gone with the Wind*?

Answers | **TV Pot Luck 5** *(see Quiz 42)*

1 Philadelphia. 2 Harry Hill. 3 Jim Nelson. 4 Julie Walters. 5 Jamie. 6 Annabel Croft. 7 General Knowledge. 8 Dolly. 9 Byker Grove. 10 Elliot. 11 Lt Commander. 12 Third Rock from the Sun. 13 Don Lang and His Frantic Five. 14 Kenny. 15 Mrs Doyle. 16 Prince Andrew. 17 Jasper Carrott. 18 Both read English at Cambridge. 19 One's green, one's brown. 20 Roseanne. 21 Bobby Davro. 22 Table Tennis. 23 Millwall. 24 Royal Canadian Airforce. 25 Bruce Willis. 26 Sir Paul McCartney. 27 Mad Men. 28 Architect. 29 Bodie. 30 Jock Weir.

Quiz 42 | TV Pot Luck 5

Answers – page 443

1 In which US city is *Cold Case* set?
2 Which stand-up comedian had a *TV Burp*?
3 In *GBH* which character played by Michael Palin was headmaster of a school?
4 Who played Marjory in *Talking Heads II*?
5 Which children's series featured Mr Zed and starred Garry Miller?
6 Who succeeded Anneka Rice on *Treasure Hunt*?
7 What was the last round on *The Krypton Factor*?
8 What kind of dealers were on *Play Your Cards Right*?
9 In which children's series did Ant McPartin appear?
10 What surname do the Chuckle Brothers share in real life?
11 What rank is Worf in *Deep Space Nine*?
12 In which sitcom do Sally and Tommy Solomon appear?
13 Who were the resident band on *Six Five Special* in the late 50s?
14 Who was Ray's brother in *Grange Hill*?
15 Who was the housekeeper in *Father Ted*?
16 *Men Behaving Badly* star Leslie Ash was born on the same day as which royal?
17 Radio and TV actress Lucy Davis is the daughter of which comedian?
18 What university studies do David Baddiel and Vanessa Feltz have in common?
19 What colour are Jane Seymour's eyes?
20 Who was described as "A bowling alley reject" in the 1989 Blackwell's Worst Dressed Women List?
21 How is TV funny man Robert Nankeville better known?
22 Paul Shane was junior champion in which sport?
23 Which soccer side does Danny Baker support?
24 Where did Hughie Green serve in WWII?
25 Which actor released a solo album *Heart and Soul* in 1990?
26 Which knight has appeared on *Baywatch*?
27 Which Mad show ended in 2015 after seven seasons?
28 Which profession did Janet Street-Porter train for before embarking on a TV career?
29 What was the western Hero Cheyenne's surname?
30 In *Z Cars* who was Fancy Smith's partner?

Answers | Movies: Music on Film (see Quiz 41)

1 Anthony Hopkins. 2 David Bowie. 3 Johnny Horton. 4 Rachel Portman. 5 Magnolia. 6 Sting, Gene Ammons & Roberta Flack. 7 Jam Session. 8 All That Money Can Buy. 9 Maurice Jarre. 10 Jazz Suite No. 2. 11 Frankie Lymon's. 12 Miklos Rozsa. 13 Monos Hadjidakis. 14 Ravel's Bolero. 15 Bruce Springsteen & Neil Young's. 16 Peggy Lee & Sonny Burke. 17 Gabriel Yared. 18 Jack Lemmon. 19 Tootsie. 20 George Harrison. 21 Sean Lennon. 22 Bob Dylan's. 23 Anton Karas's. 24 Miklos Rozsa. 25 Stravinsky's Rite of Spring. 26 Benny Andersson. 27 Prague. 28 Zimmer. 29 Alfred Newman. 30 Max Steiner.

Quiz 43 — Football: FA Cup Finals

Answers – page 446

1 Who were the first team to beat Tottenham Hotspur in an FA Cup Final?
2 Which 1990s final had opposing players with the same surname?
3 In which decade was the trophy won by a team not from England?
4 Which team were the first to arrive at Wembley by helicopter?
5 Kevin Reeves hit a final goal for which club?
6 Bramall Lane, Goodison Park and Villa Park – which of these grounds has not staged an FA Cup Final replay?
7 In the 1980s and 1990s, which player appeared in four finals and was on the losing team each time?
8 What was the first FA Cup Final to be drawn at Wembley?
9 Which Arsenal defender brought Paul Allen down from behind in 1980 when he was clear on goal?
10 In which decade could the crowd at a final correctly name the referee by shouting, "The referee's a Bastard!"?
11 What is the biggest victory in a final, and who were the teams?
12 Who was in goal for Spurs when they won the trophy in 1981?
13 Where were finals played immediately before the opening of Wembley?
14 Which club captain played in the Brighton v Manchester Utd replay but not in the first game?
15 In 1978, which spectator said, "I thought the No 10 Whymark played exceptionally well", when in fact he hadn't played at all?
16 Who were the first side to lose a Wembley FA Cup Final?
17 Which brothers played together in a 1970s final?
18 In which decade was extra time first played?
19 Who scored an own goal for Blackburn in 1960?
20 Andy Lochhead played in a final for which club?
21 Who was the last player-manager to play in an FA Cup Final?
22 Who, in 2004, became the youngest player to appear in a Cup Final?
23 Who first failed to convert a penalty in an FA Cup Final penalty shoot-out?
24 Which England international was a Portsmouth substitute in the 2008 Cup Final?
25 How many Welsh players were in Cardiff's 16 for the 2008 final?
26 Which team was the first to lift the FA Cup at the Millennium Stadium, Cardiff?
27 The 2015 FA Cup Final was the _____ final of the FA Cup?
28 Which two bitter rivals contested the 1986 and 1989 FA Cup Finals?
29 Name the player who scored a goal just 96 seconds after coming on as a sub.
30 Who was the last player to score in an FA Cup Final at the Millennium Stadium?

Answers	Movies Pot Luck 5 (see Quiz 44)

1 Five. 2 69 minutes. 3 Buscemi. 4 The Bridges of Madison County. 5 Penny Marshall. 6 95 minutes. 7 Steve McQueen. 8 Colour cinematography. 9 Yves Montand. 10 Paul McCartney. 11 Wayne's World. 12 Hugh Grant. 13 Knox Overstreet. 14 Zimmer. 15 Frances McDormand. 16 1980. 17 Bryan Singer. 18 Woody Allen. 19 Ellar Coltrane. 20 Teri Hatcher. 21 Peter Cushing. 22 Planet of the Apes. 23 158 minutes. 24 John Goodman. 25 Michael Caine. 26 Doctor. 27 Heath Ledger. 28 Sunset Boulevard. 29 Glen Campbell. 30 Francis.

1 How many dollars did Eve Marie Saint tip the waiter to seat Cary Grant near her in *North by Northwest*?
2 Within fifteen minutes, how long does *Bambi* last?
3 Which Steve featured in *Armageddon*?
4 A character named Robert Kincaid appeared in which film?
5 Who directed *Awakenings*?
6 Within five minutes, how long does *When Harry Met Sally* last?
7 Who would not be billed below Paul Newman, so refused the part of Sundance?
8 For what did W. Howard Greene and Harold Rosson win a Special Award in 1936?
9 Which actor was born Ivo Livi in 1921?
10 Which singer appeared in *Eat the Rich*?
11 Jimi Hendrix's "Foxy Lady" featured in which 90s movie?
12 Which actor links *Impromptu* and *Bitter Moon*?
13 Which character was played by Josh Charles in the film *Dead Poets Society*?
14 Which Laurie featured in *Assault on Precinct 13*?
15 In the 1990s who won the Best Actress Oscar the year before Helen Hunt?
16 In which year did Alfred Hitchcock die?
17 Who directed *The Usual Suspects*?
18 In the 1980s who said, "The baby's ... only problem is he looks like Edward G. Robinson"?
19 Who played the boy in 2014's *Boyhood*?
20 Who played Paris Carver in *Tomorrow Never Dies*?
21 Which British actor said, "Teeth are a vitally important part of an actor's equipment"?
22 A character named Dr Zira appeared in which film?
23 Within ten minutes how long does *Amadeus* last?
24 Who played the professional exterminator in *Arachnophobia*?
25 Which British actor married a former Miss Guyana in 1973?
26 What title did Harrison Ford's character Richard Kimble have in *The Fugitive*?
27 Which actor's last completed role was the Joker in *The Dark Knight*?
28 In which 1950 movie did Cecil B. De Mille appear on screen playing himself?
29 Which singer appeared at the Lion Dollar Cowboy Bar in *Any Which Way You Can*?
30 What is the first name of "Baby" Houseman in *Dirty Dancing*?

Answers | Football: FA Cup Finals *(see Quiz 43)*

1 Coventry City. 2 1992, Liverpool, Rush (Ian) v Sunderland, Rush (David). 3 1920s (Cardiff). 4 Brighton. 5 Manchester City. 6 Villa Park. 7 Paul Bracewell. 8 Chelsea v Leeds (1970). 9 Willie Young. 10 1870s (S. R. Bastard). 11 Bury 6 v Derby County 0. 12 Milija Aleksic. 13 Stamford Bridge. 14 Steve Foster. 15 Margaret Thatcher. 16 West Ham. 17 Brian and Jimmy Greenhoff. 18 1870s. 19 Mick McGrath. 20 Leicester City (1969). 21 Dennis Wise. 22 Curtis Weston. 23 Paul Scholes. 24 David Nugent. 25 Three. 26 Liverpool. 27 134. 28 Everton and Liverpool. 29 Teddy Sheringham. 30 Steven Gerrard.

1 Amy Poehler led which US TV comedy from 2009 to 2015?
2 What was the name of Dylan Moran's character in *Black Books*?
3 Which composer conducted Eric Morecambe on the piano?
4 Which comedian played Al Johnson?
5 Who owned a dog called Fanny?
6 Who was the animator in the *Monty Python* team?
7 Who played a female driver in *Taxi*?
8 What are Lily Savage's "children" called?
9 Which star of *Seinfeld* was the voice of Hugo in Disney's *The Hunchback of Notre Dame*?
10 What is Cliff's job in *Cheers*?
11 Which sport did Sam Malone play as a professional?
12 What was the nickname of the Inspector in *On the Buses*?
13 Which Carla created the *Liver Birds*?
14 Who created *Curry and Chips*?
15 Who was the star of *Ripping Yarns*?
16 In *No Place Like Home*, who starred as Arthur Crabtree?
17 Which actress appeared as Sid's wife in *Bless This House*?
18 What was Arthur Askey's catchphrase?
19 Where was *Get Well Soon* set?
20 Who used to say "She knows you know"?
21 Who played Bill in *Love Thy Neighbour*?
22 Who created the show *The Comedians*?
23 Patrick Cargill played the father in which family sitcom?
24 What was Arkwright's affliction?
25 Which comic trio dodged the traffic on a three-seater bike?
26 Who played Mrs Cravat opposite Tony Hancock?
27 What was Joe McGann's character in *The Upper Hand*?
28 Which comedian appeared in the TV play *An Evening with Gary Lineker*?
29 Who played Thora Hird's husband in *Meet the Wife*?
30 Which actor played Spike in *Hi-De-Hi!*?

Answers	**Football Pot Luck 5** *(see Quiz 46)*

1 Steve Stone. 2 Arbroath. 3 Chris Woods. 4 Southampton. 5 1900s. 6 Bradford City. 7 Coventry City. 8 Burnley. 9 Newcastle Utd. 10 11. 11 Everton. 12 Ferguson. 13 Manchester City. 14 Graham Taylor. 15 Chris Sutton. 16 Arsenal. 17 West Ham Utd. 18 Reading. 19 Bristol Rovers. 20 Preston North End. 21 Mike Phelan. 22 Norway. 23 Heath. 24 Lincoln City. 25 1890s. 26 Burnley. 27 Oxford United. 28 Alex Rae. 29 1970. 30 Five.

1 Which England player went to the same school as Gazza?
2 In Scotland, which club has its ground nearest to the sea?
3 Who was in goal when Sheffield Wednesday lost the FA Cup Final in 1993?
4 At which club did Andy Townsend make his League debut?
5 In what decade did Manchester Utd first win the championship?
6 Which club had a fanzine called *City Gent*?
7 Bobby Gould followed Dave Sexton as manager of which club?
8 Steve Davis's move to Luton in August 1995 set a club record for a transfer fee received at which club?
9 Which club, formed in 1881, were originally known as Stanley?
10 To one each way, how many international goals did John Barnes score?
11 Neil McDonald and Adrian Heath were in the same team at which club?
12 Which Bobby was Ipswich Town boss from 1982 to 1987?
13 Paul Power first played in an FA Cup Final for which team?
14 Who, at Lincoln in 1972, aged 28 became the youngest ever League manager?
15 Who spent a night in a police cell two days before breaking the British transfer record?
16 Who won, Arsenal or Aston Villa, on May 30, 2015?
17 Which present-day club used to play at the Memorial Recreation Ground, Canning Town?
18 What was the first club that Ian Branfoot managed?
19 Stuart Taylor set a League appearance record at which club?
20 Bill Shankly played for which FA Cup-winning side?
21 Which ex-player did Manchester United promote to replace Carlos Queiroz in 2008?
22 In which country would you watch Tromso playing SK Brann?
23 Which Adrian moved to Espanol from Everton in the 1980s?
24 At which club did Mick Harford make his League debut?
25 In what decade did Sheffield United first win the championship?
26 Which club had a fanzine called *Forever and a Day*?
27 Brian Horton followed Mark Lawrenson as manager of which club?
28 Who moved to Sunderland from Millwall in 1996 for what was a club record transfer fee?
29 To five years each way, when did Swansea Town become Swansea City?
30 To two each way, how many international goals did Trevor Brooking score?

Answers | TV: Comedy 1 *(see Quiz 45)*

1 Parks and Recreation. 2 Bernard Black. 3 Andre Previn. 4 Brian Conley. 5 Julian Clary. 6 Terry Gilliam. 7 Marilu Henner. 8 Bunty and Jason. 9 Jason Alexander. 10 Postman. 11 Baseball. 12 Blakey. 13 Carla Lane. 14 Johnny Speight. 15 Michael Palin. 16 William Gaunt. 17 Diana Coupland. 18 "Hello Playmates". 19 1940s TB sanatorium. 20 Hylda Baker. 21 Rudolf Walker. 22 Jonny Hamp. 23 Father, Dear Father. 24 A stammer. 25 The Goodies. 26 Patricia Hayes. 27 Charlie. 28 Paul Merton. 29 Freddie Finton. 30 Jeffrey Holland.

1 Which band was started with a loan from the alleged Mafia member James Martorano?

2 Which band presented the 1994 Christmas edition of *Top of the Pops*?

3 Who did the 52-year-old manager Rene Angelil marry in 1994?

4 Who went on a *Zoo TV Tour* in 1992?

5 Where was it suggested Elton John be listened to through headphones otherwise noise regulations could be broken?

6 Who was the album *No Prima Donna* a tribute to?

7 Why didn't Englandneworder make a follow-up to the 1990 "World in Motion"?

8 What are the first names of the original Spice Girls?

9 Which album was Madonna's "Vogue" taken from?

10 Which band included Keymaster Snow and MC Golden Voice?

11 Who was named as executive producer of "Itsy Bitsy Teeny Weeny Yellow Polka Dot Bikini"?

12 Who was the first female vocalist with Beautiful South?

13 Which two movies did "The One and Only" feature in?

14 How is Jim Moir better known?

15 Who, in the early 1990s, would make records only in aid of charities?

16 Who featured on the soundtrack of *In the Name of the Father*?

17 How many weeks was Wet Wet Wet's "Love Is All Around" at No. 1?

18 Which 90s band included Wanya and Nathan Morris?

19 Who made the album *Growing Up in Public*?

20 Whose suicide note said, "It's better to burn out than to fade away"?

21 What were New Kids on the Block doing in early 1990?

22 Which north-eastern television actor/singer had a No. 1 with "Ain't No Doubt"?

23 Which was the Spice Girls' first No. 1 without Geri?

24 How many No. 1s did Cliff Richard have in the 1990s?

25 What advice did Celine Dion give in 1995?

26 In 2016, which band celebrated the 20th anniversary of their Knebworth concerts?

27 What "Partners" had their only UK No. 1 hit with "Turtle Power" in 1990?

28 Who did the drugs fail to work for in September 1997?

29 Which three-letter band band pleaded with us "Please Don't Go" in May 1992?

30 Which girl band took "C'est La Vie" to No. 1 in June 1998?

Answers | Movies Pot Luck 6 *(see Quiz 48)*

1 Steven Spielberg. 2 James Cole. 3 75 minutes. 4 Guffrey. 5 Robert. 6 Dennehy. 7 Norma Shearer. 8 It's a Wonderful Life. 9 Warren Beatty. 10 Delbert Mann. 11 The Joker is Wild. 12 Time Bandits. 13 The Fastest Guitar Alive. 14 John Goodman. 15 1985. 16 Norman Mailer. 17 Desperately Seeking Susan. 18 Miles Teller. 19 Turturro. 20 Texas. 21 The Hucksters. 22 A newscaster. 23 Jan De Bont. 24 Silent Running. 25 The Color Purple. 26 Tony Stark. 27 Cary Grant. 28 Taps. 29 Terry Gilliam. 30 Kissy Suzuki.

1 Who said in 1985, "When I grow up I still want to be a director"?
2 What was the name of Bruce Willis's character in *Twelve Monkeys*?
3 Within five minutes, how long does *Sleeping Beauty* last?
4 Which Cary featured in *Close Encounters of the Third Kind*?
5 What is the first name of Oliver Reed, who used his middle name in the movies?
6 Which Brian featured in *Cocoon*?
7 Who won the Best Actress Oscar for *The Divorcee*?
8 Which movie starts, "I owe everything to George Bailey"?
9 Which actor was originally set to play Robert Redford's role in *Indecent Proposal*?
10 Who won the Best Director Oscar for *Marty*?
11 The song "All the Way" came from which movie?
12 Which 1980 movie visited Sherwood Forest and the *Titanic*?
13 Which 1966 film did rock star Roy Orbison star in?
14 Which actor links *The Big Easy* and *Punchline*?
15 In which year did Orson Welles die?
16 Which writer directed *Tough Guys Don't Dance* in 1987?
17 In which film did a character named Roberta Glass appear?
18 Who drummed his way to success in 2014's *Whiplash*?
19 Which Jon featured in *The Color of Money*?
20 Steve Martin was born in which American state?
21 In which movie did Clark Gable play Vic Norton?
22 What part does director Steve Miner play in *Friday the Thirteenth, Part 3*?
23 Who directed *Twister*?
24 In which film does a character named Freeman Lowell appear?
25 Which had the longest running time – *Dirty Dancing*, *Men in Black* or *The Color Purple*?
26 What was Robert Downey Jr's character's name in *Iron Man*?
27 John Cleese played Archie Leach in *A Fish Called Wanda* in homage to whom?
28 In which 1981 movie did Sean Penn make his screen debut?
29 Who directed *The Fisher King*?
30 What was the name of the Bond girl in *You Only Live Twice*?

Answers	Pop: The 1990s *(see Quiz 47)*

1 New Kids on the Block. 2 Take That. 3 Celine Dion. 4 U2. 5 Hong Kong. 6 Van Morrison. 7 They did not qualify for the 1994 World Cup. 8 Mel B., Mel C., Victoria, Geri and Emma. 9 I'm Breathless. 10 Partners in Kryme. 11 Andrew Lloyd Webber. 12 Briana Corrigan. 13 Buddy's Song, Doc Hollywood. 14 Vic Reeves. 15 George Michael. 16 Sinead O'Connor. 17 15. 18 Boyz II Men. 19 Jimmy Nail. 20 Kurt Cobain. 21 Hangin' Tough. 22 Jimmy Nail. 23 Viva Forever. 24 Two. 25 Think Twice. 26 Oasis. 27 Partners In Kryme. 28 The Verve. 29 KWS. 30 B*Witched.

1 Gabriel Kent claimed to be the son of which *Sun Hill* Sergeant?
2 Who played Tess in the 2008 series of *Tess of the D'Urbervilles*?
3 What was the trade in the drama series *A Respectable Trade*?
4 From 2005 to 2013, Steve Carrell injected a poignancy to which character?
5 Where in Provence did Peter Mayle recount his Year?
6 Who played Dr Edward Roebuck, head of a psychiatric unit, in the 80s drama *Maybury*?
7 What was the name of the lead character in *Nanny*, played by Wendy Craig?
8 Which two actresses played Emma Harte in Barbara Taylor Bradford's mini-series *A Woman of Substance*?
9 Which prison featured in *Within These Walls*?
10 Which character was the hero of *When the Boat Comes In*?
11 Which role did Oscar winner Colin Welland play in *Z Cars*?
12 Who played the Dietrich-like character Bertha Freyer in the comic drama, *Private Schulz*?
13 What was the name of Robert Lindsay's pensioner mum in *GBH*?
14 What was the title of the 110-minute conclusion of the series *Tenko*?
15 Which actor played Randolph Churchill in *Winston Churchill – The Wilderness Years*?
16 In *Upstairs Downstairs* how did Lady Marjorie die?
17 In which city was the serial *World's End* set?
18 Which Roy played Jack Ruskin in the drama *Airline*?
19 Where was the BBC1 drama *Beau Geste* actually shot?
20 Who tried to solve the Laura Palmer mystery in *Twin Peaks*?
21 What were subsequent series of *Mogul* called?
22 Who played Chrissy in *Boys from the Blackstuff*?
23 Which father of a *This Life* star played James Brant in Trainer?
24 Who played the Smiley role in the ITV's *A Murder of Quality* in 1991?
25 In *Foxy Lady*, what was Daisy Jackson's job?
26 How many singles were there in the first series of *Thirtysomething*?
27 Who played the character Brown in the political thriller *Harry's Game*?
28 Who did Bruce Willis play on TV opposite Cybill Shepherd?
29 Which TV detective was a reluctant George Cross recipient?
30 Why was the final episode of *I Remember Nelson* held over for six months before airing?

Answers | **The Great Races** (see Quiz 50)

1 Reims. 2 Alberto Ascari. 3 Jose Froilan Gonzalez. 4 Juan Manuel Fangio. 5 A Maserati. 6 Mike Hawthorn. 7 A Ferrari. 8 The last one. 9 Thillois straight. 10 Juan Manuel Fangio. 11 Mike Hawthorn. 12 Nurburgring. 13 A Ferrari. 14 Peter Collins. 15 Juan Manuel Fangio. 16 Maserati. 17 His planned pit stop was very slow. 18 Penultimate. 19 Luigi Musso. 20 Stirling Moss. 21 Jarno Trulli. 22 Bus Stop. 23 Three. 24 15th. 25 Jordan. 26 Phil Hill. 27 Three (Jim Clark, Graham Hill and John Surtees). 28 Peter Gethin. 29 Ronnie Petersen. 30 Nico Rosberg.

1 At which circuit was the 1953 French Grand Prix held?
2 Name the reigning world champion who qualified on pole for Ferrari.
3 Who led the early laps for Maserati?
4 Another Argentinian took the lead. Who was that?
5 What make of car was he driving?
6 He was then joined at the front in a slipstreaming duel with which British driver?
7 What make of car was he driving?
8 At which corner did this British driver take the lead for good on the final lap?
9 This corner was at the end of which straight?
10 Who finished second?
11 Which British driver led the opening laps of the 1957 German Grand Prix?
12 At which circuit was it held?
13 What make of car was he driving?
14 Name his teammate who was up there with him.
15 Who started from pole position?
16 For which team was he driving?
17 Why did his race plan go wrong?
18 When did the race-winner take the lead, on the final or the penultimate lap?
19 Name the third Ferrari driver who finished fourth?
20 And who was the best-placed Vanwall driver, in fifth?
21 Which Italian driver won the 2004 Monaco Grand Prix?
22 What is the name of the chicane where Lewis Hamilton had trouble at Spa in 2008?
23 How many other drivers were on the lead lap when Jenson Button won his first Grand Prix?
24 What was Fernando Alonso's grid position when he won the 2008 Singapore Grand Prix?
25 For which team did Giancarlo Fisichella win the 2003 Brazilian Grand Prix?
26 Who qualified his Ferrari in pole position for the 1961 French Grand Prix?
27 How many drivers arrived at the 1964 Mexican Grand Prix, the season's finale, with a chance of the title?
28 Who won the 1971 Italian Grand Prix for BRM?
29 Who qualified on pole position for Lotus at the 1973 British Grand Prix?
30 In 2016, who took the victory at the Russian F1 GP?

1 At which three clubs did the Futcher twins play together?
2 Who were the first brothers to win European Championship medals?
3 At which club did the Laudrup brothers begin their careers?
4 Who were the only brothers to play on the same side in a 60s FA Cup Final?
5 Which brothers Graham and Ron were at Oxford Utd in the 1960s?
6 In the 1980 Luton v QPR game, which brothers Martyn and Viv were opponents after coming on as subs?
7 Liam Brady's elder brothers Ray and Pat were together at which club?
8 What was the surname of 1950s Newcastle Utd brothers Ted and George?
9 Jimmy and John Conway were at which club together in the 1970s?
10 Mike Gatting's brother Steve played in an FA Cup Final for which team?
11 In the 50s which brothers each reached 200 League goals on the same day?
12 Which brother was at Aston Villa with Bruce Rioch?
13 The Linighan boys – Andy and David – started out at which club?
14 Which brothers were together at Villa for 18 years from the late 1930s?
15 Who were the goalkeeping brothers to be exchanged in the 60s?
16 What was the surname of dad Ken and son Peter both of Manchester City?
17 Which cousins played together in an FA Cup losing team in the 1980s?
18 Which member of a footballing family became the first non-British Scottish PFA Footballer of the Year?
19 Which Manchester City boss bought his own son Kevin?
20 What was the first name of George Eastham's father who played for England in 1935?
21 At which club was Gary & Phil Neville's father Neville a director?
22 Which Fulham and England Paul is the brother-in-law of John Terry's brother Paul?
23 How many times did two Ferdinand family members play together at West Ham?
24 Which cousin of Frank Lampard Jr played 17 times for England?
25 What relation is midfielder Craig Burley to 2008 Scotland coach George Burley?
26 Who signed his son for Newcastle United after he took charge of the club in 1997?
27 Which "Finn" played for Brondy IF and had two sons who also played for the club?
28 Who tried out for his dad's ex-team Man. Utd but opted for a career in modelling?
29 Name the ex-Man. City legend whose son played for Sunderland.
30 Which Liverpool legend's father played for Everton from 1966 to 1970?

Answers	Pop Pot Luck 7 *(see Quiz 52)*

1 Debbie Harry. 2 Denmark. 3 Joe Walsh. 4 "Pretty Flamingo". 5 Neil Sedaka. 6 Jimmy Page. 7 Bruno Mars. 8 Bryan Ferry. 9 A beach. 10 Frank Zappa. 11 Sold. 12 Ray Davies. 13 Village People. 14 Gene Vincent. 15 1921. 16 Jailhouse Rock. 17 David Bowie. 18 Great-great-great-great-grandson. 19 Salford. 20 Stanley Road (album title). 21 Edele & Keavy Lynch. 22 15. 23 Austria. 24 Charlie Watts. 25 Mary MacGregor. 26 Slim Whitman. 27 "Baby I Love You". 28 Bob Dylan. 29 Kate Bush. 30 Tony Hatch and Jackie Trent.

1 Whose stabbed head appears on the cover of her first solo album?
2 Which country pioneered pirate radio ships in the late 1950s?
3 Which guitarist went from Barnstorm to the Eagles?
4 What was Manfred Mann's last single with Paul Jones on vocals?
5 Who started his career with "I Go Ape" in 1959?
6 Who composed the soundtrack for *Deathwish II*?
7 Mark Ronson and _____ released 2015s "Uptown Funk"?
8 Who did Jerry Hall have a long relationship with before Mick Jagger?
9 What is Mike Oldfield standing on, on the *Incantations* album cover?
10 Who formed the Straight and Barking Pumpkin labels?
11 What was Boy George's debut album called?
12 Whose autobiography was called *X-Ray*?
13 Who were made up of a cowboy, an Indian, a policeman, a biker, a GI and a builder?
14 How was Vincent Eugene Craddock better known?
15 In which year was Bert Weedon born?
16 In which film did Elvis play the role of Vince Everett?
17 In 1997 who issued bonds in his name for people to invest in?
18 What relation is Pat Boone to the Western pioneer Daniel Boone?
19 In which part of Manchester was Elkie Brooks born?
20 In which immortalized road in Woking did Paul Weller live as a child?
21 Which twin sisters formed half of B*Witched?
22 How old was Billie (Piper) when she first topped the UK charts?
23 In which country are the Beatles skiing in *Help*?
24 Who drew the cartoons on the back cover of the Stones album *Between the Buttons*?
25 Who was "Torn Between Two Lovers" in 1977?
26 Who was the first country singer to tour Britain and appear at the London Palladium?
27 What was a hit for the Ronettes, Dave Edmunds and the Ramones?
28 Which singer celebrated his Bar Mitzvah in Minnesota in May 1954?
29 Who was voted Capital Radio's Best Female Singer from 1978 to 1980?
30 Who wrote "Where are You Now (My Love)"?

Answers | Football: Famous Families *(see Quiz 51)*

1 Chester, Luton, Manchester City. 2 Erwin and Ronald Koeman. 3 Brondby. 4 Allan and Ron Harris. 5 Atkinson. 6 Busby. 7 Millwall. 8 Robledo. 9 Fulham. 10 Brighton. 11 Arthur and Jack Rowley. 12 Neil. 13 Hartlepool Utd. 14 Moss Brothers. 15 The Springetts (Ron and Peter). 16 Barnes. 17 Clive and Paul Allen. 18 Brian Laudrup. 19 John Bond. 20 George. 21 Bury. 22 Konchesky. 23 Never. 24 Jamie Redknapp. 25 Nephew. 26 Kenny Dalglish (signed Paul). 27 Finn Laudrup (sons, Michael & Brian). 28 Calum Best. 29 Mike Summerbeee (son, Nicky). 30 Michael Owen (father, Terry).

1 Star of *Born on the Fourth of July*, when is his birthday?
2 What does he have in common with Robert De Niro and Charlie Chaplin?
3 What is his full real name?
4 What is the name of his character in *Days of Thunder*?
5 Who sang the title song of his first movie?
6 How old was he when he had his first movie role?
7 On which novel was *Taps* based?
8 Which 1999 movie was the last for its director?
9 Who directed him in the 1983 "brat pack" movie with Matt Dillon, Rob Lowe and others?
10 For which movie immediately after *Mission: Impossible* was he Oscar-nominated?
11 Who or what won an Oscar for *Top Gun*?
12 He received his first Oscar nomination for playing which role?
13 With which star of *Risky Business* did he have an off-screen romance?
14 Which 1986 movie won an Oscar for his co-star?
15 What is his job in the film which won his co-star Dustin Hoffman an Oscar?
16 Who was his wife prior to Nicole Kidman?
17 In which part of which state was he born?
18 Where did he spend a year before deciding to become an actor?
19 Which writer whose book a film was based on said, "He's no more my Vampire Lestat than Edward G. Robinson is Rhett Butler"?
20 What "award" did he win at high school?
21 What was his second film?
22 For which TV show did he make his directorial debut?
23 What was his next film after *Rain Man*?
24 What was the first movie he produced and starred in?
25 What was the first film he starred in with Nicole Kidman after their marriage?
26 In 2017, Tom Cruise starred in what movie as Barry Seal.
27 What is the name of his daughter, born in April 2006?
28 Which actress and competitive poker player did Tom marry in 1987?
29 What film studio did Tom and Paula Wagner take control of in 2005?
30 What did Tom train for and aspire to become before taking up a career in movies?

Answers | TV Pot Luck 6 (see Quiz 54)

1 Animal. 2 Matt LeBlanc. 3 Chris Kelly. 4 Jessica. 5 Hinge and Bracket. 6 Nationwide. 7 Ernest. 8 Orbit City Earth. 9 This Morning. 10 Tarby's Fame Game. 11 Gregory Sumner. 12 Esther. 13 Terry Wogan. 14 Tracy Ullman. 15 Give Us a Clue. 16 The Flintstones. 17 Points of View. 18 Voyage to the Bottom of the Sea. 19 Magnus. 20 Gymnastics. 21 Yates. 22 Television studio. 23 Edna Everage. 24 Parkinson. 25 Chester. 26 Peter Cook. 27 Anthony Newley – he appeared in The Upper Hand and was married to Joan Collins. 28 Richard Wilson. 29 Softly, Softly. 30 Z Cars.

1 Who was *The Muppets'* drummer?
2 Which Friend found success in *Episodes*?
3 Who presented *Clapperboard*?
4 Who was Chester Tate's wife in *Soap*?
5 How are George Logan and Patrick Fyffe better known?
6 Which early-evening programme was presented by Michael Barrett?
7 In *Dangermouse,* what was Penfold's first name?
8 Where do *The Jetsons* live?
9 Which daytime show moved from Liverpool docks to London?
10 Which game show did Jimmy Tarbuck go on to present when he left *Winner Takes All*?
11 Who was William Devane's character in *Knots Landing*?
12 What was Grandma Walton's first name?
13 Who named Lucy Ewing "The Poison Dwarf"?
14 Which of the cast of *Three of a Kind* had her own US series?
15 In which series did Liza Goddard take over a captain's role from Una Stubbs?
16 In which series was the local newspaper *The Daily Slate*?
17 Which series has had three Robinsons as presenters?
18 In which futuristic series was the character Admiral Nelson?
19 What was TV presenter and scientist Dr Pike's christian name?
20 At which sport did presenter Suzanne Dando represent Britain?
21 What was the surname of TV presenters Jess and Paula?
22 Where would you find Dollies and Cue Cards?
23 Which Australian character had a husband Norm?
24 On whose chat show was Harry Stoneham musical director?
25 What was the name of the deputy in *Gun Law*?
26 Which satirist had a hit with *The Ballad of Spotty Muldoon*?
27 Which actor/singer connects *The Upper Hand* to *Dynasty*?
28 Who played Dr Thorpe in *Only When I Laugh*?
29 In which series was there a detective named Harry Hawkins?
30 Leonard Rossiter played a detective sergeant in which series?

Answers | **Movies: Tom Cruise** *(see Quiz 53)*

1 3rd July. 2 Left-handed. 3 Thomas Cruise Mapother IV. 4 Cole. 5 Lionel Richie ("Endless Love"). 6 18. 7 Father Sky. 8 Eyes Wide Shut (Stanley Kubrick). 9 Francis Ford Coppola. 10 Jerry Maguire. 11 Song ("Take My Breath Away"). 12 Ron Kovic (Born on the Fourth of July). 13 Rebecca De Mornay. 14 The Color of Money. 15 Salesman. 16 Mimi Rogers. 17 Syracuse, New York. 18 Franciscan monastery. 19 Anne Rice (Interview with the Vampire). 20 Least Likely to Succeed. 21 Taps. 22 Fallen Angels. 23 Cocktail. 24 Mission: Impossible. 25 Far and Away. 26 American Made. 27 Suri. 28 Mimi Rogers. 29 United Artists. 30 A Catholic priest.

1 Which team entered Qualifications for the very first time at the Euros 2016?
2 Which country was the first to appear in three consecutive finals?
3 In what year was the first European Championship Final played?
4 Which country hosted the 1992 competition?
5 In which year did Spain win the trophy?
6 The home countries, except Scotland, entered the second tournament. When was this?
7 Name the first two cities to have hosted finals twice.
8 When did Italy win the trophy?
9 Which country won the Championship on penalties in 1976?
10 Who were the Dutch scorers in their final victory over Russia?
11 Who scored the two goals to win Euro 96?
12 How many games were there in Euro 96?
13 When Andy Sinton went off, who was the last player to come on as a substitute for England in Euro 92?
14 Which French player finished as the top scorer in 1984?
15 At which two grounds were the Euro 96 semi-finals held?
16 Which English headmaster was a referee in Euro 96?
17 Who scored England's first ever European Championship goal?
18 Who inspired the starting of the Championship?
19 Who contested the first ever Championship final?
20 Who were the first host country to win the European Championship?
21 How many matches were played in the finals at Euro 2008?
22 Who was England's top scorer at Euro 2004?
23 Croatia and which other country went out on penalties at Euro 2008?
24 In which city did England beat Germany 1–0 in Euro 2000?
25 What was the surname of Greece's goalkeeper at Euro 2004?
26 Which two countries will play host to the finals in 2012?
27 In which Dutch city did France beat Italy 2–1 (after extra time) in the final of Euro 2000?
28 Which country made a record 10th appearance at Euro 2008?
29 Name the French star who holds the record for most number of goals in the finals.
30 Name the two losing semi-finalists of Euro 2008.

Answers | **Pop Pot Luck 8** *(see Quiz 56)*

1 Tab Hunter. 2 Linda McCartney 3 Sheffield. 4 Clifford T. Ward. 5 Duran Duran's Nick Rhodes. 6 Never a Dull Moment. 7 Cooleyhighharmony. 8 Coronation Rag. 9 His tonsils. 10 Ten. 11 "What a Fool Believes". 12 Marti Pellow. 13 Stealing car tyres. 14 David Coverdale. 15 New Edition. 16 Liberace. 17 1,670,386,368. 18 Kate Bush – they both wrote a "Wuthering Heights". 19 Canned Heat. 20 George Michael. 21 Offspring. 22 Kevin Richardson. 23 Creedence Clearwater Revival. 24 "Cantare ... oh, oh, oh, oh". 25 "Dance to the Music". 26 John Lennon. 27 Bay City Rollers. 28 Jonathan King. 29 "As Time Goes By". 30 She was declared bankrupt.

1 Who had a No. 1 hit with "Young Love" 16 years before Donny Osmond?
2 Who took the cover photo for Paul McCartney's first solo album?
3 In which city was Joe Cocker born?
4 Who had a 1973 hit with "Gaye"?
5 Who married the heiress Anne Friedman in 1984?
6 Which Rod Stewart album cover features him sitting in an armchair?
7 What was Boyz II Men's debut album called?
8 What rag was Winifred Atwell celebrating in 1953?
9 What did Ringo Starr have removed in November 1964?
10 How many albums did David Bowie have in the charts in July 1983?
11 Which Doobie Brothers song was Grammy Record of the Year in 1979?
12 An imitator of which pop star won the 1996 *Stars in Their Eyes*?
13 Why was Barry White imprisoned in 1960?
14 Which vocalist links Deep Purple and Whitesnake?
15 Who backed Mike Batt on "Summertime City"?
16 Who said, "Too much of a good thing is simply wonderful"?
17 How many YouTube views had Adele's 2015 song "Hello" had in its first ten months – 1,670,386,368 or 1,236, 643, 213?
18 Which singer shares her birthday with Emily Bronte?
19 Which band included Bob "The Bear" Hite and Al "Blind Owl" Wilson?
20 Who was the youngest-ever recipient of the Songwriter of the Year trophy at the Ivor Novello awards in 1985?
21 Who were "Pretty Fly (for a White Guy)"?
22 Who left the Backstreet Boys in 2006?
23 Whose debut album was *Green River*?
24 What follows "Volare ... oh, oh!"?
25 What was Sly and the Family Stone's debut single?
26 Which Beatle looks directly at the camera on the cover of *Rubber Soul*?
27 Whose final 1970s UK No. 1 was "Give a Little Love"?
28 Who wrote "Johnny Reggae"?
29 Which song title links Jason Donovan and Dooley Wilson?
30 Which problem did Cyndi Lauper have in 1983?

Answers | Football: European Championship *(see Quiz 55)*

1 Gibraltar. 2 West Germany (1972, 1976, 1980). 3 1960. 4 Sweden. 5 1964.
6 1964. 7 Paris and Rome. 8 1968. 9 Czechoslovakia. 10 Gullit and Van Basten.
11 Oliver Bierhoff. 12 31. 13 Paul Merson. 14 Michel Platini. 15 Old Trafford
and Wembley. 16 David Elleray. 17 Ron Flowers. 18 Henri Delauney. 19 Soviet
Union and Yugoslavia. 20 Spain (In 1964). 21 31. 22 Wayne Rooney. 23 Italy. 24
Charleroi. 25 Nikopolidis. 26 Poland and Ukraine. 27 Rotterdam. 28 Germany. 29
Michel Platini (9). 30 Russia and Turkey.

Quiz 57

Movies: Disaster Movies

Answers – page 460

1 What is the body count of *Die Hard 2* said to be?
2 Who played Ellis in *Die Hard*?
3 Who wrote the score for *Airport*?
4 Who directed *The Poseidon Adventure*?
5 Which Rock took the lead in Brad Peyton's *San Andreas* in 2015?
6 Who directed the 50s movie *Invasion USA*?
7 Who produced *Armageddon*?
8 Where does the character Jenny die in *Deep Impact*?
9 What is the occupation of the character played by Bill Paxton in *Titanic*?
10 Which company provided the computer-generated images for *Twister*?
11 Who directed *Apollo 13*?
12 Who plays the grandmother of the Mayor's children in *Dante's Peak*?
13 Within ten minutes, how long does *Towering Inferno* run?
14 Who wrote *Die Hard with a Vengeance*?
15 Who was Oscar-nominated for *Earthquake*?
16 *The Swarm* is based on a novel written by whom?
17 Who directed *Avalanche*?
18 Where is *Daylight* set?
19 Who wrote the score for *Meteor*?
20 Which David featured in *A Night to Remember*?
21 Which actor received an Oscar nomination for *San Francisco*?
22 Who wrote the novel that *The Devil at Four O'Clock* is based on?
23 For what did *Krakatoa, East of Java* receive an Oscar nomination?
24 Upon whose novel is *The Hindenburg* based?
25 Which two studios made the movie based on *The Tower* and *The Glass Inferno*?
26 In which year was the spoof *Disaster Movie* released?
27 What type of disaster occurs in *Dante's Peak*?
28 Which 1996 movie offers a fictional account of the invention of bubble fusion?
29 In what movie does a group of teenagers cheat death by avoiding a plane crash?
30 Who played Jim Scott in the 1997 movie *Danger Zone*?

Answers | **TV Pot Luck 7** *(see Quiz 58)*

1 Milkshake. 2 Last Man. 3 Michael Grade. 4 The Academy Awards. 5 Bessie.
6 Niece. 7 Psychiatrist. 8 Diane Keen. 9 The High Street. 10 Paul Merton. 11
Newcastle. 12 Chief O'Brien. 13 Jaye Griffiths. 14 Les Dennis. 15 Miranda. 16
The Dick Van Dyke Show. 17 Local Heroes. 18 Nancy Bartlett. 19 Harriet Thorpe. 20
The Simpsons. 21 Kiss Kiss Bang Bang. 22 Channel 4. 23 Sebastian. 24 American
Football. 25 A Grand Day Out. 26 Wishbone. 27 King of the Hill. 28 Antiques,
including toys and teddy bears. 29 Anthony Newley. 30 Peter Dimmock.

1 What drink is Channel Five's early-morning general entertainment show?
2 Since 2015, Will Forte has starred as the _____ On Earth?
3 Which former Head of Channel 4 was born on the same day as Lynn Redgrave?
4 Billy Crystal won an Emmy in 1998 for hosting which annual event?
5 What was the name of Lord Belborough's steam engine in Chigley?
6 What relation, if any, is Bramwell star Jemma Redgrave to actress Vanessa Redgrave?
7 What was Lilith Crane's profession in Cheers?
8 Who was the Foxy Lady played by?
9 Where did Helen give birth in The Brittas Empire?
10 Whose show had a regular sketch set in a newsagent and tobacconist's kiosk in an Underground station?
11 Kate Adie is a former student of which university?
12 Who was the Head Engineer on Star Trek: Next Generation?
13 Which star of Bugs played D.I. Sally Johnson in The Bill?
14 How is TV presenter Leslie Heseltine better known?
15 What is the name of Hollin and Shelly's baby in Northern Exposure?
16 In which 60s sitcom did Richard Deacon play Mel Cooley?
17 Which series featured Adam Hart Davis seeking out inventors and inventions?
18 What was Sandra Bernhardt's character in Roseanne?
19 Who played Fleur in Absolutely Fabulous?
20 Side Show Bob featured in which cartoon series?
21 Which cinema magazine programme was presented by Charlie Higson?
22 On which channel was the motoring series Driven transmitted?
23 What is Rowan Atkinson's middle name?
24 Bill Cosby was offered a professional trial in which sport?
25 In which episode did Wallace and Grommit go to the moon?
26 Who was Paul Brinegar's character in Rawhide?
27 In which cartoon series are the neighbours called "Khan"?
28 What kind of expert is Bunny Campione?
29 Which actor, singer, songwriter made a guest appearance in EastEnders as a used car dealer?
30 Who was the original presenter of Sportsview?

Answers	**Movies: Disaster Movies** (see Quiz 57)

1 264. 2 Hart Bochner. 3 Alfred Newman. 4 Ronald Neame. 5 Dwayne Johnson. 6 Alfred E. Green. 7 Jerry Bruckheimer. 8 On the beach. 9 Salvage hunter. 10 Industrial Light and Magic. 11 Ron Howard. 12 Elizabeth Hoffman. 13 158 mins. 14 Jonathon Hensleigh. 15 Philip Lathrop. 16 Arthur Herzog. 17 Corey Allen. 18 New York to New Jersey tunnel. 19 Laurence Rosenthal. 20 McCallum. 21 Spencer Tracy. 22 Max Catto. 23 Special effects. 24 Michael M. Mooney's. 25 Fox & MGM (Towering Inferno). 26 2008. 27 A volcano. 28 Chain Reaction. 29 Final Destination. 30 Robert Downey Jnr.

Quiz 59 | Football: Early Days | Answers – page 462 | LEVEL 3

1 Who were the first team to lose an FA Cup Final?
2 William McGregor, who pushed for the formation of a League, was a director of which club?
3 Which club did Alf Common move from in the first £1,000 transfer?
4 Who were the first team to win the FA Cup three times in a row?
5 From 1895 to the First World War where were FA Cup Finals played?
6 Leeds United were formed following the demise of which team?
7 Samuel Widdowson of Nottingham Forest is credited with which innovation?
8 Who were the first team to score six goals in an FA Cup Final?
9 Which important spectator created a first at the Burnley v Liverpool 1914 FA Cup Final?
10 Which player turned out in nine of the first 12 FA Cup Finals?
11 Preston North End's 26 goals in an FA Cup game was against which team?
12 In 1904, which giant keeper made the first of 564 Notts County appearances?
13 Which club was the first to win promotion and the First Division in successive seasons?
14 What was formed in Paris on May 21, 1904?
15 At which ground did terracing collapse in 1902 killing 25 people?
16 Who was the first professional to play for England against Scotland?
17 In 1911 a new FA Cup was made in – and then won by the team from – which place?
18 In footballing terms what was a "Scottish professor"?
19 How many games did Preston North End lose in the first League season?
20 Who were the first team to lose a Scottish FA Cup Final?
21 When Notts County won the FA Cup in 1894, what was their home ground?
22 Which Southern League team lost the 1902 FA Cup Final?
23 Which country was the third to play international football?
24 What achievement belongs to Alexander Bonsor?
25 How many goals did Steve Bloomer score in his 23 England internationals?
26 On average how much did it cost to watch a nineteenth-century Football League match?
27 Prior to 1891 where did the referee actually officiate the match from?
28 Which Lancashire club moved to their current ground in 1910?
29 Which team won the inaugural Football Championship without losing a game?
30 In 1893 how much did Derby County propose the maximum wage should be?

Answers | **Pop Pot Luck 9** *(see Quiz 60)*

1 Argentina. 2 Coral. 3 32. 4 "For Your Love". 5 Brian Eno. 6 Belinda Carlisle. 7 David Bowie's. 8 Beggars' Banquet. 9 The Bell Boys. 10 Atlantic. 11 Life's a Riot with Spy Vs. Spy. 12 5th Dimension. 13 The Who. 14 Kim Wilde. 15 Joni Mitchell. 16 Birmingham. 17 Marillion. 18 Ziggy (real name David). 19 "Brandy". 20 Manhattan Transfer's "Chanson d'Amour". 21 Smoke and Mirrors. 22 Italian. 23 Harvey Goldsmith. 24 Manhattan Transfer. 25 "The Chicken Song". 26 Bras. 27 The Honeycombs. 28 Rod Stewart. 29 They were all by the Beatles. 30 Jo Stafford.

1 In which country was Chris de Burgh born?
2 What label did Buddy Holly record on?
3 How old was Bobby Darin when he found out that the woman he thought was his mother was his sister?
4 What is the Yardbirds' only hit to get in the Top 10 in the US and UK?
5 Who left Roxy Music to form Obscure Records?
6 Who left the Go-Go's to go solo?
7 Whose alter ego was the Thin White Duke?
8 Which Stones album commences with "Sympathy for the Devil"?
9 Who backed Freddy Bell on "Giddy-Up-A-Ding-Dong"?
10 What record label was founded by Ahmet Ertegun and Herb Abramson?
11 What was Billy Bragg's debut album called?
12 Who won the Grammy Record of the Year in 1967 with "Up Up and Away"?
13 Who were called the High Numbers in their early days?
14 Which UK vocalist joined Michael Jackson on his *Bad* tour in Europe?
15 How is Roberta Anderson better known?
16 In which city was Steve Winwood born?
17 Which band had Fish on lead vocals?
18 What is Bob Marley's eldest son called?
19 What was Barry Manilow's "Mandy" originally called in the US?
20 Which 1977 chart-topper was sung in French?
21 In 2015, Imagine Dragons released which sophomore album?
22 What nationality were Eiffel 65, who topped the charts with "Blue (Da Ba Dee)"?
23 Who was the promoter of Live Aid?
24 Which group has included Alan Paul, Tim Hauser, Janis Siegel and Cheryl Bentyne among its members?
25 What was the No. 1 produced by Fluck and Law creations in 1986?
26 What is being modelled on the back cover of the Rolling Stone album *Some Girls*?
27 Which group with a 1964 No. 1 hit had a girl drummer?
28 Who was lead singer on Python Lee Jackson's "In a Broken Dream"?
29 What was unique about the top five in the US singles chart on 4 April 1964?
30 Who was the first female singer to top the UK charts?

Answers | Football: Early Days (see Quiz 59)

1 Royal Engineers. 2 Aston Villa. 3 Sunderland. 4 Wanderers. 5 Crystal Palace. 6 Leeds City. 7 Shinguards. 8 Blackburn Rovers. 9 George V was the first monarch at a final. 10 Lord Arthur Kinnaird. 11 Hyde United. 12 Albert Ironmonger. 13 Liverpool. 14 FIFA. 15 Ibrox. 16 James Forrest. 17 Bradford. 18 Professional player (a Scot paid to play in England). 19 None. 20 Clydesdale. 21 Trent Bridge. 22 Southampton. 23 Wales. 24 First international goal. 25 28. 26 6d. 27 The touchline. 28 Manchester United. 29 Preston North End (1888–89). 30 £4 per week.

1 What was his middle name?

2 Under which star sign was he born?

3 Which studio did he sign with when he first went to Hollywood?

4 What was the first movie where he was cast opposite Marlene Dietrich?

5 For which film was he nominated for his second Oscar?

6 With whose troupe did he go to America in 1920?

7 Which short saw his screen debut?

8 What did the studio want to change his name to when he first arrived at Paramount?

9 Which 1948 movies both featured the then Mrs Cary Grant?

10 Which of his co-stars mimicked him in the subsequent film he made?

11 Which of his movies was a remake of *The More the Merrier*?

12 He was a director of which cosmetics company after his retirement from the big screen?

13 After 1958 what percentage of the takings did he receive in lieu of salary in his films?

14 His second wife was heiress to which empire?

15 For which movie did he donate his salary to war relief?

16 Who was the only winner of an Oscar for *Suspicion*, in which he starred?

17 In which film did he say, "Insanity runs in my family. It practically gallops"?

18 Mae West's invitation to Cary Grant to "come up some time and see me" came from a movie based on which play?

19 Who played his wife in the first movie for which he was Oscar-nominated?

20 Who won Best Actor for the year Grant was given a special Oscar?

21 In 1937–38 he was under joint contract to which studios?

22 Who was the mother of his only child?

23 Who did he play in *Night and Day*?

24 What was his first film for Hitchcock?

25 Which wife survived him?

26 How old was Cary Grant when his last movie was released?

27 Who played Cary Grant in *The Aviator*?

28 In which South West English city was Cary born?

29 Which English funnyman played Archie Leach in *A Fish Called Wanda*?

30 In which 2004 movie does Kyle MacLachlan play a caricature of Grant?

1 *Smack The* what was an all-woman sketch show?
2 Which *CSI* criminalist had a personal relationship with Gil Grissom?
3 What is the theme for *Blue Peter* called?
4 Who did Griff Rhys Jones replace in the *Not the Nine o'Clock News* team?
5 What was the name of Brian Wilde's character in *Porridge*?
6 Which "Man Behaving Badly" narrated *Red-Handed*?
7 Who links *Scrapheap* to *Red Dwarf*?
8 Who presented the quiz show *Pass the Buck*?
9 What does Mark Freden talk about on *GMTV*?
10 Which US comedienne has her own C5 chat show?
11 Who on Channel 5 is *The Antique Hunter*?
12 How is Ray Burns better known?
13 Who said "What a beautiful pair of knockers" on *Blue Peter*?
14 Who presented *Bookworm*?
15 Melanie and Martina Grant assist Pat Sharp on which game show?
16 Mike Yarwood had soccer trials with which clubs?
17 Which former page 3 girl presented the game show *Fort Boyard*?
18 Which Gladiator produced a fitness video called *Summer Circuit*?
19 Joanna Lumley and Jennifer Saunders were asked to edit which UK magazine?
20 Which medal did commentator Kenneth Wolstenholme win in WWII?
21 What was the subject of the *Grange Hill* song *Just Say No*?
22 Who played a womanizing PR man in the 70s sitcom *Casanova*?
23 What was Miriam Stoppard's profession?
24 Who originally was the voice of Mr Kipling in the cake ads?
25 What was the name of the series where Robbie Coltrane was a Majestic?
26 Which TV star duetted with Barbra Streisand on *Till I Loved You* in 1988?
27 Which actor has played Captain Hillio, Butler and the Governor in *Doctor Who*?
28 Sicne 2016, Dominic Cooper has starred as what profession in *Preacher*?
29 Who had a ventriloquist's dummy named Chuck?
30 What kind of food was advertised by Alf Roberts?

Answers | **Movies: Cary Grant** *(see Quiz 61)*

1 Alexander. 2 Capricorn. 3 Paramount. 4 Blonde Venus. 5 None but the Lonely Heart.
6 Bob Pender's. 7 Singapore Sue. 8 Cary Lockwood. 9 Mr Blandings Builds His Dream
House; Every Girl Should be Married. 10 Tony Curtis (Some Like It Hot). 11 Walk Don't Run.
12 Faberge. 13 75%. 14 Woolworths. 15 The Philadelphia Story. 16 Joan Fontaine.
17 Arsenic and Old Lace. 18 Diamond Lil. 19 Irene Dunne. 20 John Wayne. 21 RKO &
Columbia. 22 Dyan Cannon. 23 Cole Porter 24 Suspicion. 25 Barbara Harris. 26 62.
27 Michael-John Wolfe. 28 Bristol. 29 John Cleese. 30 A Touch of Pink.

1 Which Scottish team are known as "The Loons"?

2 What was the nickname of Brazil's Garrincha?

3 Who was known as "Pele" in his Ipswich Town days?

4 Which great international forward became known as "The Little Canon"?

5 How was Austria's goal machine of the 1930s Franz Binder known?

6 Which Scottish team are known as Wee Jays?

7 United isn't the most original nickname, but how many teams could that apply to in the Premiership and English League sides in 1996–97?

8 What was Alan Kennedy's nickname at Liverpool?

9 Bauld, Conn and Wardhaugh formed "The Terrible Trio" at which club in the 1950s?

10 What is the nickname shared by clubs situated in Crieff Road, Perth, and Milton Road?

11 Which Scottish team are known as the Ton?

12 What was the nickname of early-20th-century keeper Bill Foulke?

13 Which Scotland and Arsenal player was "The Wee Wizard"?

14 Which Manchester Utd player was known as "The Black Prince"?

15 Which international keeper of the 1990s rejoices in the nickname "El Loco"?

16 Which Scottish team are known as the Sons?

17 "The Famous Five" helped which Scottish club to the championship just after the Second World War?

18 Which Liverpool player was "The Flying Pig"?

19 Who is nicknamed "Choccy"?

20 What was the nickname of Manchester Utd's early-20th-century player Enoch Walker?

21 Who is sometimes called "Calamity" because of his blunders?

22 Who are the Shrimps?

23 Which club is nicknamed El Submarino Amarillo (the Yellow Submarine)?

24 Who is the Sultan of the Stepover?

25 Which Scottish League club is known as the Galabankies?

26 Can you recall the nickname given to Zinedine Zidane?

27 Can you name the English side formerly known as "The Glaziers"?

28 Which former England player was nicknamed "Donkey"?

29 During their early days this team was known as "The Invicibles". Can you name them?

30 Name the Italian nicknamed "Braveheart" during his time in British football.

Answers	**Pop Pot Luck 10** (see Quiz 64)

1 13. 2 Shirley Owens. 3 Apple. 4 His Rockets. 5 Ray Hildebrand and Jill Jackson. 6 "Bad". 7 Marc Bolan. 8 The Rolling Stones. 9 A train. 10 Lonnie Donegan. 11 Ropin' the Wind. 12 Phil Collins. 13 "Wipe Out" by the Surfaris. 14 5 Seconds of Summer. 15 Little Richard. 16 Bo Diddley. 17 Glasgow. 18 King Creole. 19 Dave Stewart. 20 Their window-cleaner. 21 Stuart Cable. 22 Pat Smear. 23 The Police. 24 Paul Ryan. 25 The Poppy Family. 26 Charisma. 27 Sonny and Cher. 28 "To have a good time". 29 The Sex Pistols. 30 Eve Boswell.

1 How many older brothers and sisters does Celine Dion have?
2 Who was the lead singer of the Shirelles?
3 Which label's first releases included Mary Hopkin and James Taylor?
4 Who backed Boyd Bennett on "Seventeen"?
5 What were the real names of Paul and Paula?
6 What is George Benson's nickname?
7 Who made his mark in the 60s act John's Children?
8 Which group's own record label uses the reference number prefixes COC and CUN?
9 What type of transport was on Elton John's Rocket record label?
10 Who had Britain's first-ever double-sided No. 1 in the 1950s?
11 What was Garth Brooks's debut album called?
12 Who won the Grammy award for Best Male Vocal Performance in 1984 and 1985?
13 What did "5-4-3-2-1" replace as theme music for *Ready Steady Go!*?
14 Released in 2015, *Sounds Good Feels Good* is the second studio album by the Australian pop punk band _____.
15 Who said, "I'm the innovator. I'm the emancipator. I'm the originator. I'm the architect of rock 'n' roll"?
16 How is Otha Ellas Bates better known?
17 In which city was Mark Knopfler born?
18 In which film did Elvis play the role of Danny Fisher?
19 Who formed the Spiritual Cowboys?
20 Who did Joe Cocker's parents name him after?
21 Who was sacked by the Stereophonics in 2003?
22 By what name is guitarist/pianist Georg Ruthenberg better known?
23 Who won the British Rock and Pop Best Band awards in 1979 and 1980?
24 Who wrote "Eloise"?
25 Of which family was Terry Jacks a former member?
26 Which record label uses the reference number prefix "CAS"?
27 Whose debut album was *Look at Us*?
28 What follows "We don't have to take our clothes off" in Jermaine Stewart's 1986 hit?
29 Which group's career is profiled in *The Great Rock 'n' Roll Swindle*?
30 Which Hungarian had her only chart entry with "Pickin' a Chicken"?

Answers | Football: Nicknames *(see Quiz 63)*

1 Forfar. 2 "The Little Bird". 3 Alan Brazil. 4 Ferenc Puskas. 5 "Bimbo". 6 Livingston. 7 16. 8 "Barney". 9 Hearts. 10 Saints (St Johnstone, Southampton). 11 Greenock Morton. 12 "Fatty". 13 Alex James. 14 Alex Dawson. 15 Rene Higuita. 16 Dumbarton. 17 Hibernian. 18 Tommy Lawrence. 19 Brian McClair. 20 "Knocker". 21 David James. 22 Morecambe. 23 Villareal. 24 Cristiano Ronaldo. 25 Annan Athletic. 26 Zizou. 27 Crystal Palace 28 Tony Adams. 29 Preston North End. 30 Gennaro Gattuso.

1 Who said, "Disney has the best casting. If he doesn't like an actor he just tears him up"?

2 In which 1932 film did he experiment with colour?

3 Where did he first meet Ub Iwerks?

4 Which movies were made as a result of a government goodwill tour of South America?

5 What was the first of the *Silly Symphonies* called?

6 A meeting with which photographers brought about the *True Life* nature films?

7 What was Disney's job during World War II?

8 What did Disney and Iwerks call their first cartoons?

9 Which actress won an Oscar for the last major film he made before his death?

10 What was his star sign?

11 Which special Oscar award did he receive for *Snow White and the Seven Dwarfs*?

12 Which animated film was he working on at the time of his death?

13 Who, with Disney, received a special Oscar for *Fantasia*?

14 What was the first of his all-live-action movies?

15 What were the first two silent Mickey Mouse cartoons called?

16 What was Goofy originally called?

17 Which morale-boosting movie did Disney make in 1943?

18 In 1923 what was the name of the animated live-action cartoons he produced with his brother Roy and Ub Iwerks?

19 What was the last film in the series which began with *Seal Island*?

20 How many Oscars did Disney win in his lifetime?

21 Which relative of Walt became chief executive of Disney in 1983?

22 Which series did Walt launch with Roy in 1927?

23 Which British child star did he bring to Hollywood in the late 50s?

24 Which musical was he working on at the time of his death?

25 Who wrote a biography of Disney, published in 1958?

26 How many Oscar nominations did Disney receive in his lifetime?

27 When did Disney open his first theme park?

28 How much did Disney buy Marvel for in 2009?

29 Name the Disney television programme first aired in the USA in 1954.

30 What did Walt Disney Productions change its name to in 1968?

---

1 Since 2015, which Mendelsohn has shined in Netflix's *Bloodline*?
2 In which California resort is the series *Two and a Half Men* set?
3 Angus Deayton had a soccer trial with which club?
4 Which Dr Who served on HMS *Hood* in WWII?
5 Which 1960s western series featured a stern wheel paddle steamer?
6 What was Sonny Jim's real name in *Coronation Street*?
7 Which Australian singer appeared in *The Newcomers*?
8 Who was the scout in *Wagon Train*?
9 Which *Mastermind* drove a train for the London Underground?
10 On which day did *Watch with Mother* feature *Andy Pandy*?
11 Who played Jodie Foster's father in *Paper Moon*?
12 Which duo co-wrote and starred in *Chelmsford 123*?
13 Whose neighbours were Fred and Ethel?
14 Who is taller – John Cleese or Richard Madeley?
15 Which TV comedian had the number plate COM IC?
16 Which *Neighbours* actor appeared in the film *L.A. Confidential*?
17 If Christopher Connelly was Norman who played Rodney?
18 Which luxury did Esther Rantzen choose on *Desert Island Discs*?
19 Actor Robert Brown appeared as which spymaster on film?
20 Which Italian Countess hosted the Eurovision Song Contest?
21 What was Thora Hird's autobiography called?
22 In which soap was there a character named George Holloway?
23 Who wore pink bow ties on *Call My Bluff*?
24 Which cowboy had the surname Layne?
25 Who composed the music for *Victory at Sea*?
26 What was *Honey Lane*?
27 Which of her possessions did Janet Street Porter sell at auction in 1997?
28 What was the alternative name of the television western series *Sugarfoot*?
29 Which soccer side does actor Robert Lindsay support?
30 Which giant actor appeared in *The Army Game*?

Answers | Movies: Walt Disney (see Quiz 65)

1 Alfred Hitchcock. 2 Flowers and Trees. 3 Kansas City. 4 Saludos Amigos; The Three Caballeros. 5 The Skeleton Dance. 6 Alfred & Elma Milotte. 7 Made training films. 8 Laugh O Grams. 9 Julie Andrews (Mary Poppins). 10 Sagittarius. 11 One large Oscar and seven small ones. 12 Jungle Book. 13 Leopold Stokowski. 14 Treasure Island. 15 Plane Crazy; Gallopin' Gaucho. 16 Dippy Dawg. 17 Victory Through Air Power. 18 Alice in Cartoonland. 19 Jungle Cat. 20 29. 21 Son-in-law. 22 Oswald the Lucky Rabbit. 23 Hayley Mills. 24 The Happiest Millionaire. 25 His daughter Diane. 26 59. 27 1955. 28 $4.2bn. 29 The Wonderful World of Disney. 30 Walt Disney Enterprises.

Quiz 67 | Horse Racing

Answers – page 470

1 Which horse gave Lester Piggott his 30th victory in an English Classic?
2 On the flat what is the most number of winners achieved by a jockey in a season in the 20th century?
3 Which horse finished first in the abandoned 1993 Grand National?
4 The Coronation Cup celebrates which coronation?
5 In the 1989 Oaks which "winning" horse was later disqualified after a post-race test?
6 Who rode Red Rum for the third Grand National triumph?
7 Aubrey Brabazon succeeded father Cecil as a trainer where?
8 How many winners did Frankie Dettori ride in his 1994 super season?
9 Which of the English Classics has Lester Piggott won least times?
10 At the beginning of the century what did Sceptre achieve in 1902?
11 Which horse gave Richard Dunwoody his first Grand National success?
12 What's the only Derby winner of last century to have a date as its name?
13 In which year did the Grand National witness Devon Loch's sensational fall 50 yards from home?
14 Which was the first English Classic to be raced in Scotland?
15 Which horse was the first on which Lester Piggott won two Classics?
16 Who sponsored the 1000 Guineas from 1984 to 1992?
17 Which horse came first at the 2014 Grand National?
18 Who trained the prolific winner Brigadier Gerard?
19 What was the name of the horse on which Geoff Lewis won his only Derby?
20 To the nearest thousand, how many rides did the legendary Willie Shoemaker make?
21 Who is the trainer for the Coolmore racing operation?
22 What was the stables complex Jonjo O'Neill left to take over at Jackdaws Castle?
23 Before Great Leighs which was the last British racecourse to open?
24 Which day of Cheltenham 2008 was abandoned?
25 When was the Breeders Cup staged outside of the United States (at Woodbine)?
26 Where did jump jockey Tony McCoy ride his 3000th winner?
27 Which horse was the first to regain the Cheltenham Gold Cup?
28 Which two-mile handicap is dubbed "The race that stops a nation"?
29 Which American champion racehorse was the inspiration for a highly acclaimed film released in 2003?
30 Where is the St Leger run?

Answers | **Football Pot Luck 6** *(see Quiz 68)*

1 John Aldridge. 2 Newcastle Utd. 3 Walsall. 4 Nigel. 5 Bournemouth. 6 Bolton Wanderers. 7 16. 8 Greenwich Borough. 9 Colchester Utd. 10 France. 11 Norwich City. 12 King. 13 Crystal Palace. 14 Wolves. 15 1940s. 16 Ipswich Town. 17 Hull City. 18 Ian Rush. 19 Cardiff City. 20 19. 21 AaB Aalborg. 22 Lawrie Sanchez. 23 Case. 24 Leicester City. 25 Reims. 26 QPR. 27 Bradford City. 28 FIFA. 29 Kevin Keegan. 30 Arthur Rowe.

Quiz 68 Football Pot Luck 6

Answers – page 469

1 Which player was involved in the substitute row in the Mexico v the Republic of Ireland 1994 World Cup game?
2 Which club boasted the fullback pairing of Ranson and Sansom?
3 Until 1990 which team used to play at Fellows Park?
4 What is Mark Atkins's middle name?
5 What was the first club that John Bond managed?
6 Brian Kidd finished his playing career in England with which club?
7 How many goals did Liverpool's mean machine defence concede in the 42 League games of 1978–79?
8 Which non-League side did Ian Wright play for?
9 Micky Cook set a League appearance record at which club?
10 In 2016, which country hosted the Euros for a record third time?
11 Andy Linighan and Mike Phelan were in the same team at which club?
12 Which Andy became boss of Mansfield in 1993?
13 Phil Barber played in an FA Cup Final for which team?
14 At which club did Tim Flowers make his League debut?
15 In which decade did Portsmouth first win the First Division championship?
16 Which club had a fanzine called *A Load of Cobbolds*?
17 Eddie Gray followed Brian Horton as manager of which club?
18 Who moved from Chester for £300,000 in 1980 to set a club record for a transfer fee received?
19 Which club was once known as Riverside Albion?
20 To two each way, how many international goals did Don Givens net?
21 Which club was 2007–08 League champions in Denmark?
22 Who resigned as an international coach to become full-time boss of Fulham in 2007?
23 Which Jimmy played in 1970s and 1980s FA Cup Finals for different teams and lost both times?
24 McIlmoyle, Keyworth and Cheesebrough played for which 1960s FA Cup finalists?
25 Who lost 4–3 to Real Madrid in the final of the 1956 European Cup?
26 Michael Robinson played in 1980s League Cup Finals for Liverpool and which other club?
27 121-goal Bobby Campbell is all-time top League scorer at which club?
28 Which organization is based at Hitzigweg 11, CH–8032 Zurich?
29 Which former Scunthorpe footballer sang solo on *Top of the Pops* in 1979?
30 Alf Ramsey was the only player bought by which Tottenham Hotspur boss?

Answers | Horse Racing *(see Quiz 67)*

1 Rodrigo de Triano. 2 269. 3 Esha Ness. 4 Edward VII. 5 Aliyssa. 6 Tommy Stack. 7 Rangers Lodge, the Curragh. 8 233. 9 1000 Guineas. 10 Won four Classics. 11 West Tip. 12 April the Fifth. 13 1956. 14 St Leger – in 1989. 15 Crepello. 16 General Accident. 17 Pineau de Re. 18 John Hislop. 19 Mill Reef. 20 40,000. 21 Aiden O'Brien. 22 Greystoke. 23 Taunton. 24 Wednesday (2nd). 25 1996. 26 Plumpton. 27 Kauto Star. 28 Melbourne Cup. 29 Seabiscuit. 30 Doncaster.

1 Who awarded Mark Knopfler an honorary music doctorate in 1993?

2 Which heavy-metal guitarist said, "If it's too loud you're too old"?

3 Who inspired Eric Clapton to write "Layla"?

4 What was Eric Clapton's No. 1 album of 1994?

5 Which guitarist's first two names were Brian Robson?

6 Which album did Mark Knopfler release with Chet Atkins in 1990?

7 Who was guest vocalist on Ted Nugent's *Free for All album*?

8 Who duetted on "Wonderful Land" on the 1993 *Heartbeat* album?

9 Which film soundtrack did Mark Knopfler work on after *Local Hero*?

10 Who asked Hank Marvin to join which band in 1970?

11 Which group has included the guitarists John Williams and Kevin Peek?

12 What did Brian May reputedly make his first guitar from?

13 What type of guitar did Jimi Hendrix use on the *Are You Experienced*? album?

14 Which two acts took "Cavatina", the theme from *The Deer Hunter*, into the top ten?

15 Where did Jimi Hendrix take part in a fund-raising "Guitar-In" in 1967?

16 Whose career history album was called *Crossroads*?

17 What did Brian May play at the end of the *Concert for Life* at Wembley in 1992?

18 What was Jeff Beck's debut solo album called?

19 What honour did Eric Clapton receive in January 1995?

20 What was the debut album by the Brian May Band?

21 Who was ranked No. 1 in *Rolling Stone* magazine's list of 100 top guitarists?

22 With whom did Eric Clapton collaborate on the album *The Road to Escondido*?

23 In which year was Jimmy Page awarded the OBE?

24 What was the name of Ry Cooder's 2008 album?

25 Who was the Red Hot Chili Peppers' guitarist on their *Stadium Arcadium* album?

26 Which guitarist was a member of Deep Purple, Dixie Dregs and Kansas?

27 Who named two of his guitars "Marielle" and "Our Lady"?

28 Which guitarist reformed Guns N Roses in 2016?

29 Which British guitarist has a species of dinosaur named in his honour?

30 Which former guitarist founded the heavy metal band Quiet Riot?

---

1 Which actor links *Tim* and *The Rest of Daniel*?
2 Which actress released the 1987 single "This Girl's Back in Town"?
3 What song is playing every time Bill Murray wakes up on *Groundhog Day*?
4 Which film was Gary Oldman's directorial debut?
5 Which Graham featured in *Dances with Wolves*?
6 A character named Harry Dalton appeared in which film?
7 David Fincher directed what Girl in 2014?
8 Who did Grant Williams play in *The Incredible Shrinking Man*?
9 Within five minutes, how long does *Sleeper* last?
10 Which animal mask does George Peppard steal in *Breakfast at Tiffany's*?
11 Who was quoted in *Newsweek* as saying, "I only direct in self-defence"?
12 What was the last film Grace Kelly made before becoming a princess?
13 What type of sweets are used in the trail that E.T. follows in *E.T.*?
14 Which Rachel featured in *The Craft*?
15 Who voiced Ariel in *The Little Mermaid*?
16 Which actor links *California Split* and *Vibes*?
17 What is John Travolta's occupation in *Look Who's Talking*?
18 Who won the Best Director Oscar for *The French Connection*?
19 Who was offered the role of Rambo in *First Blood*, but turned it down?
20 In 1990 Eric Brevig won a Special Award for visual effects on which film?
21 What was the name of Geena Davis's character in *The Fly*?
22 Which Jeremy featured in *Dante's Peak*?
23 Who won the Best Actor Oscar for *Disraeli*?
24 Who directed *Car Wash*?
25 To the nearest hour, how long does the 30s movie *Frankenstein* last?
26 In 2006, James Franco and Sophia Myles played which famous lovers?
27 Which Irish actor received an Honorary Oscar in 2003 after seven nominations?
28 Who directed *The Fifth Element*?
29 Who won the Best Actor Oscar for *Charly*?
30 Which actor appeared in both *Superman* and *Nixon*?

Answers	Pop: Guitar Greats *(see Quiz 69)*

1 Newcastle University. 2 Ted Nugent. 3 Patti Harrison. 4 From the Cradle. 5 Hank Marvin. 6 Neck and Neck. 7 Meat Loaf. 8 Hank Marvin and Mark Knopfler. 9 Cal. 10 Roy Wood, the Move. 11 Sky. 12 19th-century fireplace. 13 Stratocaster. 14 The Shadows, John Williams. 15 Royal Festival Hall. 16 Eric Clapton. 17 "God Save the Queen". 18 Beck-ola. 19 OBE. 20 Live at the Brixton Academy. 21 Jimi Hendrix. 22 J. J. Cale. 23 2005. 24 I, Flathead. 25 John Frusciante. 26 Steve Morse. 27 John McLaughlin. 28 Slash. 29 Mark Knopfler (Masiakasaurus Knopfleri). 30 Randy Rhoads.

1 Which Corrie character was named by *TV Weekly* as the Sexiest Soap Siren ever?

2 Who was shot when Carl and Anthony held up the Dog in *Hollyoaks*?

3 Which breakfast TV presenter starred as himself on *Brookside*?

4 Which three North Sea ports were visited by the ferry in *Triangle*?

5 What was the name of the ferry company in *Triangle*?

6 Which soccer expert was a consultant on the 60s soap *United!*?

7 Whose sister did Paula Wilcox play in *Coronation Street*?

8 Who was the narrator in *The Waltons*?

9 Which 60s soap followed the goings on at a large West End department store?

10 Jean Harvey, Nicholas Selby and Gareth Davies were editors of which fictional magazine?

11 Which soap shared its theme music with *The Upper Hand*?

12 Who played Gregory Sumner in *Knots Landing*?

13 Which former soap star hosted *The Saturday Banana* in her teens?

14 Who as well as Grant claimed to be Courtney's father in *EastEnders*?

15 Which former Queen Vic owner turned 79 in 2016?

16 Which *Coronation Street* actor's real name is William Piddington?

17 In *Heartbeat*, what is Sergeant Blaketon's first name?

18 Which twins from *Neighbours* were Des O'Connor's assistants on *Take Your Pick*?

19 In which year did the story of *The Sullivans* begin?

20 Which musical star appeared as a dodgy car dealer in *EastEnders* in 1998?

21 Luke Perry portrayed which character in *Beverley Hills 90210*?

22 In *Home and Away*, where did Joey live before moving in with Irene?

23 Which former *Coronation Street* actor played Jack Gates in *Family Affairs*?

24 Who has starred in *Emmerdale Farm*, *Coronation Street* and *Crossroads* but is most famous for her role in a long-running sitcom?

25 What was the subtitle of the 1998 Albert Square video *The Mitchells*?

26 How were Justine and Aaron related in *Home and Away*?

27 In *The Bill* what was Tosh Lines's real first name?

28 In which Valley was *Falcon Crest* first filmed?

29 Which *EastEnders* star was Mrs Dale's milkman in the days of the classic radio soap?

30 With which family did *Home and Away*'s Aaron live?

1 Who was 18 years and 14 days old when he played in the Brighton v Manchester Utd FA Cup Final?

2 Sir Stanley Matthews was manager of which English club?

3 Who got into bother for calling referee Robbie Hart a "Muppet"?

4 At which club did Tim Sherwood make his League debut?

5 In which decade did Ipswich Town first win the championship?

6 Which 92nd-placed League club won the Johnstone's Paint Trophy final at Wembley in 2009?

7 John Neal followed Geoff Hurst as manager of which club?

8 Who moved from Bury to Southampton for £375,000, in October 1991 to set a club record for a transfer fee received?

9 Which club was once known as Christ Church FC?

10 To one each way, how many international goals did Kevin Beattie score?

11 Mike Newell and Gary McAllister were in the same team at which club?

12 Which Pat became boss of Leyton Orient in 1995?

13 Jim Beglin first played in an FA Cup Final for which team?

14 What was the first name of ex-WBA and Ipswich Town player Zondervan?

15 Which defender was making his Leeds Utd debut in the same game as Gordon Strachan's first appearance?

16 Who was in goal when Tottenham Hotspur won the FA Cup Final in the 1987?

17 What was the first club that Billy Bremner managed?

18 Who created a record for Derby County by playing 486 League games?

19 What was Le slogan used to advertise the 2016 Euros?

20 Which club used to play at Steeles Field and Ravenshaws Field?

21 In which country would you be if watched Ararat Yerevan playing Mika Ashtarak?

22 Which Italian became Chairman of QPR in 2008?

23 Which country lost just once in 48 matches between 1950 and 1956?

24 At which club did Phil Neal make his League debut?

25 In which decade did Huddersfield Town first win the championship?

26 Which club had a fanzine called *The Thin Blue Line*?

27 Dave Stringer followed Ken Brown as manager of which club?

28 Blackburn Rovers established a record of going how many FA Cup games without defeat?

29 Which club was once known as Heaton Norris Rovers?

30 To two each way, how many international goals did Trevor Francis score?

Answers	TV: Soaps 1 *(see Quiz 71)*

1 Michelle Connor. 2 Darren. 3 Eamonn Holmes. 4 Felixstowe, Gothenburg and Amsterdam. 5 Triangle Line. 6 Jimmy Hill. 7 Ray Langton's. 8 John Boy. 9 Harpers West One. 10 Compact. 11 Knots Landing. 12 William Devane. 13 Susan Tully. 14 Tony Hills. 15 Babs Windsor. 16 William Tarmey (Jack Duckworth). 17 Oscar. 18 Gayle and Gillian Blakeney. 19 1939. 20 Anthony Newley. 21 Dylan McKay. 22 The commune. 23 Ken Farrington. 24 Kathy Staff. 25 Naked Truths. 26 Sister and brother. 27 Alfred. 28 Napa Valley, California. 29 Bill Treacher (Arthur Fowler). 30 With the Stewarts.

1 What are Madonna's two middle names?
2 What was her first major film role?
3 What name was given to the clothing outlet in Macy's US stores?
4 Which album included the song "Rain"?
5 Who did Madonna describe as "the coolest guy in the universe"?
6 Which knight did Madonna star with in *Who's That Girl*?
7 Who was said to have beaten Madonna to the *Evita* role in 1988?
8 Which role did Madonna play in *Dick Tracey*?
9 Who designed her clothes for the *Blonde Ambition* tour?
10 Why was Madonna sued by her neighbour in 1990?
11 Which 1991 video shows a steamy bedroom scene filmed in black and white?
12 Where was Madonna when she was interviewed on *Wogan*?
13 What was the name of her company founded in 1992?
14 What was her first album on her own record label?
15 Which controversial "sport" features in her "Take a Bow" and "You'll See" videos?
16 Which two roles did Carlos Leon have in Madonna's life?
17 Who directed Madonna in *Evita*?
18 Which instrument did Madonna play in the rock band Breakfast Club?
19 Who produced "Shanghai Surprise"?
20 Which album was "Papa Don't Preach" originally on?
21 What is the name of the son Madonna had with Guy Ritchie?
22 In which year was Madonna inducted into the Rock and Roll Hall of Fame?
23 For which James Bond movie did Madonna record the title song?
24 What international tour did Madonna do to promote her *Hard Candy* album?
25 What was Madonna's role for the first time in the 2008 movie *Filth and Wisdom*?
26 In what "City" in Michigan was Madonna born?
27 What is the name of the song Madonna released in May 2007 ahead of *Live Earth*?
28 Name Madonna's 2012 album.
29 Which actor did Madonna begin an affair with working on the movie *Dick Tracy*?
30 Can you recall the name of her Tour she began in May 2006?

Answers | **Movies Pot Luck 8** *(see Quiz 74)*

1 Yul Brynner. 2 Red. 3 Marie Dressler. 4 Peanut stall. 5 Frank Borzage. 6 Cromwell. 7 The Jazz Singer. 8 David Levinson. 9 Give My Regards to Broad Street. 10 Wes Anderson. 11 The Living Daylights. 12 Robinson. 13 "Under the Sea". 14 Terry Hayes. 15 Dirk Bogarde. 16 1980. 17 John Cleese. 18 1930s. 19 105 minutes. 20 Dysart. 21 F. Murray Abraham. 22 A mood ring. 23 Bree Daniels. 24 Terry Gilliam. 25 Oates. 26 Nightcrawler. 27 Casino Royale. 28 Elliott. 29 1954. 30 Tom Reagan.

1 Which great actor died on the same day as fellow star Orson Welles?

2 What colour is Deborah Kerr's suit in the final scene of *An Affair to Remember*?

3 Who won the Best Actress Oscar for *Min and Bill*?

4 What sort of stall does Chico have in *Duck Soup*?

5 Who won the Best Director Oscar for *Seventh Heaven*?

6 Which James starred in *Babe*?

7 What movie is shown within the film *Goodfellas*?

8 Who did Jeff Goldblum play in *Independence Day*?

9 What was the name of the last film that Ralph Richardson ever made?

10 *The Grand Budapest Hotel,* released in 2014, was directed by who?

11 In which film did Caroline Bliss replace Lois Maxwell as Miss Moneypenny?

12 Which Amy featured in *Mean Streets*?

13 Which song won Best Song Oscar for *The Little Mermaid*?

14 Who wrote the screenplay for *Mad Max Beyond Thunderdome*?

15 Which actor's memoirs include the volume *Snakes and Ladders*?

16 In which year did Peter Sellers die?

17 Who voiced Cat R. Ward in *An American Tail: Fievel Goes West*?

18 In which decade was *Morocco* released?

19 Within five minutes, how long does *Shine* last?

20 Which Richard featured in *The Hospital*?

21 Who won the Best Actor Oscar for *Amadeus*?

22 What kind of ring does Vada have in *My Girl*?

23 What was the name of Jane Fonda's character in *Klute*?

24 Who directed *Twelve Monkeys*?

25 Which Warren featured in *Badlands*?

26 Jake Gyllenhaal starred as Louis Bloom in what 2014 film?

27 "You Know My Name" was the theme to which 2006 blockbuster movie?

28 Which Sam featured in *Tombstone*?

29 In which year was the Billy Wilder-directed version of *Sabrina* released?

30 What was the name of Gabriel Byrne's character in *Miller's Crossing*?

Answers	**Pop: Madonna** *(see Quiz 73)*

1 Louise Veronica. 2 Desperately Seeking Susan. 3 Madonnaland. 4 Erotica. 5 Former husband Sean Penn. 6 Sir John Mills. 7 Meryl Streep. 8 Breathless Mahoney. 9 Jean-Paul Gaultier. 10 Her hedge blocked his view. 11 "Justify My Love". 12 Cannes Film Festival. 13 Maverick. 14 Erotica. 15 Bullfighting. 16 Personal trainer, father to her daughter. 17 Alan Parker. 18 Drums. 19 George Harrison. 20 True Blue. 21 Rocco. 22 2008. 23 Die Another Day. 24 Sticky & Sweet Tour. 25 Director. 26 Bay City. 27 Hey You. 28 MDNA. 29 Warren Beatty. 30 Confessions Tour.

1 Where was *Countdown* recorded when the Leeds studios were renovated?
2 What completes the title of the game show *Alan Carr's Celebrity ____*?
3 Which game show started with the words "My name is ____"?
4 Which 80s arts quiz was hosted by Bamber Gascoigne?
5 Who originally hosted *Password*?
6 In *The $64,000 Question,* how were the questions secured?
7 George Layton hosted which game show?
8 Which quiz was hosted by Paul Daniels's son?
9 What object was given to winning guests on *Through The Keyhole*?
10 Who was the original host of *Chain Letters*?
11 Which Bob Monkhouse game show was based on bingo?
12 Who hosted *The Man Who Got Away*?
13 On which channel was *Cyberzone* broadcast?
14 What is British TV's longest-running quiz show?
15 What giant object featured on *All Clued Up*?
16 Who replaced Eamonn Andrews as chairman of *What's My Line?* in 1970?
17 Which show required guests to sign in?
18 On *Bullseye* what score was required to win the star prize?
19 Angela Rippon hosted which master quiz?
20 Which soap character appeared in the fictional quiz show *Cat and Mouse*?
21 Which show is hosted by Alexander Armstrong and Richard Osman?
22 What couples game show was presented by Gloria Hunniford?
23 How many children appeared in each episode of *Ask the Family*?
24 Which *Good Life* star presented *What's My Line*?
25 On which show were questions asked by Sue Robbie?
26 Which game show assistant won a Miss Longest Legs contest judged by her future husband?
27 Who were the original captains on *A Question of Sport*?
28 Who announced the prizes in the early years of *Take Your Pick*?
29 Chris Kelly chaired which kids' TV quiz?
30 Princess Anne was a contestant in which TV quiz?

1 Dennis Wise joined Wimbledon after which club released him?

2 Which club had 19 points deducted in 1968 for making illegal payments to players?

3 Which manager brought Dwight Yorke to Villa Park?

4 Which Mel was with Sheffield Wednesday when he made his only England appearance in 1988 against Saudi Arabia?

5 What is Nick Barmby's middle name?

6 Which London team used to play at Northumberland Park?

7 With 448 League games in the 1950s and 1960s, Keith Jobling set an appearance record at which club?

8 Which non-League club did Stuart Pearce leave to go into the League?

9 Which club in the north of England did Ossie Ardiles play for?

10 What was the first club that Brian Clough managed?

11 Paul Warhurst and Earl Barrett were in the same team at which club?

12 Which Colin became boss of Middlesbrough in 1990?

13 Steve Hodge first played in an FA Cup Final for which team?

14 At which club did Robert Fleck make his English League debut?

15 In what decade did Dumbarton first win the championship?

16 Which club had a fanzine called *Tiger Rag*?

17 Peter Taylor followed Barry Fry as manager of which club?

18 Jermain Defoe moved to which team in 2015?

19 Which club was once known as Shaddongate United?

20 To two each way, how many international goals did Leighton James score?

21 How many points did Derby collect in the 2007–08 season?

22 Which club was 2007–08 League champions in Wales?

23 Who did Cameroon beat in the 1990 World Cup opener?

24 Which Liverpool skipper said of compatriot Bill Shankly, "His motivation could move mountains"?

25 Which Second Division side reached the Final of the League Cup and the semis of the FA Cup in the same season?

26 Gates and McCall scored Euro goals in the same game for which club?

27 Ashley Grimes played in 1980s League Cup Finals for which team?

28 When was the Football League's Centenary Season?

29 With 195 goals scored in the 1960s and 1970s Chris Chilton became all-time top League scorer at which east coast club?

30 Who lost 1–0 to Liverpool in the final of the 1981 European Cup?

Answers | TV: Quiz & Game Shows 1 *(see Quiz 75)*

1 Newcastle. 2 Ding Dong. 3 Tell the Truth. 4 Connoisseur. 5 Gordon Burns. 6 In a safe. 7 Pass the Buck. 8 Lingo. 9 A gold key. 10 Jeremy Beadle. 11 Bob's Full House. 12 Larry Grayson. 13 Channel 4. 14 University Challenge. 15 A giant typewriter. 16 David Jacobs. 17 What's My Line. 18 100. 19 Masterteam. 20 Arthur Fowler in EastEnders. 21 Pointless. 22 The Newly Wed Game. 23 Four. 24 Penelope Keith. 25 Connections. 26 Anthea Redfern. 27 Henry Cooper and Cliff Morgan. 28 Bob Danvers Walker. 29 Clapperboard. 30 A Question of Sport.

1 Which song has a line based loosely on one from Shakespeare's *As You Like It*, "You know someone said that all the world's a stage"?

2 What does Celine Dion sing after "I think of all the friends I've known" in "All by Myself"?

3 How many times does Gabrielle sing "Walk On By" in the first chorus?

4 Which song has the line "Will all those having relatives on Flight 1203 please report to the chapel across the street"?

5 Which 1960s song has the line "Wearing smells from lab'ratories, facing a dying nation of moving paper fantasy"?

6 Who does Bob Dylan tell "Don't block up the hall" in "The Times They are A-Changin'"?

7 Which song starts, "What goes up must come down."?

8 Which month is it in Paul Simon's "I Am A Rock"?

9 In "My Way" what goes before "I did what I had to do."?

10 Which song says "I love your chin-ey chin chin"?

11 Which line follows the unforgettably tasteless "I'm as serious as cancer"?

12 Which island does Madonna lament in "La Isla Bonita"?

13 What colour did Vincent "paint his palette" in the Don McLean hit?

14 Which song goes "I've never done good things, I've never done bad things"?

15 Where would you find the lines "Ev'ry summer we can rent a cottage in the Isle of Wight"?

16 Which song has the lines "I got up to wash my face, When I come back to bed, Someone's taken my place"?

17 Which song starts "When I was a little girl I had a rag doll"?

18 Where will you hear the line "Tried to hitch a ride to San Francisco"?

19 Which song says "The world is like an apple whirling silently in space"?

20 What is the answer to "What do you see when you turn out the light?"?

21 In "Love Shack", what car "seats about 20, so hurry up & bring your jukebox money"?

22 Losing what "Is like the sun going down on me"?

23 To whom does Cher open with "They say we're too young and we don't know"?

24 What will happen according to Shania Twain, "If you're not in it for love"?

25 "But it's time to face the truth, I will never be with you" ends which mega-hit?

26 The eyes belonging to which actress featured in a Kim Carnes hit?

27 What song features "If you don't eat your meat you can't have any pudding"?

28 Where did Wings have "Smiles in the sunshine, And tears in the rain"?

29 In which Frank Sinatra song do we find "I've loved, I've laughed and cried"?

30 Love was "written in the wind and everywhere I go" in which former No. 1?

Quiz 78

Movies Pot Luck 9

Answers – page 479

1 What colour was the dress that Scarlett O'Hara made from her curtains?
2 What was Marlon Brando's first film, in 1950?
3 Within five minutes, how long does *Se7en* last?
4 Who directed the film *Body of Evidence*?
5 Which Jon featured in *Miller's Crossing*?
6 Who won the Best Actor Oscar for *The Champ*?
7 Who directed *Total Recall*?
8 In which film did a character named Leeloo appear?
9 What is Ted's middle name in *Bill & Ted's Excellent Adventure*?
10 Who did Joan Collins describe as, "Short, myopic, not good looking"?
11 Which Pam starred in *Jackie Brown*?
12 Who was set to play Sofia Coppola's role in *The Godfather, Part III*, but pulled out on doctor's advice?
13 In which film did a pilot named Klaatu appear?
14 Who wrote the screenplay for the film *Billy Bathgate*?
15 Within fifteen minutes, how long does *Planet of the Apes* last?
16 Who directed *An Affair to Remember*?
17 Which Fiona featured in *The Avengers*?
18 In which film did Marisa Tomei make her debut?
19 Who wrote the screenplay for *The Bodyguard*?
20 For what did Ben Burtt win a Special Award in 1981?
21 What was the name of Spencer Tracy's character in *Father of the Bride*?
22 The song "Secret Love" came from which movie?
23 Which Joan featured in *The Ice Storm*?
24 What movie is playing on a car radio in *The Flight of the Navigator*?
25 Who won the Best Director Oscar for *Cavalcade*?
26 How many of the crew of the "Andrea Gail" survive in *The Perfect Storm*?
27 Who directed his wife Kate Winslet in 2009's *Revolutionary Road*?
28 Which actress won the Best Actress Oscar for her role in *Johnny Belinda*?
29 In which movie does Jeff Bridges play the Dude?
30 Working with which director did Tom Cruise describe as "Like watching Bruce Springsteen live for the first time"?

Answers | **Pop: Karaoke** *(see Quiz 77)*

1 "Are You Lonesome Tonight"? 2 "When I dial the telephone, nobody's home". 3 Three. 4 "Ebony Eyes". 5 "Let the Sunshine in". 6 Senators, Congressmen. 7 "Spinning Wheel". 8 December. 9 "Regrets, I've had a few, but then again, too few to mention". 10 "Cinderella Rockefella". 11 "'Cause rhythm is a dancer". 12 San Pedro. 13 Blue and grey. 14 "Ashes to Ashes". 15 "When I'm Sixty-Four". 16 "Cecilia". 17 "River Deep Mountain High". 18 "Massachusetts". 19 "Windmills of Your Mind". 20 "I can't tell you but I know it's mine". 21 Chrysler. 22 Everything. 23 Sonny. 24 I'm Outta Here. 25 You're Beautiful. 26 Bette Davis. 27 Another Brick in the Wall. 28 Mull of Kintyre. 29 My Way. 30 Love is All Around.

1 In *Arthur*, what sport did Francine love to play?
2 In *Clifford the Big Red Dog* what colour is Clifford's friend T-Bone?
3 Which two footballers presented *Junior Sportsview*?
4 What was the catchphrase of Yogi Bear's girlfriend?
5 Who played Dolly Clothes-Peg to Jon Pertwee's Worzel Gummidge?
6 What were the Woodentop twins called?
7 Which Doctor Who played the Judge in the 1946 adaptation of *Toad of Toad Hall*?
8 Who was Toad in the 80s animation *The Wind in the Willows*?
9 *Larry the Lamb* first appeared on TV in which year?
10 Which song was the closing theme to *Stingray*?
11 Which animated characters have a family TV guide in *Radio Times*?
12 Which coin had magical powers in *The Queen's Nose*?
13 What was the subject of *Wham Bam Strawberry Jam!*?
14 Which former Gladiator presented *Finders Keepers*?
15 Who hosted *All Your Own*, a series of children's interests demonstrated by children?
16 Charlie Drake and Jack Edwards appeared as which children's TV duo in the 1950s?
17 Who was the voice of the computer SID in *Galloping Galaxies*?
18 Which Doctor Who was a presenter of *Vision On*?
19 Which Maid Marion presented the children's TV's *Picture Book*?
20 The name of which producer appeared at the end of the early *Tom and Jerry* cartoons?
21 Who designed *Blue Peter's* Italian sunken garden?
22 Who replaced Ringo Starr narrating *Thomas the Tank Engine and Friends*?
23 Whose magic ray had transformed Granny Smith into Supergran?
24 In *Supercar*, what was Jimmy's talking monkey called?
25 What was the name of the special Christmas reunion episode of *The Appleyards* in1960?
26 What was the name of Billy Bunter's frustrated school master?
27 Which came first – *Andy Pandy* or *The Flowerpot Men*?
28 Who provided the voices for *Bill and Ben*?
29 *Rag, Tag and Bobtail* were glove puppets operated by which duo?
30 Whose Busy World has featured on BBC?

Answers	**Football Pot Luck 9** *(see Quiz 80)*

1 Blue and white. 2 Hereford Utd. 3 Phil Parkes. 4 Shrewsbury Town. 5 1970s.
6 Bristol Rovers. 7 Blackburn Rovers. 8 Nathan Blake. 9 Bournemouth. 10 Jordan Henderson. 11 Leeds Utd. 12 Beck. 13 Coventry City. 14 Sunderland. 15 Dean.
16 Bristol Rovers. 17 Failed to qualify. 18 Peter Reid. 19 Hungary, Spain. 20 Reading. 21 Macedonia. 22 Gary McAllister. 23 Dundee United. 24 Luton Town.
25 1900s. 26 Southampton. 27 Stoke City. 28 Neil Cox. 29 Scunthorpe United. 10 Six.

1 What colour are FC Porto's shirts?
2 Mel Pejic set a League appearance record at which club?
3 Who was in goal when West Ham Utd won the FA Cup in 1980?
4 At which club did John McGinlay make his League debut?
5 In what decade did Derby County first win the championship?
6 Which club had a fanzine called *Trumpton Times*?
7 Jim Smith replaced Gordon Lee as manager of which club?
8 Who moved from Cardiff to Sheffield Utd for £300,000 in 1994 to set a club record for a transfer fee received?
9 Which club was once known as Boscombe St Johns?
10 Who became captain of Liverpool in 2015, following Stevie's departure?
11 Haddock and Swan were in the same team at which club?
12 Which John became boss of Lincoln City in 1995?
13 Greg Downs played in an FA Cup Final for which team?
14 Who used to play at Abbs Field, Fulwell?
15 What is Warren Barton's middle name?
16 What was the first club that Bobby Gould managed?
17 Where did Portugal finish in the 1994 World Cup?
18 Which manager was dismissed by Manchester City 12 days into the 1993–94 season?
19 Ferenc Puskas played international soccer for which two countries?
20 John Arlott, the voice of cricket, was a fan of which club?
21 In which country would you watch Metalurg take on Vardar Skopje?
22 Which former player succeeded Dennis Wise as manager of Leeds United?
23 Who lost to Gothenburg in the 1987 UEFA Cup Final?
24 At which club did Garry Parker make his League debut?
25 In which decade did Sheffield Wednesday first win the championship?
26 Which club had a fanzine called *The Ugly Inside*?
27 Alan Durban followed Alan A'Court as manager of which club?
28 Which defender went from Scunthorpe to Aston Villa in 1991 to set a club record for a transfer fee received?
29 Which club dropped Lindsey from its name in the 1950s?
30 To one each way, how many international goals did Chris Waddle score?

Answers | **TV: Children's TV 1** *(see Quiz 79)*

1 Soccer. 2 Yellow. 3 Billy Wright & Danny Blanchflower. 4 "Ah do declare". 5 Lorraine Chase. 6 Jenny and Willy. 7 Jon Pertwee. 8 David Jason. 9 1947. 10 Aquamarina. 11 Wallace and Gromit. 12 50p. 13 Poetry for children. 14 Diane Youdale. 15 Huw Wheldon. 16 The Adventures of Mick and Montmorency. 17 Kenneth Williams. 18 Sylvester McCoy. 19 Patricia Driscoll. 20 Fred Quimby. 21 Percy Thrower. 22 Michael Angelis. 23 Inventor Black. 24 Mitch. 25 Christmas with the Appleyards. 26 Mr Quelch. 27 Andy Pandy. 28 Peter Hawkins. 29 Sama and Elizabeth Williams. 30 Richard Scarry.

1 Who were originally called the Saxons?

2 Which group was Keith Potger in and which group did he form?

3 What was the home country of Bachman-Turner Overdrive?

4 What was the Boomtown Rats' first hit?

5 Whose songs are on Deacon Blue's 1990 EP?

6 Vince Clarke left one successful band for another in 1981–82. Which?

7 Whose single "The Cover of *Rolling Stone*" was banned by the BBC because they said it was advertising?

8 What did the group change the title to?

9 Who is Hot Chocolate's lead vocalist?

10 Who links Bananarama and Shakespear's Sister?

11 What was the home town of the Housemartins?

12 Which band took its name from *The Hitch-Hiker's Guide to the Galaxy* and the answer to the question "What is the meaning of life?"?

13 Whose first top ten hit was "Love Missile F1–11"?

14 How many Stray Cats were there?

15 Whose first album was called *Boy*?

16 Who signed a deal to sponsor Clydebank Football Club in 1993?

17 Roland Gift was lead singer with which group?

18 Which group released "Songs in the Key of X" in 1996?

19 Who first performed as Ripples and Waves Plus Michael?

20 What did REO Speedwagon name themselves after?

21 Foo Fighters was formed by Dave Grohl after which band dissolved?

22 How many members of McFly were still in the band after four years?

23 From which American state does the group Orson originate?

24 Who was the last original member of Sugababes still with the group?

25 Which group's first album was *Parachutes*?

26 Which band's No. 1 hit in 2000 was deleted on the day it was released?

27 Fifth Harmony released what album in 2015?

28 Name the girl band who enjoyed a No. 1 hit song from the movie *The Beach*.

29 Which manufactured band made "Pure and Simple" a massive No. 1 hit?

30 Name the British animated band who claimed the No. 1 slot in 2005.

Answers | Movies Pot Luck 10 *(see Quiz 82)*

1 Pallenberg. 2 Sally Field. 3 Louisa. 4 Grady Tripp. 5 Paul Hogan. 6 185 minutes. 7 Stormare. 8 Roger Spottiswoode. 9 Jackie Collins. 10 The Hospital. 11 Roy Rogers. 12 Papa's Delicate Condition. 13 Lock Martin. 14 Tilly. 15 Visual effects. 16 Georgia. 17 Luise Rainer. 18 Misery's Child. 19 Mayron. 20 79 minutes. 21 1943. 22 Lionel Barrymore. 23 Cliffhanger. 24 Leo McCarey. 25 Farnsworth. 26 Baccarat. 27 Robert Zemeckis. 28 White. 29 The Imitation Game. 30 Charles.

1 Which Anita featured in *Barbarella*?

2 Who won the Best Actress Oscar for *Norma Rae*?

3 What is the name of the third eldest child in *The Sound of Music*?

4 Who did Michael Douglas play in *The Wonder Boys*?

5 *Flipper* and *Almost an Angel* starred which actor?

6 Within five minutes, how long does *Schindler's List* last?

7 Which Peter featured in *Fargo*?

8 Who directed *Tomorrow Never Dies*?

9 Which author appeared in *All at Sea*?

10 In which film did a character named Herbert Bock appear?

11 Which Roy said, "There's not much to acting as far as I'm concerned"?

12 "Call Me Irresponsible" won an Oscar when it was used in which movie in 1963?

13 Who was Gort the robot in *The Day the Earth Stood Still*?

14 Which Jennifer featured in *The Fabulous Baker Boys*?

15 Richard Edlund won a Special Award for what in *Return of the Jedi*?

16 Burt Reynolds was born in which American state?

17 Who was the first woman to win consecutive best actress Oscars?

18 What novel does Paul Sheldon write while under the "care" of Annie Wilkes?

19 Which Melanie featured in *Missing*?

20 How long does the 60s movie *101 Dalmatians* last?

21 In which year was *Shadow of Doubt* released?

22 Who won the Best Actor Oscar for *Free Soul*?

23 In which film did a character named Gabe Walker appear?

24 Who won the Best Director Oscar for *Going My Way*?

25 Which Richard featured in *Misery*?

26 In 2006's *Casino Royle*, the card game was poker, but what was it in 1967?

27 Who directed Goldie Hawn in *Death Becomes Her*?

28 What colour is James Dean's T-shirt during the car race in *Rebel without a Cause*?

29 Benedict Cumberbatch starred as Alan Turing in which 2014 film?

30 What is the actual first name of the actor Robert Redford?

Answers	Pop: Groups (see Quiz 81)

1 Bay City Rollers. 2 The Seekers, the New Seekers. 3 Canada. 4 "Looking After No. 1". 5 Bacharach and David. 6 Left Depeche Mode for Yazoo. 7 Dr Hook. 8 The Cover of Radio Times. 9 Errol Brown. 10 Siobhan Fahey. 11 Hull. 12 Level 42. 13 Sigue Sigue Sputnik. 14 Three. 15 U2. 16 Wet Wet Wet. 17 Fine Young Cannibals. 18 R.E.M. 19 Jackson Five. 20 A fire engine. 21 Nirvana. 22 All four. 23 California. 24 Keisha Buchanan. 25 Coldplay. 26 Manic Street Preachers. 27 Reflection. 28 All Saints. 29 Hear'Say. 30 Gorillaz.

1 Who owned a monkey called Marcel?
2 Who recounts a steamy film career in a series of spoof shorts *A Life in Film*?
3 Who wrote *An Evening with Gary Lineker*?
4 Which important character does Barry Bostwick play in *Spin City*?
5 For which role is Ardal O'Hanlon best known?
6 What was the first comedy shown on Channel 4?
7 Who links Rhoda with *The Simpsons*?
8 What was the name of Robert Guillame's butler?
9 Who kidnapped Burt Campbell in *Soap*?
10 Name Jimmy Nail's character in *Auf Weidersehen Pet*?
11 Who married Alice Tinker in the *Vicar of Dibley*?
12 Who appeared in *Men Behaving Badly* but was not recognized by Gary and Tony?
13 Who starred in *Stand Up for Nigel Barton*?
14 In 1979, the last episode of which sitcom netted 24 million viewers, the highest of that year?
15 Jennifer Aniston's husband stars in which TV show, since 2014?
16 Who had a pet hamster called SPG?
17 How is the sometime comic actor Michael Smith better known?
18 Which magician married comedienne Victoria Wood?
19 In which comic series did Joe Lynch play a tailor?
20 Which David starred in *A Sharp Intake of Breath*?
21 Which Goodie turned Twitcher?
22 Who starred in the title role in *I Dream of Jeannie*?
23 Which former PM's secretary was a consultant on the first two series of *Yes Minister*?
24 In which series did Harry Worth play himself as a brass band conductor?
25 Who was played by Jamie Farr in *M*A*S*H*?
26 In which comedy did Ted Bovis appear as an entertainer?
27 Whose son was called Spud-U-Like?
28 Which part did Liza Tarbuck play in *Watching*?
29 What career did Jo Brand follow before being a successful comedy performer?
30 What is Ben's trade in *Two Point Four Children*?

Quiz 84

Football Pot Luck 10

Answers – page 485

LEVEL 3

1 In which decade did Chester add City to their name?
2 Which Nigel went on from non-League St Blazey to play for England?
3 How many points did Newcastle Utd take from their first 10 games of the 1995–96 League season?
4 What is Peter Beagrie's middle name?
5 Which club used to play at the Antelope Ground?
6 Which Brian of Burnley made his only England appearance in 1961?
7 What was the first club that Arthur Cox managed?
8 Peter Allen set a League appearance record at which London club?
9 Gerry Ryan took temporary charge of which club in November 1991?
10 Manchester City in 1995 and Blackburn in 1996 both played how many League games before a win?
11 David Seaman and Peter Reid were in the same team at which club?
12 Which John first became boss of Millwall in 1986?
13 Clive Goodyear played in an FA Cup Final for which team?
14 At which club did England's Mark Wright make his League debut?
15 In what decade did Dundee first win the championship?
16 Which club had a fanzine called *Marching Altogether*?
17 Dave Bassett followed Billy McEwan as manager of which club?
18 Rufus Brevett moved for £250,000 to QPR in 1991 to set a record for a transfer fee received at which club?
19 Which club was once known as Singers FC?
20 To two each way, how many international goals did John Toshack score?
21 Which club was 2007–08 League champions in the Czech Republic?
22 Who left the board of Manchester United to join the board of Chelsea in 2004?
23 Marvin Hinton and Peter Houseman played for which 1970s FA Cup finalists?
24 What is Darren Huckerby's middle name?
25 What year did John terry hang up his international boots?
26 Who lost on penalties to Steaua Bucharest in the final of the 1986 European Cup?
27 Who holds the record for the fastest-ever England goal?
28 Which Arsenal player was booked for the first time in his career in the 1993 FA Cup Final replay?
29 Viv Anderson was player/manager of which club in 1993–94?
30 Ray Graydon scored a League Cup Final winner for which club?

Answers	TV: Comedy 2 *(see Quiz 83)*

1 Ross Geller. 2 Sir Leslie Quint. 3 Arthur Smith. 4 The mayor. 5 Father Dougal McGuire. 6 The Comic Strip Presents: Five Go to Dorset. 7 Julie Kavner (played Brenda opposite Rhoda & was the voice of Marge Simpson). 8 Benson. 9 Aliens. 10 Oz. 11 Hugo. 12 Kylie Minogue. 13 Keith Barron. 14 To The Manor Born. 15 The Leftovers. 16 Rick (The Young Ones). 17 Michael Crawford. 18 The Great Surprendo. 19 Never Mind the Quality, Feel the Width. 20 David Jason. 21 Bill Oddie. 22 Barbara Eden. 23 Lady Falkender. 24 Oh Happy Band. 25 Cpl Klinger. 26 Hi-De-Hi! 27 Wayne and Waynetta Slob's. 28 Brenda. 29 Psychiatric nurse. 30 A plumber.

1 Which Bowl was awarded to the winner of the Oxford–Cambridge Varsity match?

2 Which former rugby powerhouse plays home matches at Old Deer Park?

3 Who joined the Brumbies in 2008, playing with his brother flanker George Smith?

4 Which Argentine Diego holds Italy's all-time points-scoring record?

5 How many points did New Zealand score against Portugal at Lyon in 2007?

6 What nationality is Murray Kidd?

7 For which club did fly half turned broadcaster Cliff Morgan play?

8 Which Irish winger was described by Bill McLaren as "an electric eel"?

9 Where was the first Rugby Union World Cup held?

10 Who did Russian Prince Obolensky play for in 1936?

11 Name the first Union club to win the John Player Cup three years in a row.

12 Who kicked six penalty goals for Scotland on his debut in 1986?

13 Which England cricket captain was capped for England at rugby?

14 Which Irish doctor was capped at Rugby Union and soccer?

15 Who preceded Steve Sale as England captain?

16 What is South Africa's inter-provincial tournament called?

17 Which member of the royal family played in a rugby international?

18 In which country do Randwick play?

19 Who captained the 1967 touring All Blacks?

20 Which team did Andy Platt and Dean Bell join after leaving Wigan?

21 How age did Jonny Wilkinson turn in 2016? 37 or 39?

22 Which country did Hugo Porta play for?

23 Who won 53 caps without missing a single game?

24 Who scored all his team's points for Scotland in the 19–14 win against France in 1996?

25 What is New Zealand's inter-provincial championship called?

26 What was France's Olivier Merle's former profession?

27 Which Welsh player was a champion hurdler?

28 What is the occupation of Scotland's Rob Wainwright?

29 Which match was Jonathan Davies's last game of League for Wales?

30 What did New Zealanders suggest should be named after Jonah Lomu following the Rugby World Cup?

---

1 What producer's label had the slogan "Tomorrow's Sound Today"?
2 What was the lady wearing on the front and back covers of Rod Stewart's *Blondes Have More Fun* album?
3 Who recorded "Daydream Believer (Cheer Up Peter Reid)" in 1996?
4 Who was the first group at No. 1 with Roman numerals in its name?
5 What did Pink Floyd's 1977 *Animals* tour feature an inflatable of?
6 Whose first album was *Natty Dread*?
7 Whose deaths were recalled in the Stones' "Sympathy for the Devil"?
8 Which group was formerly Linda Ronstadt's backing band?
9 Who wrote Lulu's hit "The Boat That I Row"?
10 Which British female singer had three song titles on the first UK chart?
11 How is Michael Lubowitz better known?
12 What do the Beverley Sisters, the Bee Gees and the Shangri-Las have in common?
13 Who links the Beatles in Hamburg, Elvis's "Wooden Heart" and "Strangers in the Night"?
14 How is the US producer Jazzie B better known?
15 What are the grandchildren called in "When I'm Sixty-Four"?
16 Who was the first female performer to have four UK No. 1s?
17 What did the Bluebells' "Young at Heart" advertise in 1993?
18 Who were John McGeoch, Steve Severin and Budgie?
19 Who are the five named people in "Fifty Ways to Leave Your Lover"?
20 Which 50s chart-topper was at one time Paul Simon's father-in-law?
21 Tre Cool is the drummer for which band?
22 *Hairless Toys* was the name of an album for which female singer in 2015?
23 What is in the middle of the Eagles' *Greatest Hits* album cover?
24 Who had a hit with "Where Will the Baby's Dimple be"?
25 Which group had a hit in 1986 with "Rage Hard"?
26 Which British rocker needed a rabies injection after biting a rat on stage?
27 From which TV soap did Sue Nicholls' "Where Will You be" come?
28 What was in John Lennon's right hand on the cover of his book *A Spaniard in the Works*?
29 Who released a live recordings album titled *Arena*?
30 Which building has been "the ruin of many a poor boy"?

Answers	**Rugby** (see Quiz 85)

1 Bowring. 2 London Welsh. 3 Tyrone Smith. 4 Dominguez. 5 108. 6 New Zealander. 7 Cardiff. 8 Simon Geoghegan. 9 New Zealand. 10 England. 11 Leicester. 12 Gavin Hastings. 13 M. J. K. Smith. 14 Kevin O'Flanaghan (Irish RFC and Arsenal). 15 Bill Beaumont. 16 Currie Cup. 17 Peter Phillips (Princess Anne's son). 18 Australia. 19 Brian Lochore. 20 Auckland Warriors. 21 37. 22 Argentina. 23 Gareth Edwards. 24 Michael Dods. 25 Ranfurly Shield. 26 Lumberjack. 27 Nigel Walker. 28 Army doctor. 29 1995 World Cup semi-final v England. 30 Small volcanic island.

1 Who was Kristin Scott Thomas's first co-star in 1986?
2 What was the first movie which teamed Gene Kelly with Frank Sinatra?
3 Who shared a 1938 Special Oscar with Mickey Rooney?
4 Which director did Theresa Russell marry?
5 For how long was James Caan married to Sheila Ryan?
6 Which married couple acted together in *Mortal Thoughts*?
7 In which movie did Mrs Michael Caine appear with him?
8 Which Mrs Ethan Hawke appeared in *Gattaca*?
9 Which husband of Robin Wright directed her in *The Crossing Guard*?
10 What was Spencer Tracy and Katharine Hepburn's penultimate film together?
11 How was Mrs Brian De Palma, star of *Dressed to Kill*, better known?
12 What was Cary Grant's second film with Hitchcock as director?
13 In which 80s movie did Mr and Mrs Harvey Keitel star?
14 What was Alan Ladd's first western opposite Veronica Lake?
15 How many real wives did the most famous Tarzan have?
16 Who played the title roles in *Sid and Nancy*?
17 Which singer/actress was Mrs Carl Dean?
18 Who co-starred with Bette Midler in *For the Boys*?
19 What was the first movie Samuel L. Jackson starred in with his wife?
20 Who played opposite Myrna Loy 13 times?
21 Which mother and daughter were in the title roles in *Rachel Rachel*?
22 Which production company was set up by Hugh Grant and Liz Hurley?
23 Who was the female triplet in the famous baby dance routine in *The Band Wagon*?
24 Which bandleader did Betty Grable marry in 1943?
25 What was the sixth Spencer Tracy/Katharine Hepburn movie?
26 Which brothers wrote *The Matrix* series of movies and *Speed Racer*?
27 Jeff and Beau Bridges played which brothers alongside Michelle Pfeiffer?
28 What was the name of the first movie starring Robert de Niro and Al Pacino?
29 Which partnership won two Oscars in 2006 for editing and directing *The Departed*?
30 Paul Greengrass and Matt Damon can't work without each other on which 2016 spy franchise?

Answers | TV Pot Luck 10 *(see Quiz 88)*

1 Third Rock from the Sun. 2 Jemima Roper. 3 Dutch. 4 Gibbons. 5 Martin Clunes.
6 We Can Work It Out. 7 Bernadette O'Farrell. 8 Brenda Blethyn. 9 Aviation. 10
Dempsey and Makepeace. 11 Jimmy Tarbuck. 12 Robert Wightman. 13 Lou Grant.
14 The Brick. 15 Oasis Publishing. 16 Leonard Nimoy. 17 Gloria Hunniford. 18
Wolverhampton. 19 Alessi. 20 Joan Greenwood. 21 Jerry Stevens. 22 Penelope Keith.
23 Jonathan Dimbleby. 24 Jerome. 25 Commander Chakotay. 26 Brookside. 27
Squadron Leader Rex. 28 Luton Town. 29 World Illustrated. 30 Beavis and Butthead.

1 The Solomon family were the main characters in which sci-fi sit-com?
2 Who plays the character Amanda Price in the 2008 ITV drama *Lost in Austen*?
3 What nationality was Carla, played by Kylie Minogue, in *The Sullivans*?
4 What is chat show host Leeza's surname?
5 Which star narrated the *Rottentrolls*?
6 Which consumer programme was presented by Judy Finnegan?
7 Who was the first actress to play Maid Marian in *The Adventures Of Robin Hood*?
8 Who starred in *The Labours Of Erica*?
9 What was the subject of the 1980 series *Diamonds in the Sky*?
10 In which series did Tony Osoba play Det. Sgt Chas Jarvis?
11 Who presented *Winner Takes All*?
12 Who succeeded Richard Thomas as John Boy in *The Waltons*?
13 In which 80's US series was there a photographer named Dennis "The Animal" Price?
14 What is the name of Holling's bar in *Northern Exposure*?
15 What was the name of the publishing company in *Executive Stress*?
16 Who played the Great Paris in *Mission: Impossible*?
17 Which Irish presenter shares a birth date with Bobby Hatfield of the Righteous Brothers?
18 Sue Lawley was awarded an honorary doctorate by which university?
19 Gayle and Gillian Blakeney played which twins in *Neighbours*?
20 Who played the landlady in *Girls on Top*?
21 Who was the host of *TV Quiz*?
22 Who played a lady MP in *No Job for a Lady*?
23 Which Dimbleby presented *First Tuesday*?
24 Is it Robson or Jerome who has starred in *Game of Thrones* since 2012?
25 Who is second in command of the Voyager in *Star Trek: Voyager*?
26 Presenter Paula Yates made a guest appearance in which soap?
27 Who did Tim Woodward play in *A Piece of Cake*?
28 Which soccer side does Nick Owen, formerly of *Good Morning with Anne and Nick*, support?
29 Which fictional magazine featured in *Shirley's World*?
30 Who duetted with Cher on *I Got You Babe* in 1994?

Answers	Movies: Partnerships *(see Quiz 87)*

1 Prince. 2 Anchors Aweigh. 3 Deanna Durbin. 4 Nicholas Roeg. 5 Three months. 6 Bruce Willis & Demi Moore. 7 The Man Who Would be King. 8 Uma Thurman. 9 Sean Penn. 10 Desk Set. 11 Nancy Allen. 12 Notorious. 13 The Naples Connection. 14 This Gun for Hire. 15 Six. 16 Gary Oldman & Chloe Webb. 17 Dolly Parton. 18 James Caan. 19 Losing Isaiah. 20 William Powell. 21 Joanne Woodward, Nell Potts. 22 Simian Films. 23 Nanette Fabray. 24 Harry James. 25 Adam's Rib. 26 Wachowski. 27 Baker. 28 Heat. 29 Martin Scorsese and Thelma Schoonmaker. 30 Jason Bourne.

1 Which three Sheffield Wednesday players were involved in the 1962 match-fixing scandal?

2 Which side resigned from the League in 1962?

3 Who followed George Swindin as manager of Arsenal?

4 Which Peterborough forward hit 52 goals in a season?

5 Who scored six for Manchester City in an abandoned FA Cup game?

6 Who managed Rotherham, QPR and Aston Villa in just six weeks?

7 What first went to Keith Peacock on the first day of the 1965–66 season?

8 Which English player was labelled "El Beatle" by the Portuguese press?

9 Which two Scottish clubs were involved in Colin Stein's £100,000 transfer?

10 In the 1960s, which club went from Division 4 to Division 1 and back again?

11 Who was Joe Mercer's assistant when Manchester City won the championship?

12 In 1960, which club hit 100 goals for a third successive season?

13 Who did England play to celebrate the centenary of the Football Association?

14 Which Portsmouth and England wing-half retired in 1965?

15 Who was leading scorer in the 1966 World Cup tournament?

16 Who took over as manager of Leeds Utd in 1961?

17 Which Newcastle Utd player hit his first goals for seven years in the 1969 Inter-Cities Fairs Cup Final?

18 Alan Ashman was manager of which FA Cup winners?

19 What was the nationality of the referee in the 1966 World Cup Final?

20 Which player took Newcastle Utd to court?

21 Which was the first FA Cup Final of the 1960s to go to extra time?

22 Which club changed their name a year before entering the Football League?

23 Who won the first League Cup Final to be played at Wembley?

24 An injury to which joint kept Denis Law out of the 1968 European Cup Final?

25 Which non-League club beat Newport County to win the 1962–63 Welsh Cup?

26 Name the captain who lifted three different trophies at Wembley in successive years.

27 In what year was the maximum wage for footballers abolished?

28 Name the Spanish side Spurs beat in the final of the 1963 Cup-Winners' Cup.

29 Which player's court case allowed greater freedom of movement between clubs?

30 Can you recall Leeds United's conquerors in the 1967 Inter-Cities Fairs Cup Final?

Answers	Pop Pot Luck 12 *(see Quiz 90)*

1 Paul Kossoff. 2 The Rolling Stones. 3 Jennifer Rush. 4 The Performing Right Society. 5 Dragnet. 6 A doll's house. 7 Russ Conway. 8 "Green Door". 9 Their feet. 10 Kalin Twins. 11 Ricky Valance. 12 "Hey Joe". 13 Canada. 14 "Punky's Dilemma". 15 Melissa Manchester. 16 Grateful Dead. 17 Paul Jones. 18 Chicago Transit Authority. 19 Ronald Reagan. 20 The National Academy of Recording Arts & Sciences. 21 Nicky Wire. 22 Selena Gomez. 23 Jet Harris & Tony Meehan. 24 Johnny Cash. 25 Mike Harding, 26 The Rolling Stones. 27 Gary Numan. 28 Bambina. 29 Norman Greenbaum. 30 Ultravox.

1 Which Free member was brought back to life after 35 minutes in 1975?
2 Which group had three members pay £5 fines for urinating against a London petrol station?
3 Who followed up her No. 1 hit with a song called "Ring of Ice"?
4 Which society collects performance royalties for British composers?
5 Which TV cop series theme tune was a hit in 1953 for Ray Anthony?
6 Which gift to the royal family inspired HMV to manufacture the world's smallest working gramophone records?
7 How is Trevor Sandford DSM better known?
8 Which song begins "Midnight, one more night without sleeping"?
9 What do drummers play the high hat cymbals with?
10 Which brothers are singing on the flip side of Cliff Richard's "Saviour's Day" in 1990?
11 How is David Spencer better known?
12 Which song title links Frankie Laine and Jimi Hendrix?
13 Which country are Crash Test Dummies from?
14 Which Paul Simon song begins "Wish I was a Kellogg's Corn Flake"?
15 Who won a 1982 Grammy as Best Pop Female Vocal Performance for "You Should Hear How She Talks About You"?
16 Which band included Ron "Pigpen" McKernan?
17 Which singer/presenter/actor is also the name of a Victorian dance?
18 What were Chicago called on their first album?
19 Who has not made an album – Ronald Reagan, Pope John Paul II or Winston Churchill?
20 Who organizes the Grammy awards?
21 By what name is Welsh-born bassist and lyricist Nicholas Allen Jones better known?
22 Who released an album *Revival* in 2015?
23 Who had hits with "Scarlett O'Hara" and "Applejack"?
24 Whose first album was called *Everybody Loves a Nut*?
25 Whose 1978 album was called *Captain Paralytic and the Brown Ale Cowboy*?
26 Which band became the first to receive royalties from the USSR?
27 Who won the 1979 British Rock and Pop Best Male Singer award?
28 To whom was Marino Marini saying "Ciao, Ciao" in 1959?
29 Who wrote "Spirit in the Sky"?
30 Whose second album was *Rage in Eden*?

Answers | Football: The 1960s *(see Quiz 89)*

1 Tony Kay, David Layne, Peter Swan. 2 Accrington Stanley. 3 Billy Wright. 4 Terry Bly. 5 Denis Law. 6 Tommy Docherty. 7 First League substitute. 8 George Best. 9 Rangers & Hibs. 10 Northampton Town. 11 Malcolm Allison. 12 Wolves. 13 Rest of the World XI. 14 Jimmy Dickinson. 15 Eusebio. 16 Don Revie. 17 Bobby Moncur. 18 WBA. 19 Swiss. 20 George Eastham. 21 1965. 22 Headington/Oxford United. 23 QPR. 24 Knee. 25 Borough United. 26 Bobby Moore. 27 1961. 28 Atletico Madrid. 29 George Eastham. 30 Dinamo Zagreb.

1 What was the first mainstream film to use the word "virgin"?

2 What was the first Royal Command Performance film?

3 Which airline showed the first in-flight movie?

4 How old was Mae West when she made her movie debut?

5 What was Fritz Lang's first Hollywood film?

6 What did Kevin Kline play on the piano in his first movie, *Sophie's Choice*?

7 What was John Boorman's US directing debut?

8 Who was the first actor to receive $1 million for a single picture?

9 VistaVision was first used in which classic movie?

10 What was the first movie shown in Aromarama?

11 What was Milos Forman's first US movie?

12 What was the first movie to feature Dracula?

13 Which movie was the first to have Sensurround?

14 In which movie did Chow Yun-Fat make his US debut?

15 What was the first western to win an Oscar for best film?

16 What was the first film that teamed Mickey Rooney and Judy Garland?

17 What was Selznick's first movie from his own independent company?

18 Who was the first American to join the Young Vic company on an American tour?

19 What was the first production from the West allowed in Beijing's Forbidden City?

20 What was Shirley MacLaine's first movie?

21 What was Hitchcock's first film for an independent producer?

22 Who was the first US singer/actor to entertain the troops in Korea?

23 What was the first in-flight movie?

24 In which movie did Harrison Ford make his screen debut as a messenger boy?

25 What were the names of the first two film magazines in the US?

26 *Plane Crazy* in 1928 was whose movie debut?

27 Whose first – and only – word on screen was "Non" in 1976's *Silent Movie*?

28 What did the famous "Hollywood" sign first read when it was erected in 1923?

29 In which year did the inaugural Academy Awards ceremony take place?

30 "Broncho Billy" was the first cowboy star but who played him?

Answers	**TV Pot Luck 11** *(see Quiz 92)*

1 Geller. 2 Out of the Blue. 3 John Cleese. 4 John Fashanu. 5 Hull City. 6 Silk underwear. 7 Kirk. 8 Michelle. 9 Hannah Gordon. 10 Just Jimmy. 11 Caleb Temple. 12 Hamish MacBeth. 13 AA. 14 Bob Monkhouse. 15 Richard Crane. 16 Lynda Carter (Wonder Woman). 17 1985. 18 Annie. 19 Charlie. 20 Richard Pasco. 21 Tony Green. 22 Sammy Davis Jr. 23 Star Trek. 24 Investigative reporter. 25 Jessica Jones. 26 BBC Breakfast Time. 27 Denis Touhy. 28 Harry. 29 They were truckers. 30 Fulvia and Desiree Zapp.

1 What was the family name of the brother and sister in *Friends*?
2 Which Australian soap was dropped by the BBC after airing only 130 episodes?
3 What is John Cleese's real name?
4 Which ex-*Gladiators* presenter is a karate black belt?
5 Which soccer side does actor John Alderton support?
6 Which luxury did Helen Mirren choose on *Desert Island Discs*?
7 What was the name of William Shatner's Doberman Pinscher dog?
8 What was the female resistance worker's name in *'Allo 'Allo*?
9 Who played the female bank manager in *Joint Account*?
10 What was the TV version of *The Clitheroe Kid* called?
11 Who was Gail Emory's cousin in *American Gothic*?
12 In which series is the local paper *The Lochdubh Listener*?
13 Which service did Anthea Turner work for before she found media fame?
14 Who presented the new *Candid Camera*?
15 Which character in *Reckless* used a dog sled team in his attempt to return to his ex-wife to tell her she was making a mistake about remarrying?
16 Which star of a 70s adventure sci-fi series was a former Miss America?
17 In which year was TV naturalist Sir David Attenborough awarded his knighthood?
18 On *That's Life*, what was the name of the little old lady who became an overnight star after being interviewed in the street?
19 What was the name of the office boy in *The Slap Maxwell Story*?
20 Who played George Drummond in *The Drummonds*?
21 Who kept the score on *Bullseye*?
22 Which entertainer died on the same day in 1990 as Muppet creator Jim Henson?
23 Harry Mudd was a character in which sci-fi series?
24 In *This is David Lauder*, what was Lauder's job?
25 Krysten Ritter has played which Netflix super-heroine since 2015?
26 Sally Jones was the sports presenter on which breakfast programme?
27 Who welcomed viewers on the opening night of BBC2?
28 What was *Hooperman's* first name?
29 What did Rollo and Bedrock do for a living?
30 Sheila Gish played which characters in *Small World*?

Answers | Movies: Famous Firsts *(see Quiz 91)*

1 Otto Preminger's The Moon is Blue. 2 A Matter of Life and Death. 3 Imperial Airways. 4 40. 5 Fury. 6 Schumann's "Scenes from Childhood". 7 Point Blank. 8 Marlon Brando. 9 White Christmas. 10 Behind the Great Wall. 11 Taking Off. 12 Nosferatu. 13 Earthquake. 14 The Replacement Killers. 15 Cimarron. 16 Love Finds Andy Hardy. 17 Little Lord Fauntleroy. 18 Richard Gere. 19 The Last Emperor. 20 Trouble with Harry. 21 Rope. 22 Al Jolson. 23 The Lost World. 24 Dead Heat on a Merry Go Round. 25 Photoplay; Motion Picture Story Magazine. 26 Mickey Mouse. 27 Marcel Marceau. 28 Hollywoodland. 29 1929. 30 G. M. Anderson.

1 Jamie Carragher was born in Bootle or Bury in 1978?
2 Where are you going if you walk down Bescot Crescent?
3 Who did Stoke sell to Chelsea in October 1993 for a club record fee?
4 Who is Burnley's most capped player?
5 Which famous Midlands side was founded by cricketing enthusiasts of the Wesleyan Chapel?
6 Before the 1990s, when did Manchester City last win the FA Cup?
7 Which club in the north west was the first outside London to install floodlights?
8 Which Wolves player moved for a £1 million to Manchester City in 1979?
9 Which side beat Hyde by a massive 26 goals to nil?
10 Who played for Blackpool, Coventry City, Manchester City, Burnley and Swansea, while clocking up 795 League appearances?
11 Which club did Martin Dobson manage between 1984 and 1989?
12 Blackburn's Colin Hendry began his career with which Scottish club?
13 Who is Blackpool's most capped player?
14 Name the trophy won by Birmingham City in 1991?
15 Who beat Stoke in the First Division play-offs in 1996?
16 Which manager took Coventry City into the First Division in the 1960s?
17 Which club's score in two FA Cup Finals is 10 for and none against?
18 How many times did Wolves' Billy Wright play for England?
19 Who was Birmingham City boss between 1965 and 1970?
20 Who was Aston Villa's two-goal hero in the 1957 FA Cup Final?
21 In which year did Christie Park, Morecambe, first stage a Football League match?
22 Who was Kidderminster Harriers' manager when they entered the Football League?
23 Between 1981 and 1998 who was the only non-ex-Evertonian to manage the team?
24 Which 1990s Blackpool manager became coach of a British national team?
25 Who beat Birmingham City in their last major cup final?
26 Which two clubs contest the "Black Country Derby"?
27 Name the winners of the 2006–07 League One play-off final.
28 Which club played its first game under both football rules and rugby rules in 1874?
29 Which team lost to SV Hamburg in the quarter-finals of the 1960–61 European Cup?
30 This Premiership club was founded as Small Heath in 1875. Name them.

Answers	Pop Pot Luck 13 *(see Quiz 94)*

1 Dawn. 2 Brian Jones. 3 Pearl. 4 Sandie Shaw. 5 Boxing gloves. 6 Tony Meehan, the Shadows. 7 Ry Cooder. 8 1989. 9 Lonnie Donegan. 10 Helen Shapiro. 11 1960s. 12 The Life and Times of David Lloyd George. 13 Oasis. 14 "I Wanna Do It with You". 15 Clark Kent. 16 Climie Fisher. 17 Keith Richards. 18 Black felt hat. 19 Johnny Kidd. 20 G.I. Blues. 21 Rob Thomas. 22 Australia. 23 Phil Collins. 24 Brook Benton. 25 Rod Stewart. 26 Pierre Cardin. 27 Cole Porter. 28 Tina Turner. 29 Sting. 30 P. J. Proby.

1 Which group's first UK hit was called "Candida"?
2 Which Rolling Stone plays dulcimer on "Lady Jane"?
3 Which Janis Joplin album was posthumously released?
4 Who was the only British girl singer to have three No. 1 hits in the 1960s?
5 What is Cliff Richard sporting on the cover of his *I'm No Hero* album?
6 Who did Brian Bennett replace in which group in 1961?
7 Whose *Bop 'Til You Drop* was the first digitally recorded rock album?
8 What was the name of Taylor Swift's 2014 album?
9 Who was the first British artist to enter the US top 20?
10 Whose debut album was called *Tops with Me*?
11 In which decade was David Bowie's "Laughing Gnome" recorded?
12 Which TV series did the 1981 No. 2 hit "Chi Mai" come from?
13 What was the name of the group made up of Mary Hopkin, Peter Skellern and Julian Lloyd-Webber?
14 What was Barry Manilow's first top ten hit?
15 What did Shakin' Stevens call himself between his real name Michael Barratt and his later stage persona?
16 Who other than Michael Ball had a hit called "Love Changes Everything"?
17 Whose first solo album was *Talk is Cheap*?
18 Which item of Jimi Hendrix's was auctioned at Sotheby's for £14,300?
19 How is Frederick Heath better known?
20 In which film did Elvis play the role of Tulsa McLean?
21 Who did Santana feature on his smash hit "Smooth"?
22 From where do pop dup Savage Garden originate?
23 Whose "A Day in Paradise" won the Grammy for Record of the Year?
24 How was Benjamin Peay better known?
25 Who was 47 years old when his fourth child, Renee, was born?
26 Which Frenchman designed the Beatles' early collarless jackets?
27 Which songwriter's last hit show in the 1950s was *Silk Stockings*?
28 Who had an album called *Acid Queen*?
29 Who played bass with the Ronnie Pierson Trip on cruise liners before having chart success?
30 Whose first chart entry, in the 1960s, was "Hold Me"?

Answers	**Football: Midlands & North West Clubs** *(see Quiz 93)*

1 Bootle. 2 Walsall. 3 Mark Stein. 4 Jimmy McIlroy. 5 Aston Villa. 6 1969. 7 Carlisle Utd. 8 Steve Daley. 9 Preston North End. 10 Tommy Hutchison. 11 Bury. 12 Dundee. 13 Jimmy Armfield. 14 Auto Windscreens Shield. 15 Leicester City. 16 Jimmy Hill. 17 Bury. 18 105. 19 Stan Cullis. 20 Peter McParland. 21 2007. 22 Jan Molby. 23 Mike Walker. 24 Nigel Worthington. 25 Liverpool. 26 WBA and Wolves. 27 Blackpool. 28 Aston Villa. 29 Burnley. 30 Birmingham City.

1 Under what star sign was she born?
2 Which Goon was her co-star in her movie produced by John Boulting?
3 What was her first TV series?
4 Where was she born?
5 Which film was advertised as "The true story of a girl who took on all of Texas and almost won"?
6 In which 1991 movie did she play an uncharacteristically serious role?
7 She made her professional debut in which role?
8 What does she have in common with Judy Garland and Marilyn Monroe?
9 Who was the female star of her first Oscar-nominated film?
10 Who did she say was the only person who had ever made her speechless?
11 Which daughter of Ingrid Bergman was a fellow co-star along with Meryl Streep?
12 What was her very first movie – for Disney?
13 Which movie had the advertising line, "If the rustlers didn't get you ... the hustlers did!"?
14 Who was her co-star in 1990 in a cast with David Carradine?
15 Who directed her in *The Sugarland Express*?
16 What was her occupation in *Foul Play*?
17 Which TV documentary did she make about elephants?
18 How was she billed in her very first film?
19 Who was she originally tipped to play opposite in *Thelma and Louise*?
20 What is the name of her son by the actor she met on the set of *The One and Only Genuine Original Family Band*?
21 For which movie did she receive her first Oscar nomination?
22 For which movie was she turned down in preference to Meryl Streep, who won an Oscar for the role?
23 Who or what are all her pets named after?
24 Who did she divorce to marry husband No. 2?
25 Which movie saw her debut as producer?
26 In which movie does she play a football (American) coach?
27 Who is Hawn's fellow groupie co-star in *The Banger Sisters*?
28 Name the actor Goldie married in 1983 and was still with in 2008.
29 In 2017, Goldie will star in her first movie in 15 years. What's it called?
30 What is the title of her 2005 autobiography?

| **Answers** | TV Pot Luck 12 *(see Quiz 96)* |

1 Short Change. 2 Betty White. 3 Breaking Bad. 4 Three Little Words. 5 Eddie Izzard. 6 Spider. 7 Andy Griffith. 8 Rowing. 9 Peter Bowles and Penelope Keith. 10 At the top of the Eiffel Tower. 11 Picture of Marilyn Monroe. 12 Character talking to viewers in an aside. 13 Robocop. 14 Persil. 15 Sledgehammer. 16 The Late Late Breakfast Show. 17 Warrington. 18 The Organized Task Force. 19 Michael Flatley (Riverdance). 20 The picture board. 21 Lesley Garrett. 22 A collie. 23 Yorkshire TV. 24 Planet 24. 25 Ian Hislop. 26 Dr Brown. 27 Clive James. 28 George Layton. 29 Great British Holiday. 30 Ipswich Town.

1 What was the BBC's children's consumer affairs programme called?

2 Which *Golden Girls* actress played a serial killer in *Boston Legal*?

3 Which horror actor's voice is heard on Michael Jackson's *Thriller*?

4 Which Bad TV show came to an end in 2013 after six seasons?

5 Who briefly replaced Paul Merton on *Have I Got News for You*?

6 How is Geoffrey David Nugent better known?

7 Who played Matlock?

8 Hugh Laurie of *Jeeves and Wooster* fame won an Oxbridge blue for which sport?

9 Name the two stars of *Executive Stress*?

10 Where in France did Penny reunite with Vince in *Just Good Friends*?

11 Which luxury did Bob Monkhouse choose on *Desert Island Discs*?

12 What does "breaking the fourth wall" mean in TV terms?

13 In which series did Richard Eden play a unconventional lawman?

14 Which soap powder did the star of *Cracker* advertise?

15 Which spoof police series features a Captain Trunk?

16 Which show featured the Whirly Wheeler with tragic consequences?

17 Where is Chris Evans's home town?

18 Who did *The Equalizer* work for?

19 Who shot to fame after the 1994 Eurovision Song Contest?

20 What is the first round on *A Question of Sport*?

21 Who tried to teach Pauline Quirke and Linda Robson to sing in *Jobs for the Girls*?

22 What breed of dog was companion to the detective Cluff?

23 Which TV company produced *First Tuesday*?

24 Which was the first production company to produce *The Big Breakfast*?

25 Who presented Channel 4's religious series *Canterbury Tales*?

26 Who is the doctor in *Hamish MacBeth*?

27 Which humourist's autobiography was called *Unreliable Memoirs*?

28 Who played Solly in *It ain't Half Hot Mum*?

29 In *GBH*, what did GBH stand for?

30 Which soccer side does Nigel Havers of *Dangerfield* support?

Answers | Movies: Goldie Hawn *(see Quiz 95)*

1 Scorpio. 2 Peter Sellers. 3 Good Morning World. 4 Washington DC. 5 The Sugarland Express. 6 Deceived. 7 Juliet. 8 Left-handed. 9 Ingrid Bergman. 10 Fred Astaire. 11 Isabella Rossellini. 12 The One and Only Genuine Original Family Band. 13 The Duchess and the Dirtwater Fox. 14 Mel Gibson. 15 Steven Spielberg. 16 Librarian. 17 In the Wild. 18 Goldy Jeanne Hawn. 19 Meryl Streep. 20 Wyatt. 21 Cactus Flower. 22 Sophie's Choice. 23 Her film characters. 24 Gus Trikonis. 25 Cactus Flower. 26 Wildcats. 27 Susan Sarandon. 28 Kurt Russell. 29 Mother/daughter. 30 A Lotus Grows in the Mud.

1 Who was the first player to score a hat-trick in a European Cup Final?
2 Which French team became the first to lose two finals?
3 Who were the first British team to compete in the European Cup?
4 Which team appeared in the final in 1993, 1994 and 1995?
5 Who scored the only goal to win the trophy for Aston Villa?
6 Which city hosted the final when Liverpool first won?
7 Who was Liverpool skipper for the 1981 triumph?
8 Which Lancashire town team represented England in 1960–61?
9 Who met in the first all-English tie in 1978–79?
10 Which team has represented Northern Ireland most times?
11 Who were the first club to eliminate Real Madrid from the competition?
12 To two years each way, when was the first final played at Wembley?
13 Who was in goal for the first British European Cup winners?
14 Which was the first club to play a European Cup Final on their own ground?
15 Which Ipswich Town player scored five goals in the European Cup?
16 Who scored an amazing 46 goals in the European Cup for Benfica?
17 Which were the first team from Holland to win the trophy?
18 Which two clubs from the same British city played in the same competition?
19 Which London club pulled out of the first competition?
20 Who scored first for Manchester Utd in the 1960s final v Benfica?
21 Which Liverpool player was substituted in both the 2005 and 2007 finals?
22 Who became his club's all-time leading appearance-maker in the 2008 final?
23 Which team was victorious at the 2013–14 UEFA Champions League final?
24 Which Turkish club reached the 2007–08 quarter-finals?
25 Ten England internationals started the 2008 final but how many were substitutes?
26 In which stadium did Arsenal lose the 2006 final to FC Barcelona?
27 Which Greek team became the first to draw all six of its group games?
28 Which two teams were the first to contest the final from the same country?
29 Name the winners of the 50th European Cup/Champions League competition.
30 How many former Champions League winners came on as a sub in the 2008 final?

Answers	Pop Pot Luck 14 (see Quiz 98)

1 Bruce Springsteen. 2 Billie Holiday. 3 James Galway. 4 Cyndi Lauper. 5 Chicago. 6 John Mayall and Eric Clapton. 7 Blue Hawaii. 8 The Beatles. 9 "Vincent". 10 Peter Asher. 11 Air Supply. 12 Clancy Brothers and Tommy Makem. 13 James. 14 All About Eve. 15 Don Black. 16 Holland. 17 Self Aid. 18 Roxy (cinema). 19 Don Everly. 20 Vic Damone. 21 Ludacris. 22 Next. 23 Thunderclap Newman. 24 19. 25 Back to the Future. 26 Holiday. 27 Van Morrison. 28 Jonathan King. 29 "Sloop John B". 30 A horse.

Quiz 98 | Pop Pot Luck 14

Answers – page 499

LEVEL 3

1 Who did Jon Landau produce in the 1970s and call the "future of rock 'n' roll"?
2 Which jazz singer died in July 1959 of liver failure?
3 Who did the Chieftains record with on their first album?
4 Who's dancing in a red dress on the LP cover of *She's so Unusual*?
5 Peter Cetera was vocalist with which band?
6 Who had a 1960s album called *Blues Breakers*?
7 Which Elvis movie featured "Can't Help Falling in Love"?
8 Which British group's US LP cover was deemed in such bad taste in 1966 that 750,000 copies were recalled?
9 Which song refers to a bloody rose lying crushed and broken in the virgin snow?
10 Who signed James Taylor to Apple in 1968?
11 Who were Graham Russell and Russell Hitchcock?
12 Whose debut album was *Isn't It Grand Boys* in 1966?
13 Which forename is shared by Paul McCartney's father and son?
14 Which group takes its name from a 1950s Bette Davis film?
15 Who is the songwriting brother-in-law of the 1960s singer Julie Rogers?
16 Which country were Teach-In from?
17 Which concert was a follow-up to Live Aid and raised funds for the unemployed in the Irish Republic?
18 What were Roxy Music named after?
19 Whose son is called Edan?
20 How is Vito Farinola better known?
21 By what name is rapper Christopher Bridges better known?
22 R. L. Huggar, Terry and Raphael Brown formed which successful pop trio?
23 Who was the first artist to take "Something in the Air" to No. 1?
24 How many years elapsed between Stevie Wonder's first UK chart entry and his first solo UK No. 1?
25 Which film uses Huey Lewis's hit "Power of Love" on the soundtrack?
26 *Ghost Stories* was the 2014 album from which band?
27 Who released a 1960s album called *Hard Nose the Highway*?
28 Who launched a record label called UK?
29 Which Beach Boys hit refers to "my grandpappy and me"?
30 In the Lonnie Donegan song, what was the Stewball?

1 *Sommersby* was a remake of which Depardieu classic?
2 What was the only movie Hitchcock remade?
3 Who was the male star of the fourth version of *Daddy Long Legs*?
4 Who starred in a 1981 remake of a 1946 film noir with Lana Turner?
5 Who won an Oscar for the 1950 George Cukor movie remade in 1993 with Melanie Griffith?
6 Which 1997 film was a remake of *Les Comperes*?
7 Whose final movie was a remake with sound of *The Unholy Three*?
8 *Move Over Darling* reworked which 40s classic with Cary Grant?
9 Which Warren Beatty movie was a remake of *Here Comes Mr Jordan*?
10 A 30s classic with Clark Gable and Claudette Colbert was remade as *You Can't Run Away from It* starring whom?
11 *Singapore Woman* was a remake of which Bette Davis Oscar-winner?
12 In which movie did Bette Midler re-create a Barbara Stanwyck role?
13 Who directed *Love Affair* and its remake *An Affair to Remember*?
14 Who played the wedding organizer in the 1991 remake of a 50s Spencer Tracy classic?
15 *The Badlanders* was a western remake of which Sterling Hayden movie which had a young Monroe in the cast?
16 *Silk Stockings* was the musical remake of which classic?
17 Which Humphrey Bogart movie was a remake of *Bordertown*?
18 What was the Julia Roberts remake of *Dr Jekyll and Mr Hyde* called?
19 Where was the 70s remake of *Invasion of the Body Snatchers* set?
20 Who played the Hayley Mills role in the 90s version of a 1961 movie about twins?
21 Which 60s movie was a remake of Bob Hope's *The Paleface*?
22 *One Sunday Afternoon* was remade twice, once with the same title and once as what?
23 Velvet Brown as a child was played by Elizabeth Taylor, but who was the adult 30 years later?
24 What was the remake of *Kid Galahad* which did not star Elvis?
25 How was *Sentimental Journey* remade with Lauren Bacall?
26 Who wrote the original screenplay for *The Out-of-Towners* remade in 1999?
27 Which city replaced Turin in the 2003 version of *The Italian Job*?
28 Which director remade Alfred Hitchcock's signature movie, *Psycho*, in 1998?
29 Which watery 2018 remake will star Channing Tatum as a merman?
30 What 2007 remake of the 1957 original stars Christian Bale and Russell Crowe?

Answers | **TV Pot Luck 13** *(see Quiz 100)*

1 Dr Tony Hill. 2 Staines. 3 Anthea Turner 4 Richard Jordan. 5 Gloria Hunniford. 6 Liz Hurley. 7 Delta City. 8 John Hurt. 9 John Hurt. 10 P. D. James. 11 Maurice. 12 Ernestine and Gwendolyn. 13 The Hitch Hiker's Guide to the Galaxy. 14 Adam Dalgleish. 15 Lisa Bonet. 16 Noel Dyson. 17 Barry Bostwick. 18 Ray MacAnally. 19 Colin Welland. 20 Ivy Unsworth. 21 Alice. 22 Pat Coombs. 23 Colonel Marea. 24 Favourite Things. 25 The Gestapo. 26 Betty. 27 John Slater. 28 The Defenders. 29 City Lights. 30 Colin Baker.

1 Which clinical psychologist does Robson Green play in *Wire in the Blood*?

2 Which Ali G home town got renamed in 2011 to _____ Upon Thames, to distance itself from the faux gangsta?

3 Who did Eamonn Holmes nickname Miss Tippy Toes?

4 Who played Harley Gage in *The Equalizer*?

5 Which TV presenter married hairdresser Stephen Way in 1998?

6 Who made her TV debut as Dennis Potter's Christabel?

7 In which city is *Robocop* set?

8 Which "Caligula" was also "Quentin Crisp"?

9 Which male has worn the most make up on *They Think It's All Over*?

10 Which former BBC Governor received a peerage in 1991 and writes detective novels?

11 Who owns KBHR, the radio station, in *Northern Exposure*?

12 What were the first names of the Snoop Sisters?

13 Magrathea featured in which series?

14 Who investigated in the TV series *Cover Her Face*?

15 Who plays Denise in *The Cosby Show*?

16 Who played the wife of Potter?

17 In *George Washington*, who played the title role?

18 Who played chief suspect Sir William Gull in *Jack the Ripper*?

19 Who played table top games in *Late Night Line Up*?

20 Who was Thora Hird's character in *In Loving Memory*?

21 Who worked as a waitress at Mel's Diner?

22 Who starred with Peggy Mount in *You're Only Young Twice*?

23 Which Scotland Yard cop was played by Boris Karloff?

24 What was the title of the TV equivalent of *Desert Island Discs*?

25 Robert Hardy played a member of what in *Jenny's War*?

26 Who served the tea at Emu's Broadcasting Company?

27 Which John assisted Pinky and Perky?

28 E. G. Marshall was a regular in which 60's American courtroom series?

29 The character Willie Melvin featured in which comedy?

30 Which Dr Who appeared in *War and Peace*?

1 George Abecassis founded and raced for which marque?
2 From which country does Kenneth Acheson hail?
3 Which team gave him his Formula One break?
4 Philippe Adams had two outings for which team in 1994?
5 Which British single-seater championship did Adams win in 1993?
6 Kurt Ahrens Jr was driving what Formula Two car when he finished seventh in the 1969 German Grand Prix?
7 In 1981, Michele Alboreto raced in Formula Two for a marque that in 1985 graduated to Formula One. Which one?
8 For which team did Alboreto drive a Lola in 1993?
9 In which 1994 grand prix did Alboreto shed a wheel in the pit lane?
10 Jean Alesi transferred to which team in 1996?
11 Who was his team-mate there?
12 Name either of the racing categories Philippe Alliot turned to after Formula One?
13 Has Alliot ever won the Le Mans 24 Hours with Peugeot?
14 For which team did Giovanna Amati attempt to qualify in 1992?
15 How old was Chris Amon when he made his world championship debut?
16 For which team did he drive from 1967 to 1969?
17 For which team did he finish second twice in 1970?
18 What nationality is Conny Andersson?
19 In 1977, four outings led to four non-qualifications for Andersson with which team?
20 What car did Mario Andretti race in 1970?
21 Who collected the only point for the Spyker team in their only F1 season?
22 Who was the first Indian to drive in a F1 World Championship race?
23 Who was the last American driver to race in the F1 championship?
24 How many Italians drove in the F1 World Championship 1950–2008?
25 Under which country's flag does Nico Rosberg drive?
26 With which F1 team did Nick Heidfeld begin his career in 2000?
27 Up to 2016, Sebastian Vettel won the Formula One World Championship four times. With which racing team?
28 Which ex-F1 World Champion sold his team to Jaguar before the 2000 season?
29 How many different drivers won a Formula One Gand Prix in 2003?
30 Who won Jordan's F1's first ever Grand Prix at Spa in 1998?

Answers	**Football Pot Luck 11** *(see Quiz 102)*

1 Belgium. 2 Eddie and Frank Gray. 3 Barnet. 4 Bristol Rovers. 5 1950s. 6 Leicester City. 7 Aston Villa. 8 Paul Stewart. 9 Everton. 10 21. 11 Derby County. 12 Chung. 13 Brighton. 14 John. 15 Walsall. 16 WBA. 17 Hillsborough. 18 Craig Johnston. 19 QPR. 20 1970s. 21 Zinedine Zidane. 22 Bulgaria. 23 Espanyol. 24 Rochdale. 25 1920s. 26 Sheffield Utd. 27 Fulham. 28 Paul Elliott. 29 QPR. 30 Two.

Quiz 102 | Football Pot Luck 11

Answers – page 503

LEVEL 3

1 Who were the opponents when Ian Rush hit his record-breaking 24th goal for Wales?
2 Which brothers played in the 1976 European Cup Final?
3 Gary Bull established a record for most League goals in a season at which club?
4 At which club did Keith Curle make his League debut?
5 In what decade did Tottenham Hotspur first win the championship?
6 Which club had a fanzine called *The Fox*?
7 Vic Crowe followed Tommy Docherty as manager of which club?
8 Who moved from Manchester City to Tottenham Hotspur for £1.7 million in 1988 to set a club record for a transfer fee received?
9 Which club was once known as St Domingo FC?
10 To two each way, how many international goals did Mike Channon score?
11 Goddard and Hebberd were in the same team at which club?
12 Which Sammy became boss of Doncaster in July 1994?
13 Tony Grealish first played in an FA Cup Final for which team?
14 What is Dave Beasant's middle name?
15 With 467 League games from 1964 to 1982 Colin Harrison set an appearance record at which club?
16 Stuart Williams won 33 of his Welsh caps while at which club?
17 Owlerton was the original name of which ground?
18 Who had been brought to Liverpool as Keegan's replacement before Kenny Dalglish's arrival?
19 Aged 29 Frank Sibley became the youngest League manager when he was at which club?
20 In which decade did Wales first win at Wembley?
21 Which Frenchman managed Real Madrid to victory at the 2016 UEFA Champions League Final?
22 In which country would you watch FC Timisoara playing Universitatea Craiova?
23 Who lost on penalties to Bayer Leverkusen in the 1988 UEFA Cup Final?
24 At which club did Geoff Thomas make his League debut?
25 In which decade did Burnley first win the championship?
26 Which club had a fanzine called *The Greasy Chip Buttie*?
27 Bill Dodgin Jnr followed Alec Stock as manager of which club?
28 Who moved from Celtic to Chelsea in 1991 to set a then club record for a transfer fee received?
29 Which club was once known as St Jude's?
30 To one each way, how many international goals did Bobby Moore score?

Answers	**Formula One: The Drivers** *(see Quiz 101)*

1 HWM. 2 Northern Ireland. 3 RAM. 4 Lotus. 5 Formula Two. 6 Porsche. 7 Tyrrell. 8 Ferrari. 9 Imola. 10 Benetton. 11 Gerhard Berger. 12 Sports car, ice racing. 13 No. 14 Brabham. 15 19. 16 Ferrari. 17 March. 18 Swedish. 19 BRM. 20 March. 21 Adrian Sutil. 22 Narain Karthikeyan. 23 Scott Speed. 24 99. 25 Germany. 26 Prost Peugeot. 27 Red Bull Racing. 28 Sir Jackie Stewart. 29 Eight. 30 Damon Hill.

1 Penny Ford and Turbo B were vocalists in which 90s dance group?
2 In which city did House Music originate?
3 Where is Perez "Guaglione" Prado from?
4 Whose first single was "Dance Stance"?
5 Which Madonna dance hit was her first No. 1?
6 What follows the Outhere Brothers' "Don't stop"?
7 Who had a party hit about "Atmosphere"?
8 Whose "Sideboard Song" was subtitled "Got My Beer in the Sideboard Here"?
9 Who sang about "Reggae Like It Used to Be"?
10 What gave the Brothers Johnson their first top ten hit?
11 Ottawan who had an 80s hit with "D.I.S.C.O." were from where?
12 Who sang "I Haven't Stopped Dancing Yet" in 1989?
13 Who are credited with "Boogie Wonderland" in 1979?
14 Who said Dance Yourself Dizzy in 1980?
15 Which disco queen's first album was *Heart and Soul*?
16 In which year did Barry White's "You're My First, My Last, My Everything" hit the top?
17 Whose first album was *Party Party 16 Great Party Icebreakers*?
18 What did the party hit "Hoots Mon" advertise when it was re-released in 1993?
19 Which disco band included Maizie Williams, Bobby Farrell and Marcia Barrett?
20 Which two stars are credited on the cover of *Dirty Dancing*?
21 What nationality is Ferry Corsten, maker of "Rock Your Body Rock"?
22 Whose "Superstar" reached No. 3 in the charts in 2003?
23 Which Fatboy Slim single's video depicts man's evolution in 31/2 minutes?
24 What was Shapeshifter's 2004 No. 1?
25 What did Another Level's only UK No. 1 do?
26 What "Brothers" took "Don't Stop (Wiggle, Wiggle)" to No. 1 in 1995?
27 Which singer encouraged you to "shake it off" in 2014?
28 Who enjoyed their only UK No. 1 with "Toca's Miracle" in April 2000?
29 What was the name of the Italian dance music outfit that had a No. 1 in 1995?
30 Name the hit Armand Van Helden took to the top of the charts in 1999.

Answers	**Movies Pot Luck 11** *(see Quiz 104)*

1 Prosky. 2 Somerset. 3 Bruce Willis. 4 Helen Hayes. 5 Nell. 6 Magee. 7 Richard White. 8 Anthony Hopkins. 9 Harrison Ford. 10 Shepard. 11 George Stevens. 12 Montana. 13 Sissy Spacek. 14 Nina. 15 How to Drain A Dragon. 16 Pee-Wee Herman. 17 Aiello. 18 Eric Stoltz. 19 Ron Howard. 20 Sound in Fantasia. 21 120 minutes. 22 Mean Streets. 23 Fierstein. 24 Singapore. 25 Peter Markle. 26 Kevin Kline. 27 Aerosmith. 28 Emily Blunt. 29 Judy. 30 Zack Snyder.

1 Which Robert featured in *Dead Man Walking*?
2 Which soap did Hollywood star Ted Danson star in?
3 Which movie star released an album called *Heart of Soul* in 1990?
4 Who won the Best Actress Oscar for *Sin of Madelon Claudet*?
5 A character named Jerome Lovell appeared in which film?
6 Which Patrick featured in *Barry Lyndon*?
7 Who voiced Gaston in the film *Beauty and the Beast*?
8 *Bookworm* and *Surviving Picasso* both starred which actor?
9 Who said, "I ask for the money I want, they pay it. It's that simple"?
10 Which Sam featured in *Days of Heaven*?
11 Who won the Best Director Oscar for *A Place in the Sun*?
12 *The Horse Whisperer* is set in which US state?
13 Who plays the brain in the film *The Man with Two Brains*?
14 What was the name of Juliet Stevenson's character in *Truly, Madly, Deeply*?
15 Hiccup and Toothless are the stars of which 2014 sequel?
16 Who plays Penguin's father in the film *Batman Returns*?
17 Which Danny featured in *Moonstruck*?
18 Who plays Rocky Dennis in *Mask*?
19 Who directed *Ransom*?
20 For what did Walt Disney win a Special Award in 1941?
21 Within five minutes, how long does *Platoon* last?
22 A character named Johnny Boy appeared in which film?
23 Which Harvey featured in *Mrs Doubtfire*?
24 What was the destination in the first *Road* film?
25 Who directed the film *Bat 21*?
26 Who played Inspector Dreyfus in the 2006 remake of *The Pink Panther*?
27 Who recorded the theme from *Armageddon*, "I Don't Want to Miss a Thing"?
28 Who had the title role in the 2009 regal biopic *The Young Victoria*?
29 What is the first name of Private Benjamin in the move of the same name?
30 Who directed the 2009 film version of the graphic novel *Watchman*?

Answers | **Dance** *(see Quiz 103)*

1 Snap! 2 Chicago. 3 Cuba. 4 Dexy's Midnight Runners. 5 "Into the Groove". 6 "Wiggle Wiggle". 7 Russ Abbott. 8 Chas and Dave. 9 Paul Nicholas. 10 "Stomp". 11 France. 12 Pat and Mick. 13 Earth, Wind and Fire and the Emotions. 14 Liquid Gold. 15 Tina Charles. 16 1974. 17 Black Lace. 18 Maynard's Wine Gums. 19 Boney M. 20 Patrick Swayze and Jennifer Grey. 21 Dutch. 22 Jamelia. 23 Right Here Right Now. 24 Lola's Theme. 25 Freak Me. 26 Outhere. 27 Taylor Swift. 28 Fragma. 29 Livin' Joy. 30 "You Don't Know Me".

1 Which part did Eddie Redmayne play in the BBC's 2008 *Tess of the d'Urbevilles*?
2 In *Merlin*, which beast made from elements of clay is brought to life by Nimueh?
3 Who played Nancy Astor's husband, Waldorf, in the drama *Nancy Astor*?
4 *A Voyage Round My Father* was the story of which writer?
5 Who played Chamberlain in *Winston Churchill, the Wilderness Years*?
6 Which 70s drama was based on the novel *The Company* by John Ehrlichman?
7 Who played Bomber Harris in the controversial drama?
8 *We'll Meet Again* was set during which war?
9 Which 80s medical drama was produced by the same company as *Hill Street Blues*?
10 In *Spender*, what were Spender's daughters called?
11 Who played secret agent *Charlie Muffin*?
12 Who played Rick Blaine in the 1980s TV remake of *Casablanca*?
13 Which Constabulary did Barlow and Watt work for in *Softly Softly Task Force*?
14 In the 1980s which actor played the traitor Guy Burgess?
15 In *The Singing Detective*, Philip E. Marlow was confined to which hospital ward?
16 Which Bond girl played Mrs Simpson in *The Woman He Loved*?
17 Which 1983 drama showed actors Paul McGann and Robert Lindsay taking on the best in the snooker halls of London?
18 Which sitcom star took on a classic role as Mercy Pecksniff in *Martin Chuzzlewit*?
19 *The Irish RM*, played by Peter Bowles, had previously retired from which army?
20 Which US actor portrayed JFK in the TV drama *Kennedy*?
21 Who scripted the controversial *Cathy Come Home* in the mid-60s?
22 Where had *Reilly – Ace of Spies* been born?
23 In *Brideshead Revisited* Jeremy Irons and Anthony Andrews played the central characters but who played their fathers?
24 In *Widows* the four women stage a robbery based on the previous plans of whom?
25 Ray Brooks played the habitual gambler Robby Box in which BBC drama?
26 What did *The Fall Guy* do to earn money in addition to being a stunt man?
27 In which episode of *Cracker* did Fitz travel to Hong Kong?
28 David Lynch's famous TV show will return in 2017. What's it called?
29 Who plays John Munch in *Homicide: Life on the Streets*?
30 Who does Barry Corbin play in *Northern Exposure*?

Answers | **Football Pot Luck 12** *(see Quiz 106)*

1 Scunthorpe Utd. 2 William. 3 Birmingham City. 4 Bolivia. 5 Leeds Utd. 6 Norwich City. 7 Hibernian. 8 Wales. 9 Notts County. 10 Qatar. 11 West Ham Utd. 12 Buxton. 13 Fulham. 14 QPR. 15 1980s. 16 Newcastle Utd. 17 Plymouth Argyle. 18 Richard Money. 19 Clapton Orient. 20 4. 21 Gary Megson. 22 Olympiakos Piraeus. 23 Blackburn Rovers & Bolton Wanderers. 24 QPR. 25 Colin Garwood. 26 WBA, Manchester City & Norwich City. 27 Bobby Charlton. 28 United States Soccer Federation. 29 Hearts. 30 Steaua Bucharest.

1 Up to the late 1980s who used to play at the Old Showground?
2 What is Ian Bishop's middle name?
3 Joe Bradford set a record for most League goals in a season at which club?
4 Which country inflicted the worst defeat on Argentina in a World Cup qualifier in 2009 (6–1)?
5 Hankin and Hart scored in the same European game for which club?
6 At which club did Dion Dublin make his League debut?
7 Keeper Andy Goram was at which club when he scored v Morton?
8 Which country did John Mahoney play for?
9 Who were the first English club to play 3,000 matches in the League?
10 The first Arab country to host the FIFA World Cup in 2022 is _____.
11 Dicks and Dickens were in the same team at which club?
12 Which Mick became boss of Scunthorpe in March 1996?
13 Peter Mellor first played in an FA Cup Final for which team?
14 At which club did Chris Woods make his League debut?
15 In what decade did Dundee Utd first win the championship?
16 Which club had a fanzine called *The Number Nine*?
17 Steve McCall followed Peter Shilton as manager of which club?
18 Who moved from Fulham to Liverpool for £333,333 in 1980 to set a club record for a transfer fee received?
19 What were Leyton Orient known as from entering the League and the end of the World Wars?
20 How many international goals did Steve Archibald score?
21 Who twice managed West Bromwich to Premiership promotion in the 2000s?
22 Which club was 2007–08 League champions in Greece?
23 Which two teams beginning with B were relegated to the Third Division for the first time ever in 1971?
24 Which London side won 6–2 at home in the first leg of a UEFA Cup game in the 1980s and were beaten 4–0 away?
25 Who was top scorer for both Portsmouth and Aldershot in 1979–80?
26 Which three teams did Asa Hartford play for in League Cup Finals?
27 Who scored for England in his 100th international?
28 What do the initials USSF stand for?
29 Baird and Levein scored Euro goals in the same 1990s game for which Scottish club?
30 Who lost 4–0 to AC Milan in the final of the 1989 European Cup?

Answers | TV: Drama 2 *(see Quiz 105)*

1 Angel Clare. 2 The Afanc. 3 James Fox. 4 John Mortimer. 5 Eric Porter. 6 Washington – Behind Closed Doors. 7 John Thaw. 8. WWII. 9 St Elsewhere. 10 Laura and Kate. 11 David Hemmings. 12 David Soul. 13 Thamesford. 14 Alan Bates. 15 The Sherpa Tensing Ward. 16 Jane Seymour. 17 Give Us a Break. 18 Julia Sawalha. 19 The British Army. 20 Martin Shaw. 21 Jeremy Sandford. 22 Russia. 23 John Gielgud and Laurence Olivier. 24 Their deceased husbands. 25 Big Deal. 26 Bounty hunter. 27 White Ghost. 28 Twin Peaks. 29 Richard Belzer. 30 Maurice.

1 Who was president of France from 1981 through to 1995?
2 In 2015, Mhairi Black became the holder of which MP's record?
3 Betws-y-Coed in the county of Clwyd lies in which national park?
4 "Amhrán na bhFiann", serves the Republic of Ireland in what capacity?
5 The Tay Rail Bridge connects the Wormit to which Scottish city?
6 In 2012, Google Chrome replaced Internet Explorer as the world's most popular what?
7 In which century did the rule of Queen Elizabeth I begin?
8 In July 2005, which British city suffered terrorist bomb attacks?
9 The Anglesey village of Llanfairpwll-gwyn-gyllgogerychwyrndrobwllllan-tysiliogogogoch holds what European record?
10 Which island was supposedly created by the giant, Finn MacCoul?
11 Ipswich is the county town of which county?
12 Which Labour MP was assassinated in 2016?
13 Which band had a 90s hit with "Stay Another Day"?
14 County Kerry includes which geographical extreme of Ireland?
15 In Irish legend, what was the three-leafed clover used to demonstrate?
16 Which British prime minister resigned in 1990?
17 Fingal's cave is on which inner Scottish archipelago?
18 Which major European country reunified in 1990?
19 What is the name of Queen Elizabeth II's third child?
20 Which is the second-largest city in Wales?
21 What is a toxophilite?
22 Operation Desert Shield was a code name for which US-led invasion?
23 Which former US president and movie star died in 2004?
24 The meat of what animal is traditionally used in Irish stew?
25 Deep Purple's best-known track talked about smoke on what?
26 Which complex of buildings was the primary target of airliner attack on september 11, 2001?
27 Samuel Richardson's 1748 novel *Clarissa, or the History of a Young Lady*, is widely regarded to hold which English language record?
28 In 2004, a huge earthquake triggered what kind of ocean-born phenomenon?
29 Which singer Gwen is the lead singer of No Doubt?
30 Reading, Slough and Eton are all to be found in which county?

| **Answers** | **Movies Pot Luck 12** *(see Quiz 108)* |

1 Steven Spielberg. 2 Garry Marshall. 3 Colin Firth. 4 Ice Hockey. 5 Robert Duvall. 6 Helen Tasker. 7 94 minutes. 8 Captain Carey. 9 Charles. 10 Madison. 11 Wild at Heart. 12 Elia Kazan. 13 Bob Hoskins. 14 Arndt. 15 Winchester '73. 16 Ghostbusters. 17 Marie. 18 Slamdance. 19 Ghostbusters. 20 Delpy. 21 Lisa Bonet. 22 Architecture. 23 87 minutes. 24 Richard Blaney. 25 Spencer. 26 The Big Lebowski. 27 Ted Striker. 28 Laurent Cantet. 29 Biggie Smalls (aka Notorious B.I.G.). 30 Andrei Tarkovsky.

1 Who said, "The most expensive habit in the world is celluloid"?
2 Who directed *Pretty Woman*?
3 Who played Tommy Judd in the film *Another Country*?
4 At what sport did Keanu Reeves excel?
5 Who won the Best Actor Oscar for *Tender Mercies*?
6 What was the name of Jamie Lee Curtis's character in *True Lies*?
7 Within ten minutes, how long does *Porky's* last?
8 "Mona Lisa" won an Oscar when it was used in which movie in 1950?
9 Which Josh featured in *Dead Poets Society*?
10 What is the name of the mermaid in *Splash*?
11 In which film does a character named Sailor Ripley appear?
12 Who won the Best Director Oscar for *Gentleman's Agreement*?
13 *The Long Good Friday* and *Zulu Dawn* both starred which actor?
14 Which Denis featured in *Basic Instinct*?
15 Lin McAdam, played by James Stewart, searched for which stolen gun of his father's?
16 Katie Dippold wrote what spooky 2016 blockbuster?
17 What is the first name of Debra Winger, who uses her middle name in the movies?
18 Which 1988 film did rock star Adam Ant star in?
19 In which movie does Bill Murray say, "OK, so she's a dog"?
20 Which Julie starred in *Before Sunrise*?
21 Who played Epiphany Proudfoot in the film *Angel Heart*?
22 Which subject did James Mason study at Cambridge?
23 Within five minutes, how long does *Pinocchio* last?
24 What was the name of Jon Finch's character in *Frenzy*?
25 Which John featured in *Presumed Innocent*?
26 For which of her husband Ethan Coen's movies is Tricia Cooke first credited as editor?
27 Who saves the day in *Airplane!* and *Airplane II: The Sequel*?
28 Who directed the 2008 award-winning French film *The Class*?
29 Who was the subject of the 2009 biopic *Notorious*?
30 Who directed the cult 1980 Russian film *Stalker*?

Answers	**Pot Luck** *(see Quiz 107)*

1 François Mitterand. 2 Youngest. 3 Snowdonia. 4 National anthem. 5 Dundee. 6 Web browser. 7 16th century AD. 8 London. 9 Longest place name. 10 Isle of Man. 11 Suffolk. 12 Jo Cox. 13 East 17. 14 West. 15 The Trinity. 16 Margaret Thatcher. 17 Hebrides. 18 Germany. 19 Prince Andrew. 20 Swansea. 21 Archer (aka bowman). 22 Gulf War. 23 Ronald Reagan. 24 Sheep. 25 The Water. 26 World Trade Centre. 27 Longest novel. 28 Tsunami. 29 Stefani. 30 Berkshire.

1 Which band was named after a character in the movie *Barbarella*?
2 Which rocker's autobiography was called *Born to Run*?
3 Which band recorded "The Hand That Feeds"?
4 Which band is known for lead singer Justin Hawkins's high tenor voice?
5 Which band had a hit with "There There"?
6 Which band's devoted fans are known as Deadheads?
7 Which Australian rock band was formed by Angus and Malcolm Young?
8 What did R.E.M. famously lose in 1991?
9 Which brother and sister duo had hits including "Please Mr. Postman"?
10 Which group released *The Lamb Lies Down on Broadway*?
11 Which band was often fronted by Bruce Dickinson?
12 Which nu metal band was named after open space in Santa Monica?
13 Which band had a massive hit album with *Different Class* in 1995?
14 "Was "Stairway to Heaven" ever released as a single?
15 Which band had an early hit with "Heart of Glass" and "Atomic"?
16 Which band won a grammy for *Dookie*?
17 Who recorded the UK's first rock and roll hit, "Move It"?
18 Which band recorded "Lola" and "You Really Got Me"?
19 Which metal band famously features a one-armed drummer?
20 "Sympathy for the Devil" was apparently inspired by which book?
21 Which hugely successful English rock band contained John Deacon?
22 Which band was named after the Archduke whose murder sparked the first world war?
23 Which quirky rocker recorded the album *Sheik Yerbouti*?
24 Which superstar US rock band was fronted by singer Dave Lee Roth?
25 Which famously beardy band had a hit with "Gimme All Your Lovin'"?
26 *Turn on the Bright Lights* was a hit album for which band?
27 Which soft rock band jokingly claimed they were named after Dorothy's dog in the Wizard of Oz?
28 Axl Rose was the vocalist of which rock band?
29 Which Toronto rock band was named after a Herman Hesse novel?
30 "Money for Nothing", "Brothers in Arms" and "Sultans of Swing" were hits for which rock band?

Answers	Football Pot Luck 13 *(see Quiz 110)*

1 Ian Maxwell. 2 Roma. 3 Wales. 4 Motherwell. 5 1950s. 6 Leyton Orient. 7 Middlesbrough. 8 Gary Pallister. 9 Gillingham. 10 Three. 11 Coventry City. 12 Fox. 13 Coventry City. 14 Blackburn Rovers. 15 Graham. 16 QPR. 17 Tommy Docherty. 18 Millwall. 19 Sam Longston. 20 Cologne. 21 Finland. 22 Sam Allardyce. 23 John Jensen. 24 Brighton. 25 1930s. 26 Scarborough. 27 Jackie Milburn. 28 Blackpool. 29 Plymouth Argyle. 30 Three.

1 In 1984, who at Derby County became the League's youngest club chairman?

2 Where did Thomas Hassler go when he left Juventus in July 1991?

3 Dick Krzywicki played for which country in the 1970s?

4 At which club did Brian McClair make his League debut?

5 In what decade did Chelsea first win the championship?

6 Which club has a fanzine called *Into the O Zone*?

7 Willie Maddren followed Malcolm Allison as manager of which club?

8 Who moved from Middlesbrough in August 1989 to set a club record for a transfer fee received?

9 Which club was once known as New Brompton?

10 To one each way, how many international goals did Terry Butcher score?

11 Speedie and Regis were in the same team at which club?

12 Which Peter became boss of Exeter in June 1995?

13 Cyrille Regis first played in an FA Cup Final for which team?

14 Ted Harper established a record for most League goals in a season at which club?

15 What is Clayton Blackmore's middle name?

16 Which club played at the White City in the 1930s and in the 1960s?

17 Mary Brown was involved in an affair with which soccer manager?

18 What was the first London club that Chris Armstrong played for?

19 Who was the Derby County chairman when Brian Clough resigned?

20 Which club claimed to have signed Gordon Strachan before he moved to Manchester Utd?

21 In which country would you watch My-Pa 47 playing Tampere United?

22 Who was sacked as Newcastle United manager in January 2008?

23 Which Arsenal midfielder of the 1990s has the middle name Faxe?

24 At which club did Eric Young make his League debut?

25 In which decade did Manchester City first win the championship?

26 Which club had a fanzine called *The Seadog Bites Back*?

27 Who followed Alf Ramsey as manager of Ipswich Town?

28 Charnley, Mudie and Perry have all hit 100+ goals for which club?

29 Which club was once known as Argyle Athletic Club?

30 To one each way, how many international goals did Ray Kennedy score?

Answers | Rock Music *(see Quiz 109)*

1 Duran Duran. 2 Bruce Springsteen. 3 Nine Inch Nails. 4 The Darkness.
5 Radiohead. 6 Grateful Dead. 7 AC/DC. 8 Religion. 9 The Carpenters.
10 Genesis. 11 Iron Maiden. 12 Linkin Park. 13 Pulp. 14 No. 15 Blondie.
16 Green Day. 17 Cliff Richard. 18 The Kinks. 19 Def Leppard 20 The Master and Margarita. 21 Queen. 22 Franz Ferdinand . 23 Frank Zappa. 24 Van Halen. 25 ZZ Top. 26 Interpol. 27 Toto. 28 Guns N' Roses. 29 Steppenwolf. 30 Dire Straits.